Upgrading to Windows 98

Charlie Russel and Sharon Crawford
464pp; 7½" x 9"
ISBN: 0-7821-2190-X
$19.99 US

This easy-to-use guide gives current users of Windows 95 and 3.1 all the information they need to upgrade to Microsoft's revolutionary new Windows 98. Step-by-step instructions tell the reader how to prepare a PC for installing the new operating system without losing their current settings or data. The book gives users all the tips and tricks they need to get the most out of Windows 98—easy networking, troubleshooting, hardware upgrading, Internet tips, and important connectivity advice. This invaluable information will save readers countless hours of frustration and confusion.

Expert Guide to Windows 98

Mark Minasi, Eric Christiansen, and Kristina Shapar
1CD
976pp; 7½" x 9"
ISBN: 0-7821-1974-3
$49.99 US

Based on Mark Minasi's $800 seminar, this book is the MIS, consultant, and power user's troubleshooting bible to the new version of Windows. Technically precise, yet enjoyable to read, this is the most accessible guide to networking, installing, and supporting Windows 98. The new Explorer/Web View shell, which integrates the Internet with the operating system and local network, is also covered in great detail. The companion CD includes animations of the book's procedures, and several commercial Windows antivirus, diagnostic, and troubleshooting utilities.

WINDOWS® 98
SECOND EDITION
COMPLETE

 SYBEX▶ SAN FRANCISCO ▶ PARIS ▶ DÜSSELDORF ▶ SOEST ▶ LONDON

Associate Publisher: Gary Masters

Contracts and Licensing Manager: Kristine O'Callaghan

Acquisitions and Developmental Editor: Tracy Brown

Compilation Editor: Emily K. Wolman

Editors: Pat Coleman, Nancy Conner, Anamary Ehlen, Ben Miller, Douglas Robert, and Shelby Zimmerman

Compilation Technical Editor: Rima Regas

Technical Editors: Maryann Brown, Peggy Brundy, Don Hergert, Doug Langston, Doug Smith, and Rima Regas

Compilation Reviser: Pat Coleman

Production Team Leader: Jennifer Durning

Book Designer: Maureen Forys, Happenstance Type-O-Rama

Electronic Publishing Specialist: Robin Kibby

Graphic Illustrator: Chris Gillespie

Proofreaders: Dave Nash, Nancy Riddiough, and Sandy Young

Indexer: Lynnzee Elze

Cover Designer: DesignSite

Screen reproductions produced with Collage Complete.
Collage Complete is a trademark of Inner Media Inc.

SYBEX is a registered trademark of SYBEX Inc.

Mastering, Expert Guide, Premium Edition, and No experience required. are trademarks of SYBEX Inc.

First Edition Copyright ©1998

Copyright ©2000 SYBEX Inc., 1151 Marina Village Parkway, Alameda, CA 94501. World rights reserved. No part of this publication may be stored in a retrieval system, transmitted, or reproduced in any way, including but not limited to photocopy, photograph, magnetic or other record, without the prior agreement and written permission of the publisher.

Library of Congress Card Number: 99-65751
ISBN: 0-7821-2617-0

Manufactured in the United States of America

10 9 8 7 6 5

TRADEMARKS:

SYBEX has attempted throughout this book to distinguish proprietary trademarks from descriptive terms by following the capitalization style used by the manufacturer.

Netscape Communications, the Netscape Communications logo, Netscape, and Netscape Navigator are trademarks of Netscape Communications Corporation.

Netscape Communications Corporation has not authorized, sponsored, endorsed, or approved this publication and is not responsible for its content. Netscape and the Netscape Communications Corporate Logos are trademarks and trade names of Netscape Communications Corporation. All other product names and/or logos are trademarks of their respective owners.

The author and publisher have made their best efforts to prepare this book, and the content is based upon final release software whenever possible. Portions of the manuscript may be based upon pre-release versions supplied by software manufacturer(s). The author and the publisher make no representation or warranties of any kind with regard to the completeness or accuracy of the contents herein and accept no liability of any kind including but not limited to performance, merchantability, fitness for any particular purpose, or any losses or damages of any kind caused or alleged to be caused directly or indirectly from this book.

Photographs and illustrations used in this book have been downloaded from publicly accessible file archives and are used in this book for news reportage purposes only to demonstrate the variety of graphics resources available via electronic access. Text and images available over the Internet may be subject to copyright and other rights owned by third parties. Online availability of text and images does not imply that they may be reused without the permission of rights holders, although the Copyright Act does permit certain unauthorized reuse as fair use under 17 U.S.C. Section 107.

Acknowledgments

This book incorporates the work of many people, inside and outside Sybex.

Gary Masters, Bonnie Bills, Richard Mills, and Tracy Brown hammered out the idea of an inexpensive showcase compilation including the widest possible range of topics for Windows 98 Second Edition users. They defined the book's overall structure and contents.

A large team of editors, developmental editors, project editors, and technical editors helped to put together the various books from which *Windows 98 Second Edition Complete* was compiled: Maureen Adams, Sherry Bonelli, Peter Kuhns, and Neil Edde handled developmental tasks; Kim Askew, Bonnie Bills, Pat Coleman, Nancy Conner, Anamary Ehlen, Ben Miller, Vivian Perry, Lee Ann Pickrell, Douglas Robert, Michael Tom, Peter Weverka, Kim Wimpsett, and Shelby Zimmerman all contributed to editing or project editing; and the technical editors were Maryann Brown, Peggy Brundy, Don Hergert, Doug Langston, Rima Regas, and Doug Smith. Ms. Regas deserves particular thanks for helping to make sure the Internet and hardware chapters reflect Windows 98 Second Edition.

Pat Coleman deserves particular thanks for updating all of the material in this book. Similarly, thanks to Emily Wolman for editing the book and tying it all together.

The *Windows 98 Second Edition Complete* production team of electronic desktop specialist Robin Kibby, production team leader Jennifer Durning, and proofreaders Dave Nash, Nancy Riddiough, and Sandy Young worked with speed and accuracy to turn the manuscript files and illustrations into the handsome book you're now reading. Liz Paulus, Dan Schiff, and Ina Ingenito also helped in various ways to keep the project moving.

Finally, our most important thanks go to the contributors who agreed to have their work excerpted into *Windows 98 Second Edition Complete*: Sharon Crawford, Charlie Russel, and Neil J. Salkind; Robert Cowart; Mark Minasi, Eric Christiansen, and Kristina Shapar; Peter Dyson; Christian Crumlish; John Ross; Gene Weisskopf and Pat Coleman; Daniel A. Tauber, Brenda Kienan, and J. Tarin Towers; and Ben Ezzell. Without their efforts, this book would not exist.

Contents at a Glance

Introduction   xxviii

Part I ▶ Windows 98 Second Edition   1

Chapter 1   Introducing Windows 98 Second Edition   3
Adapted from Upgrading to Windows 98

Chapter 2   Installing Windows 98 SE on Your Computer   15
Adapted from Upgrading to Windows 98

Chapter 3   Visiting the Windows 98 Desktop   35
Adapted from ABCs of Windows 98

Chapter 4   Shortcuts Galore   57
Adapted from ABCs of Windows 98

Chapter 5   Windows Explorer and the Recycle Bin   73
Adapted from Windows 98: No Experience Required

Chapter 6   Installing and Running Programs   97
Adapted from Windows 98: No Experience Required

Chapter 7   Customizing Windows 98 SE with the Control Panel   113
Adapted from Mastering Windows 98 Second Edition

Chapter 8   Printers and Printing   175
Adapted from Mastering Windows 98 Second Edition

Chapter 9   Windows Multimedia   203
Adapted from Mastering Windows 98 Second Edition

Chapter 10   Hardware Mastery   263
Adapted from Windows 98: No Experience Required

Chapter 11	Maintaining the System	287
	Adapted from *Windows 98: No Experience Required* and *The ABCs of Windows 98*	
Chapter 12	System Troubleshooting	319
	Adapted from *Windows 98: No Experience Required*	
Chapter 13	Remote Access with Windows 98 SE	329
	Adapted from *The Expert Guide to Windows 98*	
Chapter 14	Windows 98 SE Applets	371
	Adapted from *The ABCs of Windows 98*	
Chapter 15	Controlling 98 SE—the Registry and .INI Files	391
	Adapted from *Expert Guide to Windows 98*	

Part II ▸ The Internet and Windows 98 Second Edition   **441**

Chapter 16	Understanding Internet and World Wide Web Basics	443
	Adapted from *The Internet: No Experience Required*	
Chapter 17	Connecting to the Internet	465
	Adapted from *Mastering Windows 98 Second Edition*	
Chapter 18	Communicating with E-Mail	491
	Adapted from *The Internet: No Experience Required*	
Chapter 19	Browsing the Web with Internet Explorer	527
	Adapted from *ABCs of Microsoft Internet Explorer 4*	
Chapter 20	Browsing with a Sense of Security	567
	Adapted from *Mastering Microsoft Internet Explorer 4*	
Chapter 21	An Alternative to Internet Explorer: Netscape Navigator	607
	Adapted from *Surfing the Internet With Netscape Communicator 4*	

Contents at a Glance

Chapter 22	Creating Web Pages with FrontPage Express	643
	Adapted from *Mastering Microsoft Internet Explorer 4*	
Chapter 23	Finding and Downloading Windows Software Online	685
	Adapted from *The Internet: No Experience Required*	

Part III ▶ Your PC and Hardware — 709

Chapter 24	A Buyer's Guide to PCs	711
	Adapted from *The Complete PC Upgrade & Maintenance Guide*	
Chapter 25	Avoiding Service: Preventive Maintenance	725
	Adapted from *The Complete PC Upgrade & Maintenance Guide*	
Chapter 26	Installing Random Access Memory	753
	Chapter written by Ben Ezzell exclusively for *PC Complete*	

Part IV ▶ Windows 98 Second Edition User's Reference — 789

Appendix A	Windows 98 SE Command and Feature Reference	791
	Adapted from *Windows 98 Second Edition Instant Reference*	
Appendix B	Windows 98 SE User's Glossary	873
	Adapted from *PC User's Essential Accessible Pocket Dictionary* And from *The Internet Dictionary*	
Appendix C	Vendors Guide	914
	Adapted from *The Complete PC Upgrade & Maintenance Guide*	

Index		*982*

Table of Contents

Introduction ... xxviii

Part I ▶ Windows 98 Second Edition ... 1

Chapter 1 ▫ Introducing Windows 98 Second Edition ... 3
What's New in Windows 98 SE? ... 4
    Internet Explorer 5 ... 4
    Bug Fixes, Security Patches, and Updates ... 7
    New Support for Technologies ... 7
How Is Windows 98 SE Different from Windows 95? ... 8
    Using Folders and Shortcuts ... 10
    Seamless Web Connections ... 11
    What About My Mail? ... 11
    Windows Update ... 12
    Other Cool Stuff That Wasn't Available in Windows 95 ... 12
What's Next? ... 13

Chapter 2 ▫ Installing Windows 98 SE on Your Computer ... 15
Easiest Approach: A Full Upgrade from an Earlier Version of Windows ... 18
Installing to a Fresh Disk or New Directory ... 24
Finding and Fixing Hard-Disk Problems during Installation ... 25
Reverting to the Previous Operating System ... 26
Removing Uninstall Files to Free Up Disk Space ... 28
Installing onto a Compressed Drive ... 28
How to Install Windows 98 SE to a Machine Running Windows NT or Windows 2000 ... 31
Multi-Booting Windows 98 SE with Linux ... 32
What's Next? ... 32

Chapter 3 ▫ Visiting the Windows 98 Desktop ... 35
The Start Button ... 36
    Programs ... 37

Table of Contents

Favorites	37
Documents	37
Settings	37
Find	38
Help	39
Run	39
Log Off	39
Shut Down	39
Taskbars Galore	40
Changing the Taskbar's Location and Size	40
Making the Taskbar Disappear	40
Also on the Taskbar	41
Selecting the Taskbar's Toolbars	41
Quick Launch Toolbar	42
Desktop Toolbar	42
Address Toolbar	42
Links Toolbar	43
Creating a Toolbar	43
Making Room for All the Toolbars	44
Configuring Toolbars	44
What My Computer Can Do for You	45
Recycling Unwanted Files and Folders	45
The Windows 98 SE Properties Dialog Box	46
Setting Up Your Desktop	47
The Background Tab	48
The Screen Saver Tab	49
The Appearance Tab	49
The Web Tab	49
The Effects Tab	50
The Settings Tab	50
Getting All the Help You'll Ever Need	51
Using Offline Help	53
Using Web Help	54
What's Next?	54

Chapter 4 □ Shortcuts Galore   57

Creating Shortcuts	59
Creating a Shortcut When You Can See the Object	60
Creating a Shortcut When You Can't See the Object	60

Table of Contents

Renaming a Shortcut	61
What to Name Shortcuts	61
Shortcut Settings	61
Finding the Target	62
Changing a Shortcut's Icon	62
Putting Shortcuts Where You Want Them	63
Putting a Start Menu Item on the Desktop	63
Adding a Program to the Start Menu	64
Adding a Shortcut to Send To	64
Starting a Program When Windows Starts	65
Starting a Program with a Keyboard Shortcut	66
Shortcuts to Other Places	67
DOS Programs	67
Disk Drives	67
Keyboard Shortcuts	68
What's Next?	70

Chapter 5 □ Windows Explorer and the Recycle Bin — 73

Using Windows Explorer	74
Viewing Extensions	75
Using Another Computer's Files	77
Sharing a Drive or Folder	80
Mapping a Drive	82
Disconnecting from Mapped Drives or Folders	83
Exploring Floppy Disks	84
Making Exact Copies	84
Formatting Floppies	84
Using the Send To Option	86
The Long...	86
...And the Short of It	87
Using the Recycle Bin	87
What It Is	88
Sending Files to the Recycle Bin	89
Recovering a Deleted File	91
Adjusting the Recycle Bin Settings	93
Doing Away with the Recycle Bin	94
Emptying the Recycle Bin	95
What's Next?	95

Chapter 6 □ Installing and Running Programs — 97

Installing a Program	98
Installing from a CD	98
Installing from Control Panel	100
Removing a Program	103
Removing a Windows 3.1 Program	104
Removing a DOS Program	104
Finding a Program	105
Program Menu	105
Shortcuts	105
Find	106
Windows Explorer	106
Making Programs Easier to Find	107
Desktop Shortcuts	108
Programs Menu Shortcuts	108
Start Menu Shortcuts	109
Toolbar Shortcuts	109
Send-To Shortcuts	110
What's Next?	111

Chapter 7 □ Customizing Windows 98 SE with the Control Panel — 113

Opening the Control Panel	114
Accessibility Options	118
Keyboard Accessibility Settings	119
Sound Accessibility Settings	121
Display Accessibility Settings	122
Mouse Accessibility Settings	123
Other Accessibility Settings	126
Adding New Hardware	127
Running the Install Hardware Wizard	128
When Your Hardware Isn't on the List	135
Adding and Removing Programs	136
Installing New Programs	137
Removing Existing Programs	138
Setting the Date and Time	139
Desktop Themes	140
Customizing Your Screen Display	142

Table of Contents xv

Setting the Background and Wallpaper — 143
Setting the Screen Saver — 147
Adjusting the Appearance — 151
Effects — 157
Web — 159
Driver Settings — 159
Adjusting the Mouse — 168
    Switching the Buttons and Setting Double-Click Speed — 168
    Setting Your Pointers — 170
    Setting the Pointer Motion — 171
What's Next? — 173

Chapter 8 □ Printers and Printing 175

A Print-Manager Primer — 177
Adding a New Printer — 178
    About Printer Installation — 178
    About Adding Printers — 179
    Running the Wizard to Add a New Printer — 181
Altering the Details of a Printer's Setup—The Properties Box — 187
How to Delete a Printer from Your Printers Folder — 189
How to Print Out Documents from Your Programs — 190
    About the Default Printer — 190
    Printing from a Program — 191
    Printing by Dragging Files onto a Printer Icon or into Its Window — 192
Working with the Print Queue — 194
    Refreshing the Network Queue Information — 196
    Deleting a File from the Queue — 196
    Canceling All Pending Print Jobs on a Given Printer — 197
    Pausing (and Resuming) the Printing Process — 198
Printing to a Disk File Instead of a Printer — 199
What's Next? — 200

Chapter 9 □ Windows Multimedia 203

Exactly What Is Multimedia? — 205
What's New in Windows 98 SE Multimedia — 207
Upgrading to Multimedia — 208
The Supplied Multimedia Applications and Utilities — 218
    Doing It All with DVD Player — 220

Table of Contents

Assigning Sounds with the Control Panel's Sound Utility	228
Playing Multimedia Files with Media Player	233
Recording and Editing Sounds with Sound Recorder	235
Playing Tunes with CD Player	240
Web TV	248
Using TV Viewer	250
Tips for Using Web TV	253
Managing Multimedia Drivers and Settings	260
What's Next?	261

Chapter 10 □ Hardware Mastery   263

Modems	264
Installing a Modem	264
Deleting a Modem	266
Modem Settings	266
Dialing Properties	270
Troubleshooting	271
Scanners and Cameras	272
Adding and Configuring Printers	273
Adding a Printer	273
Uninstalling a Printer	275
Printer Settings	275
Troubleshooting	276
Changing a Mouse	276
Game Controllers	278
Using Infrared Devices	279
Setting the Display Adapter	280
Changing a Video Card	280
Changing a Video Driver	281
Optimizing Video Settings	283
What's Next?	285

Chapter 11 □ Maintaining the System   287

Running ScanDisk	288
Starting ScanDisk	288
Changing ScanDisk Settings	289
Fixing Disk Fragmentation	291
Disk Cleanup	293

Doing a System Tune-Up	295
Using Task Scheduler	297
Windows Update	297
Using Space Efficiently	299
FAT32	299
Compressing Hard Drives	303
Backing Up and Restoring Files	308
Getting Started	308
Tape Drive or Floppies	309
Deciding on a Type of Backup	310
Deciding What to Back Up	310
Defining a File Set	311
Creating a Backup	312
Choosing Backup Options	314
Restoring Files	315
What's Next?	316

Chapter 12 □ System Troubleshooting   319

Using the System Information Utility	320
Meet Dr. Watson	321
Checking System Files	322
Using System Monitor	323
Using the Resource Meter	325
Troubleshooting Tools	326
What's Next?	327

Chapter 13 □ Remote Access with Windows 98 SE   329

What Is Remote Access?	331
So Near, and Yet So Far	331
What Are the Setup Options for Dial-Up Networking?	332
What Connection Protocols Are Supported by Dial-Up Networking?	333
What Are the Different Combinations for Connection Protocols and Network Protocols?	334
How Do I Install Dial-Up Networking?	335
Installing Dial-Up Networking on the Network	335
Configuring the DUN Connection	336
Installing Dial-Up Networking on the Client Machine	337

Table of Contents

Configuring a DUN Client Connection	342
How Do I Test the DUN Connection?	347
Using the Internet Connection Wizard	349
Altering an Internet Connection	351
Sample ISP Information	352
Using WINS to Connect to an NT Domain over an Existing Internet Connection	352
Troubleshooting a WINS Connection	357
Regular DUN vs. WINS vs. PPTP	359
Installing the Windows 98 SEDial-Up Server	359
What About Security?	364
Password Authentication Protocol (PAP)	364
Challenge-Handshake Authentication Protocol (CHAP)	366
Remote Access to Resources with DUN	366
What's Next?	369

Chapter 14 □ Windows 98 SE Applets — 371

A World of Applets	371
Using Notepad	372
What Notepad Has	372
Working with WordPad	372
Opening WordPad	373
Making and Formatting Documents	373
Page Setup and Printing	374
What's on the Clipboard	375
Taking a Look	375
Saving the Clipboard's Contents	375
Drawing with Paint	376
Creating Original Art	376
Modifying the Work of Others	376
Entering New Characters	377
Entering Characters	377
Phone Dialing for Fun	378
Speed Dialing	379
The Telephone Log	380
Using the Calculators	380
Just the Basics	381
Or One Step Beyond	381
Pasting in the Numbers	382

Communicating with
  HyperTerminal 382
    How to Use It 383
    Sending Files 385
    And Receiving Them Too 387
    Saving a Session 387
    Using a Connection 388
  Using My Briefcase 388
    How It Works 388
  What's Next? 389

Chapter 15 ◻ Controlling 98 SE—the Registry and .INI Files 391

The Limited New Roles of AUTOEXEC.BAT and CONFIG.SYS 392
  Loading Real-Mode Drivers and TSRs 393
  Creating Your Own DOS Environments 393
What Is the Registry? 398
  Why Have a Registry? 400
  What's in the Registry? 401
  What's Not in the Registry? 402
  The Windows 98 SE Registry Is Not the Same As the
    Windows NT Registry 403
  Cautions About Working with the Registry 404
The Registry: Pieces of the Puzzle 405
  Subtree Functions 406
  Opening the Registry 407
  Navigating in the Registry 408
Editing the Local Registry 409
  Backing Up the Registry 409
  SCANREGW.EXE 413
  Exporting a Registry with REGEDIT.EXE 414
  Reducing the Size of Your Registry 416
  Editing the Registry's Contents 418
  Restoring the Registry Using REGEDIT.EXE 421
  What About Duplicate Entries? 423
  Preparing to Administer a Remote Computer 424
  Connecting to the Remote Computer 426
  Troubleshooting a Remote Registry Connection 427

Permitting Other Groups to Administer Remote Registries 428
Editing the Remote Registry 430
WIN.INI and SYSTEM.INI under Windows 98 SE 431
   Contents of .INI Files 431
   The New Look of .INI Files 432
   Why Do I Have .INI Files? 434
Some Neat Registry Tips 435
   Saving Your Desktop Settings 435
   Remove the Shut Down Option from the Start Menu 436
   Preventing Windows Menus from Following Your Mouse 437
Zooming Windows 437
   Changing Your System's Shell Folders 438
Hiding Your Machine from Your Network's Browse List 439
What's Next? 440

Part II ▶ The Internet and Windows 98 Second Edition 441

Chapter 16 □ Understanding Internet and World Wide Web Basics 443

Introducing the Internet 444
   Communicating through E-Mail or Discussion Groups 444
   What's the Difference between the Web and the Internet? 446
   Discovering What's New on the Net 450
Getting on the Internet 452
   Cruising the Net at Work 452
   Cruising the Net at Home 453
   The Anatomy of an Internet Address 456
What You Can Do on the Net 459
   Downloading Files from the Internet 460
   Using Web Sites to Gather Information about the Internet and the Web 461
What's Next? 462

Chapter 17 □ Connecting to the Internet 465

What Kind of Connection? 466
Choosing a Service Provider 469

Using a National ISP	471
Using a Local ISP	472
Connecting through an Online Service	473
Getting Directly on the Internet—Finding a Local ISP	475
Setting Up Windows 98 SE Dial-Up Networking	478
Loading the Software	479
Creating a Connection Profile	480
Changing the Default Connection	482
Sharing Your Internet Connection with Networked Computers	485
Setting Up Internet Connection Sharing	486
What's Next?	489

Chapter 18 □ Communicating with E-Mail — 491

E-Mail Basics	492
Running an E-Mail Program	493
Sending Mail	493
Reading Mail	497
Replying to Mail	498
Deleting Mail	500
Using Proper E-Mail Netiquette	500
Exiting an E-Mail Program	502
Trying Out Microsoft Outlook Express and Netscape Messenger	502
Microsoft Outlook Express	502
Netscape Messenger	503
Using E-Mail More Effectively	505
Sending Mail to More Than One Person	505
Sending Files via E-Mail	506
Forwarding Mail to Someone Else	508
Enhancing Your E-Mail with HTML Formatting	509
Writing E-Mail with Your Word Processor	511
Checking Your Spelling	512
Attaching a Signature	513
Filing Your Messages	515
Filtering Messages as They Come In	517
Dealing with E-Mail from Several Accounts	522
Managing an Address Book	522
Finding Internet E-Mail Addresses	524
Use Search Tools on the Web	524
Say "Send Me E-Mail"	525

Table of Contents

Send Mail to Postmaster@	525
What's Next?	525

Chapter 19 □ Browsing the Web with Internet Explorer — 527

Starting Internet Explorer	528
The Internet Explorer Screen	528
Changing the Toolbars' Appearance	531
Using and Customizing the Links Bar	531
Moving around the Web	534
Typing an Address	534
Using Hot Links	536
Returning to Sites You've Recently Visited	537
Explorer Bars	538
Moving Forward and Backward	542
Using More Than One Window at a Time	543
Home Pages	543
Choosing a Home Page	544
Changing Your Home Page	544
Using Internet Search Tools	545
Focusing Your Searches	549
Returning to Favorite Web Pages	549
Working with the Favorites List	550
Making Your Own Hot List	557
Viewing Web Pages Offline	558
Creating and Using Web Shortcuts	559
Changing the Default Browser: A Warning	564
What's Next?	565

Chapter 20 □ Browsing with a Sense of Security — 567

Guarding Your Privacy on the Web	568
Staying Secure with Passwords	569
Saying "No Thank You" to Cookies	571
Retaining Your Privacy with the Profile Assistant	572
Keeping Transactions Secure with Microsoft Wallet	576
Filtering Sites with the Content Advisor	580
Avoiding www.offensive	581
The Content Advisor	582
Cooperation between Web-Page Authors, Rating Systems, and Parents	583

Determining the Ratings for Pages You Author	584
Enabling the Content Advisor	584
Setting the Ratings Criteria in the Content Advisor	587
What to Do When a Page Is Disallowed	588
Adding Another Rating System	590
Assigning Trust through Security Zones	592
Dividing the Web into Security Zones	593
Changing the Security Level for a Zone	595
Assigning a Site to a Zone	596
Encrypting Transfers over a Secure Connection	597
Verifying Identity with Certificates	600
Software Publisher Certificates	601
Site Certificates	604
Personal Certificates	604
What's Next?	605

Chapter 21 □ An Alternative to Internet Explorer: Netscape Navigator   607

Launching Netscape Navigator	608
What You See: The Navigator Interface	610
Opening Your First Document	615
Following Hot Links	615
Opening a Document Using Its URL	617
Changing the Size and Color of Displayed Text	620
Changing Fonts and Type Sizes	620
Changing Colors	622
Saving Stuff to Your Local Machine	624
Saving Stuff You Can See	625
Saving Stuff That's Not in View	627
Viewing Documents You've Saved	628
Jumping Back and Forth While Viewing a Document	629
Getting Around in Frames	631
Caching and Reloading	633
Error Messages Demystified	636
Printing a Document or a Single Frame	638
Quitting Netscape Navigator	640
What's Next?	640

Chapter 22 ▫ Creating Web Pages with FrontPage Express — 643

- Starting Out in FrontPage Express — 644
  - Starting FrontPage — 644
  - Navigating in FrontPage — 645
- Editing a Web Page — 646
  - Inserting Line Breaks and Special Characters — 647
  - Finding and Replacing Text — 648
  - Adding Comments — 649
  - Seeing the HTML Source Code — 649
  - Previewing Your Work in Internet Explorer — 650
  - Printing Your Work — 651
- Creating New Pages and Saving Your Work — 652
  - Creating a New Page — 653
  - Opening an Existing Page — 655
  - Saving Your Work — 657
- Adding Structure to a Page — 658
  - Separating Sections with a Horizontal Line — 658
  - Creating Headings to Subdivide a Page — 661
  - Organizing Data with Bulleted and Numbered Lists — 661
- Formatting Pages — 663
  - Setting Character Properties — 663
  - Setting Paragraph Properties — 666
  - Setting Page Properties — 668
  - Creating Meta Page Information — 671
- Creating Links — 672
  - Creating a New Hyperlink — 672
  - Revising and Deleting a Hyperlink — 674
  - Working with Bookmarks — 675
- Working with Images — 677
  - Getting the Picture — 677
  - Creating an Inline Image — 678
  - Setting Image Properties — 679
- What's Next? — 683

Chapter 23 ▫ Finding and Downloading Windows Software Online — 685

- What's New with Searching? — 686

Searching the Web	686
Searching through a Directory	687
Searching with a Search Engine	690
Refining Your Search	693
Visiting a Central Search Page	693
Some Search Addresses	695
Downloading and Decompressing Files	695
Compression Programs	698
Downloading WinZip	698
Shareware.com	703
Buying Things Online	704
What's Next	707

Part III ▸ Your PC and Hardware   709

Chapter 24 □ A Buyer's Guide to PCs   711

Parts of a Generic PC	712
Problems with Proprietary PCs	713
Choosing a Market Niche	715
Choosing PC Parts	716
CPU	716
"Upgradable" PCs	717
Bus	717
RAM	718
ROM BIOS	718
Motherboard/System Board	718
Disk Drives	719
Floppy Disks	719
Video Board	719
Video Monitor	719
Mice	719
Printers	720
Serial Ports	720
Parallel Ports	720
Universal Serial Bus (USB)	720
From Whom Should You Buy?	720
What's Next?	722

Chapter 25 □ Avoiding Service: Preventive Maintenance 725

- Heat and Thermal Shock 726
  - Removing Heat with a Fan 726
  - Removing Heat with a Heat Sink 727
  - Good and Bad Box Designs 727
  - Dead Fans 728
  - Heat Sensor Devices 729
  - Safe Temperature Ranges for PCs 729
  - Duty Cycles 730
  - Thermal Shock 731
  - Sunbeams 731
- Dealing with Dust 732
- Magnetism 733
- Stray Electromagnetism 735
  - Electromagnetic Interference 735
  - Power Noise 739
  - Electrostatic Discharge 743
- Avoiding Water and Liquids 747
  - Corrosion 748
- Making the Environment "PC Friendly" 749
- What's Next? 750

Chapter 26 □ Installing Random Access Memory 753

- How Much Memory Is Enough? 754
  - Windows Swap Files 757
  - How Much Memory Is Installed? 758
- Types of Memory Modules 761
  - Memory Packaging 761
  - Memory Speed 762
  - Memory Blocks 762
  - Memory Types 763
  - SIMM and DIMM Memory Sockets 765
  - Using Older Memory Modules in Newer Machines 769
  - Planning Memory Requirements 770
- Installation 771
  - Static Electricity—IMPORTANT! 771
  - Opening the Computer 772
  - Locating the Memory Sockets 775

Is Space Available?	781
Before You Buy	782
Adding New Memory	784
Success!	786
What's Next?	787

Part IV ▸ Windows 98 Second Edition User's Reference — 789

Appendix A ▫ **Windows 98 SE Command and Feature Reference** — **791**

Appendix B ▫ **Windows 98 SE User's Glossary** — **873**

Appendix C ▫ **Vendors Guide**

Index — *982*

Introduction

Windows 98 Second Edition Complete is a one-of-a-kind computer book—valuable both for the breadth of its content and for its low price. This thousand-page compilation of information from more than a dozen Sybex books provides comprehensive coverage of the Windows 98 Second Edition operating environment and related Internet and PC hardware topics. This book, unique in the computer book world, was created with several goals in mind:

- To offer a thorough guide covering all the important user-level features of Windows 98 SE at an affordable price.
- To help you become familiar with the essential Windows 98 SE topics so you can choose your next Windows 98 SE book with confidence.
- To acquaint you with some of our best authors—their writing styles and teaching skills, and the level of expertise they bring to their books—so you can easily find a match for your interests as you delve deeper into Windows 98 SE and the realms of software and hardware it opens up to you.

Windows 98 Second Edition Complete is designed to provide all the essential information you'll need to get the most from Windows 98 SE and your computer, while at the same time inviting you to explore the even greater depths and wider coverage of material in the original books.

If you've read other computer "how-to" books, you've seen that there are many possible approaches to the task of showing how to use software and hardware effectively. The books from which *Windows 98 Second Edition Complete* was compiled represent a range of the approaches to teaching that Sybex and its authors have developed—from the quick, concise No Experience Required. style to the wide-ranging, thoroughly detailed Mastering style. These books also address readers at different levels of computer experience, from ABCs to Expert Guide. As you read through various chapters of Windows 98 Second Edition Complete, you'll see which approach works best for you. You'll also see what these books have in common: a commitment to clarity, accuracy, and practicality.

You'll find in these pages ample evidence of the high quality of Sybex's authors. Unlike publishers who produce "books by committee," Sybex authors are encouraged to write in individual voices that reflect their own experience with the software at hand and with the evolution of today's personal computers. Nearly every book represented here is the work of a single writer or a pair of close collaborators. When Mark Minasi, for example, says, "I once helped troubleshoot a network that had been installed...," you know you are getting the benefit of *his* direct experience. Likewise, all the Windows 98 SE chapters are based on their authors' firsthand testing of prerelease software and subsequent expertise with the final product.

In adapting the various source materials for inclusion in *Windows 98 Second Edition Complete*, the compiler preserved these individual voices and perspectives. Chapters were edited only to minimize duplication, omit coverage of non-Windows tools, and update or add cross-references so that you can easily follow a topic across chapters. A few sections were also edited for length so that other important Windows 98 SE subjects could be included.

Who Can Benefit from This Book?

Windows 98 Second Edition Complete is designed to meet the needs of a wide range of computer users working with the newest version of Microsoft's operating system. Windows 98 is an extraordinarily rich environment, with some elements that everyone uses, as well as features that may be essential to some users but of no interest to others. Therefore, while you could read this book from beginning to end—from installation through the features and on to expert tuning and tinkering—all of you may not need to read every chapter. The table of contents and the index will guide you to the subjects you're looking for.

Beginners Even if you have only a little familiarity with computers and their basic terminology, this book will start you working with Windows 98. You'll find step-by-step instructions for all the operations involved in running application programs and managing your computer system, along with clear explanations of essential concepts. You may want to start with chapters from the ABCs or No Experience Required titles.

Intermediate users Chances are, you already know how to do routine tasks in Windows 3.1, 95, or 98. You know your way around a few productivity applications, use e-mail extensively, browse the Web a little, and maybe have a favorite game or two. You also know there is always more to learn about working more effectively, and you want to get up to speed on the new Windows 98 SE features. Throughout this book you'll find instructions for just about anything you want to do. Nearly every chapter has nuggets of knowledge from which you can benefit.

Power users   Maybe you're a hardcore multimedia freak looking to upgrade your hardware to take advantage of Windows 98 SE's expanded capabilities, or the unofficial guru of your office network, or an Internaut ready to try HTML authoring. There's plenty for you here, too; particularly in chapters from the Mastering books, *Expert Guide to Windows 98*, and the two *PC Upgrade and Maintenance* titles.

This book is for people using Windows 98 SE in any environment. You may be a SOHO (small-office/home-office) user, working with a stand-alone computer or a simple peer-to-peer network with no administrators or technical staff to rely on. In that case, you'll find plenty of information about maintaining, troubleshooting, and upgrading your computer and about sharing resources. Or you may be working within a larger network and simply want to get a leg up, quickly and inexpensively, as your office migrates to the new operating system. If you belong to both camps, with a home or laptop computer as well as one at work, you may be especially interested in Chapter 13's coverage of Dial-Up Networking, a tool for telecommuting and for connecting via modem to the Internet.

How This Book Is Organized

Windows 98 Second Edition Complete has four parts, consisting of 26 chapters and four appendices.

Part I: Windows 98 Second Edition   Not surprisingly, the biggest portion of the book is devoted to Windows 98 SE itself. The 15 chapters in Part I cover all the Windows essentials—installing Windows 98 SE, touring the Desktop, creating shortcuts to programs and files you use frequently, using the Control Panel to customize your computer system, working with printers, and much more. You'll learn about Windows 98 SE's extensive support for multimedia and about its tools for keeping your computer trouble-free. Anyone moving from a previous Windows version (3.1, 95, or 98) will want to start with Chapter 1's summary of the new features.

Part II: The Internet and Windows 98 Second Edition   One of the most significant features of Windows 98 (and 98 SE) is the integration of Internet Explorer with Windows Explorer and the Desktop. The extensive Sybex library of Internet books has already helped guide hundreds of thousands of users into cyberspace. Part II of this book takes an in-depth look at the Internet and the tools you've just acquired for browsing the Web, exchanging e-mail, subscribing to channels, and even building your own Web site. You'll also learn about Netscape Communicator, the most popular alternative to Internet Explorer, and about security issues such as screening inappropriate content and maintaining privacy for financial transactions.

Part III: Your PC and Hardware   If you're responsible for maintaining your own computer and for deciding what components to upgrade and when, you'll appreciate the last three chapters of this book. You'll learn how to protect your computer from physical hazards, and you'll get some guidelines for buying a new computer. If you don't want to spend thousands of dollars to get a system that's ready for Windows 98 SE and the Internet, check out the chapter on adding RAM. With very little money and the expertise you'll gain here, you just might give your current PC another couple of years of useful life.

Part IV: Windows 98 Second Edition User's References   The appendices here are designed for quick lookup—or casual browsing. There's an alphabetical reference to the essential commands and features of Windows 98 SE, a glossary of Windows and Internet terminology you may encounter, and a listing of Internet contact information for vendors of hardware and utility software.

A Few Typographical Conventions

When a Windows operation requires a series of choices from menus or dialog boxes, the ➤ symbol is used to guide you through the instructions, like this: "Select Programs ➤ Accessories ➤ System Tools ➤ System Information." The items the ➤ symbol separates may be menu names, toolbar icons, checkboxes, or other elements of the Windows interface—anyplace you can make a selection.

`This typeface` is used to identify Internet URLs and HTML code, and **boldface type** is used whenever you need to type something into a text box.

You'll find these types of special notes throughout the book:

TIP
You'll see a lot of these Tips—quicker and smarter ways to accomplish a task, which the authors have based on many, many months spent testing and using Windows 98 SE.

NOTE

You'll see these Notes, too. They usually represent alternate ways to accomplish a task or some additional information that needs to be highlighted.

WARNING

In a very few places you'll see a Warning like this one. There are few because it's hard to do irrevocable things in Windows 98 SE unless you work very hard at it. But when you see a warning, do pay attention to it.

YOU'LL ALSO SEE "SIDEBAR" BOXES LIKE THIS

These boxed sections provide added explanation of special topics that are noted briefly in the surrounding discussion, but that you may want to explore separately. For example, Chapter 9, on Windows 98 SE's multimedia features, includes a look at the likely future of Web TV technology; and Chapter 19, on security issues for Internet users, includes a sidebar explaining how the SSL (Secured Sockets Layer) method of security works. Each sidebar has a heading that announces the topic so you can quickly decide whether it's something you need to know about.

For More Information...

See the Sybex Web site, www.sybex.com, to learn more about all the books that went into *Windows 98 Second Edition Complete*. On the site's Catalog page, you'll find links to any book you're interested in. Also be sure to check the Sybex site for late-breaking developments about Windows 98 SE itself.

We hope you enjoy this book and find it useful. Happy computing!

PART I
WINDOWS 98 SECOND EDITION

Chapter 1

INTRODUCING WINDOWS 98 SECOND EDITION

Windows 98 Second Edition (SE) is an upgrade to Windows 98. In the past, Microsoft has released upgrades and bug fixes in the form of Service Packs, so Windows 98 SE is a somewhat new development in the life cycle of an operating system.

If you recently purchased a new Windows computer, you most likely have Windows 98 SE on that machine. Windows 98 SE is also available on a retail CD and on an upgrade CD that you can order from Microsoft's Web site (www.microsoft.com). In addition, you can download some new features from the Windows Update Web site (choose Start ➤ Windows Update).

In the first part of this chapter, we're going to take a look at the new features in Windows 98 SE, and then in the second part, we'll talk about how Windows 98 SE differs from Windows 95—just in case some of you are upgrading directly from Windows 95 to Windows 98 SE.

• •

Adapted from *Upgrading to Windows 98*
by Charlie Russel and Sharon Crawford
ISBN 0-7821-2190-X   464 pages $19.95

What's New in Windows 98 SE?

If you upgraded to Windows 98 SE from Windows 98, you won't notice many differences at first glance. The basic user interface is the same, but you'll find that you access some features in new ways. For example, the Accessories menu now includes an item called Internet Tools, and you can use it to open the Internet Connection Wizard, NetMeeting, Personal Web Server, and the Web Publishing Wizard.

The new features are in three primary categories:

- Internet Explorer 5
- Bug fixes, security patches, and updates
- New support for technologies

In this section, we'll look at all of these categories briefly and then point you to the related chapters in this book where you'll find the details.

Internet Explorer 5

Windows 98 and Internet Explorer 4 were described as "tightly integrated," and this is also the case with Windows 98 SE and Internet Explorer 5. A difference in this integration, however, is that Active Desktop and the Channel bar are no longer installed by default. If you already had these features on your computer, they will still be there after you install Internet Explorer 5, but they are not available otherwise.

If you noodle around with Internet Explorer 5 a bit, you'll soon discover features that exemplify the primary design goal for this new browser version: to simplify and provide step-savers. For example, in addition to using the Address bar to go to an Internet resource and open a file on your local system, you can now also enter a word or phrase and initiate a search. When you enter a search term and click the Search button, the Search bar opens, as shown in Figure 1.1.

NOTE
For more on searching, see Chapter 23, *Finding and Downloading Windows Software Online*.

Introducing Windows 98 Second Edition 5

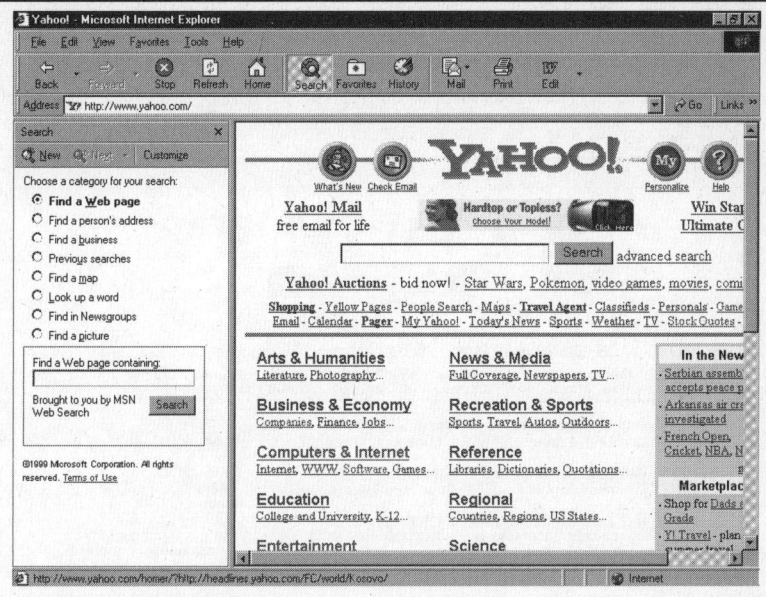

FIGURE 1.1: The Search bar in Internet Explorer

Choose View ➢ Toolbars ➢ Radio to take a look at another new feature: Windows Radio. Internet Explorer adds the Radio toolbar (see Figure 1.2), which you can use to tune in to live programming from radio stations around the world.

> **NOTE**
>
> For more on Windows Radio, see Chapter 19, *Browsing the Web with Internet Explorer*.

Also included with Internet Explorer 5 is Outlook Express 5, which is shown in Figure 1.3. The most prominent new feature of Outlook Express is Identities, which you can use to share a single Outlook Express installation with multiple people. This is a handy feature for a family or for someone who wants to customize messages for business use, personal use, and so on.

6 Chapter One

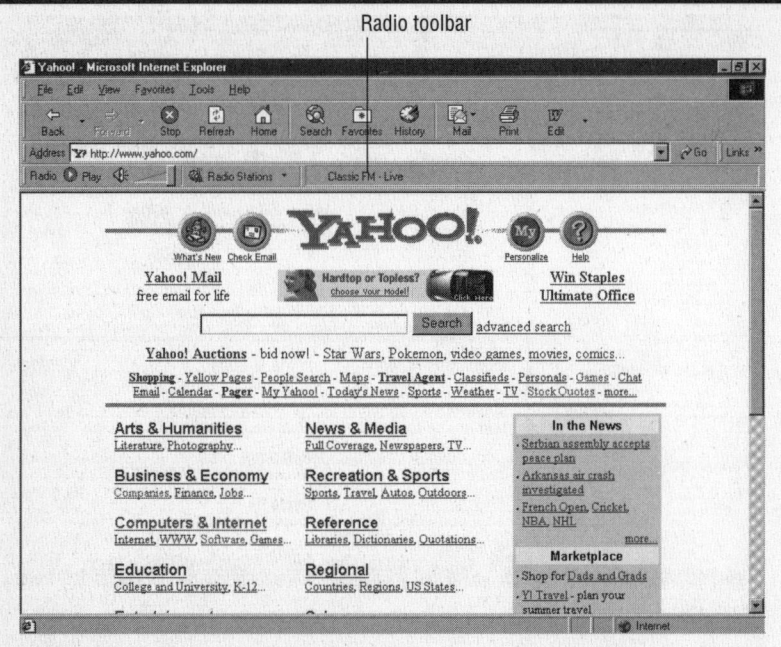

FIGURE 1.2: Windows Radio is a new feature in Internet Explorer 5.

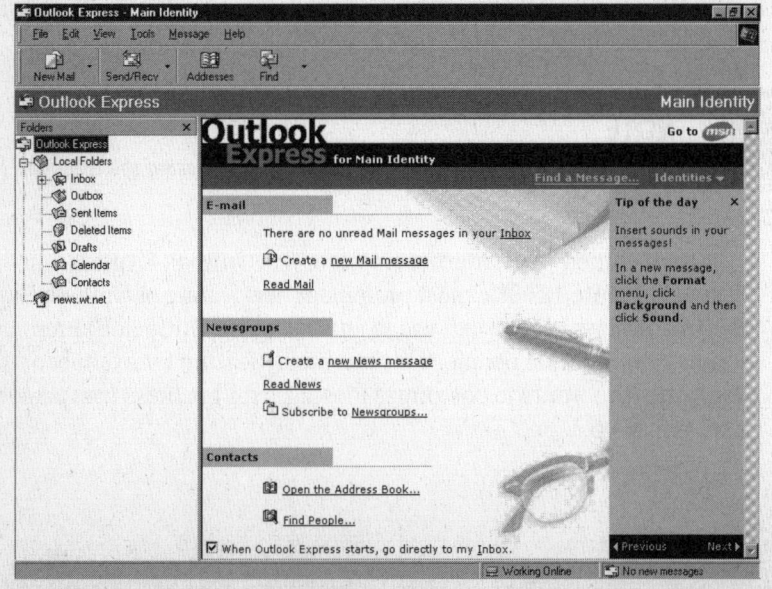

FIGURE 1.3: Outlook Express 5 is new with Internet Explorer 5.

> **NOTE**
> For much more on these and other features of Internet Explorer 5, see the chapters in Part II, *The Internet and Windows 98 Second Edition*.

Bug Fixes, Security Patches, and Updates

The Windows 98 Service Pack is part of Windows 98 SE and contains bug fixes, security patches, and updates, including fixes for known Year 2000 issues. Dial-up networking has been enhanced to further protect connections with strengthened password management and data encryption.

New Support for Technologies

Although most users will probably agree that the main advantage in upgrading to Windows 98 SE is access to Internet Explorer 5 and its components, such as Outlook Express and NetMeeting, Windows 98 SE includes new support for a number of technologies. If any of the following are important to the way you work or use your computer, you'll want to know about these upgrades:

- Active Accessibility, which allows software developers to develop operating system and application aids for users with disabilities
- Distributed Component Object Model (DCOM), which allows you to distribute applications across networks, including the Internet
- Device Bay Support, which allows you to add or upgrade peripherals with opening your hardware.
- WebTV for Windows, which allows your computer to display both standard and interactive television broadcasts
- Wake-On-LAN, which allows a computer on a network to "wake" another computer that is in a low power state

In addition, Windows 98 SE includes several fonts that support the euro glyph, the symbol for the single European Union currency.

> **NOTE**
> For information on fonts and printing, see Chapter 8, *Printers and Printing*.

Internet Connection Sharing (ICS) is another new feature, which you can use to configure a network so that all computers can share a single connection to the Internet. For all the details, see Chapter 17, *Connecting to the Internet.*

How Is Windows 98 SE Different from Windows 95?

We know that some of you have been using Windows 95 (and probably even Windows 3.1) and so are totally new to the Windows 98 environment. If you've jumped from Windows 3.1 to Windows 98 SE, you've made a huge leap. The following sidebar is just for you.

> **FOR WINDOWS 3.1 USERS: WHAT'S DIFFERENT ABOUT WINDOWS 98 SE**
>
> The introduction of Windows 95 brought some major improvements over Windows 3.1. Here's a rundown of some of these features, which haven't changed in Windows 98 SE.
>
> One of the most crucial improvements is the change from a 16-bit operating system to one using 32-bit pieces of information. You don't really have to know anything about the jump to a 32-bit system other than that it makes lots of good things possible.
>
> Because this is a 32-bit system and built with today's computers in mind, other features and refinements are possible. One of the biggest is the switch to what's called *32-bit memory addressing*, which is a way of identifying locations in memory. You probably know that computers work with information in the form of binary numbers—ones and zeros. A binary number 32 digits (bits) wide can have 2^{32} possible values, so 32-bit addressing means that the computer can work with up to 2^{32} pieces of information in its memory.
>
> Intel introduced a microprocessor that allowed 32-bit addressing back in 1988, but DOS and Windows 3.*x* were limited by a peculiar system that managed to encompass a sort of 20-bit addressing. One result of this poor construct is that only 640 kilobytes are available for DOS programs. Another is that only 64 kilobytes were available for Windows 3.1 resources. This explains how you can have multi-megabytes of RAM and still run out of Windows resources.
>
> CONTINUED →

Introducing Windows 98 Second Edition

With Windows 95, 98, and 98 SE, we have full 32-bit addressing. This means, among other things, that a 32-bit application running in Windows has access to essentially unlimited amounts of memory—in fact, up to 2 gigabytes.

Although Windows 3.1 could multitask—sort of—Windows 95, 98, and 98 SE *really* can. This means the system makes decisions about priorities and doesn't depend on an application to release its hold on the CPU before taking care of other business. In actual practice, it means that even if the hourglass is showing for one of your programs, you can usually switch to another program and do something useful. You can copy or format disks while printing a document. Or you can download your e-mail from the Internet while writing letters or entering information into a database.

You will also notice that multitasking works much better than it ever did in Windows 3.1. For one thing, it's faster; and most important, a disagreement between programs is much less likely to bring your whole system to a halt.

Another improvement with Windows 98 SE is the introduction of long filenames. Everyone coming from the world of DOS and Windows 3.1 has had to deal with the burden of the MS-DOS 8.3 file-naming restrictions. With only eight characters (often the extension was used by the program itself), your files ended up with names that were cryptic at best. What are you to make of a file called SSCRANRL.DOC? Six months down the road, were you likely to remember what it stood for?

Windows 95 brought relief in the form of long filenames. Now instead of SSCRANRL.DOC, you can call the file `Susan Stamberg's Cranberry Relish Recipe`. Filenames can be up to 255 characters long, can include spaces, and can include both capital and lowercase letters.

The change from Windows 3.1 to Windows 95 was a radical one. It wasn't just the exterior that changed; the plumbing and wiring were completely redone to give the system important new capabilities such as true multitasking.

The step up from Windows 95 to Windows 98 or Windows 98 SE is less drastic. Although the core operating system code has been tuned for better performance, it remains the same basic plumbing and wiring.

Using Folders and Shortcuts

Windows 95 introduced the concepts of folders and shortcuts. *Folder* is really just a new name for what used to be called a *directory*—a division of a hard drive or other storage device in which files and other folders can be stored. Though it took a while, the new name is catching on. Earlier versions of Windows, as well as other operating systems, have long used a file folder icon to represent a directory. Referring to directories as folders makes the name consistent with the image, and more accessible to users with little technical knowledge.

> **NOTE**
> Because folders and directories are the same thing, the various authors who have contributed to *Windows 98 Second Edition Complete* use both terms interchangeably.

Shortcuts were genuinely new with Windows 95, and they are unchanged in Windows 98 and Windows 98 SE. Many users, however, are still learning how to make the best use of them. Windows 98 made a significant improvement in one of the shortcuts set up during installation. Microsoft's Office 95 and Office 97 suites attempt to force users to keep their work in a folder called My Documents, an approach that might not suit everyone. Windows 98 rescued the idea of a standard location for documents, without attempting to force the user to give it a particular name. The My Documents icon on the Windows 98 or 98 SE Desktop is a system icon, but you can modify it to point to any folder you wish.

> **FOR WINDOWS 3.1 USERS: SHORTCUTS IN WINDOWS 98 SE**
>
> Shortcuts are similar in some ways to the icons in a Program Manager group, but they are so much more flexible that the comparison could be misleading. Shortcuts are small files that serve as pointers. *Opening* a shortcut actually opens the object that the shortcut points to. That can be a program, as in Windows 3.1, but it can also be a document, a folder, or another resource available to your computer, such as a printer.
>
> In addition, shortcuts can be placed anywhere you want them: on your Desktop, on the Start menu, or in any folder. Details about shortcuts are in Chapter 4, *Shortcuts Galore*.

Seamless Web Connections

Even though millions more people now use computers than when Windows 95 was released, many are still intimidated when faced with using the Internet. Windows helped make PCs easier to use, but the Internet remained a whole different world. The Internet's most popular features are those on the World Wide Web, accessible with browser software. As you know from reading the first part of this chapter, the Internet Explorer browser is an integral part of Windows 98 SE and makes accessing and using the Internet as easy as clicking the mouse.

And if you aren't connected to the Internet yet, Windows 98 SE can help you correct that lamentable situation! After installing Windows 98 SE, you will find an Online Services folder on your Desktop. Opening it will reveal shortcuts to setup programs for several major online services and Internet Service Providers. These include America Online, AT&T WorldNet, CompuServe, and Prodigy Internet. You'll also find a separate shortcut to set up access to MSN.

As long as your machine includes a modem, all you have to do is choose a service, and Windows 98 SE will install the software and allow you to connect and set up an account.

What About My Mail?

Windows 98 and Windows 98 SE both include Outlook Express, a program for handling Internet e-mail. It's much less complex and easier to use than the Exchange/Windows Messaging system that was part of Windows 95. This is mostly good news for home users and those working in small offices who don't have their own e-mail systems. Offices and companies that do have their own e-mail system based on either a local area network or an intranet can, of course, continue to use it.

Besides handling Internet e-mail, Outlook Express allows you to make use of Internet newsgroups. This is a big advance, as Windows 95 had no built-in access to newsgroups. Now you can sign on to an Internet news server and participate in discussions on any imaginable topic. The Internet has tens of thousands of newsgroups, with topics ranging from assassination conspiracies to software support.

> **NOTE**
> The uses of Outlook Express are described in Chapter 18, *Communicating with E-Mail*.

> **WARNING**
> The switch from Exchange to Outlook Express has one big drawback: Windows 98 and Windows 98 SE have no built-in fax capability. If that's important, you might want to continue using Exchange. To do that, you should install Windows 98 SE as an upgrade as discussed in Chapter 2, *Installing Windows 98 SE on Your Computer*.

Windows Update

One of the big problems faced by many computer users is keeping their whole hardware/software system up-to-date. You may be one of the millions who have installed a new game or other video-intensive program, only to find it won't run because your system doesn't have the latest driver for the video display. Drivers for video, sound, and many other types of hardware are constantly being updated, but few companies send these updates out routinely, even if you have registered your hardware.

The Windows Update program included with Windows 98 SE is designed to compare the drivers and other system software you are using with a master database stored on Microsoft's Web site. When it finds that a newer version is available, it will offer you the option of upgrading.

Other Cool Stuff That Wasn't Available in Windows 95

The Windows 98 SE package has lots more goodies, from system tools to new hardware support to a new file system that makes better use of large hard drives. Here are some of the most important ones:

System tools Windows 98 SE includes several system tools to keep your computer running at its best and to help avoid problems. These are discussed in Chapter 11, *Maintaining the System*.

Input and output devices Details on such treats as digital cameras and force-feedback joysticks, among others, are in Chapter 10, *Hardware Mastery*.

Power management functions Newer computers can go on standby, with greatly reduced power consumption, and still carry out scheduled tasks such as hard-disk maintenance and the downloading of Web pages. The computer can restart quickly, with programs running just as you left them.

FAT32 This is a method of storing information on hard drives that uses larger drives more efficiently. It is an important upgrade to the hard drive file system that came preinstalled on some Windows 95 computers, but it was "not available in stores" until Windows 98.

What's Next?

Now that Charlie Russel and Sharon Crawford have given you an overview of Windows 98 Second Edition, they and the other contributors of this book will start digging into just what you can do with it. The next chapter shows you how to install Windows 98 SE on your computer.

Chapter 2

INSTALLING WINDOWS 98 SE ON YOUR COMPUTER

Chances are good that your computer came installed with Windows 98 Second Edition already, in which case reading this chapter isn't necessary for you. On the other hand, if you are still using Windows 3.x, Windows 95, or the first edition of Windows 98, or if you have no version of Windows on your computer at all, you'll want to read this chapter. If at some point after you install Windows you discover that you are missing some of the components discussed in this book, you can install them later from the Windows Control Panel's Add/Remove Programs applet, as explained in Chapter 7, *Customizing Windows 98 SE with the Control Panel*.

Adapted from *Mastering Windows 98 Second Edition*
by Robert Cowart
ISBN 0-7821-2618-9   928 pages $39.99

There are several basic scenarios when installing Windows 98 SE:

- Installing on a new or newly formatted hard disk
- Installing over Windows 3.x
- Installing over Windows 95
- Installing over Windows 98 (first edition)

NOTE
Not sure which version of Windows 98 you have? Right-click My Computer and choose Properties from the shortcut menu that appears. On the General tab of the System Properties dialog box, you should see a version listed. If you already have Windows 98 SE, you'll see the words "Second Edition" under System. The version number for Second Edition is 4.10.2222 A.

Within each scenario, there are sub-scenarios, based on the source of the installation programs:

- Local CD-ROM or hard disk
- Installation files copied to your hard disk
- Network CD-ROM or hard disk

In the vast majority of cases, you'll be installing from a local CD-ROM drive, over an existing Windows installation.

NOTE
If you have a previous version of Windows on your computer, you can install from a DOS prompt, but Microsoft recommends installing from within Windows.

Although I don't recommend it, you can choose to install Windows into a directory other than the existing Windows directory. This lets you install a "clean" version of Windows 98 SE, with no settings pulled in from the earlier installation. Although this assures you of having a fresh Registry and might make you feel safer about trying out the new version, it will be a hassle in the long run.

What I *do* recommend is upgrading *over* your existing Windows directory, by which I mean installing into the same directory; typically this would be `C:\Windows`. Besides, when you install over an existing version of Windows, you are offered the option of saving your old system

Installing Windows 98 SE on Your Computer

files, so you can effortlessly revert to the old system if you want. (But be warned that if you're currently running Windows 95 or 98, it can take as much as 110 MB of additional space to perform this save.)

When you opt to install over an existing Windows version (that is, 3.x, 95, or 98—see the note below about Windows NT), various important settings—such as program INI settings, file locations, program associations, program groups, and so forth—are transferred into your new version. The most important advantage of this approach is that you won't have to install all your applications (such as Microsoft Office) again for Windows 98 SE. (If you install to a separate directory, things get pretty complicated, because with two separate versions of Windows on the same computer, the changes you make in one version don't carry over to the other.)

> **NOTE**
> If you are installing on a computer that has Windows NT on it, read the NT section at the end of this chapter. You cannot install *over* NT, though 98 SE can coexist *with* NT on the same drive.

Microsoft has done a laudable job of making the Windows 98 SE installation process pretty painless, thanks to the Setup Wizard, which provides a pleasant question-and-answer interface. It's been made even simpler than in Windows 95 by asking only a few questions up front, and then doing the rest of the work on its own without your intervention. Therefore, I'll spare you the boredom of walking you through *every* step here on paper. Rather, I'll get you going and discuss some of the decisions you'll have to make along the way.

> **TIP**
> Setup requires approximately 210 MB of hard disk space to complete. The exact amount will vary depending on the setup options you choose, as well as on the configuration of the hard drive on which you are installing Windows. For additional information about space requirements, see the file \Win98\setup.txt on the Windows 98 Second Edition CD-ROM before you begin installation.

> **WARNING**
> Microsoft strongly suggests that you back up any important existing data and programs before you install Windows 98 SE, just to be safe. Also, be sure to take Setup's advice about making a new Startup disk. Startup disks that you may have created with earlier versions of Windows are not compatible with some features of Windows 98 SE.

Easiest Approach: A Full Upgrade from an Earlier Version of Windows

First off, you'll need to decide whether you are going to install from CD-ROM or from your local area network. I highly recommend using a CD (or networked CD or hard disk if one is available). If you choose to copy the installation files to your hard disk, see `\Win98\setup.txt` on the Windows 98 Second Edition CD-ROM for special instructions.

Before beginning, make sure you have at least 210 MB of free hard-disk space on the drive onto which you're going to install Windows. You can use Windows Explorer or the DOS **dir** command to check this.

To begin the setup process:

1. Boot your computer into Windows.
2. Insert the CD into the CD-ROM drive.

> **TIP**
>
> As I mentioned earlier, if you're using the CD, the CD-ROM drive needn't be on your local computer. Furthermore, you can install over a local area network or dial-up connection from a shared directory or drive that contains the CD (or a copy of all of its files). You simply switch to that directory (via File Manager in Windows 3.*x* or Windows Explorer in Windows 95 or 98) and run `Setup.exe`.

3. I recommend you read through three text files that contain last-minute information about Windows 98 SE. These files, which might provide special tips about your brand of computer or cards, printers, and other accessories, are called `readme.txt`, `setuptip.txt`, and `setup.txt`. The first two can be found in the root directory of the CD-ROM, and `setup.txt` can be found in the `\Win98` directory. To read these files, just get to them via the File Manager or Windows Explorer, and then double-click on them.

4. If you're in Windows 3.*x*, switch to the File Manager or Program Manager, open the File menu, and choose Run. If you're

Installing Windows 98 SE on Your Computer 19

running Windows 95, go to Start ➢ Run. Then enter whichever of the following commands is appropriate for your circumstance (i.e., depending on whether you're installing from a CD-ROM, hard disk, or network):

- If installing from a CD, enter **d:\win95\setup**.

- If installing from a network, click Browse and navigate to the network computer and CD-ROM drive where the disk is located.

(You may have to replace d: in the above statement with the appropriate drive letter for your machine.) Alternatively, in File Manager or Windows Explorer you can look around for setup.exe and double-click it. In a few seconds, you'll be greeted with a fancy blue screen and some directions about installation (as in Figure 2.1).

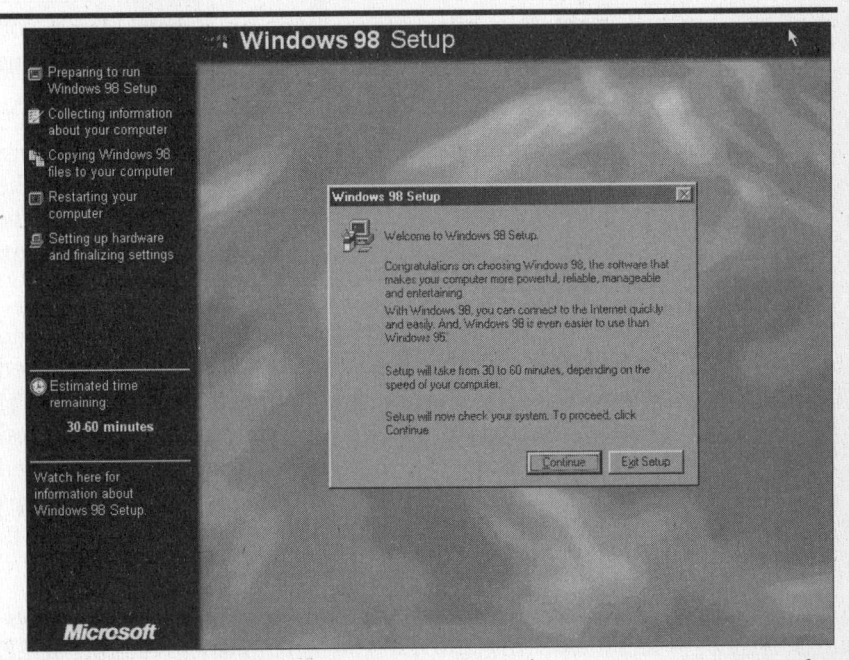

FIGURE 2.1: The first welcome screen when installing over an existing version of Windows

> **NOTE**
>
> If you install from the DOS prompt instead of from Windows, you will have more questions to answer than the ones you're asked from this series of screens, relating to your choice for the destination directory for Windows and concerning which components to install. If you're interested in this approach, see the upcoming section, "Installing to a Fresh Disk or New Directory."

5. Click Continue to let Setup check out your computer. If you have too little disk space, you'll be alerted.

   ▶ You'll also be alerted to quit other programs if they are running. This is because Setup might bomb, in which case any work you have open in those programs could be lost. Switch to any program in which you have open work, save the work, close the program, and switch back to Setup.

   ▶ If you see a warning pertaining to your anti-virus software, follow the instructions on screen. Ideally you should disable the anti-virus software before proceeding with the installation.

6. Next, you'll see a license agreement. If you agree to the terms, click Yes, then click Next. You will be prompted to enter the Product Key, which is a 25-digit number you should have received with your Windows 98 SE CD. Click Next again when you have entered it.

7. Setup now checks out what hardware is in your computer, and initializes the system's Registry file. It will check for installed components if you are upgrading from a previous version of Windows, and it will check to see that you have enough hard disk space. Assuming there is enough disk space (you checked for that earlier, didn't you?), you won't see any error messages about that. If you do, see the "Removing Uninstall Files to Free Up Disk Space" section later in this chapter.

   You'll also be asked at this point if you want to save your "system files." This is so that you can uninstall Windows 98 SE if it doesn't work, or if you decide you don't like it, or if for some other reason you want to be able to go back to your old operating system. (See the "Reverting to the Previous Operating System" section later in this chapter.) Click Yes or No. If in doubt, click Yes, then Next. If you have more than one

Installing Windows 98 SE on Your Computer 21

hard drive, you will also be asked which disk you want the uninstall files saved on.

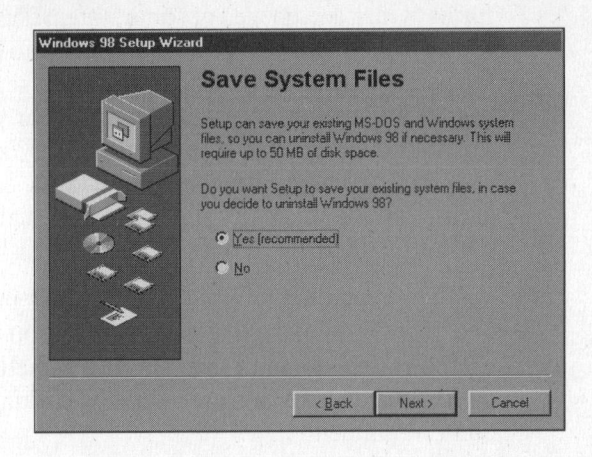

8. Your current system files will be backed up to a hidden, compressed file. If doing that would leave too little space for installation of Windows 98 SE, you'll be alerted and given the option of skipping the backup in order to save disk space.

9. Next, you're asked about your location. This will allow Windows to more easily set you up to receive local news and information via the Internet "channels." For now, just click the country you are in, and then click Next. (Scroll the list if necessary.)

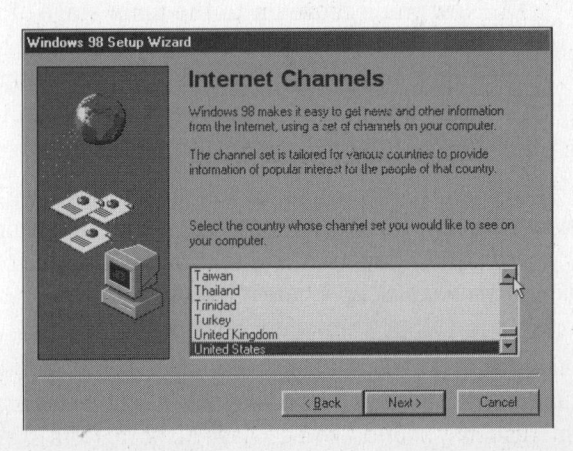

10. At this point, Setup offers the opportunity to create an emergency startup disk. This is for starting your computer in case the hard disk is damaged or some system files get lost or corrupted. Since these are problems that could happen to even the best of machines, it's a good idea to make such a disk and keep it in a readily accessible drawer near your computer. This disk is also necessary for uninstalling Windows 98 SE in case the installation bombs. Just read the screen and then click Next. Setup creates the list of files that will be put on the startup disk, but it doesn't make the disk yet.

11. You'll be prompted to insert a floppy disk in the disk drive and click OK to make the disk. Anything on the floppy disk will be erased, so don't use one with something important on it. You can skip this procedure by clicking Cancel, but I don't recommend it.

    ▶ For reasons given earlier, it's a very good idea to proceed with the creation of the startup disk now. However, if you don't have a floppy with you, you can cancel this process for now and continue with the rest of the installation. You can always return to Setup at some other time (even after you've been using Windows 98 SE for months) to make a startup disk later. However, if Setup crashes for some reason, you could be left with a computer that won't boot.

12. Now you'll move on to the main stage of the installation process: the copying of files from the source to your hard disk. This is the portion that takes the most time. Click Next to start this process. A status bar keeps you abreast of the progress of the file copying operation.

At this point, your computer will reboot. Remove the floppy disk if you haven't already, and let the computer restart. If nothing happens for an extended period, you may have to turn the machine off and then on again. It *should* pick up where it left off.

Upon restarting, a Windows 98 SE screen appears with blue clouds on it along with the words "Getting ready to run Windows for the first time." This screen may stay there a *long time* (15 minutes or more) and your hard disk may sound like a garbage disposal (lots of activity), but that's okay. Really. Setup is doing some major housekeeping, and possibly defragmenting your hard disk. Just sit tight.

Installing Windows 98 SE on Your Computer   23

> **NOTE**
> I've actually had to sit for 20 minutes while waiting for Windows to do its initial housecleaning. As long as the hard disk light is still lighting up, or you hear hard disk activity, all is well. Don't despair unless everything goes silent for several minutes.

Now you're in the phase in which hardware drivers are installed. Plug-and-Play devices are detected first, and then older, non–Plug-and-Play hardware is detected.

Then the system may reboot again in order to load the hardware drivers it just set up. Devices such as PCMCIA cards should initialize. Again, if the system hangs (nothing happens for a long period of time), turn the computer off and on again using the power switch.

Next, a number of other things are adjusted:

- ▶ Control Panel options are set up.
- ▶ Programs on the Start menu are set up.
- ▶ Windows Help is installed.
- ▶ MS-DOS program settings are adjusted.
- ▶ Applications are set to start faster.
- ▶ Some system configuration is optimized.

The last activity, updating system settings, can take a bit of time, like five to ten minutes. But a progress bar lets you know how it's going. A few files may be copied from the CD at this time, so make sure the CD is still available.

Again, the system restarts. The blue clouds will appear. It may take a couple of minutes for the Windows Desktop to appear. If you are updating from a previous version of Windows, you should see the same Desktop background or wallpaper you had before. You'll be prompted to enter your username and password.

> **TIP**
> You may choose a username and password now and enter it if you like. Remember the password for the next time you log into Windows 98 SE. If you don't enter a password, you won't be prompted for a name and password during startup in the future.

After that, the computer may even restart one more time. Once it does, you're up and running. Turn to Chapter 1 to begin learning what's new and exciting about Windows 98 Second Edition.

INSTALLING TO A FRESH DISK OR NEW DIRECTORY

You may prefer to install Windows 98 SE into a new directory for one of three reasons:

- ▶ You have no version of Windows on the machine.

- ▶ *Or* you have an existing version of Windows on the machine, but want to keep that version and set up Windows 98 SE, too. Then, by changing directory names or using some third-party utility program such as Partition Magic or BootCom, you can choose which version boots up. (This option is for confident, advanced users.)

- ▶ *Or* you want to control which components of Windows get installed. When you install to a new directory you have many more options than when upgrading over an existing installation.

To control the destination directory, you must (1) run Setup from a DOS prompt, and (2) boot in such a way as to have access to the CD-ROM drive, or, if you're installing across a network, to the network drive. If you have Windows 95 on the machine, the best way to do this is to create a Windows 95 emergency startup disk and boot from that. (To create this disk, go to Control Panel ➢ Add/Remove Programs ➢ Startup Disk.) If you had a CD-ROM drive available to you when you created the startup disk, it should have CD driver support files on them. Once you've booted to DOS, switch to the Setup source disk and run `setup.exe`.

When running Setup from DOS, ScanDisk runs first, checking the hard disk media. Assuming that all is okay (see the following section if it's not), exit ScanDisk by typing X (for Exit) when prompted. Setup will proceed, temporarily in character mode, then in a GUI mode with graphics, blue background, and mouse functionality.

After accepting the terms of the license agreement, you'll be given the option of choosing a hard disk directory for your Windows 98 SE installation. The default will be the existing Windows directory if there is one, but you can create a different directory at this point by typing a name for

Installing Windows 98 SE on Your Computer

it. Next, you'll see a series of screens asking for your input or verification concerning the following tasks:

- Choose which set of Windows 98 SE components to install: Typical, Portable, Compact, or Custom (your choice).
- Provide your name and company name.
- Select specific components.
- Provide or verify your network ID: computer name, workgroup, and workstation description.
- Verify your computer settings: Keyboard, Language, Regional Variants, and User Interface (Windows 98 or 3.1).
- Choose your Location. (You can simply choose the country at this point.)
- Create a Windows 98 SE emergency startup disk.

The rest of the installation will go as explained in the previous section.

> **TIP**
> If you have a situation that requires additional setup options—for example, you may be a LAN administrator and want remote setup capabilities—refer to the Microsoft Windows 98 Resource Kit.

FINDING AND FIXING HARD-DISK PROBLEMS DURING INSTALLATION

The Setup program automatically runs ScanDisk to check for problems on your hard disk before proceeding. If it finds problems on your hard disk, the setup process won't continue until they are fixed. It's also possible that you'll see a message during a later stage of the setup process that says you have to run ScanDisk to fix the problems.

> **WARNING**
> The MS-DOS–based version of ScanDisk that Setup runs may detect long-file-name errors, but it can't correct them. These errors will not prevent Setup from proceeding, but once it completes, you should run the new Windows version of ScanDisk from within Windows 98 SE to correct these errors.

To run ScanDisk most effectively:

1. Exit from the Setup program (and quit Windows if it's running).

2. Boot to a DOS prompt that offers access to the drive you're installing from.

3. Insert the CD into the drive, and from a DOS prompt, type the following:

   `d:scandisk.exe /all`

   (replacing the "*d*" with the letter for the drive that contains the Setup disk; for example, "`e:`" if that is the letter for your CD-ROM drive).

4. Follow the instructions on your screen to fix any problems that ScanDisk finds.

5. Run Setup again (from Windows if it's available on your machine; otherwise, run it from a DOS prompt).

> **TIP**
> If you have problems or questions about Setup that are not covered in this chapter, check out the file called `setup.txt` on the CD. On the CD, you'll find it in the `Win98` **directory.**

Reverting to the Previous Operating System

Assuming you opted during your Windows 98 SE setup to save your previous version's system files, you can revert to that version of Windows in case of a failed or unappreciated installation. (For exceptions to the "Saving System Files" scenario, see the upcoming sidebar.)

To uninstall Windows 98 SE and completely restore your system to its previous versions of MS-DOS and Windows 3.*x* or Windows 95 or 98, follow these steps:

1. Choose Start ➤ Settings ➤ Control Panel.

2. Double-click Add/Remove Programs.

Installing Windows 98 SE on Your Computer

3. On the Install/Uninstall tab, click Windows 98, and then click Remove.

If you can't even get to the Start menu to begin the steps above (because of problems starting Windows 98), use your startup disk to start your computer and, from a DOS prompt, type **a: UNINSTAL** and press Enter. Here are a few notes to be mindful of when running `Uninstal`:

- The uninstall program needs to shut down Windows 98 SE. If your computer starts to run Windows 98 SE again on reboot, try restarting it again and this time quickly pressing F8 when you see the message "Starting Windows 98." (Note, though, that you might only have a fraction of a second to do this, depending on how fast your machine is. Another approach that may work, depending on your computer, is to hold down the Shift key during the bootup process.) Then choose Command Prompt Only and run `Uninstal` from this command prompt.

If you've misplaced your startup disk but can get to the DOS prompt, you can run `Uninstal` from the hard disk instead. There should be a copy of the `Uninstal` program in your `Windows` directory on the hard disk.

- If you saved your files on a drive other than C, you can use the /w option to specify the drive where the files are located. For example, if your system files were saved to drive E during installation, type **Uninstal /w e:** to access them on that drive.

WHY YOU CAN'T ALWAYS SAVE YOUR SYSTEM FILES

The option of saving your system files for a future uninstall is not always offered during setup. Here are some situations where Setup does not offer the option:

- You are upgrading over an earlier version of Windows 98 itself.
- *Or* you are installing to a new directory (in which case you don't need to *revert* to your previous version; instead, you can simply boot to the previous version's directory to run that version).
- *Or* you are running a version of MS-DOS earlier than 5 (in which case your system is automatically updated with the version of DOS that is used in Windows 98).

CONTINUED ➡

> In most other situations, you are given the option to save your system files. When you choose this option, Setup saves your system files in a hidden, compressed file on your local hard drive. (They cannot be saved to a network drive or a floppy disk.) If you have multiple local drives, you will be able to select the one you want to use.
>
> If you are not in one of the above exception situations but you see a message during setup about not being able to save your system files, refer to the "Setup Error Messages" section of the setup.txt file in the CD's Win98 directory or on the floppy installation disk.

Removing Uninstall Files to Free Up Disk Space

If you want to free up an additional 50 to 100 MB of disk space, you can remove the Uninstall files by following the steps below. Please note, however, that without the Uninstall files, you will no longer be able to uninstall Windows 98 SE. In short, save this operation until you're sure you're going to keep Windows 98 SE.

Here are the steps for removing the Uninstall files. Note that Windows 98 SE must be running to perform this operation.

1. Choose Start ➢ Settings ➢ Control Panel.
2. Double-click Add/Remove Programs.
3. On the Install/Uninstall tab, click Old Windows/MS-DOS System Files, and then click Remove.

Installing onto a Compressed Drive

If you have used compression software to compress your hard disk, or if a host drive or partition for your startup drive is compressed, you may get a message during setup that there is not enough space on the host partition of the compressed drive. If you get this message, you should free up some space on the specified drive, and then run Setup again. Note that if the drive was compressed with SuperStor or Stacker, you'll have to decompress the drive and remove the compression program before you can install Windows 98 SE. If you used Microsoft DriveSpace, you were smart: You don't have to decompress in order to free up extra space—you just tell it to free up the space.

Here are some other steps to freeing up space for your installation:

- If you are setting up Windows on a compressed drive, try setting it up on an uncompressed drive if possible.
- Delete any unneeded files on your host partition.
- If you are running Windows 3.1 and have a permanent swap file, try making it smaller. In the Control Panel, click the 386 Enhanced icon, and then click Virtual Memory. Then modify the size of your swap file.
- Use your disk compression software to free up some space on the host drive for the compressed drive.

And don't forget to check out the following subsections concerning particular compression programs.

WARNING
If you create a startup disk during setup, make sure you do *not* use a compressed disk for the startup disk.

SuperStor or Stacker Compressed Drive

If you have compressed your hard disk by using SuperStor, Setup may not be able to find your startup drive and install Windows 98 SE. If you get a message about this during setup, uncompress your disk, remove SuperStor, and then run Setup again.

Windows 98 Second Edition will not run on a Stacker-compressed hard drive. If you currently have Stacker v. 4.1 installed on your computer, uninstall Stacker before you upgrade to Windows 98 SE.

DriveSpace or DoubleSpace Compressed Drive

To free up some space on a compressed drive using DriveSpace or DoubleSpace, follow these steps:

1. Quit Windows and get to a DOS prompt.
2. Run `Drvspace.exe` or `Dblspace.exe` (probably in your DOS or Windows directory).
3. Select the compressed drive on which you want to free up some space.
4. On the Drive menu, select Change Size.

> **NOTE**
> If you notice a discrepancy between the amount of free space reported by Setup and the amount of space you *think* is available on your host drive, it may be because Windows is reserving some space for a swap file.

XtraDrive Compression

If you have compressed your hard disk by using XtraDrive and you are upgrading over a previous version of Windows, you'll have to turn off XtraDrive's *write cache* before doing the install. Here's how to do that:

1. Exit Windows and get to DOS.
2. Run `Vmu.exe` (XtraDrive's Volume Maintenance Utility).
3. Click Advanced Options, and then press Enter.
4. Set the EMS cache size to **0**.
5. Set the Conventional cache size to **1** (the minimum).
6. Set Allow Write Caching to **No**.
7. At the confirmation prompt, click Yes. You will see a message saying that you must restart your computer for the changes to take effect.
8. Quit the Volume Maintenance Utility, and then restart your computer.
9. Start Windows, and then run Windows 98 Setup again.

How to Install Windows 98 SE to a Machine Running Windows NT or Windows 2000

Although you can install Windows 98 SE to a machine that is already running Windows NT or Windows 2000, you must install it to a separate partition—you cannot install 98 or 98 SE *over* NT, or vice versa. (You may remember that you could install NT over Windows 3.*x* and share settings, associations, and so forth; Windows 98 SE does not work this way.) As a result, though you can have NT or 2000 and Windows 98 SE on the same computer and boot either operating system as you like, they won't share INI settings, installed applications, and other settings. This may change in the future, but in the meantime, it's simply an annoyance, because it means you'll have to install most applications twice—once for NT and once for Windows 98 SE.

If you're configured to multi-boot MS-DOS and Windows NT or Windows 2000   Boot to MS-DOS, and then run Windows 98 SE Setup from either MS-DOS, Windows 95, or Windows 98. You will not be able to install Windows 98 to a partition with a shared Windows 95/Windows NT configuration; you will need to install Windows 98 SE to a different partition.

If you're not configured to multi-boot MS-DOS and Windows NT or Windows 2000   You must first configure your computer to multi-boot MS-DOS and Windows NT, and then follow the instructions above.

If you were planning to boot to MS-DOS from a floppy disk and then run Windows 98 SE Setup   This approach permits you to install Windows 98 SE as you wish; however, you will no longer be able to boot to Windows NT or Windows 2000. You can *restore* Windows NT, however, by booting from the Windows NT boot/repair disk and then selecting the Repair option.

> **NOTE**
> Windows 98 SE Setup will not run on OS/2. You need to boot to MS-DOS and then run Setup from the MS-DOS prompt. For more about installing over OS/2, see the `setup.txt` file on floppy disk 1 or in the `readme` directory on the CD.

Multi-Booting Windows 98 SE with Linux

If you currently have a version of Linux installed on your computer and want to be able to multi-boot Windows 98 SE, you must install Windows on its own DOS partition. Create the partition using Disk Druid, and then run a normal MS-DOS prompt installation of Windows as described earlier.

When the installation is complete, reboot using your Linux boot floppy. The Windows 98 SE setup program erased LILO (the Linux Loader program), so you will have to reinstall it by running /sbin/lilo. LILO can then be configured to ask you which operating system you want to boot during startup.

What's Next?

Now that you've installed Windows 98 SE and have it running successfully, in the next chapter, Sharon Crawford and Neil Salkind give you a quick tour of the operating system's Desktop.

Chapter 3

Visiting the Windows 98 Desktop

In this chapter, we'll take a quick tour of the screen you see when Windows 98 SE first starts up. There'll be a description of each item you see on the Desktop as well as how to get more information on each item. Of course, everything can't be covered in detail here, so there are frequent references to later chapters—but we'll try not to bounce around any more than necessary.

Adapted from *ABCs of Windows 98*
by Sharon Crawford and Neil J. Salkind
ISBN 0-7821-1953-0   384 pages $19.99

The Start Button

The opening screen in Windows 98 SE (see Figure 3.1) is a mostly blank Desktop with a Taskbar running along the bottom of the screen and two or more icons located along the left side of the screen. Fortunately, there's a clear signal where to begin in the form of a Start button in the lower-left corner.

FIGURE 3.1: The Windows 98 SE Desktop displays the Taskbar and various icons.

> **NOTE**
> Your Desktop can contain many icons, depending on how Windows 98 SE was originally configured when it was installed. If you purchased a computer with Windows 98 SE already installed on it, there are probably items on the Start menu, the Programs submenu, and the Desktop in addition to the items that appear on your Desktop by default.

Click the Start button once to open a menu of choices. (To close the Start menu, click somewhere else on the Desktop.) Initially there will be only a few items, but they're enough to get you going. Starting from the top, the next few pages discuss what you'll see.

Programs

Slide the mouse pointer to Programs and you'll get a cascading menu that includes all the programs currently installed plus access to a DOS prompt used to launch programs from a command line, the Internet Explorer used to browse the Internet (covered in Chapter 19, *Browsing the Web with Internet Explorer*), and Windows Explorer used to work with files and folders (addressed in Chapter 5, *Windows Explorer and the Recycle Bin*).

Favorites

Want to find out the score of the Yankees game? Where to have dinner in Cleveland? How about the latest reviews of a Disney movie or the most recent stock quotes? These are just some of the options that are available on the Favorites portion of the Start menu.

Documents

Windows 98 SE remembers the files you recently worked on and puts them on this menu. To clear all the entries on the Documents menu, follow these steps:

1. Click the Start button.
2. Point to Settings and select Taskbar & Start Menu.
3. Select the Start Menu Programs tab.
4. Under the Documents menu, click the Clear button.
5. Click OK or Close.

There's no way to clear this menu selectively. It's all or nothing.

Settings

Branching off this item, you'll find the Control Panel folder, the Printers folder, the Taskbar & Start Menu settings, Folder Options, an Active Desktop submenu, and Windows Update. The Control Panel (explored in detail in Chapter 7, *Customizing Windows 98 SE with the Control Panel*) allows you to customize the way that Windows 98 SE looks and works. The Printers folder (refer to Chapter 8, *Printers and Printing*) is the place to go to add or modify the way a printer operates. You already know that the Taskbar & Start Menu option help you customize what appears on both the Programs menu and the Start menu. Folder Options allow you to determine which items you want on your Desktop and how you want them to appear; and Active Desktop allows you to switch the Desktop view, including whether you want to view the Desktop as a Web page, and to customize the Desktop appearance. If you are connected to the Internet, selecting Windows Update opens the Microsoft Windows Update page, where you can download and install the latest product updates and access support information.

Find

This is a neat little program that will let you search for files (and folders) or even a particular piece of text within a file. You can search your whole computer, just a particular drive, or just selected drives. If you're on a network, you can search for a particular computer by name. You can even search for something on the Microsoft Network or the Internet or e-mail a long-lost friend.

Select Find and then Files Or Folders to begin a search for one of these items. Figure 3.2 shows the dialog box that appears if you select to find files.

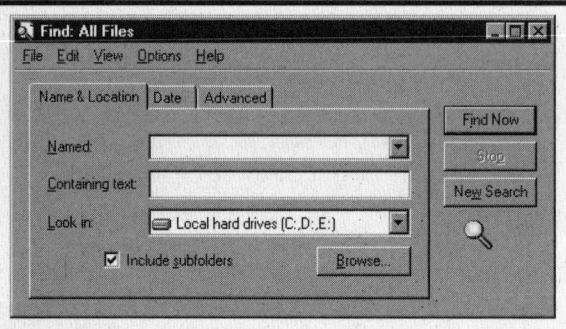

FIGURE 3.2: The Find All Files dialog box

As you can see from the tabs, you can search by name and location and by the date a file was created or modified. The Advanced tab has an option for searching for a particular type of file. The menus include options to make your search case sensitive or to save the results of a search.

The really nice thing about Find is that once you locate the file or folder you want, you can just click to open it, or you can drag it to another location. In other words, the file or list of files displayed at the end of a search is "live," and you can act on it accordingly.

Visiting the Windows 98 Desktop

> **TIP**
> To launch a search when the Desktop is visible, press the F3 key.

You can also use the Browse button on the Name & Location tab to look around for the file you want. And if you click the downward arrow on the Named box, you get a drop-down list of all the recent programs you've run from this box.

Help

The Help option on the Start menu is where you want to go to get help with anything and everything about Windows 98 SE. When you click Help, you have the option of going to the help files that were installed along with Windows 98 SE or using the Internet to access help. Help is so important that we'll spend extra time on it later in this chapter in the section called "Getting All the Help You'll Ever Need."

Run

Those who loved the command-line option popular in earlier versions of Windows will be equally happy here. Select Run from the Start menu, and you can type the name of any program you want to launch. Or use the Browse button to go to the specific location. You can even enter an Internet site and Windows 98 SE will see to it that Internet Explorer takes you there.

Log Off

Log Off closes all programs, disconnects your computer from the network (if you're connected), and prepares your computer to be used by someone else. It does not shut down the computer.

Shut Down

This Start menu option is only used when you want to shut down your computer, restart it, or restart it in MS-DOS mode.

Taskbars Galore

The Taskbar appears at the bottom of your screen and contains the Start menu button and other helpful tools. Every open program has a button on the Taskbar associated with it. This is extremely handy because it means you don't have to close windows or move them aside to find other ones. Just click the button, and the corresponding open item will become active.

You can modify the Taskbar's appearance and location to make its use even more convenient.

Changing the Taskbar's Location and Size

To change the location of the Taskbar, drag it to the top of the screen or to either side. (Make sure your cursor isn't over a button when you drag it.) To increase its size (so you can fit more buttons), position the mouse pointer at the edge of the Taskbar, and when you see a double-headed arrow, drag the border to where you want it.

Making the Taskbar Disappear

If you have a smallish monitor, you may want the Taskbar to disappear except when you need it. This gives you more room on the Desktop. To try this look, follow these steps:

1. Click the Start button, and choose Settings ➤ Taskbar & Start Menu.

2. In the Taskbar Properties dialog box, click the Auto Hide checkbox.

3. If you want to access the Taskbar even when you're running a full-screen program, select Always On Top as well.

4. Click Apply to preview the changes, or click OK to accept them and close the dialog box.

Now the Taskbar will only appear as you move the mouse pointer toward the bottom of the screen. Once you move the mouse pointer away from the bottom, the Taskbar will no longer be visible. You can reverse this by deselecting the Auto Hide checkbox in the Taskbar Properties dialog box.

Visiting the Windows 98 Desktop   41

> **TIP**
> You can also quickly get to the Taskbar Properties dialog box by right-clicking between Taskbar buttons and selecting Properties.

Also on the Taskbar

The Taskbar contains the all-important Start menu and buttons for each open item, but it also contains other items to make your Windows 98 SE activities easier.

To the right of the Start button is the Quick Launch toolbar with buttons that can be used to access Internet Explorer (the Windows 98 SE Internet browser, discussed in Chapter 19), launch Outlook Express (the Windows 98 SE e-mail program, discussed in Chapter 18), change the view of the Desktop, and view Channels to access information.

The right corner of the Taskbar is interesting as well. That's where you'll find active bits of hardware. If you have a sound card and it's working, there'll be a little speaker icon on the Taskbar. Also, when you're printing or faxing, a miniature printer appears in the same area. Position the mouse pointer over the clock display, and a box showing the day and date will pop open. To change this, either double-click or right-click and select Adjust Date/Time. If you install software that opens when you start Windows 98 SE and remains available at all times, a corresponding icon will appear as well in this area of the Taskbar.

Selecting the Taskbar's Toolbars

The Taskbar can contain a series of toolbars. To display a toolbar, point to a blank place on the Taskbar, and click the right mouse button. Select Toolbars, and then select the toolbar you want to use. The menu includes ready-made toolbars plus the opportunity to make your own.

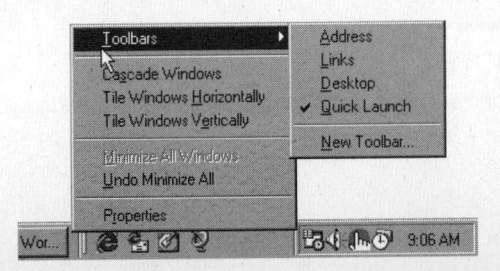

Quick Launch Toolbar

The Quick Launch toolbar is on the Taskbar by default. It consists of icons representing Internet Explorer, Outlook Express, the Desktop, and Channels.

A single click will open Internet Explorer or any of the other programs represented. When you have a bunch of windows open and you want to get at something on your Desktop, simply click the Show Desktop icon to minimize the current windows. Click the icon again to return the open windows to their original positions.

Desktop Toolbar

Select the Desktop toolbar, and every icon on your Desktop will be represented in the Taskbar. Click any of the icons to open the file or program it represents.

Address Toolbar

Select Address to open a toolbar that allows you to enter a Web address without having to open an Internet browser first. The address can be on your own computer, on your intranet, or on the Internet.

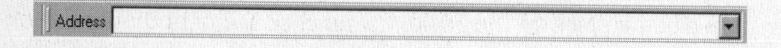

Type an address or click the drop-down arrow to select a recently visited site.

NOTE
For more on using Web addresses, see Chapter 19.

Links Toolbar

The Links toolbar is another Web-based toolbar. It contains all the shortcuts to Web sites that are listed in the folder `Windows\Favorites\Links` (or in Start ➤ Favorites ➤ Links). You can add shortcuts and delete the ones you don't want (see Chapter 4, *Shortcuts Galore*).

| Links | Best of the Web | Microsoft | Product News | Today's Links | Web Gallery |

Right-clicking the Taskbar allows you to select the toolbars option and choose which toolbars are displayed on the Desktop.

> **NOTE**
> The Address and Links toolbars may not be available on your computer, depending on whether you have established an Internet connection.

Creating a Toolbar

After right-clicking the Taskbar, select Toolbars ➤ New Toolbar to create a toolbar of your own design. In the New Toolbar window (see Figure 3.3), select a folder and then click the OK button. The items in the folder you selected will appear as a toolbar.

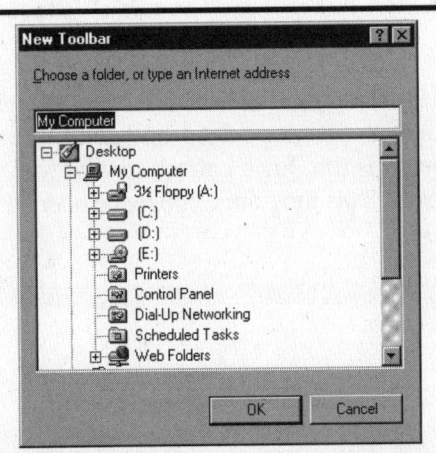

FIGURE 3.3: Selecting a folder that will become a toolbar

Making Room for All the Toolbars

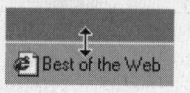

Opening even two toolbars at the same time will surely overcrowd the Taskbar. To make more room for an individual toolbar, point to the top of the Taskbar so your cursor looks like this vertical bar. When your pointer grows two heads, click once and drag the vertical sizing bar to the position you want.

If you want even more room, point to the right or left edge of a toolbar, and when the pointer turns to a double-headed arrow, click and drag to make it wider. Now you can have all the toolbars you want!

Configuring Toolbars

Are the icons on the toolbar too small? Right-click a blank part of the toolbar, and choose View ➢ Large. You can make one toolbar large and leave the others at their default setting.

WARNING

It's a big help that each of the toolbars can be adjusted. It can be a challenge to find a truly blank spot to right-click once you have several toolbars on the Taskbar.

To change the contents of a toolbar, right-click it and choose Open. In the window that opens, delete items you don't need, and add shortcuts to files or programs you want. Below is the Quick Launch toolbar with the addition of a shortcut to Quicken. This program can now be opened by single-clicking it on the Taskbar.

What My Computer Can Do for You

The My Computer icon is on every Windows 98 SE Desktop. Double-click the icon to display icons for all your drives, plus a folder for Control Panel and a Printers folder, as well as folders used in creating dial-up connections. My Computer is one of several ways to access information about the drives on your computer and your printer. It's the perfect place to go to highlight a hard drive and then right-click to find out about some of the drive's properties, such as how much space is available through its Properties option.

Right-click the My Computer icon and select Properties for a look at your hardware.

Click the My Computer icon and choose View ➤ Folder Options. On the General tab, you can select whether you want Web Style, Classic Style, or a combination of the two. In Classic Style, only one window is displayed at a time, which is probably preferable unless you have a very large monitor. On the average monitor, having every click open a new window (with all the old ones remaining) can turn your Desktop into a crowded mess very quickly.

> **NOTE**
> If the name My Computer is just too cute for your tastes (and it is for ours), right-click the icon and select Rename from the menu. Then edit the existing name or type an entirely new one.

Recycling Unwanted Files and Folders

The Recycle Bin, as you might imagine, is where old, deleted files hang out until you may need them again or until you send them to a quick and painless death (meaning they are no longer recoverable).

Despite the name, the deleted files aren't actually recycled unless you rescue them from the bin before they're deleted permanently. Nevertheless, the Recycle Bin gives you a nice margin of safety. When you delete a file, you have days or even weeks (depending on how you set things up) to change your mind and retrieve it.

You need to know two very important things about the Recycle Bin:

- You cannot rename or delete the Recycle Bin icon.

- Files that you delete using DOS programs or any program that is not part of Windows 98 SE are not sent to the Recycle Bin. They're just deleted, so be careful.

The Windows 98 SE Properties Dialog Box

Sometimes it's important to have information about files, folders, and programs. For example, you might be having trouble running a certain program and need the size and location of a particular file. In Windows 98 SE, it's a snap to use Properties dialog boxes and find out about objects that appear on your Desktop. You can try it by right-clicking the object you want to learn more about and selecting Properties.

When you select Properties, you open what's called a *Properties dialog box* (shown in Figure 3.4). Properties dialog boxes vary, of course. Some types of files will have multiple tabs in the Properties dialog box; others will have only one tab and very few options. The one you see in Figure 3.4 is a simple Properties dialog box for a file created using Microsoft Word.

Properties dialog boxes contain valuable information about files, programs, devices, and virtually anything else that can be represented by an icon. So when you find yourself with a program or a piece of hardware that isn't working the way you want it to, right-click it, select Properties, and then examine the contents of the Properties dialog box.

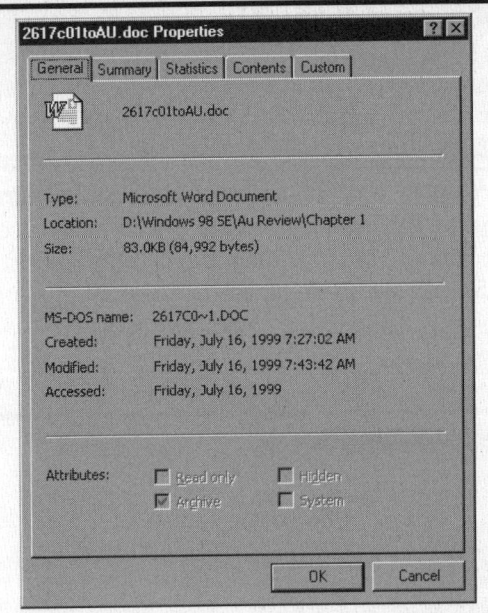

FIGURE 3.4: A Properties dialog box for a simple Microsoft Word file

Setting Up Your Desktop

The default Windows 98 SE Desktop screen you saw in Figure 3.1 probably does not elicit cries of joy on first glance. But this can be easily changed. One of the most convenient and friendly features that Windows 98 SE offers is that you can change the appearance of the Desktop and almost any of the elements it contains, such as the color of the display or the resolution of the objects.

> **WARNING**
> When you begin changing default Windows 98 SE settings, it's a good idea to write down the old settings just in case you end up with something you like less than the original. This will make it fairly easy to switch back to the original settings should you need to do so.

Remember that you can use the entire area of your monitor's screen in Windows 98 SE. You can have many folders, a few, or none at all. You can have all your programs on menus that fold out of the Start button's menus, or you can have program icons on the Desktop so that you can open them with a mouse click. You can also have colors, fonts, and Desktop wallpaper of many types. You can do just about anything you can imagine, so experiment until you find a setup that works the way you do. Here's how to get at all the settings that affect the Desktop.

To get to the Properties dialog box that controls the Desktop, move the pointer to a blank spot on the Desktop and right-click the mouse. Select Properties from the pop-up menu to open the Display Properties dialog box (see Figure 3.5) with six labeled tabs.

Next, we'll explore the contents of each individual tab that is part of the Display Properties dialog box.

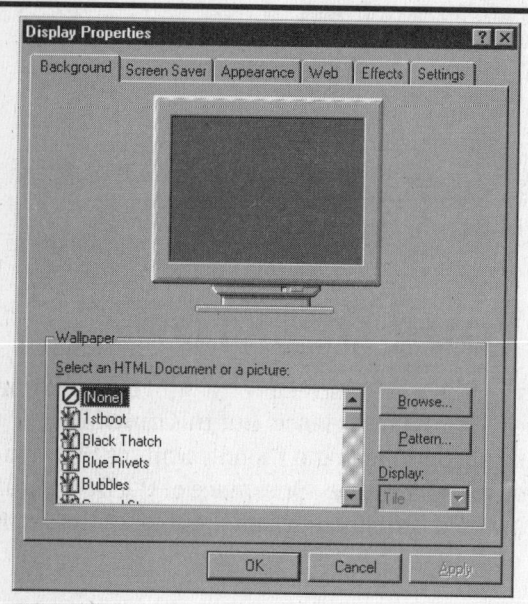

FIGURE 3.5: Use the Display Properties dialog box to change the appearance of your Desktop.

The Background Tab

The wallpaper and background pattern is what appears as your Desktop. On the Background tab, you can set both elements. If you have a special type of pattern, you can use the Browse button to locate that file and use it as your wallpaper. Any file that is in a bitmap format (.BMP) or device-independent bitmap file format (.DIB) can be used as wallpaper.

Visiting the Windows 98 Desktop

WARNING

When Windows 98 SE is installed, it uses the minimal amount of memory necessary to maintain the Desktop display. Changes, such as adding complex patterns to the Desktop, use valuable memory. If you don't want to use memory resources, minimize the number of Desktop settings you change.

TIP

The Apply button lets you see how a setting will work without having to close the Display Properties dialog box. It also allows you to try several different settings before deciding which one you want to use.

The Screen Saver Tab

When personal computers were relatively new, monitors could be damaged if the same image was left on the screen for an extended period of time. Screen savers, a constantly moving and repetitive display, came to the rescue. If you installed a screen saver—the one that comes with Windows 98 SE or some other one—you can adjust the settings on this page. All the installed screen savers are in the Screen Saver drop-down list. Click the Preview button to get a full-screen view of the selected screen saver. Move your mouse or press any key on the keyboard to return to the Display Properties dialog box.

The Appearance Tab

You use this tab to change the color scheme of the Desktop elements, such as the title bar and how text will appear on the Desktop. Click any of the elements in the window at the top of the Appearance tab, and the name of the element appears in the Item box as well as the colors and any other settings. Change the size or color or both. If there's a font that can be changed, the current one will appear in the Font box. And if you're just not in a very creative mood, select one of the many color schemes ranging from Desert to Lilac. How pretty.

The Web Tab

The Web tab gives you the opportunity to create different configurations of items on the Windows 98 SE Active Desktop, and to open a series of

Channels or links, which you can go to using Internet Explorer (see Chapter 19), with a click. You can also place other active resources (such as links to other Internet sites) on your Desktop and change the way you click the Desktop icons using the Folder Options button.

The Effects Tab

You use the options on this tab to work with the various icons that represent files and folders on the Windows 98 SE Desktop, and it even allows you to hide all the icons on the Desktop if you are viewing it as a Web page. You can also adjust visual effects such as the size of the icons on the Desktop, and you can even smooth the edges of those pesky fonts that refuse to cooperate.

The Settings Tab

Of all the tabs in the Display Properties dialog box, this one offers the changes that have the most direct impact on your working environment. Here's where you can change how your screen actually looks (as well as what Windows 98 SE knows about your display hardware).

You can change the number of colors that are used (which is limited by the type of monitor you have and the capability of the video driver), the size of the fonts used on the Desktop (by clicking the Advanced button), and most important, the area of the Desktop that is used by Windows 98 SE (also limited by your hardware and software capabilities).

Changing Resolutions

Displays are described in terms of their resolution—that's the number of dots (or pixels) on the screen and the number of colors that can be displayed at the same time. The resolutions you can choose using the slider under the Screen Area are limited by the hardware and software you have. You can't make your monitor and video card display more than is built into them. As the resolution increases, objects become more defined, but they become smaller as well. Also, as the resolution increases, more of your computer's memory is devoted to appearance rather than performance.

Most computers and most people are happy with the 800×600 setting. Resolution choices are based on what you like to look at—constrained by the capabilities of your monitor and video card. At the lowest resolution, you may not be able to see all the elements of some programs, so try the next higher resolution. At the highest resolutions, screen elements are very small, so you may want to try Large Fonts from the Font Size box (by clicking the Advance button). That will make the icon captions on the Desktop easier to see.

Here are the most likely display settings:

- **640×480**   A standard VGA display that's 640 pixels wide by 480 pixels high.
- **800×600**   A typical SVGA display (super VGA).
- **1024×768**   This is the upper limit of SVGA and the beginning of more advanced systems such as 8514/A and XGA. This is a very fine (that is, non-grainy) resolution; but if your monitor is 15 inches or smaller, you'd better have very good eyes.
- **1280×1024**   A very fine resolution but one that requires a large monitor. Even with a 17-inch screen, you'll need good eyes.

You'll notice as you move the slider toward higher resolutions that the number of colors displayed in the Colors box changes. As resolution numbers go up, color numbers have to go down because they're both competing for the same video memory. That's why, if you want the most realistic color represented on your screen, you'll need a video card (also called a display adapter) with 2, 4, or more megabytes of its own memory.

> **NOTE**
> If you change your screen resolution, you may end up with some peculiar icon arrangements. They may be way too far apart or so close together that they're difficult to use. The Appearance tab contains controls for the spacing of icons. Pull down the Item drop-down list and select one of the Icon Spacing choices, and then adjust the spacing using the Size box.

Getting All the Help You'll Ever Need

Who needs help with Windows 98 SE? Sooner or later, almost everyone. Windows 98 SE provides extensive help that is easily accessible and easily understood.

Chapter Three

The most direct way to get Windows 98 SE help is from the Start menu. Click the Start button and then click Help. The initial Windows 98 SE help screen shown in Figure 3.6 opens.

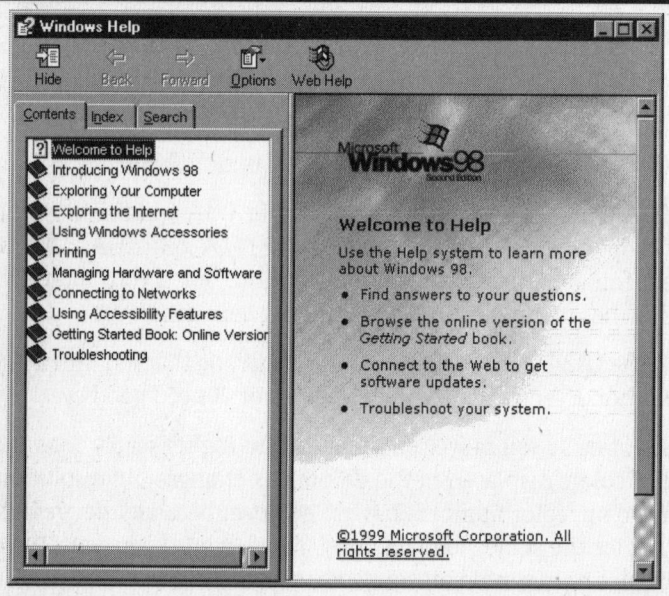

FIGURE 3.6: From the Help menu, you can select local Help or the Web Help button from the Internet browser.

You can elect to access offline help or access Web help through your Internet connection. Offline, Windows 98 SE will use the files stored on your computer to provide you with assistance on the topic of your choice. If you click the Web Help button, Windows 98 SE will use your Internet connection to make a direct connection to Microsoft and you can access help there.

Which help should you use? The offline option is great for most common problems, and you can probably find the help you need. But if you have a fast Internet connection and want to access all the help and services at your disposal, try the Web Help option. In a nutshell, offline is faster, but the Web Help option is more comprehensive.

TIP

Earlier versions of Windows allowed the user to press the F1 key and get help on the selected dialog box option. This easiest of help approaches is still alive and well. At any time in any Windows 98 SE dialog box, you can press F1 and get help on the Desktop or the current action. It's quick, it's handy, and it works.

Using Offline Help

Offline Help allows you to select from three ways of getting help (see Figure 3.7). One is through a search of the Contents of Windows 98 SE, which includes general help categories. Here you click the category in which you are interested (such as Printing) and then work your way through the selection of options until you find the topic on which you need help. Just follow the instructions provided to get the assistance you need.

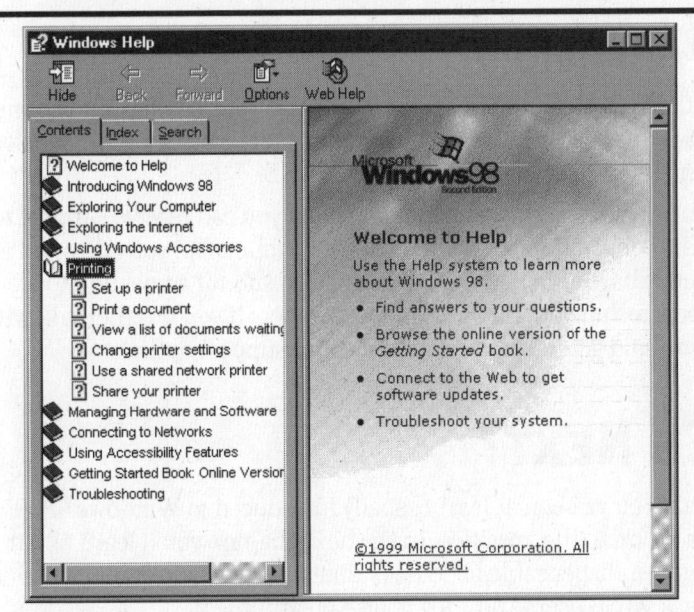

FIGURE 3.7: Use local Help to find out about printing documents.

A second way to get help is through clicking the Index tab. This action produces a list of all the topics contained in Windows 98 SE Help; you can scroll through the list or type a keyword or a phrase to find the topic on which you need assistance.

The third way of using offline Help is to use the Search tab to look for a particular term or operation you want to perform. Windows 98 SE will find terms that relate to whatever you enter and provide you with help on that topic.

One of the nicer features of Windows 98 SE help is that you can continue performing those help steps without worrying about the help screen retreating to the background as you click a new Window or select a menu option. The help screen only disappears when you close out of it.

> **NOTE**
> Clicking in the right frame of help allows you to perform many different operations, including printing the contents of the help topic. You can then make up your own little book of special help tips. You can also save help screens as wallpaper, copy them as graphic files, or create a shortcut for a particular topic.

Using Web Help

Using the Web Help option allows you to use your browser and connect to the Microsoft Personal Support Center. Here, you can get extensive help on almost any aspect of Windows 98 SE.

There are just too many topics for which you can receive support to go through them all here, but when you use online help, you access an entire knowledge base of help topics. You can also submit a question to a Microsoft technician, find out phone numbers if you'd rather talk with someone, and get information about other support options.

What's Next?

Now that you've been at least casually introduced to Windows 98 SE, we'll move on to the specifics. In the next chapter, you'll learn about *shortcuts*—indispensable little tools that will make you a more efficient Windows 98 SE user. And they're also great fun!

Chapter 4

SHORTCUTS GALORE

You can accomplish the same task in many different ways in Windows 98 SE. For example, you can open the Windows Explorer and click the application program you want to start. Or you can create a shortcut for that program, place it on the Desktop, and click it when you're ready to use it. Shortcuts are meant to be convenient ways to get at all the things on your computer or network: documents, applications, folders, printers, and so on. In this chapter, we'll cover all the ways to make and modify a shortcut and how to place the shortcuts you want where you want them.

> **NOTE**
> At the end of the chapter, you'll find a different type of shortcut—a set of keyboard combinations you can use to perform many of the most important functions in Windows 98 SE.

Adapted from *ABCs of Windows 98*
by Sharon Crawford and Neil J. Salkind
ISBN 0-7821-1953-0   384 pages $19.99

58 Chapter Four

A shortcut is identified by the small arrow in its lower-left corner. The arrow isn't there just to be cute. It's important to know (particularly before a deletion) whether something is a shortcut or a real object. You can delete shortcuts at will. You're not deleting anything that you can't re-create in a second or two. But if you delete an actual file or folder, you'll have to reinstall it or rummage around in the Recycle Bin to retrieve it. And if it's a while before you notice it's missing, the Recycle Bin may have been emptied in the meantime, and the object may be gone.

Here's an example. Let's say that on your hard drive you have a folder called NetMeeting (and you do, unless you've deleted it). On the Desktop, you can put a shortcut to that folder just like the shortcuts in Figure 4.1. You can get to the contents of the folder by clicking the shortcut. If you delete the shortcut folder on the Desktop, the folder on the hard drive remains untouched.

FIGURE 4.1: A sample of shortcuts representing various files and applications

If you delete the folder on the hard drive but not the shortcut on the Desktop, the shortcut will still be there, but it will be pointing to nothing. When you click the shortcut, you will get a dialog box telling you that Windows 98 SE is looking for the file to which the shortcut refers. But if you've deleted the file or folder it's looking for, Windows won't be able to locate it and neither will you. The best thing to do in this situation is delete the shortcut from the Desktop.

Shortcuts are an excellent tool for configuring your Desktop to suit you. You can create shortcuts to folders, to programs, and to individual files. In fact, you can create shortcuts to any Windows 98 SE objects. Arrange them any way you want on the Desktop, inside other folders, or on menus.

Creating Shortcuts

The Create Shortcut option can be found in many places, including:

- An object's pop-up menu (see Figure 4.2)
- Various drop-down menus
- The Desktop pop-up menu, where it appears as New ➤ Shortcut

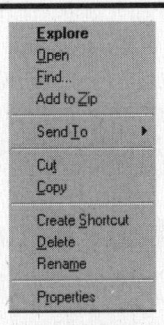

FIGURE 4.2: Create Shortcut is an option almost every time you use the right mouse button to click an object.

Shortcuts are pointers to objects. So you need to either find the object you want to create a shortcut to or be able to tell Windows 98 SE where the object is located.

The easiest way to create a shortcut is to use My Computer or the Windows 98 SE Explorer to locate the object for which you want to create the shortcut. Then, right-click the object and click Create Shortcut. A new icon named "Shortcut to..." appears.

> **NOTE**
> There are some special circumstances you need to keep in mind depending on where the original object is located. The next few sections address this issue.

Creating a Shortcut When You Can See the Object

To create a shortcut when you have the original object in view inside the Explorer or My Computer window, follow these steps:

1. Right-click the object for which you want to create a shortcut.

2. Click the Create Shortcut option on the pop-up menu.

The new shortcut is created with the name "Shortcut to *Name*" (where *Name* is the name of the program or file). For example, the shortcut shown here, when clicked, will open Microsoft Word. You can now drag the shortcut to any location you choose, including another folder, the Start menu, or the Desktop.

Creating a Shortcut When You Can't See the Object

If the original object isn't handy or you can't remember where it is, you can still create a shortcut by following these steps:

1. Right-click on the Desktop and select New ➤ Shortcut.

2. In the Create Shortcut dialog box, type the location and name of the original object. If you don't know the path (and who ever does?), click the Browse button.

3. Using the Browse window, mouse around until you find the file or object you want to link to. You may have to change the Files Of Type item in the Browse window to the All Files option.

4. Highlight the file with the mouse (the name will appear in the File Name box) and click Open. The Command Line box will now contain the name and location of the object.

5. Click Next and either accept or change the name for the shortcut.

6. Click Finish and the shortcut appears on your Desktop.

Renaming a Shortcut

To rename a shortcut from the default name assigned by Windows (for example, to change "Shortcut to Winword.exe" to simply "Word"), right-click the icon and select Rename from the menu that opens. Type the name you want. Click a blank spot on the Desktop when you're through.

What to Name Shortcuts

When you name or rename a shortcut, take full advantage of the long file name feature (up to 255 characters) that Windows 98 SE makes available. No need to get carried away, but you might as well call a folder "March Budget Reports" rather than "MAR BUD."

As with naming any file, certain characters aren't allowed in shortcut names, including:

Backslash	\
Forward slash	/
Greater-than sign	<
Less-than sign	>
Pipe symbol	|
Colon	:
Double quotation mark	"
Question mark	?
Asterisk	*

Just be a bit creative, and learn to live without these characters in your shortcut names.

Shortcut Settings

Like other Windows 98 SE objects, each shortcut has a Properties dialog box associated with it that you can see by right-clicking the shortcut icon and selecting Properties from the pop-up menu. For shortcuts to Windows objects (as opposed to DOS programs), the most interesting tab is the one labeled Shortcut (shown in Figure 4.3).

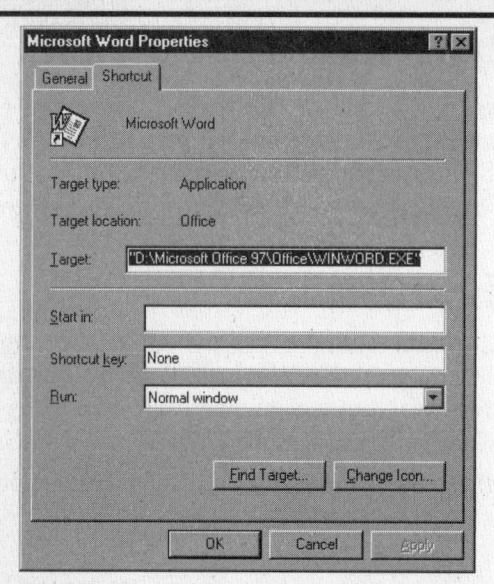

FIGURE 4.3: The Shortcut tab of the Properties dialog box

Finding the Target

Forget what object is represented by the shortcut and where it's located? The path or address for the target, or the object from which the shortcut was created, can be found in the Target text box on the Shortcut tab of the Properties dialog box.

If you want to find out what the shortcut is pointing to and be delivered to that location, click the Find Target button. When you click this button, a window opens into the folder containing the application or file the shortcut is for. You can then click the file or application to open it.

Changing a Shortcut's Icon

Shortcuts to programs will usually display the icon associated with that program. You can, however, change the icon for any shortcut by following these steps:

1. Right-click the shortcut icon and select Properties from the pop-up menu.

2. Select the Shortcut tab and click the Change Icon button.

3. Use the Browse button to look in other files. Click the icon you want to use.

4. Click OK twice, and the new shortcut icon will be displayed, taking the place of the old shortcut icon.

TIP
Many icons are available from icon libraries that are distributed as shareware, and an especially great place to find them is on the Internet. Just use the Search tools found in Internet Explorer or any other browser. Learn more about this in Chapter 19, *Browsing the Web with Internet Explorer*.

Putting Shortcuts Where You Want Them

The point of shortcuts is to save time and effort. Indiscriminately placing a bunch of shortcuts on the Desktop may help you, but it also may just clutter up the Desktop. There are a number of other ways and places shortcuts can be made useful, including placing them at locations other than the Desktop.

Putting a Start Menu Item on the Desktop

When you click the Start menu and follow the Programs arrow, you'll see a hierarchical display of programs installed on your system. All those menu items are just representations of shortcuts. To create the shortcuts you want on your Desktop, you'll need to (if you'll pardon the expression) go Exploring:

1. Right-click the Start button and select Open or Explore.

2. Click the Programs icon.

3. Find the programs you want here. (You may have to go down another level by clicking one of the folders.)

4. Right-click the shortcut you want and drag it to the Desktop, selecting Create Shortcut(s) Here from the menu that opens when you release the mouse button:

Adding a Program to the Start Menu

You undoubtedly have some objects that you'd like to get at without having to go through the menus or without searching around the Desktop.

To add a program to the top of the Start menu, just click a shortcut and drag and drop it on the Start button. Then when you click the Start button, the program will be instantly available.

You can remove programs from the Start menu by selecting Start ➢ Settings ➢ Taskbar & Start Menu. Click the Start Menu Programs tab and then the Remove button. Highlight the program you want to remove and then click the Remove button. Then select Close and OK. Once again, the shortcut (which appeared on the Start menu) is removed, but the actual program to which the shortcut refers remains.

Adding a Shortcut to Send To

When you right-click most things in Windows 98 SE, one of the choices on the pop-up menu is Send To. By default, the Send To menu includes shortcuts to your floppy drive (or drives) and also may include (depending on your installation) shortcuts to mail and fax recipients.

A great example of using shortcuts effectively is to add one that represents a printer to the Send To folder. That way, all you need to do is right-click a file icon and then select the printer. The application associated with the icon will open and the document will print. Pretty nifty.

To add a shortcut to Send To, follow these steps:

1. Choose Start ➢ Programs ➢ Windows Explorer.

2. Locate the Windows folder in the left pane of Explorer and open it.

3. Locate the Send To folder and click it.

4. Now drag any item you want to appear on the Send To menu into the Send To folder.

   You may have to open a second instance of Explorer to get at other folders if the shortcuts you want are not on the Desktop.

> **TIP**
> When you use Send To, you're actually doing the equivalent of drag-and-drop. The item you highlighted will be dropped on the selection you make in Send To.

STARTING A PROGRAM WHEN WINDOWS STARTS

You may have programs you want to have ready to run when you start Windows—for example, your calendar or another application to which you want immediate access. Windows 98 SE includes a StartUp folder for just such purposes.

To start a program when Windows 98 SE starts, you must first create a shortcut for that program and then place it in the Windows 98 SE StartUp folder. Here's how:

1. Right-click the Start button and select Open or Explore from the pop-up menu.

2. Click the Programs icon and then click the StartUp folder icon.

3. Drag whatever shortcuts you want to start to the StartUp folder.

> **NOTE**
> If you want to leave the original shortcut where it is, drag with the right mouse button and choose Copy Here from the menu that pops up when you release the button.

Now that you've got the shortcut in the StartUp folder, how do you want the window to appear when it starts? It can appear as minimized (on the Taskbar), normal (as it would if normally opened), or maximized (using the entire Desktop area).

To specify how you want programs to look when Windows 98 SE starts:

1. Right-click the shortcut and select Properties.
2. Click the Shortcut tab.
3. In the Run box, select Minimized (or Normal Window or Maximized).
4. Click OK when you're done.

Starting a Program with a Keyboard Shortcut

You can click a shortcut placed anywhere on the Desktop to work with a file, a folder, or an application. And you can also use a keystroke combination as a shortcut.

What's great about this Windows 98 SE feature? Imagine having a maximized window on your Desktop where all you can see is the document. You need to open another application. Even if you have a shortcut to what you need, you can't use it because you can't see it! A keyboard shortcut is just what you need. If you have a keyboard shortcut, you can use that to open the application without any other fuss.

To create a keyboard shortcut, follow these steps:

1. Right-click the shortcut and select Properties.
2. On the Shortcut tab, click in the Shortcut Key field.
3. Type a letter, and Windows will add Ctrl+Alt. (So if you enter a W, the keyboard combination will be Ctrl+Alt+W.)
4. Click OK when you're finished.

Now whenever you want to use the shortcut to access the application, just use that key combination.

TIP
To remove a keyboard shortcut, open the Properties dialog box again, click in the Shortcut Key field, and press the Backspace key.

> **NOTE**
> It's best to limit keyboard shortcuts to just a few programs or folders because shortcuts assigned in Windows have precedence over those in Windows application programs. For example, Microsoft Word uses the Ctrl+Alt+T combination as a shortcut to insert the trademark (™) symbol; if you assign these keystrokes to a new Windows shortcut, you won't be able to use them for the Word shortcut.

Shortcuts to Other Places

Shortcuts quickly become a normal way of accessing files and programs on your own computer, but they're a much more powerful tool than you'd first suspect.

DOS Programs

Shortcuts to DOS programs are made in the same way as other shortcuts. Find the program file in the Explorer and do a right-mouse drag to the Desktop.

> **WARNING**
> Windows 98 SE will always try to find the target for a shortcut, even if you move the target to another location. But you might not be so lucky with DOS programs. So if you move your game to another drive or rename a batch file, plan on making a new shortcut.

Disk Drives

Right-click a disk drive in Explorer or My Computer, and drag it to the Desktop to create a shortcut to the contents of a drive. When you click the shortcut, you'll see its contents almost instantly—it's much quicker than opening the entire Explorer.

Keyboard Shortcuts

The mouse is the mouse, but some people prefer to keep their hands on the keyboard and perform as many Windows 98 SE operations as possible from there. In fact, you can perform practically every Windows 98 SE function using either the mouse or the keyboard.

Of course, you probably can't be bothered memorizing all these keyboard combinations, but you may want to consider a few for your memory bank (the one in your head), particularly if there are actions that you do repeatedly and find the mouse too clumsy for. The more you use keyboard shortcuts that best fit your needs (such as Ctrl+S for Save or Ctrl+X for Cut), the easier they will be to remember, and the more proficient you'll be as a Windows 98 SE user.

Table 4.1 includes the most useful (and in many cases, undocumented) keyboard shortcuts.

TABLE 4.1: Windows 98 SE Keyboard Shorcuts

Key	Action
Alt+Esc	Switch between open applications.
Alt+F4	Close the current application. If no application is open, it will activate the Shut Down window.
Alt+PrintScreen	Copy the active window to the Clipboard.
Alt+Tab	Cycle through open files and folders (see Figure 4.4).
Alt+Shift+Tab	Move the cursor through the open items in the opposite direction from Alt+Tab.
Alt+Spacebar	Open the Control menu (same as clicking the icon at the upper-left corner of the application or folder window).
Alt+Enter	View the selected Desktop item's properties.
Alt+hyphen	Open the Control menu (in Office applications).
Alt+*underlined letter*	Select the menu item.
Backspace	Move up one level in the folder hierarchy.
Ctrl+A	Select all.
Ctrl+X	Cut.
Ctrl+C	Copy.
Ctrl+V	Paste.

Table 4.1 continued: Windows 98 SE Keyboard Shorcuts

Key	Action
Ctrl+Z	Undo.
Ctrl+F4	Close the current window in programs that allow several windows to be open (like Word or Excel).
Ctrl+Esc	Open the Start menu.
F1	Get help.
F10 or Alt	Put the focus on the menu bar. To move between menus, use the left and right arrow keys (← and →). The ↓ or ↑ key will open the menu.
F2	Rename the file or folder that's highlighted.
F3	Open Find.
F4	Open the drop-down list in the Address toolbar. Press F4 a second time and the drop-down list will close.
F5	Refresh the view in the active window.
Left arrow (←)	Collapse the highlighted folder. If it's already collapsed, move up one level in the folder hierarchy.
Print Screen	Copy the current screen to the Clipboard, from which it can be pasted into Paint or another graphics application.
Right arrow (→)	Expand the highlighted folder. If the folder is already expanded, go to the subfolder.
Shift+Del	Delete immediately and do not place in the Recycle Bin.
Shift+F10	View the shortcut menu for the selected item.
Shift+Tab	Move the selection cursor in the opposite direction from Tab.
Tab or F6	In Explorer view, toggle the focus between the drop-down window in the left pane toolbar and the right pane.

> **NOTE**
> The Clipboard mentioned above is not an actual application; it's a special place in memory. However, there is a Clipboard Viewer (available under Programs ➢ Accessories ➢ System Tools) that can see whatever you copy. If it's not installed, go to Add/Remove Programs in Control Panel. Select Windows Setup and then Accessories.

FIGURE 4.4: Use the Alt+Tab key to scroll through active programs. Here, the program that will become active is Microsoft Word.

What's Next?

Shortcuts can really speed things up and make you a better and more efficient Windows 98 SE user. Whether you create shortcuts and place them on your Desktop or in a dedicated folder, they do their job very well. Now let's move on to working with Windows Explorer.

Chapter 5

Windows Explorer and the Recycle Bin

At this point you've been introduced to Windows 98 SE, seen how to install the system if necessary, toured the Desktop, and learned how to create and use shortcuts. That's a good start, but of course, there's more to the Windows interface.

In this chapter, we'll cover Windows Explorer, the Recycle Bin, and other Desktop elements. You'll also learn how to use important features such as the Send To menu, and you'll learn the basics of working with floppy disks. As you'll see, Windows Explorer is probably the single most important tool for any Windows user.

Adapted from *Windows 98: No Experience Required*
by Sharon Crawford
ISBN 0-7821-2128-4   544 pages $24.99

Using Windows Explorer

Windows Explorer offers the easiest way of viewing folders, files, and other resources located on your machine (see Figure 5.1). The default Explorer is a two-pane window. When you click an item in the left window pane, the right pane displays the contents. You can choose different viewing options from the View menu.

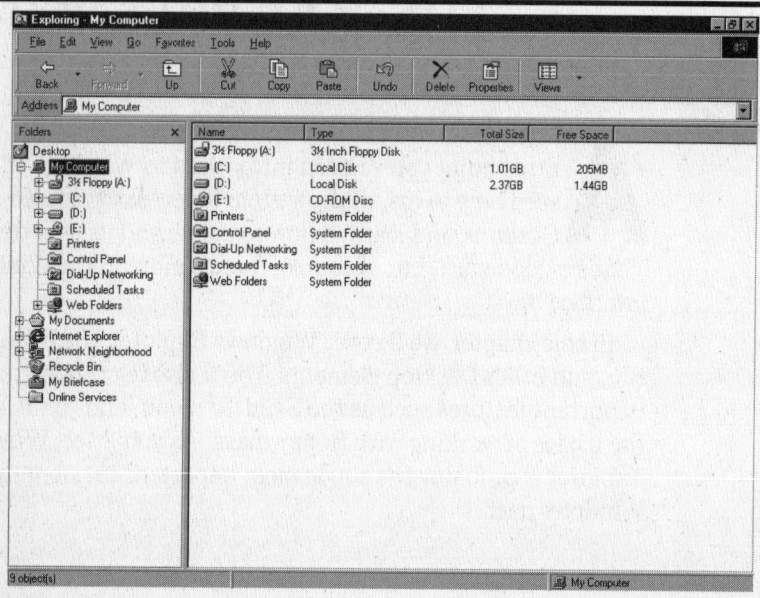

FIGURE 5.1: Windows Explorer at its most informative: the Details view

> **TIP**
> You can open more than one Windows Explorer window at a time. In fact, that's often the easiest way to move files from one place to another.

The Explorer is always available from the Start menu. Click the Start button, slide the pointer to Programs and then to Windows Explorer, and click.

Windows Explorer and the Recycle Bin

If you use Windows Explorer a lot, as most people do, you may want to put a shortcut to the Windows Explorer on your Desktop. Here's a quick way:

1. Begin as if you were opening Windows Explorer: Click Start and slide the mouse pointer to Programs, then Windows Explorer. Don't click just yet.

2. Using the right mouse button, drag the Windows Explorer shortcut icon out onto your Desktop.

3. When you release the right mouse button, a pop-up menu appears. Choose Copy Here or Create Shortcut Here. (Since it's a shortcut you're dragging, the results are the same.)

```
Move Here
Copy Here
Create Shortcut(s) Here
Cancel
```

Inside Windows Explorer, folders are organized in a fashion that doesn't look all that different from Windows 3.1 or DOS, except that the top level folder/directory is called Desktop, and the filenames look peculiar.

> **NOTE**
> Notice the plus and minus signs next to folders. A plus sign means there's at least one more layer of folders that you can see if you click the plus icon. Click the minus sign to collapse the lower level into the upper level.

Viewing Extensions

If you are upgrading from Windows 3.1, you'll probably notice first that most files shown in Windows Explorer's right pane are missing their extensions. The thinking behind this is that these files are registered (in other words, the system knows what they are and where they came from) and can be activated with a click—so why would you need to know the extension?

In a perfect world, of course, you wouldn't. But the Explorer screen shown in Figure 5.2 demonstrates how confusion can arise.

There are two files named CAPTURE and two named IMGMGR. If you know what the icons mean or expand the window to show the file types,

Chapter Five

you can figure out which file does what. But if you prefer to see file extensions, here's how to do it:

1. Click the Start button and choose Programs ➤ Windows Explorer to open Explorer.

2. Choose View ➤ Folder Options.

3. In the Folder Options dialog box, click the View tab, and then click the box next to Hide File Extensions For Known File Types to remove the check mark. Click OK when you're done.

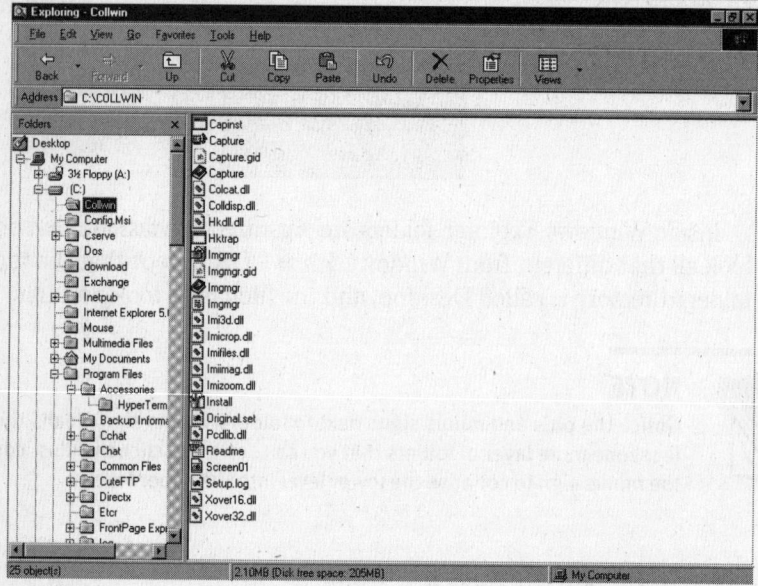

FIGURE 5.2: The lack of extensions can prove confusing when there is more than one file with the same name.

TIP
If you really want to see everything, look under Hidden Files and select Show All Files, so even hidden and system files are displayed in Windows Explorer.

Of course, many, if not most, of the programs you'll be using will be started using the Start menu or from the Desktop itself, so the file extensions are less important as time goes on.

Using Another Computer's Files

If your computer is connected to others in a local area network (LAN), the Network Neighborhood icon will appear on your Desktop and in the left window of Windows Explorer. You can see a list of computers on your network when you click Network Neighborhood in the left window of Windows Explorer (or when you click the Network Neighborhood icon on the Desktop). To see the contents of other computers' hard drives, the drives have to be *shared*. There are two steps to this. First, the network itself has to be set up for file and printer sharing. See the accompanying box if you need to do that.

A QUICK GUIDE TO SETTING UP A NETWORK

Obviously, there's more to planning and setting up a peer-to-peer local area network (the type best suited to a small office of no more than about 10 computers) than we can summarize in a couple of pages. You'll need to decide on the network *topology*, or layout; the type of cabling; the type of network card; and the type of network connector. You'll also need to buy all the network hardware. *Windows 98: No Experience Required* devotes most of a chapter to reviewing these choices, and there are many good books on networking.

Once you've decided what you're going to implement and have made the physical connections, here's what you'll need to do in Windows 98 SE:

1. **The Add New Hardware Wizard** When you physically install the network card, Windows 98 SE will notice the change the next time it boots up, and it will run the Add New Hardware Wizard to configure it. This process should happen automatically, but you can do it manually if for some reason it doesn't happen by itself. Just click the Add New Hardware icon in Control Panel.

    The Add New Hardware Wizard will walk you through the process of adding your new network card to your system. In addition, it will automatically install the minimal level of network support—adding the Microsoft client layer, so you can use

CONTINUED ➡

Chapter Five

files on someone else's Windows 95, 98, or 98 SE computer — and both the NetBEUI protocol and the IPX/SPX compatible protocol. (NetBEUI is an older Microsoft protocol that still has merit in small network systems or where the primary access is over slower dial-up lines. IPX/SPX is the protocol used on Novell NetWare networks and is installed by default by Windows 98 SE.)

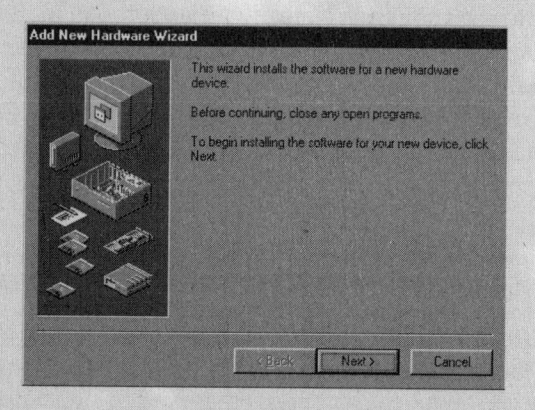

2. **The Network Wizard** If the Add New Hardware Wizard doesn't open the Network dialog box shown here, you can run it yourself. Just open Control Panel and double-click the Network icon.

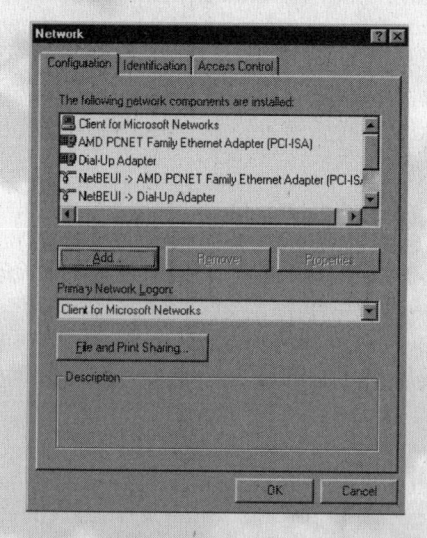

CONTINUED ➡

Windows Explorer and the Recycle Bin 79

Some network components may have been added in already when you installed the new network card. Additional client protocols, hardware adapters, networking "stacks" or protocols, and networking services can be added here.

3. **Client Choices** Network clients let you use the services being provided by another machine on your network. The default network configuration includes clients for both Microsoft Networks and Novell NetWare Networks. If you're just using Windows 98 SE as a peer-to-peer network, you can delete the Client for NetWare choice since you will only be using the built-in Microsoft networking. (To remove the NetWare client, just highlight it, and then click the Remove button. Don't worry, you can always add it back in later if you need to.)

If you don't see the Client for Microsoft Networks listed in the Network dialog box under the heading The Following Network Components Are Installed, click the Add button, and then double-click the Client icon in the Select Network Component Type box:

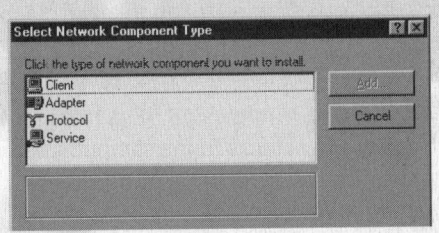

Clicking the Client icon opens the Select Network Client dialog box. Highlight Microsoft, select Client for Microsoft Networks, and then click OK.

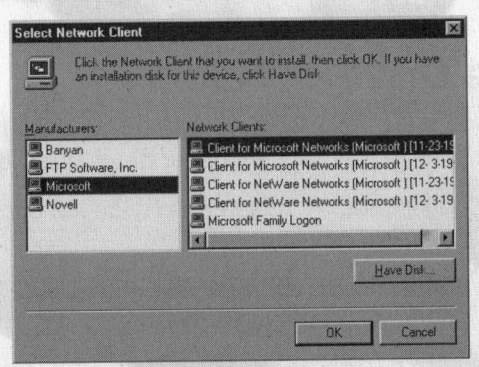

CONTINUED ➡

4. **Service Choices** The default installation doesn't install any services at all, which is fine if you never want anyone else to be able to use the resources of your computer. If you were setting up your local network to have one main machine everyone else would share—the one with the fax modem, the big hard drive, the printer, and such—then you could leave this choice alone. But if you are going to distribute your resources across the network, you will need to add services to all the workstations to allow them to share their resources with others.

Double-click the Service icon in the Select Network Component Type box. In the Select Network Service dialog box, select File And Printer Sharing For Microsoft Networks, and click OK. This will add the necessary network services to allow others on the network to use your documents and folders as well as any printers or fax modems attached to your computer.

These steps should be enough to get your network configured and ready to go. You will need to reboot each machine after you add the necessary hardware and software components, since these changes are more than Windows 98 SE can do on the fly.

A new feature in Windows 98 SE is Internet Connection Sharing, which you use to set up a home computer network to share a single connection to the Internet. For all the details, see Chapter 17, *Connecting to the Internet*.

Once this has been done, you can choose to share some or all of your files with others on the network, and they can, in turn, share with you.

Sharing a Drive or Folder

How do you give others access to drives or folders on your computer? Once the network has been set up for file sharing, just follow these steps:

1. Choose Start ➢ Programs ➢ Windows Explorer to open Windows Explorer.

2. Right-click the drive or folder you want to share, and choose Sharing from the pop-up menu.

3. On the Sharing tab of the Properties dialog box, select Shared As, as shown in Figure 5.3.

4. Accept the default Share Name, or change it to something that others will understand. Share names are limited to 12 characters.

5. Indicate what type of access you want others to have, and enter a password if you want to limit access. Remember that if you grant full access, others will be able to change the files on your computer.

6. Click OK to accept the revised Properties dialog box.

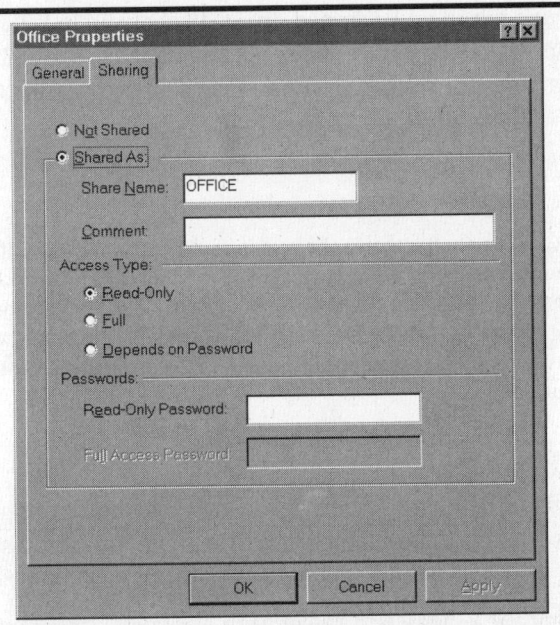

FIGURE 5.3: Sharing a drive with other users on your network

The drive or folder you have chosen to share will now appear under the name of your computer when others on your network open their Network Neighborhood. If you specified a password, they will need to know it to gain access.

> **TIP**
>
> If you don't want others to be able to make changes to your drive or folder, choose the Read-Only access type on the Sharing tab of the Properties dialog box. Read-only also means that others will be unable to *add* any new files to the shared drive or folder. Use passwords for only the most sensitive files.

Mapping a Drive

If you find yourself often going through Network Neighborhood or Explorer to get to a particular drive, you may want to *map* it. You can make any shared drive or folder on another computer appear just as if it were a drive on *your* computer. A mapped drive will show up in Windows Explorer as another hard drive. For example, if you have a C drive plus a CD-ROM drive that uses the letter D, you can map a shared network drive as letter E.

> **TIP**
>
> A mapped drive is even better than a shortcut in one important respect: If you're using older programs, they're not going to recognize things like Network Neighborhood, and they will flat-out refuse to open or save files to anywhere other than your own computer. Map a drive, and the program will cooperate because now the drive on the other computer will appear (to the program at least) to be on your computer.

Here's how it's done:

1. Click Network Neighborhood in Windows Explorer or the Network Neighborhood icon on the Desktop, and find the folder or drive you want to show as one of your local drives.

2. Right-click the object, and select Map Network Drive from the pop-up menu to open the Map Network Drive dialog box shown in Figure 5.4.

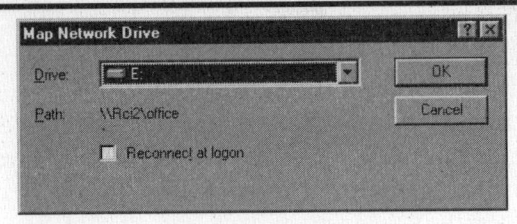

FIGURE 5.4: Mapping the Office folder to be Drive E

3. Click OK when you're done. Open Explorer or My Computer and look.

> **NOTE**
> The Reconnect At Logon box should be checked if you want the connection to the mapped drive to be made every time you start your computer. If the computer where the mapped drive resides is turned *off* when you log on, you'll get an error message.

Disconnecting from Mapped Drives or Folders

To get rid of a mapped drive or folder, you can highlight it and right-click. Select Disconnect from the pop-up menu:

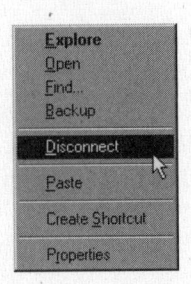

When you disconnect a mapped drive, you're just removing it from the list of drives shown on your computer. It has no other effect on the drive. You can always go back and remap it if you need to.

Exploring Floppy Disks

Click the floppy drive icon in Explorer's left window to see the contents of the diskette currently in the drive. Windows Explorer also provides the graphical interface for the care and maintenance of floppy disks. If you yearn for DOS, you can also open a DOS window to copy, format, and label a floppy disk.

Making Exact Copies

To make an exact copy of your floppy disk, put the disk in the drive and open Windows Explorer. Right-click the icon for the floppy drive, and select Copy Disk to open the dialog box shown in Figure 5.5. It doesn't say so, but these selections must be the same type of disk. For most people, that means the same drive (unless you have two identical diskette drives or two Zip drives).

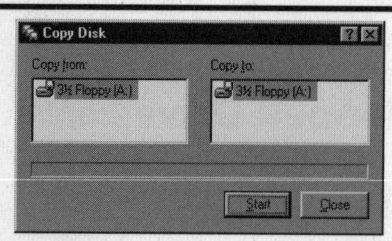

FIGURE 5.5: Windows 98 SE's direct route to copying a floppy disk

TIP
If you do much work with floppies, you may want to put a shortcut to the drive on your Desktop. Just drag the floppy drive icon from the left window of the Explorer to your Desktop.

Formatting Floppies

Here's how to format a floppy disk:

1. Put the floppy disk you want to format into your A or B drive as appropriate.
2. Choose Start ➤ Programs ➤ Windows Explorer.

Windows Explorer and the Recycle Bin

3. In the left pane of the Explorer window, right-click the floppy drive icon. Do not open the floppy drive. A pop-up menu will appear.

4. Select Format from the menu to open the Format dialog box:

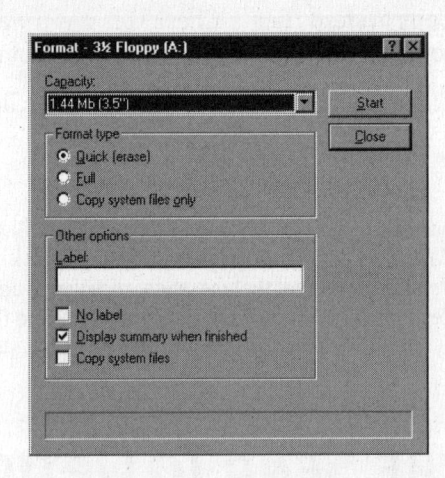

5. In the Format Type and Other Options sections, select the options you want:

   Quick   A quick format changes the names of any files on the disk so that they "disappear" as far as the operating system is concerned. This format is very fast (hence the name), but it doesn't check to make sure that the floppy disk is undamaged. It also doesn't work on new, unformatted disks.

   Full   A full format is necessary for new floppies and desirable for old ones because it checks for errors and defects on the disk. It's a lot slower, though.

   Copy system files only   This copies system files to a disk that's already formatted without removing any of the files already present. This allows you to turn any floppy into a bootable floppy—providing there's room available on the floppy disk for the system files.

   Label   This will let you provide a label for the floppy.

Display summary when finished This option is on by default. When the formatting is complete, it opens a window showing the details of the formatted disk. Clear the box if you don't want to be bothered with this information.

Copy system files Check this if you want system files copied to the disk to make the disk bootable.

6. When you're finished selecting options, click the Start button.

> **TIP**
> If Windows Explorer (or any open window) is showing the contents of the floppy disk, Windows 98 SE concludes that the floppy disk is in use and therefore can't be formatted. If you get that message, click your C drive icon in Explorer or close the Desktop window showing the contents of the floppy. Then right-click the floppy icon, and select Format from the pop-up menu.

Using the *Send To* Option

When you're working in Explorer (or any other folder for that matter) and you right-click an object, the menu that opens includes an option called Send To. When you first start using Windows 98 SE, the system will put your floppy drive and other removable media such as a Zip drive on the Send To submenu automatically.

This is pretty handy, as you might guess. But it can be even handier. You can add any application or device you choose. For example, you can select a file and send it to your word processor or your printer.

The Long...

As an example, here's how to add the Notepad applet to the Send To menu:

1. Choose Start ➢ Programs ➢ Windows Explorer.

2. Click your Windows folder, and then click Start Menu, Programs, and Accessories, and then right-click Notepad. Select Create Shortcut from the pop-up menu. The shortcut will appear in Explorer.

3. Right-click the shortcut you've just made and select Cut from the menu.

4. Scroll to the SendTo folder (it's a subfolder under the main Windows folder).

 5. Right-click the SendTo folder and select Paste.

...And the Short of It

If you want to be able to add stuff to the Send To menu without going through all the previous steps every time, just do the following once:

 1. Choose Start ➢ Programs ➢ Windows Explorer, and then click the Windows folder.

 2. Right-click the SendTo folder and drag it to the Desktop. Release the mouse button and select Create Shortcut Here from the pop-up menu.

 3. Go back to the Explorer and open the SendTo folder under Windows.

 4. Drag and drop the shortcut you just made to the SendTo folder.

Now when you highlight an object and open the Send To menu (the right-mouse-button menu), there's a shortcut to Send To as an option on the menu. Select that option, and the item you've selected will be instantly added to the Send To menu.

When the menu gets too crowded, open the SendTo folder in the Explorer and delete any extra clutter.

> **TIP**
> For a quicker way to find the SendTo folder, single-click the Start button and select Run. In the Open box, type **Sendto** (all one word) and press Enter. The SendTo folder will open on your Desktop.

USING THE RECYCLE BIN

In the bad old days of computing, it was far too easy to accidentally delete a file from your system—and there was no going back. There were, of course, tools you could buy such as the Norton Utilities. Norton included a program that could retrieve deleted files—providing you acted quickly enough. And DOS itself, starting with version 5, included a program to undelete files. The weakness of both approaches was that if you didn't undelete right away, your file could easily be overwritten by another file, and then there was *no way* to recover.

The Recycle Bin, introduced in Windows 95, retains all your deleted files for as long as you want, and you can adjust the amount of security from "just a little" to "all I can get" to match your own personal comfort level.

What It Is

The Recycle Bin is a reserved space on your hard drive. When you delete a file or drag it to the Recycle Bin icon:

the file is actually moved to that reserved space. If you have more than one hard drive, each drive has its own reserved space. There's an icon that represents the Recycle Bin on each drive—though the contents displayed when you click any icon will be the same as the Recycle Bin on any other drive. If you want a deleted file back, you can click the Recycle Bin icon to open it and retrieve any file.

The Recycle Bin functions as a first-in, first-out system. That is, when the bin is full, the oldest files are the first ones deleted to make room for the newest ones.

As configurable as the rest of Windows 98 SE is, the Recycle Bin cannot be

- ▶ Deleted
- ▶ Renamed
- ▶ Removed from the Desktop

though you can change a number of settings to make the Recycle Bin suitable for your use.

> **NOTE**
> See "Adjusting the Recycle Bin Settings" later in this chapter for information on how to determine the amount of disk space used by the Recycle Bin as well as other settings.

Sending Files to the Recycle Bin

By default, Windows 98 SE is set up to deposit all deleted files into the Recycle Bin. When you right-click a file and select Delete, or highlight a file and press the Delete key, you'll be asked to confirm if you want to send the file to the Recycle Bin. After you click Yes, that's where the file is moved. Deleted shortcuts are also sent to the Recycle Bin.

> **TIP**
> If you delete an empty folder, it's not sent to the Recycle Bin but you can recover it by immediately selecting Undo Delete from the Recycle Bin's Edit menu. If the folder came from the Desktop, just right-click a blank spot on the Desktop and select Undo Delete from the pop-up menu.

Sending a Floppy Disk's Files to the Recycle Bin

Normally, files that you delete from a floppy drive are *not* sent to the Recycle Bin. They're just deleted. However, if that strikes you as just a little too impetuous, there's an easy way to make sure that the files on your floppy do go to the Recycle Bin.

1. Choose Start ➢ Programs ➢ Windows Explorer.
2. Use the scroll bar for the left pane to move up so that you can see the entry for your floppy drive.
3. Click (with the left mouse button) the floppy drive icon. In the right pane, select the file(s) you want to delete but still want in the Recycle Bin.
4. Right-click the file(s), and select Cut from the pop-up menu. Then, right-click the Desktop and select Paste.

5. Highlight the file on the Desktop. (If there's more than one, hold down the Shift key while you click each one in turn.) Right-click a highlighted file, and select Delete. You'll be prompted to confirm that you want to send the file(s) to the Recycle Bin.

There's no more direct way to do this function because the Recycle Bin stubbornly refuses to accept any files that are sent directly from a floppy.

> **TIP**
> You can also use this method when you're deleting files from any external drive (such as a Zip drive) and you want the security of having the files safely stashed in the Recycle Bin for a while.

Bypassing the Recycle Bin

If you've got a file that you know for sure you want to delete and that you don't want taking up space in the Recycle Bin, just hold down the Shift key when you select Delete. But be sure that's what you want to do, because there's no way in Windows 98 SE to recover a deleted file that's bypassed the Recycle Bin.

> **NOTE**
> If you have the Norton Utilities for Windows, you can use the Unerase program to recover deleted files that are not in the Recycle Bin—again, you must do this very quickly before another file overwrites the one you want to recover.

Files That Won't Go Willingly

Some older programs (not written specifically for Windows 95 or later) allow you to delete files from within the program. Files deleted this way will not be sent to the Recycle Bin. Similarly, files you delete at the DOS prompt will also disappear into never-never land rather than into the Recycle Bin.

Therefore, you should make all your deletions through the Windows Explorer or My Computer or on the Desktop. If Windows 98 SE knows about the deletion, the file will automatically go to the Recycle Bin.

Recovering a Deleted File

Retrieving a file from the Recycle Bin is remarkably easy. Just click the Recycle Bin icon. The Recycle Bin window can be set up in any of the choices on the View menu. The Large Icons view (see Figure 5.6) is useful because it lets you identify which programs made which files.

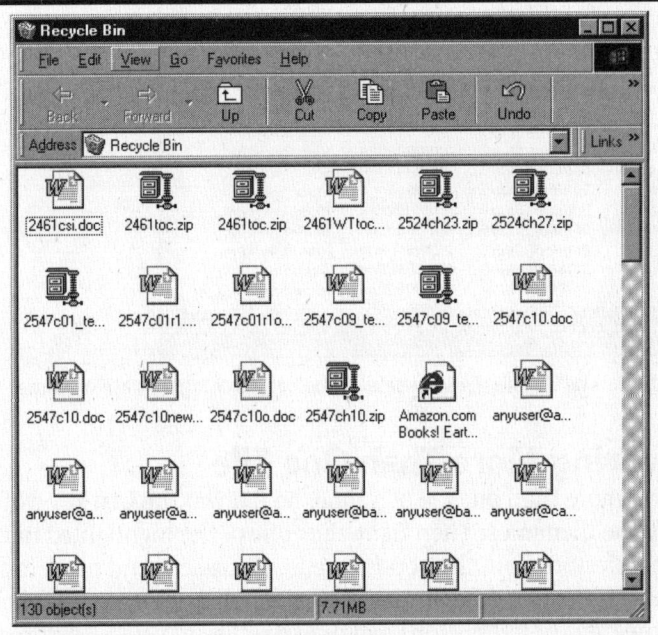

FIGURE 5.6: In the Large Icons view, you can quickly identify files that were made by a particular program.

The Details view (see Figure 5.7) is the best view if you're looking for a file recently deleted. Just click the Date Deleted bar to arrange the files in date order. A second click will reverse the order. Similarly, if you know the name of the file, a click on the Name bar will list the files in alphabetical order.

To retrieve a single file, click it with either the left or the right button and drag it to a folder or the Desktop. If you just want to send it back to its original location, right-click the filename and select Restore from the pop-up menu.

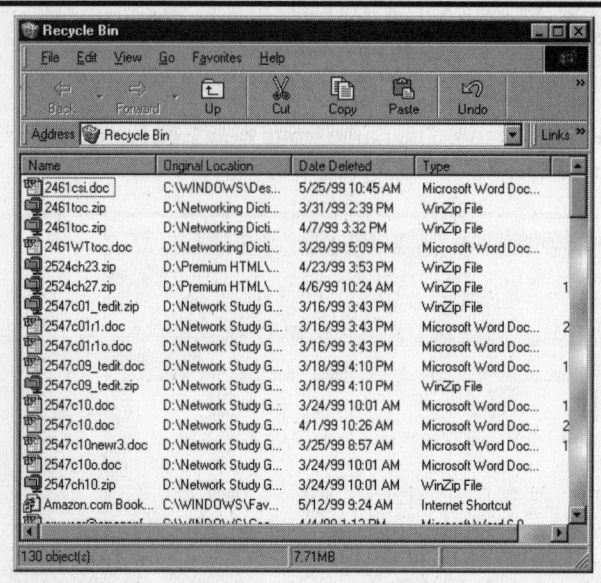

FIGURE 5.7: The Details view is useful if you're searching by date or name.

Recovering More Than One File

To recover more than one file at a time, hold down the Ctrl key while selecting the filenames. Then right-click one of the highlighted names and select Restore from the pop-up menu. Or use cut and paste to send the whole bunch to a different location. And of course, you can click (either the right or left button) and drag the files to your Desktop or another open folder.

To retrieve a number of files all in a series, click the first one and then hold down the Shift key while selecting the last one in the series.

Let's say you deleted a whole folder and the only thing all the items in the folder have in common is that all were deleted at the same time. Here's how to recover them:

1. Open the Recycle Bin by clicking the icon.
2. Choose View ➤ Details.
3. Click the Date Deleted bar. Use the scroll bar to move through the list until you find the group of files you want to retrieve.
4. Click the first one's name, and, then, while holding down the Shift key, click the name of the last one you want. All the files from the first to the last selection will be highlighted.

5. Right-click one of the highlighted files and select Recover from the pop-up menu.

All the files will be returned to their original homes, and although the original folder were not listed in the Recycle Bin, the files will be in their original folders.

Adjusting the Recycle Bin Settings

You can adjust the amount of space the Recycle Bin claims and change other settings that affect how the Recycle Bin works. Mostly you have to decide just how much safety you want and are comfortable with.

How Much Space?

Right-click the Recycle Bin icon and select Properties from the pop-up menu to open the Recycle Bin Properties dialog box, as shown in Figure 5.8.

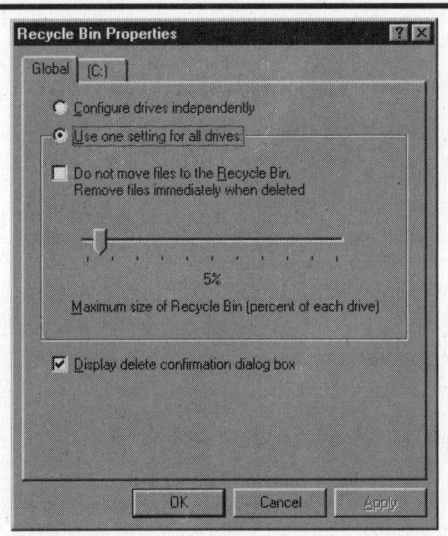

FIGURE 5.8: The Recycle Bin Properties dialog box

As you can see, you can set the amount of space reserved for the Recycle Bin for each hard disk drive individually, or you can make a global setting. By default, 10 percent of each drive is set aside for the Recycle Bin. On a large drive, that's a lot of megabytes, so you may want to reduce the size a bit.

Click the radio button for Configure Drives Independently, and then click each drive tab in turn. Click the sliding arrow and move it to the right or left until the space reserved is to your liking.

> **NOTE**
> There's also a field below the slider, showing the percentage of the drive that is reserved. If your drives are different sizes, you might want to make things easier for yourself by just reserving the same percentage on each drive.

Remember that the Recycle Bin is first-in, first-out, so if you make the reserved space very small, deleted files may pass into oblivion faster than you wish.

Getting Rid of Confirmations

On the Global tab of the Recycle Bin Properties dialog box, a checkbox controls the confirmation notice that opens every time you delete a file or folder:

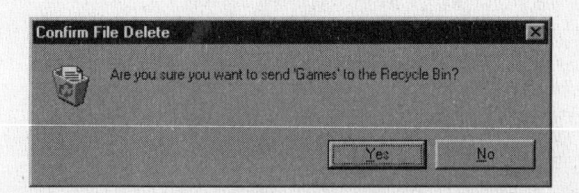

If you like the comfort of being consulted about every deletion, leave the check mark in the box. If you clear the check mark, files you choose to delete will move to the Recycle Bin without any further notice.

Doing Away with the Recycle Bin

You can't exactly do away with the Recycle Bin completely. As mentioned before, you can't delete it or remove it from the Desktop. However, you can check this box:

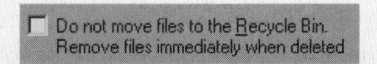

in the Recycle Bin Properties dialog box. If you have the Recycle Bin space configured separately for each drive, you can choose which drives to apply this to.

> **WARNING**
> Bypassing the Recycle Bin is generally a very bad idea unless you have another program for undeleting files. Files that are deleted and not sent to the Recycle Bin are gone beyond recall.

Even if you do have a program that will rescue files deleted in error, it's still not a good idea to bypass the Recycle Bin completely. Most such programs are dependent on your getting to the deleted file before it is overwritten by something else. And that can easily happen in Windows 98 SE, where something is usually going on behind the scenes.

> **TIP**
> If you begrudge large portions of your hard drive, make the reserved space on the hard drive very small—maybe 5 or 10MB. Check the box in the Properties dialog box to disable the confirmation requests. Then the Recycle Bin will be quite unobtrusive, but you'll still have some margin for safety.

Emptying the Recycle Bin

To get rid of everything in the Recycle Bin, right-click the Recycle Bin icon and select Empty Recycle Bin. There's also an Empty Recycle Bin option on the File menu in the Recycle Bin dialog box.

To remove only *some* of the items in the Recycle Bin, in the Recycle Bin dialog box, highlight the filenames, right-click one of them, and select Delete from the pop-up menu. You'll be asked to confirm the deletion (assuming you have the confirmation option turned on), and when you say Yes, the files will be deleted permanently.

What's Next?

In the first five chapters of this book, you've learned quite a bit about setting up and working with the Windows 98 SE interface. By now, you probably want to start doing something productive with your Windows 98 SE computer. The next chapter talks about installing and running programs.

Chapter 6

INSTALLING AND RUNNING PROGRAMS

Programs—also called *applications*—have become easier and easier to install in recent years, but there are still occasional pitfalls. In this chapter, we'll cover the steps for installing programs, whether or not the program is designed for Windows 98 SE. Later in the chapter, you'll find information on how to set up the programs you use most so that they are available when you want them.

Adapted from *Windows 98: No Experience Required*
by Sharon Crawford
ISBN 0-7821-2128-4   544 pages $24.99

Chapter Six

Installing a Program

In general, computer programs are easy to install. If you're going to have a problem, it's most likely to happen when you try to *run* a program. Programs that are genuinely compatible with Windows 98 SE, Windows 98, or Windows 95 are the easiest to install.

Installing from a CD

If the program is supplied on a CD-ROM, it may almost install itself. Some CDs are self-starting. Put the CD-ROM in the drive, and in a few seconds you'll see a window like the one shown in Figure 6.1.

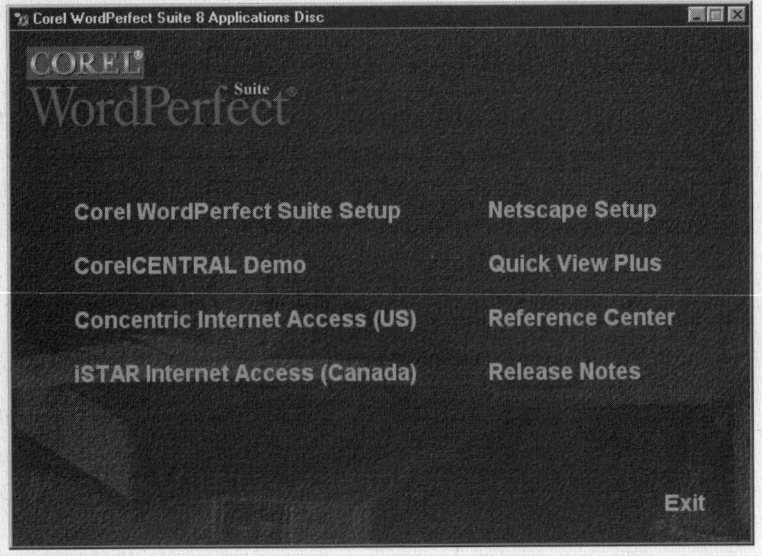

FIGURE 6.1: Corel's WordPerfect Suite on a CD-ROM automatically starts and lets you choose what to install.

In the window that opens, you choose what you want to install from the choices presented. After that, you answer the questions that are asked as you go along. You're often asked to supply your name, approve the location for files, and perhaps supply other information.

> **TIP**
> If you put the CD-ROM in the drive and nothing happens, go to "Installing from Control Panel" later in this chapter.

Most applications will copy some files to your hard drive, and when the setup procedure is completed, you remove the CD-ROM. You won't need it again unless you need to reinstall or you later decide to install some piece of software on the CD that you skipped the first time.

Running from a CD

Some programs are so large that you may not be able to install all of their data files for space reasons. Or you use them only infrequently and don't want to clutter your hard drive with a zillion graphics files. In that case, you can often *run* the program from the CD. For example, WordPerfect (see Figure 6.2) offers the option of running the program from the CD.

Installation Type

Select the type of installation you want, and then click Next.

- ○ **Typical** — Performs a standard installation (recommended). Default size: 108.94 MB
- ○ **Compact** — Performs a minimum installation (for laptops or low disk space configurations). Default size: 38.75 MB
- ○ **Custom** — Lets you choose which components to install. Default size: 110.18 MB
- ○ **Run from CD-ROM** — Installs files to your hard disk that let you run the applications from the CD-ROM. (Runs slower.) Default size: 53.16 MB

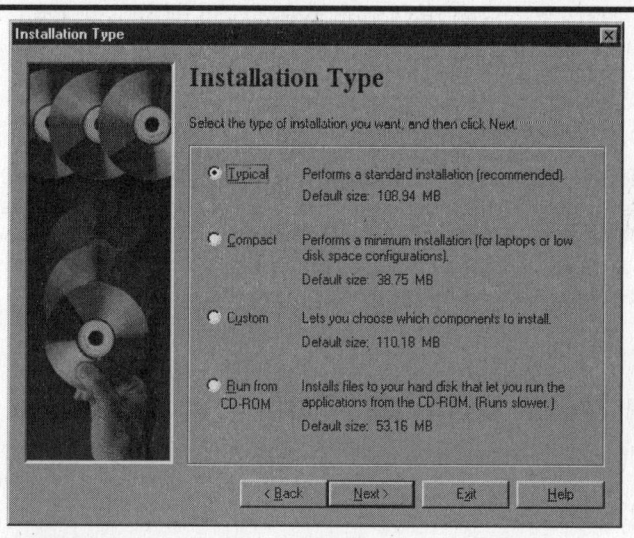

FIGURE 6.2: Selecting the installation type for WordPerfect

Although this type of installation uses only minimal hard drive space, it will also cause the program to run much slower. For a word processing program, which you presumably use for extended periods, this will be both annoying and frustrating. Getting and using files from the hard drive is much faster than even the fastest CD-ROM drive. And you won't be able to run the program at all unless the CD is in the CD-ROM drive.

> **TIP**
> If your hard drive space is severely limited, try a laptop installation rather than running a frequently used application from the CD-ROM drive.

Many programs that are designed to be run from the CD-ROM don't give you any other option. These are often games and reference works (dictionaries, encyclopedias, catalogs of graphics, and the like). These programs will set up by copying some files to your hard drive, but they will still require the CD-ROM to be in the CD-ROM drive in order to work.

For example, The Encarta World Atlas copies about 10MB to your hard drive. These are the files used, for the most part, to make accessing the CD-ROM faster. The Encarta World Atlas runs speedily enough from the CD-ROM drive because you're looking at a series of maps with at least a second or two between each. This is a positively restful pace for acquiring images from a CD. In the case of games, where such delays would be unacceptable, perhaps 80MB or more will be copied to the hard drive. All the files necessary to keep the action moving will be on your hard drive, with only backgrounds or help files retrieved from the CD.

> **TIP**
> If you have plenty of space, you can copy the entire contents of a CD to your hard drive and run the program from there. For example, I speeded up searches through the Encyclopedia Britannica by copying all 601MB to my local hard drive. With hard drive space selling at an average of 4 cents per megabyte, that isn't as much of an extravagance as it might seem.

Installing from Control Panel

All programs, whether on a CD or on floppy disks, can be installed using Add/Remove Programs in Control Panel. Have the CD or the first floppy disk handy and follow these steps:

1. Choose Start ➢ Settings ➢ Control Panel.
2. In Control Panel, click the Add/Remove Programs icon.

Add/Remove Programs

Installing and Running Programs

3. In the Add/Remove Programs Properties dialog box, click the Install button. Click Next.
4. Insert the first floppy or the CD-ROM, and click Next.
5. The application will search for a setup program, first in the floppy drive and then in the CD-ROM drive. Usually it will find Setup and proceed with the installation. If it doesn't, you'll see a dialog box like the one in Figure 6.3.

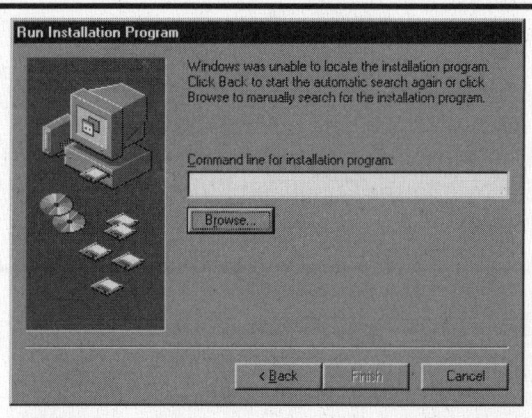

FIGURE 6.3: Add/Remove Programs is unable to find the new program's setup file.

6. If you know exactly where the setup program is on the CD or the floppy disk, you can, of course, type the path into the Command Line text box. But more likely, you'll need to click the Browse button.
7. The Browse window opens showing your C drive. Use the Look In drop-down box to move to your floppy drive or CD-ROM drive.
8. Find the setup file (the program's documentation will be helpful here) and select it (see Figure 6.4). Click the Open button.

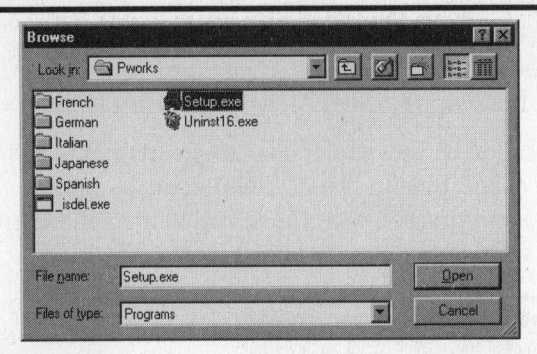

FIGURE 6.4: This program's setup file is in a subdirectory on the CD-ROM.

9. You'll return to the installation process with the path for the setup file shown in the Command Line text box (see Figure 6.5). Click Finish.

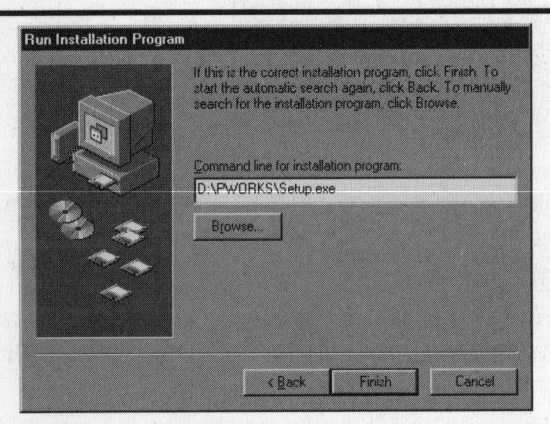

FIGURE 6.5: With the setup file located, you can click Finish to move on in the installation process.

The Setup program will run, and the actual installation of the new program will start.

TIP

Programs downloaded from the Internet or other sources are installed in a similar fashion. You can use Add/Remove Programs, pointing to the setup file location on your hard drive. Or you can click the setup file directly to start the installation process.

Removing a Program

The process of removing a program (also called *uninstalling*) varies depending on whether the program is a true 32-bit program written for Windows 95, Windows 98, Windows 98 SE or something older.

A software producer who wants the license to put a Windows 98, 98 SE, or 95 logo on a product is required to make sure the program can uninstall itself. This proviso is intended to correct a problem in Windows 3.1. When using Windows 3.1, it was very difficult to completely get rid of some programs because their files could be spread all over the hard drive. The average person has no way of knowing whether a file called, let's say, `fxstl.dll` is disposable because it belonged to a long gone program or whether deleting it will cause the entire system to fail!

A few programs that claim to have been written for Windows 95, 98, or 98 SE can be uninstalled and still leave bits of themselves cluttering your hard disk. How the major programs written for Windows 98 or 95 handle Add/Remove varies widely. Some will just uninstall themselves without a fuss; others give you the option of removing all or just part of the program. *Nothing* will be uninstalled without your OK.

To remove a Windows 98 SE, Windows 98, or Windows 95 program, follow these steps:

1. Choose Start ➣ Settings ➣ Control Panel.
2. Click the Add/Remove Programs icon.
3. In the dialog box that opens (shown in Figure 6.6), you'll see a list of programs that can be automatically removed. If the program you want to uninstall is in the list, highlight it and then click the Add/Remove button.

Sometimes after the removal, you'll get a message to the effect that not all parts of the program could be deleted. Since you're not told *which* parts, this is something less than helpful. For the ultimate in hard drive tidiness, look into one of the third-party programs like Uninstaller or WinDelete; these are very good at getting rid of stray files with safety.

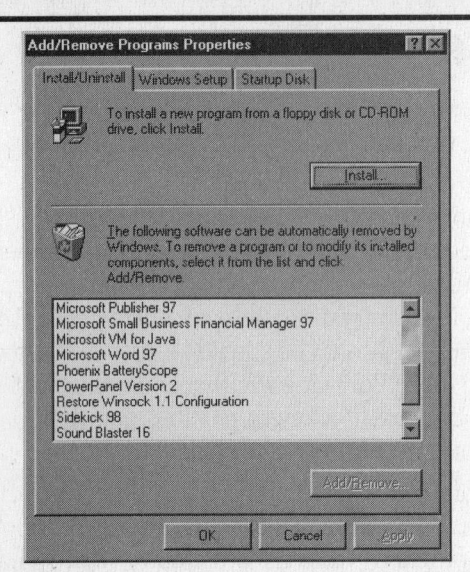

FIGURE 6.6: In this window, select a program to uninstall.

Removing a Windows 3.1 Program

Programs written for Windows versions prior to Windows 95 don't have an uninstall capability. These programs aren't hard to get rid of—at least superficially. Just find the directory for the program and delete it. Delete shortcuts relating to the program. Unfortunately, these early Windows programs have an unhappy tendency to deposit files in the main Windows directory, the System subdirectory, and anywhere else that the program's designers thought appropriate.

Getting rid of every trace of such a program is very difficult unless you have a program such as Uninstaller. Most of the time, however, it's not absolutely necessary to track down and delete every stray .dll file. You can survive quite well even if bits and pieces of a program remain.

Removing a DOS Program

Removing a DOS-based program is the easiest of all. Find the program's folder and delete it. DOS programs don't have roaming files, so if you delete the folder, you delete everything.

Installing and Running Programs 105

The only exception to the non-wandering file is if you have a shortcut to the program on the Desktop or elsewhere. Delete the shortcuts at the same time you delete the program folder.

Finding a Program

There are times when you've installed a program only to be abruptly returned to the desktop with your new application nowhere in sight. Or you inherit a computer that you know has certain programs on it—but they're likewise nowhere in sight.

Starting with the easiest method, here are some ways to find a program hiding on your system.

Program Menu

Your application may be in the easiest place of all. Click the Start button and select Programs. If it's not in the first menu, look for something that might be a "parent" to the one you want. For example, Figure 6.7 shows the Encarta World Atlas under the more general heading of Microsoft Reference.

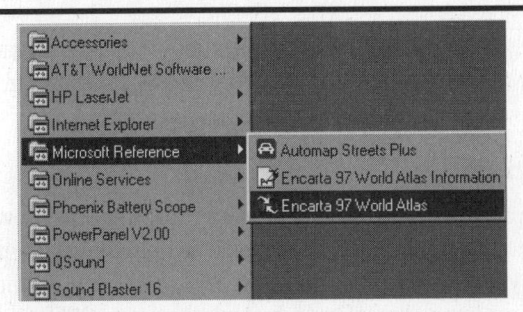

FIGURE 6.7: Finding the Encarta World Atlas program under a more general heading

Shortcuts

Look for a shortcut on your Desktop. If all you want to do is launch the program, clicking the shortcut should do the job. If you want to find the physical location for the program's files, right-click the shortcut and select Properties from the pop-up menu. In the Properties dialog box, click the Find Target button. The folder containing the program will open.

Find

Knowing the name of the program is usually enough to use the Find feature. Click the Start button and choose Find ➤ Files Or Folders. In the Named text box, type in what you know. In Figure 6.8, I'm looking for a program made by Starfish. Sure enough, the search turns up a folder called Starfish, and inside is the program I'm looking for.

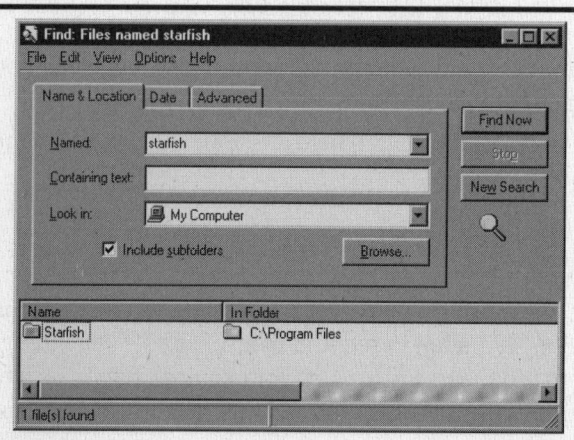

FIGURE 6.8: The Find function turns up a folder named Starfish.

I could just as easily search using a partial filename or program name. Sometimes it takes two or three tries to find what you're looking for.

Windows Explorer

When all else fails, you can simply open Windows Explorer and browse. Be sure to look in the Program Files folder as well as any Temp folders. The folder may or may not be clearly named. In Figure 6.9, it's not hard to figure out what might be in PhotoDraw, but what about 1033? Once you get to this stage of searching, you'll just have to poke around.

> **TIP**
>
> If you're in an unhelpfully named folder looking at even more unhelpfully named files, look for a file that really might help (it'll have the .hlp extension) and click it. You'll be looking at a help file that—if its authors were at all thoughtful—should tell you what program you're dealing with.

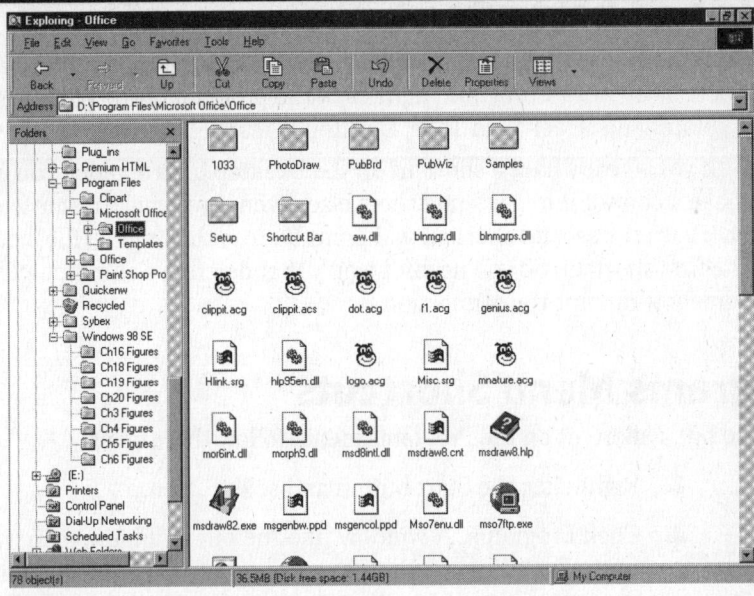

FIGURE 6.9: Searching for program files in Windows Explorer

Making Programs Easier to Find

Once you've been through a few searches like the ones just described, you realize the importance of making your programs easy to find. In the next sections, you'll see how to put your programs in convenient locations. When you're deciding, do give some consideration to how often you use a given application. If you put shortcuts to all your programs on the Start menu or on the Desktop, the resulting clutter will immediately cancel out any gain.

To make a shortcut to a program on the Programs menu, you need to first locate the program file. This is the file you click to start running the program. In general, this file will have the extension .exe and will have the same name (or a shortened version) as that of the overall program. As an example, the program file for Word 97 is Winword.exe, and that for WordPerfect 8 for Windows is wpwin8.exe. On the other hand, the program file for Quicken for Windows is qw.exe, and for InfoSelect it's is.exe.

Desktop Shortcuts

As described in Chapter 4, *Shortcuts Galore*, shortcuts are easily made. For a shortcut to a program, right-click the program file in Windows Explorer and select Send To ➢ Desktop (Create Shortcut).

If you already have a shortcut on the Desktop or in a folder, you can make a copy of it to use somewhere else. Even if you make a shortcut to a shortcut, the second shortcut will point back to the original file, *not* to the first shortcut. So you needn't worry that deleting a shortcut will somehow disrupt the connection.

Programs Menu Shortcuts

To put a shortcut on the Programs menu, follow these steps:

1. Right-click the Start button and select Open.
2. Click Programs. A window like the one in Figure 6.10 will open. Each item on this list corresponds to an entry on the Programs menu. Items that appear as a folder in the window are the items on the Programs menu with an arrow (➢) next to them—indicating that there are additional items to be found if you follow the arrow.

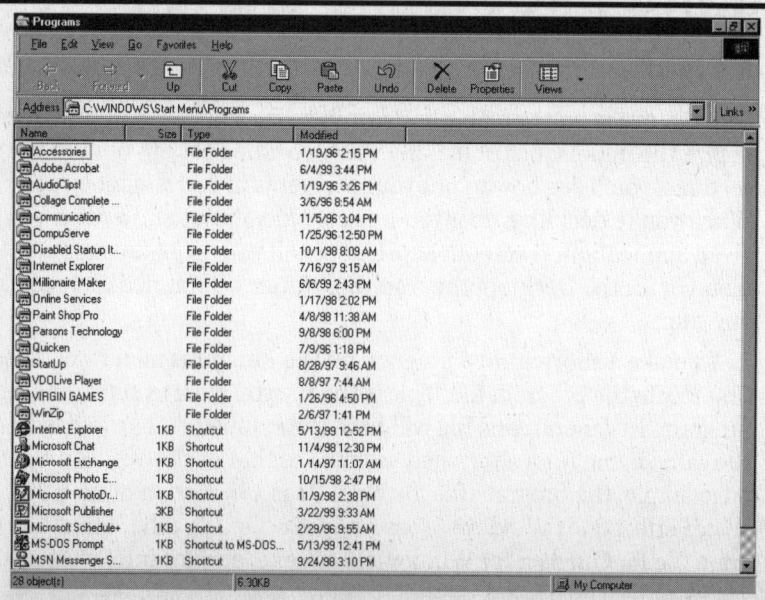

FIGURE 6.10: Compare the Programs window and the Programs menu.

Installing and Running Programs 109

3. If the shortcut is to be at the first level of the Programs menu, drag and drop the shortcut you've made into the Programs window.

4. To put the shortcut at the next level down, drag it into one of the folders in the Programs window. For example, drag and drop a shortcut to a game in the Accessories folder.

You can also easily move a program that's a level or two down up to the first Programs menu level:

1. In the Programs window, find the shortcut you want to move.

2. Right-click on the shortcut and select Cut from the pop-up menu.

3. Click the Up icon on the Programs window toolbar to move up one level in the Programs menu.

4. Right-click in a blank area of the new window and select Paste from the pop-up menu.

The program shortcut will move to its new location.

Start Menu Shortcuts

Adding a shortcut to the Start menu is as easy as drag and drop. In fact, that's what you do. Drag the shortcut to the Start button and drop it. When you open the Start menu, your shortcut will be listed among the programs at the top.

Toolbar Shortcuts

Even quicker access to a program can be had if you add a shortcut to the Quick Launch toolbar. By default, the Quick Launch toolbar comes with shortcuts to Internet Explorer, Outlook Express, the Desktop, and Channels already in place.

Add any shortcut to the toolbar by right-clicking, dragging the shortcut to the toolbar and dropping it there. Choose Move Here from the shortcut menu. You can remove shortcuts from the toolbar by reversing the procedure. Right-click the icon on the toolbar and, holding the mouse button down, drag the icon to the Desktop. When you release the mouse button, choose Move Here from the shortcut menu.

> **TIP**
>
> The Show Desktop icon on the Quick Launch toolbar acts as a "minimize all" button—minimizing all open windows to the Taskbar, even dialog boxes that won't ordinarily minimize. If you'd like to have other copies, right-click the icon and drag it to the Desktop (or to an open folder). Release the mouse button and select Copy Here from the pop-up menu.

Send-To Shortcuts

A right-click on a file or almost any other object will produce a menu that includes the option Send To ➤. When you follow the arrow, you'll see a list of shortcuts to possible file destinations such as the floppy drive, mail recipient, or My Briefcase.

To modify the Send To list, follow these steps:

1. Right-click the Start button and select Explore from the menu.

2. In the Windows Explorer window that opens, look for the SendTo folder in the left pane (see Figure 6.11).

3. Click the SendTo folder to open it.

4. Add to, delete, or rename any of the shortcuts. The changes will be shown as soon as they're made.

> **NOTE**
>
> If a program—any program—doesn't want to run or hangs or crashes, see Chapter 12, *System Troubleshooting*, for troubleshooting tips.

Installing and Running Programs

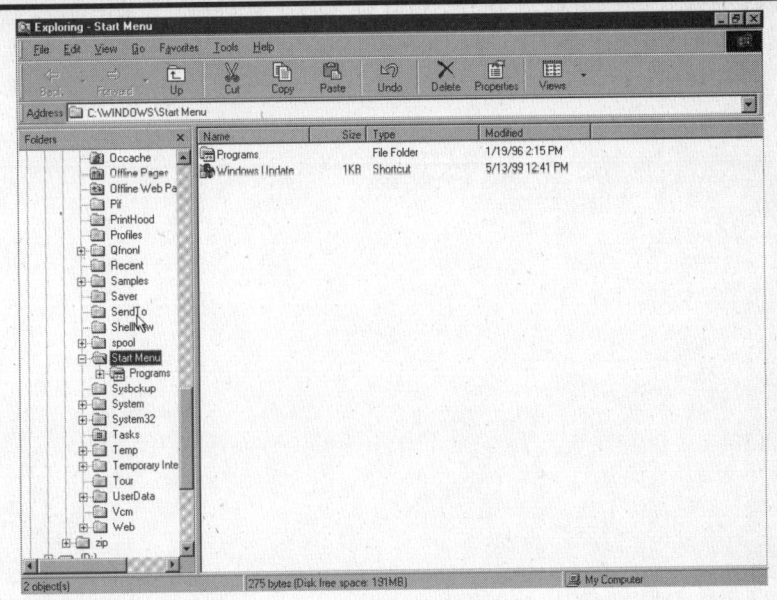

FIGURE 6.11: The mouse pointer shows the location of the SendTo folder.

What's Next?

In the next three chapters, we'll call upon another Windows 98 SE expert, Bob Cowart, to take you through some topics related to hardware. First, we'll look at customizing your configuration with the Control Panel, and then we'll explore printers and printing. Finally (here's the fun stuff), we'll check out the extensive support for multimedia in Windows 98 SE.

Chapter 7
Customizing Windows 98 SE with the Control Panel

There are numerous alterations you can make to customize Windows to your liking—adjustments to screen colors, modems, mouse speed, passwords, key repeat rate, fonts, and networking options, to name just a few. Most of these adjustments are not necessities as much as they are niceties that make using Windows just a little easier. Others are more imperative, such as setting up Windows to work with your brand and model of printer, setting up Windows Messaging preferences for your e-mail, or getting your mouse pointer to slow down a bit so you can reasonably control it.

Preferences of this sort are made through Windows 98 SE's Control Panel. Once you change a setting with the Control Panel, alterations are stored in the Windows configuration Registry. The settings are reloaded each time you run Windows and stay in effect until you change them again with the Control Panel.

Adapted from *Mastering Windows 98 Second Edition*
by Robert Cowart
ISBN 0-7821-2618-9   928 pages $39.99

A few Control Panel settings can be altered from other locations throughout Windows. For example, you can set up printers from the Start ➢ Settings ➢ Printers command, you can make Internet settings from within Internet Explorer, and you can change your screen's settings by right-clicking the Desktop. However, such approaches essentially run the Control Panel option responsible for the relevant settings, so the Control Panel is still doing the work. Running the Control Panel to make system changes is often easier because it displays in one place all the options for controlling your system. This chapter discusses how you run and work with the Control Panel and delves into what the multifarious settings are good for.

OPENING THE CONTROL PANEL

You open the Control Panel by clicking the Start button, choosing Settings, and choosing Control Panel. The Control Panel window then opens, as shown in Figure 7.1.

> **NOTE**
> The Control Panel can also be reached from My Computer or from Explorer. From Explorer, scroll the left pane to the top and click the My Computer icon. Then click the Control Panel in the right pane.

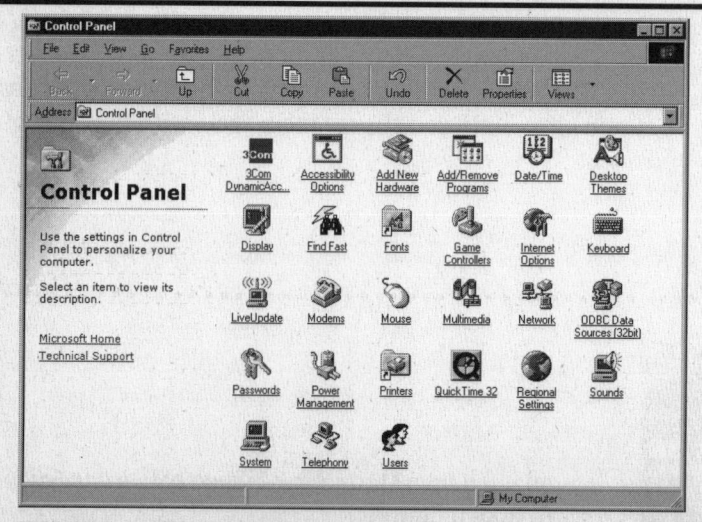

FIGURE 7.1: The Control Panel window. Each item opens a window from which you can make adjustments.

Customizing Windows 98 SE with the Control Panel 115

In your Control Panel there will be as many as twenty or so items to choose from, depending on the hardware in your computer and which items you opted for during installation of Windows 98 SE. As you add new software or hardware to your system, you'll occasionally see new options in your Control Panel, too. Or your mouse icon might look different from the one you see in the figure. One of my computers has a Microsoft Ballpoint mouse, so the icon looks like a trackball rather than a tabletop mouse.

Each icon in the Control Panel runs a little program (called an *applet*) when you open it, typically bringing up one or more dialog boxes for you to make settings in. Below is a list of all the standard Control Panel applets and what they do. For more on these programs, also see Chapter 14, *Windows 98 SE Applets*.

Accessibility Options   Lets you set keyboard, mouse, sound, display, and other options that make a Windows 98 SE computer easier to use by those who are visually, aurally, or motor impaired.

Add New Hardware   Installs or removes sound, CD-ROM, video, MIDI, hard- and floppy-disk controllers, PCMCIA sockets, display adapters, SCSI controllers, keyboard, mouse, printers, ports, and other device drivers.

Add/Remove Programs   You can add or remove modules of Windows 98 SE itself and sometimes add or remove other kinds of programs. Also lets you create a start-up disk to start your computer with in case the operating system on the hard disk gets trashed accidentally.

Date/Time   Sets the current date and time and which time zone you're in.

Desktop Themes   These combine custom sounds, color schemes, screen savers, and cursors into easily chosen groups of settings.

Display   Sets the colors (or gray levels) and fonts of various parts of Windows' screens, title bars, scroll bars, and so forth. Sets the background pattern or picture for the Desktop. Also allows you to choose the screen saver, display driver, screen resolution, and energy-saving mode (if your display supports it).

Fonts   Adds and deletes typefaces for your screen display and printer output. Allows you to look at samples of each of your fonts.

Game Controllers   Adds, removes, and adjusts settings for "joysticks" and other types of game controllers.

Infrared   Configures and monitors infrared (wireless) communications.

Internet Options   Settings for all Internet-related activities such as Web, mail, newsgroups, your home page location, and so on.

Keyboard   Sets the rate at which keys repeat when you hold them down, sets the cursor blink rate, determines the language your keyboard will be able to enter into documents, and lets you declare the type of keyboard you have.

Modems   Lets you add, remove, and set the properties of the modem(s) connected to your system.

Mouse   Sets the speed of the mouse pointer's motion relative to your hand motion and how fast a double-click has to be to have an effect. You can also reverse the functions of the right and left buttons, set the shape of the various Windows 98 SE pointers, and tell Windows that you've changed the type of mouse you have.

Multimedia   Changes the audio, MIDI, CD music, and other multimedia device drivers, properties, and settings.

Network   Function varies with the network type. Typically allows you to set the network configuration (network card/connector, protocols, and services), add and configure optional support for Novell, Banyan, Sun network support, and network backup hardware, change your identification (workgroup name, computer name), and determine the manner in which you control who gains access to resources you share over the network, such as printers, fax modems, and folders.

ODBC Data Sources   If you are connected to a network and use an ODBC (Open Database Connectivity) compliant database program such as Oracle or Access, this applet allows you to control your connections and modify driver settings. You can also specify data sources on your own machine for sharing on the network.

Customizing Windows 98 SE with the Control Panel

Passwords   Sets up or changes log-on passwords, allows remote administration of the computer, and sets up individual profiles that go into effect when each new user logs onto the local computer.

PCMCIA   Lets you stop PCMCIA cards before removing them, set the memory area for the card service shared memory (very unlikely to be needed), and disable/enable the beeps that indicate PCMCIA cards are activated when the computer boots up. This icon only appears on laptops or on desktop machines configured with PCMCIA slots.

Power Management   If you have a battery-powered portable computer or an energy-efficient desktop machine, this applet provides options for setting the Advanced Power Management details and viewing a scale indicating the current condition of the battery charge.

Printers   Displays the printers you have installed on your system, lets you modify the property settings for those printers, and lets you display and manage the *print queue* for each of those printers. Use this applet to install *printer drivers*.

Regional Settings   Sets how Windows displays times, dates, numbers, and currency.

Sounds   Turns off and on the computer's beep or adds sounds to various system events if your computer has built-in sound capability. Lets you set up sound *schemes*—preset collections of sounds that your system uses to alert you to specific events.

System   Displays information about your system's internals—devices, amount of RAM, type of processor, and so forth. Also lets you add to, disable, and remove specific devices from your system, set up hardware profiles (for instance, to allow automatic optimization when using a docking station with a laptop), and optimize some parameters of system performance such as CD cache size and type. This applet also provides a number of system-troubleshooting tools.

Telephony   Lets you delete your location, your dialing prefixes for an outside line, and other attributes relating to telephone-dependent activities that rely on the TAPI interface.

Users Enables your computer to be set up for use by other people, allowing each of them to have their own Desktop icons, background, color choices, and other settings.

> **NOTE**
> All the Control Panel setting dialog boxes have a ? button in their upper-right corner. You can click this button, then on an item in the dialog box that you have a question about. You'll be shown some relevant explanation about the item.

I'll now discuss the Control Panel applets in detail. Aside from the Accessibility settings, the applets here are the ones you're most likely to want to adjust.

Accessibility Options

Accessibility means increasing the ease of use or access to a computer for people who are physically challenged in one way or another. Many people have difficulty seeing characters on the screen when they are too small, for example. Others have a disability that prevents them from easily typing on the keyboard. Even those of us who hunt and peck at the keyboard have it easy compared with those who can barely move their hands, are limited to the use of a single hand, or who may be paralyzed from the neck down. These people have gotten the short end of the stick for some time when it came to using computers unless they had special data-entry and retrieval devices (such as speech boards) installed in their computers.

Microsoft has taken a big step in increasing computer accessibility to disabled people by including in Windows 98 SE features that allow many challenged people to use Windows and Windows programs without major modification to their machines or software. (Accessibility add-ons for older versions of Windows have been available for some time, but as add-ons.)

The Accessibility applet lets you make special use of the keyboard, display, mouse, sound board, and a few other aspects of your computer. To run the Accessibility option, double-click its icon in the Control Panel. The resulting dialog box looks like Figure 7.2.

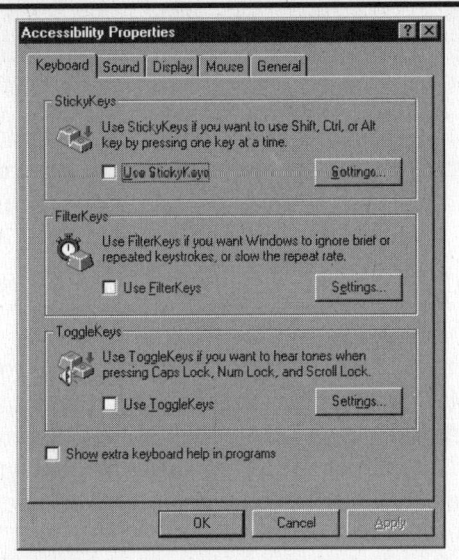

Customizing Windows 98 SE with the Control Panel

FIGURE 7.2: Accessibility dialog box

> **NOTE**
>
> As of Windows 98 SE, several new accessibility features have been added, including support for screen readers, larger high-contrast font displays, screen magnification, and more. Most of these features are available via the Accessibility Wizard, which is an entry point and interface for the settings described in this section. To reach this wizard, click Start ➢ Programs ➢ Accessories ➢ Accessibility Wizard. For more information about Microsoft's ongoing advancements in accessibility support, and for API information, please see http://microsoft.com/enable.

Keyboard Accessibility Settings

Probably all of us have some difficulty keeping multiple keys depressed at once. Settings here help with this problem and others.

1. Click the Keyboard tab (if it's not already selected). There are three basic setting areas:

    StickyKeys   Keys that in effect stay pressed down when you press them once. Good for controlling the Alt, Ctrl, and Shift keys.

FilterKeys	Lets you filter out quickly repeated keystrokes in case you have trouble pressing a key cleanly once and letting it up. This prevents multiple keystrokes from being typed.
ToggleKeys	Gives you the option of hearing tones that alert you to the Caps Lock, Scroll Lock, and Num Lock keys being activated.

2. Click the box of the feature you want your Windows 98 SE machine to use.

3. Note that each feature has a Settings button from which you can make additional adjustments. To see the additional settings, click the Settings button next to the feature, fine-tune the settings, and then click OK. The most likely setting changes you'll make from these boxes are to turn on or off the shortcut keys.

4. After you have made all the keyboard changes you want, either move on to another tab in the Accessibility box or click OK and return to the Control Panel.

> **TIP**
> You can turn on any of these keyboard features—StickyKeys, FilterKeys, or ToggleKeys—with shortcuts at any time while in Windows 98 SE. To turn on StickyKeys, press either Shift key five times in a row. To turn on FilterKeys, press and hold the right Shift key for eight seconds (it might take longer). To turn on the ToggleKeys option, press the Num Lock key for five seconds.

When StickyKeys or FilterKeys are turned on, a symbol will appear on the right side of the Taskbar indicating what's currently activated. For example, here I have the StickyKeys and FilterKeys both set on. StickyKeys is indicated by the three small boxes, representative of the Ctrl, Alt, and Shift keys. FilterKeys is represented by the stopwatch, the different key timing that goes into effect when the option is working.

> **TIP**
> Turning on FilterKeys will make it seem that your keyboard has ceased working. You have to press a key and keep it down for several seconds for the key to register. If you activate this setting and want to turn it off, the easiest solution is to use the mouse or switch to Control Panel (via the Taskbar), run the Accessibility applet, turn off FilterKeys, and click OK.

Customizing Windows 98 SE with the Control Panel

Unless you disable this feature from the Settings dialog box, you can turn off StickyKeys by pressing two of the three keys that are affected by this setting. For example, pressing Ctrl and Alt at the same time will turn StickyKeys off.

Sound Accessibility Settings

There are two Sound Accessibility settings—Sound Sentry and Show-Sounds (see Figure 7.3). These two features are for the hearing impaired. What they do is simply cause some type of visual display to occur in lieu of the normal beep, ding, or other auditory alert that the program would typically produce. The visual display might be something such as a blinking window (in the case of Sound Sentry), or it might be some kind of text caption (in the case of ShowSounds).

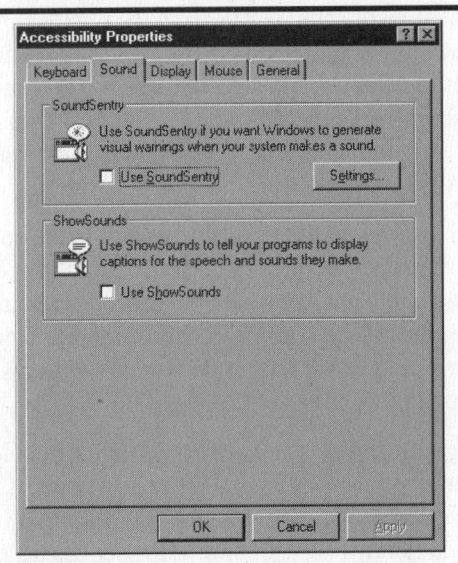

FIGURE 7.3: The two Sound Accessibility settings

The Settings button for Sound Sentry lets you decide what will graphically happen on screen when a program is trying to warn you of something. For example, should it flash the window, flash the border of the program, or flash the whole screen? If you really don't want to miss a beep-type warning, you might want to have it flash the window. (Flashing the whole screen doesn't indicate which program is producing the warning.)

> **NOTE**
> Not all programs will work cooperatively with these sound options. As more programs are written to take advantage of these settings, you'll see more *closed captioning*, for example, wherein sound messages are translated into useful captions on the screen.

Display Accessibility Settings

The Display Accessibility settings (see Figure 7.4) pertain to contrast. These settings let you set the display color scheme and font selection for easier reading. This can also be done from the normal Display setting, described below, but the advantage to setting it here is that you can pre-set your favorite high-contrast color scheme, then invoke it with the shortcut key combination when you most need it. Just press Left-Alt+Left-Shift+Prnt-Scrn. This might be when your eyes are tired, when someone who is sight impaired is using the computer, or when you're sitting in an adverse lighting situation. To establish Display Accessibility setting, follow these steps:

1. Turn on the High Contrast option box if you want to improve the contrast between the background and the characters on your screen. When you click Apply or OK, this will kick in a high-contrast color scheme (typically the Blue and Black scheme), which will put black letters on a white work area. (You can't get much more contrast than that!)

2. Click the Settings button if you want to change the color scheme that'll be used for high contrast or if you want to enable or disable shortcut-key activation of this feature. This option may come in handy because some of the schemes have larger fonts than others and some might show up better on your screen than will others.

> **TIP**
> You can experiment more easily with the schemes in the Display applet than here. You can even create your own custom color scheme with large menus, title bar lettering, and dialog box lettering if you want. I explain how to do all this in the Display section.

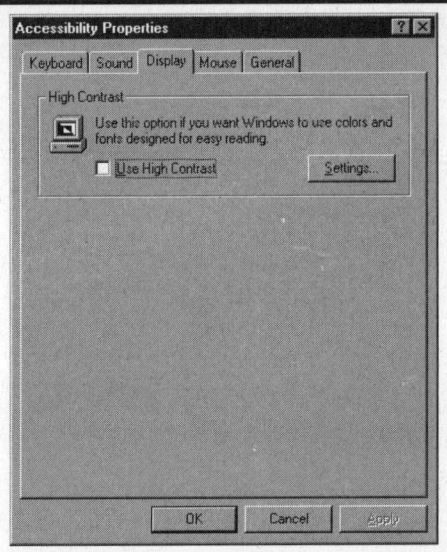

Customizing Windows 98 SE with the Control Panel

FIGURE 7.4: The dialog box for setting Display Accessibility

3. Click Apply if you want to keep making more settings from the other tab pages, or click OK to return to the Control Panel.

Mouse Accessibility Settings

If you can't easily control mouse or trackball motion, or simply don't like using a mouse, this dialog box is for you. Of course, you can invoke most commands that apply to dialog boxes and menus throughout Windows and Windows programs using the Alt key in conjunction with the command's underlined letter. Still, some programs, such as those that work with graphics, require you to use a mouse. This Accessibility option turns your arrow keys into mouse-pointer control keys. You still have to use the mouse's clicker buttons to left- or right-click things, though. Here's what to do:

1. Click the Mouse tab in the Accessibility dialog box. You'll see the box displayed in Figure 7.5.

> **TIP**
> This is a great feature for laptop users who are on the road and forgot the mouse. If you have to use a graphics program or other program requiring more than simple command choices and text entry, use the Mouse Accessibility tab to turn your arrow keys into mouse-pointer keys.

Chapter Seven

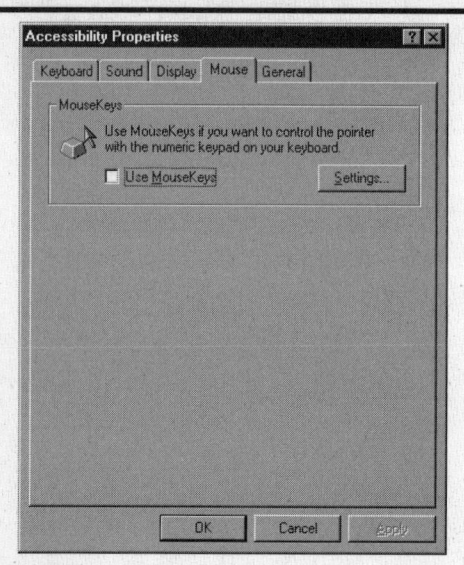

FIGURE 7.5: The Mouse Accessibility dialog box

2. Turn on the option if you want to use the arrow keys in place of the mouse. You'll probably want to adjust the speed settings for the arrow keys, though, so the pointer moves at a rate that works for you. The Settings button brings up the box you see in Figure 7.6. Note that you can also set a shortcut key sequence to activate MouseKeys.

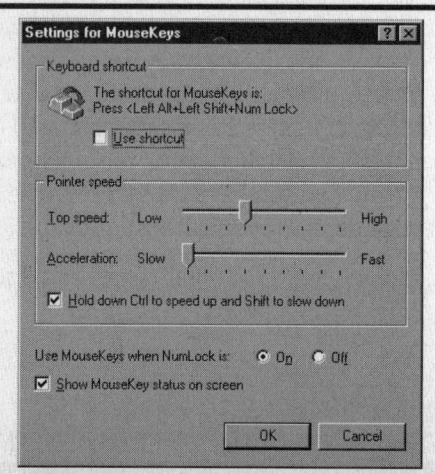

FIGURE 7.6: Additional Mouse Accessibility settings

Customizing Windows 98 SE with the Control Panel

3. Play with the settings until you like them. The Top Speed and Acceleration settings are going to be the most important. And note that you have to set them, click OK, then click Apply in the Mouse dialog box before you can experience the effect of your changes. Then go back and adjust your settings if necessary. Notice that one setting lets you change the tracking speed on the fly while using a program, by holding down the Shift key to slow down the pointer's motion or the Ctrl key to speed it up.

4. Click Apply if you want to keep making more settings from the other tab pages, or click OK to return to the Control Panel.

TIP

The pointer keys that are used for mouse control are the ones on a standard desktop computer keyboard's number pad. These are the keys that have two modes—Num Lock on and Num Lock off. These keys usually have both an arrow and a number on them; for example, the 4 key also has a ← symbol on it. Most laptops don't have such keys because of size constraints. However, many laptops have a special arrangement that emulates these keys, providing a ten-key numeric keypad (and arrows when Num Lock is off).

WHEEL MOUSE SUPPORT

One particularly crucial accessibility improvement in Windows 98 is the inclusion of support for the Microsoft "wheel mouse" (a.k.a. the Intellimouse™). That's a mouse with a little wheel sticking up between the mouse buttons. When you spin the wheel with some newer programs it scrolls the contents of the active window; it relieves you of having to position the pointer on the scroll bar. Spinning the wheel one increment causes text to scroll several lines (default: three) per wheel detent.

Just because a window has a scroll bar doesn't mean it will work with the wheel. The program has to be "wheel aware." Some wheel-aware programs, including the programs in Office 2000, will zoom in or out (cause the document to be displayed larger or smaller) if you rotate the wheel and hold down the Ctrl key at the same time.

CONTINUED ➞

> Some wheel-aware applications (such as Internet Explorer or an Office 2000 program) also offer "panning mode": you press down on the wheel to enter this special mode. When in panning mode, the mouse cursor changes to a special panning cursor, and just moving the mouse forward or backward will start the document scrolling in its window. The scroll speed is determined by how far you pull the mouse away from the position where you activated panning mode. When you want to exit the panning mode, simply press any mouse button.

Other Accessibility Settings

The last tab in the Accessibility box is called General (see Figure 7.7).

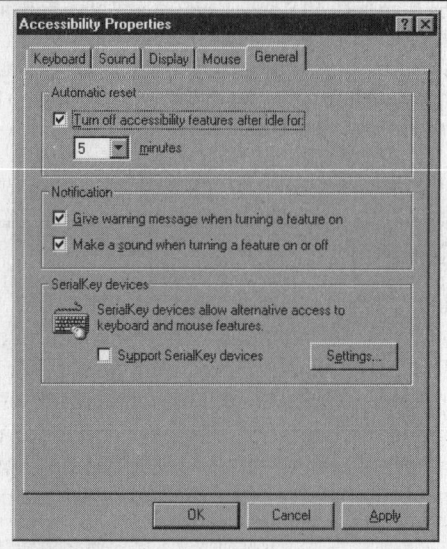

FIGURE 7.7: The last of the Accessibility settings boxes

The box is divided into three sections pertaining to:

- ▶ When Accessibility functions are turned on and off. Notice that you can choose to turn off all the settings after Windows has been idle for a period of time.

Customizing Windows 98 SE with the Control Panel 127

- How you are alerted to a feature being turned on or off. You have the choice of a visual cue (a little dialog box will appear) and/or a sound.

- Acceptance of alternative input devices through the serial (COM1 through COM4) ports on your computer:

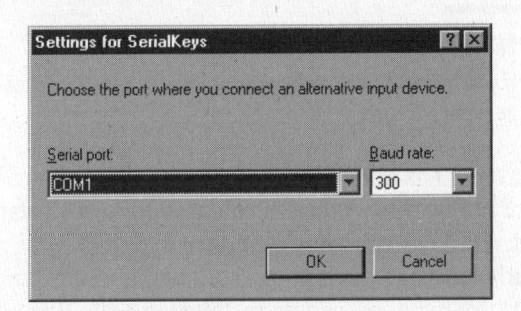

Adding New Hardware

If you have a computer that is Plug-and-Play compatible, this section won't be of a lot of use to you, and you should celebrate. That's because Plug and Play ensures that by simply plugging a new card or other device into your computer, it will work. The Plug and Play software in Windows 98 SE—in concert with software coding in the computer and add-on cards and devices—takes care of installing the appropriate hardware device driver file and making the appropriate settings so your new device doesn't conflict with some other device in the system. That's the good news.

> **NOTE**
> Of course, there are a limited number of IRQs, ports, and DMAs. Plug in enough Plug-and-Play cards, and one or more is guaranteed not to be installed by the system because Plug and Play will not enable a device unless resources are available for it.

The bad news is that there are a zillion non–Plug-and-Play PC cards and devices floating around in the world and just as many pre–Plug-and-Play PCs. This older hardware isn't designed to take advantage of Windows 98 SE's Plug-and-Play capabilities. The upshot of this is that when you install such hardware into your system, many computers won't detect the change. This will result in disappointment when you've carefully installed some piece of new and exciting gear (such as a sound card) and it just doesn't work—or worse, it disables things that used to function just fine.

> **NOTE**
> If you're installing a new printer, please read Chapter 8, *Printers and Printing*, as well.

Microsoft has added a nifty feature that tries its best to install a new piece of hardware for you. All you have to do is declare your new addition and let Windows run around and try to detect what you've done. Luckily, the Add Hardware applet is pretty savvy about interrogating the hardware you've installed—via its Install Hardware Wizard—and making things work right. You can also tell it exactly what you have in order to save a little time and ensure that Windows gets it right.

> **NOTE**
> Notice the applet is only for adding new hardware, not for removing hardware and associated driver files. Removing drivers is done through the System applet. Note that there are other locations throughout Windows for installing some devices, such as printers, which can be installed from the Printers folder via My Computer. However, the effect is the same as installing these devices from this applet.

> **TIP**
> Microsoft maintains a Windows 98 driver library that contains new, tested drivers as they are developed for printers, networks, screens, audio cards, and so forth. You can access these drivers through the Microsoft Web site, CompuServe, GEnie, or the Microsoft Download Service (MSDL). You can fax MSDL at (425) 936-6735. You can also order the entire library on disk by calling Microsoft at (800) 426-9400.

Running the Install Hardware Wizard

If you've purchased a board or other hardware add-in, first read the supplied manual for details about installation procedures. There may be

Customizing Windows 98 SE with the Control Panel 129

installation tips and an install program supplied with the hardware. If there are no instructions, then install the hardware and follow the steps below (but *only* if there are no instructions).

> **NOTE**
>
> I strongly suggest you install the hardware before you run the Wizard, or Windows 98 SE won't be able to validate that the hardware is present. Also, unless you follow these procedures, simply putting new hardware into your computer usually won't change anything. This is because Windows has to update the Registry containing the list of hardware in your system, it has to install the appropriate device-driver software for the added hardware, and it often has to reboot before the new hardware will work.

1. Close any programs you have running. You're probably going to be rebooting the machine, and it's possible that the detection process will hang up the computer, possibly trashing work files that are open.

2. Look up or otherwise discover the precise brand name and model number/name of the item you're installing. You'll need to know it somewhere during this process.

3. Run the Control Panel and double-click the Add New Hardware applet. You'll see its dialog box, looking like the one in Figure 7.8.

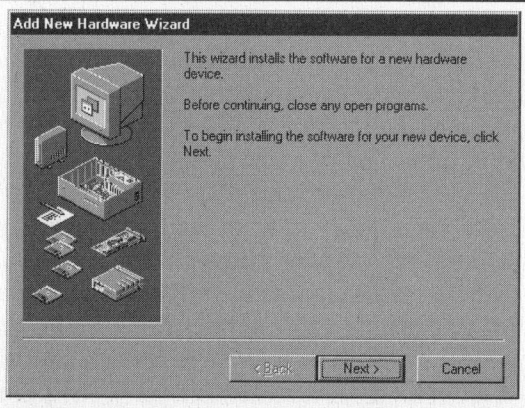

FIGURE 7.8: The Add Hardware Wizard makes installing new hardware easy—usually.

Chapter Seven

4. There's nothing to do but click Next. The wizard looks for any new Plug-and-Play hardware, and will list anything new that it finds. The next box, as shown in Figure 7.9, requires some action on your part, though.

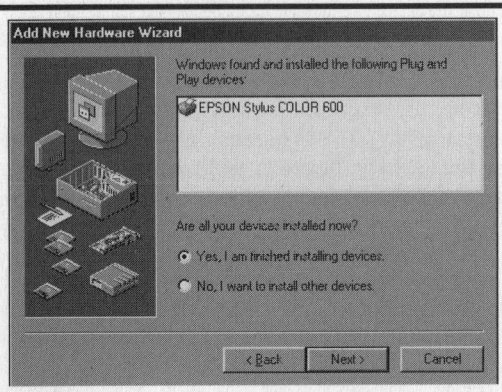

FIGURE 7.9: Choose the type of hardware you want to install.

5. If the item(s) list looks complete, click Yes, I Am Finished Installing Devices, and click Next. Follow instructions on screen. If you are not satisfied with the list and want some other stuff installed, click No, I Want To Install Other Devices, then Next, and move to step 7.

6. Now, if you want the Wizard to run around, look at what you have, and notice the new item you installed, just leave the top option button selected and click Next. You'll be warned that this could take several minutes and be advised to close any open programs and documents. Keep in mind that the Wizard is doing quite a bit of sleuthing as it looks over your computer. Many add-in cards and devices don't have standardized ID markings, so identifying some hardware items isn't so easy. The Microsoft programmers had to devise some clever interrogation techniques to identify myriad hardware items. In fact, the results may even be erroneous in some cases. Regardless, while the hardware survey is underway, you'll hear a lot of hard-disk activity, and you'll see a gauge apprising you of the progress:

Customizing Windows 98 SE with the Control Panel

In rare cases, the computer will hang during this process, and you'll have to reboot. If this happens repeatedly, you'll have to tell the Wizard what hardware you've added, as explained in the next section.

7. When completed, you'll either be told that nothing new was found or you'll see a box listing the discovered items, asking for confirmation and/or some details. Respond as necessary. You may be prompted to insert one of your Windows 98 SE diskettes or the master CD-ROM so the appropriate driver file(s) can be loaded. If nothing new was found, click Next, and the Wizard sends you on to step 2 in the section below.

Telling the Wizard What You've Got

If you're the more confident type (in your own abilities rather than the computer's), you might want to take the surer path to installing new hardware. Option two in the previous Wizard box lets *you* declare what the new hardware is. This option not only saves you time, but even lets you install the hardware later, should you want to. This is because the Wizard doesn't bother to authenticate the existence of the hardware: It simply installs the new driver.

1. Follow steps 1 through 5 above.
2. Now choose the second option button, Install Specific Hardware.
3. Scroll through the list to get an idea of all the classes of hardware you can install via this applet. Then click the category you want to install. For this example, I'm going to install Creative Lab's Sound Blaster sound card because that's a popular add-in item.

> **TIP**
> If you don't know the class of the item you're installing, you're not sunk. Just choose Other Devices. Find and click the manufacturer's brand name in the left-hand list; most popular items made by that manufacturer will be displayed in the right-hand list. Then choose your new hardware from this list.

Chapter Seven

4. Click Next. This brings up a list of all the relevant drivers in the class you've chosen. For example, Figure 7.10 lists the sound cards from Creative Labs, the people who make the Sound Blaster cards.

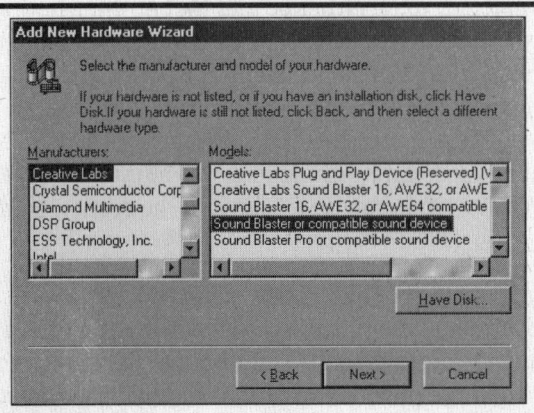

FIGURE 7.10: After choosing a class of hardware, you'll see a list of manufacturers and models.

5. First scroll the left list and click the manufacturer. Then find the correct item in the Model list and click that.

6. Click Next. What happens at this point depends on the type of hardware you're installing:

    ▶ If the hardware is Plug-and-Play compatible, you'll be informed of it, and the Wizard will take care of the details.

    ▶ For some non–Plug-and-Play hardware, you'll be told to simply click Finish, and the Wizard will take care of installing the necessary driver.

    ▶ In some cases, you'll be shown the settings that you should adjust your hardware to match. (Add-in cards often have switches or software adjustments that control the I/O port, DMA address, and other such geeky stuff.) For example, Figure 7.11 shows the message I got about the Sound Blaster card. Your job is to read the manual that came with the hardware and figure out how to adjust the switches, jumpers, or other doodads to match the settings the Wizard gives you.

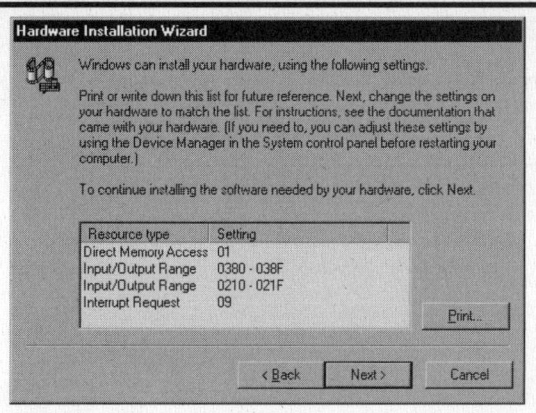

Customizing Windows 98 SE with the Control Panel

FIGURE 7.11: For hardware that has address or other adjustments on it, you may be told which setting to use to avoid conflicts with other hardware in the system.

TIP

If for some reason you don't want to use the settings suggested by the Wizard, you can set the board or device otherwise. Then you'll have to use the System applet's Device Manager to change the settings in the Windows Registry to match those on the card.

▶ In some cases, you'll be told there's a conflict between your new hardware and what's already in your computer (see Figure 7.12). Despite the dialog box's message, you have *three* choices, not two. In addition to proceeding or canceling, you could also back up and choose a different piece of hardware, such as a different model number or a compatible make or model that might support a different port, DMA address, or whatnot. If you decide to continue, you'll have to resolve the conflict somehow, such as by removing or re-addressing the conflicting board or device. In that case you'll be shown a dialog box that lets you run the *conflict troubleshooter*. This is a combination of a Help file and the System applet's Device Manager. The Help file walks you through a series of questions and answers.

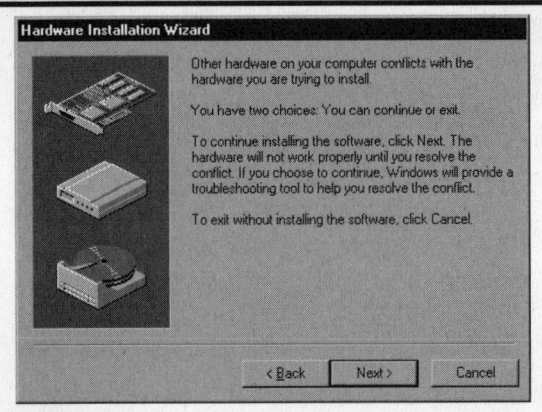

FIGURE 7.12: You have three options when the Wizard detects a conflict: the two choices offered and the Back button to try another piece of hardware.

7. Next, you may be prompted to insert a disk containing the appropriate software driver. Windows remembers the disk drive and directory you installed Windows 98 SE from, so it assumes the driver is in that location. This might be a network directory, your CD-ROM drive, or a floppy drive. In any case, just supply the requested disk. If the driver is already in your system, you will be asked if you want to use the existing driver. This is okay assuming the driver is up to date and you aren't trying to install a new one.

8. Finally, a box will announce that the necessary changes have been made and you can click Finish. If you haven't physically installed the hardware already, you'll see this message:

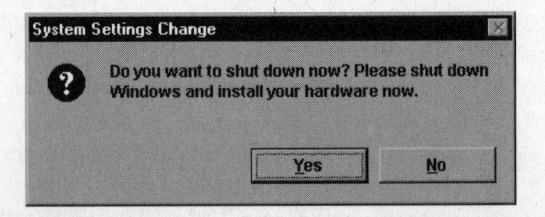

If the hardware is already installed, you'll probably see a message asking you to shut down and restart.

When Your Hardware Isn't on the List

Sometimes your new hardware won't be included in the list of items the Wizard displays. This means that Microsoft hasn't included a driver for that device on the disks that Windows 98 SE came on. This is probably because your hardware is newer than Windows 98 SE, so it wasn't around when the disk went out the door from Microsoft. Or it could be that the manufacturer didn't bother to get its product certified by Microsoft and earn the Windows "seal of approval." It's worth the few extra bucks to buy a product with the Windows 95 or 98 logo on the box rather than the cheapie clone product. As mentioned above, Microsoft makes new drivers available to users through several channels. However, manufacturers often supply drivers with their hardware, or you can get hold of a driver from the Internet, an information service such as CompuServe, or Microsoft Network.

If you're in this boat, you can just tell the Add New Hardware Wizard to use the driver on your disk. Here's how:

1. Run the Add New Hardware applet and choose the correct class of hardware, as explained above.

2. Click the Have Disk button:

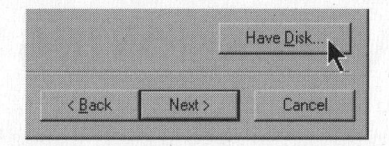

3. Enter the location of the driver (you can enter any path, such as a directory on the hard disk or network path) in this box:

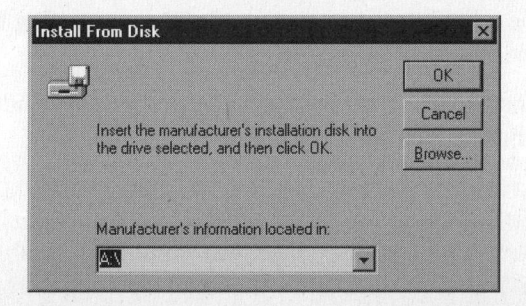

Often, you'll be putting a disk in drive A, in which case you'd use the setting shown here. However, don't type the filename for the driver, just its path. Usually this will be just A:\ or B:\. If the driver is on a hard disk or CD-ROM and you don't know which letter drive or which directory it is, use the Browse button and subsequent dialog box to select the source drive and directory. When the path is correct, click OK.

4. Assuming the Wizard finds a suitable driver file (it must find a file called OEMSETUP.INF), choose the correct hardware item from the resulting dialog box and follow on-screen directions (they'll be the same as those I described above, beginning with step 6).

NOTE

If you're not sure which ports and interrupts your other boards are using, rather than use the old trial-and-error method, Windows 98 SE comes with a great tool for sleuthing this out—the Control Panel's System applet. Double-clicking the Computer icon at the top of the Device Manager page in that applet will reveal a list of IRQs and ports that are currently in use.

Adding and Removing Programs

If you want to install a new piece of software or install and remove Windows features, this is the place to go. The applet has three functions:

- Installing and uninstalling programs that comply with Windows 98's API for these tasks. The API ensures that a program's filenames and locations are recorded in a database, allowing them to be reliably erased without adversely impacting the operation of Windows 98 SE.

- Installing and removing specific portions of Windows 98 SE itself, such as Web TV for Windows.

- Creating a start-up disk that will start your computer in case the operating system gets trashed beyond functionality for some reason. With a start-up disk, you should still be able to gain access to your files and stand a chance of repairing the problem that prevents the machine from starting up.

Installing New Programs

The applet's first tab page is for installing new programs.

1. Run Control Panel, then the Add/Remove Programs applet. You'll see the box shown in Figure 7.13.

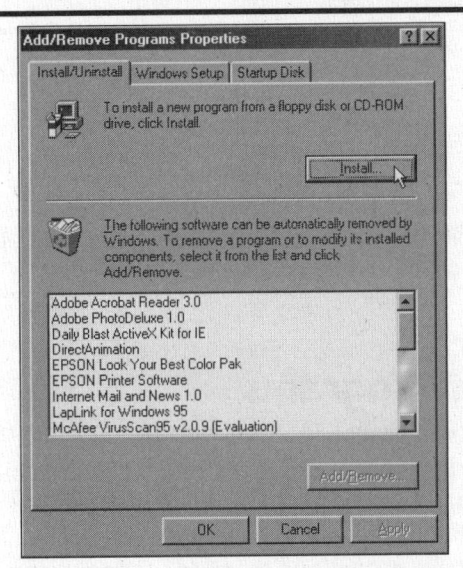

FIGURE 7.13: The Wizard for adding and removing software can be reached from the Add/Remove Programs applet (only programs that comply with Windows 98 SE installation standards).

2. Click Install. Now a new box appears, telling you to insert a floppy disk or CD-ROM in the appropriate drive and click Next. Assuming an appropriate program is found (it must be called *install* or *setup* and have a .BAT, .PIF, .COM, or .EXE extension), it'll be displayed as you see in Figure 7.14.

3. Click Finish to complete the task. The new software's installation or setup procedure will now run. Instructions will vary depending on the program. If your program's setup routine isn't compatible with the applet, you'll be advised of this. After installation, the new program will appear in the list of removable programs only if it's compatible with Windows 98 SE's install/remove scheme.

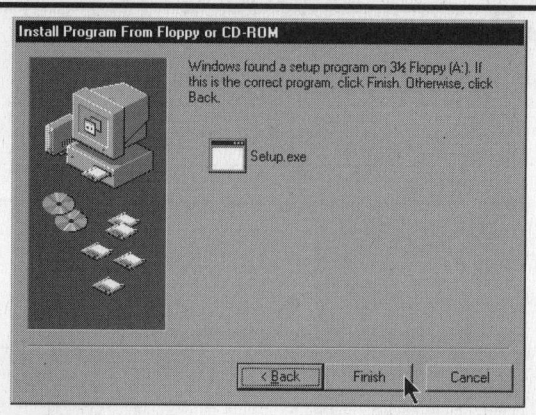

FIGURE 7.14: The Wizard looks for a likely installation program on your CD-ROM or floppy, and displays the first one it finds.

Removing Existing Programs

With time, more programs will be removable via the Control Panel. This is because the PC software industry at large has heard much kvetching from users and critics about tenacious programs that once installed are hard to remove. Some ambitious programs spread themselves out all over your hard disk like olive oil in a hoagie, and there's no easy way of reversing the process to return your system to a pristine state. The result is often overall system slowdown, unexplained crashes, or other untoward effects.

To this end, aftermarket utilities such as Uninstaller or Quarterdeck Cleansweep have become quite popular. Uninstall utility programs monitor and record just exactly what files a new software package adds to your hard disk and which internal Windows settings it modifies. It can then undo the damage later, freeing up disk space and tidying your Windows system.

In typical fashion, Microsoft has incorporated such a scheme into Windows 98 SE itself. Often it is not as effective as the aftermarket utilities, but some programs will not work properly if an uninstall utility monitored the installation. Keep in mind that not all programs that claim to make Windows 98 SE work better actually do. Programmers are writing installation routines that work with Windows 98 SE's Add/Remove Programs applet, so it looks like we're in luck.

Customizing Windows 98 SE with the Control Panel

Use of the uninstall feature of the applet is simple:

1. In the bottom pane, select the program(s) you want to uninstall.
2. Click Remove.
3. Answer any warnings about removing an application as appropriate.

> **NOTE**
> Once removed, you'll have to reinstall a program from its source disks to make it work again. You can't just copy things out of the Recycle Bin to their old directories because settings from the Start button—and possibly the Registry—will have been deleted.

> **TIP**
> Always check a program's disk or program group (from the Start button) for the possible existence of its own uninstall program. Such programs are frequently more thorough than the Windows Add/Remove Programs approach.

Setting the Date and Time

The Date/Time icon lets you adjust the system's date and time. The system date and time are used for a number of purposes, including date- and time-stamping the files you create and modify, scheduling fax transmissions, and so on. All programs use these settings, regardless of whether they are Windows or non-Windows programs. (This applet doesn't change the format of the date and time—just the actual date and time.)

> **NOTE**
> You can also adjust the time and date using the TIME and DATE commands from the DOS prompt, or by double-clicking the time in the System Tray on the end of the Taskbar.

1. Double-click the Date/Time applet. The dialog box in Figure 7.15 appears.

140 Chapter Seven

2. Adjust the time and date by typing in the corrections or clicking the arrows. Note that you have to click directly on the hours, minutes, seconds, or AM/PM area before the little arrows to the right of them will modify the correct value.

3. Next, you can change the time zone you are in. Who cares about the time zone, you ask? Good question. For many users, it doesn't matter. But because people fax to other time zones, and some programs help you manage your transcontinental and transoceanic phone calling, it's built into Windows 98 SE. These programs need to know where in the world you and Carmen Sandiego are. So, use the Time Zone drop-down menu to select the time zone that you are in.

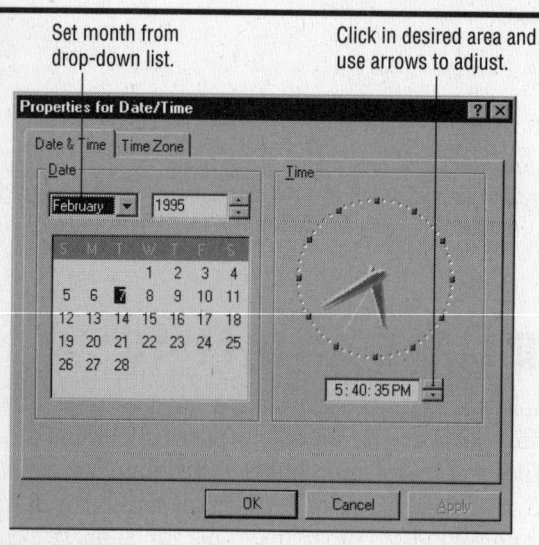

FIGURE 7.15: Adjust the date, time, and local time zone from this dialog box. A shortcut to this box is to double-click the time in the Taskbar.

Desktop Themes

The Desktop Themes applet combines sound schemes, color schemes, screen savers, and cursors for your Windows 98 SE system. It isn't much different from what you can achieve using the Sounds, Display, and Mouse applets from the Control Panel. The advantage of Desktop Themes is that settings from these three areas are pulled into one applet called Desktop Themes, making it easy to recall many settings at once. If you've installed Desktop Themes (use Control Panel's Add/Remove Programs applet and

Customizing Windows 98 SE with the Control Panel 141

then choose Windows Setup), you'll have several preset themes to choose from, some of which are fairly artistic.

Desktop Themes isn't just a tool for organizing your own settings into groups. You also get some great sounds and Desktop backgrounds; you also get cute new icons for My Computer, the Recycle Bin, and Network Neighborhood.

Running the applet brings up the dialog box shown in Figure 7.16.

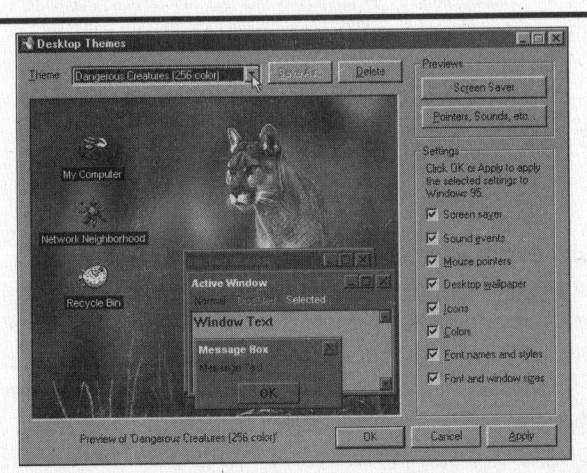

FIGURE 7.16: Desktop Themes provides a means for coordinating various elements of the Windows 98 SE environment and saving them under a single name. An interesting variety of Desktop Themes is supplied with the Microsoft Plus! package.

You can create your own schemes by setting up the screen saver, sounds, cursor, and Desktop the way you like and then saving them using the Save As button at the top of the box. However, you might find that the supplied themes give you all the variation you need. Choose a theme from the drop-down list box to see what it looks like. You can preview the screen saver, pointers, and sounds using the two Preview buttons in the upper right corner.

> **TIP**
> Because some of the visuals are actually photo-realistic, some of the schemes may look pretty bad on your monitor, even in 256 colors, if you don't switch to a high-color or true-color setting. High-color themes are marked as such. If you *don't* have a high-color video driver, you might as well remove these schemes; it will save a significant amount of disk space (about 9MB).

In the Settings portion of the box, you'll see eight checkboxes for things like Screen Saver, Sound Events, and so on. Each scheme includes settings for all these options. However, you might not want to load all these features when you change schemes; for example, you might like the sounds you already have but want everything else from one of the Desktop Themes. To do this, turn off the Sound Events option before clicking Apply or OK.

To switch back to the ordinary Windows 98 SE settings, choose the Windows Default master theme at the bottom of the list of themes.

Customizing Your Screen Display

The Display applet packs a wallop under its hood. For starters, it incorporates what in Windows 3.*x* were the separate Color and Desktop Control Panel applets for prettying up the general look of the Windows screen. Then, in addition, it includes the means for changing your screen driver and resolution—functions heretofore (in Windows 3.*x*) available only from the Setup program. If you were annoyed by getting at all these areas of display tweaking from disjunct venues, suffer no more. Microsoft has incorporated all display-related adjustments into the unified Display applet. If you are among the blessed, you will even have the option of changing screen resolution on the fly. If you've been using Windows 95, well, there's new stuff here for you, too.

> **TIP**
> The Display applet is accessible either from the Control Panel *or* from the Desktop. Right-click an empty area of the Desktop and choose Properties.

Here are the functional and cosmetic adjustments you can make to your Windows 98 SE display from this applet:

- Set the background and wallpaper for the Desktop.
- Set the screen saver and energy conservation.
- Set the color scheme and fonts for Windows elements.
- Set the display device driver and adjust resolution, color depth, and font size.

Customizing Windows 98 SE with the Control Panel

- Change the icons you want to use for basic stuff on your Desktop such as My Computer and the Recycle Bin.
- Set color management compatibility so that your monitor and your printer output colors match.
- Decide which Web goodies you want alive on your Desktop, such as stock quotes, news, and so forth.

Let's take a look at this dialog box page by page. This is a fun one to experiment with and will come in handy if you know how to use it.

First run the applet by double-clicking it.

Setting the Background and Wallpaper

The pattern and wallpaper settings simply let you decorate the Desktop with something a little more festive than the default screen. Patterns are repetitious designs, such as the woven look of fabric. Wallpaper uses larger pictures that were created by artists with a drawing program. You can create your own patterns and wallpaper or use the ones supplied. Wallpapering can be done with a single copy of the picture placed in the center of the screen or by tiling, which gives you multiple identical pictures covering the whole screen. Some of the supplied wallpaper images cannot be used if you are low on memory. This is because the larger bit-mapped images take up too much RAM.

Loading a Pattern

To load a new pattern, follow these steps:

1. Click the Background tab of the applet's dialog box.
2. Scroll the Wallpaper list to a pattern you're interested in and highlight it. A minuscule version of your choice will show up in the little screen in the dialog box (see Figure 7.17).
3. To see the effect on the whole screen, click the Apply button. This keeps the applet open and lets you easily try other patterns and settings. (If you want to leave it at that, click OK. Then the applet will close, and you'll be returned to the Control Panel.)

Chapter Seven

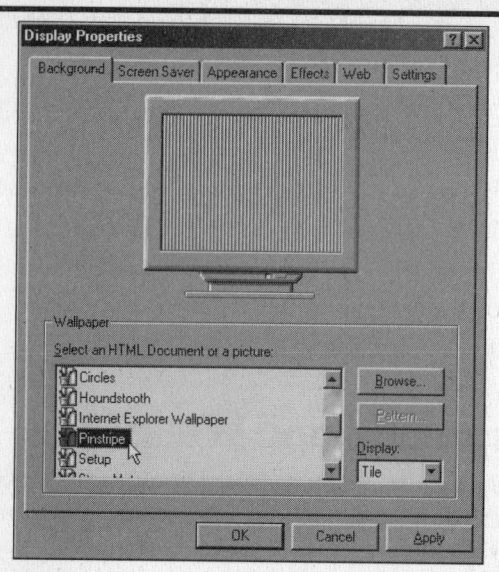

FIGURE 7.17: Simply highlighting a pattern will display a facsimile of it in the dialog box's tiny monitor screen.

Open the Display drop-down list and choose Center, Tile, or Stretch to position the chosen item. If the picture is rather large, you'll want to use Center. Tile repeats the graphic across the screen in a mosaic, so that every inch is covered. Stretch will ensure that a single copy of the graphic fills the entire screen. This can look pretty ghastly, since usually the dimensions of the graphic become disproportional.

You can have a *pattern* on your Desktop rather than wallpaper, if you want. Patterns give the Desktop a nice texture rather than placing a whole picture there. And they easily fill up the whole Desktop if you use the Tile setting.

To choose a pattern, follow these steps:

1. Select None in the list on the left.
2. Click Pattern.
3. From the resulting list, choose a pattern you like.
4. Click OK.

Customizing Windows 98 SE with the Control Panel

NOTE
For a pattern to show up, wallpaper has to be set to None or be smaller than the full-screen size. This is because wallpaper always sits on top of the Desktop's pattern.

Editing a Pattern

If the supplied patterns don't thrill you, make up your own with the built-in bitmap editor. You can either change an existing one or design your own. If you want to design your own, choose None from the Name drop-down list before you begin. Otherwise, choose a pattern you want to play with:

1. Click the Edit Pattern button. A new dialog box appears.

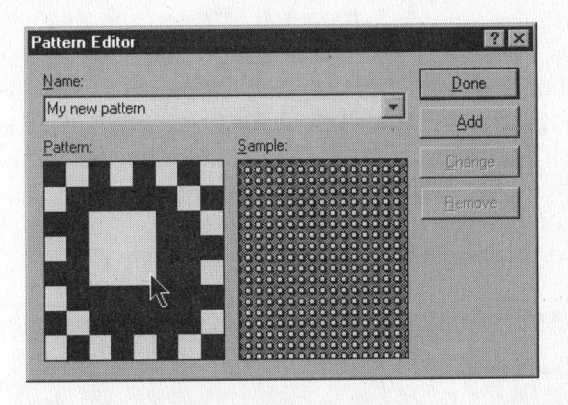

2. In the Name text box, type in a name for the new pattern.

3. Create the pattern by clicking in the box on the left. What you are doing is defining the smallest element of the repeated pattern (a cell). It is blown up in scale to make editing easier. Each click reverses the color of one pixel. The effect when the pattern is applied across a larger area and in normal size is shown in the Sample section to the right.

4. When you like the pattern, click Add and the pattern will be added to your list of patterns.

5. Click Done when you're through creating new patterns.

If you later want to remove a pattern, select the pattern while in the editor and click Remove. If you want to edit an existing pattern, get into the editor, select an existing pattern, make changes to it, and click Change.

> **TIP**
> If you want to abandon changes you've made to a pattern, click the Close button (X) and answer No to the question about saving the changes.

Loading a New Slice of Wallpaper

If you don't like the wallpaper you see, you can go hunting. Click Browse, and look around for something else to use. A nice improvement over Windows 95 is that you can use pictures other than BMP (Microsoft Paint) files. So in addition to BMP files, GIF and JPG files will work. HTML files (a.k.a. Web pages) will also display as wallpaper on your Desktop. Well, most of them will. They may not link properly or scroll correctly, but they'll show up. With all these file types accepted as Desktop wallpaper, the sky's the limit. For example, you could use a scanned color photograph of your favorite movie star, a pastoral setting, some computer art, a scanned Matisse painting, or a photo of your pet lemur. Figure 7.18 shows an example of a custom piece of wallpaper.

FIGURE 7.18: A custom piece of wallpaper. This is a .BMP file of the Apollo 11 base cam on the moon.

> **NOTE**
> In Microsoft Paint's File menu, there's a choice for setting the currently open bit-mapped file to Wallpaper.

> **TIP**
> If you have some other form of picture file, such as a .TIF or .PCX file that you want to use, you can, but you'll have to convert the file to .BMP, .JPG, or .GIF format first using another graphics program such as Collage Image Manager, Publisher's Paintbrush, Paintshop Pro, or other.

Setting the Screen Saver

A Screen Saver will blank your screen or display a moving image or pattern if you don't use the mouse or keyboard for a predetermined amount of time. Screen savers can prevent a static image from burning the delicate phosphors on the inside surface of the monitor, which can leave a ghost of the image on the screen for all time no matter what is being displayed. They can also just be fun.

Many modern computer monitors have an EPA Energy Star, VESA, or other kind of energy-saving strategy built into them. Because far too many people leave their computers on all the time (although it's not really true that they will last longer that way), efforts have been made by power regulators and electronics manufacturers to devise computer–energy-conservation schemes. If your monitor has an Energy Star rating and your video board supports this feature, the screen saver in Windows 98 SE can power the monitor down after it senses you went out to lunch or got caught up at the water cooler for a longer-than-expected break.

The screen-saver options allow you to choose or create an entertaining video ditty that will greet you when you return to work. You also set how much time you have after your last keystroke or mouse skitter before the show begins. And a password can be set to keep prying eyes from toying with your work while you're away.

Chapter Seven

> **NOTE**
>
> For an energy-saving screen saver to work properly, you'll have to set the Energy Star options from the Control Panel ➤ Display ➤ Settings ➤ Advanced Properties ➤ Monitor tab. Also, the monitor must adhere to the VESA Display Power Management Signaling (DPMS) specification or to another method of lowering power consumption. Some LCD screens on portable computers can do this. You can assume that if your monitor has an Energy Star emblem, it probably supports DPMS. Energy Star is a program administered by the U.S. Environmental Protection Agency (EPA) to reduce the amount of power used by personal computers and peripherals. If you notice that your screen freaks out or the display is garbled after your power-management screen saver turns on, you should turn off this check box.

Loading a Screen Saver

Here's how it's done:

1. Click the Screen Saver tab. The page appears as you see in Figure 7.19.

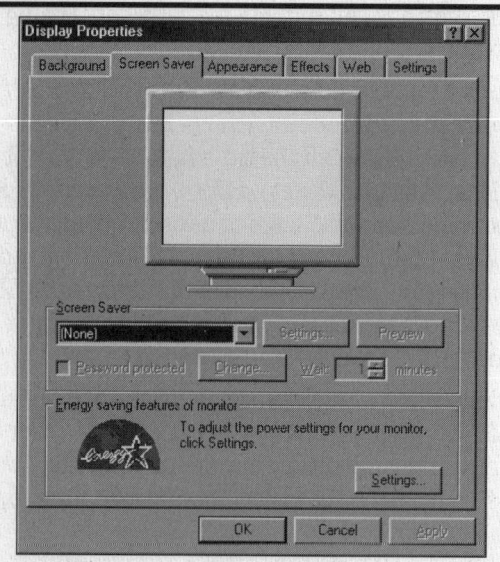

FIGURE 7.19: Setting up a screen saver

2. Choose a name from the drop-down list. The saver will be shown in the little screen in the dialog box. (The 3-D Pipes are particularly dazzling.)

Customizing Windows 98 SE with the Control Panel

3. Want to see how it will look on your whole screen? Click Preview. Your screen will go black and then begin its antics. The show continues until you hit any key or move your mouse.

4. If you want to change anything about the selected screen saver, click Settings. You'll see a box of settings that apply to that particular screen saver. For example, for the Mystify Your Mind saver, this is the Settings box:

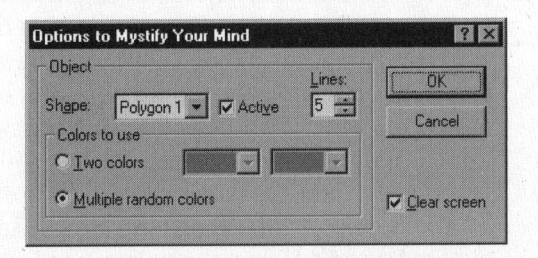

![Options to Mystify Your Mind dialog box showing Object settings with Shape (Polygon 1), Active checkbox, Lines (5), Colors to use (Two colors / Multiple random colors), OK, Cancel, and Clear screen options]

Most of the option boxes have fun sliders and stuff you can play with to get an effect you like. Depending on which screen saver you chose, you'll have a few possible adjustments, such as speed, placement, and details pertinent to the graphic. Play with the settings until you're happy with the results and OK the Setting box.

5. Back at the Screen Saver page, the next choice you might want to consider is Password Options. If you set password protection on, every time your screen saver is activated you will have to type your password into a box to return to work. This is good if you don't want anyone else tampering with your files or seeing what you're doing. It can be a pain, though, if there's no particular need for privacy at your computer. Don't forget your password, either, or you'll have to reboot to get back to work. Of course, anyone could reboot your computer to get to your files, so this means of establishing security is somewhat bogus. Click the Password Protected checkbox if you want protection and go on to the next two steps. Otherwise skip them.

6. Click the Change button to define or change your password. In the dialog box that appears, type in your new password.

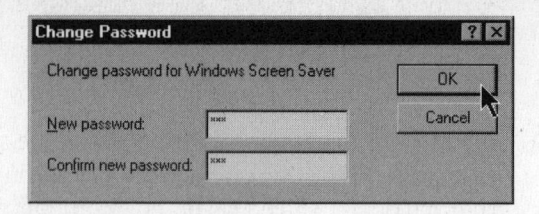

You won't see the letters, just an asterisk for each letter (to preserve confidentiality). For confirmation that you typed it correctly, type it again (don't copy the first one and paste it; a mistake in the first one can result in your being locked out of your computer) in the Confirm New Password text box. If there is a discrepancy between the two, you'll get an error message. Reenter the password. (If you're changing a password, the steps will be approximately the same. Enter your old password first, then the new one and its confirmation.) When it is correct, click OK.

7. Back at the Desktop dialog box, set the number of minutes you want your computer to be idle before the screen saver springs into action. Next to Wait, either type in a number or use the up and down arrows to change the time incrementally.

8. Next you have the Energy Star options. Energy Star monitors need an Energy Star-compatible video card in the computer. If your screen setup supports this, the options will not be grayed out. Otherwise they will be. Assuming you can gain access to the settings, click Configure. That will bring you to the Power Management dialog box. Here you have two choices: when the low-power mode kicks in and when total power off kicks in. You don't want total power down to happen too quickly because the screen will take a few seconds (like about ten) to come back on when you move the mouse or press a key, which can be annoying. So make the two settings something reasonable, such as 15 minutes and 30 minutes.

9. When all the settings are correct, click Apply or OK.

TIP
Some Energy Star displays require the "Blank Screen" screen saver in order to shut down.

Adjusting the Appearance

The Appearance page lets you change the way Windows assigns colors and fonts to various parts of the screen. If you're using a monochrome monitor (no color), altering the colors may still have some effect (the amount will depend on how you installed Windows).

Windows sets itself up using a default color scheme that's fine for most screens—and if you're happy with your colors as they are, you might not even want to futz around with them.

However, the color settings for Windows are very flexible and easy to modify. You can modify the color setting of just about any part of a Windows screen. For those of you who are very particular about color choices, this can be done manually, choosing colors from a palette or even mixing your own with the Custom Colors feature. Once created, custom colors and color setups can be saved on disk for later use or automatically loaded with each Windows session. For more expedient color reassignments, there's a number of supplied color schemes to choose from.

On clicking the Appearance tab, your dialog box will look like that shown in Figure 7.20. The various parts of the Windows graphical environment that you can alter are shown in the top portion and named in the lower portion. As you select color schemes, these samples change so you can see what the effect will be without having to go back into Windows proper.

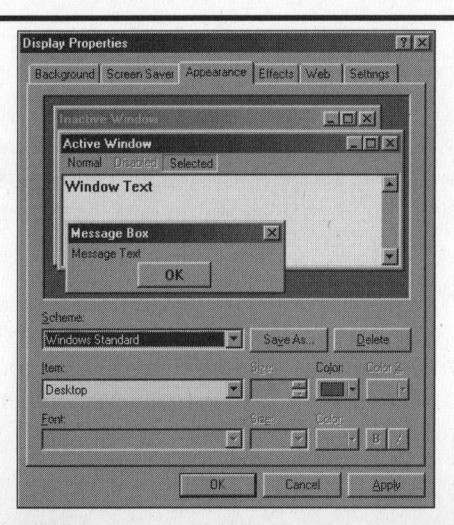

FIGURE 7.20: The dialog box for setting the colors, font, and metrics of the Windows environment

Loading an Existing Color Scheme

Before playing with the custom color palette, first try loading the supplied ones; you may find one you like:

1. Click open the drop-down Color Schemes list box.

> **TIP**
> You can always toggle a drop-down list box open and closed from the keyboard by pressing Alt+↓ or Alt+↑.

2. Choose a selection whose name suits your fancy. The colors in the dialog box will change, showing the scheme. Try them out. Some are garish, others more subtle. Adjusting your monitor may make a difference, too. (You can cycle through the different supplied color schemes without selecting them from the drop-down list: with the Color Schemes space highlighted, just press the ↑ and ↓ keys. The sample screen elements will change to reflect each color scheme as its name appears in the Color Schemes box. There is an amazing variety!)

3. Click Apply or OK to apply the settings to all Windows activities.

Microsoft has incorporated a few color schemes that may enhance the operation of your computer:

▶ On LCD screens that you'll be using in bright light, you might try the setting called High-Contrast White.

▶ If your eyes are weary, you may want to try one of the settings with the words Large or Extra Large in the name. These cause menus, dialog boxes, and title bars to appear in large letters.

Choosing Your Own Colors and Other Stuff

If you don't like the color schemes supplied, you can make up your own. It's most efficient to start with a scheme that's close to what you want and then modify it. Once you like the scheme, you may save it under a new name for later use. Here are the steps:

1. Select the color scheme you want to modify.

2. Click the Windows element whose color you want to change. Its name should appear in the Item area. You can click menu

Customizing Windows 98 SE with the Control Panel

names, title bars, scroll bars, buttons—anything you see. You can also select a screen element from the Item drop-down list box rather than by clicking directly on the item.

3. Now click the Color button to open up a series of colors you can choose from.

4. Click the color you want. This assigns it to the item. Repeat the process for each color you want to change.

5. Want more colors? Click the Other button. This pops up another 48 colors to choose from. Click one of the 48 colors (or patterns and intensity levels, if you have a monochrome monitor) to assign it to the chosen element.

6. Once the color scheme suits your fancy, you can save it. (It will stay in force for future Windows sessions even if you don't save it, but you'll lose the settings next time you change colors or select another scheme.) Click Save Scheme.

7. Type in a name for the color scheme and click OK.

TIP
If you want to remove a scheme (such as one you never use), select it from the drop-down list and click the Delete button.

Before I get into explaining custom colors, there are two other major adjustments you can make to your display—the fonts used for various screen elements, and Windows metrics, which affect how big or small some screen elements are.

In Windows 3.x this wasn't possible, but since Windows 95 you can choose the font for elements such as title bars, menus, and dialog boxes. You can get pretty wacky with this and make your Windows 98 SE setup look very strange if you want. Or, on the more practical side, you can

Chapter Seven

compensate for high-resolution monitors by making your menus more easily readable by using large point sizes in screen elements. In any case, you're no longer stuck with boring sans serif fonts such as Arial or MS Sans Serif. For an example, see Figure 7.21.

1. On the Appearance page, simply click the element whose font you want to change, such as the words "Message Box."

2. In the lowest line of the dialog box, the current font for that element appears. Just open the drop-down list box and choose another font if you want. You may also change the size, the color, and the style (bold or italic) of the font for that element.

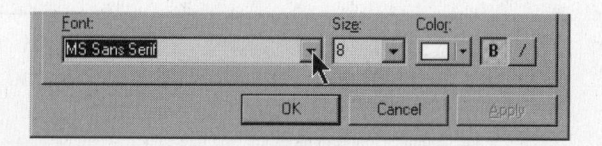

3. Be sure to save the scheme if you want to keep it.

FIGURE 7.21: You can use any installed fonts when defining your screen elements.

Customizing Windows 98 SE with the Control Panel 155

Finally, consider that many screen elements—such as the borders of windows—have a constant predetermined size. However, you might want to change these settings. If you have trouble grabbing the borders of windows, for example, you might want to make them larger. If you want icons on your Desktop and in folders to line up closer or farther apart, you can do that, too.

1. Simply open the list and choose the item whose size you want to adjust. Some of the items are not represented in the upper section of the dialog box. They're things that appear in other parts of Windows, such as vertical icon spacing or selected items. You'll have to experiment a bit to see the effects of these items.

2. Click the up or down size buttons to adjust.

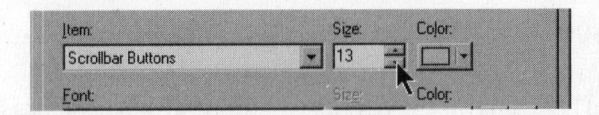

3. Click Apply to check out the effects of the changes. You might want to switch to another application via the Taskbar to see how things look.

4. If you don't like the effects of the changes you've made, click Cancel and return to the Control Panel. Or you can just select another color scheme, because the screen metrics are recorded on each color scheme.

Making Up Your Own Colors

If you don't like the colors that are available, you can create your own. There are 16 slots at the bottom of the larger color palette for storing colors you set using another fancy dialog box called the color refiner. Here's how:

1. Click the Color button and then choose Other. This opens the enlarged color-selection box.

2. In that box, click Define Custom Colors. Now the Color Refiner dialog box appears (see Figure 7.22).

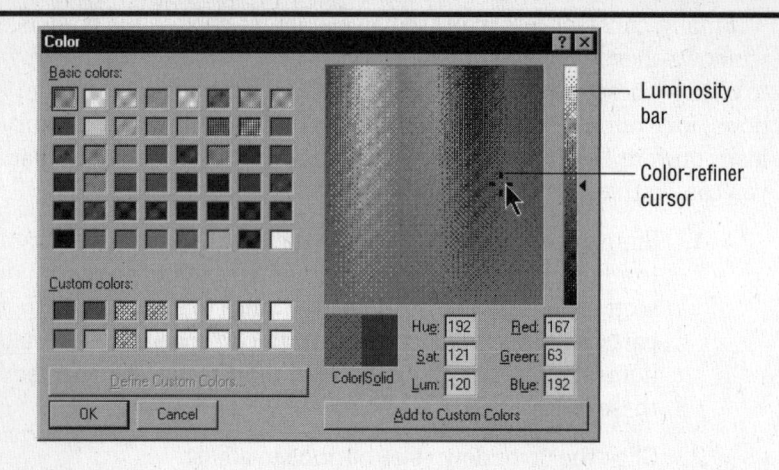

FIGURE 7.22: The custom color selector lets you create new colors.

There are two cursors that you work with here. One is the luminosity bar, and the other is the color-refiner cursor. To make a long story short, you simply drag these around one at a time until the color in the box at the lower left is the shade you want. As you do, the numbers in the boxes below the color refiner will change. *Luminosity* is the amount of brightness in the color. *Hue* is the actual shade or color. All colors are composed of red, green, and blue. *Saturation* is the degree of purity of the color; it is decreased by adding gray to the color and increased by subtracting it. You can also type in the numbers or click the arrows next to the numbers if you want, but it's easier to use the cursors. When you like the color, click Add Color to add the new color to the palette.

You can switch between a solid color and a color made up of various dots of several colors. Solid colors look less grainy on your screen but give you fewer choices. The Color|Solid box shows the difference between the two. If you click this box before adding the color to the palette, the solid color closest to the actual color you chose will be added instead of the grainier composite color.

Once a color is added to the palette, you can modify it. Just click it, move the cursor around, and then click Add Color again. Click Close to close the dialog box. Then continue to assign colors with the palette. When you are content with the color assignments, click OK. If you decide after toying around that you don't want to implement the color changes, just click Cancel.

Customizing Windows 98 SE with the Control Panel 157

Effects

The settings on this tab page were inherited from the Plus! program that used to be sold as an add-on for Windows 95 (not to be confused with Plus! for Windows 98). Among other creature comforts like font smoothing and full-window drag, Plus! lets you install what Microsoft calls Desktop "themes."

> **TIP**
>
> Full-window drag and font smoothing are included in Windows 98 SE; they just aren't settable from the Display applet. Open any folder window, choose View ➢ Options ➢ Advanced, and look for the options Smooth Edges Of Screen Fonts and Show Windows Contents While Dragging.

Themes were combinations of color settings, wallpaper, and icons designed for your Desktop. The fancy icons are what this option is about. Instead of being stuck with the same boring icons as everyone else, you can change them to something more your style.

1. Click Effects from the Display Properties dialog box (see Figure 7.23).

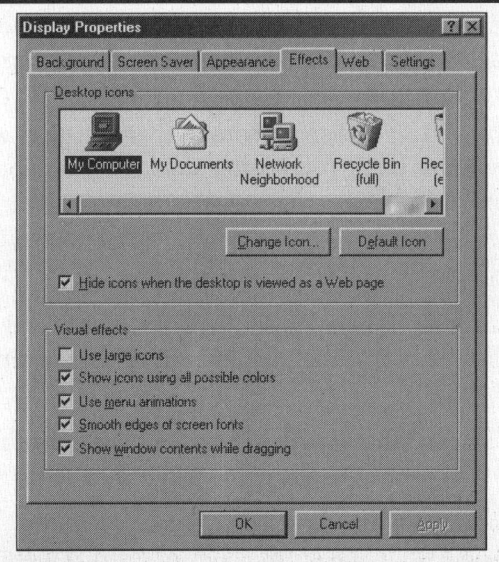

FIGURE 7.23: Change the look of your Desktop icons from here.

2. Click the icon you want to alter, then click Change Icon or Default Icon (to return to the factory setting). You'll get a resulting list of icons you can choose from, and you can also browse for icon replacements. (Where to look? Use the Browse box's "Files of type" selector to set the type of file as you're cruising. You can pick up an icon from an existing program [.EXE], library [.DLL], or icon [.ICO] file.

> **TIP**
> The Internet is a good source of icons. One way to find them is to do a search for the phrase *Icons* or *.ICO*.

> **TIP**
> The file Windows Explorer.exe (in the Windows directory) contains a bunch of icons. In fact, these are the old Windows 95 default icons, the ones you get if you click the Default Icon button when reassigning icons. To get back to the newer Windows 98 SE icons, use the file \windows\system\cool.dll.

The Visual Effects portion of the Effects tab page offers an assortment of other options. If you want your icons to be larger and more easily seen, set the Large Icons checkbox on. You can click Apply to see the results. If you don't like them looking large on your Desktop horizon, just turn off the checkbox and click Apply again.

You can force Windows 98 SE to display icons in their full glory with the last checkbox, Show Icons Using All Possible Colors. This is normally on, so there typically isn't a problem.

In addition to the icon settings, this portion of the Effects tab also offers the following settings:

Use menu animations When this setting is on, menus will open up in a little more artistic manner. Instead of just popping up, they'll slide open.

Smooth edges of screen fonts Makes larger fonts look smoother on the screen.

Show window contents while dragging Keeps each window's contents visible while you are dragging or resizing it on screen.

Web

This tab page lets you set up your Active Desktop. Active Desktop is the feature in Windows 98 SE that lets you pull in stuff from the Web and have it display on the Desktop.

Driver Settings

The last tab page of the Display applet tweaks the video driver responsible for your video card's ability to display Windows. These settings are a little more substantial than those that adjust whether dialog boxes are mauve or chartreuse because they load a different driver or bump your video card up or down into a completely different resolution and color depth, changing the amount of information you can see on the screen at once (see Figure 7.24).

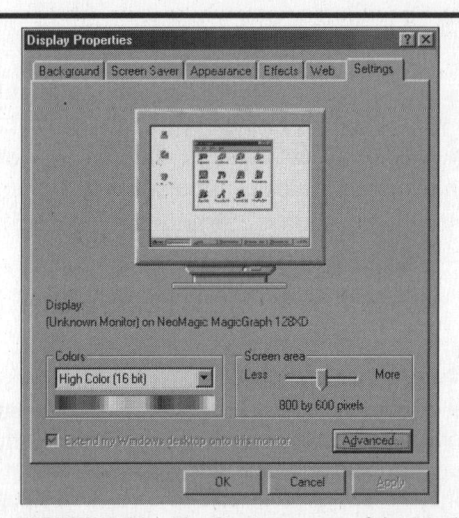

FIGURE 7.24: The Settings page of the Display applet controls the video card's device driver. With most video systems, the slider lets you adjust the screen resolution on the fly.

NOTE

This option is also the one to use for installing a Windows 3.x video driver for your video card just in case there isn't a Windows 98 SE driver for it.

> **NOTE**
> Changing the color depth or palette on some systems requires rebooting before the changes will take effect.

Color Palette

Let's start with the color palette. Assuming your video card was properly identified when you installed Windows 98 SE, this drop-down list box will include all the legitimate options your card is capable of. As you may know, different video cards are capable of displaying differing numbers of colors simultaneously. Your monitor is not the limiting factor here (with the exception of color LCD screens like those on laptops or flat panel monitors, which do have limitations); the limitations have to do with how much RAM is on your video card. All modern analog color monitors for PCs are capable of displaying 16 million colors, which is dubbed True Color.

It's possible that the drop-down list box will include color amounts (called depths) that exceed your video card's capabilities, in which case such a choice just won't have any effect. On the other hand, if your setting is currently 16 colors and your screen can support 256 or higher, Windows will look a lot prettier if you choose 256 and then choose one of the 256-color schemes from the Appearance tab page.

> **TIP**
> When you move the Desktop Area slider to the right, the resolution setting increases, right? True, but usually this will also lower the color palette setting to 256 or 16 colors (unless you have a really fancy display card). If after this you choose a lower resolution, such as 640 by 480, and you want to return to the richer color depth, you'll have to reset the color palette to a higher setting manually, by opening the color palette drop-down list.

Screen Area

The Screen Area setting is something avid Windows users have been wanting for years. With Windows 3.x, changing this parameter (essentially the screen resolution) meant running Windows Setup, choosing a different video driver, and rebooting the machine and Windows. Windows 95 made this much easier. Now, with the right video card, you can change the resolution as you work. Some jobs—such as working with

Customizing Windows 98 SE with the Control Panel 161

large spreadsheets, databases, CAD, or typesetting—are much more efficient with more data displayed on the screen. Because higher resolutions require a tradeoff in clarity and make on-screen objects smaller, eyestrain can be minimized by going to a lower resolution, such as 640-by-480 pixels (a pixel equals one dot on the screen). Note that there is a relationship between the color depth and the resolution that's available. This is because your video card can only have so much RAM on it. That RAM can be used to display extra colors or extra resolution, but not both. So, if you bump up the colors, you won't have as many resolution options. If you find the dialog box won't let you choose the resolution you want, try dropping the color palette setting to 16 colors.

To change the Desktop area:

1. Run Control Panel and run the Display applet.
2. Choose the Settings tab page.
3. Grab the slider and move it right or left. Notice how the little screen in the box indicates the additional room you're going to have on your real screen to do your work (and also how everything will get relatively smaller to make this happen, because your monitor doesn't get any larger!). Figure 7.25 illustrates.

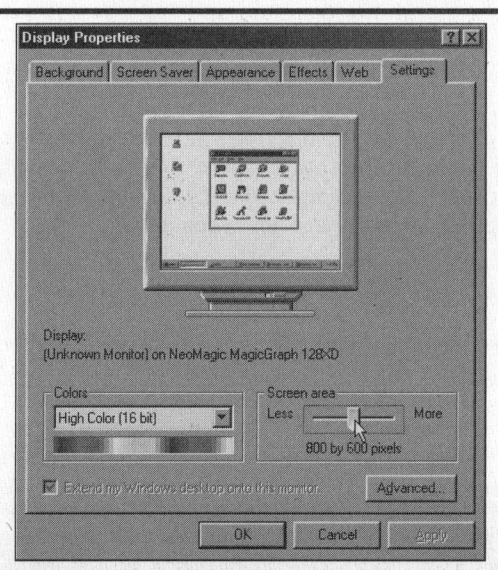

FIGURE 7.25: Change your screen resolution by dragging the slider. Here I've chosen 800 by 600.

4. Click Apply. You'll now see this message:

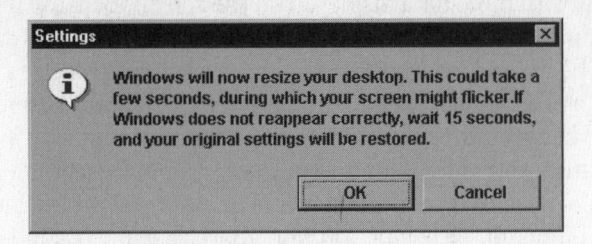

> **Settings**
>
> Windows will now resize your desktop. This could take a few seconds, during which your screen might flicker. If Windows does not reappear correctly, wait 15 seconds, and your original settings will be restored.
>
> [OK]   [Cancel]

Go ahead and click OK to try the setting. If your screen looks screwy and you can't read anything, don't worry. It will return to normal in about 15 seconds. If, on the other hand, you like what you see, there will be another dialog box asking you to confirm that you want to keep the current setting. Confirming that box makes the new setting permanent until you change it again.

Advanced Properties

Finally, the Advanced... button in the Settings box leads you to the Advanced Settings page, which allows you to actually change a bunch of nitty-gritty stuff like the type of video card and monitor that Windows thinks you have, the refresh rate, and some performance factors. If you install a new video card or monitor, you should update this information.

TIP
You may have noticed on the Advanced Settings page the option "Show settings icon on Taskbar." Turn this checkbox on, and you'll get a little monitor icon next to the clock in the Taskbar. Click the icon and you're able to immediately choose the color depth and Desktop area from a popup menu.

NOTE
If your screen is flickering, you'll want to check the refresh rate for sure!

WARNING
If you specify a refresh rate that is too high for your monitor, trying to expand the Desktop area to a larger size may not work. You'll just get a mess on the screen. If this happens, try using a setting with a lower refresh rate, such as 60Hz or *interlaced*. The image may flicker a bit more, but at least it will be clearly visible.

Customizing Windows 98 SE with the Control Panel 163

> **TIP**
> If you have just received a new driver for your video adapter card or monitor and want to use that instead of the one supplied with Windows 98 SE (or Windows 98 SE doesn't include a driver), click the Have Disk button and follow the directions.

Click the Advanced Properties button, and you'll see something like Figure 7.26.

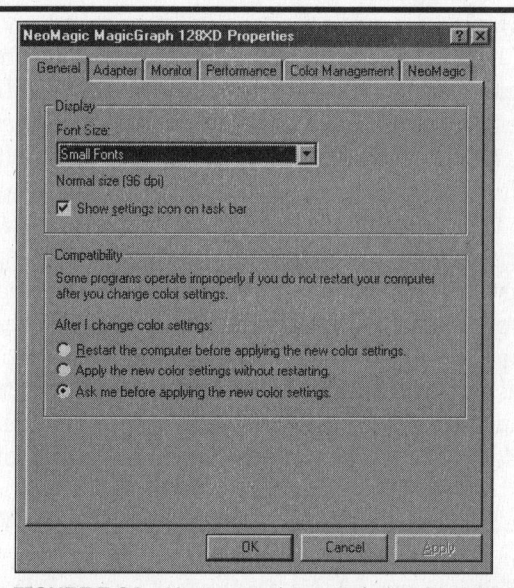

FIGURE 7.26: You can make some hairy alterations to your monitor setup from here. You should investigate all the tab pages. If you're into monitors, you'll really like what's available from this box.

This stuff isn't for the novice, but if you're like me, you've waited a long time for settings like these to be easily available. Windows NT started the trend, and now it's migrated to Windows 98 SE. The first tab page allows you to make some "basic" advanced settings changes, such as displaying font sizes and setting application procedures. As you may know, some screen drivers use different size fonts for screen elements such as dialog boxes and menus. When you switch to a high screen-area resolution, such as 1,280 by 1,024, these screen elements can get quite small, blurry, and difficult to read. For this reason, you can adjust the font size. Of course, you can do this via the Fonts settings on the Appearance page as discussed earlier. But doing it here is a little simpler. If you select a Desktop area above 640 by 480, you'll have the choice of Small Fonts or Large Fonts. Especially for resolutions of 1,024 by 768 or above, you might want to check out the Large Fonts selection from this drop-down list box. If you want, you can also choose a custom-size font by clicking the Custom button, which lets you declare the amount that you want the fonts scaled up. The range is from 100 to 200 percent.

The Adapter tab tells you more stuff about your display card than you may have wanted to know, such as the chipset and DAC (Digital to Analog Converter) type, which exact driver files are being used, and amount of RAM on your card. Useful, maybe. Boring, definitely. But the refresh rate, now that's a biggie in my book. In case you don't know, the refresh rate is how many times per second the screen is redrawn by the electron gun in the back of the monitor. Translation: It determines whether the screen appears to be flickering like an old-fashioned movie or not, and whether your eyes get tired looking at the screen for hours on end. Anything under 70Hz is too slow, say the experts, and I agree. In fact, I prefer 72Hz or above. But beware! Not all monitors can work that fast (that electron gun has to move really fast to paint all those dots on the screen), especially at resolutions above 800 by 600. Even if your display card can put out the right refresh signal, the monitor might not be able to handle it. And this can fry a monitor after some time. So if after setting the correct monitor on the Monitor tab page, you don't have the desired refresh available from the Refresh Rate drop-down list, take heed—your monitor probably can't cut the mustard, and Windows is trying to save you from damaging the monitor. Try living with a slower refresh like 70, or get a new monitor (or possibly just a new card). Or choose Optimum. The Adapter Default setting will accept whatever speed the display card is currently set to, or boots up in. This is more than likely not an optimal setting.

THINKING OF BUYING A NEW MONITOR OR DISPLAY CARD?

If you're thinking about purchasing a new monitor or card, check the specs on both the monitor *and* the card. For both the monitor and the card, you'll want to ensure that you can:

▶ display at 72Hz or above, while

CONTINUED ➡

Customizing Windows 98 SE with the Control Panel

- displaying your favorite resolution (a.k.a. Desktop size, such as 1024 × 768), while
- displaying your favorite color depth (such as 64,000 colors or 16 million colors). At least 64,000 colors are necessary for photo-like display.

Make sure the monitor has a dot pitch value smaller than .28, preferably .26. If you have a big wallet, check out the new flat-panel displays just coming out from the likes of NEC and Viewsonic. These are *super* sharp and clear, and refresh isn't even an issue with them.

If you notice that the adapter setting for your computer is wrong, click the Change button on the Adapter tab page. This will run a wizard. Depending on your choices here you may see a list of compatible boards. For example, on my computer the adapter is listed as S3. The S3 is a popular video chip, installed on my display adapter. But hey, my adapter is a Diamond Stealth 64 PCI. My guess is that the driver that Windows 98 SE assigned is some generic S3 chipset driver. When I clicked on Change, I saw this:

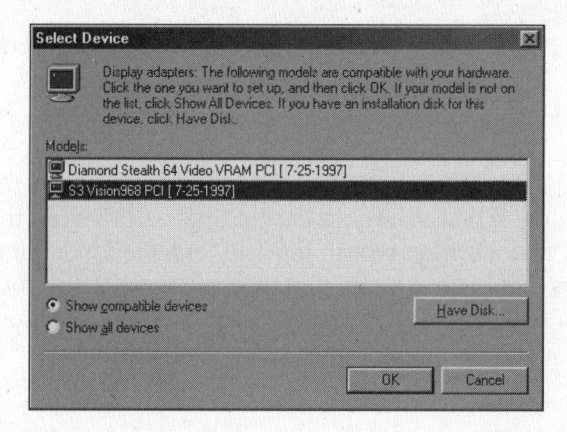

Looks like the Diamond Stealth is compatible, and there is a later date on the driver, so I think I'll try that. This driver was provided by the Diamond company and sent to Microsoft for inclusion in Windows 98 SE.

If you want to see all the possible drivers to choose from (including ones that *won't* work with your card), click Show All Devices. But typically this won't be useful unless you're planning to install another driver, power down, change display cards, and then boot up again.

Monitor Tab

Bought a new monitor? Here's the place to tell Windows 98 SE about it. Or at least to see what monitor it *thinks* you have. Click the Monitor tab on the Advanced Display Properties dialog, and you'll see something like Figure 7.27.

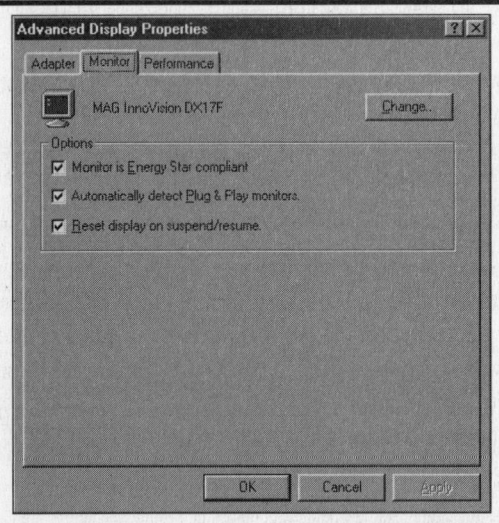

FIGURE 7.27: The Monitor tab of the Advanced Display Properties box

Click Change if the monitor is reported wrong. Then choose the correct monitor. You might have to use Show All Devices to see your brand. What's that? You say your monitor isn't listed, or you have a no-name monitor? If that's the case, choose Show All Devices, then select the topmost manufacturer type in the list ("Standard monitor types"), and choose the generic brand that most closely matches your monitor's maximum screen resolution and refresh rate at that resolution. You may have to look in your monitor's manual to figure this out.

> **NOTE**
> Notice there is a *Television* choice in the Standard monitor types. This may seem a little strange at first. But more and more computers are now equipped with a video output that can drive a TV set as your monitor.

Customizing Windows 98 SE with the Control Panel 167

The other options on this tab are also interesting:

Monitor is Energy Star compliant If yours fits this description, set this. It affects other Power Management settings in your computer.

Automatically detect Plug & Play monitors Windows runs around and detects Plug & Play hardware once in awhile (when booting up, for example). In some cases this can cause PnP monitors to flash wildly. If yours does this, try turning off this checkbox.

Reset display on suspend/resume Does your computer have the ability to go into a suspended state (low power state)? I mean the whole computer, not just the screen. If it does, and your screen flickers or freaks out when your computer "wakes up," turn this checkbox off. It may help.

Performance

When you click the Performance tab, you'll see a dialog box that looks like Figure 7.28.

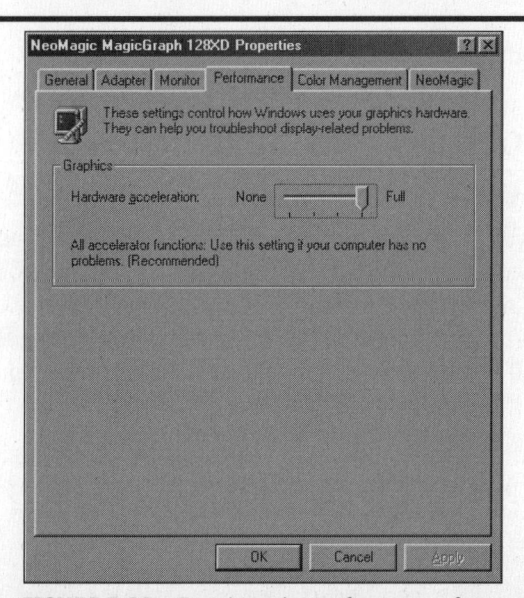

FIGURE 7.28: Tweaking the performance of your monitor/card duo can be achieved from this box.

If speed is your concern (and who isn't concerned with their computer's speed?), make sure the slider is set to Full. This is recommended for most computers. Occasionally a computer/card combo (the monitor has nothing to do with this) won't be able to take advantage of all the graphics speed-up routines that Windows is capable of for things like moving lots of graphics around the screen quickly ("bit blitting") and such. If you're seeing display anomalies, you might try slowing this setting down a bit, clicking OK, and closing the Display Properties box. Then see if anything improves.

Adjusting the Mouse

You can adjust six aspects of your mouse's operation:

- left-right button reversal
- double-click speed
- look of the pointers
- tracking speed
- mouse trails
- mouse type and driver

Switching the Buttons and Setting Double-Click Speed

If you're left-handed, you may want to switch the mouse around to use it on the left side of the computer and reverse the buttons. The main button then becomes the right button instead of the left one. If you use other programs outside of Windows that don't allow this, however, it might just add to the confusion. If you only use the mouse in Windows programs and you're left-handed, then it's worth a try.

1. Run the Control Panel and double-click Mouse. Then click the first tab page of the dialog box (Figure 7.29).

Customizing Windows 98 SE with the Control Panel 169

2. Click the Left-handed button as shown in the figure. Then click Apply to check it out. Don't like it? Revert to the original setting and click Apply again.

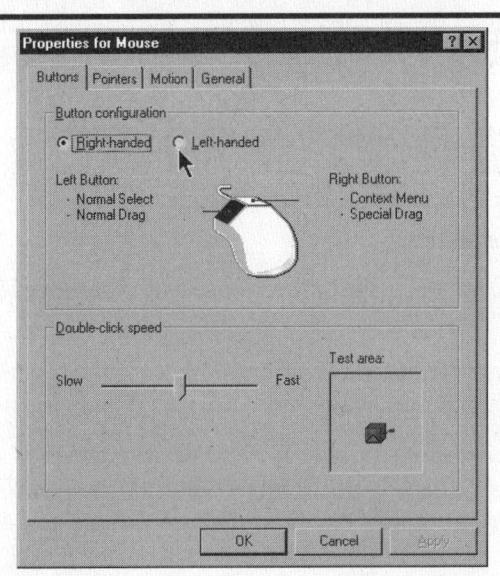

FIGURE 7.29: First page of the Mouse setting. Here you can reverse the buttons for use by left-handed people. You can also adjust the double-click speed.

On the same page, you have the double-click speed setting. Double-click speed determines how fast you have to double-click to make a double-click operation work (that is, to run a program from its icon, to open a document from its icon, or to select a word. If the double-click speed is too fast, it's difficult for your fingers to click fast enough. If it's too slow, you end up running programs or opening and closing windows unexpectedly. Double-click the Jack-in-the-box to try out the new double-click speed. Jack will jump out or back into the box if the double-click registered. If you're not faring well, adjust the slider and try again.

> **NOTE**
> You don't have to click Apply to test the slider settings. Just moving the slider instantly affects the mouse's double-click speed.

Setting Your Pointers

Your mouse pointer's shape changes depending on what you are pointing at and what Windows 98 SE is doing. If you are pointing to a window border, the pointer becomes a two-headed arrow. If Windows 98 SE is busy, it becomes an hourglass. When you are editing text, it becomes an I-beam, and so on.

You can customize your cursors for the fun of it or to increase visibility. You can even install animated cursors that look really cute and keep you amused while you wait for some process to complete.

To change the cursor settings:

1. Click the Pointers tab page of the Mouse dialog box (see Figure 7.30).

2. The list shows which pointers are currently assigned to which activities. To change an assignment, click an item in the list.

3. Next, if you've changed the shape and want to revert, click Use Default to go back to the normal pointer shape that Windows 98 SE came with. Otherwise, choose Browse and use the Browse box to load the cursor you want. When you click a cursor in the Browse box, it will be displayed at the bottom of the box for you to examine in advance—a thoughtful feature. Even animated cursors will do their thing right in the Browse box. (Cursors with the .ANI extension are animated ones.)

4. Click Open. The cursor will now be applied to the activity in question.

You can save pointer schemes just as you can colors. If you want to set up a number of different schemes (one for each person in the house, for example), just get the settings assigned the way you like, enter a name in the scheme area, and click Save As. To later select a scheme, open the drop-down list box, select the scheme's name, and click Apply or OK.

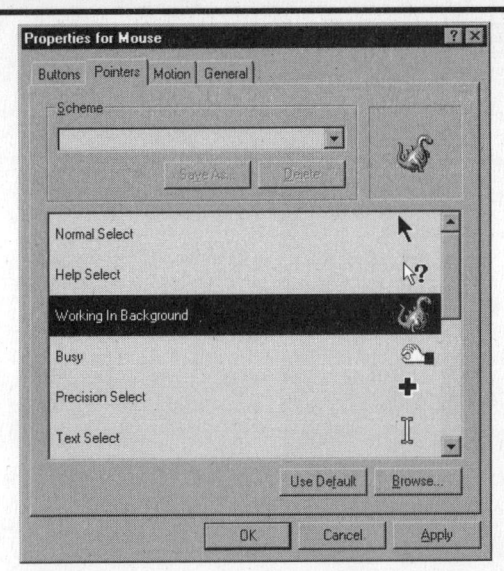

Customizing Windows 98 SE with the Control Panel 171

FIGURE 7.30: Choose pointer shapes for various activities here. As you can see, I have a couple of weird ones installed, such as the walking dinosaur instead of the hourglass.

Setting the Pointer Motion

Two very useful adjustments can be made to the way the mouse responds to the motion of your hand—speed and trails (see Figure 7.31).

Pointer speed is the speed at which the mouse pointer moves relative to the movement of the mouse. Believe it or not, mouse motion is actually measured in *Mickeys*! (Somebody out there has a sense of humor.) A Mickey equals 1/100 of an inch of mouse movement. The tracking-speed setting lets you adjust the relationship of Mickeys to pixels. If you want to be very exact in your cursor movement, you'll want to slow the tracking speed, requiring more Mickeys per pixel. However, this requires more hand motion for the same corresponding cursor motion. If your desk is crammed and your coordination is very good, then you can increase the speed (fewer Mickeys per pixel). If you use the mouse with MS-DOS programs that use their own mouse driver, you might want to adjust the Windows mouse speed to match that of your other programs so you won't need to mentally adjust when you use such non-Windows programs.

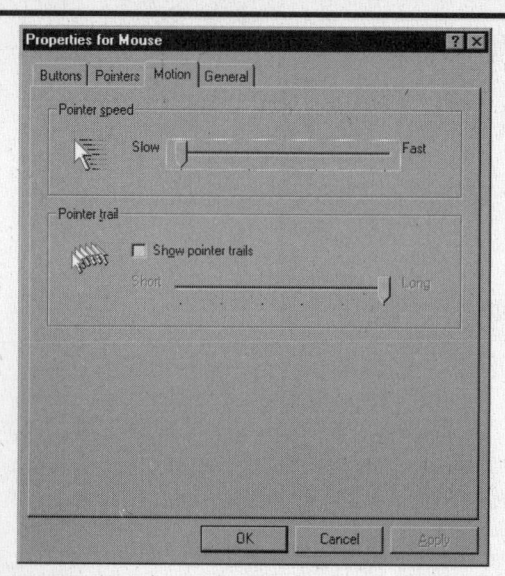

FIGURE 7.31: You can adjust the speed at which the mouse pointer moves and whether you'll see trails.

Incidentally, if you think the mouse runs too slowly in your non-Windows applications, there may be a fix. Contact your mouse's maker. For example, if you're using a Logitech mouse, a program called Click that is supplied with the Logitech mouse lets you easily control its tracking. See the Logitech manual for details.

The other setting—Mouse trails—creates a shadow of the mouse's path whenever you move it. Some people find it annoying, but for those who have trouble finding the pointer on the screen, it's a blessing. Mouse trails are particularly helpful when using Windows on passive-matrix or dual-scan laptop computers, where the pointer often disappears when you move it.

Here are the steps for changing these items:

1. Drag the speed slider one way or another to increase or decrease the motion of the pointer relative to your hand (or thumb in the case of a trackball) motion. Nothing may happen until you click Apply. Adjust as necessary. Try aiming for some item on the screen and see how well you succeed. Having the motion too fast can result in straining your muscles and holding the mouse too tight. It's ergonomically more

Customizing Windows 98 SE with the Control Panel

sound to use a little slower setting that requires more hand motion.

2. If you want trails, click the option box on and adjust the slider. You don't have to click Apply to see the effects.

3. Click OK or Apply to make it all official.

What's Next?

The next chapter continues our tour of Windows 98 SE's hardware support with a detailed look at printers and printing.

Chapter 8

PRINTERS AND PRINTING

If your printer is of the Plug-and-Play variety, your Windows system will probably have a so-called default printer driver already installed. This means you'll be able to print from any Windows program without worrying about anything more than turning on the printer, checking that it has paper, and choosing the File ➢ Print command from whatever programs you use. If your printer isn't Plug-and-Play compatible, wasn't plugged in at the time of installation, or you weren't upgrading over a previous version of Windows for which you had printers set up already, you'll have to manually set up your printer before you can print. This chapter tells you how to do that and how to manage the use of your printer to get your work done.

As with Windows 3.1, Windows 95, Windows 98, and Windows NT, unless you specify otherwise, Windows programs hand off data to Windows 98 SE, which in turn *spools* the data to a specified printer. Spooling means temporarily putting on the hard disk the information that's really headed for the

Adapted from *Mastering Windows 98 Second Edition*
by Robert Cowart
ISBN 0-7821-2618-9   928 pages $39.99

printer. Your document then gets sent out to the printer at the slowest speed that the printer can receive it. This lets you get back to work with your program sooner. You can even print additional documents, stacking up a load of jobs for the printer to print. This stack is called a *queue*.

In Windows 3.*x*, a program called Print Manager was responsible for doing the spooling and managing the print jobs. Windows 98 SE nomenclature dispenses with the term "Print Manager," even though the same functionality is provided. Now you simply look at what's "inside" a printer by clicking the printer's icon. This opens a window and displays the print queue for that printer. In reality, however, there *is* a spooler program and Print Manager-like thing in Windows 98 SE, and that is how I'll refer to the window that displays and works with the print queue.

> **NOTE**
> Unlike Windows NT, Windows 98 SE doesn't always prevent a program from writing directly to the printer port. (In Windows NT, any such attempt by programs to directly write to hardware, such as an LPT port, is trapped by the security manager.) Windows 98 SE offers less security in this regard. Applications can directly access a port. Also, if you shell out of Windows 98 SE and run MS-DOS mode, direct port access is allowed.

> **NOTE**
> MS-DOS programs can also be spooled so you can get back to work with your DOS or Windows programs while printing happens in the background.

When you print from a Windows program, Print Manager receives the data, queues up the jobs, routes them to the correct printer, and, when necessary, issues error or other appropriate messages to print-job originators. You can use the Print Manager user interface to manage your print jobs, making it easy to check out what's printing and see where your job(s) are in the print queue relative to other people's print jobs. You may also be permitted to rearrange the print queue, delete print jobs, or pause and resume a print job so you can reload or otherwise service the printer.

Each printer you've installed appears in the Printers folder, along with an additional icon called Add Printer that lets you set up new printers. Printer icons in the folder appear and behave like any other object: You can delete them at will, create new ones, and set their properties. Double-clicking a printer in the folder displays its print queue and lets you manipulate the queue. Commands on the menus let you to install, configure, connect, disconnect, and remove printers and drivers.

This chapter explains these features, as well as procedures for local and network print-queue management. Some basics of print management also are discussed, providing a primer for the uninitiated or for those whose skills are a little rusty.

A Print-Manager Primer

Windows 98 SE's Print Manager feature mix is quite rich. Here are the highlights:

- You can add, modify, and remove printers right from the Printers folder (available from My Computer, Explorer, the Start button, or Control Panel).

- An object-oriented interface using printer icons eliminates the abstraction of thinking about the relationship of printer drivers, connections, and physical printers. You simply add a printer and set its properties. Once added, it appears as a named printer in the Printers folder.

- Once set up, you can easily choose to share a printer on the network so others can print to it. You can give it a useful name such as *LaserJet in Fred's Office* so people on the network know what it is.

- If you're on a network, you can manage network-printer connections by displaying available printers, sharing your local printer, and connecting to and disconnecting from network printers.

- Because of Windows 98 SE's multithreading and preemptive multitasking, you can start printing and immediately go back to work; you don't have to wait until spooling is finished. (This won't be true for older 16-bit programs.)

- While one document is printing out, other programs can start print jobs. Additional documents are simply added to the queue and will print in turn.

- Default settings for such options as number of copies, paper tray, page orientation, and so forth are automatically used during print jobs so you don't have to manually set them each time.

- For the curious, a window can be opened displaying jobs currently being printed or in the queue waiting to be printed, along with an indication of the current print job's progress.

- You can easily rearrange the order of the print queue and delete print jobs.

- You can choose whether printing begins as soon as the first page is spooled to the hard disk or after the last page of a document is spooled.

- You can temporarily pause or resume printing without causing printer time-out problems.

Adding a New Printer

If your printer is already installed and seems to be working fine, you probably can skip this section. In fact, if you're interested in nothing more than printing from one of your programs without viewing the queue, printing to a network printer, or making adjustments to your current printer's settings, just skip down to the "Printing from a Program" section. However, if you need to install a new printer, modify or customize your current installation, or add additional printers to your setup, read on to learn about how to:

- Add a new printer
- Select the printer port and make other connection settings
- Set preferences for a printer
- Install a printer driver that's not listed
- Set the default printer
- Select a printer when more than one is installed
- Delete a printer from your system

About Printer Installation

Before installing hardware, including printers, you should read any last-minute printed or on-screen material that comes with Windows 98 SE. Often such material is full of useful information about specific types of hardware, including printers. Open the files `Setup.txt` and `Printers.txt` on your Windows 98 SE CD-ROM, then look through the files for information about your printer.

With that said, here is the overall game plan for adding a new printer. It's actually a really easy process thanks to the Add Printer Wizard that walks you through it.

1. Run Add Printer from the Printers folder.
2. Declare whether the printer is local (directly connected to your computer) or on the network.
3. Declare what kind of printer it is.
4. Select the printer's port and relevant port settings.
5. Give the printer a name.
6. Print a test page.
7. Check and possibly alter the default printer settings, such as the DPI (dots per inch) setting and memory settings.

About Adding Printers

Before running the wizard, let's consider when you'd need to add a new printer to your Windows 98 SE configuration:

- You didn't tell Windows 98 SE what kind of printer you have when you first set up Windows.

- You're connecting a new printer directly to your computer.

- Someone has connected a new printer to the network and you want to use it from your computer.

- You want to print to disk files that can later be sent to a particular type of printer.

- You want to set up multiple printer configurations (preferences) for a single physical printer so you can switch between them without having to change your printer setup before each print job.

Notice that a great deal of flexibility exists here, especially in the case of the last item. Because of the modularity of Windows 98 SE's internal design, even though you might have only one physical printer, you can create any number of printer definitions for it, each with different characteristics.

> **NOTE**
> These definitions are actually *called* printers, but you can think of them as printer names, aliases, or named virtual devices.

For example, you might want one definition set up to print on legal-sized paper in landscape orientation while another prints with normal paper in portrait orientation. Each of these two "printers" would actually use the same physical printer to print out on. While you're working with Windows 98 SE's manual, online help, and this book, keep this terminology in mind. The word "printer" often doesn't really mean a physical printer. It usually means a printer setup that you've created with the wizard. It's a collection of settings that typically points to a physical printer, but it could just as well create a print file instead.

About Printer Drivers

And finally, consider that a printer can't just connect to your computer and mysteriously print a fancy page of graphics or even a boring old page of text. You need a *printer driver*. The printer driver (actually a file on your hard disk) translates your text file to commands that tell your printer how to print your file. Because different brands and models of printers use different commands for such things as *move up a line, print a circle in the middle of the page, print the letter A*, and so on, a specialized printer driver is needed for each type of printer.

> **NOTE**
> Because some printers are actually functionally equivalent, a driver for a popular brand and model of printer (for example, an Epson or a Hewlett-Packard) often masquerades under different names for other printers.

> **NOTE**
> DOS programs require a print driver for the application, too. For instance, WordPerfect 5.1 running in a DOS session under Windows 98 SE will use a DOS printer driver *and* a Windows 98 SE printer driver to work under Windows 98 SE.

When you add a printer, unless you're installing a Plug-and-Play–compatible printer, you're asked to choose the brand and model of printer. With Plug-and-Play printers, if the printer is attached and turned on, Windows queries the printer and the printer responds with its make and model number. Virtually all new printers are Plug-and-Play compatible, but if yours isn't, you'll have to tell Windows what printer you have so it will install the correct driver.

A good printer driver takes advantage of all your printer's capabilities, such as its built-in fonts and graphics features. A poor printer driver might succeed in printing only draft-quality text, even from a sophisticated printer.

If you're the proud owner of some offbeat brand of printer, you may be alarmed when you can't find your printer listed in the box when you run the Wizard. But don't worry, the printer manufacturer might be able to supply one. The procedure for installing manufacturer-supplied drivers is covered later in this chapter.

> **TIP**
>
> Some printers now come with special software to replace the Windows print queue or to perform special maintenance procedures like cleaning or print-head alignment. Check your printer's documentation to ensure it doesn't require a different installation procedure from what is described here.

> **NOTE**
>
> If your printer isn't included in the list, consult "When You Don't Find Your Printer in the List," later in this chapter.

Running the Wizard to Add a New Printer

Microsoft has made the previously arduous chore of adding a printer something that's much more easily mastered by a majority of computer users. Here's what you have to do:

1. Open the Printers folder by clicking the Start button and choosing Settings ➢ Printers. Two other paths are from My Computer and from Control Panel.

> **NOTE**
>
> Depending on the type of access control you stipulate from the Access Control tab of the Network applet in the Control Panel, you may want to password-protect your printer when you share it on the network. This helps guard against a printer being continually tied up with print jobs from an unauthorized user somewhere on the network.

2. Double-click Add Printer, as shown in Figure 8.1.

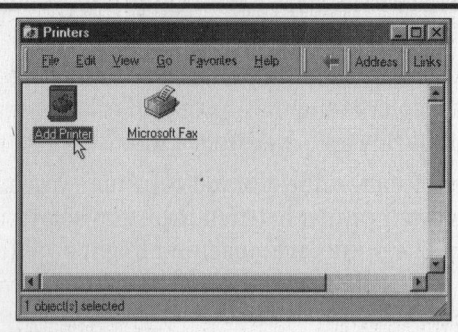

FIGURE 8.1: Run the Wizard to add a printer.

3. Click Next in the first dialog box that appears.
4. You're asked whether the printer is Local or Network. Because here I'm describing how to install a local printer, choose Local, then click Next.
5. You're presented with a list of brands and models. In the left column scroll the list, find the maker of your printer, and click it. Then in the right column choose the model number or name that matches your printer. Be sure to select the exact printer model, not just the correct brand name. Consult your printer's manual if you're in doubt about the model. What you enter here determines which printer driver file is used for this printer's definition. Figure 8.2 shows an example for an HP LaserJet 4.

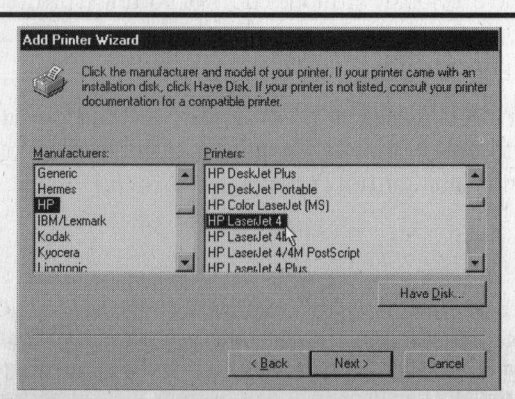

FIGURE 8.2: Choosing the printer make and model. Here I'm choosing a Hewlett-Packard LaserJet 4.

Printers and Printing   183

6. Click Next. Now you'll see a list of ports. You have to tell Windows which port the printer is connected to. (A port usually refers to the connector on the computer—but see Table 8.1 for the "file" exception.) Most often, the port will be the parallel printer port called LPT1 (Line Printer #1). Unless you know your printer is connected to another port, such as LPT2 or a serial port (such as COM1 or COM2), select LPT1 as in Figure 8.3.

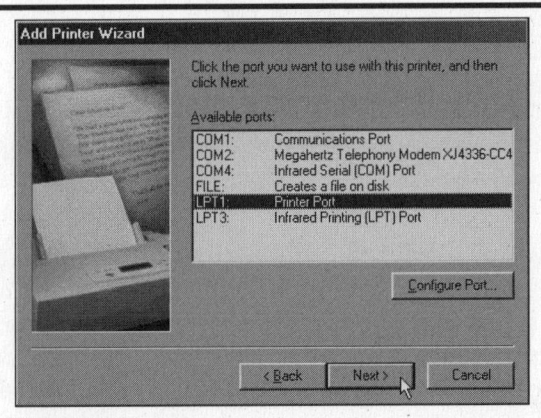

FIGURE 8.3: Choosing the port the printer's connected to is the second step in setting up a local printer.

7. Click Next. Now you can give the printer a name (see Figure 8.4).

NOTE

If the printer will be shared with DOS and 16-bit Windows users (such as people running Windows for Workgroups 3.11), you might want to limit this name to twelve characters because that's the maximum length those users will see when they are browsing for printers.

8. Also set whether the printer will be the default printer for Windows programs.

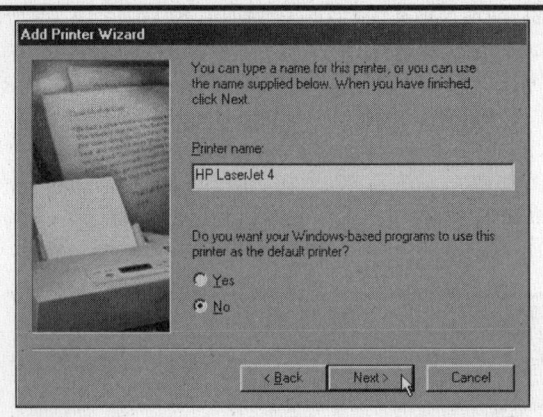

FIGURE 8.4: Give your new printer a name that tells you and other people something about it.

9. Finally, you're asked if you want to print a test page. It's a good idea to do this. Turn on the printer, make sure it has paper in it, and click Finish. If the driver file for your printer is in the computer, you'll be asked if you want to use it or load a new one from the Windows 98 SE CD-ROM or floppy disks. It's usually easier to use the existing driver. If the driver isn't on your hard disk, you'll be instructed to insert the disk containing the driver.

10. The test page will be sent to the printer. It should print out in a few minutes, and then you'll be asked if it printed OK. If it didn't print correctly, click No, and you'll be shown some troubleshooting information containing some questions and answers. The most likely fixes for the malady will be described. If the page printed OK, click Yes, and you're done. The new icon for your printer will show up in the Printers folder now.

> **NOTE**
> Windows 98 SE remembers the location you installed Windows 98 SE from originally. If you installed from a CD-ROM, it's likely that the default location for files is always going to be the CD-ROM drive's logical name (typically some higher letter, such as E or F). If you have done some subsequent installs or updates from other drives or directories, those are also remembered by Windows 98 SE and will be listed in the drop-down list box.

TABLE 8.1: Printer Ports

Port	Notes
LPT1, LPT2, LPT3	The most common setting is LPT1 because most PC-type printers hook up to the LPT1 parallel port. Click Configure Port if you want to turn off the ability to print to this printer from DOS programs.
LPT3 Infrared printing port	If your computer is equipped with an infrared port, you may have this option.
COM1, COM2, COM3, COM4	If you know your printer is of the serial variety, it's probably connected to the COM1 port. If COM1 is tied up for use with some other device, such as a modem, use COM2. If you choose a COM port, click Configure Port to check the communications settings in the resulting dialog box. Set the baud rate, data bit, parity, start and stop bits, and flow control to match those of the printer being attached. Refer to the printer's manual to determine what the settings should be.
File	This is for printing to a disk file instead of to the printer. Later, the file can be sent directly to the printer or sent to someone on floppy disk or over a modem. When you print to this printer name, you are prompted to enter a filename. (See "Printing to a Disk File Instead of a Printer" later in this chapter.)

When You Don't Find Your Printer in the List

When you're adding a local printer, you have to supply the brand name and model of the printer because Windows 98 SE needs to know which driver to load into your Windows 98 SE setup to use the printer correctly. (When you are adding a network printer, you aren't asked this question because the printer's host computer already knows what type of printer it is, and the driver is on that computer.)

What if your printer isn't on the list of Windows 98 SE–recognized printers? Many off-brand printers are designed to be compatible with one of the popular printer types, such as the Apple LaserWriters, Hewlett-Packard LaserJets, or the Epson line of printers. Refer to the manual that came with your printer to see whether it's compatible with one of the printers that *is* listed. Some printers require that you set the printer in compatibility mode using switches or software. Again, check the printer's manual for instructions.

Finally, if it looks like there's no mention of compatibility anywhere, contact the manufacturer for their Windows 98 SE–compatible driver. If you're lucky, they'll have one. It's also possible that Microsoft has a new driver for your printer that wasn't available when your copy of Windows was shipped. Contact Microsoft at (425) 936-6735 and ask for the Windows 98 Driver Library Disk, which contains all the latest drivers, or, better yet, check the Microsoft Web site support.microsoft.com/support/printing.

> **NOTE**
> All existing printer setups should actually have been migrated from Windows 95 to Windows 98 SE when you upgraded, so if it was working under Windows 95, it will probably work fine under Windows 98 SE. This is true for other types of drivers, too, such as video display cards, sound boards, and so on.

Also remember that Windows 98 SE can use the 16-bit drivers that worked with Windows 3.x. So, if you had a fully functioning driver for your printer in Windows 3.x (that is, your printer worked fine before you upgraded from Windows 3.x to Windows 98 SE), you should be able to use that driver in Windows 98 SE.

Locate the Windows 3.x driver disk supplied with your printer or locate the driver file. (Sometimes font or other support files are also needed, incidentally, so it's not always as simple as finding a single file.)

Assuming you do obtain a printer driver, do the following to install it:

1. Follow the instructions above for running the Add Printer Wizard.

2. Instead of selecting one of the printers in the Driver list (it isn't in the list, of course), click the Have Disk button. You'll see this box:

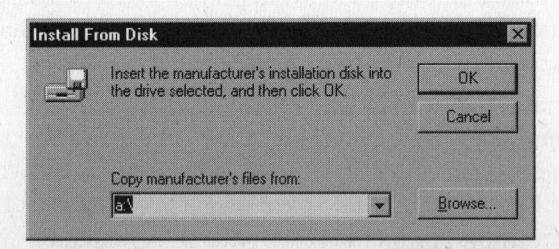

3. The Wizard is asking you to enter the path where the driver is located (typically a floppy disk). Insert the disk (or make

sure the files are available somewhere), enter the path, and click OK. Enter the correct source of the driver. Typically, it'll be in the A or B disk drive.

> **NOTE**
> The Wizard is looking for a file with an .INF extension, incidentally. This is the standard file extension for manufacturer-supplied driver information files.

4. Click OK.
5. You might have to choose a driver from a list if multiple options exist.
6. Continue with the Wizard dialog boxes as explained above.

> **NOTE**
> If none of the drivers you can lay your hands on will work with your printer, try choosing the Generic *text-only* driver. This driver prints only text—no fancy formatting and no graphics. But it will work in a pinch with many printers. Make sure the printer is capable of or is set to an ASCII or ANSI text-only mode, otherwise your printout may be a mess. PostScript printers typically don't have such a text-only mode.

ALTERING THE DETAILS OF A PRINTER'S SETUP— THE PROPERTIES BOX

Each printer driver can be fine-tuned by changing settings in its Properties dialog box. This area is difficult to document because so many variations exist due to the number of printers supported. The following sections describe the gist of these options without going into too much detail about each printer type.

The settings pertaining to a printer are called *properties*. Properties abound in Windows 98 SE. Almost every object in Windows 98 SE has properties that you can examine and change at will. When you add a printer, the Wizard makes life easy for you by giving it some default properties that usually work fine and needn't be tampered with. You can change them later, but only if you need to. It may be worth looking at the properties for your printer, especially if the printer's acting up in some way when you try to print from Windows 98 SE.

1. Open the Printers folder.

2. Right-click the printer's icon and choose Properties. A box such as the one in Figure 8.5 appears.

TIP
You can also type Alt+Enter to open the Properties box. This is true with many Windows 98 SE objects.

3. Notice that there is a place for a comment. This is normally blank after you add a printer. If you share the printer on the network, any text that you add to this box will be seen by other users who are browsing the network for a printer.

4. Click the various tab pages of your printer's Properties box to view or alter the great variety of settings. These buttons are confusing in name, and there's no easy way to remember what's what. But remember that you can get help by clicking the ? in the upper-right corner and then on the setting or button whose function you don't understand.

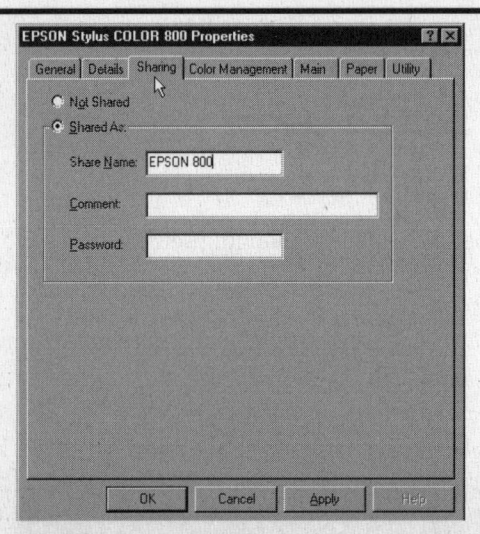

FIGURE 8.5: Each printer has a Properties box such as this, with several tab pages. Options and tabs differ from printer to printer.

How to Delete a Printer from Your Printers Folder

You might want to decommission a printer after you've added it, for several reasons:

- You've connected a new type of printer to your computer and you want to delete the old setup and create a new one with the correct driver for the new printer.
- You want to disconnect from a network printer you're through using.
- You've created several slightly different setups for the same physical printer and you want to delete the ones you don't use.

In any of these cases, the trick is the same:

1. Open the Printers folder (the easiest way is using Start ➢ Settings ➢ Printers).
2. Right-click the icon for the printer setup you want to delete and choose Delete (or just press Del). You will see at least one confirmation box before the printer is deleted. You may see another warning if there are print jobs in the queue for the printer.

NOTE
If you have stipulated that the computer can keep separate settings for each user (via Control Panel ➢ Passwords ➢ User Profiles), the removal process removes only the printer setup from Windows 98 SE's Registry for the currently logged-in user. Also note that the related driver file and font files are not deleted from the disk. Therefore, if you want to re-create the printer, you don't have to insert disks, and you won't be prompted for the location of driver files. This is convenient, but if you're tight on disk space, you might want to remove the printer fonts and drivers. To remove fonts, use the Fonts applet in the Control Panel, as described in Chapter 7, *Customizing Windows 98 SE with the Control Panel*.

How to Print Out Documents from Your Programs

By now your printer(s) is(are) added and ready to go. The procedure for printing in Windows 98 SE is simple. Typically, you just open a document, choose File ➢ Print, and make a few settings, such as which pages to print, and click OK. (You might have to set the print area first or make some other settings, depending on the program.) If you're already happy with the ways in which you print, you might want to skim over this section. However, there *are* a couple of conveniences you might not know about, such as using drag and drop to print or right-clicking a document to print it without opening the program that created it.

About the Default Printer

Unless you choose otherwise, the output from Windows programs are routed to the Print Queue for printing. If no particular printer has been chosen (perhaps because the program—for example, Notepad—doesn't give you a choice), the default printer is used.

> **NOTE**
> The default printer can be set by right-clicking a printer icon and choosing Set as Default.

Exactly how your printed documents look varies somewhat from program to program because not all programs can take full advantage of the capabilities of your printer and the printer driver. For example, simple word-processing programs like Notepad don't let you change the font, while a full-blown word-processing program such as Microsoft Word can print out all kinds of fancy graphics, fonts, columns of text, and so forth.

When you print from any program, the file is actually printed to a disk file instead of directly to the printer. The Print Queue then spools the file to the assigned printer(s), coordinating the flow of data and keeping you informed of the progress. Jobs are queued up and listed in the Print Queue window, from which their status can be observed; they can be rearranged, deleted, and so forth.

Printing from a Program

To print from any program, including Windows 3.*x* and Windows 95 programs, follow these steps (which are exact for Windows programs but only approximate for other environments):

1. Check to see that the printer and page settings are correct. Some programs' File menus provide a Printer Setup, Page Setup, or other option for this. Note that settings you make from such a box temporarily (sometimes permanently, depending on the program) override settings made from the Printer's Properties dialog box.

2. Select the Print command on the program's File menu and fill in whatever information is asked of you. For example, in WordPad, the Print dialog box looks like that in Figure 8.6.

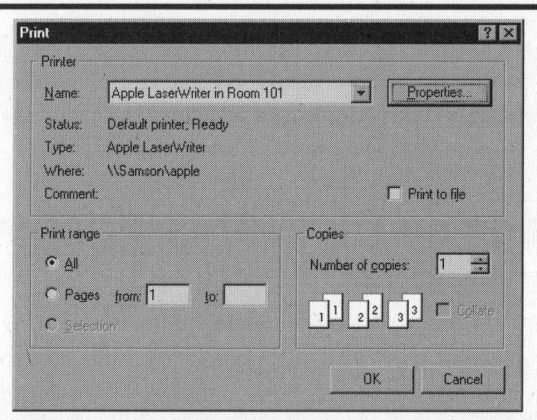

FIGURE 8.6: When you choose Print from a Windows program, you often see a dialog box such as this that allows you to choose some options before printing. This one is from WordPad, a program supplied with Windows 98 SE.

Some programs have rather elaborate dialog boxes for choosing which printer you want to print to, scaling or graphically altering the printout, and even adjusting the properties of the printer. Still, you can normally just make the most obvious settings and get away with it:

- ▶ Correct printer
- ▶ Correct number of copies

- Correct print range (pages, spreadsheet cells, portion of graphic, etc.)
- For color printers, which ink cartridge you have in (black and white or color)

3. Click OK (or otherwise confirm printing). Windows 98 SE intercepts the print data and writes it in a file, then begins printing it. If an error occurs—a port conflict, the printer is out of paper, or what have you—you'll see a message.

Check the paper supply, check to see that the printer is turned on, that it's online (there may be a switch on the printer for this). If it's a network printer, make sure it's shared and that the computer it's connected to is booted up and has shared the printer for use.

> **TIP**
> When printing commences, a little printer icon will appear in the Taskbar next to the clock. You can double-click this icon to see details of your pending print jobs.

Printing by Dragging Files onto a Printer Icon or into Its Window

You can quickly print Windows program document files by dragging them onto a printer's icon or window. You can drag from the Desktop, a folder, the Find box, or the Windows Explorer window. This will only work with documents that have an association with a particular program. To check if a document has an association, right-click it. If the resulting menu has an Open command on it (not Open With), it has an association.

1. Arrange things on your screen so you can see the file(s) you want to print as well as either the printer's icon or its window (you open a printer's window by double-clicking its icon).

> **TIP**
> You can drag a file into a shortcut of the Printer's icon. If you like this way of printing, keep a shortcut of your printer on the Desktop so you can drag documents to it without having to open up the Printers folder. Double-clicking a shortcut provides an easy means of checking its print queue, too.

Printers and Printing 193

2. Drag the document file(s) onto the Printer icon or window (as Figure 8.7 illustrates). The file is loaded into the source program, the Print command is automatically executed, and the file is spooled to Print Queue. The document isn't actually moved out of its home folder, it just gets printed.

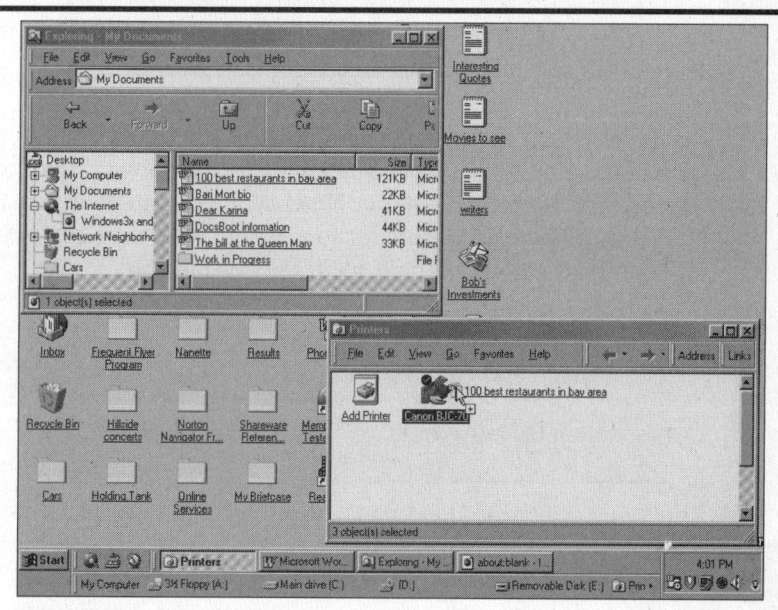

FIGURE 8.7: You can print a document by dragging it to the destination printer's icon or window.

If the document doesn't have an association, you'll see an error message:

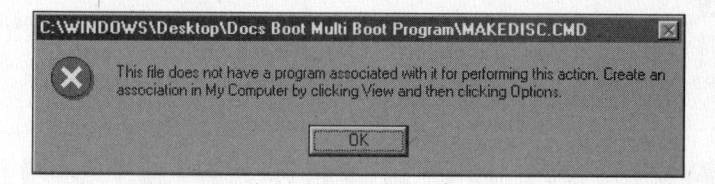

Also, a nice feature of this approach is that you can drag multiple files onto a printer's icon or open window at once. They will all be queued up for printing, one after another, via their source programs. You'll see this message asking for confirmation before printing commences:

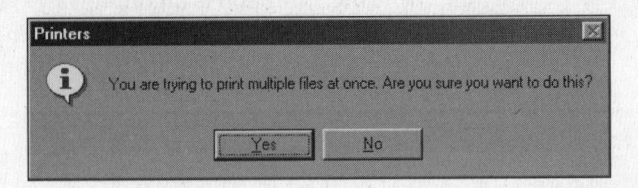

> **Printers**
> You are trying to print multiple files at once. Are you sure you want to do this?
> [Yes] [No]

One caveat about this technique: As you know, some programs don't have a built-in facility for printing to a printer other than the default one. Notepad is a case in point: Try to drag a Notepad document to a printer that isn't currently your default printer, and you'll see this message:

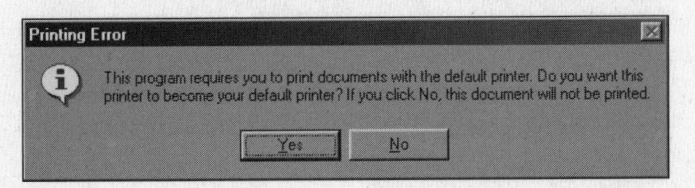

> **Printing Error**
> This program requires you to print documents with the default printer. Do you want this printer to become your default printer? If you click No, this document will not be printed.
> [Yes] [No]

TIP
The drag-and-drop method can be used with shortcuts, too. You can drag shortcuts of documents to a printer or even to a shortcut of a printer, and the document will print.

TIP
In addition to using drag and drop, you can also right-click many documents and choose Print from the context menu that appears.

Working with the Print Queue

If you print more than a few files at a time, or if you have your printer shared for network use, you'll sometimes want to check on the status of a printer's print jobs. You also might want to see how many jobs need to print before you turn off your local computer and printer if others are using it. Or you might want to know how many other jobs are ahead of yours.

You can check on these items by opening a printer's window. You'll then see:

Document Name   Name of the file being printed and possibly the source program

Status   Whether the job is printing, being deleted, or paused

Owner   Who sent each print job to the printer

Progress   How large each job is and how much of the current job has been printed

Start at   When each print job was sent to the print queue

To see the queue on a printer:

1. Open the Printers folder.

2. Double-click the printer in question.

3. Adjust the window size if necessary so you can see all the columns.

NOTE

If the print job originated from a DOS program, the Document Name will not be known. It's listed as Remote Downlevel Document, meaning that it came from a workstation that doesn't support Microsoft's RPC (Remote Procedure Call) print support. Additional cases in point are Windows for Workgroups, LAN Manager, Unix, and NetWare.

TIP

If the printer in question is a network printer, and the printer is offline for some reason, such as its computer isn't turned on, you'll be forced to work offline. An error message will alert you to this, and the top line of the printer's window will say "User intervention required—Work Offline." Until the issue is resolved, you won't be able to view the queue for that printer. You can still print to it, however.

Refreshing the Network Queue Information

The network cabling connecting workstations and servers often is quite busy, so Windows usually doesn't bother to add even more traffic to the net by polling each workstation for printer-queue information. This is done when necessary, such as when a document is deleted from a queue. So, if you want to refresh the window for a printer to get the absolute latest information, just press F5. This immediately updates the queue information.

Deleting a File from the Queue

After sending a file to the queue, you might reconsider printing it, or you might want to re-edit the file and print it later. If so, you can simply remove the file from the queue.

1. Open the printer's window.
2. Select the file by clicking it in the queue.

> **NOTE**
> I have found, especially with PostScript laser-type printers, that after deleting a file while printing, I'll have to reset the printer to clear its buffer or at least eject the current page (if you have a page-eject button). To reset, you'll typically have to push a button on the printer's front panel or turn the printer off for a few seconds, then on again.

3. Choose Document ➢ Cancel Printing, press Delete, or right-click and choose Cancel Printing. The document item is removed from the printer's window. If you're trying to delete the job that's printing, you might have some trouble. At the very least, the system might take some time to respond.

> **NOTE**
> Of course, normally you can't delete someone else's print jobs on a remote printer. If you try to, you'll be told that this is beyond your privilege and that you should contact your system administrator. You *can* kill other people's print jobs if the printer in question is connected to *your* computer. But if you want to be able to delete jobs on a remote computer, someone has to alter the password settings in the remote computer's Control Panel to allow remote administration of the printer.

NOTE
Pending print jobs will not be lost when computers are powered down. Any documents in the queue when the system goes down will reappear in the queue when you power up. When you turn on a computer that is the host for a shared printer that has an unfinished print queue, you will be alerted to the number of jobs in the queue and asked whether to delete or print them.

Canceling All Pending Print Jobs on a Given Printer

Sometimes, because of a megalithic meltdown or some other catastrophe, you'll decide to bail out of all the print jobs that are stacked up for a printer. Normally you don't need to do this, even if the printer has gone wacky. You can just pause the queue and continue printing after the problem is solved. But sometimes you'll want to resend everything to another printer and kill the queue on the current one. It's easy:

1. Select the printer's icon or window.

2. Right-click and choose Purge Print Documents, or from the printer's window choose Printer ➤ Purge Print Documents. All queued jobs for the printer are canceled.

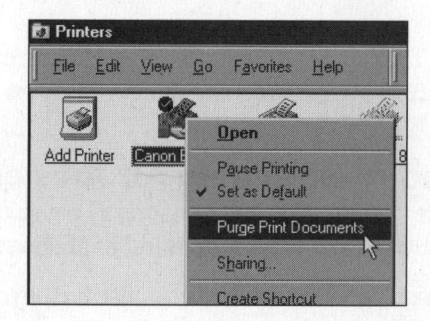

WARNING
Make sure you really want to cancel the jobs before you do this. This is a good way to make enemies if people on the network were counting on their print jobs being finished any time soon.

Pausing (and Resuming) the Printing Process

If you're the administrator of a printer with a stack of jobs in the print queue, you can temporarily pause a single job or all jobs on a particular printer at any time. This can be useful for taking a minute to add paper, take a phone call, or have a conversation in your office without the noise of the printer in the background. The next several sections explain the techniques for pausing and resuming.

Pausing or Resuming a Specific Print Job

You can pause documents anywhere in the queue. Paused documents are skipped, and subsequent documents in the list print ahead of them. When you feel the need to pause or resume a specific print job:

1. Click the document's information line.
2. Choose Document ➤ Pause Printing (or right-click the document and choose Pause Printing). The current print job is temporarily suspended, and the word "Paused" appears in the status area. (The printing might not stop immediately because your printer might have a buffer that holds data in preparation for printing. The printing stops when the buffer is empty.)
3. To resume printing the document, repeat steps 1 and 2 to turn off the check mark next to Pause Printing.

Pausing or Resuming All Jobs on a Printer

In a similar fashion, you can temporarily pause all jobs on a given printer. You might want to do this for a number of reasons including:

- ▶ To load paper or otherwise adjust the physical printer
- ▶ To alter printer settings from the printer's Properties dialog box

Follow these steps to pause or resume all jobs for a printer:

1. Deselect any documents in the printer's window; press the spacebar if a document is selected.
2. Choose Printer ➤ Pause Printing. The printer window's title bar changes to say "Paused."

3. To resume all jobs on the printer, choose Printer ➤ Pause Printing again to turn off the check mark next to the command. The *Paused* indicator in the title bar disappears, and printing should resume where the queue left off.

Printing to a Disk File Instead of a Printer

There are times when you may want to print to a disk file rather than to the printer. When you print to a disk file, the codes and data that would normally be sent to the printer are shunted off to a disk file—either locally or on the network. The resulting file typically isn't just a copy of the file you were printing; it contains all the special formatting codes that control your printer.

Why would you want to create a disk file instead of printing directly to the printer? Printing to a file gives you several options not available when you print directly to the printer:

- Print files are sometimes used by programs for specific purposes. For example, printing a database to a disk file might allow you to more easily work with it in another application.

- You can send the file to another person, either on floppy disk or over the phone lines, with a modem and a communications program such as HyperTerminal. That person can then print the file directly to a printer (if it's compatible) with Windows or a utility such as the DOS copy command. The person doesn't need the program that created the file and doesn't have to worry about any of the printing details—formatting, setting up margins, and so forth.

- It allows you to print the file later. Maybe your printer isn't hooked up, or there's so much stuff on the queue that you don't want to wait. Later, you can use the DOS copy command or a batch file with a command such as copy *.prn lpt1 /b to copy all files to the desired port. Be sure to use the /b switch. If you don't, the first Ctrl+Z code the computer encounters will terminate the print job because the print files are binary files.

In some programs, printing to a disk file is a choice in the Print dialog box. If it isn't, you should modify the printer's configuration to print to a file rather than to a port. Then, whenever you use that printer, it uses all the usual settings for the driver but sends the data to a file of your choice instead of to the printer port.

1. In the Printers folder, right-click the printer's icon and choose Properties.
2. Select the Details tab page.
3. Under Print To The Following Port, choose FILE:

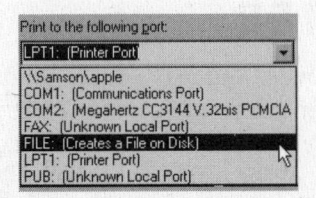

4. Click OK. The printer's icon in the Printers folder will change to indicate that printing is routed to a disk file.

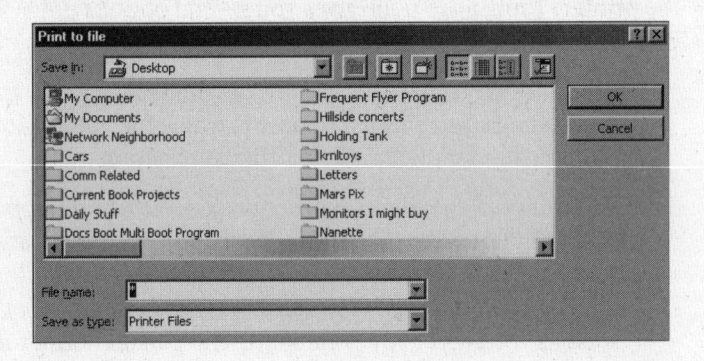

Epson LX-80

Now when you print a file from any program and choose this printer as the destination for the printout, you'll be prompted for a filename.

What's Next?

In the next chapter, we'll continue looking at Windows 98 SE's extensive hardware support, digging into its particularly rich multimedia features. You'll learn about working with everything from the Windows Media Player to the latest-and-greatest gizmos like the DVD player.

Chapter 9
WINDOWS MULTIMEDIA

Windows 98 SE is more *multimedia-ready* than any previous version of Windows. Gone are the days when upgrading your PC for multimedia meant days of intense hardware analysis. And because Windows 98 SE has built-in, high-performance, 32-bit support for digital video, digital audio, MIDI, game controllers, and even TV, developers and users no longer need to worry about installing special drivers and programs to squeeze maximum multimedia out of their Windows machines.

PC-based multimedia has grown dramatically in the last several years. Not only do practically all mainstream software packages (including Windows 98 SE itself) now come to us on CD-ROMs, many of them also have online multimedia tutorials to teach basic skills. These often include music, video, or animation, as well as voice coaching. Thanks to the cooperative efforts of many hardware and software engineers, we've come a long way from the old days when a program consisted of a single

Adapted from *Mastering Windows 98 Second Edition*
by Robert Cowart
ISBN 0-7821-2618-9   928 pages $39.99

floppy disk and a big, boring manual. And this is just the tip of the multimedia iceberg. Internet-based multimedia games, music education programs, video telephone conferencing, 360-degree panoramic-view Web sites, and streaming audio and video Web sites are some of the nifty features that are becoming common.

Improvements in Plug-and-Play (PnP) technology have decreased the hassle of upgrading your system to add stuff like CD-ROMs, audio cards, microphones, and speakers. Nowadays, you're almost guaranteed that any new PnP multimedia device you add will install itself with little or no hassle. You're also more likely to meet with success when plugging in some older piece of gear, due to improved detection of "legacy" (a.k.a. old) hardware by Windows 98 SE.

With few exceptions, today's PCs are multimedia PCs, complying with standards that were primarily developed by Microsoft and a few other industry giants. The "multimedia PC standard," proposed a few years back, has been widely adopted by PC makers, partly by design and partly as the result of mass popularity of specific pieces of hardware. (For example, most PC sound systems are SoundBlaster compatible. Manufactured by Creative Labs, Inc., SoundBlaster was one of the first add-in sound cards. Even without being endorsed by other hardware and software companies, it has become a de facto industry standard thanks to the sheer number of installed units in the field.) Windows 98 has helped solidify the standards for multimedia by adding multimedia APIs (Application Program Interface) that serve as a set of building blocks for anyone making multimedia programs for Windows. By writing their code around the APIs, software developers only have to write one version of a program regardless of the hundreds of possible combinations of video, audio, MIDI, or other multimedia hardware that may be included in users' computer systems. Windows and the installed device drivers take care of the rest.

A multimedia PC equipped with Windows 98 SE can:

- ▶ Display cable and broadcast television in a resizable window or full-screen with better-than-TV quality, and even capture the closed-captioning text of a show to a text file for later perusal.

- ▶ Play DVD movies, complete with display of embedded textual or other material that the producer may add.

- ▶ Record, edit, and play sounds in a variety of formats from highly compressed monaural voice grade to CD-quality stereo.

- ▶ Play MIDI sequences on your synthesizer or other MIDI device.

- Play fancy CD-ROM titles such as interactive encyclopedias that talk or adventure games such as Myst.
- Display streaming video and audio from Web broadcasts such as live concerts or news shows.
- Display live video and audio teleconferencing over the Internet using NetMeeting or other compatible programs.

All such capabilities, and the hardware and software that make them work, fall into the category of *Windows multimedia*. This chapter will answer your questions about Windows 98 SE's multimedia abilities and how you can best take advantage of them. Please keep in mind while reading this chapter that talking about Windows multimedia is like shooting at a moving target. Changes are taking place so rapidly in the field that book publishers would need unrealistically brisk turnaround times (akin to that of magazines) to accurately reflect the state of the industry. Therefore, to spare you the annoyance of reading out-of-date material, I'll focus this chapter on the multimedia features of Windows 98 SE itself, and deal only fleetingly with issues of secondary, aftermarket products.

EXACTLY WHAT IS MULTIMEDIA?

Multimedia—alias *interactive media* or *hypermedia*—is difficult to define, which accounts for much general confusion on the topic. The practical definition changes each time I write a book about Windows, and that's about every year or so. Actually, multimedia simply means two or more simultaneous types of display. Regular old TV is a good example—it's a multimedia device since it integrates audio and video. Computers are capable of even more advanced levels of multimedia, amalgamating animation, graphics, video, MIDI, digitally recorded sounds, and text. Computers can also interact with people as they view the presentation.

It's interesting to chronicle the breakneck rate of multimedia advancements. Just a few years ago, updating a system to multimedia meant adding a CD-ROM drive. Today, any decent PC (even most laptops) has one built in, along with speakers and even accelerated video display cards capable of 30 frame-per-second high-speed animation and texture mapping.

Some multimedia programs are *interactive* and some are not. Interactivity means that through some input device such as keyboard, mouse, voice, or external controller—for example, a Musical Instrument Digital Interface (MIDI) keyboard—you interact with the system to control aspects of the presentation. Most of today's software is still primarily based on text display, though it's increasingly permeated with graphics, charts, and clip art. With the added capabilities of stereo sound, animation, and video, multimedia computing offers a rich and efficient means of conveying information. As an example of a simple interactive program, consider the Windows tour, which demonstrates Windows fundamentals for the newcomer. (You launch it by choosing Start ➤ Programs ➤ Accessories ➤ System Tools ➤ Welcome To Windows. Then click Discover Windows 98.) The tutorial demonstrates rudimentary multimedia, integrating animation, text, and voice. It does not incorporate live-action video clips. Now imagine expanding such a tutorial to include music, realistic 3-D animation, and moving video images just as if you were watching TV. As you probably know by now, animators, musicians, designers, writers, programmers, audio engineers, industry experts, and video producers have joined forces to create multimedia applications such as:

- A word processing document that lets you paste in video clips (with audio); instead of displaying just a still graphic, the document will be "alive" with sight and sound.

- A music-education program on a CD-ROM from Microsoft that plays Beethoven's Ninth Symphony while displaying informative and educational text about each passage and about the composer.

- A dictionary, thesaurus, book of quotations, and encyclopedia on a CD-ROM from Microsoft that not only contains a huge amount of textual information but actually pronounces the dictionary entries; reads quotations aloud in the voices of Robert Frost, Carl Sandburg, T.S. Eliot, e.e. cummings, Dylan Thomas, and John F. Kennedy; and illustrates scientific phenomena with animation.

- Programs that teach you how to play the piano using a MIDI keyboard connected to your PC. The computer senses whether you play the lesson correctly and responds accordingly with a recorded high-quality voice. Similar programs teach music theory.

- Interactive company annual reports, product demonstrations, presentations, or corporate training manuals for new employees.

- *Moving catalogs* from mail-order houses, displaying everything from cars to coats via high-quality video and audio.

- An interactive geography test used at the National Geographic Society Explorer's Hall in Washington, D.C.

- Interactive high-speed, random-access books, newspapers, or catalogs for the blind, using high-quality voice synthesis or recorded voices.

- Interactive training for hard-to-teach professions such as medical diagnosis, surgery, auto mechanics, and machine operation of various types.

- Complex interactive games and children's learning programs that incorporate stereo sound effects, flashy visuals, and the ability to move through synthetic virtual worlds.

These multimedia products and more already exist. The explosion of multimedia CD titles has been enormous in the last few years.

What's New in Windows 98 SE Multimedia

Windows 98 SE adds a number of new features as well as enhancing some of the better features of Windows 95 multimedia:

- Built-in support for compressed video allows playback of video files (such as AVI and QuickTime) without installation of additional licensed drivers.

- AutoPlay support lets users simply insert a CD and it will begin to run, eliminating the need to enter the correct command or find and click the correct program icon in the CD's file directory.

- 2-D and 3-D graphics support is now provided through improved DirectX, a set of tools that help developers take advantage of new capabilities of Windows 98, such as multiple monitors, Intel Pentium MMX extensions, use of the USB (Universal Serial Bus) interface for gaming device input, faster texture mapping, and anti-aliasing.

- DirectShow, a streaming media player technology, allows Windows 98 SE to efficiently play back a variety of multimedia file types: AVI video, MPEG compressed video, Apple QuickTime video, and WAV audio. MPEG-compressed video can be played back on PCs that have no decompression hardware; Windows 98 SE can achieve decompression quickly enough.

- NetShow, a streaming media player, plays unicast and multicast streaming audio and video that comes over the Web. It's compatible with existing RealAudio and RealVideo formats as well as with Microsoft's own NetShow format.

- A DVD (Digital Video Disk) player program is included. If you have a (hardware) DVD player attached to your system, you can play DVD, CD-sized disks that contain huge amounts of data, such as audio, several hours of video, and optional text.

- Surround Video allows software developers an easy way to create programs that let users interact with objects, images, patterns, and live action video in a 360-degree view in a synthetic environment.

- Windows 98 SE includes 32-bit drivers for support of faster CD-ROM drives, while still supporting older drives and 16-bit Windows 3.*x* drivers (MSCDEX). Also supported is the new CD-PLUS specification developed by Sony and Phillips, which puts text (including biographies and music program notes), video, and other enhancements on the same CD with the usual audio material. These new CD titles can be played on a Windows 98 SE machine.

- Windows 98 SE "broadcast-enables" your computer. You can receive Web pages that contain video and audio content, and, with the right hardware, view television programming from cable, over-the-air, and satellite networks.

- Smoother 32-bit multitasking and better codec (compression/decompression) software make it possible to display even full-screen video simultaneous with MIDI or audio playback, something not possible only a few years ago. Even modest-priced laptops have fast enough electronics to support this.

Upgrading to Multimedia

With Windows 3.*x*, working with multimedia required purchasing Microsoft's Multimedia upgrade kit or buying an expensive and hard-to-find MPC (multimedia PC). Beginning with Windows 95, Microsoft started to bundle multimedia drivers with their operating systems and include related utility programs (such as Sound Recorder) in the hope that this would accelerate the development of multimedia Windows applications. Setting up the MPC specification helped set some standards for what a multimedia PC should look and act like, and the PC add-on market did the rest. A vast profusion of multimedia hardware, applications, and utilities have subsequently become prevalent, many of which are now incorporated into Windows 98 SE.

Magazines now inundate us with ads for newer and faster CD-ROM and DVD-ROM drives, 128-bit co-processed video cards, high-resolution energy-efficient monitors, and fancy sound cards—some even have samples of real orchestral instruments built in. The MPC moniker has fallen by the wayside, and now what's really more important is whether a system is fully Windows 98–compatible or not. After that, the rest is icing on the cake: How big is the screen, how good do the speakers sound, how clear is the image, and overall, how fast does the *whole system* perform (not just the CPU chip)? You'll have to rely on the magazines for these kinds of test comparisons. Don't rely on the guys in the store. One brand of 400MHz Celeron machine might actually be faster than another one that's got a 450MHz Pentium II under the hood, because of the vagaries of hard-disk controllers, type of internal bus, memory caching, or speed of the video card.

If you already own a multimedia-ready machine with a couple of speakers and a CD-ROM drive, you might as well skip this section and move down to the next major section in this chapter, "Supplied Multimedia Applications and Utilities." But if you don't have such a machine, and you're thinking about endowing your machine with the gift of gab, some fancy video graphics capabilities, and the ability to watch TV or play DVDs, stay on track here.

There are three basic ways to upgrade your computer: buy a whole new computer, buy an "upgrade-in-a-box," or mix and match new components that exactly fit your needs (see Table 9.1 for a comparison of the three approaches). As of this writing, there were about twenty upgrade-in-a-box products to choose from. You'll typically get a CD-ROM drive, speakers, a sound card, a microphone, and maybe some CDs in the package. The sound card has the SCSI (Small Computer Systems Interface, pronounced "scuzzy") connector that hooks the CD-ROM drive to the computer. Mixing and matching is for us total control-freak geeks, who must have the best or who don't like the idea of other people controlling our purchase decisions. The obvious downside is that sorting through the sea of components in the marketplace is a big waste of time. I've spent too many hours testing video boards, trying to get a SCSI upgrade to my sound card to work with my CD-ROM drive, or running around listening to speakers. In any case, here are a few points about the pros and cons of the three upgrade routes.

In your shopping, you may wonder what the minimal requirements of a multimedia system should be. With the technology changing so quickly, it's hard to predict what the pickings will look like a year from now; or what the latest and greatest version of Riven (or some other multimedia game you'll want as your major distraction from work) will crave in the way of MM nuts and bolts. Still, here's Bob's rule of thumb about buying new computer stuff: The best balance between price and performance lies just in the wake of the technology wave.

That is, if price is an issue, eschew the cutting edge! State-of-the-art gear is too expensive and usually still has some bugs to be worked out, or ends up becoming an "industry standard" with a half-life of about nine months before being dropped like a hot potato. When a product hits the mainstream, that's the time to buy; prices usually take a nosedive at that point, often about 50 percent.

TABLE 9.1: Approaches to Multimedia Upgrading

QUESTION	NEW COMPUTER	KIT IN A BOX	MIX AND MATCH COMPONENTS
What is it?	A whole computer system that is designed for multimedia Windows 98 from the ground up and includes a fairly zippy computer, color screen, speakers, microphone, sound card, fast video display card capable of TV tuning and video capture, built-in Zip drive, and a CD-ROM drive. Options will be CD writers and DVD players.	A box of stuff you get at a computer store or by mail order. Everything works together and costs less than $200. Includes a sound card, CD-ROM drive, microphone, and speakers. (For more money you can get a DVD drive instead of a CD-ROM drive. Most DVD drives can play normal CDs as well as DVD disks.)	CD-ROM drive, optional DVD drive, sound board, speakers, microphone, cabling, and possibly necessary software drivers. Purchase parts separately. $200–$400. Add an additional $150 minimum for a CD writer.

TABLE 9.1 continued: Approaches to Multimedia Upgrading

Question	New Computer	Kit in a Box	Mix and Match Components
Who should buy?	Owner of an older computer who has already decided to purchase a new computer either because existing computer isn't worth upgrading to a faster CPU and larger hard disk, or because an additional computer is needed.	Average owner of non-multimedia computer that's acceptably endowed in terms of the CPU and hard-disk (e.g., a Pentium and 2GB hard disk or larger) but needs multi-media capability to run multi-media games and standard productivity applications.	Power user who wants the best selection of components—or who already has one or two essential components, such as a CD-ROM drive, and now wants the rest. May be a professional (such as a musician, application developer, or graphic artist) who needs one element of the multimedia upgrade to be of very high quality.
How much hassle?	No hassle. Everything is installed and working. Get the system with Windows 98 SE installed and working if you can, and you're really set.	You'll have to remove the cover to the computer, remove some screws, insert a couple of cards, hook up some cables and the CD-ROM drive (if the drive is the internal type), and then hook up the speakers. If the cards and computer are not Plug-and-Play compatible, you'll have to make IRQ and DMA settings. This may take some homework. You might have conflicts with existing hardware; if so, you should have Windows 98 detect and install drivers for the new hardware, or use supplied drivers.	About the same amount of hassle as a box upgrade, but you'll have to deal with separate documentation for each component and figure out how to get everything working together, unless they are Plug-and-Play components. IRQ and DMA conflicts are likely otherwise.
Advantages?	Low hassle factor. You can start getting work done instead of poring over magazines and manuals. Your church (or kid) gets your old computer (which means you get an easy tax write-off), and you get more sleep, and have only one vendor to deal with at service time.	You don't have to sell your existing computer. You might even get some free CD-ROM software in the box.	You can have exactly what you want. 24-bit True-Color graphics, direct video capturing, video conferencing, great sound, superfast display at 1600 by 1280—you name it.

TABLE 9.1 continued: Approaches to Multimedia Upgrading

Question	New Computer	Kit in a Box	Mix and Match Components
Disadvantages?	You have to buy a whole new system. You'll probably be compromising somewhat on the components for the low hassle factor.	It will take some work to install it, unless it comes from the same people who made your computer (e.g., a Dell upgrade to a Dell computer). Again, some compromise on the components is likely. You may not have the best-sounding speakers, fastest video, greatest color depth, or CD-ROM drive.	Price and installation hassle can be high, but PnP is making things much easier. Multiple dealers to reckon with at service time.
Price?	Less than $1500 for most systems, which is not much more for a multimedia system than for those without multimedia. A few hundred additional dollars is typical. Tricked-out systems with all options and lots of memory and large hard disk will be between $2500 and $4000.	Typically between $100 and $250 for fast CD-ROM or DVD drive, 3D sound card, speakers, and a few extras.	Difficult to predict. Bottom-of-the-line but functional clone parts could run you as little as a few hundred dollars. Or you could pay well into the thousands for the best brands.

What does this mean in the current market? Well, the now old and crusty MPC specification requires at least a machine with 4MB of RAM, a 130MB hard disk, and a fast processor such as a 486 or Pentium. But that's now a joke. You won't find a PC with that little RAM these days. On the next few pages are my suggestions to keep in mind when you're shopping for multimedia components and systems.

Computer   I'd suggest at *least* a Pentium MMX CPU, a local bus video card, and a 2GB hard disk (EIDE or SCSI), with 32MB (preferably 64MB) of RAM. A SCSI hardware interface is even better because you can also hook up as many as seven devices to most SCSI controllers, not just hard disks, and they run faster. But the bulk of machines these days have EIDE hard disks, and they are fast enough for most purposes short of doing real-time video capture. Remember, this is a minimum configuration.

Of course, if you're buying a new computer, you're probably going to get at least a Pentium II or Celeron 400 (or equivalent) with a 4 GB hard disk. For any serious work (or play) I'd recommend that kind of speed or faster.

CD-ROM Drive   Get at least a 16x speed drive. (The x means how many times faster the data can be read from the disk relative to the first CD drives, which are considered 1x.) As of this writing, affordable 40x drives are common. Windows 98 SE caches your CD-ROM drive data, so that it will help slower drives keep up with the data-hungry demands of applications that display video, for example.

If you want to be able to connect to a laptop or move the drive between computers, get a lightweight portable external job, maybe even a Zip or Jaz drive. Many computer manufacturers offer optional Zip drives for less than $100. Make sure the drive supports multisession Kodak photo format. This lets you not only view photographs in CD-ROM format on your computer but also take an existing photo CD-ROM to your photo developer and have them add new pictures to it. You might want up-front manual controls on the player so you can listen to audio CDs without running the CD Player program that comes with Windows.

PHOTOS AND WINDOWS 98 SE

If you're among the gadget happy, you'll probably be procuring yourself a digital camera soon, or at least want your photos on disk or in your computer somehow. That way, you can futz with your pictures using nifty software such as Adobe PhotoShop, Goo Power Tools, or other programs that let you make art out of common photographs. Or, so you can e-mail pictures of your pet iguana to your friends back home.

The easiest way to get your pix into the computer is to take your next roll of film down to the photo finisher's and request your snaps back on disk as well as on paper. Though some will give them to you on floppies, most services will provide the shots on CD. The standard format is the Kodak CD format.

CONTINUED ➞

Once you get the CD, check it for the info that tells you how to view the pictures. If all else fails, you may be able to simply click the picture files using Windows Explorer, but better to use some software front-end to do it. The pictures usually show up as JPG or GIF files, and there may be numerous resolutions for each picture (thus, a set of files for each picture).

Digital cameras always come with Windows software that you can load up, and instructions for getting your pictures from the camera into your computer. I like using the cameras that have a pop-out memory card that I can plug into the PC card slot on my laptop. Then I don't have to hassle with wires (and thus the relatively slow download speed of the pictures over a wire). Two of the cameras I've tested (Panasonic Cool Shot and Kodak DC 210) used these cards, and they were interchangeable. I just took some pictures and then popped the card out of the camera and then into the computer. Windows 98 SE recognizes the card automatically and treats it like a disk drive, which makes it easy to display the contents in Windows Explorer or in a Browse box from a photo display program or other imaging program.

NOTE
There are two flavors of Photo CD you should know about: *single-session* and *multi-session*. With a multi-session Photo CD, you can just bring in your existing CD to your photo finisher's shop and ask them to add your new pictures to the same disk. Single-session doesn't let you do that; it's a write-once format.

CD Writer Among the latest goodies in the CD-ROM drive market are the now-affordable writers that will "burn" (record) a custom CD for you. These used to cost thousands of bucks, and were affordable by only recording and software magnates. Now, creating your own music CDs (I create CD compilations of my fave dance tunes for parties), or backing up tons of data on CDs is something anyone can do. All you need is a CD-R (CD Recordable) or CD-RW (CD ReWritable) drive. The blank disks cost only a few dollars, and you can put 650MB on one. The drives that record them, though, are about three times the price of a standard CD-ROM reader.

I bought a CD-R kit recently (called the "Smart and Friendly" kit) for just a few hundred dollars at Costco/Price Club. Such a deal. It installed with only a little hassle, and the bundled Adaptec Easy CD Pro software was simple to use. Check the magazines and get a kit that has everything you might need, right in the box. You might be buying more than you need, but you'll be avoiding headaches in the long run. For example, I paid for the extra SCSI card they bundle with the drive (I already have a faster one), just so I knew I had a complete one-stop solution. Also note that CD-R drives tend to be slower at reading CD-ROMs than regular read-only drives. Mine reads at only 6x and writes at a measly 2x. So I have two CD-drives: a regular 24x and the CD-R at 2x/6x. Many CD-Rs require a SCSI interface, but not all do. Many EIDE units are also available. Most of the SCSI units come with a simple SCSI adapter card. It doesn't have to be a fancy fast SCSI card (fast/wide/ultra or any of that), since speed isn't an issue. If you already have a SCSI card, it will likely work with a CD-R drive.

> **NOTE**
> The CD-R format allows you to record once, and that's all. Once a CD is written, it can't be erased and rewritten. With some formats you can add more data later, until the disk is full, but you can't erase. Another format, CD-RW (rewritable) uses slightly more expensive media to allow you to write and rewrite disks again and again.

DVD DVD drives are the new hot item on the market. However, DVD is a technology in such an emerging state that manufacturers can't even agree what DVD stands for. (Some say Digital Video Disk while others say Digital Versatile Disk.) Regardless, we're seeing a lot more of them every day. Many households in the US have DVD players in their computers and on their TV set tops already. As of this writing, set-top DVD players run about $250 and support lots of nifty features such as:

- 500 lines of horizontal resolution (more than twice as sharp as standard TV)
- Eight sound tracks (for different languages, instruction, and so on)
- 32 sets of subtitles
- Multiple movie viewing formats (standard, letterbox) and angles
- Theater sound

- Two hours of video per side (up to four hours max)
- Dolby digital sound

Adding a DVD drive to your PC lets you view movies and educational titles on the PC, with the superior resolution of your computer's monitor (instead of the pretty funky resolution of a standard TV). In addition, you'll be able to interact with DVD titles designed for computers. Windows 98 SE supports DVD drives and has a DVD Player program (similar to its CD Player program) for playing DVD titles.

A number of DVD add-in kits are available today for your PC. More and more PCs come equipped with DVD as an option or standard fare, and writable DVDs should appear soon. Currently they are expensive. But once those appear, editing your own homebrew movies will be a snap.

Speakers The larger the better, usually. Little speakers will sound tinny, by definition. Listen before you buy if possible. Listen to a normal, speaking human voice—the most difficult instrument to reproduce. Does it sound natural? Then hear something with some bass. If you're going to listen to audio CDs, bring one with you to the store and play it. Speakers that are separate (not built into the monitor) will allow a nicer stereo effect. Separate tweeter and woofer will probably sound better, but not always. It depends on the electronics in the speaker. Magnetic shielding is important if the speakers are going to be within a foot or so of your screen; otherwise, the colors and alignment of the image on the screen will be adversely affected. (Not permanently damaged, though. The effect stops when you move the speakers away.)

Of course, instead of buying speakers you can use your stereo or even a boom box if it has high-level (sometimes called *auxiliary*) input. Some boom boxes and virtually all stereos do have such an input. Then it's just a matter of using the correct wire to attach your sound card's *line* output to the stereo's or boom box's AUX input and setting the volume appropriately. The easiest solution is to purchase a pair of amplified speakers designed for small recording studios, apartments, or computers. For about $100 you can find a good pair of smaller-sized shielded speakers (4- or 5-inch woofer, separate tweeter) with volume, bass, and treble controls. For $300 you can get some that sound very good. If you like real bass, shell out a little more for a set that comes with a separate larger subwoofer you put under your desk.

Sound Board This should have 64-bit sound capability for CD-quality sound. You'll want line-in, line-out, and microphone-in jacks at least. Typical cards also have a joystick port for your game controller. The card should be compatible with Windows 98 SE, with the General MIDI specification, and with SoundBlaster so it will work with popular games. This means it should have protected-mode 32-bit drivers for Windows 98 SE, either supplied with Windows 98 SE or with the card. If it doesn't, you'll be stuck using 16-bit drivers that take up too much conventional memory space, preventing many DOS-based games and educational programs from running. I've seen this problem with cards, such as the Sound-Blaster Pro, that prevent a number of games such as the Eagle-Eye Mystery series from running. Fancy cards such as those from Turtle Beach don't sound like cheesy synthesizers when they play MIDI music because they use samples of real instruments stored in *wave tables* instead of using synthesizer chips, but you'll pay more for them. Wavetable cards are easy to find now for less than $40.

Video Card and Monitor The video card goes inside the computer and produces the signals needed to create a display on the monitor. A cable runs between the video card and the monitor. For high-performance multimedia, you'll want a *local bus* video card (typically VLB or PCI) capable of at least 256 colors at the resolution you desire. If your motherboard has an AGP (Accelerated Graphics Port) adapter, get an AGP video card for best performance.

> **TIP**
> Local bus cards only work in computers that have a local bus connector slot, so check out which kind of slots your computer has before purchasing a video card upgrade.

Standard resolution (number of dots on the screen at one time, comprising the picture) for a PC is 640 (horizontal) by 480 (vertical). Most new video cards these days will support that resolution at 256 colors. If you have a very sharp 15-inch screen or a 17-inch screen, you may opt for a higher resolution, such as 800 by 600 or 1024 by 768. When shopping for a video card, make sure it displays at least 16-bit color (and preferably 24-bit) at the resolution you want *and has at least a 70Hz noninterlaced refresh rate at that resolution and color depth.* The correct refresh rate prevents screens from flickering, which can cause headaches and/or eye fatigue. Video cards with graphics coprocessor chips on them will run faster than those that don't. High speed is necessary when you move objects around on the screen or display video clips.

Make sure the board will work well with Windows 98 SE, preferably with the 32-bit video driver that comes with Windows 95/98/98 SE, not an old driver designed for Windows 3.x. You don't have to worry about any monitor's ability to display colors, because any color monitor will display all the colors your card can produce. What you *do* have to check on are a monitor's dot pitch, controls, and refresh rate. The monitor should ideally have a dot pitch of .25 or .26, be at least 17 inches (though 15 inches will do), and run all your desired resolutions at 70Hz refresh or higher to avoid flicker. Beware of the refresh-rate issue: False or misleading advertising is rampant. Many monitors and video cards advertise 72-Hz or higher refresh rates, but the fine print reveals that this is only at a low resolution such as 640 by 480. Bump up the resolution, and the refresh rate on cheaper cards or monitors drops to a noticeably slow 60Hz. Get a monitor that has low radiation emissions, powers down automatically when it isn't being used (a so-called green monitor), and has a wide variety of controls for size, picture position, brightness, contrast, color, and so forth.

> **TIP**
>
> If you expect to view lots of TV or play the latest games, get a video card with 2D and 3D acceleration, video capture, a TV tuner, and video in and out. The ATI All-In Wonder card is currently my card of choice. It works well with Windows 98 SE's TV tuner programs, has a slew of video resolutions, and works right out of the box with Windows 98 SE. It's about $140, street price.

That's the basic rundown on multimedia upgrading. Now let's look at what's supplied with Windows 98 SE in the way of multimedia programs and utilities.

THE SUPPLIED MULTIMEDIA APPLICATIONS AND UTILITIES

Here's what you get in the way of multimedia programs and utilities with Windows 98 SE:

Sound Settings   This Control Panel applet lets you assign specific sound files (stored in the `.wav` format) to Windows system events such

Windows Multimedia

as error messages, information dialog boxes, and when starting and exiting Windows.

Media Player   This application, which you'll find in the Start ➤ Programs ➤ Accessories ➤ Multimedia folder, lets you play a variety of multimedia files on the target hardware. In the case of a device that contains data, such as a CD-ROM or video disk, Media Player sends commands to the hardware, playing back the sound or video therein. If the data is stored on your hard disk (as are MIDI sequences, animation, and sound files), Media Player will send them to the appropriate piece of hardware, such as a sound board, MIDI keyboard, or other device.

> **NOTE**
> The Media Player only works with MCI (Media Control Interface) devices and thus requires MCI device drivers.

Sound Recorder

This is a simple program for recording sounds from a microphone or auxiliary input and then editing them. Once recorded, sound files can be used with other programs through OLE. Sound files also replace or augment the generic beeps your computer makes to alert you to dialog boxes, errors, and so forth. Sound Recorder is also the default program used to play back WAV files.

> **TIP**
> You can find more elaborate WAV file editors. For my CD recording projects, I use a shareware program called Cool Edit, which you can find and download from the Web. Another capable shareware WAV file program is called WaveWorks.

CD Player   Assuming your computer's CD-ROM drive and controller card support it (most do), this accessory program lets you play back standard audio CDs. This can be a great boon on long winter nights when you're chained to your PC doing taxes or writing that boring report. You'll find coverage of this program later in the chapter.

DVD Player   If the DVD drive you purchase, whether by upgrade or built-in, says it is Windows 98 SE–compatible, then it will have a DVD Player program supplied. Whether you choose to use that player or the one supplied with Windows 98 SE is up to you; they all work similarly. You just have to compare their respective features, as some have more bells and whistles than others. In this chapter I'll cover the player that comes with Windows 98 SE.

Adding Drivers　　The System and Add New Hardware applets in the Control Panel let you install drivers for many add-in cards and devices such as CD-ROMs, MIDI interface cards, and video-disk controllers if they are not detected automatically once you plug them in. Drivers for most popular sound boards such as the SoundBlaster (from Creative Labs, Inc.) and Ad Lib (Ad Lib, Inc.) and popular MIDI boards such as the Roland MPU-401 (Roland Digital Group) are supplied. Other drivers can be installed from manufacturer-supplied disks using this option. Even if your hardware is physically installed, it won't work unless the proper driver is loaded.

A few programs have either been covered elsewhere in this book or were seen in Windows 3.x but have been dropped from Windows 95. They are:

> **Volume Control**　　The volume control accessory, available from the Taskbar, simply lets you control the balance and volume levels of the various sound sources that end up playing through your computer's speakers.
>
> **MIDI Mapper**　　This was included as a separate Control Panel applet in Windows 3.1 and NT, but has been hidden in Windows 98 SE because it is rarely used. Its purpose was to declare settings for your MIDI device, such as channel assignment, key remapping, and patch-number reassignment for nonstandard MIDI instruments. The assumption now is that most MIDI instruments comply with the General MIDI standard for these parameters and thus the Mapper is rarely needed. If you have a nonstandard MIDI instrument that you're running from Windows programs (this won't affect DOS programs), check out Control Panel ➣ Multimedia ➣ MIDI ➣ Custom Configuration ➣ Configure. It will lead you to the rather complex remapping facilities.

Doing It All with DVD Player

As mentioned earlier in the chapter, Windows 98 includes support for DVD (Digital Versatile Disk/Digital Video Disk) drives. DVD and

CD-ROM use very much the same technology (micro laser to read the disk), so besides being able to play DVD disks on your computer, you should be able to use a DVD drive to read your current CD-ROM and audio CD disks (this depends, however, on how early you buy; first-generation DVD drives could not read as many CD formats as the current generation). Price wise, this will be an almost unnoticed transition, at least for new system buyers. A computer equipped with a DVD drive will probably cost only $100 to $150 more than one equipped with a CD-ROM drive instead. (If it weren't for the need for a decoder card to play DVD movies on your computer, the difference would be less.) DVD drives are now offered as standard equipment in many PCs, as they begin to replace CD-ROM drives.

Some DVD Specifics

I already sang the praises of DVD earlier in the chapter. However, as there is some confusion about different generations of DVDs, I want to make sure we have the basics understood before I discuss the DVD Player program supplied with Windows 98 SE. DVD is becoming the content-providing medium of choice. Sure, CDs will still be around, but even with the giganto capacity of 650MB on a CD, some programs (such as Microsoft's own Office 2000) actually require multiple CDs! In addition, mega-databases such as national phone directories, the catalog of the Library of Congress, the complete Oxford English Dictionary, photo stock house collections, museum and gallery holdings photographed in high resolution, and fonts packages, span multiple CD-ROMs. These are all prime candidates for appearing on DVD.

And then, of course, we've got movies—the hands-down winners of the disk-consumption sweepstakes. With a maximum capacity of 17GB (yes, gigabytes), an innocent DVD (which looks almost identical to a CD) can store two hours of video that displays more clearly (and has groovier options) than VHS, LaserDisk, or video CD-ROMs. DVD movies boast multichannel surround sound, subtitles, multiple alternative audio tracks (for different languages), multiple video playback formats, and even, in some cases, user-selectable camera angles.

How does a DVD pack all that information onto a five-inch disk? Well, first, the optical pits on a DVD disk are stuffed in twice as close to one another as on a CD, and so are the tracks. Also, more of the surface is recorded on. *And* error correction is more rigorous! All this increases the data storage capacity from a CD's 650MB to a DVD's 4.3GB. But wait! That's only for one layer! DVDs can have *two* layers per side. By focusing the read laser carefully, a second layer can be used, adding another 4.3GB, for a one-side total of approximately 8.4GB. But wait! DVDs can have data written on *both sides*, so by flipping the disk over, the 8.4GB is doubled.

Another compelling point about DVD is its versatility. CD-ROM suffers from a plethora of competing and often incompatible formats: multisession, Photo CD, Mode 1, Mode 2, Joliet, CD-I, and CD+, to name but a few. The DVD spec is, well, versatile (as the name implies: Digital Versatile Disk). A new disk file format that was devised for DVD, called Universal Disk Format (UDF), ensures compatibility between disk and player, regardless of content. (Well, almost. As the saying goes, some limitations apply.) A single DVD drive should be able to read most existing CDs, as well as text, data, and video DVD formats. Even CD-R (recordable CDs) and CD-RW (rewritable CDs) disks should be readable by most second-generation DVD drives.

Shop Carefully!

If you're thinking about buying a DVD, check the specs thoroughly, and ask around before you drop your cash. Third generation drives are widely available, so you'll probably want to skip buying a first- or second-generation drive. The differences lie mostly in the formats they can read. Second-generation drives can read CD-R and CD-RW, whereas first-generation drives can't. Third-generation drives read a greater variety of recordable and re-recordable formats.

As for speed, don't worry. As long as they can play back a movie, you'll have speed to burn. The latest crop of DVD drives (5x DVD) plays CDs at the equivalent speed of a 32x CD-ROM drive.

Installation of DVD can be tricky. I suggest you purchase a complete upgrade kit or purchase a computer with the DVD built in. I upgraded piece by piece. It cost me more, and was a hassle to get working. Read the requirements for an upgrade carefully. Typically you'll need at least a 166MHz Pentium with 16MB of RAM; you'll also need a bus-mastering PCI slot, an empty drive bay for the drive, and an open EIDE connector. (Although some DVDs are SCSI drives, most are EIDE. Besides, most motherboards support four EIDE drives, and you probably don't have four hard disks connected; so why buy a SCSI disk controller if you don't need it?) Most DVD drives don't care whether they are "slave" or "master" drives.

> **TIP**
> As a rule, just look for a kit or computer that is Windows 98–compatible, and follow the instructions supplied with the unit.

In addition, until you can buy a video card that is tailored to support DVD video playback, you'll need a *decoder card* to be able to watch DVD movies on your computer. (If you aren't planning to play video DVD disks, neither of these is necessary.) The decoder card plugs into the PCI bus (typically) and connects to your existing video card (via a ribbon cable) to translate the video data into the analog signals needed for display on your monitor. Among other things, such as decoding Dolby Surround-Sound audio, and handling copy-protection schemes, the decoder decompresses the MPEG-1 or MPEG-2 compressed video in real time. This takes some serious computing speed. Some DVD drives come with "software" decoders which they say can be used instead of a decoder card, but don't expect smooth performance from them, even on a fast Pentium 266 machine. The computer's CPU just can't keep up with the data stream very well, and ends up dropping frames to keep up.

Running the DVD Player

Typically the DVD player that comes with the drive will have all the basic controls found on a VCR, plus some number of additional bells and whistles, such as searching tools, audio controls for bass, treble, and volume, a viewing angle selector, child-proofing locks, video format selector, "chapter" and "title" features, and so on. Most of them are used in similar ways; you'll just have to compare the features of each. In this section, I'll provide the basic instructions for running the player that comes with Windows 98 SE.

First, I'll assume that you've got your hardware installed (or someone at the factory did it for you), as discussed earlier. If your drive is in working order, then here are the basics of running the Microsoft DVD Player:

1. Insert a DVD disk as you would insert a disk into any other drive, and shut the door. Windows will detect the disk; if the disk is a video disk, the DVD Player will start; if it's an audio

Chapter Nine

disk, the CD Player will start (as discussed earlier in this chapter).

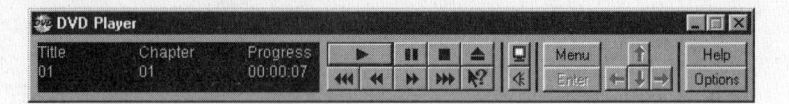

2. If a disk has been inserted and nothing happens, run the DVD Player explicitly by choosing Start ➤ Programs ➤ Accessories ➤ Entertainment ➤ DVD Player. Then click the Options button and choose Select Disk. You'll see this dialog box:

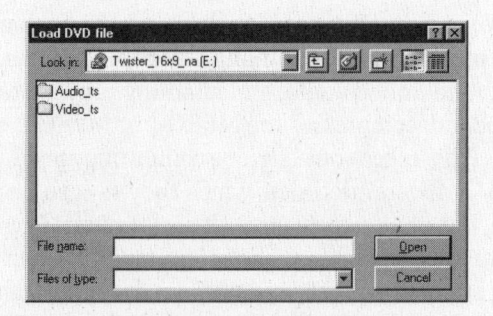

3. If you've set the option that prevents someone from running a movie without authorization (see the Tip following this step), you'll see a logon dialog box:

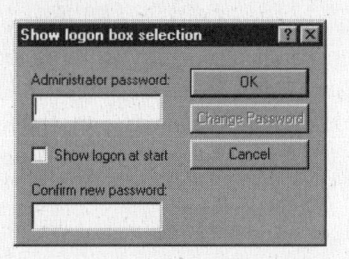

TIP
You can create a new logon password by choosing the Options button on the player. Typically, you might create a password to prevent children from playing your disks.

Windows Multimedia

4. To start playing a disk, click the ➤ button on the player toolbar. You should experiment with the other various controls by clicking them as well, just as you might in the CD Player application or on a VCR. You can play, stop, pause, fast forward, fast rewind, eject, and so on. (There are also buttons here for "very fast forward" and "very fast rewind.") If you're better with words than icons, you can display a textual list of all of the commands available from the player toolbar by right-clicking any one of the controls:

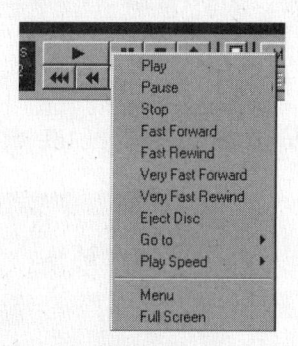

```
Play
Pause
Stop
Fast Forward
Fast Rewind
Very Fast Forward
Very Fast Rewind
Eject Disc
Go to          ▶
Play Speed     ▶
Menu
Full Screen
```

To see a full-screen view of the movie you are watching, click the little icon of the television set in the toolbar. The toolbar disappears. You can access the tools again by right-clicking anywhere on the screen. That action pops up the following menu:

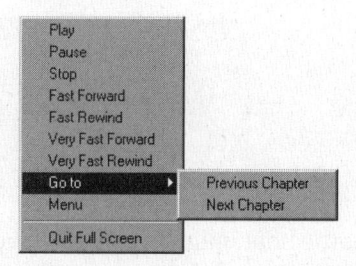

```
Play
Pause
Stop
Fast Forward
Fast Rewind
Very Fast Forward
Very Fast Rewind
Go to          ▶   Previous Chapter
Menu               Next Chapter
Quit Full Screen
```

Choose the Quit Full Screen command to see the toolbar again, or choose any of the other commands as you wish. Alternatively, to cancel this menu and return to full-screen view, click anywhere outside of the menu.

Chapters and Titles Typically you'll watch video DVDs just as you would a VHS tape; that is, you'll start it, pause it once in a while to get up for more popcorn, then sit down and click Play to start it up again. But as more interesting DVDs start to hit the market, you may want to jump to specific *titles* and *chapters*. Think of a title as, say, one of several shows on the disk. A chapter, then, is a subset of a title: perhaps a lesson, a scene in the movie, or a section of a tutorial, for example. Once a disk is inserted, you can quickly choose to search for sections by title or chapter by right-clicking the display, as shown below.

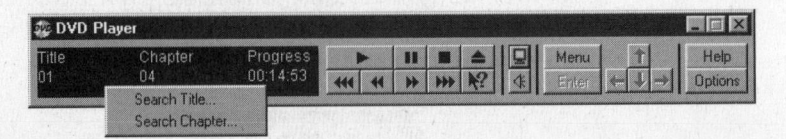

▶ If you choose Title, this handy little box lets you jump to a specific title and to any portion of the title track by entering its time value:

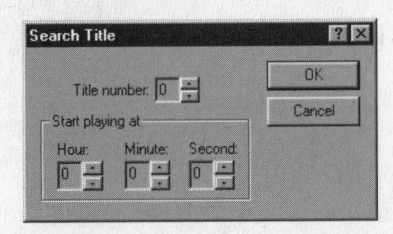

▶ If you choose Chapter, you'll see the following box, which also expects you to enter a time value:

Just enter the hour, minute, and second of the spot you want to jump to (and if you're in the Title box, enter the title number), and click OK.

Selecting Language and Subtitles Some disks will have subtitles (nice for when you're talking on the phone; that way nobody can hear what's distracting you), and some disks will have multiple languages (i.e., multiple alternative audio tracks), as I mentioned earlier. You can make choices for these features from the Options button:

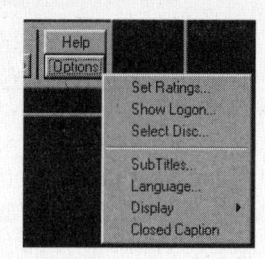

The procedure is a no-brainer:

1. Click Options.
2. Choose SubTitles or Language.
3. Set the subtitle or language option as desired, and click Close.

For example, suppose I wanted to see English subtitles (assuming my disk offered them). The Options ➤ SubTitles command might show the following choices:

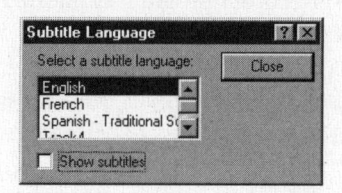

I'd just click English, then on the Show Subtitles checkbox. For language choice, I might see the following little box. I'd just choose the audio language I'm interested in listening to:

Ending a DVD Session When you're finished listening to, using, or viewing the disk, you can either press the Eject button on the front of the drive or click the Eject button on the DVD Player toolbar. Then close the DVD Player program.

Assigning Sounds with the Control Panel's Sound Utility

You can use the Control Panel's Sound utility for assigning sounds to system events, such as warning dialog boxes, error messages when you click in the wrong place, and so on. Once you've installed a sound board, you can personalize your computer's beep to something more exciting. If your computer had a sound card when you installed Windows 98 SE, it's likely Windows established a default set of rather boring sounds for your system, most of which you're probably tired of already. Besides making life more interesting, having different sounds for different types of events is also more informative, because you can assign sounds to many more events than Windows does by default. You know when you've made an error as opposed to when an application is acknowledging your actions, for example.

Of course, to add basic sounds to your Windows setup, you need a Windows 98 SE–compatible sound card. The sounds you can use must be stored on disk in the .WAV format. Most sounds that you can download from the Internet or get on disk at the computer store are in this format. Also, the Sound Recorder program explained later in the chapter records sounds as WAV files. Windows 98 SE comes with more than a few sound files. In fact, just as with the color schemes you can create and save with the Control Panel's Display applet, you can set up and save personalized sound schemes to suit your mood. Microsoft has supplied us with several such schemes, running the gamut from happy nature sounds to futuristic, mechanistic robot utterances to the sonorities of classical musical instruments.

> **NOTE**
> You have to do a Custom installation to get all the sound schemes loaded into your computer. You can do this after the fact by running Control Panel ≻ Add/Remove Programs ≻ Windows Setup. Then click Multimedia to select it and click the Details button. The Multimedia Sound Schemes are located near the bottom of the list.

Despite this diverse selection, you may still want to make or acquire more interesting sounds yourself or collect them from other sources.

To record your own, you'll need a sound board that handles digital sampling. I have messages in my own voice, such as, "You made a stupid mistake, you fool," which—for a short time—seemed preferable to the mindless chime. If your system lets you play audio CDs, you should be able to directly sample bits and pieces from your favorite artists by popping the audio CD into the computer and tapping directly into it, rather than by sticking a microphone up to your boom box and accidentally recording the telephone when it rings. Check out the Volume Control applet and adjust the slider on the mixer panel that controls the input volume of the CD. Then use the Sound Recorder applet to make the recording.

> **TIP**
>
> Any time your sound isn't working correctly (if there's no sound, for example), check the following: Are your speakers connected and turned on? Is the volume control on them (if they have it) turned down? Has the sound worked before? If so, it's probably the mixer settings that are wrong. Right-click the speaker icon near the clock in the TaskBar and choose Open Volume Controls. Check the settings. Don't forget to choose Options ➤ Properties and poke around. Don't change the mixer device, but notice that you can choose to see the Recording mixer controls, and choose which sliders are on either the recording or playback controls. Make sure the source that isn't working properly isn't muted.

Like any good sound-o-phile, I'm always on the lookout for good WAV files. You'll find them everywhere if you just keep your eyes open: cheap CDs at the local Compu-Geek store, on the Internet, on CompuServe, even on other people's computers. Usually these sound files aren't copyrighted, so copying them isn't likely to be a legal issue. Most WAV files intended for system sounds aren't that big, either. But do check out the size, using the Explorer or by showing the Details view in a folder, before copying them. Sound files *can* be super large, especially if they are recorded in 16-bit stereo (about 172 kilobytes per second of CD-quality audio). As a rule you'll want to keep the size to a minimum for system sounds because it can take more than a few seconds for a larger sound file to load and begin to play.

Once you're set up for sound and have some WAV files, you assign them to specific Windows events. Here's how:

1. Open the Control Panel and run the Sounds applet. The dialog box shown in Figure 9.1 appears.

2. The top box lists the events that can have sounds associated with them. There will be at least two classes of events—one for Windows events and one for Explorer events. (Scroll the

list to the bottom to see the Explorer events.) As you purchase and install new programs in the future, those programs may add their own events to your list. An event with a speaker icon next to it already has a sound associated with it. You can click it and then click the Preview button to hear the sound. The sound file that's associated with the event is listed in the Name box.

3. Click any event for which you want to assign a sound or change the assigned sound.

4. Open the drop-down Name list and choose the WAV file you want to use for that event. Some of the event names may not make sense to you, such as Asterisk, Critical Stop, or Exclamation. These are names for the various classes of dialog boxes that Windows displays from time to time. The sounds you're most likely to hear often will be Default sound, Menu Command, Menu Popup, Question, Open Program, Close Program, Minimize, Maximize, Start Windows, and Exit Windows.

TIP
The default directory for sounds is the \Windows\Media directory. That's where the WAV files that come with Windows 98 are stored. If you have WAV files stored somewhere else, you'll have to use the Browse button to find and assign them to an event. I find it's easier to copy all my WAV files into the \Windows\Media directory than to go browsing for them when I want to do a lot of reassigning of sounds.

5. At the top of the list of available sounds there is an option called <none> that has the obvious effect—no sound will occur for that event. Assigning all events to <none> will effectively silence your computer for use in a library, church, and so forth. You can also quickly do this for all sounds by choosing the No Sounds scheme as explained below.

6. Repeat the process for other events to which you want to assign or reassign sounds.

7. Click OK.

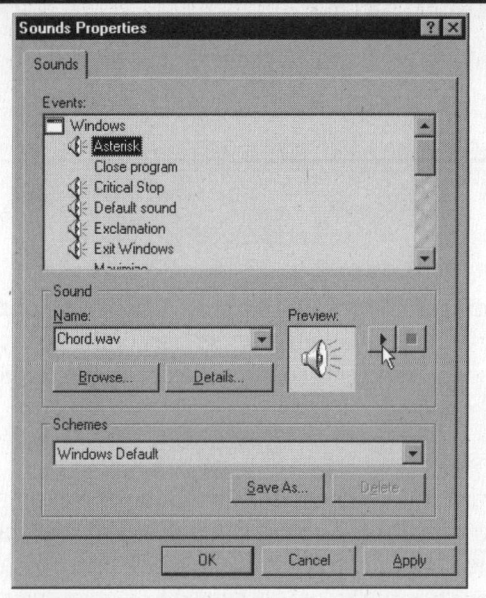

FIGURE 9.1: Use this dialog box to choose which sounds your computer makes when Windows events occur.

Keep in mind that different applications will use event sounds differently. You'll have to do some experimenting to see when your applications use the default beep, as opposed to the Asterisk, Question, or the Exclamation.

Clicking the Details button displays information about the WAV file, such as its time length, data format, and copyright information (if any).

Loading and Saving Sound Schemes

Just as the Control Panel's Display applet lets you save color schemes, the Sounds applet lets you save sound schemes so you can set up goofy sounds for your humorous moods and somber ones for those gloomy days—or vice versa. The schemes supplied with Windows 98 SE are pretty nice even without modification.

To choose an existing sound scheme:

1. Click the drop-down list button for schemes, down at the bottom of the box:

2. A list of existing schemes will appear. Choose a sound scheme. Now all the events in the upper part of the box will have the new sound scheme's sounds. Check out the sounds to see if you like them.

3. If you like the sound scheme, click OK.

You can set up your own sound schemes by assigning or reassigning individual sounds, as I've already explained. But unless you *save* the scheme, it will be lost the next time you change to a new one. So, the moral is: once you get your favorite sounds assigned to system events, save the scheme. Then you can call it up any time you like. Here's how:

1. Set up the sounds the way you want. You can start with an existing scheme and modify it or start from scratch by choosing the No Sounds scheme and assigning sounds one by one.

2. Click the Save As button.

3. In the resulting dialog box, enter a name for the scheme. For example, here's one I made up and saved:

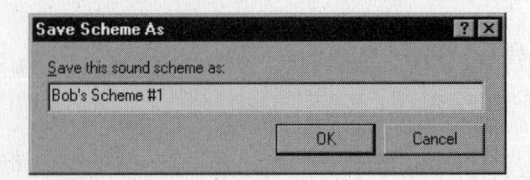

4. Click OK in the little dialog box, and your scheme is saved. Now you can create additional schemes and save them or just OK the large dialog box to activate the new scheme.

You can delete any existing sound schemes by choosing the doomed scheme from the list and then clicking the Delete button. You'll be asked to confirm the deletion.

Playing Multimedia Files with Media Player

Media Player is a little application that plays multimedia files, such as digitized sounds, MIDI music files, and video files. It can also send control information to multimedia devices such as audio CD players or video disk players, determining which tracks to play, when to pause, when to activate slow motion, and so on.

The capabilities of Windows Media Player has been upgraded for Windows 98 Second Edition, primarily to allow it to handle a wider variety of media formats than previous versions. Microsoft now claims that the Media Player can play virtually all standardized formats of audio, video, and streaming signals, but some media providers may still require you to use a specific player. This is especially true for streaming audio, which most often uses RealNetwork's RealPlayer (www.real.com), and for streaming video which often utilizes QuickTime 4 from Apple (www.apple.com).

Obviously, you can only use Media Player on devices installed in your system and for which you've installed the correct device drivers (see "Installing New Drivers," below), so first see to that task. Then follow these instructions for playing a multimedia file:

1. Run Media Player from the Start ➤ Programs ➤ Accessories ➤ Entertainment ➤ Windows Media Player. The Media Player's control panel appears, as shown here:

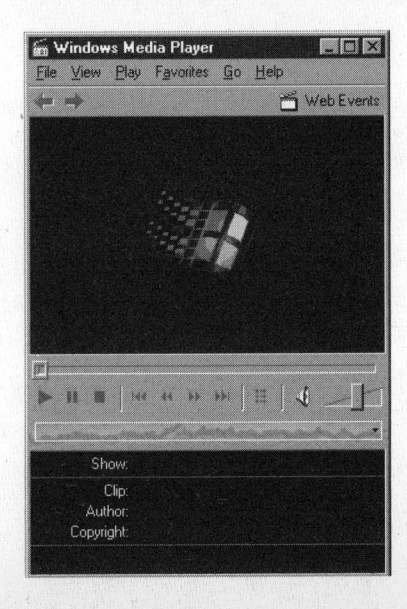

2. Open the media file you want to play by giving the File ➤ Open command.

3. In the special Open dialog box that appears, type the address (or path) of the file. It it's located on disk, it will probably be easiest to click Browse and navigate to the file from there. When the correct file address appears in the Open dialog box, click OK. The Media Player's appearance will change slightly based on the type of media file you opened. In the example shown below, a WAV sound file has been opened. Since the file contains only sound, the video playback section of the Media Player is automatically hidden.

TIP
You can jump to a particular location in the piece by dragging the scroll bar, clicking at the desired point in the scroll bar, or using ↑, ↓, ←, →, PgUp, and PgDn. Also, check the Device menu for options pertaining to the device you are using.

4. Now you can use the buttons in the dialog box to begin playing the piece. The buttons work just as on a VCR or cassette deck; if in doubt, the buttons have pop-up descriptions.

5. When you're done playing, close the application from the File menu.

Media Player has a few options worth noting. Check out the View ➤ Options dialog box. Choose Repeat Forever to keep playing the media file over and over.

Recording and Editing Sounds with Sound Recorder

Sound Recorder is a nifty little program that lets you record your own sounds and create WAV files. To make it work, you need a digital sampling card such as the SoundBlaster and some kind of input, such as a microphone. The program also lets you do some editing and manipulation of any WAV files you might have on disk. You can do this even if you don't have a microphone.

The resulting WAV files can be put to a variety of uses, including assigning them to system events or using them with other multimedia applications, such as Media Player. Once a file is recorded, you can edit it by removing portions of it. Unfortunately, you cannot edit from one arbitrary spot to another, only from one spot to either the beginning or the end of the file. You can also add an echo effect to a sample, play it backwards, change the playback speed (and resulting pitch), and alter the playback volume.

Playing a Sound File

Follow the steps below to play a sound file:

1. Make sure your sound board is working properly. If it's been playing sounds, such as the one that plays when Windows starts up, it probably is. If not, check that you've installed the correct driver and that your sound board works (Chapter 7 discusses how to add new hardware and drivers).

2. Run Sound Recorder by choosing Start ➢ Programs ➢ Accessories ➢ Entertainment ➢ Sound Recorder. The Sound Recorder window appears, as shown here:

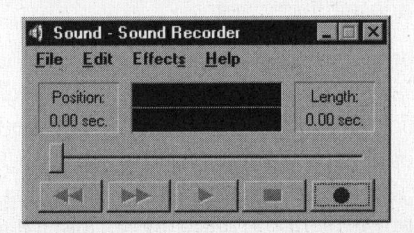

3. Choose File ➢ Open and choose the file you want to play. Notice that the length of the sound appears at the right of

the window and the current position of the play head appears on the left.

4. Click the Play button or press Enter to play the sound. As it plays, the wave box displays the sound, oscilloscope style. The Status Bar also says Playing. When the sound is over, Sound Recorder stops and the Status Bar says Stopped. Press Enter again to replay the sound. You can click Stop during a playback to pause the sound, and then click Play to continue.

5. Drag the scroll button around (see below) and notice how the wave box displays a facsimile of the frequency and amplitude of the sample over time.

You can also click the rewind and fast-forward buttons to move to the start and end of the sample or press the PgUp and PgDn keys to jump the play head forward or backward in longer increments.

Recording a New Sound

This is the fun part, so get your microphone (or line input) ready. Suppose you want to make up your own sounds, perhaps to put into an OLE-capable application document such as Wordpad or Word so that it talks when clicked on. Here's how:

1. Choose File ≻ New.

2. You may want to check the recording format before you begin. Choose File ≻ Properties. Select Recording Formats, then click Convert Now. A dialog box appears, showing some details about the recording format. Click the Convert Now button to see the dialog box shown in Figure 9.2. A combination of data-recording format (e.g., PCM, Microsoft's ADPCM, and so forth) and sampling rate (e.g., 8KHz 4-bit mono) are shown. Together these comprise a format scheme.

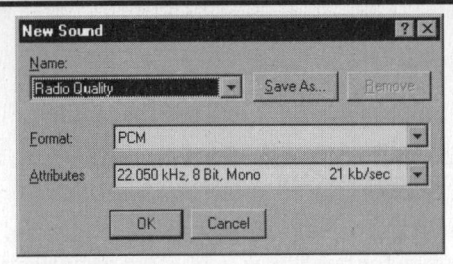

FIGURE 9.2: Choosing a data scheme for a new sound recording

> **NOTE**
>
> The Attributes list shows the amount of disk space consumed per second of recording. You'll want to consider this when making new files, as recording in high-fidelity stereo can suck up precious disk room, rendering sound files quite unwieldy. Also, for most purposes, you are best served by choosing one of the preexisting sound schemes—CD-Quality, Radio Quality, or Telephone Quality—for your recordings. All three use the PCM recording technique but employ different sample rates. If you are recording only voice, use either the Radio or Telephone setting. The CD-quality setting will only use up more disk space than you need to. If you are planning to record from an audio CD player, you'll probably want to choose the CD-quality setting unless you want to conserve disk space. If you accidentally record at a higher quality level than you wanted to, don't worry. You can convert to a lower quality and regain some hard disk space via the File ➢ Properties ➢ Convert Now button. You can save recording and playback settings with the Save As button in the dialog box.

3. Click the Record button. The clock starts ticking, counting the passing time. Begin talking into the microphone that's plugged into your sound card, playing whatever is connected to your AUX input (a.k.a. *line in*) on the sound card, or playing the audio CD that's in the CD-ROM drive. You'll have to use the volume control applet to set the relative balance of the various devices. Typically you'll be able to mix these disparate audio sources into a single recording if you use the mixer deftly. The maximum recording time will vary, depending on your recording format. In the default setting (PCM, 22.050KHz 8-bit mono) you can record for up to one minute. Be cautious about the length of your sounds, as they tend to take up a large amount of disk space. For example, a one-second sample at CD Quality in stereo consumes about 172K.

4. Click Stop when you are finished recording.
5. Play back the file to see if you like it.
6. Save the file with File ➤ Save As. You'll see the familiar File dialog box. Enter a name (you don't have to enter the WAV extension; the program does that for you).

When recording a voice narration, make sure to speak loudly and clearly, particularly if you notice that playback is muffled or buried in noise.

> **TIP**
> A simple way to create a new sound file is to right-click the Desktop and choose New ➤ Sound File. Name the file, then double-click it. Then click the Record button.

Editing Sounds

You can edit sound files in several ways. For instance, you can:

- Add echo to a sample.
- Reverse a sample.
- Mix two samples together.
- Remove unwanted parts of a sample.
- Increase or decrease the volume.
- Increase or decrease the speed and pitch.
- Convert it to another format for use by a particular program.

> **NOTE**
> You may run out of memory if your file becomes very long because of inserting files into one another. The amount of free physical memory (not virtual memory) determines the maximum size of any sound file.

To edit a sound file:

1. Open the sound file from the File menu.
2. Open the Effects menu to add echo, reverse the sound, increase or decrease volume, or increase or decrease speed. All the set-

tings except echo can be undone, so you can experiment without worry. You undo a setting by choosing its complementary setting from the menu (e.g., Increase Volume instead of Decrease Volume) or by choosing Reverse. Some sound quality can be lost by doing this repeatedly, however.

3. To cut out the beginning or ending of a sound—i.e., to eliminate the lag time it took you to get to the microphone or hit the Stop button—determine the beginning and ending points of the sound, get to the actual starting position of the sound, and choose Edit ➢ Delete Before Current Position. Then move the scroll button to the end of the desired portion of the sample and choose Edit ➢ Delete After Current Position.

4. To mix two existing sounds, position the cursor where you'd like to begin the mix, choose Edit ➢ Mix with File, and choose the file name. This can create some very interesting effects that are much richer than single sounds.

5. To insert a file into a predetermined spot, move to the spot with the scroll bar, choose Edit ➢ Insert File, and choose the file name.

6. To put a sound on the Clipboard for pasting elsewhere, use Edit ➢ Copy.

7. To return your sound to its original, last-saved state, choose File ➢ Revert.

Note that not all sound boards have the same features. Some won't let you save a recording into certain types of sound files. Also, the quality of the sound differs from board to board. Some boards sound "grainy," others less so. This is determined by the sampling rate you've chosen, the quality of the digital-to-analog converters (DAC), and the analog amplifiers on the board.

Some programs require a particular sound file format to use sounds. For example, the Voxware plug-in for Web browsers (which lets you put sound clips on your Web pages) expects sound files in its proprietary Voxware format. You can convert an existing sound file by opening it in Sound Recorder. Then choose File ➢ Properties. Click Convert Now and choose the correct setting from the Format list. Then click OK. Then save the file. It should be in the new format.

> **NOTE**
> Typically programs that require proprietary sound formats supply their own conversion tools, and it's often better to use those tools when they are available than a little accessory such as Sound Recorder.

Playing Tunes with CD Player

The CD Player accessory turns your computer's CD-ROM drive into a music machine. With it, you can play standard audio CDs with all the controls you'd expect on a "real" CD player, and then some. Of course, you'll need speakers (or at least a pair of headphones) to hear the music. Here's what CD Player looks like:

With CD Player, you can:

- Play any CD once through or continuously while you work with other programs.

- Play the tracks in sequential or random order, or play only the tracks you like.

- Move forward or in reverse to any desired track.

- Fast forward or rewind while a track is playing.

- Stop, pause, and resume playback, and (if your CD-ROM drive has the capability) eject the current CD.

- Control play volume if you're playing the CD through a sound card (this only works with some CD-ROM drives).

- Control the contents of the time display (you can display elapsed time, time remaining for the current track, or time remaining for the entire CD).

▶ Catalog your CDs (after you've typed in the title and track list for a CD, CD Player will recognize it when you load it again, displaying the titles of the disk and the current track).

Getting Started with CD Player

To run CD Player, begin from the Start menu and choose Programs ➤ Accessories ➤ Entertainment ➤ CD Player. Load your CD-ROM drive with an audio CD, turn on your sound system or plug in the headphones, and you're ready to go.

CD Player can tell when your CD-ROM drive is empty or doesn't contain a playable audio CD. In this case, it will display the message:

```
Data or no disc loaded
Please insert an audio compact disc
```

in the Artist and Title areas in the middle of the window.

Basic Playing Controls

The CD Player window looks much like the front panel of a typical CD player in a sound system. The large black area at the top left displays track and time information. On the left, the faux LED readout tells you which track is currently playing, while on the right it keeps a running tally of how many minutes and seconds have played in the track. You can change the contents of the time display as detailed below:

If you've ever worked a standard CD player, the control buttons (to the right of the track and time display) should be immediately familiar.

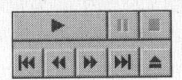

On the top row are the essential stop/start controls:

Play The largest button with the big arrow starts or resumes play.

Pause The button with the two vertical bars pauses play at the current point in the track.

Stop The button with the square stops play and returns you to the beginning of the current track.

On the second row, the first four buttons have double arrows pointing to the left or right. These let you move to other parts of the disc.

> **TIP**
> You can move directly to a specific track by choosing it from the list in the Track area near the bottom of the CD Player window. See "Playing Discs with the Play List" later in the chapter.

Previous and Next Track At either end of this set of four buttons, the buttons with the vertical bars move to the beginning of the previous or next track. The one at the left end—with the left-pointing arrows—moves to the beginning of the previous track (or if a track is playing, to the beginning of the current track). The one at the right—with the right-pointing arrows—moves to the beginning of the next track.

Skip Backward and Skip Forward The two center buttons in the set of four have double arrows only; these are for moving quickly through the music while the disc plays in the reverse or forward direction.

Eject This is the last button at the far right of the second row, with the upward-pointing arrow on top of a thin rectangle. Click here to pop the current disc out of your CD-ROM drive. Of course, this will only work if your drive is capable of ejecting automatically.

Display Options

Like other Windows programs, CD Player has a Toolbar with buttons for other common commands (we'll cover these in a moment). The Toolbar may not be visible when you first run the program; choose View ➤ Toolbar to turn it on and off. Here's how the CD Player window looks with the Toolbar visible:

When the Toolbar is on, you can get a brief description of each button's function by placing the mouse pointer over the button.

Two other elements of the CD Player window can also be turned off and on via the View menu. These are the Status Bar and the area displaying the artist and disc and track titles.

When visible, the Status Bar runs along the bottom of the window. It offers Help messages when the mouse pointer passes over a menu choice or rests over a button on the Toolbar for a few moments. Otherwise, it displays the total play time for the disc and current track. To turn the Status Bar off or on, choose View ➤ Status Bar.

Once you've cataloged a disc, CD Player displays the artist, disc title, and title of the current track in the middle of its window. If you want to hide this information, perhaps to make the window small enough to stay on your screen while you work with another program, choose View ➤ Disc/Track Info.

> **TIP**
> You can choose between two font sizes for the numerals in the track and time readout. See "Setting CD Player Preferences" later in this discussion.

You can also control the display of time information in the main readout of the CD Player window. The standard setting shows elapsed time for the track currently playing. If you prefer, you can instead see the time remaining for the current track or for the entire disc. To select among these options, open the View menu and choose one of the three relevant options: Track Time Elapsed, Track Time Remaining, or Disc Time Remaining. The currently active choice is checked on the View menu. Or, if the Toolbar is visible, you can click the button corresponding to your time-display choice.

Other Play Options

You have several commands for determining the play order for a disc's tracks. Three of these are available as items on the Options menu or as buttons on the Toolbar:

Random Order Plays the tracks randomly. This is often called shuffle mode on audio-only CD players.

Continuous Play Plays the disc continuously rather than stopping after the last track.

Intro Play Plays only the first section of each track. You can set the length of this intro with the Preferences command, covered below.

> **NOTE**
> If you have a multiple-disc CD-ROM drive, you'll find an additional Multidisc Play choice on the Options menu. Select this if you want to hear all the discs loaded in the drive rather than just the currently active disc.

You can select these playback options in any combination. To turn them on or off, open the Options menu and choose the desired item; they are active when checked. Alternatively, click the button for that command (the button appears pressed when the command is active). Here are the buttons you use:

If none of these commands are active, CD Player plays the tracks in full and in sequence, stopping after the last track.

Other play options include whether or not the current disc keeps playing when you close CD Player (covered in "Setting CD Player Preferences," below) and playing a custom list of tracks, covered in the next section.

Cataloging Your CDs and Creating Play Lists

If you're willing to do a little typing, CD Player will keep a "smart" catalog of your disc collection. Once you've entered the catalog information, such as the disc title, the artist, and the track titles, CD Player automatically displays these details whenever you reload the disc:

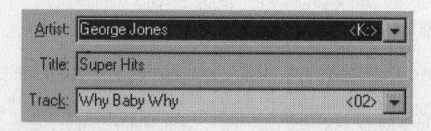

Note that if you have a multidisc CD-ROM drive (or more than one unit), you can choose from the available drives by letter, using the list in the Artist area.

Cataloging a Disc When you load a disc that hasn't been cataloged, CD Player displays generic disc information. The Artist area reads *New Artist*, and the Title area says *New Title*. Tracks are titled by number (*Track 1*, *Track 2*, and so on).

To enter the actual information for the current disc, choose Disc ≻ Edit Play List, or, if the Toolbar is visible, click the corresponding button (the one at the far left, shown here on the left). The dialog box shown in Figure 9.3 will appear.

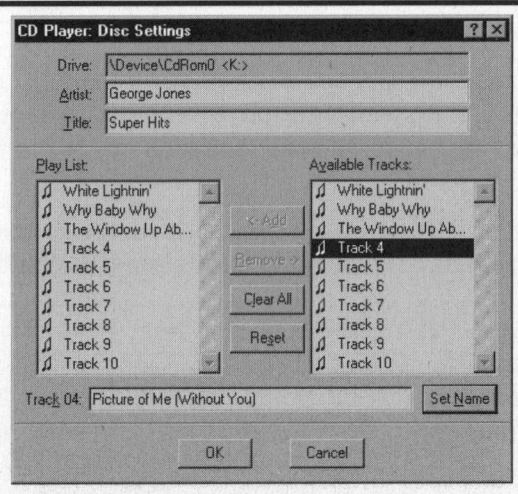

FIGURE 9.3: The Disc Settings dialog box

The top area in this dialog box, labeled Drive, identifies the location of the disc being cataloged. If you have a multidisc player, you can double-check whether you're working with the correct disc here.

Type in the artist and title of the CD in the appropriate areas at the top of the dialog box. To type in track titles:

1. Select a track in the Available Tracks box (the one at the *right* of the dialog box).

2. Type in the track title in the Track area at the bottom of the dialog box.

3. Click the Set Name button to change the current name.

You can change any of this information at any time. When you're satisfied with your entries, go on to create a play list as described below or click OK to return to CD Player. The disc information will appear in the appropriate areas of the window.

Creating a Play List   The typical CD has some great songs, a few that are good to listen to but aren't favorites, and one or two that are just terrible. CD Player lets you set up a custom play list for each disc so you never have to hear those dog songs again. If you like, you can even play your favorites more often than the others (be careful, you might get sick of them).

Here's how to create a play list:

1. In the Disc Settings dialog box (Figure 9.3), the Play List box on the left side of the window displays the tracks in the play list. Initially, the box displays all the tracks on the disc in order.

2. If you just want to remove one or two tracks, drag each track off the list as follows: Point to the track's icon (the musical notes) in the Play List box, hold down the mouse button, and drag to the Available Tracks box. Alternatively, you can highlight each track in the Play List box and click the Remove button. To remove all the tracks and start with an empty list, click Clear All.

3. You can add tracks to the play list in two ways:
   - Drag the track (or tracks) to the Play List box using the same technique for deleting tracks but in the reverse direction: Starting from the Available Tracks box, drag the track to the desired position in the play list. You can add a group of tracks by dragging across them to highlight them, releasing the mouse button, and then dragging from the icon area to the play list.
   - Use the Add button: Highlight one or more tracks in the Available Tracks box and click Add. In this case, the added track always appears at the end of the list.

4. If you want to start again, click Reset. The Play List box will again show all the tracks in order.

5. Click OK when you've finished your play list to return to the main CD Player window.

Playing Discs with the Play List CD Player always selects the tracks it plays from the play list. Before you make any modifications, the play list contains all the tracks on the disc, and you'll hear every track when you play the disc. Once you've created your own play list, though, CD Player plays only the tracks on the list. If you select Random Order play, the program randomly selects tracks from the play list, not from all the tracks on the disc.

The play list tracks are accessible individually in the Track area near the bottom of the CD Player window. To move to a particular track, just select it in the list. If the disc is already playing, the selected track will start. Otherwise, click the Play button to start it.

Setting CD Player Preferences

Use the Preferences dialog box to change miscellaneous CD Player settings. To display it, choose Options ➤ Preferences. Here's what the Preferences dialog box looks like:

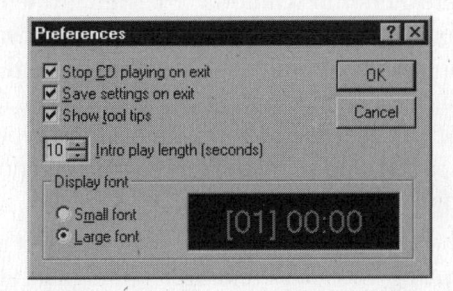

Here are the available preference settings and their effects:

Save Settings On Exit When this box is checked, the settings you make on the View and Options menu and in the Preferences dialog box are saved when you close the program. If you clear this box, changes in settings affect only the current session—the previous settings are restored the next time you start CD Player.

Show Tool Tips Check this box if you want pop-up descriptions (also known as tooltips) and Help messages in the Status Bar when the mouse pointer rests on a button for a few moments. Clear it if you find these messages annoying.

Intro Play Length Use the arrow controls to set the number of seconds at the beginning of each track that CD Player will play when you activate the Intro Play command.

Display Font Choose a large or small font for the LED-like track and time readout by choosing the appropriate radio button.

Web TV

One of my favorite multimedia applications in Windows 98 Second Edition is Web TV, formerly known as the TV Viewer. It's probably not installed in your system, because it's an option. To install it from the CD, run Control Panel ➢ Add/Remove Programs ➢ Windows Setup ➢ Web TV for Windows. You may be prompted to reboot the computer several times before the installation is complete, so close up any work in advance.

Web TV works in conjunction with special TV cards and video capture cards/drivers that are compatible with DirectShow 2.0 and WDM (drivers that are built into Windows 98). Even if you don't have a video capture card or TV display card, you can still take advantage of the program listing guide, which downloads TV listings from the Web and displays them in various formats that put *TV Guide* (even the online version) to shame. You can search for shows, times, show types (sci-fi, drama, specials, and so on), and set reminders so your computer reminds you not to miss a show.

With the appropriate hardware, you can select and tune among hundreds of analog (broadcast and cable) or digital satellite television programs, and navigate to Web channels and other information broadcast through these networks. For satellite reception, drivers specifically written for the Broadcast Architecture are required. Check with your satellite TV provider to see whether their service is compatible with Web TV.

You will need a PC system capable of running Microsoft Windows 98 or Windows 2000 Professional, including:

- A Pentium-class PC with at least 24MB RAM
- An additional 65MB of free hard disk space
- Television or standard VGA monitor (large screen monitor optional)
- Supported TV tuner and video card(s)

Windows Multimedia

- Wireless remote control device (optional)
- Modem and Internet connection (optional)

TIP
For more information on supported hardware, search the Microsoft Web site for Broadcast Architecture. (When I wrote this chapter, the information was in a password-protected area of the site for registered beta-testers, but it should be publicly accessible by the time you read this.) For the latest information about Microsoft's plans to integrate digital TV, the Web, and your PC, visit http://www.microsoft.com/windows/tv/home.htm.

What's So Cool About Web TV?

For starters, you watch TV either on the whole screen or in a window while you work, and the quality is very high. The picture is much sharper than on a standard TV; and some of the TV cards perform "line doubling," drawing twice as many lines on the screen as on a normal TV. This results in a better-looking picture, especially since you are typically watching from just a couple of feet from your screen. Most TV tuner cards decode stereo sound, so the sound will be good as well. Further, you also get the benefit of *enhanced TV* viewing. Here are some of the potential benefits of enhanced TV viewing (once this technology is more firmly developed):

- News and weather reports can be accompanied by local or other specialized information that satisfies the needs of limited audiences.
- Educational programs could spice things up with references and links to other programs and locations on the Web.
- When watching dramas and comedies, you could read cast information, recaps of past episodes, links to related Internet and bulletin board sites, and other such background information.
- When watching sporting events, you could read statistics, or even create your own data sheets for personalized tracking of favorite players or teams. You could hear or read additional syndicated commentary.
- Music-only channels can add background graphics containing song title, album, and artist information, so you know what you are listening to and how to find it again.

- Shows can be enhanced by letting the viewer respond and interact. Viewers can then play along with game shows, enter contests, take quizzes, vote on issues presented in the show, express opinions, and take part in polls. Consumers using a back channel can actually investigate and purchase things from the comfort of their living rooms.

> **NOTE**
> Of course, your Internet connection must be correctly configured and working to download Program Guide information from the Web and to interact with shows. To verify your connection, confirm that you can successfully view content from some popular Web pages such as www.microsoft.com with Internet Explorer.

How It Works

At its simplest, Web TV simply picks up TV signals from an antenna or cable TV input plugged into your TV tuner card and displays the result in a resizable window. Windows 98 SE provides the TV tuner program to make this happen. If your TV tuner card is supported, Windows 98 SE also supplies all the drivers. If not, you'll get them in the box with the card.

Going a step beyond that, if you're on a digital satellite system, you'll probably have to get a special accompanying card (either external or mounted inside the PC) that decodes the digital signals and then pumps them into the TV card.

You can download your program listings either from a broadcast channel or over the Web. It's much faster over the Web. The Web TV program is set up to decode the broadcast listings from Gemstar and load them into the Program Guide.

Using TV Viewer

To run the program, first install it as I explained above. Then run it either by clicking the TV set icon in the Quick Launch bar or choose Start ➢ Programs ➢ Accessories ➢ Entertainment ➢ Web TV For Windows. The first thing you'll notice upon running the program is that it takes a bit of time to load. You'll see the TV Viewer "splash screen" first and after a little wait you'll be walked through setting up the program the first time.

There will be a man's voice telling you what to do. Just listen and follow the instructions.

If you're already hooked up to a good TV source (antenna, cable, satellite), have the wizard scan for channels. I have found that when I'm using a cheesy antenna, I have to input the channels manually or they don't get registered because the signals aren't strong enough. (I'll show you how to do that shortly.) And if you have a Web connection, choose that as the source for your Program Guide data, not the broadcast option, which can take hours to download, though you may be able to do this in the background. If you download from the Web, you'll have to answer a few questions about your zip code and perhaps specify what your source of TV signal is (which cable company, which local broadcast area), as in Figure 9.4.

After a few minutes of downloading, the Web page should tell you that the process is now complete. You can start using the program, and you'll see something like what I have in Figure 9.5. It looks totally unlike anything else in Windows 98, so get ready, since the interface is completely new and a little annoying at first. But it's pretty easy to learn, so don't worry.

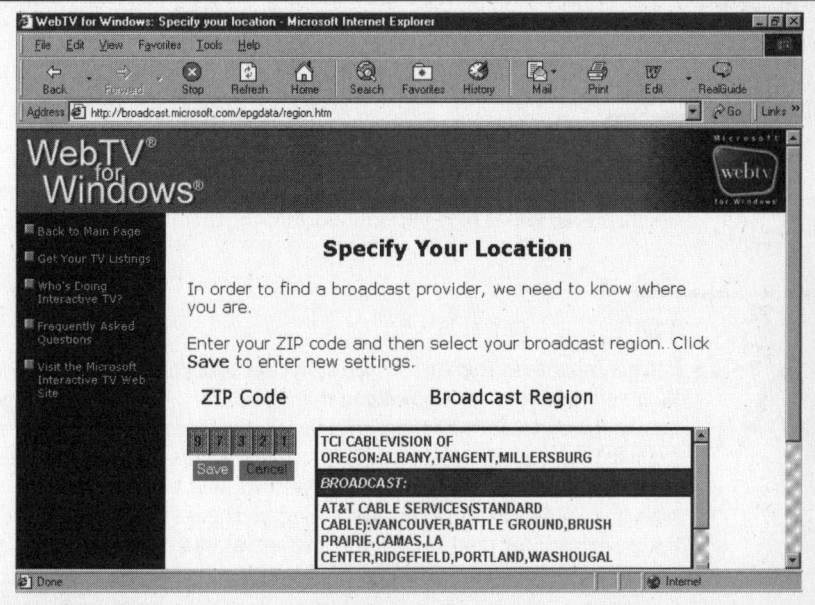

FIGURE 9.4: Specifying your broadcast medium when using the Gemstar Program Guide Web download

Chapter Nine

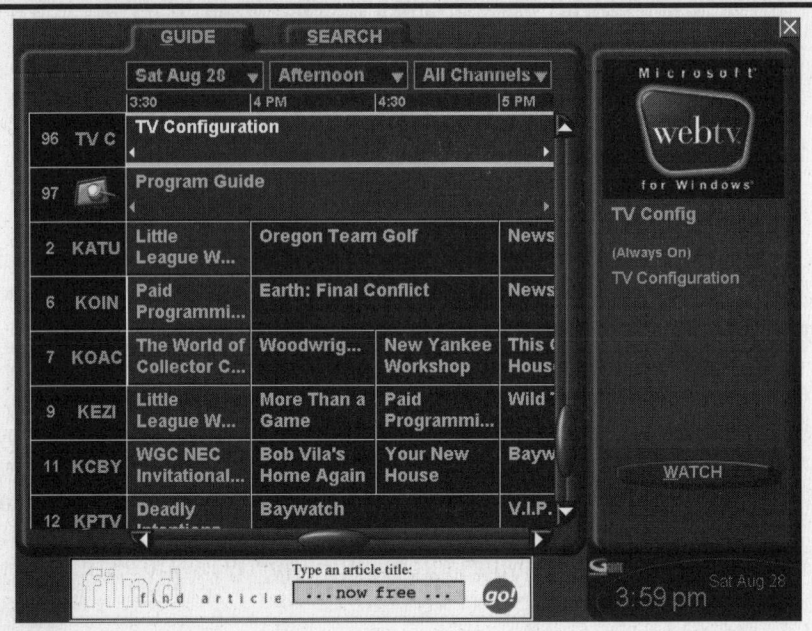

FIGURE 9.5: Typical Program Guide appearance. Click a green area to preview a show on the right.

> **NOTE**
> Only the shows displayed in green are being broadcast currently. Other times are displayed with a blue background. Clicking them does nothing.

> **TIP**
> You may not have program listings, either because you aren't connected to the Web and therefore can't download them from the Net, or you don't live in an area that broadcasts the listings over the air. Not to worry. If you don't have program listings you can still watch TV. You just click the TV channel number over to the left, or press the PageUp and PageDown keys to change channels. If you have no channels except 1 and 99 showing, you have to add your channels manually. See "Adding (and Removing) Channels Manually" below.

Windows Multimedia

Adding (and Removing) Channels Manually

Just like when you set up a new TV or VCR, the automatic scan option can add channels you don't want, or can skip over weak channels and not add them. To manually add or remove channels, do this:

1. With the Web TV window active (or full screen) Press Alt or F10. This brings up a big toolbar with a few icons on it.

2. Click Settings in the toolbar. In the resulting dialog box, click Add Channels. Add and enter the number, as you see in Figure 9.6. To remove a channel, select it and click Remove.

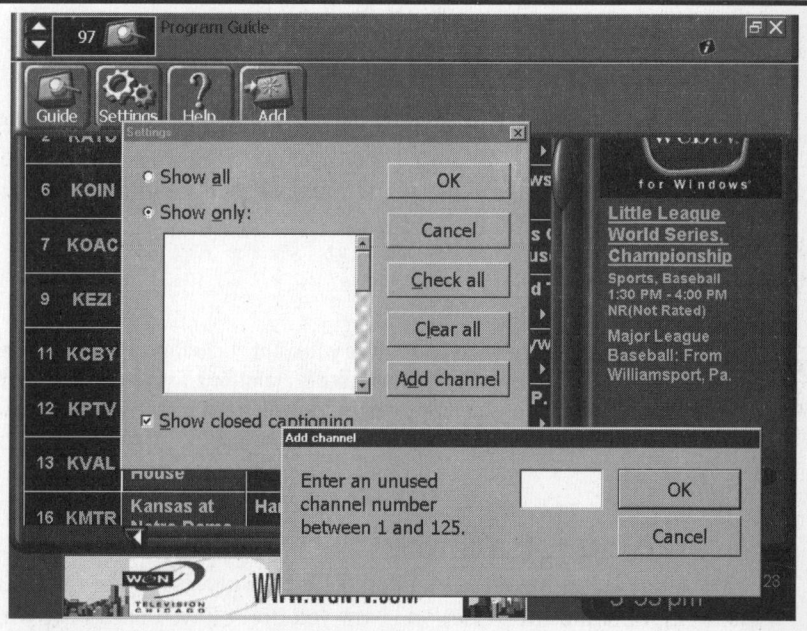

FIGURE 9.6: You can add or remove channels using the Settings box. You also choose which channels to display in the Program Guide.

Tips for Using Web TV

Here are some tips to make using Web TV easier.

Online Documentation

Use the online help. It's pretty good. Just press F1 while you're in Web TV.

Avoid Channel 1

Channel 1 is the Setup channel. Choosing it by clicking it, or (more likely) by landing on it while pressing PgUp and PgDn to channel-surf, runs the wizard again and starts talking you through the setup routine. Unless you want to hear all that and download the Program Guide again, or choose your video options (like for assigning a VCR or camera to a channel), just skip to another channel quickly.

> **TIP**
> Channel 99 is always the Program Guide.

Scrolling the Display

Note the scroll buttons on the display. You can grab them and slide just as you do with other windows. When you do so, you'll see an indication of where you're headed. They work in both the horizontal (time) and vertical (channel) directions. See Figure 9.7.

> **TIP**
> You can size the display to any size you want, including full screen. The correct height/width proportion of the image is maintained as you resize. See the keystroke table below for how to toggle between full screen and a window. While in a window, size it just as you would any other.

Searching for a Show

How many times have you wondered, "Hey, when is *X-Files* (or the *Price Is Right*, or something else) on? Now you don't have to scan the whole *TV Guide*. Just use the Search option.

1. Click the Search tab near the top of the TV Viewer window.
2. Click in the Search area at the bottom left.
3. Enter the show you're looking for. Then click Search.

Windows Multimedia

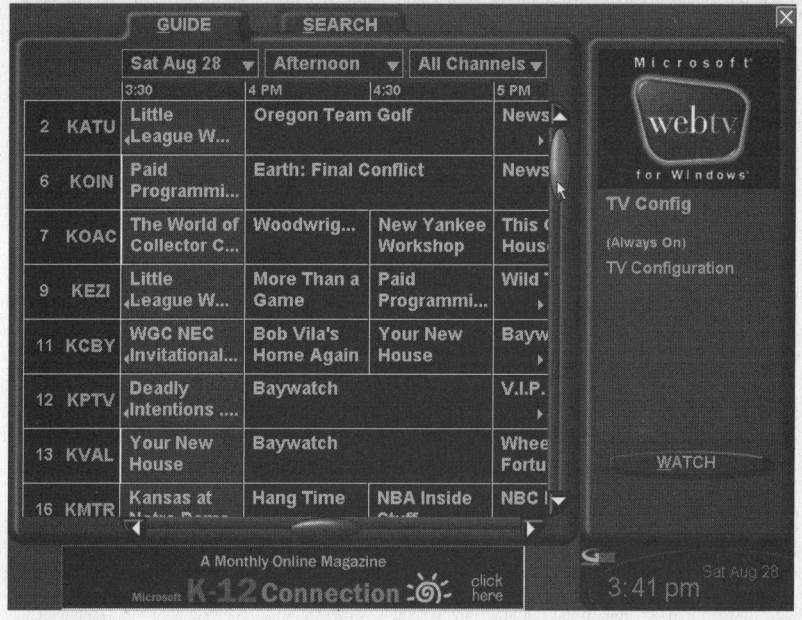

FIGURE 9.7: Use the scroll bars to get around your Program Guide.

You'll see shows that match the name, on all stations in your area. You can then choose to set reminders (see below), or tune to it immediately. You can also click Other Times to see a list of other times and channels when the same program is going to be on.

Looking for a Category of Shows

Looking for a drama, something educational, maybe a musical? Instead of just channel surfing and taking pot luck with a regular TV remote control, why not search by category and get what you're really looking for, like when you go to the video store?

1. Click the Search tab.
2. Click the desired category in the left pane.
3. Pull down the left time menu at the top:
4. Choose the time slot you're thinking of.

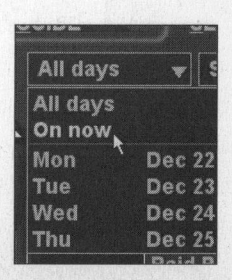

TIP

After choosing a time slot, you'll only see listings for that time. The time slot you choose stays active until you change it or go back to the Guide Page by clicking the Guide tab. So, clicking other categories will also display only shows in the chosen time slot.

Reading about a Program

Wondering if you've seen the program before? A spiffy feature of the Program Guide is that it also contains lots of information about shows it lists. You can click a show in the Program Guide, and over to the right, under the preview screen you'll see some stuff about the show, such as the rating, whether it's a rerun, a synopsis of the content, and more. Figure 9.8 shows an example. Note the location of the pointer.

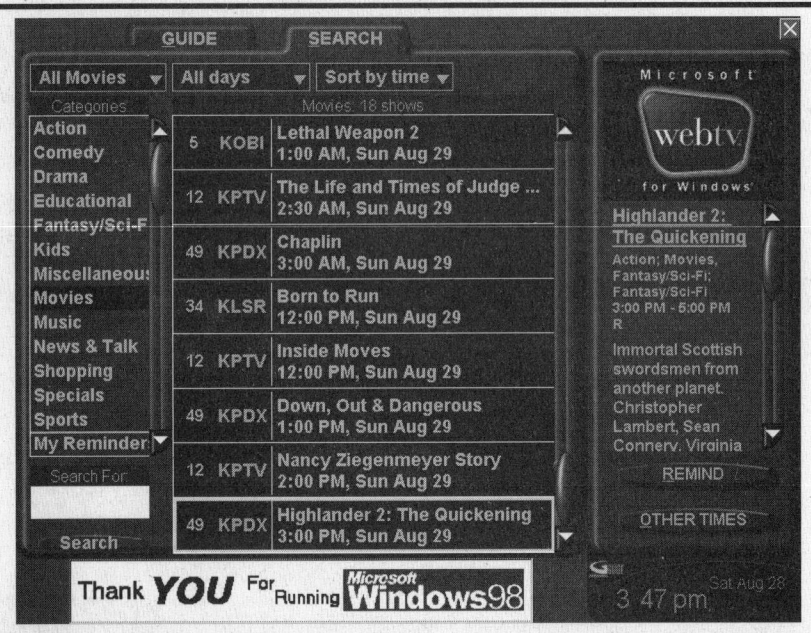

FIGURE 9.8: You can read about a program or movie by clicking it. Click the link (if you're online) to search for Web pages that contain the name.

If you're online with the Internet, you can click the name of the program just under the preview window to quickly conduct a search of pages that contain the name of the show. Sometimes you get useful information about the show, fan pages, and so on.

Setting Reminders

Want to be alerted before a show comes on, so you can tape it or watch it? Easy. You just set a reminder:

1. Click a program in Program Guide.

2. Click the REMIND button in the lower right. You'll see a dialog box:

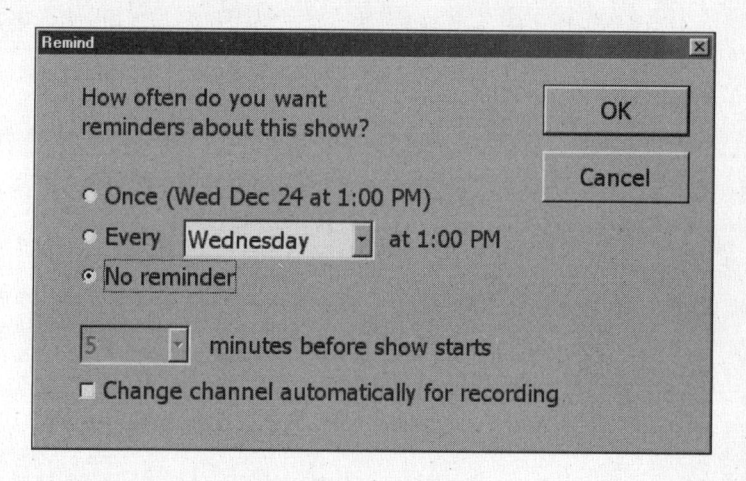

```
Remind
How often do you want
reminders about this show?            OK

                                      Cancel
  ○ Once (Wed Dec 24 at 1:00 PM)
  ○ Every  Wednesday  ▼  at 1:00 PM
  ● No reminder

  [5 ▼]  minutes before show starts
  ☐ Change channel automatically for recording
```

3. Fill in the relevant info and click OK.

A dialog box will appear on the screen to remind you of the upcoming show, at the time(s) you choose.

> **NOTE**
> The Web TV program has to be running in order to give you reminders.

Adding Favorite Channels to Your Toolbar

You can have up to five favorite channels in your toolbar, making it easy to switch between favorite channels. If you have five and add another, the oldest one disappears and is replaced by the new one.

1. Display the toolbar.
2. Select a channel you want, using one of the various techniques.
3. Click Add:

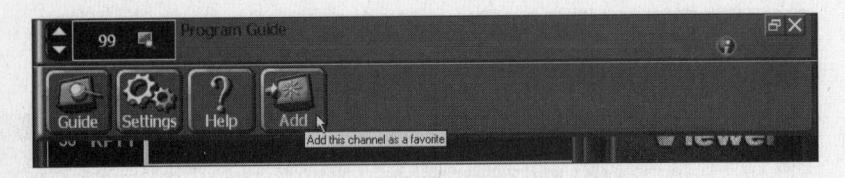

The new channel appears on the toolbar. Click it now to switch to that channel.

> **TIP**
> When you're viewing full-screen, just move the pointer to the top of the screen and wait a second. The toolbar will appear. If you then move it away from the top of the screen, the toolbar will disappear after a few seconds. Pressing Esc always makes the toolbar go away, too.

Remote Controls and Special Keys while Watching

Web TV is designed to work with remote controls available (or to-be-available) from your computer manufacturer. (Not your standard TV remote!) If you don't have a computer remote control, you're not alone. As an alternative, you can use the keystrokes listed in Table 9.2 with Web TV; the most frequently used keys are listed first.

Windows Multimedia

> **TIP**
> If you have a Gateway Destination entertainment system, your remote control will work with Web TV. The only exception is that the Recall button on the Gateway remote control has no function.

TABLE 9.2: Keystroke Controls for Web TV

Keystroke	Action
F10	Brings up toolbar menu (favorites, guide, logins, preferences, and other options are accessible from the toolbar).
F6	Toggles windowed/full screen mode. Windowed mode is useful for displaying video while using Desktop applications.
0-9	Changes channels. Channels are three digits.
Enter	Confirms selection.
↑, ↓, ←, →	Scrolls up/down when viewing programming grid.
Win	Brings up Start menu.
Win+Ctrl+Shift+Z	Shows the Program Guide (grid view).
Win+Ctrl+Z	Brings up Web TV if not yet started, otherwise toggles between desktop and full screen.
Win+Ctrl+V	Volume Up (on Master Mixer).
Win+Shift+V	Volume Down (on Master Mixer).
Win+V	Toggle Mute (on Master Mixer).
Win+Ctrl+Alt+Z	Channel Up.
Win+Ctrl+Alt+Shift+Z	Channel Down.
Win+Ctrl+Alt+Shift+F	Arrow Left (some apps may interpret as REWIND).
Win+Ctrl+Alt+Shift+P	Arrow Up (some apps may interpret as PLAY).
Win+Ctrl+Alt+F	Arrow Right (some apps may interpret as FORWARD).
Win+Ctrl+Alt+Shift+G	Recall (some apps may interpret as EJECT).
Win+Ctrl+Alt+P	Arrow Down (some apps may interpret as STOP).
Win+Ctrl+Alt+G	PAUSE.

* "Win" means the Windows key on your keyboard if it has it. Older keyboards do not have this key.

Managing Multimedia Drivers and Settings

When you add a new piece of hardware to your system, such as a sound board, CD-ROM controller, MIDI board, or other piece of paraphernalia, you'll have to alert Windows to this fact by installing the correct software device driver for the job. Some drivers simply control an external player as though you were pushing the buttons on the device's control panel by hand. These types of devices are called Media Control Interface (MCI) devices and include audio CD players, video disc players, MIDI instruments, and others. Other drivers actually send the sound or video data to the playback card or hardware, as well as control the playback speed and other parameters.

You use the Add New Hardware option in the Control Panel to install the device driver. Drivers for popular multimedia items are included with Windows and will often be detected when you've added the hardware, especially if the hardware is Plug-and-Play compatible.

> **TIP**
> As a rule, when you're purchasing new stuff, avoid non–Plug-and-Play hardware like the plague.

If you are having trouble running your multimedia hardware or need to make adjustments to it, you'll have to examine the Properties of the item and its driver. Device property dialog boxes can be reached from several locations. For example, the Edit menu in the Sound Recorder applet will take you to your sound card's Properties settings, though you could also use the System applet in the Control Panel to get there.

When in doubt, always contact the manufacturer of your multimedia hardware to obtain drivers and driver updates for use with Windows 98 SE. You can often download new drivers over the Web, but not always. Sometimes a phone call is required.

What's Next?

In the next chapter, you'll learn about Windows 98 SE's features for installing and working with various types of hardware. As you'll see, Plug-and-Play technology and the New Hardware Wizard make adding new devices almost as easy as plugging them in.

Chapter 10

Hardware Mastery

Imagine that you've bought a new kitchen appliance from Blenders 'R Us, and it turns out that different manufacturers are the sources for the glass container, push buttons, blade, and motor. Each piece comes with an instruction booklet and its own warranty card. After assembling all the pieces, you go to make yourself a milkshake, and a message pops out: "Sorry, the Framjit 34ExY894 blade isn't sharp enough to cut frozen products. You need to upgrade to the Framjit 34ExY894 Plus." (And incidentally, the new blade exerts additional torque, requiring a new shaft—but you don't find that out until after you've bought the blade upgrade and spent several fruitless hours trying to install it.)

Welcome to the world of computers! Except to actually resemble computers, the blender's new blade must not fit on the new shaft, and the manufacturers blame each other. But don't worry—a new blade-shaft adapter will be available by spring at the latest.

OK, so I exaggerate for effect. But not by much.

Adapted from *Windows 98: No Experience Required*
by Sharon Crawford
ISBN 0-7821-2128-4   544 pages $24.99

Fortunately, starting with Windows 95, sanity has begun to triumph in the world of computer hardware. The sanity goes by the name of the *Plug-and-Play* standard. Forget that the standard used to be called Plug and Pray—these days, "PnP" in Windows 98 SE really works. Nevertheless, there are so many manufacturers and so much new hardware, not everything will go perfectly. This chapter addresses the possible problems and their solutions.

Modems

Installing and configuring a modem in Windows 98 SE is fairly simple (almost as simple as it should be). When you first install Windows 98 SE, the modem that's physically installed in your computer or connected to it should be detected automatically. You'll only need to deal with the following steps if the modem wasn't detected or if you later change modems.

Installing a Modem

> **NOTE**
> In the context of this chapter, "installing" a modem or other hardware means setting up the device to work with Windows 98 SE (and your other software) once it has been physically attached to your computer. See Chapter 26, *Installing Random Access Memory*, for general instructions about opening your computer case and adding hardware internally. Also, Chapter 7, *Customizing Windows 98 SE with the Control Panel*, describes another tool for telling Windows 98 SE about hardware that's not Plug-and-Play, the Add New Hardware applet.

Before starting any modem procedure, make sure the modem is plugged in and turned on (if it's an external modem) and that the telephone wire is plugged into the modem and into the wall receptacle (for both internal and external modems). To install a modem (where none has been before), follow these steps:

1. Choose Start ➢ Settings ➢ Control Panel.

2. Click the Modems icon to open the Modems Properties dialog box.

3. Click Add to start the Install New Modem Wizard (see Figure 10.1).

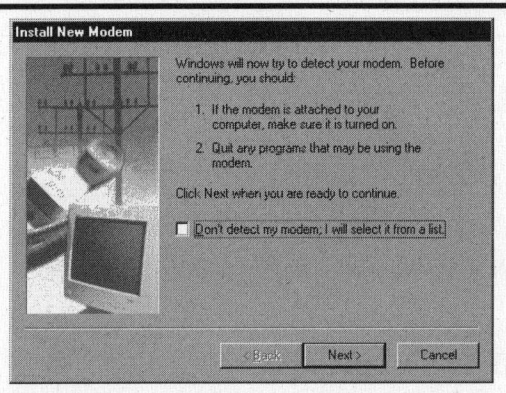

FIGURE 10.1: A Wizard steps you through the process of installing a modem.

4. You can let Windows 98 SE search for the modem, or you can select your modem directly. As a rule, let Windows try first—it's the easiest way. If Windows 98 SE has difficulty, you can always specify your particular modem on a second go-round. Windows will search around your communications ports and try to find a modem. When it finds one, you'll see a Verify Modem dialog box. If the modem isn't correct, or if the designation seems too generic, click the Change button and continue with the next step.

5. If Windows 98 SE fails to find the modem (or if you click Change in the Verify Modem page), you'll be asked to get specific. Figure 10.2 shows the dialog box in which you select a manufacturer in the left box and the particular model in the right box. If your modem isn't listed, but you have an installation disk that came with it, click Have Disk.

6. Keep clicking OK, Next, or Finish until the installation is complete.

[Figure 10.2 screenshot of "Install New Modem" dialog]

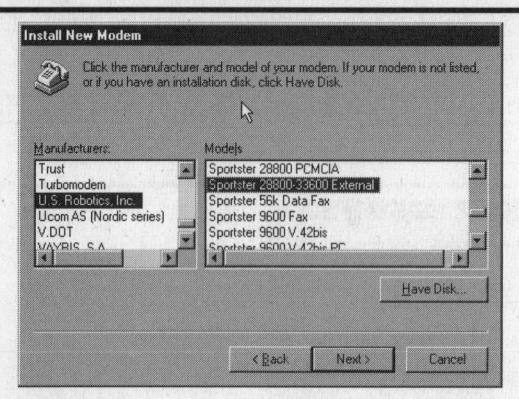

FIGURE 10.2: If Windows 98 SE doesn't find your modem, you can install a modem by selecting a particular manufacturer and model.

Deleting a Modem

If you change modems (or install the wrong one), it's easy to correct the situation:

1. Choose Start ➢ Settings ➢ Control Panel.
2. Click the Modems icon in the Control Panel to open the Modems Properties dialog box.
3. On the General tab, highlight the modem name.
4. Click the Remove button, and it's gone!

Modem Settings

To find the hardware-type settings for your modem, choose Start ➢ Settings ➢ Control Panel and click the Modems icon to open the Modems Properties dialog box. Highlight your modem (if it isn't highlighted already) and click Properties to open the modem's Properties dialog box (see Figure 10.3).

The General Tab
On the General tab are:

- The full name of the modem
- The port to which it's connected

- A slider for setting the volume of the modem speaker
- A drop-down box for setting the maximum speed

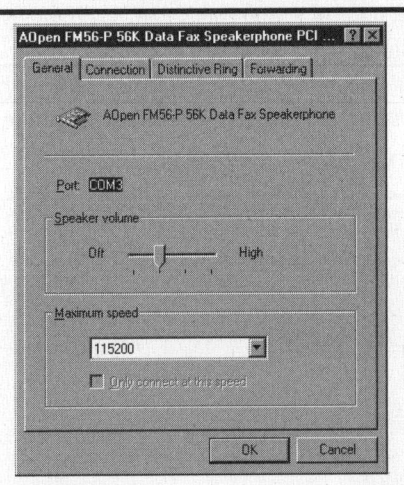

FIGURE 10.3: This is the place to check up on the settings for your modem.

> **NOTE**
> These settings (except for volume, which is strictly a matter of preference) rarely need to be fooled with. That's because they come from what Windows 98 SE knows about your specific modem. Only change the settings when you've had some difficulty with your modem being recognized and you're sure a particular setting is wrong.

INSTALLING A REPLACEMENT MODEM

When the time comes to replace your modem with something faster, the process is easy. Just delete the old modem using the procedure described above. Unplug the old modem and plug in the new one at the same location. Make sure the modem is turned on and that all connections—including the one to the phone line—are made; then follow the steps described under "Installing a Modem."

The Connection Tab

More of the hardware settings are on the Connection page (see Figure 10.4). Again, unless you have a good reason for changing the Connection Preferences, leave them alone. The Call Preferences can be changed if you find the default ones unsuitable. In particular, you may want to set a time to disconnect a call if the line is idle for an extended time. Although many online services will disconnect an inactive line, they may take quite a long time to do it.

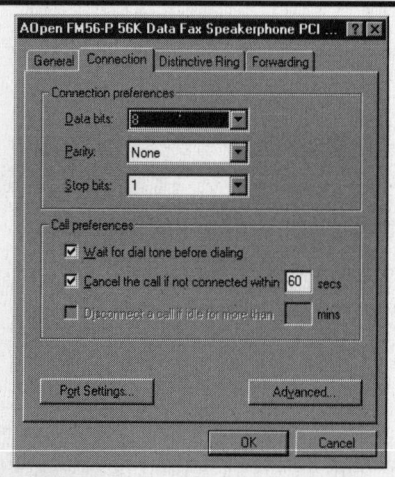

FIGURE 10.4: The properties for the modem's connection

Advanced Settings

If you click the Advanced button on the Connection tab, you'll see the dialog box shown in Figure 10.5. These settings are rarely anything to be concerned about. They're just here for those odd and infrequent times when it might be necessary to force error correction or use software for error control. The one thing on this page that you might use more often is the log file. If you're troubleshooting a bad connection, click View Log to open a text file containing a log of the last connection (or attempt). Normally, this file is overwritten with the new log each time you connect. If you want to keep an ongoing log, check the Append To Log checkbox.

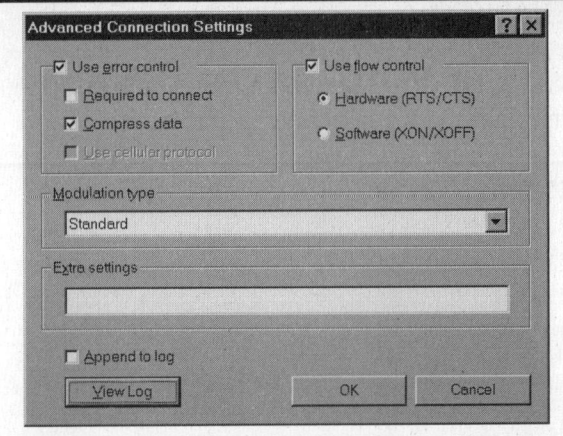

FIGURE 10.5: You might try these advanced settings with a connection that's otherwise difficult.

The Distinctive Ring Tab

Some telephone companies offer a distinctive ringing service, which provides specific ring patterns for different kinds of calls. For example, you might specify that one long ring indicates that someone is calling your main number (if you have more than one line).

Using the Distinctive Ring tab, you can check the This Phone Line Has Distinctive Ring Services checkbox and then specify ring patterns and the types of calls using the drop-down boxes, as shown in Figure 10.6.

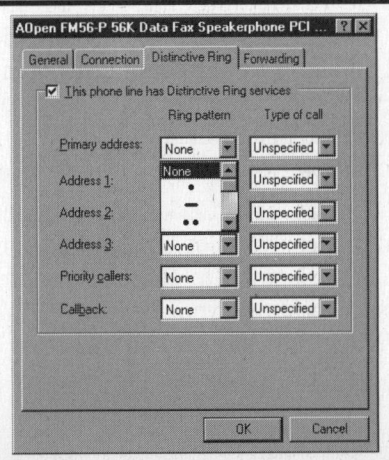

FIGURE 10.6: Use the Distinctive Ring tab to set up distinctive ringing on your modem.

The Forwarding Tab

If you have call forwarding, you can use the Forwarding tab (see Figure 10.7) to configure your modem to automatically forward calls to a number that you specify when you are away from your computer.

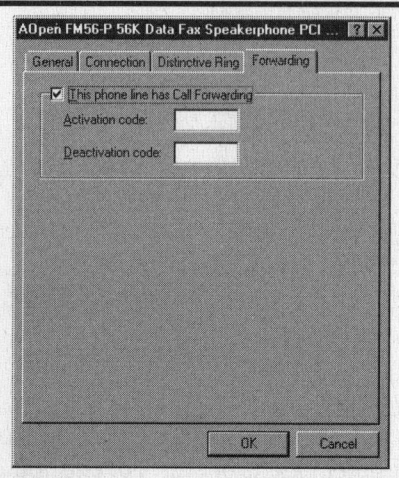

FIGURE 10.7: Contact your telephone company for information on how to activate call forwarding.

Dialing Properties

In addition to centralizing the modem's hardware and software settings, you also want to enter information about how you're dialing and where you're dialing from. Windows 98 SE allows for the configuring of multiple dialing locations, so if you travel with your computer, you can make calls from your branch office (or the condo in Maui where you take your vacations) without making complex changes every time you change locations.

Click the Modems icon in the Control Panel. Click Dialing Properties on the General tab of the Modem Properties dialog box, and fill out the information for your location. Click the New button to supply additional locations. When you change physical locations, you need only tell Windows 98 SE where you are (see Figure 10.8), and all your necessary dialing information will be loaded.

Hardware Mastery 271

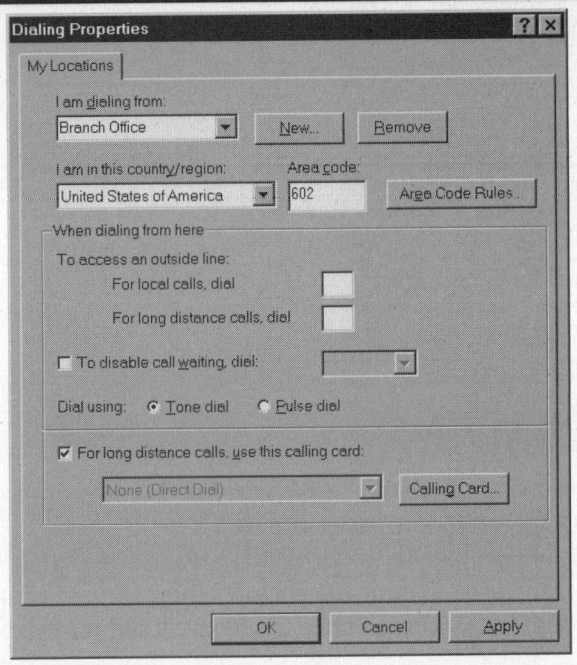

FIGURE 10.8: If you travel with your computer, you don't have to redo your communications settings when you change locations.

Troubleshooting

As a rule, when your modem is uncooperative, it's for obvious reasons:

- It's not plugged into a phone line.
- The modem's turned off, or it's not plugged into an active electrical socket (external modems).
- One or more programs have confused the settings.

After you check the first two items, click the Modems icon in the Control Panel. On the Diagnostics tab, highlight the port your modem is connected to, and click More Info. The resulting dialog box (see Figure 10.9) tells you that the system recognizes the modem and describes it in terms of speed, interrupt, memory address, and the modem's response to various internal commands.

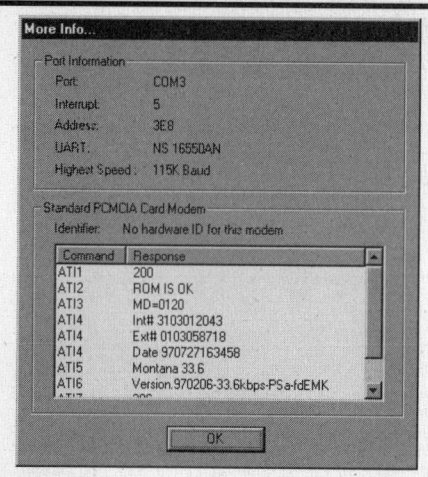

```
More Info...
Port Information
  Port:           COM3
  Interrupt:      5
  Address:        3E8
  UART:           NS 16550AN
  Highest Speed:  115K Baud

Standard PCMCIA Card Modem
  Identifier:    No hardware ID for this modem

  Command   Response
  ATI1      200
  ATI2      ROM IS OK
  ATI3      MD=0120
  ATI4      Int# 3103012043
  ATI4      Ext# 0103058718
  ATI4      Date 970727163458
  ATI5      Montana 33.6
  ATI6      Version.970206-33.6kbps-PSa-fdEMK

              [ OK ]
```

FIGURE 10.9: Here's where you verify that the system can find the modem and that the modem is responding correctly.

If you receive a message that the system can't communicate with the modem, the modem is not plugged into a usable port, not turned on, or defective.

> **NOTE**
> ATI2 is a check of the modem's read-only memory (ROM); if the response isn't "OK," the modem may be defective. The other information in the More Info window is of little interest except to someone with an advanced degree in modemology. Depending on your modem, however, some actual information may filter through.

If your modem isn't recognized, go back to the main Modem Properties dialog box and click the Remove button. After the modem's removed, close everything and reboot your system. Then go back to the Modems icon in the Control Panel and add your modem back.

Scanners and Cameras

Most scanners and digital cameras come with their own installation programs. If you have a scanner or a digital camera installed, you'll see a Scanners and Cameras icon in the Control Panel. Click this icon to troubleshoot a problem with either a scanner or camera or to set logging options. Color profiles can also be added or removed. Color profiles are issues best addressed to the manufacturer or a photography expert.

Adding and Configuring Printers

As in earlier versions of Windows, printers are set up to use a common set of drivers so that you don't have to configure each program independently for printing. Adding or removing a printer is as easy as pointing and clicking, and sharing printers over a network is painless.

You can access your printers in any of the following ways:

- ▶ Click My Computer and select the Printers folder.
- ▶ Choose Start ➢ Settings ➢ Printers.
- ▶ Choose Start ➢ Settings ➢ Control Panel and select the Printers folder.

And of course, you can drag a shortcut to the folder (or to any of the printers in it) onto your Desktop or to any folder where you'd like it.

Adding a Printer

You probably installed a printer when you installed Windows 98 SE, but if you didn't or you want to add another or a network printer, it's very easy to do.

Adding a Local Printer

To add a printer that's connected directly to your computer, open the Printers folder as described above and follow these steps (clicking the Next button after each entry):

1. Select Add Printer.

2. When the Add Printer Wizard starts, click Next, and check the Local Printer entry.

3. Highlight the printer's manufacturer and the model name.

4. Select the port you want to use. Unless you know of some special circumstances, choose LPT1, the standard connection point for printers.

5. Type in the name you want to use for the printer and indicate whether it is the default printer for all your Windows programs. If this is the printer you plan to use practically all the time, select Yes. Otherwise say no—you'll still be able to select the printer when you want to use it. In the Printers folder, the default printer will have a check mark by it.

6. Print a test page to verify all is well. Then click Finish.

Adding a Network Printer

A network printer is one that's plugged into someone else's computer—a computer to which you have access via a network. A networked printer shows up in the Printers window with a drawing of a network cable attached.

To tell your computer about a network printer that you want to use, open the Printers folder as described above and follow these steps (clicking Next after each entry):

1. Select Add Printer. When the Add Printer Wizard starts, click Next, and then select Network Printer.

2. You'll need to tell the system the address of the printer. Click on the Browse button to look for available printers. Highlight the printer (as shown in Figure 10.10) and click OK.

3. If you expect to print from DOS programs, click Yes so that the system can add the necessary information to the printer setup.

4. Enter the name you want to call the printer, and check whether you want this printer to be the default printer. Only check Yes if you expect to be using the network printer for the majority of your printing.

5. Print a test page to make sure everything's running properly; then click Finish.

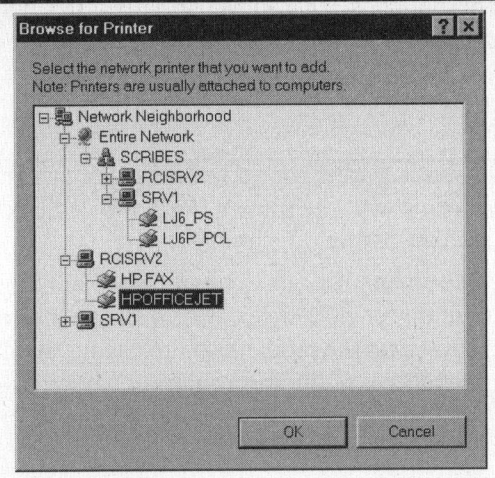

FIGURE 10.10: Here's where you select a printer on the network.

> **NOTE**
> To use a printer set up this way, the printer and the computer it's connected to must both be switched on.

Uninstalling a Printer

Sometimes you may need to uninstall a printer, which is quite easily done. Just right-click the printer's icon in the Printers folder, and select Delete. You'll be asked to confirm the deletion. You may also be asked if you want to delete files associated with this printer that won't be necessary if the printer is gone. If you're getting rid of the printer permanently, select Yes. If you're planning on reinstalling the same printer soon, select No.

Printer Settings

To get at the settings for a printer, right-click the printer's icon in the Printers folder, and select Properties. In the Properties dialog box for that printer, you can set details about fonts, paper, how the printer treats graphics, and so on.

The printer driver that installs with Windows 98 SE makes most of these settings. Change those that you need to change, but avoid changing settings if you're not clear what the setting does. You can inadvertently disable your printer. If this happens, you can usually cure it by uninstalling the printer (see the previous section) and then installing it again.

Troubleshooting

If you're not having any success getting your printer to print, or there appears to be something wrong with the printer, Windows 98 SE comes with excellent tools for troubleshooting the problem.

Select Help from the Start menu. On the Contents tab, open Troubleshooting. Then open Windows 98 Troubleshooters and select Print. The guide is interactive: You select the problem you're having, and then you're stepped through the process of finding a solution.

> **TIP**
> For a more extensive discussion of installing and working with printers in Windows 98 SE, see Chapter 8, *Printers and Printing*.

Changing a Mouse

Usually, you can change the pointing device on your computer by simply turning the computer off, unplugging the old mouse, plugging in the new mouse, and then rebooting your computer.

Sometimes you'll see a window informing you that Windows 98 SE has found new hardware and is installing it, but more often than not, the new mouse will simply *work*. However, if your mouse needs a new (or different) driver, you can install it manually by following these steps (described in terms of keyboard commands because you can hardly use your mouse if the mouse isn't functional):

1. Use the Tab and arrow keys to move the highlight to the My Computer icon. Press Alt+Enter to open the System Properties dialog box. (The Tab key cycles from Start through any open program buttons and the last icon used, back to Start again. Once the focus is on an icon, you can use the arrow keys to move around the Desktop icons.)

2. Press the Tab and arrow keys to move the focus to the Device Manager page.

Hardware Mastery 277

3. Press the Tab key twice to move the focus to the list of devices, then use the down arrow to highlight Mouse.

4. Press the right arrow to display the devices under Mouse. Then press the down arrow to highlight the device (see Figure 10.11).

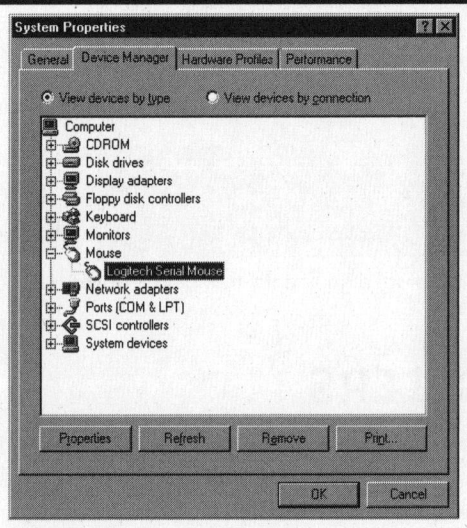

FIGURE 10.11: Selecting the mouse

5. Press the Tab key once to move the focus to the Properties button; then press Enter. This will open the mouse's Properties dialog box.

6. Keep tabbing until the Update Driver button is selected, and then press Enter. The Update Device Driver Wizard will start.

From here on you can let the Wizard do the work. Use the default settings except when you get to the window shown in Figure 10.12. This window is where you specify the location for the new driver. It may have been supplied to you on floppy or CD; if not, it may be on a drive somewhere on your network. Or you can tell the Wizard to try the online Windows Update site, discussed in Chapter 11, *Maintaining the System*. You can check more than one box if you want to search in multiple locations.

278   Chapter Ten

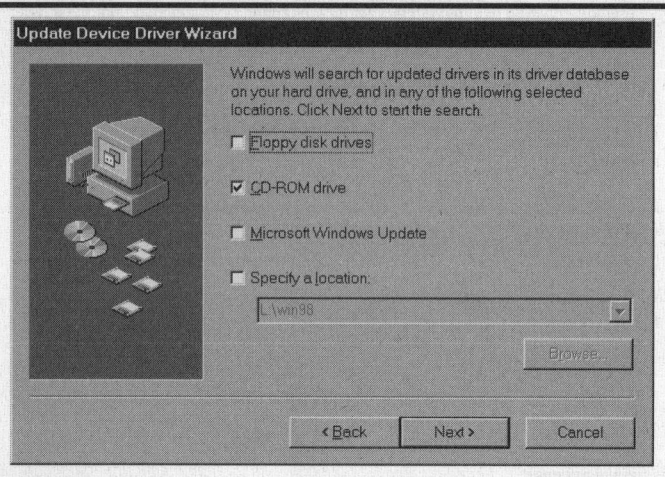

FIGURE 10.12: Telling Windows where to find the new device driver file

Game Controllers

Game controllers are what used to be called joysticks. It's possible that the name changed because not all game controllers are sticks, but I think it's because joystick sounds too much like fun.

Click the Game Controllers icon in the Control Panel to open a Properties dialog box for adding a controller to the setup. Click Add to display a list of more than two dozen types that are ready to go (shown in Figure 10.13) or highlight Custom to specify another type altogether.

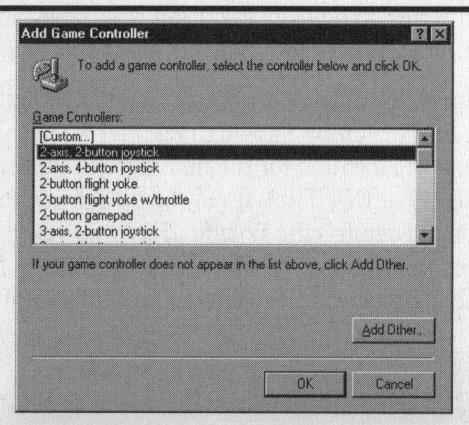

FIGURE 10.13: Game devices for all occasions

Using Infrared Devices

Many new computers—particularly laptops—have infrared ports that allow for wireless communication. To communicate with a printer, for example, your computer needs an infrared port and the printer must have a corresponding infrared port and be within range. "Within range" means that the two ports must have an unobstructed "view" of each other. (Think of a television or VCR remote control.)

To set up the device, click the Infrared icon in the Control Panel. (This icon is available only if you have an infrared device.) On the Status tab, you'll see what (if any) devices are in range (see Figure 10.14).

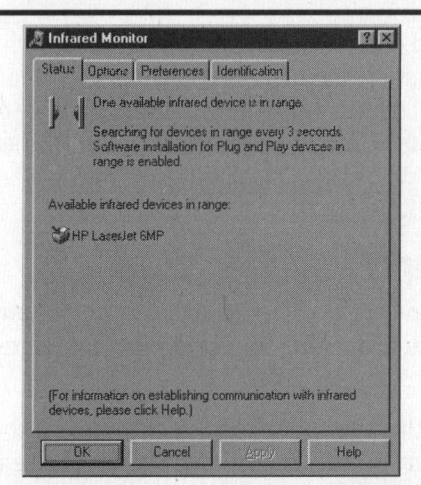

FIGURE 10.14: Infrared devices are reported on the Status tab of the Infrared Monitor dialog box.

On the Options tab, specify the port on which you want to enable communications. It's important to understand that infrared communications are, shall we say, still developing. Depending on the devices involved, you may be able to communicate easily, or you may have to experiment with settings—at length—before you get results. Be prepared to call the manufacturer of the devices involved.

Setting the Display Adapter

The performance of the video system is absolutely critical to all versions of Windows. A slow video system makes your whole computer seem painfully slow—regardless of the processor or amount of RAM on your motherboard. Windows 95 increased the pressure on your video card and monitor, and Windows 98 SE continues to up the ante.

> **TIP**
> If your video card has 1MB of memory or less, you'll want to upgrade. You'll also have to consider whether your monitor can handle the increase in resolution and colors that the video card promises.

There are three video-related chores that you may have to deal with at some point in your Windows career. You may have to change a video card, change a video driver, or, most commonly, optimize the appearance of the video system that you already have. All three are addressed in the next sections.

Changing a Video Card

Installing a new video card is one of the easiest computer chores—providing you're not completely averse to opening your computer box. Here are the steps:

1. Open the box with the new video card, make sure all the pieces are there, and read the instructions. Handle the card only by its edges. Don't handle the edge with the gold contacts.

2. With the computer turned off, unplug the monitor cable from the main computer box and then open the case.

3. Remove the screw holding in the video card (the one the monitor was plugged into). Save the screw.

4. Using a gentle rocking motion, remove the video card from the slot.

5. Put the new video card in the same slot—again, using the same gentle rocking motion. Make sure the card is firmly seated into the slot.

6. Replace the screw holding the card in place. Replace the monitor cable.

7. Close the computer case and restart the computer.

8. After the initial boot process, Windows 98 SE will start. The system will detect the new hardware and install it.

Video cards that were in production at the time Windows 98 SE was released will have drivers included with Windows 98 SE. If you are installing a new card a year or more after the release of Windows 98 SE, you may need to supply the floppy disk or CD that came with the new card to get the best driver.

Changing a Video Driver

Often the manufacturer of a video card will release new drivers some time after the card has been in production. This may be to take advantage of a feature in a new operating system (such as Windows 98 SE) or to fix a bug that wasn't apparent at the time the card was manufactured.

To install a new video driver, just follow these steps:

1. Choose Start ➤ Settings ➤ Control Panel and click the Display icon.

2. Click the Settings tab, and then click the Advanced button. This opens even more settings. Click the Adapter tab here.

3. The Adapter tab (shown in Figure 10.15) shows the name of the video card and something about its features. Click the Change button.

4. The Update Device Driver Wizard will launch and search for updated drivers.

Use the default settings except as shown in Figure 10.16, where you can be specific about the location of the new driver. As with other devices, you may have the driver file on floppy disk, CD-ROM, or a network drive; or you may want the Wizard to check the Windows Update site (see Chapter 11). If you want, you can let the Wizard search all the locations.

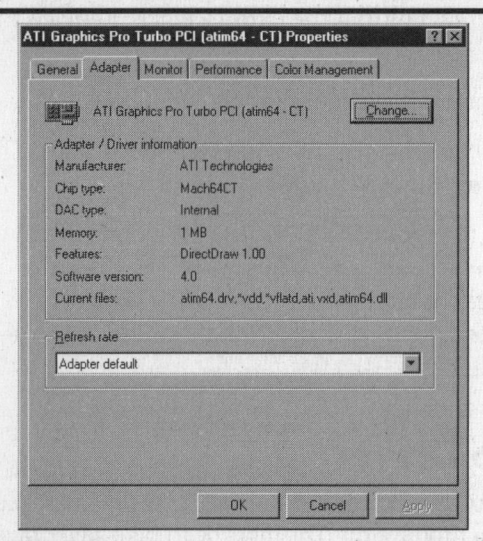

FIGURE 10.15: The Adapter tab describes the characteristics of the video card.

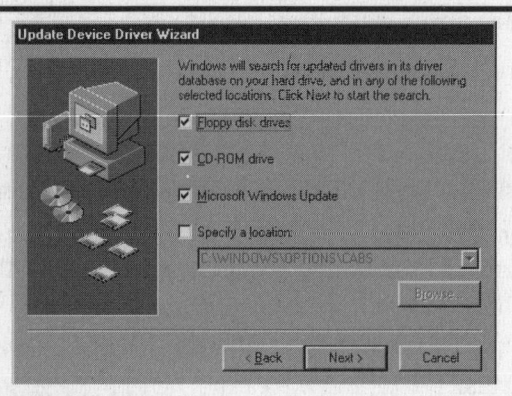

FIGURE 10.16: Places that the system should search for the new video driver

> **NOTE**
>
> Deselect the floppy disk drive option if you don't have a floppy disk. Likewise, if you want the system to search the CD-ROM drive, make sure there's actually a CD in the drive. It won't do any harm, but you'll receive error messages that will slow the process.

Optimizing Video Settings

The video settings you can make are limited only by the capacity of your video card and monitor. Also, some settings—such as very high resolutions on small monitors—are aesthetically unappealing, not to mention rendering icons practically invisible. Feel free to experiment; you can't do any harm (except as noted below).

To modify your video settings, you need to open the Display Properties dialog box. You can do this by clicking the Display icon in the Control Panel. Or you can right-click on a blank spot on the Desktop and select Properties from the pop-up menu. Then click the Settings tab.

Changing Resolutions

Displays are described in terms of their resolution—the number of dots on the screen and the number of colors that can be displayed at the same time. The resolutions you can choose using the slider under Screen Area are determined by the hardware you have (see Figure 10.17). Resolution choices are based on what you like to look at—constrained by the capabilities of your monitor and video card. Chapter 3, *Visiting the Windows 98 Desktop*, describes the resolution options in detail.

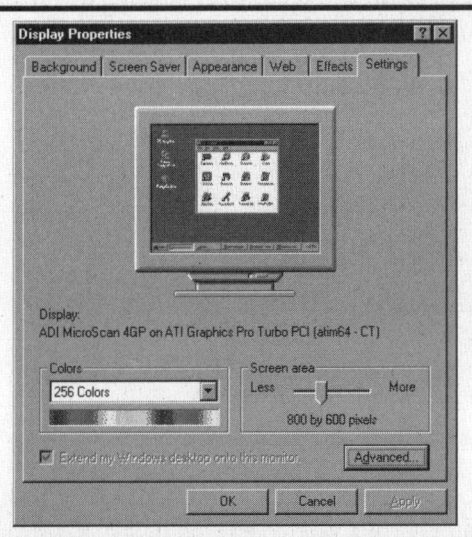

FIGURE 10.17: Colors and resolution are configured on the Settings page.

Making Advanced Changes

Also on the Settings page is a button labeled Advanced. Click this button to get to additional tabs for video configuration. Different types of video cards will have different effects on these tabs. You may have other tabs in addition to the ones described below. Consult the documentation for your video card and monitor for information on how these additional pages are to be used.

General   If you're using a very high resolution, the Desktop elements can be very small. Try Large Fonts under Display to see if that works better for you. (Under the Display Properties' Effects tab, you can also choose to use Large Icons.) This way you can preserve the higher resolution *and* have objects on the Desktop that are legible.

The default setting under Compatibility is to be prompted whenever you make new color settings. While it's true that some programs require a reboot after colors and resolution have changed, most do not. If you don't have a problem program and you change color settings frequently, choose Apply The New Color Settings Without Restarting.

Likewise, if you change display settings often, put a check mark next to Show Settings Icon On Task Bar. This will place a miniature Display icon on the Taskbar. Click the icon to display the following menu and change your display on the spot.

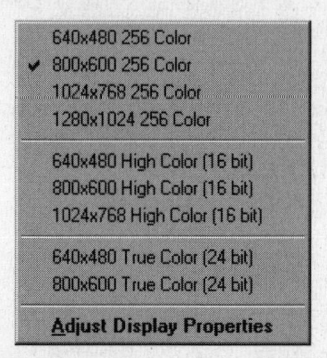

```
  640x480 256 Color
✓ 800x600 256 Color
  1024x768 256 Color
  1280x1024 256 Color

  640x480 High Color (16 bit)
  800x600 High Color (16 bit)
  1024x768 High Color (16 bit)

  640x480 True Color (24 bit)
  800x600 True Color (24 bit)

  Adjust Display Properties
```

Monitor   If you change your monitor, you usually only need to plug it in and start Windows 98 SE. The monitor will be detected and correctly installed. If the monitor isn't correctly detected, you'll have to provide the right information. Click the Change button, and then supply the name of the manufacturer and the model.

> **NOTE**
> There's no reason to change settings if everything is functioning. Sometimes Windows will report "Unknown Monitor," and yet the monitor appears to work perfectly well.

Also on the Monitor tab are options relating to power management and Plug and Play. These are probably set correctly. However, if you have display problems such as a flashing screen after the monitor returns from Suspend mode, click the Help button (the one with the question mark), click an option, and read the description. Try checking or unchecking these options to see if your problem is solved. If you don't *have* a problem, leave the settings in their default state.

> **TIP**
> If weird things are happening to your screen—particularly a laptop screen—sometimes merely disabling the screen saver will set everything right. Screen savers often conflict with Power Management settings on laptops and computers with EnergyStar monitors.

Performance   The Performance tab lets you adjust graphics acceleration. Again, if your display is working fine, leave the Hardware Acceleration set to Full. If your mouse pointer disappears frequently, try moving the slider down one notch.

Color Management   Many color profiles are included with Windows 98 SE, and you can choose one or many. Click Add and select a profile. Add as many as you like. Highlight one and click Set As Default.

> **NOTE**
> See the previous section "Changing a Video Driver" for information on the Adapter tab.

What's Next?

Windows 98 SE provides extensive tools for keeping your computer and its software running smoothly. In Chapter 11, Sharon Crawford and Neil Salkind show how to use ScanDisk, Disk Defragmenter, and other utility programs for system maintenance.

Chapter 11

Maintaining the System

Computers appear to be intelligent but, as we all know, they're only as smart as their software. Computers still have problems with internal errors—frequently caused by conflicts among programs—and require regular maintenance to operate at their best. This chapter covers the tools that perform that maintenance. In addition, you'll learn about the merits and demerits of FAT32, a file system introduced with Windows 98 that can make efficient use of your available hard drive space.

Adapted from *Windows 98: No Experience Required*
by Sharon Crawford
ISBN 0-7821-2128-4   544 pages $24.99

and

The ABCs of Windows 98
by Sharon Crawford and Neil J. Salkind
ISBN 0-7821-1953-0   384 pages $19.99

Running ScanDisk

Whenever a computer is turned on and operating, a lot of complicated tasks are going on inside. Fortunately, you're spared specific knowledge of these goings on, but you still have to deal with the consequences. As in most complex systems, errors are made, and, if not corrected, they tend to pile up into serious problems.

ScanDisk is protection against the accumulation of serious problems on your hard drive. It's a direct descendant of the CHKDSK utility in DOS, with many added features much like those in the justly famous Norton Disk Doctor.

You should run ScanDisk frequently—at least weekly. Once a month you should run its Thorough testing procedure, so the hard disk surface is checked for problems in addition to the standard checking of files and folders.

> **NOTE**
> You may have seen ScanDisk when you installed Windows 98 SE, because part of the installation routine is to do a quick check of the hard drive to look for errors. Also, if you turn the computer off or reboot without the proper sign-off routine, ScanDisk runs automatically when the computer starts up again.

Starting ScanDisk

To run ScanDisk, follow these steps:

1. Choose Start ➤ Programs ➤ Accessories ➤ System Tools ➤ ScanDisk to open the ScanDisk dialog box, as shown in Figure 11.1.
2. Highlight the drive you want tested.
3. Select the type of test and whether you want ScanDisk to fix all errors automatically or prompt you.
4. Click Start.

> **NOTE**
> If the Automatically Fix Errors box is checked, ScanDisk will repair most errors without consulting you again. Such corrections are made based on the settings you can review by clicking the Advanced button.

Maintaining the System 289

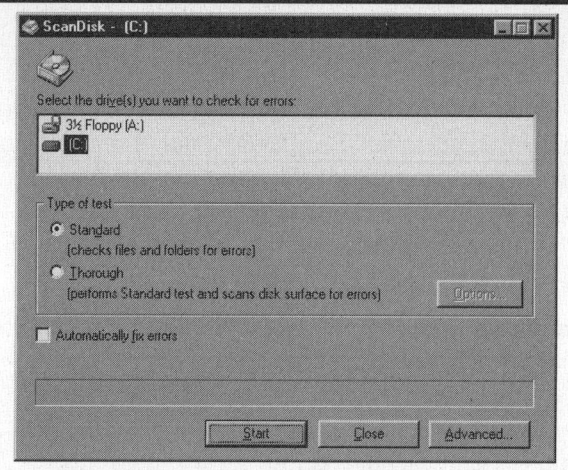

FIGURE 11.1: The basic ScanDisk dialog box

Changing ScanDisk Settings

Click the Advanced button to see (and change) the settings that Scan-Disk uses.

Display summary This setting controls whether you see a summary of ScanDisk's findings after a check (see Figure 11.2).

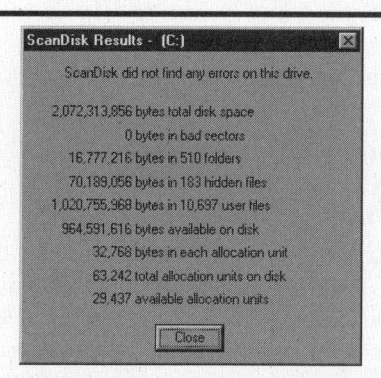

FIGURE 11.2: This is ScanDisk's summary report on the drive just scanned.

Log file By default, ScanDisk creates a new log detailing its activities every time it's run. If you want one long continuous log or no log at all, change the setting.

Cross-linked files   A cross-link occurs when more than one file tries to use the same area (cluster) on the hard drive. The information in the cluster is probably correct only for one file (although it might not be correct for either of them). The Make Copies setting attempts to make some order out of the mess by copying the information in the cluster to both of the files that are contending for the space. This is the best of the three settings—it may not save your data, but the other two options definitely won't.

Lost file fragments   File fragments are a fact of computer life. You can leave the default setting to convert them to files. (They'll be given names like FILE0001 and FILE0002 and deposited in your root directory.) The odds are very high that these fragments aren't useful, and they do take up valuable disk space. I always set this to Free, and I have never lost anything valuable—but you can be extra cautious and leave it at Convert to Files. (Just remember to go look at these files periodically and delete the junk.)

WHY SCANDISK RUNS AUTOMATICALLY

When you turn off your computer using the Start ➣ Shut Down procedure, Windows 98 SE goes through an orderly process of closing open files, deleting temporary files, and ending its own internal operations. That's what is going on between the time you order the shut down and the time you see the screen telling you it's OK to turn off the computer.

However, if you turn the computer off without going through the shut down procedure, when you start up again, ScanDisk will run automatically *before* Windows 98 SE is launched.

You may have turned the computer off by accident or because applications caused a lock-up; either way, the results will undoubtedly be file fragments, lost files, and other detritus left on the hard drive. It's even possible that a crash could produce errors that could prevent a normal reboot. ScanDisk finds and fixes those sorts of serious errors *and* minor problems that could accumulate and cause trouble in the future.

Check files for   The default is to look just for invalid names, although you can add dates, times, and duplicate filenames if you want. It will slow down ScanDisk's progress, but not dramatically.

Check host drive first   If you have a compressed drive, errors are sometimes caused by errors on the host drive. Leave this box checked so the host drive will be examined first.

Report MS-DOS mode name length errors   What with the mixture of long filenames and the eight-plus-three filenames used in MS-DOS mode, errors can result. Check this box for a report on name length errors.

Fixing Disk Fragmentation

Windows 98 SE is like its Windows and DOS predecessors in that when it writes a file to your disk, it puts it anywhere it finds room. As you delete and create files, over time a single file can have a piece here, a piece there, another piece somewhere else. When a file is spread over multiple places, it's said to be *fragmented*.

This isn't a problem for Windows 98 SE—it always knows where these pieces are. But it will tend to slow file access time because the system has to go to several locations to pick up one file. The Disk Defragmenter in Windows 98 SE addresses this problem, plus it can rearrange the files on your hard disk to improve the speed at which programs start up.

> **NOTE**
> If you are upgrading from a previous version of Windows, you'll notice that Disk Defragmenter no longer reports the fragmentation percentage of a drive. Some specific fragmentation of program files may be desirable for better performance, so the percentage of fragmented files is less important.

As a matter of good housekeeping, you should probably run Disk Defragmenter about once a month. Here's how it's done:

1. Choose Start ➤ Programs ➤ Accessories ➤ System Tools ➤ Disk Defragmenter to open the Select Drive dialog box.

2. Click the drop-down arrow to select the drive you want to defragment. You can also select All Hard Drives from the list.

Chapter Eleven

3. Click OK to start Disk Defragmenter. Once the process starts, you can click Show Details to get a cluster-by-cluster view of the program's progress. Or you can just minimize Disk Defragmenter and do something else. If you write to the hard drive, Disk Defragmenter will start over—but in the background and without bothering you.

If you want to check out Disk Defragmenter options, click the Settings button to open the Disk Defragmenter Settings dialog box as shown in Figure 11.3. Here's what the options mean:

Rearrange program files so my programs start faster. Windows 98 SE keeps track of how often you start each program on your machine and what files are required. Disk Defragmenter can use this information to optimize the location of program files for faster startup. In the process, it deliberately fragments some program files, so you should not use a third-party disk defragmenter (such as Norton Utilities) if you select this option.

Check the drive for errors. Disk Defragmenter checks the drive before defragmenting. If it finds errors, you'll be advised of this fact, and Defragmenter won't continue.

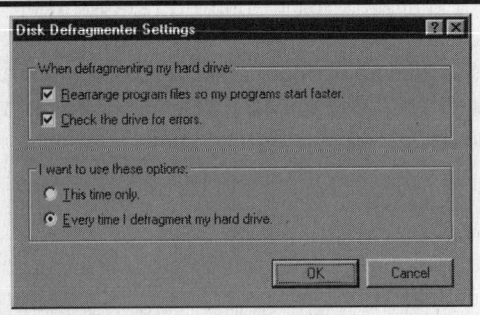

FIGURE 11.3: The Disk Defragmenter options

> **NOTE**
> When Disk Defragmenter finds an error on your disk, run ScanDisk to repair the problem, and then run Defragmenter again.

Select whether these options are for this session only or should be saved for future sessions.

Disk Cleanup

The Windows operating system creates a mass of temporary files and cached files—all designed to speed up the performance of the graphical interface. These files do a pretty good job of it, too, but there are too many of them, and they often don't get deleted when they should be. The result is a lot of files cluttering up your hard drive—files that have inscrutable names and an unknown purpose.

Disk Cleanup is aptly represented as a small broom. When you run it, Disk Cleanup checks for files that can be safely deleted and then presents a listing of such files.

To start Disk Cleanup, choose Start ➤ Programs ➤ Accessories ➤ System Tools ➤ Disk Cleanup to open the Select Drive dialog box. Choose the drive you want to clean up, and click OK. The program runs a check on the selected drive and then opens the Disk Cleanup dialog box, as shown in Figure 11.4.

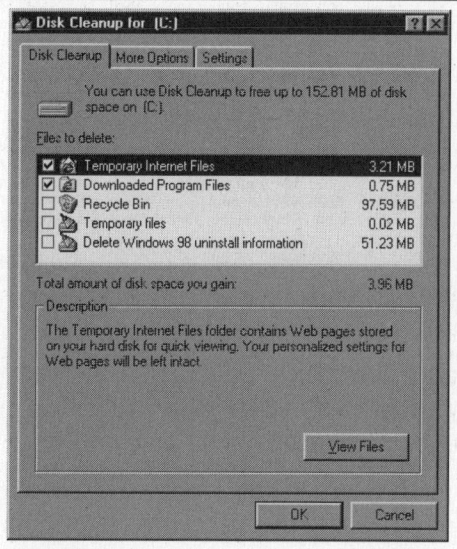

FIGURE 11.4: Disk Cleanup reports on files that can be deleted.

Understand that just because a file *can* be deleted doesn't necessarily mean it *should* be deleted. It all depends on your needs. Some of the categories that Disk Cleanup finds are listed below. Options will vary in each Cleanup window.

Chapter Eleven

Temporary Internet Files These are from various Web sites that you've visited, and they can make reconnecting to a Web site much faster. But there's no point in keeping them around forever. Click the View Files button. Choose Details from the View menu, then click Last Accessed (see Figure 11.5). Delete anything with a Last Accessed date of more than six months ago.

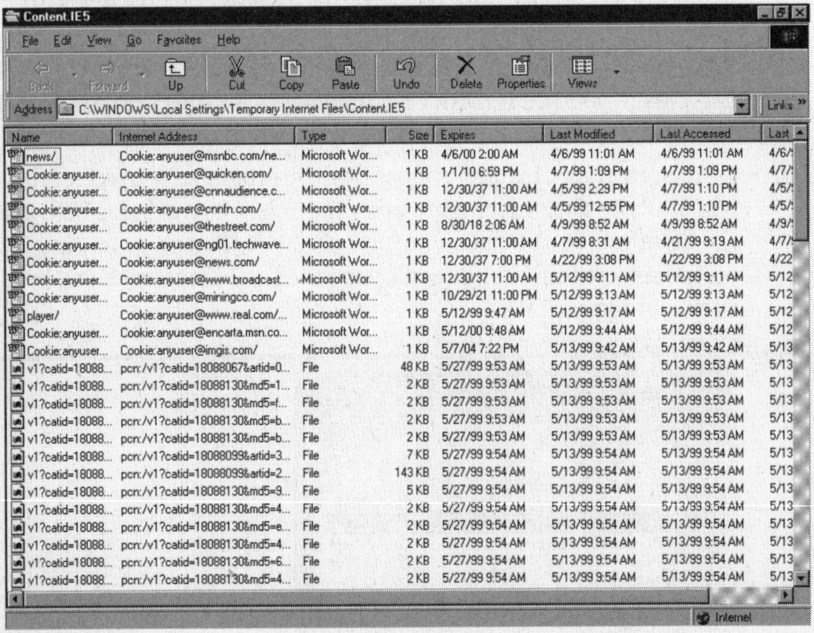

FIGURE 11.5: Select and delete Web files that you haven't used for a long time.

Downloaded Program Files These are also files downloaded from Web sites. They are ActiveX or Java applets that produce effects on the Web pages you've visited.

Old ScanDisk Files in the Root Folder These are the recovered file fragments converted into files described under "Running ScanDisk."

Recycle Bin If the Recycle Bin settings are correctly configured, you shouldn't need to empty the bin to clear space on your hard drive. If the Recycle Bin is too large, reset it to some smaller size (see Chapter 5, *Windows Explorer and the Recycle Bin*).

Temporary Files   These are files created by Windows and Windows programs. In the normal course of events, these are routinely deleted by the operating system. Any that remain to be found by Disk Cleanup can be safely deleted. If you're at all unsure, use Windows Explorer to look at the files in the Temp folder inside your Windows folder. Any files older than a few days are strays and should be deleted.

Temporary Setup Files   Along with Windows setup files, these can be deleted, because a process long since finished created them.

Delete Windows 98 Uninstall Information   These are files you can obviously clear away once you have Windows 98 SE installed and running.

Put a check mark next to the categories you want to delete. The zealousness with which you delete whole categories of files is largely dependent on the amount of hard drive space you can afford to squander. If your available free space consistently hovers at 50MB or less, use Disk Cleanup with as much ruthlessness as you can muster. If you have a more recent multi-gigabyte hard drive, and you have hundreds and hundreds of megabytes of free space, run Disk Cleanup every two or three months just to get rid of the totally useless stuff.

TIP
Click the Settings tab to set Disk Cleanup to run automatically if the drive runs low on space.

NOTE
The More Options tab in Disk Cleanup just offers you alternate paths to the Add/Remove Programs program in the Control Panel (see Chapter 7, *Customizing Windows 98 SE with the Control Panel*) and to FAT32 Drive Conversion (covered later in this chapter).

DOING A SYSTEM TUNE-UP

We're all fallible. We promise ourselves to faithfully do our computer maintenance tasks, and yet they often, in the press of events, don't get done. Fortunately, Windows 98 SE comes with a tune-up application called Maintenance Wizard that—run once—will set up Scan Disk, Disk Defragmenter, and Disk Cleanup to run automatically on a schedule you specify.

To start the Maintenance Wizard, follow these steps:

1. Choose Start ➢ Programs ➢ Accessories ➢ System Tools ➢ Maintenance Wizard.

2. Select the Express option, and click Next. Choose one of three daily time slots for the tune-up process. The easiest, if you don't mind leaving your machine on all the time, is Nights. If you have an older machine that can't go to standby mode to conserve power, you may want to choose a different schedule.

3. Click Next, and the Wizard lists the three tasks to be performed, as shown in Figure 11.6.

   Speed up your most frequently used programs. Disk Defragmenter will run weekly, processing all of your hard drives with the option Rearrange Program Files So My Programs Start Faster.

   Check hard disk for errors. ScanDisk will run weekly with its default settings, checking all your hard drives.

   Delete unnecessary files from hard disk. Disk Cleanup will run at the beginning of each month. It will remove temporary Internet files, downloaded program files, old ScanDisk files in the root directory, and temporary files.

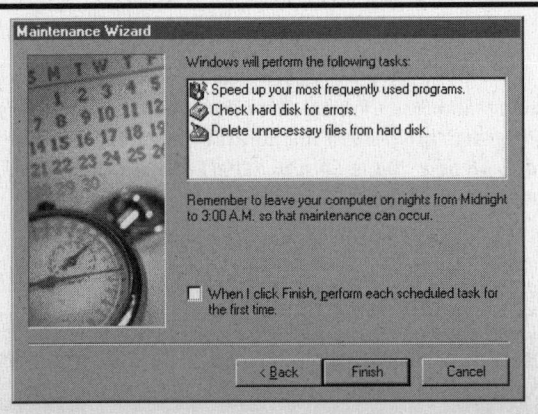

FIGURE 11.6: Here's what the Maintenance Wizard can do for you.

Maintaining the System

4. Click the checkbox at the bottom of the dialog box if you want all the maintenance operations to run for the first time immediately after finishing the setup.

5. Click Finish. Now all you have to do is remember to leave the computer on at the appropriate times so that the programs can run.

You can also choose a custom setup that allows you to make very specific settings for when the programs will run and what their individual settings will be.

Using Task Scheduler

The Task Scheduler icon appears in the System Tray at the right end of the Taskbar on your Desktop. Double-click the icon to open the Scheduled Tasks system folder. If you have already run the Windows Maintenance Wizard, you'll find a list of scheduled tasks already in the folder.

Click the Add Scheduled Task item to run the Scheduled Task Wizard, which will start any program on your computer according to a schedule you decide. The Wizard is simple and straightforward. You choose from a list of all the programs on your computer and then set the schedule. Schedule options include When My Computer Starts and When I Log On, so you can use Task Scheduler to start programs that you always want running when you work.

Windows Update

In years past, bugs or other problems in software were yours to live with until a new version of the software came out. If the maker of your printer or modem didn't produce satisfactory drivers for a particular operating system, you could even be forced to buy new hardware or do without. If you were very knowledgeable, you might be able to download bug fixes from the manufacturer's bulletin board system or, later, their site on the Internet. However, this was an avenue all but closed to the average user.

Windows Update is Microsoft's attempt to resolve this problem of keeping up-to-date by providing a single site for bug fixes, program patches, and hardware drivers.

Chapter Eleven

Choose Start ➤ Windows Update to launch Internet Explorer and connect to the Windows Update Web site (see Figure 11.7). To check for updated drivers or system files, click the Product Updates link.

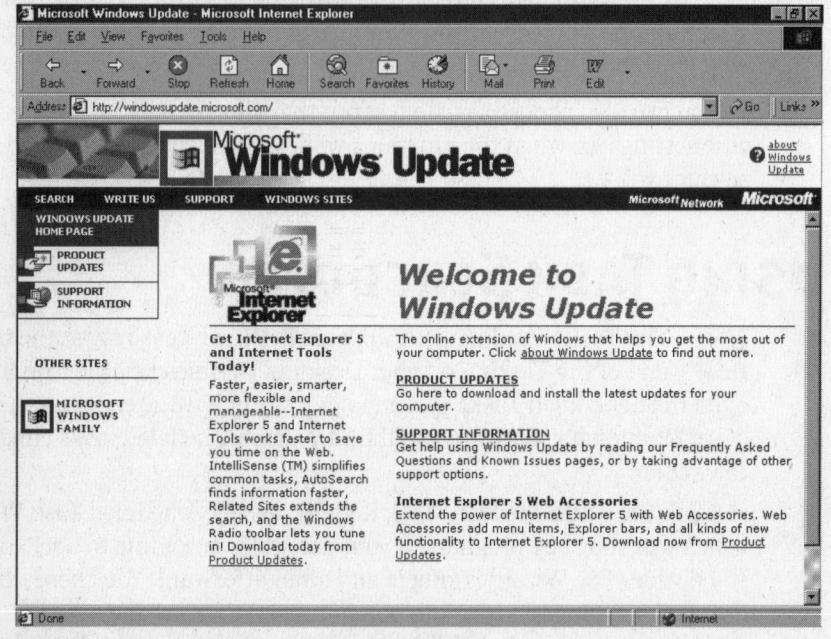

FIGURE 11.7: The Windows Update home page

Before you can upgrade your system, some active components must be downloaded and run by Internet Explorer on your system.

After the necessary components are downloaded, you will see a message that your system needs to be checked to see what files need to be updated, and you are asked if you want your system checked now. Click Yes. When the check is complete, you'll see a list of available updates for your system. To install an update, click it and then click the Download button.

> **TIP**
> A system update requires that the update site communicate with your computer. This means you may have to bypass some security warnings. You are not going to receive any viruses or Trojan horses or other vermin from a Microsoft Web site. However, if you're at all squeamish about letting an automated program scan your system, don't use Windows Update.

Using Space Efficiently

Windows 98 SE takes hundreds of megabytes of hard disk space, and some applications nearly reach that scale. Space can soon be at a premium, even on a large hard drive. Windows 98 SE includes two features that can effectively expand your hard drive by using the space on it more efficiently:

Drive Converter FAT32 Makes more efficient use of drives and partitions over 512MB by reducing wasted space.

DriveSpace 3 Compresses files so they take up less space.

The two systems are unrelated *and* mutually exclusive: You can't use DriveSpace on a FAT32 hard drive.

FAT32 is generally more useful on newer computers, which tend to have hard drives over one gigabyte (1000MB), often in the two to three gigabyte range. DriveSpace is more useful on machines with hard drives of about a gigabyte or less.

> **NOTE**
> A *partition* is a section of a hard drive. Windows 98 SE, like other operating systems, sees partitions as separate drives, although they are located on the same physical hard drive. The drive sizes referred to in discussing FAT32 and DriveSpace actually refer to the size of individual partitions, not the whole physical drive. However, most computer manufacturers format hard drives as one giant partition, so it usually amounts to the same thing.

FAT32

FAT is an acronym for file allocation table. From their beginnings, MS-DOS and Windows have used the FAT system for keeping track of the contents of hard drives. Basically, the directory (or folder) tells the operating system where to look in the FAT, and the FAT stores the list of hard drive clusters, or allocation units, where the file is located.

The system used by DOS in the 1990s, and by the original version of Windows 95, is now called FAT16. It could divide a hard drive into, at most, 65,536 allocation units, which meant that as hard drives got bigger, allocation units also had to get bigger, and large allocation units waste space.

The FAT32 system allows for a much larger file allocation table, which means smaller allocation units and much less wasted space. On a drive in the one to two gigabyte size range, containing about 7500 files (which is typical for a Windows 98 SE machine), the saved space amounts to about 100MB.

Conversion Facts

Microsoft introduced FAT32 in 1996 as an interim improvement to Windows 95, but made it available only to computer manufacturers, to be installed on new machines. So, although you couldn't buy the FAT32 version of Windows 95 in a store, the system has now been installed on millions of computers and is known to be reliable.

There are several limitations on the use of FAT32. The first is that it is not designed for use on hard drives smaller than 512MB, or about 537 million bytes, the units by which hard drive sizes are stated by the manufacturers.

NOTE
The second limitation, described below, does not apply to the Windows 2000 family of operating systems. Windows 2000 can run on and access a FAT32 drive.

The second important limitation has to do with the use of operating systems other than Windows 98 and Windows 98 SE. No other operating system (OS) can read a hard drive formatted with FAT32. If you run other operating systems on your computer (such as Windows NT, Windows 95, DOS, or Unix), they will have no access to drives that you have converted to FAT32. It also means that you cannot dual-boot Windows 98 or Windows 98 SE and any other OS if your C drive is FAT32, nor will you be able to share removable hard drives unless all parties have FAT32.

About the only way to make effective use of FAT32 on a machine that needs to run multiple operating systems is to use a third-party utility, such as System Commander, to choose the OS at start-up time. In that case, you can use FAT32 on the drive where Windows 98 or Windows 98 SE is installed, as long as you don't store any files on that drive that you need to get to when running another OS.

> **NOTE**
> If your computer is connected to a network, other machines on the network still have access to hard drives that you choose to share even if you're using FAT32 and they are not.

Another thing to think about before converting to FAT32 is third-party disk utilities. Most have now been upgraded to work with FAT32, but if you have older versions, you will not be able to use them.

Briefly put, if your hard drive is larger than 512MB, and you plan to run only Windows 98 or Windows 98 SE, you should convert to FAT32. Use only Windows 98 or Windows 98 SE disk utilities or others that specify they are compatible with FAT32.

Converting to FAT32

If you install Windows 98 SE to a newly formatted (empty) hard drive, FAT32 can be part of the installation process. If you install Windows 98 SE over Windows 95 or Windows 3.1, FAT32 will not be used. After Windows 98 SE is installed and running, you can convert your hard drive to FAT32 by using the Drive Converter program.

> **TIP**
> If your computer came from the manufacturer with Windows 95, Windows 98, or Windows 98 SE installed, it may already be using FAT32. To find out, open My Computer and right-click the drive. Choose Properties. On the General tab, you will see File System; it will show either FAT (meaning FAT16) or FAT32.

To convert a partition to FAT32, just follow these steps:

1. To start Drive Converter, choose Start ➤ Programs ➤ Accessories ➤ System Tools ➤ Drive Converter (FAT32).

2. Click Next to open the dialog box shown in Figure 11.8. On many machines, this dialog box will show only drive C. Make your choice, and click Next.

Chapter Eleven

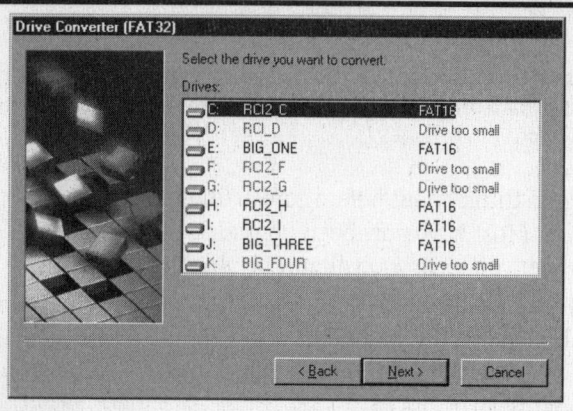

[Drive Converter (FAT32) dialog box showing drives C: through K: with labels RCI2_C (FAT16), RCI_D (Drive too small), BIG_ONE (FAT16), RCI2_F (Drive too small), RCI2_G (Drive too small), RCI2_H (FAT16), RCI2_I (FAT16), BIG_THREE (FAT16), BIG_FOUR (Drive too small), and Back/Next/Cancel buttons.]

FIGURE 11.8: Choose the drive you want to convert to FAT32.

3. Windows 98 SE will then check your system for antivirus programs and disk utilities that are not compatible with FAT32. Once this is resolved, you can click Next.

4. The Wizard will now offer to start Backup so that you can back up your files before converting the drive.

WARNING
Although converting a drive to FAT32 is considered a safe operation, you should always back up important data before starting any task that tampers with your hard drive.

5. After creating the backup, click Next again to see the last dialog box before actual conversion of your drive. Be sure you have closed all running programs, and then click Next.

6. Your machine will reboot to MS-DOS mode and run the conversion. If you use System Commander or another multiboot system, make sure the machine reboots to your Windows 98 SE partition.

> **TIP**
> Although the dialog box in step 5 says the process might take a few hours, the basic conversion to FAT32 actually takes only a few minutes. What *may* take several hours is running Disk Defragmenter, which starts automatically after your drive is converted to FAT32. You can interrupt the defragmentation process if you wish. However, performance of the FAT32 drive will probably be poor until you run Disk Defragmenter and allow it to completely defragment the drive.

Returning to FAT16

Windows 98 SE does not include a converter for going from FAT32 to FAT16. If you find you need to do this, you have two options:

- Back up all your data files on the FAT32 drive. Run FDISK on the partition and choose No to the option to enable large disk support. Then format the drive and reinstall Windows 98 SE and any applications that were on the drive. For more details, see the installation appendices.

- Get a program called Partition Magic, which can convert FAT32 to FAT16 without losing the content. There has to be enough unused space on the drive to allow for the extra space the files will occupy using FAT16. If not, you can first use Partition Magic to change the partition size.

> **TIP**
> Not only can Partition Magic do FAT 32 to FAT16 conversion and resize partitions, it can also move programs from one partition to another without a reinstallation.

Compressing Hard Drives

Another way to make more efficient use of hard drive space is to use disk compression. Disk compression is helpful if you have a serious shortage of space—but in this era of super-cheap hard drives, it's a lot of trouble for a fairly modest return.

Windows 98 SE comes with DriveSpace 3. It will let you:

- Compress and uncompress a hard drive partition or a diskette

- Upgrade a DoubleSpace or DriveSpace compressed drive to DriveSpace 3
- Use your free space to create a new, empty, compressed partition

> **NOTE**
> You cannot use DriveSpace 3 to compress a FAT32 drive; you must use a third-party utility to do so.

Compressing an Existing Drive

To compress a drive, you need only follow these steps:

1. Choose Start ➤ Programs ➤ Accessories ➤ System Tools ➤ DriveSpace.

2. Highlight the drive you want to compress, and select Compress from the Drive menu.

3. The next screen (shown in Figure 11.9) will show before-and-after pie charts for the selected drive.

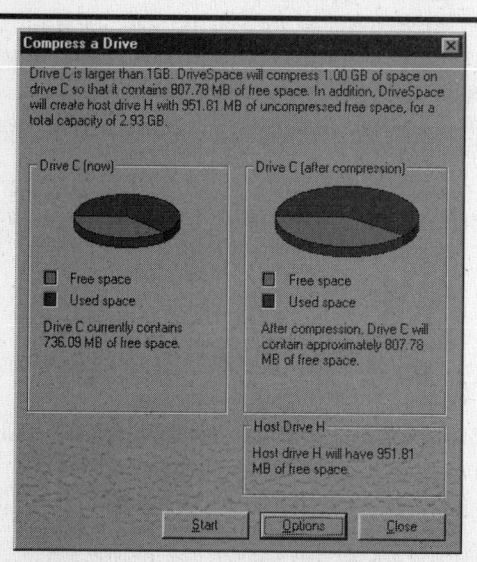

FIGURE 11.9: A drive before and after compression

4. Click Start. You'll be asked if you have an updated Windows 98 SE Startup disk. If you don't have a recent version of the Startup disk, make one now.

5. If you haven't backed up the files on the drive you want to compress, click the Back Up Files button and follow the instructions.

6. Click Compress Now.

7. The drive will be checked for errors, and then, if it's your C drive that's being compressed, you'll be advised that your computer needs to restart. Once you click Yes here, there's no stopping, so be sure you've done all the preparatory steps correctly, and you have something else to do during the time the compression is going on. This process can't be run in the background.

> **WARNING**
> If you're running more than one operating system, be sure the reboot is into Windows 98 SE. This applies equally to reboots that are part of other Drive-Space conversion operations, such as uncompressing, creating a new partition, and adjusting free space.

The compression can take quite a while, especially on the older machines that are most likely to need it because of their limited hard disk space. For example, on a 75MHz 486 laptop with 16MB RAM, compressing 230MB of files took about 90 minutes. At the end of the compression cycle (an on-screen progress bar is displayed), you get a before-and-after report showing the previous space on the disk and new statistics on free space and used space.

How Compression Works

When you compress a drive—let's say your C drive—the whole thing ends up as one big file on a "new" drive called H (by default—though you can give it a later letter in the alphabet). The "new" drive H is called a *host* drive.

When you boot your machine, a DriveSpace command is loaded first. This tells the system to look for this big file and load it, so it looks to all the world like a regular boot into the C drive. Any other compressed drives present when you boot your machine are also recognized and interpreted.

In the Properties dialog box for the host drive, there's an option to hide this drive from view. This is a good option to select, because there's not a thing you can do in a host drive. There's a little bit of free space, but this big compressed file that you can't read and mustn't fool with takes up the rest.

DriveSpace 3 Settings

Choose Advanced ➢ Settings in DriveSpace if you want to control how DriveSpace does its job. You can either set the degree of compression to be used when saving new files or limit the circumstances where compression is used. For a more complete description of each option, click the ? button in the top-right corner, and then click the item for which you want more information.

> **TIP**
> To see the status of compression on a drive, right-click the drive in My Computer. Choose Properties, and then look at the information on the Compression tab.

Uncompressing a Drive

Providing you have room for the data once it's all uncompressed, you can get rid of the compression on a drive at any time. Just follow these steps:

1. Choose Start ➢ Programs ➢ Accessories ➢ System Tools ➢ DriveSpace and highlight the drive you want to uncompress.

2. Select Uncompress from the Drive menu.

3. You'll see a window showing the drive as it is now and as it will be after uncompressing. Click Start to proceed.

4. You'll see a warning about backing up your files. If you haven't backed up the files on the compressed drive, click the Back Up Files button and follow the instructions.

5. Click Uncompress Now.

6. After a while, if this is the only compressed drive on your system, you'll be asked if you want to remove the compression driver at the end of the procedure. Choose:

No If you're still going to be reading compressed removable media (that is, floppies or removable hard drives).

Yes If you're through using any compressed drives for the foreseeable future.

The drive will be checked for errors, and then the computer will restart. Uncompressing will be completed, and the computer will have to restart yet again (if drive C is involved).

> **NOTE**
> Uncompressing takes even longer than compressing. So it's not a task to undertake when you're in a hurry.

Creating a New Partition

DriveSpace can take the free space on your drive and make it into a new partition. This partition will be compressed and will provide more storage space than the amount of space it uses.

To make a new drive in this way, follow these steps:

1. Choose Start ➤ Programs ➤ Accessories ➤ System Tools ➤ DriveSpace.

2. Highlight the drive that contains the free space you want to use, and select Create Empty from the Advanced menu.

3. Accept the suggested settings or make changes as you wish.

4. When you're finished, click Start.

Compression Agent

Compression Agent works with DriveSpace 3 to control and change the degree of compression used on your files. For example, you could improve performance on file save operations by telling DriveSpace to use No Compression (choose Advanced ➤ Settings in DriveSpace). Then you can have Compression Agent compress these files when your computer is not in use.

Open Compression Agent from the System Tools menu. Click Settings to choose the compression options you want. The Overview button in Compression Agent takes you to the DriveSpace Help file, which explains all the options.

Changing the compression method used on files can take a substantial amount of time, so Compression Agent is best run on a regular basis by making use of the Task Scheduler, as described earlier in this chapter.

Backing Up and Restoring Files

Your hard disk has (or will soon have) a lot of material on it that's valuable to you. Even if it's not your doctoral dissertation or this year's most important sales presentation, you'll have software (including Windows 98 SE) that you've set up and configured just so.

Hard disk crashes are really quite rare these days, but if you are unlucky enough to have a crash, not having a recent backup can change your whole perspective on life. So resolve now to do frequent backups of your important files. If you are lucky and/or cautious enough to have a tape drive or other high-capacity backup system, you should also make less-frequent backups of your entire system.

> **NOTE**
> Don't forget, there are two types of computer users. Those who have lost their data and those who back up their files! With the Backup feature, you'll be able to tell Windows 98 SE what to back up, how to do it, where to back it up to, and when to do it. So make sure you are a computer user who backs up your files.

Getting Started

To start the Backup program, click the Start button, then select Programs ≻ Accessories ≻ System Tools ≻ Backup. Your first decision is whether you want Backup to create a set of emergency disks for you to use should your hard drive crash. Creating an emergency set takes lots of disks and will take some time, but it's well worth the effort. Click OK if you want to create a set of emergency disks, and follow the onscreen instructions. Click No if you do not want to create such a set, and continue with the backup.

Maintaining the System

> **NOTE**
> If the Backup program isn't on the menu, you'll need to install it. Go to Add/Remove Programs in the Control Panel and use Windows Setup to add Backup.

Figure 11.10 shows the opening window you'll see when you open Backup the first time.

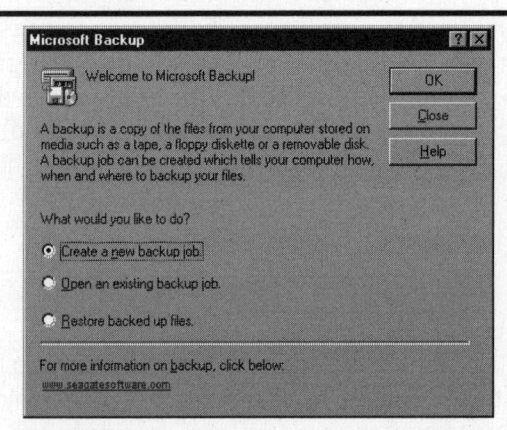

FIGURE 11.10: Your introduction to Backup

Tape Drive or Floppies

If you have a tape drive and it's been installed properly, Backup will find it and prepare to back up to it.

> **WARNING**
> Not all tape drives are supported.

If Windows 98 SE doesn't find a tape drive, it will present you with a message telling you that if you really do have a tape drive, it isn't working and what to do about it. If you don't have a tape drive, just click OK. You'll be backing up to floppies (which you already know about).

> **NOTE**
> If you have two hard drives, backing up from one to the other is as safe as any other method. But you must use two physically separate hard drives, not just different partitions on a single hard drive.

Deciding on a Type of Backup

When you decide that you need to make a backup, it's important to know what you need to back up and where you want the backup to be created. There are three ways to perform a backup. In the Microsoft Backup dialog box, you can create a new backup job (if this is your first backup), open an existing backup job (which you created earlier), or restore files (previously backed up) that you no longer have immediate access to on your hard drive. Click OK when you're done.

Deciding What to Back Up

Before you create a backup, you should know that you don't have to back up your entire system at once. You can back up a group of files or folders or a specific drive on your computer.

> **NOTE**
> When you back up, don't select applications. You should have them on disk or CD anyway. If your computer came with the programs already installed, you may not have the original disks. Contact the manufacturer and ask for a set, or in that case, you may have to make a set for yourself. Better yet, if you can afford it, buy a CD-ROM player you can write to and make your backups there.

Backing Up Everything

You can back up all the files and folders on the local drive or back up just selected files. This means that everything that is on your hard drive will be duplicated on a set of disks or on whatever medium you back up to.

TIP

If your hard disk suddenly sounds like it's full of little pebbles, there's nothing more comforting than having a Full System Backup on your shelf. You should make a Full System Backup when you first install Windows 98 SE, after you install new applications, and occasionally thereafter. But keep in mind, if you do back up to floppy disks, the number of disks you use will be very large—possibly 30 or 40.

You need to tell Backup which folders need to be backed up every day or every week. Once you have a solid backup of your entire hard disk, you'll want to back up only certain folders on a regular basis.

Backing Up Selected Files

Regular backups involve less than the entire hard drive and will probably depend on how valuable certain files are, how difficult they would be to re-create (probably very difficult if it's a document like a college paper or a business plan), and how often they change.

Defining a File Set

If you want to back up all the files and folders on your computer, you need not specify anything else. Backup will back up everything. There's no need to define a set of files or folders. But, if you just want to back up selected files, Backup will create a *file set*.

What is a file set? Backup is based on the idea that you have a large hard disk with perhaps thousands of individual files and perhaps hundreds of different folders. You don't usually want to back up everything on the disk. Usually you'll be backing up a few folders—the folders containing your Corel drawings, your Excel spreadsheets, your WordPerfect documents, your appointment book, your customer database, and so on. A file set is a collection of files that is backed up as a unit and has a unique name. When you use Backup, you create such file sets.

TIP

You might want to make several file sets for backups of different depths. Back up really important folders at the end of every work day (or at lunch) and less important ones at the end of major projects. How to create a backup file set is covered in the following section.

Creating a Backup

In this section we'll create a backup to demonstrate how it's done. If Backup isn't running, start it now. (See the instructions in the "Getting Started" section earlier in this chapter.) Once you get through the initial dialog boxes, you should see the Backup Wizard window shown in Figure 11.11.

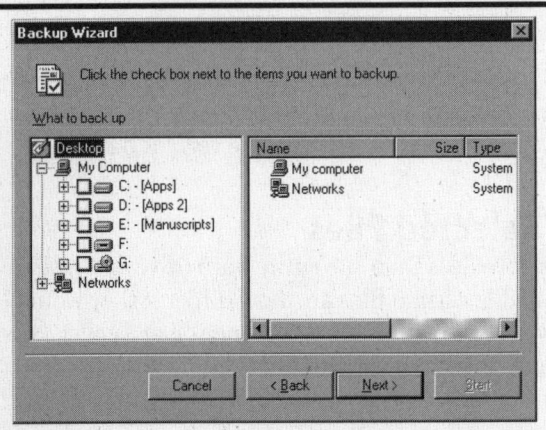

FIGURE 11.11: Designing your backup

Clicking the objects in the section on the left tells Backup which device, folders, or individual files you want to back up.

> **NOTE**
> Each of the drives shown in the Backup window has a tiny checkbox next to it. If you want to back up the entire device—every file and folder from the root to the farthest branch—click this box to automatically select everything. This, in itself, may take several minutes.

Backing Up Particular Files or Folders

Here's how you can back up particular files or folders. For the sake of this example, we'll back up a single file using the Backup Wizard, which is already open on your screen if you've been following along at your computer.

1. Click the plus sign next to the disk that contains the file you want to back up.

Maintaining the System

2. Scroll down the list until you find the file, and then click it to place a check in the box next to it. Your screen will look similar to that in Figure 11.12. Click Next.

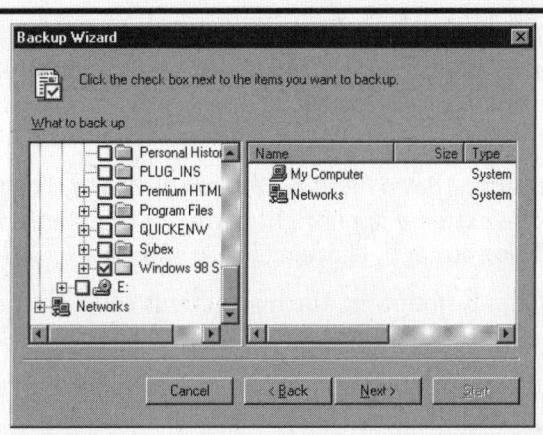

FIGURE 11.12: An individual file ready to be backed up.

3. Specify whether to back up all selected files or only new and changed files, and click Next.

4. Select where you want the backup stored and click Next.

5. Specify backup options. By default, Backup verifies that the data of backed up successfully and compresses the data. Click Next.

6. Enter a name for this backup, and click Start to back up the file.

If you prefer not to use the Backup Wizard, follow these steps to back up a single file:

1. At the first Microsoft Backup dialog box, click Close.

2. Click the plus sign next to the disk that contains the file you want to back up.

3. Scroll down the list and click the file to place a check in the checkbox.

4. In the Where To Back Up section, specify where you want to store the backup.

5. Select options in the How To Back Up section.

6. In the Backup Job box, enter a name for the backup.

7. Click Start.

Backing Up an Existing File Set

Let's do a backup of an existing file set. You'll do this once you've backed up files and folders and made changes that need to be backed up. Here's what to do:

1. Begin by shutting down Backup. (You can do this by clicking the X at the extreme upper-right corner of the Microsoft Backup dialog box or by choosing File ➤ Close.)

2. Start Backup by following the instructions earlier in this chapter in the section "Creating a Backup."

3. When you get to the Backup window, pull down the Backup Job drop-down menu and click the name of the file set.

4. Click Start. Make sure your backup medium (floppy disk or tape) is in the device selected.

Choosing Backup Options

To use Backup's options, click Options to open the Backup Job Options dialog box, which has six tabs:

General   This tab is used to set verification of the backup to the original, determine if data will be compressed to save space or time, and to determine whether backup files will be appended or written over.

Password   This tab is used to assign a password for any backup job.

Type   This tab allows you to specify whether you want all selected files or only new and changed files backed up.

Exclude   This tab lets you set which files should be excluded from the backup. This is a very handy feature because it allows you to exclude hungry, space-eating files, such as those with a .GIF or .AVI extension.

Report This tab provides options for you to design how you want Backup to report the results.

Advanced This tab allows you to back up the Windows Registry.

Drag-and-Drop Backup

You can also drag-and-drop files that you want backed up by first placing Backup on your Desktop as an icon. You can then back up a file by dragging it to the Backup icon and dropping it. Here's how to place Backup on your Desktop as an icon:

1. Choose Start ➤ Programs ➤ Accessories ➤ System Tools.
2. Right-click Backup and drag it to the Desktop.
3. Choose Create Shortcut(s) Here.

When you're ready to back up a particular file, you can find it in Explorer or My Computer and then drag-and-drop it on the Backup icon on the Desktop. This will start Microsoft Backup. Another way to back up a file is to make a folder called Backup. Put shortcuts to your file sets and to Backup inside the folder. If you want, put a shortcut to the folder on your Desktop. Then all you have to do is open the folder and drag the appropriate file to the Backup icon to start a backup.

> **TIP**
> Want some help backing up? Use the Backup Wizard on the Tools menu.

Restoring Files

Restoring is useful for more than recovering from disaster. It's a good way to restore large files that were backed up from your hard disk when they were no longer immediately needed. Now you can restore them and use them again.

Specify where you want files restored from, what files you want restored, where you want the file restored to, and how you want the restore done. Here are the specific steps:

1. Start Backup, and click the Restore tab.
2. If you are asked if you want to refresh the current view, click Yes.

3. In the Select Backup Sets dialog box, click the file that you want to restore, and then click OK.

4. In the Where To Restore section, click the drop-down arrow to specify where you want the file restored to. The default is the file's original location.

5. Click Start.

Options for Restoring

To specify options for the restore, click the Options button in the Restore tab to open the Restore Options dialog box, which has three tabs (whose names and functions are similar to those listed in the "Choosing Backup Options" section earlier in this chapter):

General This tab lets you determine how and when you want files restored that already exist.

Report This tab provides options for you to design how you want to report the results of a restoration.

Advanced This tab allows you to restore the Windows Registry.

WHAT'S NEXT?

As you've seen in this chapter, Windows 98 SE is well equipped with tools for automatically detecting and fixing problems with your computer. The preventive maintenance techniques you've learned here should keep your system running smoothly. But as we all know, "stuff happens." In the next chapter, you'll learn about using the tools that Windows 98 SE provides for troubleshooting your system.

Chapter 12
System Troubleshooting

In general, Windows 98 SE is pretty good at fixing itself. When a problem is detected, ScanDisk or some Plug-and-Play utility jumps into action, finds out the extent of the trouble, and notifies you what action needs to be taken. However, there are occasions when *you* must be the active party. Windows 98 SE includes enough system information and troubleshooting capability so that no fact about the system is hidden, if you're willing to look for it.

Adapted from *Windows 98: No Experience Required*
by Sharon Crawford
ISBN 0-7821-2128-4   544 pages $24.99

Using the System Information Utility

Support technicians require specific information about your computer when they are troubleshooting your configuration. Using the System Information utility, you can quickly find the data to answer their questions, so they can resolve your system problem.

System Information collects your system configuration information and provides a menu for displaying the associated system topics. To access System Information, choose Start ➢ Programs ➢ Accessories ➢ System Tools ➢ System Information. The display is organized into three sections:

> **Hardware Resources** These are hardware-specific settings, namely DMA, IRQs, I/O addresses, and memory addresses. Click Conflicts/Sharing to see devices that are sharing resources or are in conflict (see Figure 12.1). This can help identify device problems.

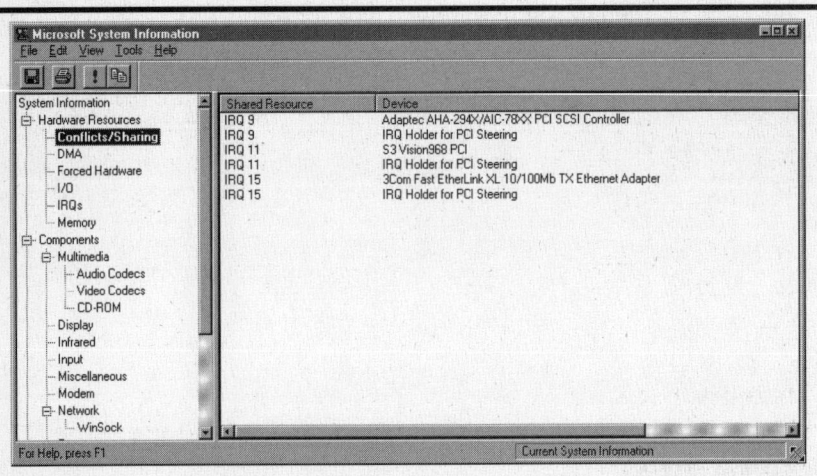

FIGURE 12.1: Checking for IRQ conflicts

> **Components** Here you'll see information about the Windows configuration. You'll see the status of your device drivers, networking, and multimedia software. In addition, there is a comprehensive driver history, which shows changes made to your components over time.

System Troubleshooting

Software Environment This is a view of the software loaded in computer memory. This information can be used to see if a process is still running or to check version information.

Depending on the individual topic, you may be presented with a choice of basic, advanced, or historical system data.

Check the Tools menu for quick access to other diagnostic tools that a technician may ask you to run, such as Dr. Watson, the System File Checker, and the System Configuration Utility.

Meet Dr. Watson

Dr. Watson is a utility that runs in the background and keeps a log of errors that occur. The output of the log may not make much sense to the average user, but it can speak volumes to a service technician.

To run Dr. Watson, follow these steps:

1. Choose Start ➢ Programs ➢ Accessories ➢ System Tools ➢ System Information.

2. Choose Tools ➢ Dr. Watson. The Dr. Watson icon will be placed in the System Tray at the end of your Taskbar.

3. Right-click the icon to open this menu:

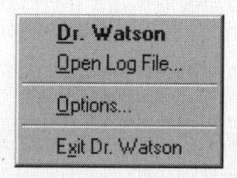

   > Dr. Watson
   > Open Log File...
   > Options...
   > Exit Dr. Watson

4. Choose Dr. Watson from the menu to get a snapshot of current conditions.

5. Choose Options to set how many error conditions Dr. Watson will record and to set the location of the log file (see Figure 12.2).

6. Choose Open Log File to see the incidents recorded by Dr. Watson.

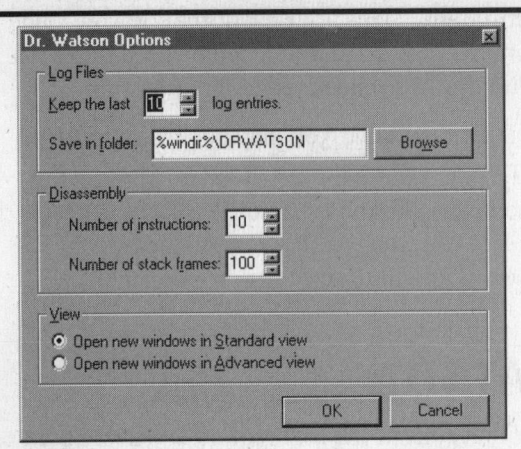

FIGURE 12.2: Settings for Dr. Watson, the system detective

Checking System Files

System File Checker is a utility that scans the system files on your machine, checking for file corruption or other errors. System File Checker maintains a data file with characteristics of your installed system files, so it can recognize unexpected changes.

Run System File Checker only if you're having otherwise inexplicable errors. If a system file turns out to be corrupted, you can also use System File Checker to extract a clean version from the Windows 98 SE installation CD.

To open System File Checker, choose Start ➢ Programs ➢ Accessories ➢ System Tools ➢ System Information to open the Microsoft System Information dialog box. Now, choose Tools ➢ System File Checker (see Figure 12.3).

Click the Settings button to make configuration settings for System File Checker.

If a system file is corrupted or missing, you can extract that file directly from the Windows 98 SE CD. Click Extract One File From Installation Disk. Type in the name of the file or click the Browse button to locate the file. (Make sure the Windows 98 SE disk is in the CD-ROM drive.)

Click Start when you're ready to extract the file.

System Troubleshooting 323

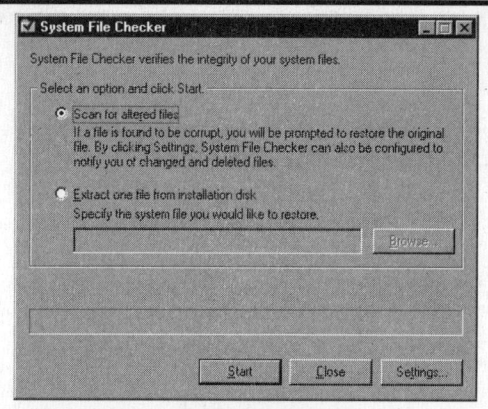

FIGURE 12.3: System File Checker

Using System Monitor

The System Monitor gives you a graphical representation of a number of processes going on inside your computer. If you know what you're looking for, sometimes the information can be helpful.

To open System Monitor, choose Start ➢ Programs ➢ Accessories ➢ System Tools ➢ System Monitor.

In the initial window (shown in Figure 12.4), System Monitor tracks the processor usage. Choose File ➢ Start Logging to display processor usage.

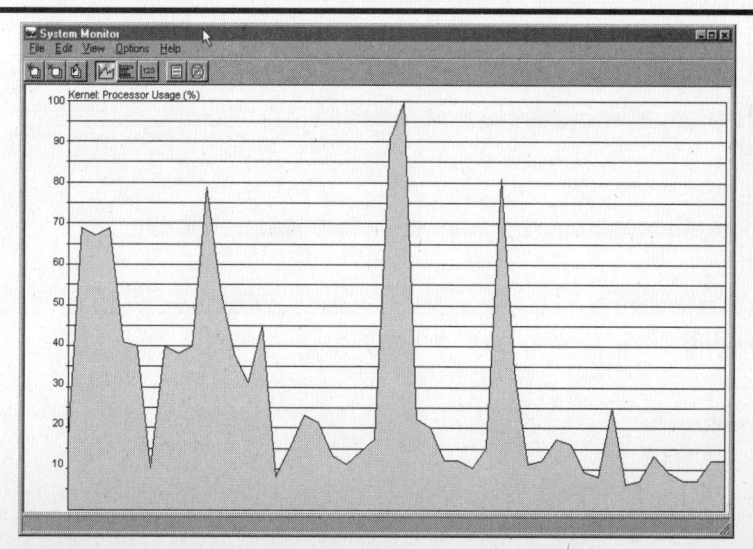

FIGURE 12.4: The System Monitor showing processor usage

324   Chapter Twelve

To track use of other system components, choose Edit ➤ Add Item. Highlight a category (see Figure 12.5), and then select the item you want to view.

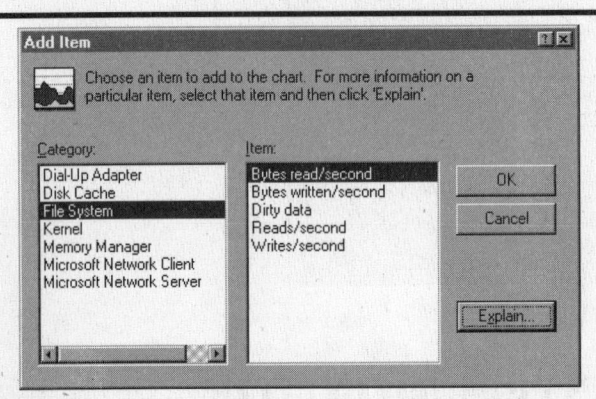

FIGURE 12.5: Choosing the items you want to monitor

On the toolbar, click the Bar Chart button to display the data as a bar chart (see Figure 12.6).

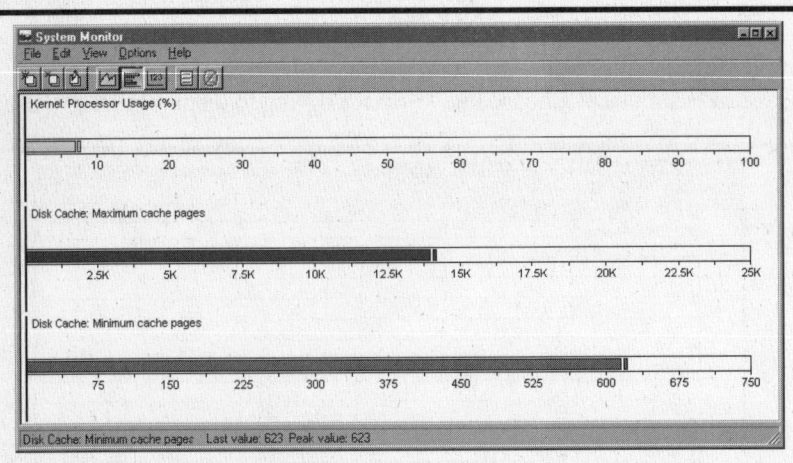

FIGURE 12.6: Viewing three kinds of data in a bar chart

TIP
A numeric graph is also available. Click the Numeric Chart button next to the Bar Chart button to see one.

Using the Resource Meter

The Resource Meter provides visual feedback on the available Windows 98 SE resources. It's pretty hard to run out of resources in Windows 98 SE, but you can get awfully low if you have enough windows open.

To put Resource Meter on the end of your Taskbar, take these steps:

1. Right-click the Start button and select Open.
2. In the window that opens, double-click Programs ➢ Accessories ➢ System Tools.
3. Right-click Resource Meter and select Create Shortcut.
4. Right-click the new shortcut and select Cut.
5. Next, go to the Windows Startup folder, using the Up icon on the toolbar at the top of the window. Click it twice to move up two levels to Programs.
6. Double-click Startup. When the Startup window opens, right-click in an empty area and select Paste from the pop-up menu.

The next time you start up your computer, a small icon will be placed on your Taskbar. Place your pointer on the icon, and a flyover box will open, showing available resources. Or right-click the icon and select Details. A window like the one in Figure 12.7 will open.

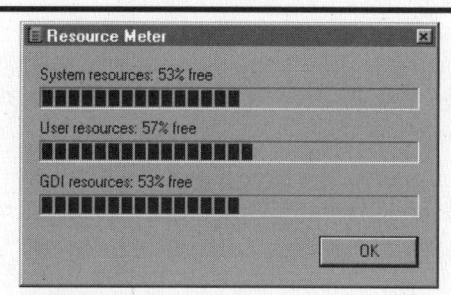

FIGURE 12.7: The Resource Meter in Details view

There's no point in trying to describe what the different resources mean, because the explanation would involve phrases such as *memory heaps* and *device contexts*. Suffice it to say that if any of these numbers starts approaching zero, it's time to close some programs to give yourself more maneuvering room.

> **TIP**
> Sometimes, through no fault of your own, resources will dwindle dangerously, even though you have only one or two programs open. This is because one of those programs—or one you've had open recently—grabbed some resources and isn't letting them go. Blame it on bad programming practices, but the only practical solution is to reboot your computer (and then complain to the maker of the program).

Troubleshooting Tools

Windows 98 SE comes with its own set of relatively smart troubleshooting tools. If you run into a problem, try these troubleshooters first. They work very well, providing you observe some simple rules:

- Make sure you can see the Help window that contains the troubleshooter text while you follow the instructions there.
- Resize the Help window and move it to one side of the screen so you can use the rest of the screen to follow the instructions.
- Always follow the troubleshooter steps *exactly*. If you don't, the troubleshooter can't do its job.
- After you complete a step in a troubleshooter, review the information in the Help window, and verify that you've followed the instructions.

To use a troubleshooter, choose Start ➢ Help. If necessary, click the Contents tab. In the left pane, click Troubleshooting, then click Windows 98 Troubleshooters. The list shown in Figure 12.8 will open.

Select one that seems most appropriate to your problem. You may have to run more than one troubleshooting application to solve the problem.

> **TIP**
> After you start the troubleshooter, click the Hide icon at the top-left corner of the Windows Help window to close the left pane and make more room on the Desktop.

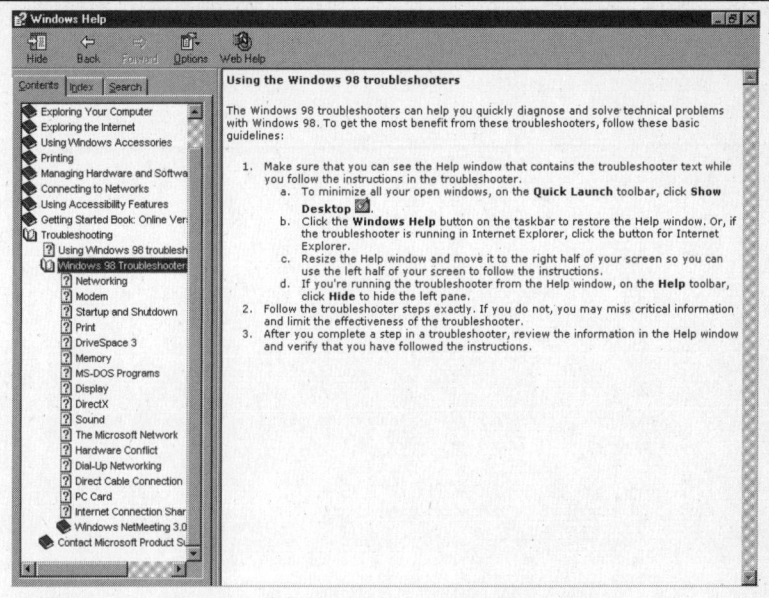

FIGURE 12.8: The list of built-in troubleshooting applications

What's Next?

With any luck, you will rarely, if ever, need to apply what you've just learned about Windows 98 SE troubleshooting.

In the next chapter, Windows expert Mark Minasi shows how you can use Dial-Up Networking (also called remote access) to connect with your Internet Service Provider and to log on to your office network from your home computer or on the road.

Chapter 13

REMOTE ACCESS WITH WINDOWS 98 SE

One of the biggest features Microsoft introduced as an integral part of Windows 95 *Dial-Up Networking* (DUN): the ability to remotely attach to a major network, including the Internet, via a telephone or leased connection. Basically, you'll find that Dial-Up Networking has two main advantages:

- It can often replace whatever software you're using to dial into the Internet.
- It gives you the ability to connect from home to the office network to retrieve data or do remote network administration, and you can even connect to your office network over the Internet, *but in a secure fashion*.

Adapted from *The Expert Guide to Windows 98*
by Mark Minasi, Eric Christiansen, and Kristina Shapar
ISBN 0-7821-1974-3   976 pages $49.99

Dial-Up Networking also has many advantages for people who want to connect with their company's network from their home computers, while on the road, and from other places when they're not at their company's physical location.

One advantage is convenience. If you leave the office and decide to continue working on a project at home, often you'll discover that files you need were not saved to the floppy disk that you brought home with you. One option is to get in your car, drive back to work, and retrieve the files from the network. But wouldn't it be so much easier and more convenient to dial up your network from home and download the files? That's what's known as *telecommuting*.

Another advantage of DUN is remote administration. If you are a network administrator with a pager (and there are very few of you without pagers), you often get that dreaded page at 2:00 A.M. If a user locked himself out of the network (for example, he was having a bad typing day and mistyped his password three times), it becomes your job to either unlock his account or give him a new password. (If someone is actively working at 2:00 A.M., this must be a *very* important project.) Without Dial-Up Networking, you must drive to the office and fix his user account. With Dial-Up Networking, all you have to do is drag yourself to your computer at home, dial up the network, and perform the administrative task. Then—and most important—you get to go back to bed.

In addition to these advantages, Dial-Up Networking is the way many business users and probably most home users connect with their Internet Service Provider (ISP) to access the Internet.

Now all of this probably sounds terrific, but you must be wondering, "How difficult is it to set up?" If you have ever worked with modems and telecommunications, you're probably fearing the adventure ahead of you. Good news! Once you get the terminology down, installing Dial-Up Networking is not that difficult.

This chapter will consider:

- How to set up, configure, and test a DUN connection, including a PPTP connection
- Using the Internet Wizard to set up a DUN Internet connection
- Using WINS to connect to a remote network
- DUN vs. PPTP vs. WINS connections
- Installing a dial-up server

- Security concerns
- Remote access to resources via DUN

Let's begin by considering what remote access actually consists of.

> **NOTE**
> Unlike other books from which we've compiled *Windows 98 Second Edition Complete*, Mark Minasi's *Expert Guide* is addressed to network administrators as well as to users. Most users will only need to read the sections of this chapter through "Using the Internet Wizard." If you need to connect to a Windows NT network, however, or if you have administrative responsibilities for a network, you should read the entire chapter.

What Is Remote Access?

Remote access (also known as *remote-node access*) makes the remote PC a node on the network, rather than the controller of a network PC. The remote PC does all the necessary processing. The remote PC should have on its hard drive all the applications that it will need, to keep the data transfer to a minimum.

So Near, and Yet So Far

Remote access to a network requires a modem, a phone line, a remote PC, and remote-access software on both ends of the connection. In effect, remote access makes the remote PC a node on the office LAN. The phone line acts as a cable that connects the remote PC to the network interface card at the office. To log on to the network, the remote user dials up the remote access server (which, depending on the type of network your company is running and how the servers are configured, may or may not be the same computer as the file server). Once connected, remote users must log on to the network just as they would if using one of the office PCs. (The security measures involved vary from product to product.)

Once logged on to the network, remote users can use the network just like any other user, according to their user rights. When a remote user accesses files, he works on them at the remote computer, only accessing the file server to save the file or to get a new one. Therefore, if the user is running Windows or other graphical user interface (GUI) applications, remote access is a faster option than remote control.

> **NOTE**
>
> *Remote control* is another form of Dial-Up Networking, in which the remote user actually runs applications located on a network server or workstation. It has a number of disadvantages, however, the most important of which is that Windows 98 SE does not support it directly. Therefore, we've omitted coverage of it in adapting this material for *Windows 98 Second Edition Complete*.

Of course, it will still take remote users longer to access files on the server than it will take local users, as remote users must use telephone lines for transmission instead of fast network cable. This is obviously more of a problem with bigger files. When accessing an 11K memo, it's no big deal. Accessing a 1MB *book*, however, will take significantly longer. Since the user is running the application on the remote PC, however, at least the GUI application screen needn't travel through the phone lines; only the data needs to make the trip.

What Are the Setup Options for Dial-Up Networking?

The most common method of implementing Dial-Up Networking will be via a modem. I strongly recommend that you use a modem that follows a useful standard, for example, Hayes compatibility. You definitely want to avoid modems that only talk to their evil twins, such as the High Speed Transmission (HST) modems, which only talk to other HST modems.

Dial-Up Networking does not limit you to connecting via modem. You can use DUN to attach a cable between two machines, which turns them into a small network. DUN supports a direct connection via parallel cable or null modem cable.

Dial-Up Networking also supports *Integrated Services Digital Network* (ISDN) connections. In order to use ISDN for a dial-up connection, you must make sure that ISDN is supported in all the locations that you will be calling to and from.

> **NOTE**
>
> Dial-up networking is the same as *Remote Access Service* (RAS), with which you are familiar if you have used Windows for Workgroups 3.1x or Windows NT. Dial-up networking in Windows 98 SE is more powerful and flexible than WfW's RAS but not as complete as Windows NT's RAS.

What Connection Protocols Are Supported by Dial-Up Networking?

PPP The protocol of choice for connecting with Dial-Up Networking is the *Point-to-Point Protocol* (PPP). Microsoft has designed most of its remote access and dial-up connectivity around this protocol. At the speeds at which most of us will conduct our Dial-Up Networking (128Kbps or less), the primary advantage of PPP is that the connection does error checking of data and data compression during the transmission process. This makes for faster and more secure data transfer. Another reason to consider using PPP is that it has pretty much become an industry-wide standard.

> **NOTE**
> If you are using PPP, you can connect to a network using IPX/SPX, TCP/IP, NetBEUI, or any combination of the three. Because of its power and flexibility, PPP is the default protocol when installing Dial-Up Networking.

PPTP A variation on PPP, through *Point-to-Point Tunneling Protocol* (PPTP), multiprotocol virtual private networks can allow remote users to access a private network via a secure connection over the Internet or other public IP networks. For example, if a user wants to access her company's computer from her laptop while she's on the road, she can connect to the Internet—if she has a local access number, she'll even avoid long-distance charges—and then use this connection to access her company's network without having to dial into it directly. PPTP works by enclosing PPP packets within *Internet Protocol* (IP) packets and sending them out over the Internet or any IP network.

NetWare Connect Novell uses software known as NetWare Connect to allow remote clients to dial up to the network. Windows 98 SE comes with a NetWare Connect client, which allows your Windows 98 SE machine to attach to a NetWare Connect server directly, without going through a Microsoft gateway of any type. Even though Windows 98 SE machines can connect to a NetWare Connect server, it is not a reciprocal relationship; NetWare Connect clients cannot dial in to a Windows 98 SE server.

RAS Dial-Up Networking supports RAS as implemented by Windows for Workgroups 3.11 and Windows NT 3.1. (Windows NT 3.5x and 4 default to using PPP.) You may see this RAS option referred to as *asynchronous NetBEUI* in some systems' help files or in network documentation.

SLIP An older protocol standard is the *Serial Line Interface Protocol* (SLIP). Unlike its PPP counterpart, SLIP does not perform error checking or data compression while transmitting data; the responsibility for performing these functions is placed on your hardware. This is not a bad thing, since most of today's modems *do* perform these functions.

> **NOTE**
> Microsoft recommends against using SLIP except when dialing up a Unix network that is using a dial-up server with TCP/IP.

What Are the Different Combinations for Connection Protocols and Network Protocols?

There are two parts to Dial-Up Networking: the dial-up *server* and the dial-up *client* (the remote user's machine). Let's take a look at the various combinations from that perspective. The information is summarized in Table 13.1.

TABLE 13.1: Various Combinations of Connection and Network Protocols

Clients	Server
TCP/IP over SLIP	Unix remote server, Internet (SLIP Router)
IPX over NetWare Connect	NetWare Connect Server
IPX, NetBEUI, and/or TCP/IP over PPP	Internet (PPP Router), Windows 98 SE, Windows 98, Windows 95, Windows NT RAS Server, and NetWare
NetBEUI over RAS (Asynchronous NetBEUI)	Windows 98 SE, Windows 98, Windows 95, Windows NT, Windows for Workgroups 3.11, and LAN Manager Servers
TCP/IP over PPTP	Windows 98 SE, Windows 98, Windows NT 4

How Do I Install Dial-Up Networking?

Installing Dial-Up Networking is a two-step process:

1. You must install the Dial-Up Networking software onto your client machine and onto your host PC or server.
2. You must configure the Dial-Up Networking software as either client or server.

Installing Dial-Up Networking on the Network

If you selected Typical when you installed Windows 98 SE, Dial-Up Networking is installed by default. If Dial-Up Networking is not installed, for whatever reason, follow these steps to install it on your company's host PC or server:

1. Click Start ➤ Settings ➤ Control Panel.
2. Select Add/Remove Programs to open the Add/Remove Programs Properties dialog box.
3. Select the Windows Setup tab, as shown in Figure 13.1.

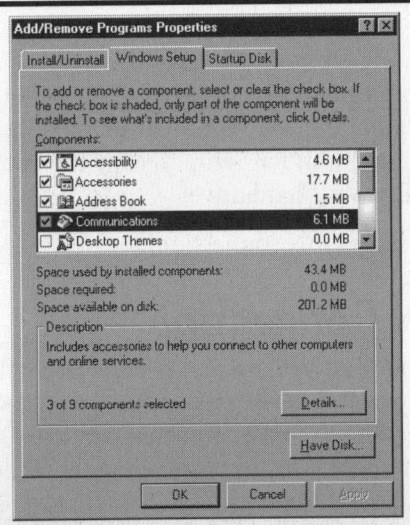

FIGURE 13.1: Going to Windows Setup to install DUN

4. Click the Communications option, and then select Details.

5. Select Dial-Up Networking from the list, as illustrated in Figure 13.2. If you want your PC to act as a dial-up server, you'll want to check Dial-Up Server, as well. If you want to set up a Virtual Private Networking (VPN) connection, check the last box on the list to install the Microsoft VPN adapter. You can also do this through the Control Panel, as described later in this chapter.

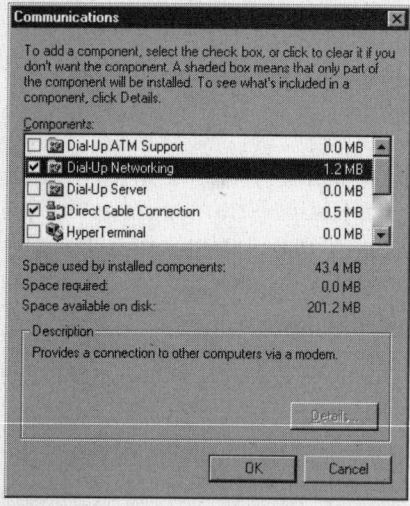

FIGURE 13.2: Adding DUN from Communications Details

6. Click OK to return to the main window to continue with the setup. Make sure your Windows 98 SE CD-ROM is in its drive; then click OK, and wait for Setup to copy the necessary files from the CD to your hard drive.

Next you'll need to configure the DUN connection.

Configuring the DUN Connection

Good news! You do not have to restart your system in order to configure Dial-Up Networking (although you will have to reboot your machine before you can use it). To configure the connection on a Windows 98 SE server, skip ahead in this chapter to the section "Installing the Windows 98 SE Dial-Up Server." To configure the connection on a Windows 98 SE client machine, read on.

Installing Dial-Up Networking on the Client Machine

The first step to installing Dial-Up Networking software on a remote machine is to install all the *protocols* the remote user might need and bind them to the *dial-up adapter*:

1. On the remote machine, go to Control Panel and choose Network to open the Network dialog box.

2. Select Dial-Up Adapter, and then click Add to open the Select Network Component type dialog box, as shown in Figure 13.3. You need to install an adapter for Dial-Up Networking, so click Adapter, and then click Add.

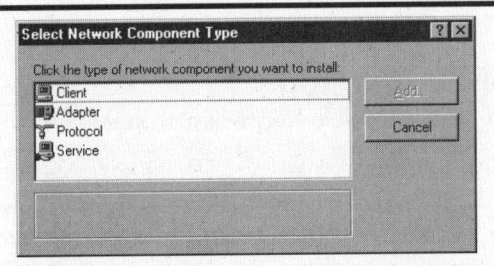

FIGURE 13.3: Different component types

3. You'll get a listing of companies whose adapters have been included in Windows 98 SE. Figure 13.4 shows the adapters supplied by Microsoft. You'd choose the top one, Dial-Up Adapter, to set up most dial-up connections. But notice the third option, Microsoft Virtual Private Networking Adapter. If you want to set up a PPTP connection, you must select this option if you haven't set up the adapter in Add/Remove Programs in the Control Panel, as described earlier.

And while you're in Control Panel, if you want to set up a DUN connection to access an NT domain, you'll need to synchronize your Windows and networking passwords using the Passwords applet and network identification (name of NT domain) in the Network applet; you can read about this later in this chapter, in the section on setting up a WINS connection.

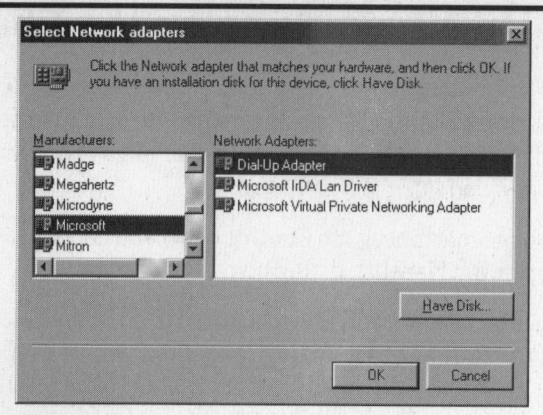

FIGURE 13.4: Microsoft network adapters

Creating a DUN Connection

The next step is to create a new Dial-Up Networking connection:

1. Go, or have the remote user go, to the DUN folder in My Computer and, within the folder, choose the Make New Connection option. As you can see in Figure 13.5, you'll be asked what you want to call this connection (I have multiple ISPs and DUN connections, so I designate each with the name of the company or ISP I'm connecting to) and the device over which the connection is to be made, in most cases via your computer's modem.

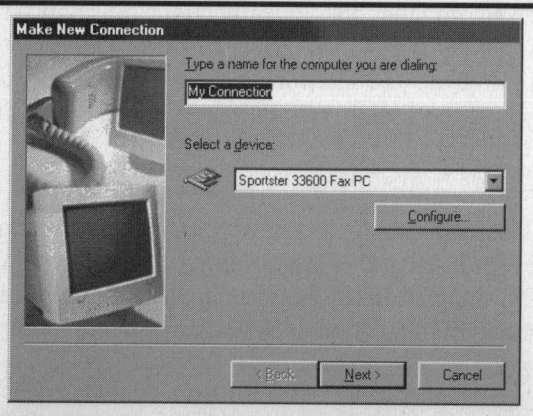

FIGURE 13.5: Setting up a DUN connection

Remote Access with Windows 98 SE

2. Then you'll be asked for the telephone number of the computer to which the connection is being made (as shown in Figure 13.6). Supply the necessary information, click Next, and then click Finish. This creates a Connection icon in the Dial-Up Networking folder.

> **TIP**
> If you have Call Waiting, you might want to use the *70 prefix to turn off this feature when making the connection.

> **NOTE**
> If you want to set up a connection to the Internet, you can use the Internet Connection Wizard instead of following the steps detailed here. You can read about this Wizard later in this chapter.

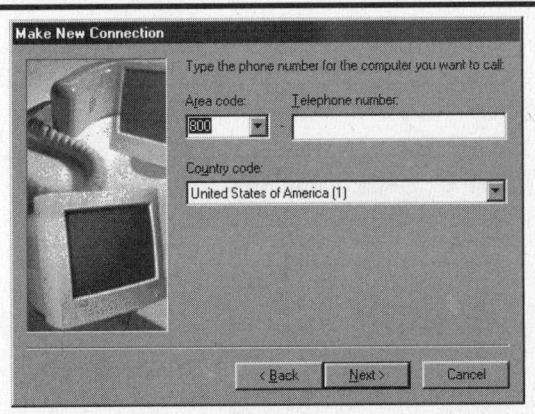

FIGURE 13.6: Entering the telephone number of the computer to be accessed

What About Setting Up a PPTP Connection?

The process is slightly different if you want to set up a PPTP DUN (ah, that acronymic alphabet soup) connection. (This assumes, of course, that the system administrator of the network you want to access via PPTP has installed a PPTP server. If in doubt, ask.) Remember that you first have to install the VPN adapter via Control Panel ➢ Add/Remove Programs ➢ Windows Setup ➢ Communications or via the Network dialog box, as described earlier. After doing this and rebooting, go into Dial-Up Networking ➤ Make New Connection, and you'll have another choice of modem type, as shown in Figure 13.7.

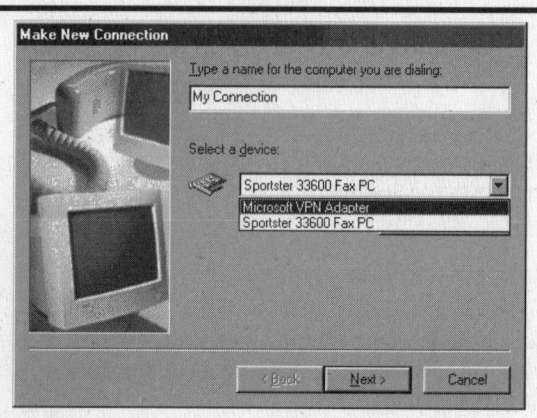

FIGURE 13.7: Setting up a PPTP connection

In the next dialog box, enter the IP address RAS server of the domain you'll be connecting to via PPTP. Figure 13.8 shows such an IP address. Enter the correct address; then click Next.

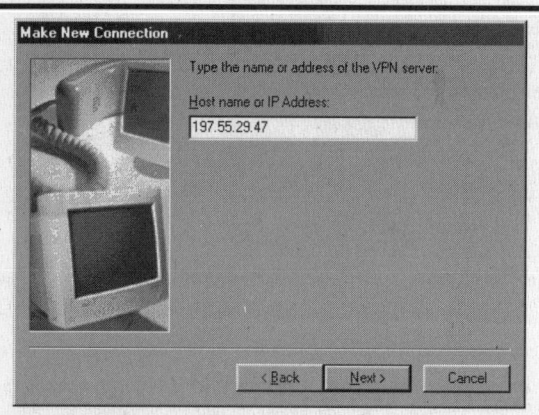

FIGURE 13.8: Specifying the IP address of the VPN server

Whether your new connection is a regular DUN or PPTP connection, the next screen, which you can see in Figure 13.9, will tell you that your new connection has been set up. If you're done, click Finish.

> **NOTE**
> Later, if you want to edit the properties of any DUN connection you've set up, you can do so by going to the Dial-Up Networking folder, right-clicking the connection you want to edit, and selecting Properties. See the section on configuring a dial-up connection for more info.

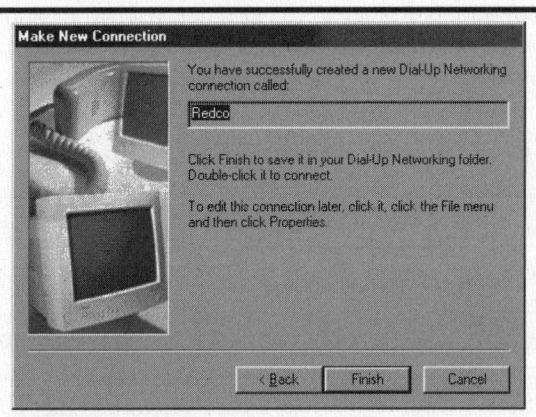

FIGURE 13.9: The connection has been set up.

> **TIP**
> If the DUN connection is to an NT domain, you must also specify the domain name in the Network applet in Control Panel, both in the Identification tab *and* in the Client For Microsoft Networks Properties dialog box. Otherwise, you may be able to connect, but you won't be able to "see" anything on the network.

Once you have created the DUN connection, you can double-click the Connection icon at any time to dial up to the network. The DUN setup program may ask for the name of the server or domain you want to log on to, as well as a password. DUN will then dial the location, verify the username and the password, and if everything checks out, allow access to the server. At this point, you can now do anything you normally could if you were local to the network (only more slowly).

Use DUN to Access Data, Not Applications

I strongly recommend that remote users do *not* attempt to run applications across the DUN connection; they should use DUN to get only data files and information. For example, if you choose to start a network copy of Microsoft Word from your remote DUN location, it could easily take more than 45 minutes for the application to begin, because the entire program would have to be transported via modem to the memory of your remote DUN machine.

> **TIP**
> DUN is designed with data in mind. The best implementation of DUN is a remote DUN machine that has its applications loaded locally and the data files on a network server.

Configuring a DUN Client Connection

To configure a DUN client connection, simply right-click the Connection icon that was created in the preceding section and select Properties.

Your first major decision here concerns the type of server you will be dialing up via this connection. If you typically dial to the same site, but you know that sometimes you'll want to connect via RAS (asynchronous NetBEUI) and other times you'll want to connect via NetWare Connect, use Make New Connection and create two separate connections. Then whenever you go to make your connection, you can choose from a pair of Connection icons.

You can see your choices for Type of Dial-Up Server in Figures 13.10 and 13.11.

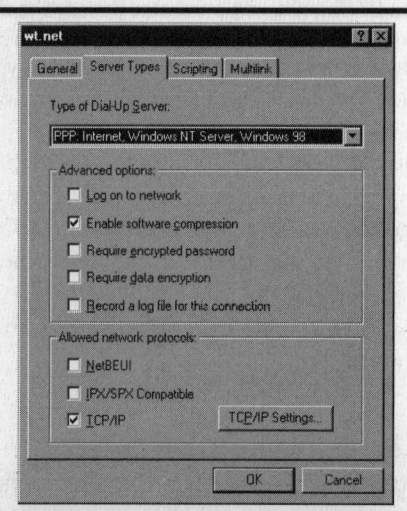

FIGURE 13.10: The Server Types tab

Remote Access with Windows 98 SE

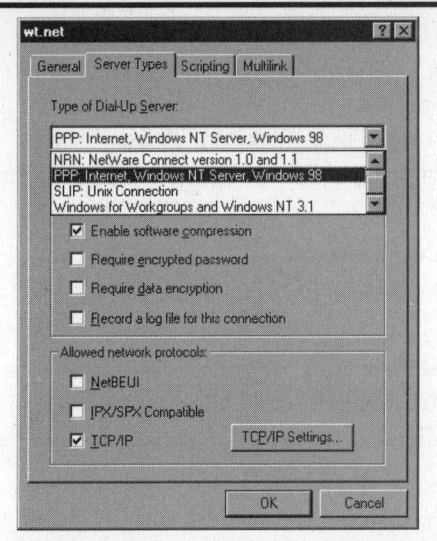

FIGURE 13.11: Types of dial-up servers

> **NOTE**
> Remember that *server* here refers to the computer you'll be connecting to, not a Windows 98 SE server you're setting up on your own machine.

Let's take a look at some of the options available on this screen:

PPP   This option is used for dialing into RAS servers that are using TCP/IP, IPX, NetBEUI, or any combination of the three. DUN will automatically detect which of the three to use, based on the protocols you select at the bottom of the screen. Use this option for dialing into a Windows 98 SE, 98, or 95 dial-up server or an NT 4 RAS server.

NRN   This option is used for connecting to a NetWare Connect server.

SLIP   This option is used for any implementation of SLIP of the TCP/IP protocol.

Windows for Workgroups and Windows NT 3.1   This option is used when dialing into a WfW RAS server or an NT 3.1 server.

Advanced options:

Log on to Network   This option will dial up and log you in to the network using the username and password you typed in when you logged in to Windows 98 SE. If this option is not selected, you will be asked for a logon name and password every time you attempt a new connection.

Enable Software Compression   This option will compress the data before it is sent to the modem (or the like) for transmission.

Require Encrypted Password   This option enables a feature known as the Challenge Handshake Authentication Protocol (CHAP). CHAP is discussed in greater detail later in this chapter.

Require Data Encryption   If you select this option, any information that is transferred using this connection must be encrypted.

Record a Log File for This Connection   Select this option if you want to keep track of when you use this connection or attempt to do so.

This screen is also where you specify the protocols that you want the DUN connection to support. If you want to configure a connection to the Internet, click the TCP/IP settings. This option, shown in Figure 13.12, will ask for information that you may need to get from your network administrator or your Internet Service Provider.

As you saw in Figure 13.11, there are other tabs with options you can select. The General tab, shown in Figure 13.13, contains pretty much the same options you chose when setting up the connection in the first place, giving you the chance to change them if necessary. The Scripting tab, shown in Figure 13.14, lets you specify the script to be run when this connection is made. The Multilink tab, shown in Figure 13.15, lets you add additional devices to make the connection. So, for example, if you want to increase the speed of the connection and you have two modems installed, you would use this tab to set up the second modem to be used in making this connection. Figure 13.16 shows how you can choose the second modem and configure it with the correct phone number for the connection.

Remote Access with Windows 98 SE 345

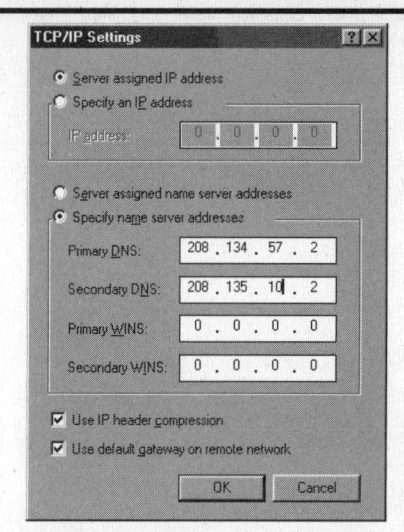

FIGURE 13.12: Specifying TCP/IP settings

FIGURE 13.13: General DUN options

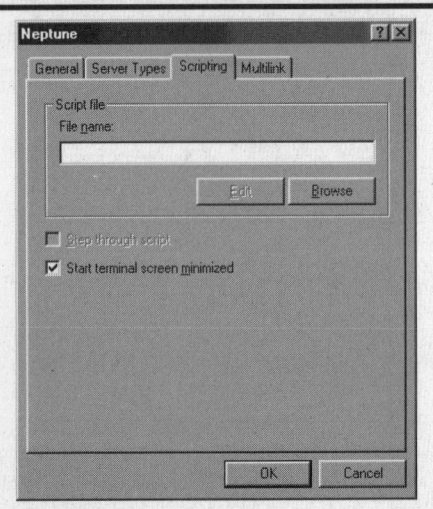

FIGURE 13.14: Specifying a DUN script

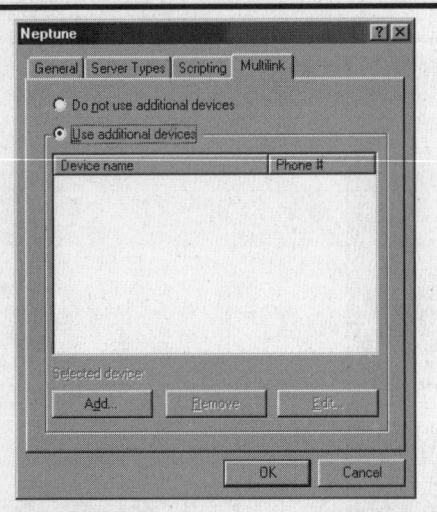

FIGURE 13.15: Setting up a multilink connection

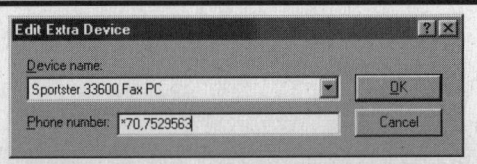

FIGURE 13.16: Specifying additional modems and telephone numbers

How Do I Test the DUN Connection?

Once you have configured your DUN connection, just double-click and the connection will be made immediately. You should see the lights of your modem flashing, and, if you have enabled the modem speaker, you should hear the lovely and distinctive squelching noise that indicates that Windows 98 SE is negotiating a connection.

Whether you're using a regular dial-up connection or a VPN connection to connect to an NT domain, you'll see a User Logon box like the one shown in Figure 13.17. Once you've filled in the boxes, click OK to make the connection. If you're using DUN to connect to your ISP, if your Windows network password is the same as you use for this connection, and if you've checked the Log On To Network box under Server Types in Properties for the connection, you'll bypass this step when logging on to your ISP. Otherwise, you'll see the same screen but without the Logon Domain line. Fill in your password, and you'll be connected.

You can then map network drives, see the other computers on the network via Network Neighborhood, and do whatever network functions you have permission to do.

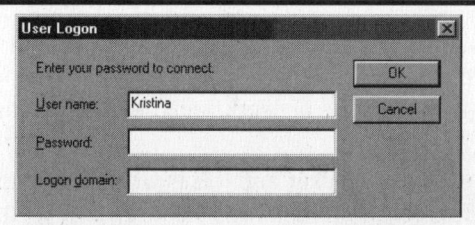

FIGURE 13.17: Logging onto an NT domain

Using Microsoft's Universal Naming Convention (UNC), you should now be able to access any network resource for which you have permission. Or, if you're connecting to your ISP, you should be able to connect to any Internet service your ISP connection allows (e-mail, the World Wide Web, and so on).

> **TIP**
> When you are connected to a network, you can go to the Connected To window and see the number of packets sent, number of packets received, and the overall status of your connection.

Once you have established a connection for the first time, Dial-Up Networking will be activated in any of the following circumstances:

- When you select a network resource that is not part of your network
- When a UNC directs you to a network resource (for example, \\server\public_)
- When an application calls for a network resource

SHORTCUTS TO POPULAR NETWORK INFORMATION

If you need to dial up to many different networks, shortcuts are a great way to organize all your frequently visited sites. Shortcuts also get you quickly to the information on those networks that you use most frequently.

Without shortcuts, I have to take the following steps every time I want to connect to my home directory at work:

1. Open the My Computer folder.
2. Open the Dial-Up Networking folder.
3. Select my connection. (In my case, it's MMCO Office.)
4. Provide a password.

At this point the system starts to negotiate the connection and to authenticate me to the network. After validation, I map a network drive to my home directory on the network, and *then* I can access my files.

All this gets a little tiresome quickly, and this is where shortcuts come to the rescue. To create a shortcut to my home directory, I still follow the above steps the very first time I connect, but I let Windows 98 SE automatically create a shortcut to the directory by clicking and dragging my network home directory folder to the Desktop.

From that point on, if I want to get to my home directory, I just double-click its shortcut. Windows 98 SE will now automatically call the network, validate me to the network (assuming my Windows 98 SE logon and network logon are identical), and take me to my home directory. If I am already connected to the network, the shortcut is still a useful way to fly directly to my home directory.

Using the Internet Connection Wizard

If you want to set up a connection to the Internet, you can also use the Internet Connection Wizard (ICW) in Windows 98 SE to configure a connection to your ISP(s). Choose Start ➤ Programs ➤ Accessories ➤ Internet Tools ➤ Internet Connection Wizard. You'll see a screen like the one shown in Figure 13.18.

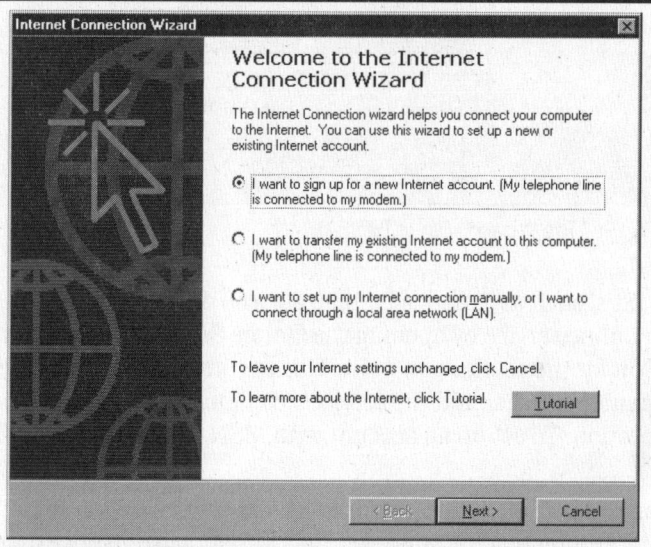

FIGURE 13.18: Using ICW to set up an Internet connection

Basically this screen gives you the chance to set up a new connection to the Internet, to transfer an existing connection to this computer, to set up a connection manually, or to connect through a LAN.

If you want to set up a new connection, select the first option and click Next. Then your computer will dial a toll-free number to get a list of the ISPs in your area or, failing that, of national ISPs, and give you a listing, similar to that shown in Figure 13.19.

To establish an account with one of the providers, click Next, and, if necessary, fill in the boxes with the appropriate information. Continue to follow the instructions on the screen to set up your account.

350 Chapter Thirteen

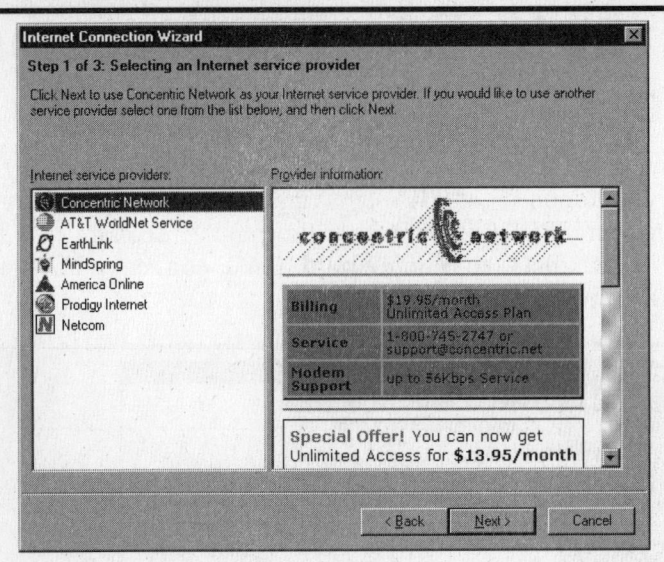

FIGURE 13.19: The Wizard's list of ISPs

Some ISPs, such as America Online, are also online services. You can set up an online service by opening the Online Services folder and clicking the icon for the service you want. This results in the same procedure: Your computer will dial into the service's computer to set up the account and connection. To set up an account with MSN, click Setup MSN Internet Access.

This option is useful if you prefer to have your connection to the Internet set up "automatically." However, the ISP listing isn't very extensive. Fortunately, setting up an Internet connection following your ISP's instructions for Dial-Up Networking and setting up your e-mail and other services is usually not difficult—many ISPs post instructions for doing this on their Web sites.

If you want to reconfigure an existing connection and you want to use Outlook Express as your e-mail, news, and Internet Directory client, you can change the details of your e-mail and news servers, and so on. (You can also change the telephone number you use to dial in with.) If you want to use other programs for these functions, such as Pegasus Mail or Netscape Navigator, don't use ICW to set them up—use the setup functions within these independent programs.

Altering an Internet Connection

If you want to alter the details of an existing connection, or if your ISP isn't on Microsoft's list and you want to use Outlook Express, click the third radio button of the initial ICW screen. You're then taken through a series of questions: Do you connect via a regular phone line or a LAN? Does your ISP's server use a proxy? Do you want to set up a new Internet mail account? A news service? and so on. You can also change the telephone number by which you connect to your ISP. You'll want to know the answers to these questions before you start.

For instance, say you want to create a new Internet mail account. You'll check the box next to that option, click Next, and then fill in your name, e-mail address, and then the mail-server info asked for in Figure 13.20. You need to get this information from your ISP. (If Windows doesn't think you've typed in a valid server name, you'll get nagged.)

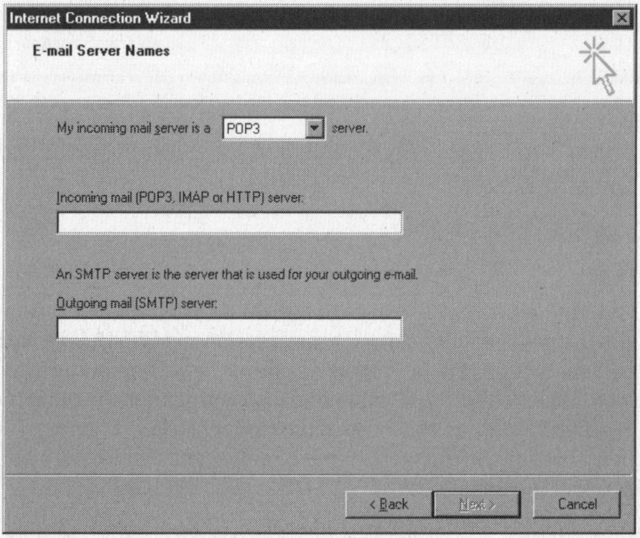

FIGURE 13.20: What type of mail server?

Next you'll be asked for your logon info (account name and password, and whether you log on using *Secure Password Authentication*, or SPA). Click Next, and then click Finish to connect to your ISP.

Sample ISP Information

If you need to fill in this information manually for your ISP(s), Table 13.2 shows an example of the information your ISP must provide so that you can do so.

TABLE 13.2: Setup Information Taken from an Actual ISP and Modified

Server	Location	Function
NNTP Server	newsdesk.worldwide.net	(News)
SMTP Server	postmaster.worldwide.net	(Outgoing Mail)
POP3 Server	postoffice.worldwide.net	(Incoming Mail)
FTP Host	ftp.worldwide.net	(Personal Sites)
FrontPage	ftp.worldwide.net	(FrontPage Sites)
Primary DNS	208.85.53.2	(Name Server #1)
Secondary DNS	198.85.50.2	(Name Server #2)

In the Server Types Tab, only Enable Software Compression and TCP/IP should be checked.

> **NOTE**
> You set up the first options in each individual program, but this last set of options, namely, enabling software compression and TCP/IP, is set up by going to the Server Types tab in Properties of the connection in the Dial-Up Networking folder. You set the telephone number and name of the connection when setting it up initially as described in the earlier section "Creating a DUN Connection," but you can change the phone number and dialing and modem properties under the General tab.

Using WINS to Connect to an NT Domain over an Existing Internet Connection

If you have an existing connection to the Internet, there's another way to connect to (and log on to) a remote NT network: by exploiting that remote network's WINS servers. If you have the right information, it's a fairly simple matter to set up a WINS connection to an NT domain, say, between your home computer and your network at work. You need the machine name of the networked computer you want to access, and the information you need to access the network it's on: password, domain name, and WINS specification of the network's domain server.

> **TIP**
> If the network you're trying to access is behind a firewall, you won't be able to connect to it via WINS. Use PPTP (described earlier in this chapter) instead. Even with PPTP, however, the people administering the firewall must have opened the firewall to PPTP before you can PPTP to a network behind the firewall.

Here are the four steps to connecting to an NT domain via WINS:

1. Set your Windows and Windows Network passwords to be identical to your password in the office. Your username should also match the username you employ in the office.

2. Point your TCP/IP software to the IP address of the WINS server in the office; this makes it easier for your computer to locate NT domain controllers in the office network. Alternatively, you can create an LMHOSTS file to achieve the same results—this often works where WINS fails.

3. Set the workgroup for your Windows 98 SE machine equal to the name of whatever NT domain your workstation at work uses.

4. Connect to the Internet, and you should be able to access the office network—again, assuming that the office doesn't use a firewall!

In step 1, you synchronize your Windows and Windows Networking passwords via the Passwords applet in Control Panel. If they differ, you won't be able to make the connection. First go to Control Panel ➢ Passwords. Since you'll probably need to change your Windows password, click the Change Windows Password button, fill in the old Windows password, and then fill in the password you need to use to access the NT domain and again to confirm the change, and click OK. You'll need to reboot for the change to take effect. (If you already have a Network password as well, you can check a box to change it to the new password at the same time. Or, if your Windows password is correct but you need to change your Network password, click Change Other Passwords and follow the instructions.)

WORKAROUND FOR POSSIBLE PROBLEMS WITH CHANGING NETWORKING PASSWORDS

When writing this section, I was dutifully changing Network and Windows passwords as necessary without trouble via the Passwords applet in Control Panel. But for some reason, one day I ran into major problems trying to change the Network password when my machine was set up for connection to a domain in the Network applet. I could change the Windows password without trouble, but I got an error message saying the Network password couldn't be changed because the authenticating server for the new domain couldn't be found.

After at least an hour of trying to get this to work, I hit upon this workaround. The basic idea is to remove the domain references before changing the Windows password, then restore them after rebooting. In this way, the Windows and Microsoft Network passwords will automatically be synchronized—without the problem of having an authenticating server validate the Network password before it can be used.

Here's how to do it:

1. Go to Control Panel ≻ Network ≻ Identification, and change the Workgroup.

2. Select Client For Microsoft Networks in the Configuration tab, and then click Properties.

3. Clear the check by Log On To Windows NT Domain and clear out the name of the domain (for some reason, merely unchecking the box didn't work).

4. Go ahead and reboot.

5. When you're back up again, go to Control Panel ≻ Passwords and change the Windows password to whatever your new network requires.

6. Go to Network and add the domain information in the same two places that you removed it above.

7. Reboot.

8. You'll be prompted for your Microsoft Network password, which will be the same in this case as your Windows password. Enter it, and you should be fine.

Remote Access with Windows 98 SE

Then you need to change your networking identification. Go to Control Panel ➢ Network, and select Client For Microsoft Networks; then click Properties. You'll see a checkbox for Log On To Windows NT Domain; click it to put a check there and fill in the name of the NT domain in the space provided. Then click OK and click the Identification tab. Fill in the name of the NT domain in the space for Workgroup. Click OK and reboot for the changes to take effect.

Next, enter the WINS address for the TCP/IP adapter by means of which you connect to the Internet. In my case, I access the Net via a cable modem, which means via a network card. So I go to Control Panel ➢ Network, and find the TCP/IP adapter for my Net connection, which is the Ethernet card. This is shown in Figure 13.21.

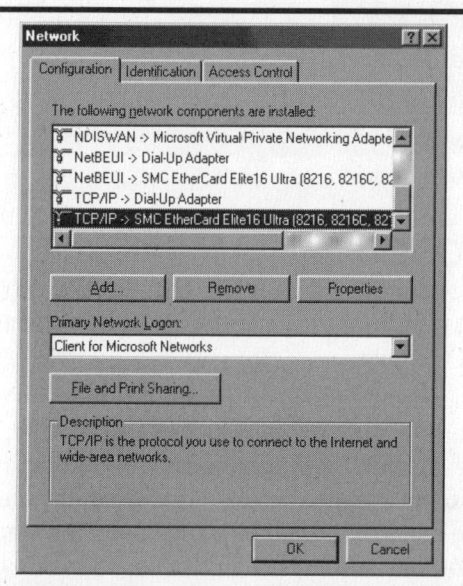

FIGURE 13.21: Changing the TCP/IP properties of the connection

Click Properties, and then go to the WINS Configuration tab shown in Figure 13.22. Click the Enable WINS Resolution radio button, and then enter the IP address in the WINS Server Search Order box. Click Add when finished; then click OK. You'll need to reboot for these changes take effect.

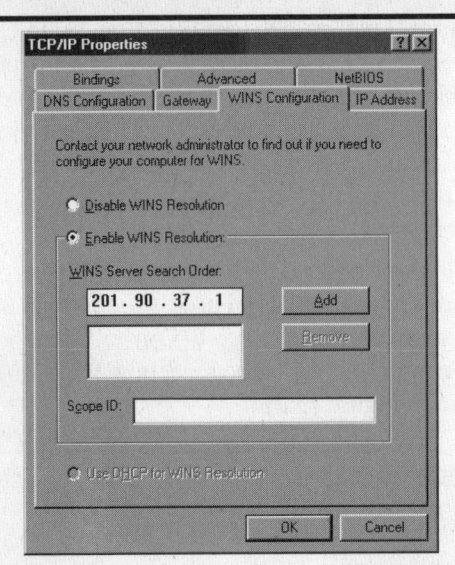

FIGURE 13.22: Specifying the WINS address

Creating an LMHOSTS File

If the network in your office doesn't have a WINS server, or if you try this entire procedure and can't get it to work, you can employ an older and simpler method: an LMHOSTS file.

To go the LMHOSTS route, you need to set up an ASCII file, lmhosts (no .TXT or other extension), in your \windows directory. This file, which can be as small as one line, must tell your machine how to locate the machine on the network you're trying to access. This means the server's DNS address, the machine name of the computer you're trying to access, and the name of the network domain. Although this only needs to be one line—for one machine—you can set it up to try other machines if the first one listed can't be reached. Here's a sample lmhosts file:

```
201.90.37.1 guava #dom:tropfruit #pre
201.90.37.2 mango #dom:tropfruit #pre
```

Here we have two different machines, *Guava* and *Mango*, both domain controllers in a domain called *Tropfruit*. The file gives the path of the signal between my home computer and my network at work. Guava can be found at the 201.90.37.1 address in the domain Tropfruit. But if Guava can't be reached, Mango can be reached in the same domain at the 201.90.37.2 address. Notice that Guava and Mango are the simple machine names for

… Remote Access with Windows 98 SE   357

those PCs; don't enter the Internet name like guava.fruits.acme.com, just enter the up-to-15-character machine name (techies call it the *NetBIOS name*, by the way).

The #pre at the end of each line is for *preload*, which speeds things up by preloading the entries preceding it into the name cache. Without this enabled, the entries are parsed only after dynamic name resolution fails. (Translation: #pre makes the whole operation faster.)

> **TIP**
>
> Just a reminder: Have you gone to Control Panel ➢ Network and set the workgroup in the Identification tab equal to the NT domain that your network is a member of back at the office, as well as filling in the same domain information under Properties For Client For Microsoft Networks? If not, do so now and reboot.

OK, now it's time to connect to the Internet. Those of you with cable modems are already on the Internet as soon as you boot your machine, but those of you who use a dial-up Internet connection need to use that to dial into your ISP and get on the Internet. If all has gone well, you should also now be accessing your office network via your WINS connection. But if all *hasn't* gone well, read on.

Troubleshooting a WINS Connection

If you can't log on to the network after you've done these things and rebooted, you should wait a few minutes, since it takes a little time for the network master browser to update the browse list. But if the network still hasn't shown up in Network Neighborhood, or if you're unable to map a network drive after several minutes and you've checked to make sure you've entered the right password and domain name, you'll want to check into a few other things using the command line (sometimes GUI networking is a little flaky):

1. Go to Start ➢ Run and enter **winipcfg**. This results in a dialog box like the one shown in Figure 13.23, which shows the details of your networking setup. If you click More Info, you'll see what WINS server, if any, you're attached to, along with the host name, DNS servers, and so on. If you have more than one TCP/IP adapter installed and you don't see any WINS server info, click the drop-down list and select the adapter that you've set up for WINS. If you see the right numbers by

Chapter Thirteen

Primary WINS Server (and Secondary if applicable), go to Step 2. If not, go back to the Network dialog box and make sure your WINS information is correctly entered for the TCP/IP adapter you plan to use.

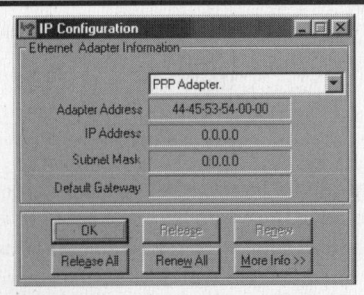

FIGURE 13.23: Using WINIPCFG to examine your networking setup

2. Go to a command prompt and type **net view ***servername*. If your server comes up, go to Step 4. If that doesn't work, try typing **net view ***ipaddress*, where *ipaddress* is the IP address of the server; for example, if NET VIEW \\\\GUAVA didn't work, I'd try NET VIEW \\\\201.90.37.1.

3. To connect to a share on the server, type **net use** *driveletter:* *****servername\sharename*, as shown in Figure 13.24. If NET VIEW with the NetBIOS name didn't work and NET VIEW with the IP address worked, use the IP address in the NET USE command as well.

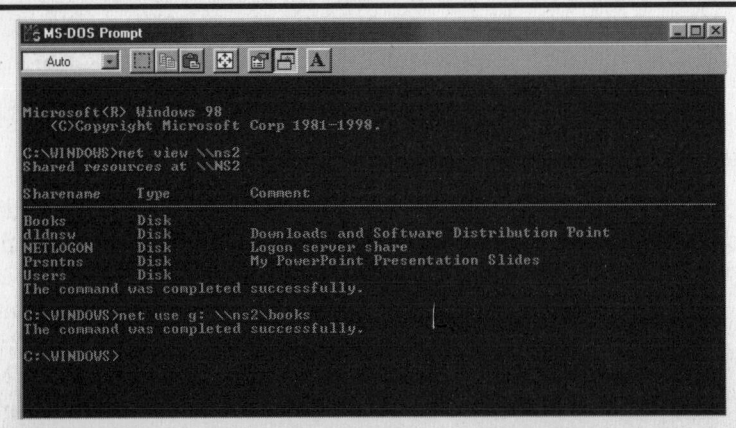

FIGURE 13.24: Connecting to a share via command prompts

4. Sometimes you can also use Find from the Start menu to find your network. Choose Start ➢ Find ➢ Computer, and fill in the IP address (for a WINS connection) or the server name with no backslash ("whack") characters (for a dial-up connection); then click Find Now. I've found that Find ➢ Computer with an IP address can work when nothing else does.

Regular DUN vs. WINS vs. PPTP

What are the advantages and disadvantages of these three kinds of remote connections?

If you're going by speed, my testing showed the regular DUN and WINS connections to be faster; the regular DUN connection (over a 33.6Kbps modem) was marginally faster than the WINS. In contrast, I found the PPTP connection extremely slow, even though I was using my one-megabit-plus cable connection to the Internet to make the connection.

Another issue is whether you want to tie up a phone line to make the connection (or indeed, whether your computer is connected to a phone line at all). A regular DUN connection requires that your computer be connected to a phone line; the other two connections don't (in my case, I just used my cable connection). However, if the network you want to access is behind a firewall, you won't be able to connect to it via WINS, but you can connect to it via a dial-up connection or via PPTP if the system administrator opens the PPTP port in the firewall for this purpose (it's port 1723 and Generic Routing Encapsulation [GRE] Protocol 47, by the way).

If security is your main concern, a PPTP connection offers encryption plus the usual RAS password protection, although this severely slows down the connection.

INSTALLING THE WINDOWS 98 SE DIAL-UP SERVER

Want outside users to be able to dial into your network, but you don't have an NT machine to act as an RAS server? No problem—a Windows 98 SE machine can be a dial-up server. Many users familiar with Windows NT Remote Access Server may be wondering, "What's the difference between NT's RAS and Windows 98 SE's server?" The major difference

Chapter Thirteen

comes down to how big or how simple the network being supported is. The Windows 98 SE server, which is designed for small LANs, supports one connection at a time. On the other hand, Windows NT is designed for much larger networks and can support up to 256 simultaneous connections. To install Windows 98 SE Server, do the following:

1. Make sure Dial-Up Server is included in your Windows 98 SE installation. Do this by going to the Add/Remove Programs applet in Control Panel, then Windows Setup ➤ Communications. Click Details, and see if there's a check in the box for Dial-Up Server (as shown in Figure 13.25). If there's not, you'll need to install the Dial-Up Server facility. With your Windows 98 SE CD in its drive, click the box by Dial-Up Server to put a check in it, then click OK twice and let your machine add the necessary files from the CD.

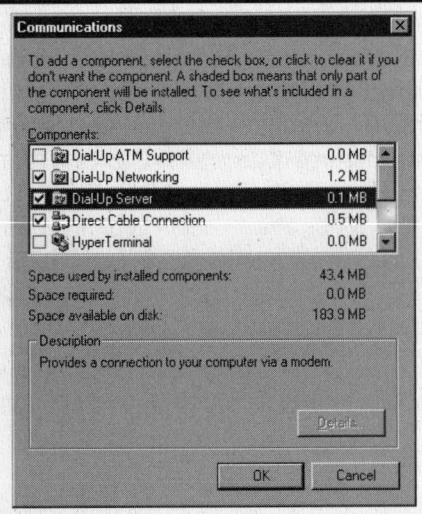

FIGURE 13.25: Looking for Dial-Up Server in Windows Setup

TIP
You can also see if you have Dial-Up Server installed on your system by going to Dial-Up Networking and seeing if there's a Dial-Up Server option in the Connections menu. If there isn't, you'll need to install one as described here.

2. Once Dial-Up Server is installed, go to Dial-Up Networking and open the Connections menu, which will have a new option, Dial-Up Server.

3. In the Dial-Up Server configuration window, shown in Figure 13.26, click Allow Caller Access. You can also describe the server if you like.

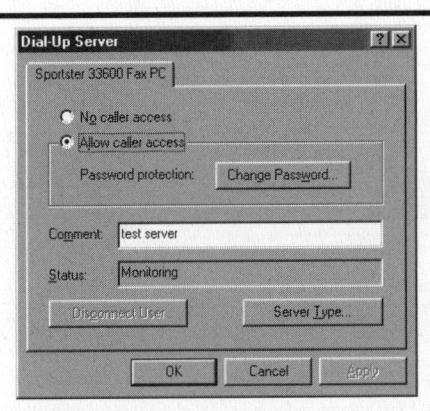

FIGURE 13.26: Allowing caller access and describing the server

4. Set the Security option: you can define a password that anyone calling to this Windows 98 SE machine must provide in order to access the shared resources of the DUN server system. This is shown in Figure 13.27.

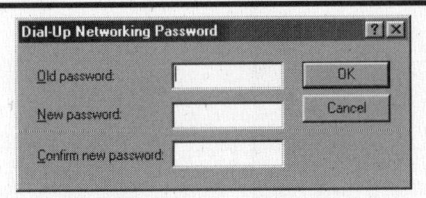

FIGURE 13.27: Setting a password

5. Alternatively, if you are implementing user-level security, you can specify the users who can access this machine. Figure 13.28 shows the Dial-Up Server screen set up for user-level security. Figure 13.29 shows adding a user from a list in a domain, and

Chapter Thirteen

Figure 13.30 shows the results. (Note that the Status is Idle instead of Monitoring, since I'm in the process of setting up a connection, not monitoring one that already exists.)

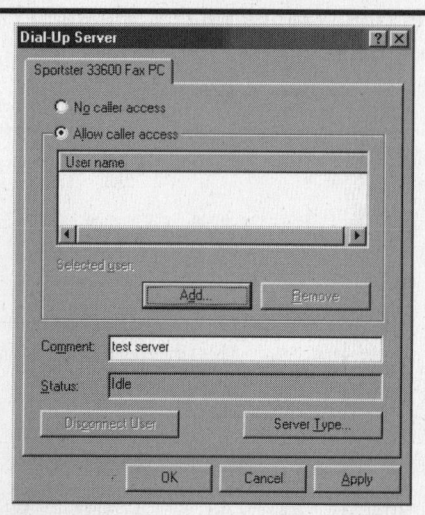

FIGURE 13.28: User-level security for Dial-Up Server

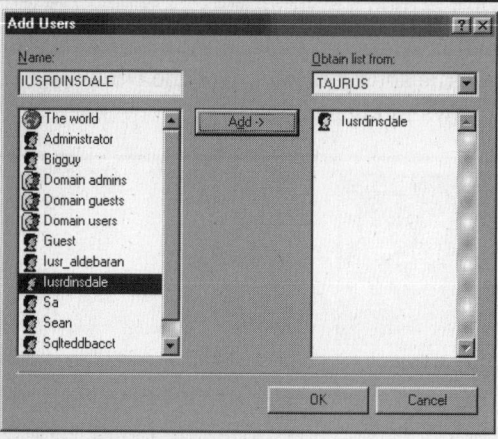

FIGURE 13.29: Adding a user

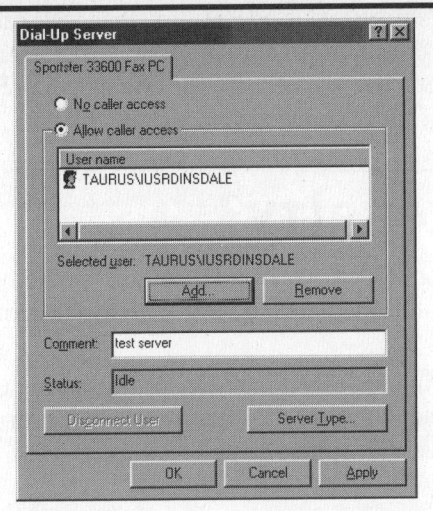

FIGURE 13.30: The user has been added.

6. Click Server Type. This option defaults to PPP, which supports TCP/IP, IPX, and NetBEUI. When you've selected this option, a determination is made during the negotiation of callers to this DUN server machine. If PPP cannot negotiate a viable connection, the DUN server will automatically switch to RAS for NT 3.1 and Windows for Workgroup clients. You can also enable software compression and require an encrypted password to access the server, as you can see in Figure 13.31.

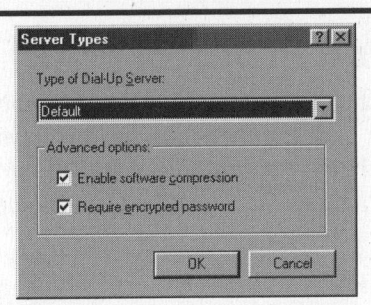

FIGURE 13.31: Setting the server type

Once you click OK, your system is now waiting to receive calls. You'll see a little server icon in your system tray, like the one shown here. If you click it, you'll see a screen like the one shown in Figure 13.26, displaying the status of connections to your server.

What About Security?

I've discussed what it takes for DUN to work and to interact properly. But once you have DUN up and running, there are a few security concerns you might want to consider.

For example, Jennifer, dialing up from home, can locate another user—say Joe, who is currently logged in to the DUN server—and kick him off. All she has to do is follow these four simple steps:

1. Go to My Computer.
2. Select Dial-Up Networking.
3. Select Dial-Up Server.
4. Click the Disconnect User button.

In the same vein, if Joe hasn't been kicked off yet, he can take a preemptive strike against everybody by remotely turning off the server! All he has to do is follow the first three of the steps above and then click No Caller Access.

Fortunately, once you have DUN working, there are a few security features you can enable.

Password Authentication Protocol (PAP)

The first level of security is established during the connection. If you have selected PPP as your server type on both the client and the server, you can utilize a technology known as the *Password Authentication Protocol* (PAP). Before the invention of PAP, the server, client, and user would hold the following conversation:

Server (to client): *Do you use PAP?*

Client (to Server): *No.*

Server (to Client): *What is the user's name?*

Client (to User): *What is your logon name?*

User (to Client): *Frank.*

Client (to Server): *The user says his name is Frank.*

Server (to Client): *Great, what is the user's password?*

Client (to User): *What is your logon password?*

User (to Client): *Doghouse.*

Client (to Server): *The client says his password is Doghouse.*

Server (to Client): *Thank you.*

This conversation would take place every single time Frank wanted to log into the network remotely. There was no encryption of information being sent back and forth. With some network servers, you might actually have had to create a script file so this conversation could be automated. In either case, it still required that the network administrator understand how to create the script file. In theory, scripts are very straightforward, but in practice the syntax can vary from hardware device to hardware device and from network operating system to network operating system.

If both your server and the client are using PAP, the conversation goes something like this:

Server: *Do you use PAP?*

Client: *Yes.*

Server: *Great, then please send over the username.*

Client: *Frank.*

Server: *Great, please send over the password.*

Client: *Doghouse.*

Server: *Thank you.*

This entire conversation took place without any interaction on the part of the user. If it took any time at all, all Frank saw was the hourglass while this conversation took place in the background. Unfortunately, just as you saw the password *Doghouse* in the first conversation, the password was sent as a simple text string across the communication line. When I last looked in Webster's dictionary under the word *security*, this wasn't part of the definition. If you are looking for a secure validation, you want to use CHAP.

> **NOTE**
> Before we discuss CHAP, I would like to mention SPAP in passing. The makers of the Shiva modem have their own authentication protocol, known as *Shiva Password Authentication Protocol* (SPAP). Windows 98 SE supports SPAP for dialing into a Shiva server.

Challenge-Handshake Authentication Protocol (CHAP)

As I said previously, CHAP allows for secure validation. If the server and client have CHAP enabled, the following conversation takes place:

Server: *Do you do CHAP?*

Client: *Yes.*

Server: *47.*

Client (to itself): *Let me factor the password by 47 and send the encrypted version across the line.*

Client (to Server): *Kjsyao7r* (representing the password *Doghouse*).

Server: *Thank you.*

Now, since the server sent a *challenge code* (47 in the example), it knows that it will use the same number as the challenge factor to decrypt the password and then validate it. The power of CHAP is that when the first client logs in, the challenge code may be 47, but when the next client logs in, the challenge code dynamically changes. Since the challenge code is constantly changing, the passwords are encrypted using a different key every time.

To enable CHAP, just select Require Encrypted Password when configuring the client *and* when configuring the server. If Server Type is PPP, DUN will attempt a PAP conversation by default, unless Require Encrypted Password is selected.

Remote Access to Resources with DUN

DUN allows you to specify how people may gain access to the DUN server.

▶ The first option is *share-level security*. This permits you to assign passwords to each resource that you share. You can set a password for read-only access and a different password for full-control access. The downside of this configuration is that a user may have to memorize many passwords. If you are looking for centralized control, you will want to set user-level permissions instead.

▶ When you set *user-level permissions*, Windows 98 SE will look for a Windows NT or NetWare server to validate a user. The user has to be a valid user of the Novell network or NT domain in order to gain access to your machine. Windows 98 SE still controls read-only or full-control access to the resource, but it enforces these security parameters by user, not by resource.

To set share-level or user-level security, go to the Network applet in Control Panel and click the Access Control tab, which you can see in Figure 13.32. If you want share-level security, make sure the first radio button is clicked. If you want user-level security, click the second radio button and fill in the name of the domain server for the network in question (*Pineapple* in the figure).

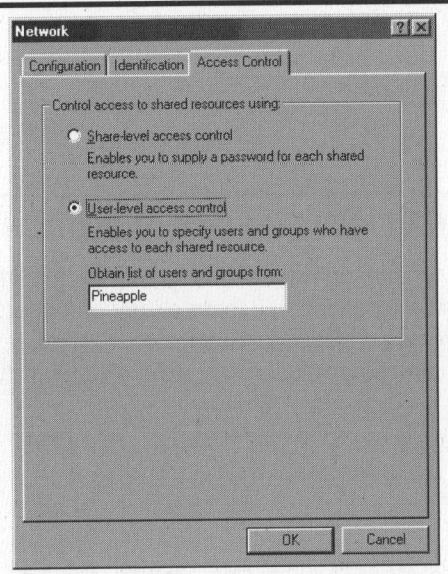

FIGURE 13.32: Changing type of access in Control Panel

If you're not connected to this network at the time you're setting this up, Windows will tell you it can't find the security provider for this domain and ask if you want to proceed, as shown in Figure 13.33. If you do, click OK. Windows will ask you for the type of authenticator used by the network: Choose between NetWare (bindery) and Windows NT domain, as shown in Figure 13.34. Select the right one, click OK, and reboot. Once you connect to the network after rebooting, your settings will take effect.

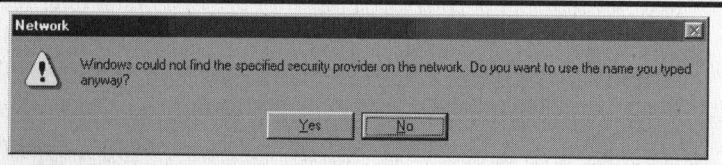

FIGURE 13.33: Can't find authenticator

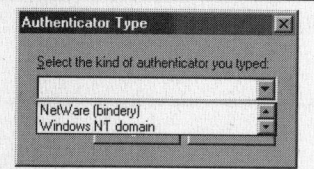

FIGURE 13.34: Choice of authenticator

HOW DO I CREATE A DIRECT SERIAL CONNECTION?

Users aren't limited to dialing in via a phone line to set up a network connection; they can connect their remote computer directly via a serial cable. To create a direct serial connection, the first thing that you need is an acceptable cable. Any of the following will do:

- Serial null modem cable
- LapLink cable
- InterLink cable
- 25-pin parallel cable (all wires must be present)

Of the four types of cables, the parallel cable will provide the fastest throughput between machines.

CONTINUED ➡

Once you have made a physical connection between the machines, take the following steps:

1. Choose Add/Remove Programs in Control Panel and then select the Windows Setup tab.
2. Select Communications in the Components list.
3. Click Details, and select Direct Cable Connection.

A new icon, Direct Cable Connection, will appear in the My Computer window. Please make sure this icon appears on both machines before attempting to establish a connection.

The first time you click Direct Cable Connection, the Direct Connect Wizard will appear and allow you to designate one machine as the host machine and the other machine as the guest machine.

What's Next?

This chapter gave you a detailed look at setting up Dial-Up Networking, the Windows tool for remote access to local area networks and for modem connections to Internet Service Providers.

In the next chapter, Sharon Crawford and Neil J. Salkind survey the *applets*, or accessory programs, supplied with the operating system.

Chapter 14

Windows 98 SE Applets

From the first, graphical operating systems have come with a complement of smallish programs such as calculators and paint programs. Because of their usually limited capabilities, these programs are called *applets* rather than applications. In many cases, these programs are just as big as they need to be, so they actually *are* full applications. But the name applet has stuck and generally applies to programs that come with an operating system. This chapter looks at the Windows 98 SE applets.

A World of Applets

The applets we'll try out in the following pages are Notepad, its "big sister" WordPad, the Clipboard Viewer, Paint, the Character Map, Phone Dialer, the Calculator, HyperTerminal, and My Briefcase—quite a selection. You'll be able to see which ones may be useful and which ones you can probably skip.

Adapted from *The ABCs of Windows 98*
by Sharon Crawford and Neil J. Salkind
ISBN 0-7821-1953-0   384 pages $19.99

> **NOTE**
> Your computer may have more or fewer applets than what we've listed here already installed when you start using Windows 98 SE. If you don't have the ones shown here, use the Add/Remove Programs icon in the Control Panel to add them to your system.

Using Notepad

Notepad is a simple text editor with very few charms except speed. Click any text file, and it will immediately load into Notepad (unless it's associated with a word processing file installed on your system or it's bigger than 64KB—in which case you'll be asked if you want to load it into WordPad instead).

To start Notepad, click Start ➢ Programs ➢ Accessories ➢ Notepad.

What Notepad Has

Notepad has the bare minimum of facilities on its menus. You can:

- Search for characters or words.
- Use Page Setup to set margins, paper orientation, customize the header and footer, and select a printer.
- Copy, cut, and paste text.
- Insert the time and date into a document.

Working with WordPad

WordPad, like Notepad, is a text editor, but it is more elaborate than Notepad. For one (important) thing, you can make format changes with WordPad, but not with Notepad. However, WordPad still falls way short of being a real word processing program. WordPad will read Write, Notepad, and Word for Windows documents, as well as text and rich-text formats.

To start WordPad, click Start ➢ Programs ➢ Accessories ➢ WordPad.

Windows 98 SE Applets 373

> **TIP**
> You can uninstall WordPad using the Add/Remove Programs function in the Control Panel. However, if you use Microsoft Fax, you'll need WordPad because it's the fax operation's text editor. If you use a different fax program such as WinFax or you don't fax from your computer at all, you can remove WordPad without worry.

Opening WordPad

When you open WordPad (see Figure 14.1), it looks like most other text editors. On the menus you'll find the usual things one associates with text editors. Pull down the menus to see the various options.

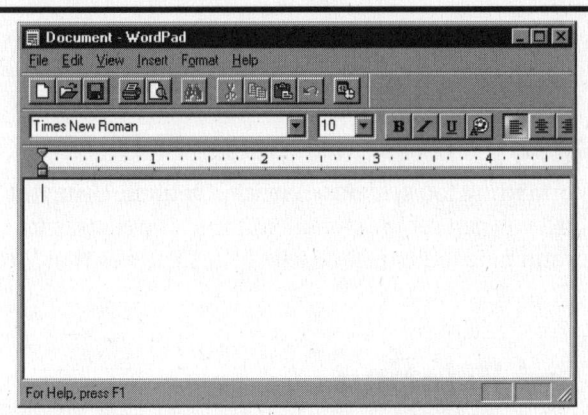

FIGURE 14.1: The opening screen for WordPad

WordPad is completely integrated into Windows 98 SE. You can write messages in color and post them to the Internet so recipients see your messages just as you wrote them—fonts, colors, embedded objects, and all. WordPad also has the distinct advantage of being able to load really big files.

Making and Formatting Documents

You can always click a document and drag it into WordPad. Documents created in Microsoft Word (.doc) and Windows Write (.wri), as well as those in text (.txt) or rich-text (.rtf) format, are all instantly recognized by WordPad. You can also just start typing away in the opening WordPad screen shown in Figure 14.1.

Formatting Tools

The toolbar (see Figure 14.2) and Format bar (see Figure 14.3) are displayed by default. You can turn either of them off by deselecting it from the list under the View menu.

FIGURE 14.2: Here are the various functions on the WordPad toolbar.

FIGURE 14.3: The WordPad Format bar lets you manipulate text in all the basic ways.

To set tabs, you use the ruler. Click the ruler at the spot where you want a tab. To remove a tab, just click it and drag it off the ruler.

Other Options

To access other formatting tools, choose View ➤ Options. Using the Options dialog box, you can set measurement units as well as word wrap and display and hide toolbars for each of the file types that WordPad recognizes.

Page Setup and Printing

The File menu has the usual Print command, but there's also a Page Setup item that you can use to set margins as well as paper size and orientation. WordPad can be used to print envelopes as well as work with varying sizes of paper.

It may take some fooling around to get envelopes lined up correctly, but fortunately there's a Print Preview choice (on the toolbar and also on the File menu). There you can see how the envelope or paper is lining up with your text. Adjust the margin in the Page Setup dialog box until you get it the way you want.

TIP
To change printers, choose File ➤ Page Setup. Click the Printer button to select any printer currently available to you.

What's on the Clipboard

When you copy or cut something, Windows needs a place to store it until you decide what to do with it. This storage place is called the Clipboard. And if you look in the Clipboard, you will see the material that has just been cut or copied.

Sometimes you want to see what's on the Clipboard and maybe save its contents. Clipboard Viewer makes it possible for you to do this.

Taking a Look

To open the Viewer, choose Start ➤ Programs ➤ Accessories ➤ System Tools ➤ Clipboard Viewer. You'll see a window like the one shown in Figure 14.4.

> **NOTE**
> Immediately before snapping the screen shot of the Clipboard Viewer, we selected and copied the text you see in the figure. You can also press the PrintScreen key (which captures the entire screen to the Clipboard) or Alt+PrintScreen (which captures the active window to the Clipboard).

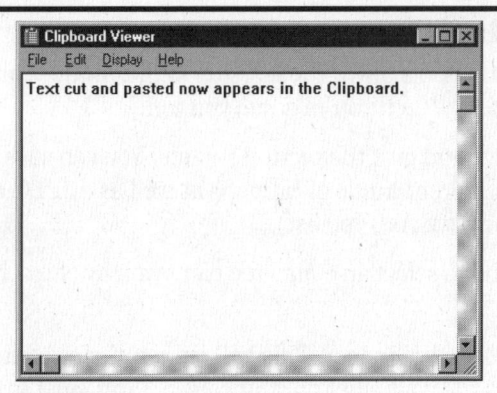

FIGURE 14.4: The Clipboard Viewer

Saving the Clipboard's Contents

To save the current contents of the Clipboard, choose File ➤ Save As. You can save files under a proprietary format identified by the .clp extension.

These files are (as far as we can tell) only used by the Windows Clipboard Viewer.

Once you've saved the contents, you can use the Clipboard to copy and paste other material, and later, you can reload what you saved by choosing File ➢ Open. Pull down the Display menu to see all your options for viewing the data on the Clipboard.

The most important thing to remember about the Clipboard is that it can only hold one thing at a time, which is always the most recently cut or copied material. So if you copy a section of text (which goes to the Clipboard) and then copy an image, the image will replace the text on the Clipboard.

Drawing with Paint

As a drawing and painting program, Paint has its limitations, but it's fine for creating and modifying simple graphics. To open Paint, choose Start ➢ Programs ➢ Accessories ➢ Paint. It may not be installed by default, so if you don't see it, use the Add/Remove Programs function in Control Panel. (It's under Accessories on the Windows Setup page.)

Creating Original Art

Open Paint and, using the tools down the left side of the window, create a drawing and/or a painting. When you're done, you can:

- ▶ Choose File ➢ Save and give the picture a name. You can save it as one of several different kinds of bitmaps as well as a JPEG or GIF image (see the Save As Type list).

- ▶ Choose File ➢ Send to select an e-mail recipient worthy of receiving your work.

- ▶ Choose File ➢ Set As Wallpaper. This will let you tile or center your work of art as the wallpaper on your screen. (You must save the file before you choose this option.)

Modifying the Work of Others

Any file with the extension .bmp, .pcx, or .dib can be opened in Paint. Use the tools to make any modifications you want, and then do any of the things listed in the section above. Once a file is modified, it is saved as a bitmap (.bmp).

> **NOTE**
> For a really good painting program at a very reasonable price, check out the excellent shareware program Paint Shop Pro. It's available for download on the major online services at www.jasc.com. Just search for Paint Shop Pro, download the program, and install it.

ENTERING NEW CHARACTERS

The fonts that show up in your word processor are very nice, but they often don't go beyond the characters found on your keyboard. What about when you need a copyright sign (©) or an e with an umlaut (ë)? With Character Map you have access to all kinds of symbols, including Greek letters and other special signs.

To start Character Map, choose Start ➢ Programs ➢ Accessories ➢ System Tools ➢ Character Map. You'll see the opening screen shown in Figure 14.5.

FIGURE 14.5: The Character Map shows all.

Entering Characters

Select the font you want to use by clicking the downward-pointing arrow at the right end of the Font list box. Each font represents a different set of symbols. To enter a character, double-click it in the window. It will appear in the text box at the top right of the window. Continue double-clicking until you have the entire string of characters you want in the text box. When you have all the characters you want in the text box, click the Copy button halfway down the right side of the window. Then return to your application using the Taskbar or by pressing Alt+Tab until your application is selected.

Position the cursor on the spot where you want to place the character, and choose Edit ➢ Paste (or just press Ctrl+V).

Phone Dialing for Fun

Do you frequently have to make a lot of telephone calls? Has your dialing finger ever felt as if it were going to fall off? If you have Windows 98 SE, you can turn over the grief of dialing to its capable, virtual hands. Phone Dialer is a handy little program that doesn't do a lot, but if you need it, it's terrific to have.

To start Phone Dialer, choose Start ➢ Programs ➢ Accessories ➢ Communications ➢ Phone Dialer. You'll see the opening screen shown in Figure 14.6 (without a phone number in the Number To Dial box).

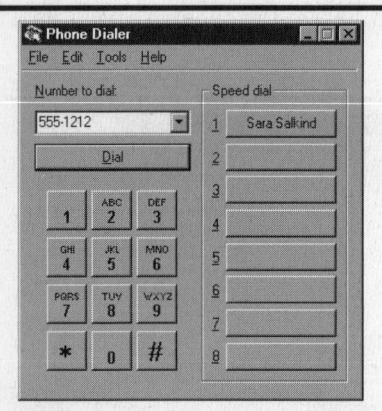

FIGURE 14.6: The Phone Dialer window can help you put an end to the heartbreak of "Digititis."

> **NOTE**
> Windows uses your installed modem to dial your telephone. In order for this scheme to work, you need to have a telephone on the same line you're using for your modem. If you have a separate phone line for data, you'll need an actual telephone on that line to use Phone Dialer. You can pick up inexpensive couplers at Radio Shack that will allow all your available phone lines to work in conjunction with your data line.

Windows 98 SE Applets 379

The Phone Dialer gives you two simple ways to make phone calls:

Speed Dial   If you have a number you need in an emergency or one you call constantly, you can enter it in the Speed Dial list.

The Telephone Log   If you have a long list of numbers you call periodically, you can simply type those numbers into the Number to Dial text box, and they will be added to a telephone log. You can access your log by clicking the downward-pointing arrow at the right end of the Number to Dial box.

Speed Dialing

To create a speed dial number, choose Edit ➢ Speed Dial to open the Edit Speed Dial dialog box shown in Figure 14.7.

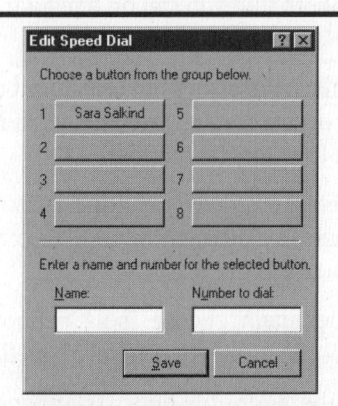

FIGURE 14.7:   Creating a Speed Dial number

Here's how to set it up:

1. Click the numbered speed dial button you want to assign.
2. In the Name text box, type the name of the person or place that you will dial with that button.
3. Type the number to dial in the Number To Dial text box.
4. Click Save. (You'll be returned to the Phone Dialer dialog box, and the name you entered in the Edit Speed Dial dialog box will appear on the numbered speed dial button you selected.)

5. To speed-dial the number, just click the button and lift your telephone handset.

> **TIP**
> When you enter a phone number in the Phone Dialer, don't forget to enter any numbers that are needed before the number, such as 1 or 70. Also, numbers can be entered separated by a dash, a space, or nothing at all, such as 555-1212 or 555 1212 or 5551212.

The Telephone Log

As mentioned at the beginning of this section, there are two ways to use the Phone Dialer. The quick and easy way is to use the speed dialer, but as you may have noticed, the speed dialer is limited to a list of eight numbers. If you have more than eight numbers that you call on a regular basis, you'll have to use your log. Here's how:

1. In the opening Phone Dialer screen, either type the number in the Number To Dial box or use the telephone keypad in the Phone Dialer dialog box to enter the number.

2. When the number is completely entered, click the Dial button and pick up your telephone. In a moment, you will be connected to the number you are calling.

3. If you need to call the number again, choose Tools ➢ Show Log. This displays a list of all the numbers you have called.

4. To redial one of these numbers, double-click its entry in the log.

You can see how the Phone Dialer can be a terrific convenience if you spend a lot of time making calls.

Using the Calculators

You actually have two calculators in Windows 98 SE: a standard calculator, the likes of which you could buy for $4.95 at any drugstore counter, and a scientific calculator.

Just the Basics

To start Calculator, choose Start ➤ Programs ➤ Accessories ➤ Calculator. You'll see the opening screen shown in Figure 14.8.

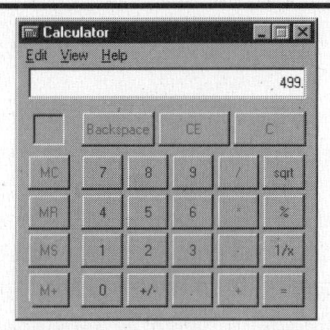

FIGURE 14.8: The standard calculator

Using the mouse, click the numbers and functions just as if you were pressing the keys on a hand-held calculator. Or, if you have a numerical keypad on your keyboard, press NumLock and then use the keypad keys to enter numbers and basic math functions.

Or One Step Beyond

To access the scientific calculator, choose View ➤ Scientific. That displays the calculator in Figure 14.9.

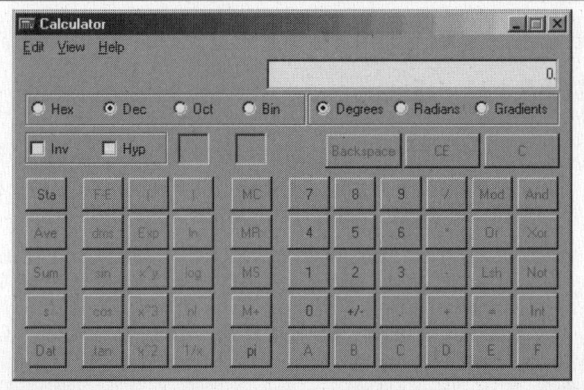

FIGURE 14.9: The much more sophisticated scientific calculator

> **TIP**
> If you're unsure of the use for a function, right-click its button. You'll see a rectangle containing the words "What's This?" Click the text to see a short explanation of the function. To close the text box, click outside it.

Pasting in the Numbers

Both calculators can be used in conjunction with the Clipboard. Type a number in any application, and select it. Press Ctrl+C (for Copy). Press Alt+Tab until the calculator is selected (or click it in the Taskbar) and then press Ctrl+V (for Paste). The number will appear in the number display of the calculator as if you had entered it from the calculator keypad.

Work your magic—adding, subtracting, multiplying, or deriving the inverse sine. You can pull down the Edit menu and select Copy, which places the contents of the display on the Clipboard, ready for you to paste into your document.

> **TIP**
> Here's a neat trick to transfer numbers from one calculator view to another. First, click the MS button to store the displayed number. Then, on the View menu, click the desired view. Finally, click the MR button to recall the stored number.

Communicating with HyperTerminal

HyperTerminal is the Windows 98 SE applet that accesses other computers, bulletin boards, and online services through your modem. For the most part, all of HyperTerminal's work will be done for you by your Internet Service Provider or your online service. But on special occasions you may need HyperTerminal to make a connection.

To start HyperTerminal, choose Start ➤ Programs ➤ Accessories ➤ Communications ➤ HyperTerminal. Then click the HyperTerminal icon (HYPERTRM.EXE) and you'll see the opening screen shown in Figure 14.10.

Windows 98 SE Applets

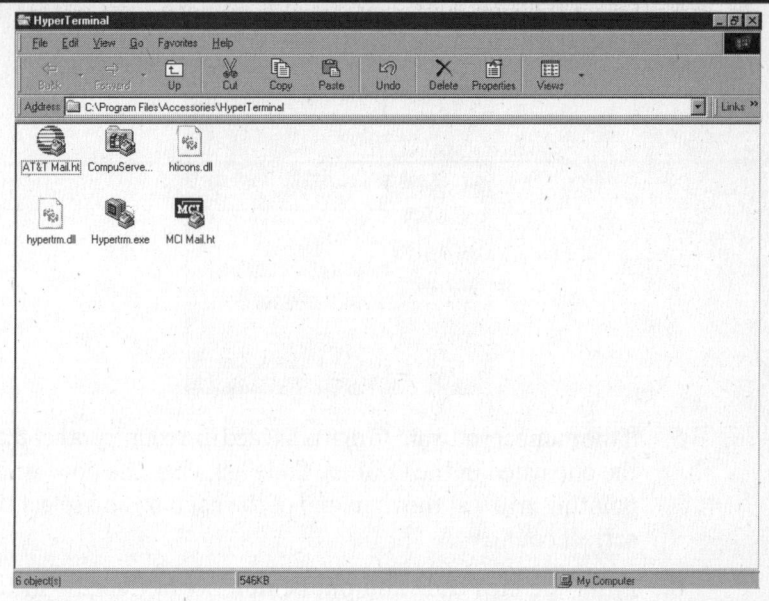

FIGURE 14.10: The HyperTerminal screen, where you begin the connection process

How to Use It

When you use HyperTerminal, each connection you make can be named and provided with an icon. That allows you to quickly identify connections so you can make them again. Once established, all it takes is a click on the icon to connect to where you want.

Let's create a fictional connection. Imagine you're a journalist working for a newspaper called *The Past Times* and you need to log on to the paper's BBS to file stories and columns.

1. Double-click Hypertrm.exe to open the Connection Description dialog box.

2. Type **The Past Times** in the Name text box.

3. Scroll through the icons until you locate an icon that resembles a briefcase and an umbrella—what better icon for a reporter?

384 Chapter Fourteen

4. Select the icon, and then click OK to open the Connect To dialog box:

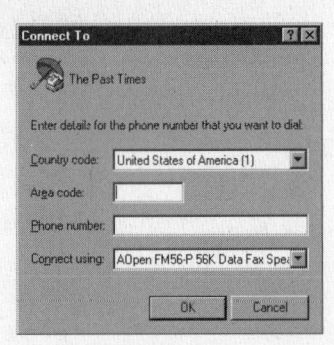

5. If the number you want to dial is located in a country other than the one listed in the Country Code list, click the downward-pointing arrow at the right end of the list box, and select the correct country.

6. Enter the area code and phone number of the BBS in the appropriate text boxes. (For our example, enter **555-1212** as the number, and click OK.)

7. The Connect dialog box opens. Since this is the first time we've run this application, click the Dialing Properties button to confirm that the connection is made properly. Look over the options in this dialog box, and make sure that they're correctly set.

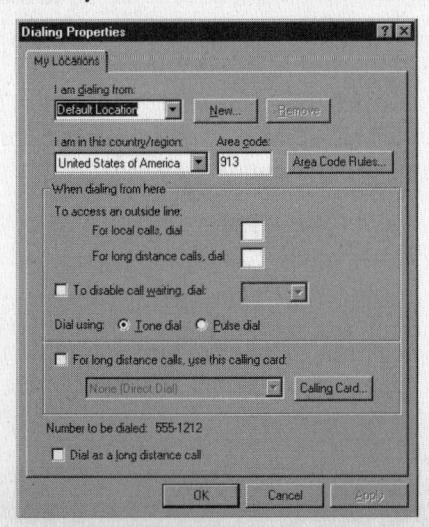

8. If you click the Calling Card button, a dialog box will open for you to enter your telephone credit card number.

9. If you have to dial a number to get out of your business or hotel phone system (typically 9 or 7), enter this number in the appropriate To Access an Outside Line text box, and enter the number (or numbers) you dial for long distance access in the text box below it.

10. When you are through filling out this dialog box, click OK. You will see the Connect dialog box again.

11. At this point, all you need to do is click Dial to make the connection. If all the settings you made in the previous dialog boxes are correct, the call will go through, and you can use the BBS software to upload your story to the newspaper. (We'll cover file transfers in a moment.)

12. When you're through placing your call, choose Call ➤ Disconnect, or click the icon that looks like a handset being hung up to break the connection.

13. When you close the window, you will be prompted to save the session.

Sending Files

Once you have connected with a remote computer, you will probably want to upload or download files. This is the principal reason for making this sort of connection. The file transfer protocols (which are the rules for transferring information) supported by HyperTerminal are:

- 1K Xmodem
- Xmodem
- Ymodem
- Ymodem-G
- Zmodem
- Zmodem with Crash Recovery
- Kermit

Binary Files

To send a binary file, follow these steps:

1. After the connection is made, choose Transfer Send File to open the Send File dialog box.

2. Using the options in this dialog box, specify the file to send. Click the Browse button to locate and identify the file to be sent.

3. Select the protocol for file transfer from the Protocol drop-down menu. Zmodem is the best choice because it combines speed and good error correction (see Figure 14.11).

4. Click the Send button. The file will be transferred.

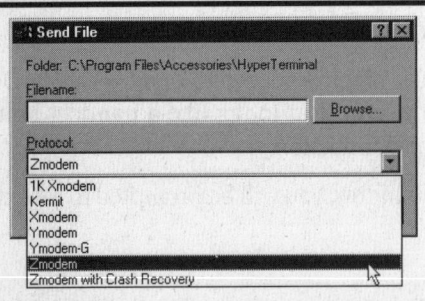

FIGURE 14.11: Here's where you select a binary file and the protocol for sending it.

Text Files

Text files are a little different from binary files. Most file transfer software distinguishes between binary files and text files—sending one in Binary mode and the other in ASCII mode or Text mode. HyperTerminal is no different.

To send a text file, follow the steps for a binary file, but choose Send Text File from the Transfer menu. When you specify the file to send and click the Open button, the file will be sent as if you had typed it into the terminal program.

> **TIP**
> Unless you're transferring files to a Unix system, you're usually better off sending every file as a binary file. Even a little bit of formatting in the file can cause a text file transfer to fail, while *any* file can be sent as a binary transfer.

And Receiving Them Too

To receive a file being sent from another computer:

1. Pull down the Transfer menu and select Receive File. That will open a dialog box like the one shown in Figure 14.12.
2. Click the Browse button to specify a filename and location for the received file.
3. Select a file transfer protocol.
4. Click the Receive button to start receiving the file from the remote location.

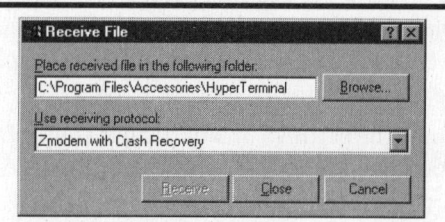

FIGURE 14.12: Receiving files using HyperTerminal

> **NOTE**
> Take the above steps when you hear the incoming call from the other computer. You have to do this yourself because HyperTerminal is not smart enough to answer the phone.

Saving a Session

To help you remember how to navigate the complexities of a service you don't use very often, terminal programs provide *logging*—a way to save everything you do in a particular session to disk and/or print it on paper.

To save everything to a file:

1. Choose Transfer ➢ Capture Text.
2. By default, all the screen information in a session will be saved in a file called `capture.txt` in the HyperTerminal folder inside the Accessories folder. Of course, you can use the Browse button to save the file in a different location. Click Start when you're ready.

3. Pull down the Transfer menu again. Now you will note that there is a tiny triangle next to the Capture Text option. Select it and you will see a submenu with Stop, Pause, and Resume options to give you control over the capture.

4. If you prefer to send the session to the printer rather than to a file on your disk, pull down the Transfer menu and select Capture To Printer.

Using a Connection

As you may recall, when we started using HyperTerminal, we created a connection with a name and an icon. This connection appears in the HyperTerminal program group. Any time you want to use this connection in the future, simply double-click its icon, and all the settings (telephone number and so forth) will be in place for you.

Any time you want to change the settings in a particular connection, open the connection, pull down the File menu, and select Properties.

Using My Briefcase

My Briefcase is not an applet in the usual sense. You won't find it listed under Accessories, but My Briefcase should be on your Desktop from the original installation of Windows 98 SE. If you don't see it there, it's probably not installed. To install it, use the Add/Remove Programs option in Control Panel (discussed in Chapter 6, *Installing and Running Programs*).

My Briefcase is designed to help those with multiple computers keep a set of files synchronized. It may be your computer at work and your computer at home. Or maybe you have a desktop computer and a laptop, and you work on the same files on both computers. When two computers are involved, it's only a matter of time before things get confused as to which version of a memo or a speech is the most current. My Briefcase helps rectify that problem.

How It Works

When you open My Briefcase and copy a file into it, a link is made between the original and the copy in My Briefcase. This is called a *sync link*. After the link is made, you can work on the copy in My Briefcase or the original file and select Update All (from inside My Briefcase), and the latest version will be copied over the earlier version, keeping both in sync.

To make use of My Briefcase, follow these steps:

1. Drag the files that are important to the My Briefcase folder on the Desktop of computer #1.

2. Copy My Briefcase to a floppy disk. Right-click and use the Send To command, which is particularly handy for this.

3. Take the floppy to computer #2. Open drive A either in Windows Explorer or My Computer.

4. Open My Briefcase. Work on the files inside My Briefcase on computer #2.

5. When you're finished, save and close the files on the floppy in the usual way.

6. Return the floppy to computer #1. Open My Briefcase on the floppy disk, and choose Briefcase Update All.

What's Next?

With a solid understanding of applets under your belt, it's time to move on to a fairly in-depth discussion of what really makes Windows 98 SE tick: the Registry and .INI files. You will learn about all kinds of configuration files as well as when and how to work with the Registry.

Chapter 15

Controlling 98 SE—the Registry and .*INI* Files

I f you've ever used DOS or Windows, you're familiar with the array of system and hardware configuration files that accompany DOS-based operating systems: AUTOEXEC .BAT, CONFIG.SYS, WIN.INI, and SYSTEM.INI, to name a few. NT users know that these files were replaced in Windows NT with a centralized configuration database called the *Registry*. Just to make life complicated, however, Windows 98 SE uses both kinds of configuration files: the DOS ones *and* an NT-like Registry. (Actually, there's more to it than just perversity on Microsoft's part, but we'll talk about the roles of the legacy configuration files in Windows 98 SE later in this chapter.)

· ·

Adapted from *Expert Guide to Windows 98* by Mark Minasi, Eric Christiansen, and Kristina Shapar
ISBN 0-7821-1974-3   976 pages $49.99

Basically, the Registry holds all configuration information for Windows 98 SE and Windows 95/98 SE–ready applications. Older 16-bit apps do not know to use the Registry, unfortunately, so you'll still have .INI files scattered all over your system if you use Windows 3.x programs. Fortunately for current Windows 95 users, the Registry structure has stayed the same—the exception being that such things as the new Desktop, active setup, and new applications have been added.

Although both the DOS configuration files and the Registry have a role to play in configuring your Windows 98 SE environment, they look and work a little differently in Windows 98 SE than they do in DOS/Windows and NT. In this chapter, we'll talk about what these configuration files look like, how you can use them to tune your system, and how to avoid bollixing up your system while trying to tune it. Specifically, I'll discuss:

▶ What to do with AUTOEXEC.BAT and CONFIG.SYS now that your system has a Registry

▶ The Registry—what it does, how to maintain it, and how to fix it when it breaks

▶ Modifying the Registry of a remote machine

▶ WIN.INI and SYSTEM.INI and how they're used by Windows 98 SE

Plus, I'll even show you some neat Registry editing tricks that'll give you an idea of how the Registry works.

The Limited New Roles of *AUTOEXEC.BAT* and *CONFIG.SYS*

You probably know that, unlike pre–Windows 95 versions of Windows, Windows 98 SE is an operating *system*, not an operating environment. It's not a GUI front end to the DOS operating system (as were versions of Windows before Windows 95), but complete unto itself.

Most DOS machines use CONFIG.SYS and AUTOEXEC.BAT to set up the system hardware and operating environment. Although these files can be pretty vanilla if all you want to do is just boot the machine, the more stuff you add to the machine, the more complicated and system-specific they get. Windows 98 SE, in contrast, does not rely on CONFIG.SYS and AUTOEXEC.BAT for system information; a file named IO.SYS and another called the Registry take care of configuring the system as the former pair of files once did.

But if you look at the root directory of your boot drive, you'll notice that you've still got a CONFIG.SYS and an AUTOEXEC.BAT. If Windows 98 SE doesn't need these files to set up your system, why are these files still there? Two reasons:

- ▶ To load any real-mode drivers and TSRs that your computer requires
- ▶ To allow you to tailor DOS sessions for specific DOS programs

Loading Real-Mode Drivers and TSRs

A few computers, but not all, need to run some real-mode (that is, DOS) programs that aren't part of Windows 98 SE. The statements corresponding to these programs appear in CONFIG.SYS and AUTOEXEC.BAT, and even if your particular computer requires no such programs, their configuration files will remain on your system, in the unlikely event the need arises in the future.

Creating Your Own DOS Environments

You can run most DOS programs from Windows 98 SE and, if necessary, set up an individual AUTOEXEC.BAT and CONFIG.SYS for each one. Thus, if you've got an application that can't run if DOS is loaded high or has some other special requirements, you can set up a custom operating environment for that application.

Now let's talk a little about how to use CONFIG.SYS and AUTOEXEC.BAT to give a DOS application a custom-made environment. Open My Computer and find the icon for a DOS program on your system. Right-click it, and choose Properties from the pop-up menu. A dialog box like the one in Figure 15.1 will appear.

(SNAP, if you're wondering, is a useful screen-capture program for DOS.) Click the Program tab, and then click the Advanced button at the bottom of the Program screen. You'll see a dialog box that looks like the one in Figure 15.2.

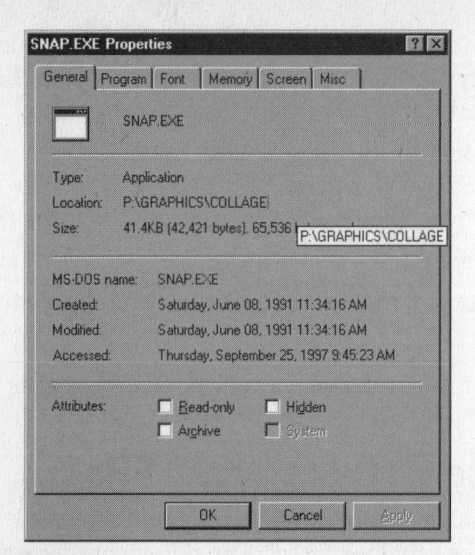

FIGURE 15.1: Properties dialog box for SNAP.EXE

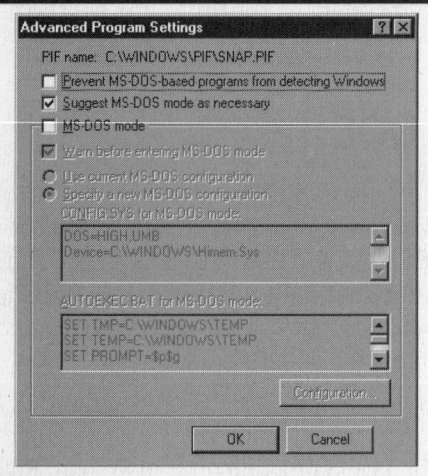

FIGURE 15.2: Advanced screen of SNAP Properties dialog box

> **TIP**
> Don't panic if you turn to the Advanced screen of the Properties tab for a particular DOS app and there's nothing in the CONFIG.SYS or AUTOEXEC.BAT files. You can't see their contents until you've selected MS-DOS mode at least once.

Controlling 98 SE — The Registry and .INI Files 395

Notice the CONFIG.SYS and AUTOEXEC.BAT files that are listed. Notice also that, by default, Suggest MS-DOS Mode As Necessary is selected, and you must use the vanilla configuration files provided. By default, these files won't do much more than define an operating environment, enable EMM386, define the temporary file directory, and provide mouse support. To change them, you'll need to set the operating environment to MS-DOS mode so that they're no longer grayed out, as you see in Figure 15.3.

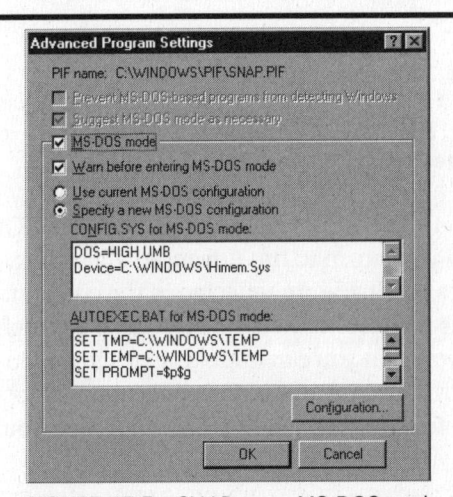

FIGURE 15.3: SNAP set to MS-DOS mode

Now, you're ready to customize the configuration files for this program's DOS session. You can type in the commands you want to load, or you can select canned configuration information from the screen available after clicking the Configuration button, as you see in Figure 15.4.

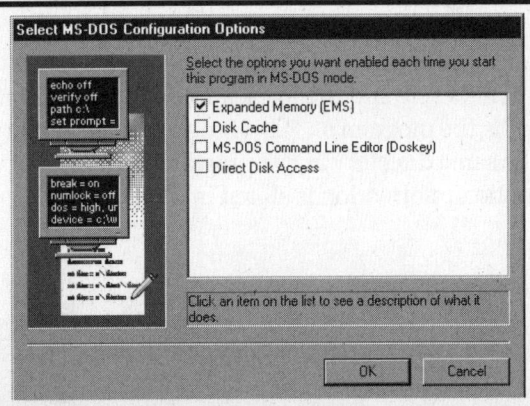

FIGURE 15.4: Canned configuration options

I like the way that this dialog box is set up: rather than providing you with a list of statements to add to or delete from CONFIG.SYS or AUTOEXEC.BAT, Windows 98 SE lists the options to activate or deactivate and then adjusts the configuration files to correspond to your choices. By default, EMM386 (the memory manager) is activated. If you're not sure of an option's function, click it to display its description in the text box below the list.

> **WARNING**
> When editing the CONFIG.SYS and AUTOEXEC.BAT files for a DOS session, watch what you're doing, and make sure you make backups before you get started. There's no Restore Defaults button.

Select the options that you want for the MS-DOS mode of the DOS session, and click OK. When you return to the Advanced dialog box, you'll notice that the changes you made are reflected in the configuration files. Notice also that there is no Restore Defaults button, so be careful what you do here. The only way that you can undo changes to a DOS session's configuration files is by canceling out of the application's Properties dialog box altogether. Once you click OK to close Properties, you're stuck with the changes that you've made.

Once you've set up CONFIG.SYS and AUTOEXEC.BAT for that DOS session, return the program's running mode to Suggest MS-DOS Mode As Necessary, the default. If DOS mode is necessary for the program to run well, the configuration files that you set up will run.

Where Are Configuration Settings Kept?

As you can set up an individual CONFIG.SYS and AUTOEXEC.BAT file for each DOS program on your system, clearly this information isn't centrally located, but is somewhere specific to each DOS program. That "somewhere specific" is the program's .PIF (Program Information File), normally stored in the same directory as the program file itself. For example, SNAP's configuration information is stored in SNAP.PIF.

> **NOTE**
> A DOS program does not need a .PIF file to run—it only needs one if you customize its setup in some way, like changing the icon or adding a line to its CONFIG.SYS.

Controlling 98 SE—The Registry and .INI Files 397

If Windows 98 SE can't find a .PIF for a DOS program, it will look in APPS.INF for the configuration for that file and create a new .PIF from that information. APPS.INF holds default information for many DOS programs, although it doesn't update itself for new applications that you add to the system. The information in APPS.INF may not be exactly to your liking (for example, if I erase 1-2-3 version 3.1's .PIF, the version stored in APPS.INF defines MS-DOS mode for the program), but once Windows 98 SE has re-created the .PIF, you can edit it via the Properties dialog box.

USING DEBUG TO LOOK AT A DOS PROGRAM'S .PIF

.PIF files are not readable in a text editor like Notepad, but you can use a DOS program called DEBUG to check out the contents of a DOS program's .PIF, if you care to go through the trouble. Before starting up, however, let me issue this warning:

It's very easy to render your machine unbootable with DEBUG. Do *not* experiment with commands other than those listed here unless you know exactly what you're doing.

I hate to sound grouchy, but I don't want my e-mail flooded with messages from people who've blown away their MBR and can't boot. Please keep your Startup disk on hand at all times when working with DEBUG.

Enough lecturing—let's check out the contents of SNAP.PIF. First, I'll need to add something distinctive to its configuration so that I can find it easily. Therefore, I'll go into SNAP's Properties dialog box, and manually add the statement

    rem elephant=pink

at the end of its CONFIG.SYS. The *rem* is so I don't mess up the configuration with junk lines.

Now, I'm ready to use DEBUG. I open the DOS prompt and type

    DEBUG_C:\UTILS\SNAP.PIF

(All underscores indicate spaces—DEBUG is very picky about syntax.) The cursor changes to a dash, indicating that DEBUG is running.

CONTINUED →

Next, I need to find out how long SNAP is. I know that the length of a file is stored in register CX, so I'll type **r** to display the contents of all of the .PIF's registers. The result looks like this:

```
AX=0000  BX=0000  CX=04F9  DX=0000  SP=FFEE  BP=0000
SI=0000  DI=0000
DS=1B6C  ES=1B6C  SS=1B6C  CS=1BPC  IP=0010  NV UP EI PL
NZ NA PO NC
1B6C:0100 007853  ADD [BX+SI+53],BH        DS:0053=00
```

As you can see, SNAP's .PIF is 04F9 bytes long (that's hex, translating to 1273 bytes in decimal). That means that I need to search memory, starting from DS 100, for a file 04F9 bytes long that contains the string "elephant." I'll do that with this command:

s_100_l_04f9_"elephant"

That nets me the following:

1B6C:05E8

This is the segment and offset for part of SNAP.PIF. Armed with this information, I can dump the contents of this part of the .PIF onto the screen with **d_1b6c:05e8**.

When you're done looking at SNAP.PIF, type **q** to quit DEBUG and exit the DOS prompt.

To view other information in the .PIF, I'd use a smaller number to describe the segment, perhaps substituting **16c0:05e8** in the dump statement. The result would be earlier lines in the configuration files, as they're stored in the .PIF, in the order in which they appear in the Properties dialog box.

What Is the Registry?

You may still have an AUTOEXEC.BAT and CONFIG.SYS, for odd drivers and configuring DOS programs, but the meat and potatoes of your Windows 98 SE configuration resides in the Registry. You control the Registry with C:\windows\regedit.exe. Let's take a look; you can see the opening screen of the Registry in Figure 15.5.

WARNING

I don't mean to keep reciting the same old rhetoric, but it can't be said enough: *be careful when using REGEDIT*. Make sure that you back up your Registry before you do *anything*. You'll thank me later. Sometimes you can get away with making a mistake or two, but it'll catch up to you and you'll be sorry.

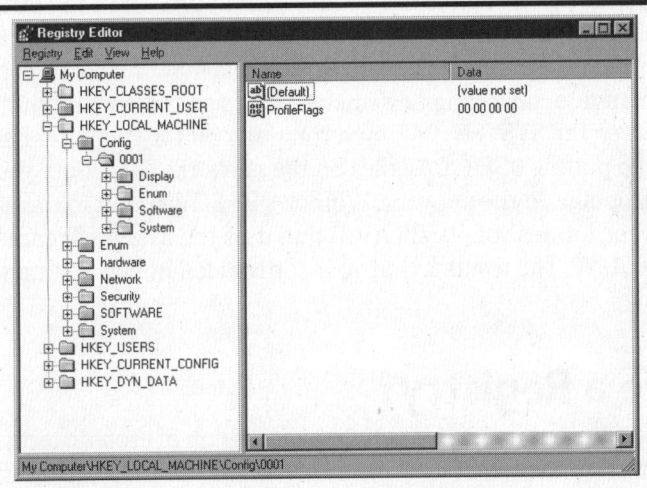

FIGURE 15.5: Registry branches, keys, and subkeys

This, by the way, is not the way your Registry will look when you first open it. I've expanded some parts of it to illustrate what you may see when working with it. Normally, when you start up REGEDIT, all you'll see are the icons labeled HKEY-something. HKEY is Microsoft-ese for "*handle* (that is, pointer) to a *key*." Keys are the folders you see.

This scary-looking database contains all the configuration information for your computer and its network connections, your session on the computer, and the sessions of any user that logs in to that computer. It's a lot of information, cryptically organized, but understanding how it works and how to get around in it is essential for working with Windows 98 SE.

The Registry is the front end for all Windows 98 SE configuration data: the system configuration, the hardware configuration, the setup information for Win32-based applications, and user preferences. The actual files where this information is stored are called USER.DAT, SYSTEM.DAT, and (if you're using the Policy Editor) CONFIG.POL, but they are not in human-readable form. To see your current user and system configurations all in one place, you'll need to run REGEDIT.

Some of the information in the Registry is always stored on disk, while other information is stored initially in RAM, and thus dynamically reflects changes. For example, if you adjust the configuration of a Plug-and-Play optical drive, that change appears immediately in the Registry.

Why is the Registry stored in two files (USER.DAT and SYSTEM.DAT) instead of one? For a very good reason: Many people use Windows 98 SE in a networked environment, and so those users may "roam" from computer to computer on a company's network. It's possible with Windows 98 SE to keep the SYSTEM.DAT for a computer on the computer itself, and then to put the USER.DAT files on the network. Then, once you log on to a computer on the network, Windows 98 SE goes out to the network servers, locates your USER.DAT, and uses the user preferences in that USER.DAT. The result is that your settings follow you around the network.

Why Have a Registry?

Before you tune out in preparation for a discussion of esoteric techie stuff, know that there is at least one characteristic of the Registry that makes understanding it worthwhile: its compactness. It used to be that you had a lot of work to do before you could safely install new software. If you wanted to be sure your system would work right after you installed a new program and didn't want to worry that the new program would introduce changes to your system that would corrupt your Windows installation, you had to back up a whole slew of files so that you could, if necessary, restore your system to the way it was before you installed the new program.

As the Registry contains all Windows 98 SE system and user information, you only need to back up USER.DAT and SYSTEM.DAT. With the Windows 98 SE Registry, all you have to do is export these files to another directory or to disk, name them something in English if you like, and then restore them when things go wrong. The only caveat I might make is this: Name the exported versions something that is easily identifiable when they are condensed to the eight-dot-three format that real-mode sessions demand.

What's in the Registry?

The Registry is an ASCII database pulling information from SYSTEM.DAT, USER.DAT, and (if set up) CONFIG.POL. These files are not in a human-readable form, so you can only see their contents or manipulate them via the Registry Editor (or, more usually, the Control Panel or, for CONFIG.POL, the System Policies Editor).

- SYSTEM.DAT contains hardware-related and computer-specific settings.
- USER.DAT contains user-specific information found in user profiles, such as user rights, Desktop settings, and so forth.
- CONFIG.POL contains policy information relating to the system and user settings. For example, you can create a system policy controlling how users may configure their displays or the devices that they can share. Any information in the system policies file overrides the information in USER.DAT and SYSTEM.DAT. (CONFIG.POL is not mandatory to a Windows installation.)

The Registry itself contains nothing—as you can see in Figure 15.6. It's just the front end to the database of your system's configuration, a way of seeing the information in a way that makes sense to humans.

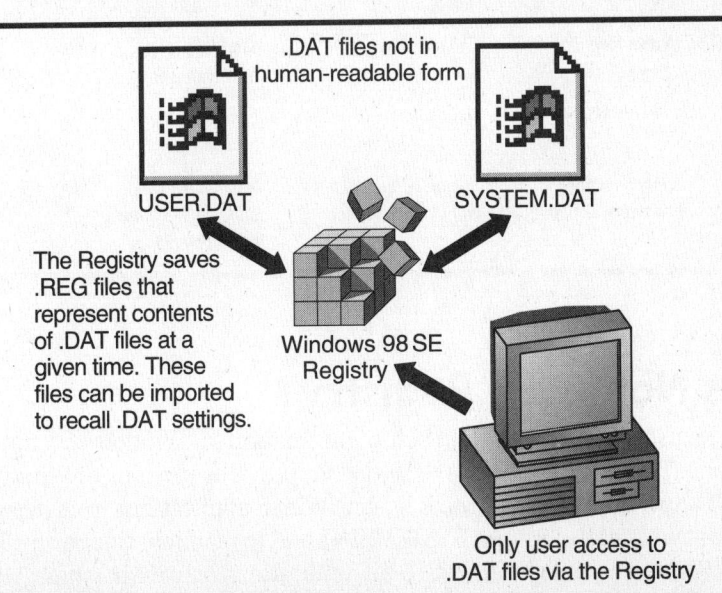

FIGURE 15.6: How the Registry allows users to access Windows 98 SE configuration files

If you export the Registry, you'll create a text file with a `.REG` extension, but this file is only a *link* to the configuration information, not the configuration itself. You can blow away all files with the `.REG` extension on your machine and nothing bad will happen; your system will just re-create another Registry from the information in the `.DAT` files. (If you do this, it won't create another `.REG` file until you export the Registry.)

> **NOTE**
> The Registry itself contains no system information—it's just the human-readable representation of the information in the `.DAT` files, which contain information that your system requires to boot, start Windows, and keep it running.

Conversely, if you erase or rename `SYSTEM.DAT` and `USER.DAT`, your system will not be able to load the Registry on bootup, and it'll have to rebuild the files from the backups it makes each time the machine boots successfully.

The contents of the Registry are described in Table 15.1.

TABLE 15.1: Overview of Registry Contents

Filename	Directory Location (Local Install)	Directory Location (Network Install)	Contents	Required for Installation?
`SYSTEM.DAT`	`C:\windows`	`C:\windows`	Machine-specific information	Yes
`USER.DAT`	`C:\windows`	User's home directory	User-specific information	Yes
`CONFIG.POL`	Logon directory of network server	Logon directory of network server	Hardware and user information determined by policy	No

What's Not in the Registry?

The Registry does *not* contain setup information for Windows 3.*x* applications. This is because apps designed for previous versions of Windows don't know how to access the Registry; Win16 applications were designed to work with `WIN.INI` and `SYSTEM.INI` and to maintain their own `.INI` files. As long as you've still got 16-bit applications on your machine, you'll use the `.INI` files.

Nor does the Registry contain program-specific setup information for DOS programs. If you edit a DOS application's `.PIF`, that information is not reflected in the Registry.

The Windows 98 SE Registry Is *Not* the Same As the Windows NT Registry

Before we go any further with this discussion, NT users should know that the Windows 98 SE Registry is *not* the same as the NT Registry that you've come to know and love. It's still the same old Registry you knew in Windows 95. When Microsoft was tailoring the Win32 API for Windows 95, it had to cripple its implementation slightly to permit the operating system to run on 4MB of RAM, as promised. Some Registry functions were among the casualties of this crippling. Windows 98 SE is no different, although you're going to need quite a bit more than the 4MB of RAM required by Windows 95 in order to get it to work at a reasonable speed.

The Windows 98 SE Registry isn't bad, it's just different. It's more like an extension of the Windows 95 Registry. It works a little differently than NT's Registry, it contains different information, the data is arranged differently, and the syntax is different. That said, your experience working with NT's Registry isn't wasted—you just can't use quite the same skills to work with the Windows 98 SE Registry that you developed for NT. For example:

- You cannot set the Windows 98 SE Registry to read-only from within the Windows 98 SE Registry Editor. To make it read-only, you must change the access settings from the USER.DAT Properties dialog box.

- You cannot set group permissions to the Windows 98 SE Registry from within the application. By default, *anyone* can edit the Registry on the local machine. (This is not a particularly smart way to leave things, as you'll see in this chapter.)

- The Windows 98 SE Registry does not keep `*.LOG` versions of important files to record changes.

- Windows NT is much better designed to support a range of national languages and character sets than is Windows 98 SE, and that affects the Registry. Like most older microcomputer operating systems, Windows 98 SE represents characters with a character set called ASCII, the American Standard Code for Information Interchange. ASCII is great for Americans, as it contains all the characters we use, but not so good for people needing other characters. That's why NT doesn't use ASCII, but instead uses *Unicode*, which allows NT to use virtually any character set. Anyway, here's what that has to do with the Registry. The NT Registry stores character data as Unicode, and the Windows 98 SE Registry stores data as ASCII. *That's* why a machine running both NT and 98 SE can't share a Registry.

Cautions About Working with the Registry

For those who haven't worked with Windows NT and so skipped the previous section, here are a few things to think about before leaping into editing the Registry:

In general, the Registry is *not* where you should be making changes. Most of the configurations that you can adjust in the Registry have a GUI front end somewhere else, with a Cancel button attached. If you can make the adjustments you want from another dialog box, it's a good idea to do so, for two reasons:

- You can cancel changes before they take effect.
- It's harder to screw up.

Know what you're editing. Before you change any values, make sure that you know what making the change will do to your system. *If you don't know, then don't change it.* The Registry *cannot* distinguish between valid and invalid entries, so, for example, you *could* change the value of the primary network provider from "Microsoft" to "goldfish" and receive no complaints from Windows 98 SE—at least not immediately.

Back up before editing. Using the Export Registry File option in the Registry menu, you can save your system configuration to disk or to another drive or directory before editing it. This is a very good idea, in case you make a mistake while editing.

'Nuff said. You know that reckless meddling with your system's configuration is dangerous. Keeping that in mind, let's discuss the anatomy of your Registry and how you can safely make changes to it.

The Registry: Pieces of the Puzzle

Like Windows Explorer, the Registry is organized in a treelike structure. It consists of trees, subtrees, keys, and values, as you can see in Figure 15.7.

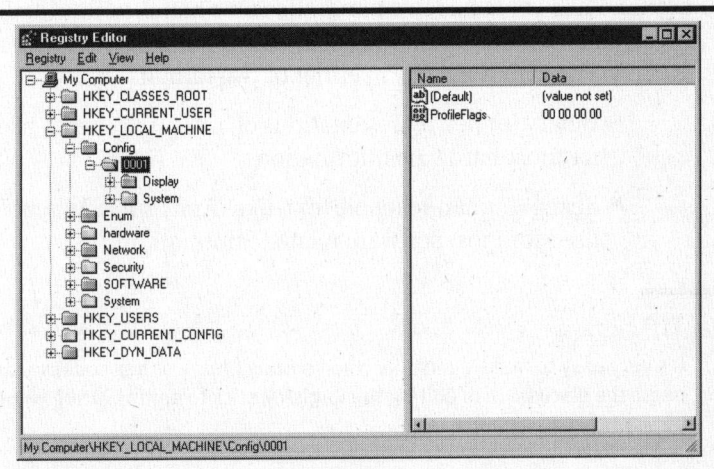

FIGURE 15.7: Anatomy of the Registry

- The *tree* is the entire Registry, called My Computer. It consists of six subtrees:
    - Hkey_Classes_Root
    - Hkey_Current_User
    - Hkey_Local_Machine
    - Hkey_Users
    - Hkey_Current_Config
    - Hkey_Dyn_Data
- Each of the *subtrees* controls a different part of your system. For example, Hkey_Local_Machine controls the hardware setup for your machine. (A complete list of the subtrees and their functions appears later.)
- Each of the folders within a subtree is called a *key* (and no, it doesn't make sense—you'd think a "subtree" would be divided

into "branches" or the like). As you'll notice, keys can contain subkeys and sub-subkeys. The keys (and subkeys) control the configuration to a specific part of the subtree's function. For example, the key called *Mouse* within the subtree Hkey_Local_Machine contains all the mouse settings.

- The actual settings within the Registry are called *values*, or *value entries*. Each value has two parts: the value name, which identifies it, and the value data, which contains the configuration information. The values may be in either of two formats:

  - Binary (or hex representations of binary numbers), used for most hardware information

  - String (human-readable text, like "Ami ProDocument"), used for most software-related information

TIP

It's very easy to make a mistake when editing binary or hex code, so, once we begin the discussion of editing the Registry, stick to editing string values.

Subtree Functions

As mentioned above, the six subtrees of the Registry divide up the configuration for your computer and where it fits into the network. Table 15.2 illustrates those divisions.

TABLE 15.2: Location of Your Computer's Configuration Information

Subtree	Description
HKEY_Classes_Root	Contains the file associations and OLE links, the information that tells your system, "When the user double-clicks a file with the extension .BMP, start up PBRUSH.EXE to display the file." Much of this information is duplicated in the Local_Machine subtree, as Root is a duplicate of Hkey_Local_Machine\Software\Classes.
HKEY_Current_User	Contains the user profile (colors, sounds, applications, etc.) for the person currently logged in to the machine. This subtree is a subset of Hkey_Users (described later in this table). User-specific applications settings (like whether or not Word should hyphenate words) *should* go in here. Some applications designers don't understand the Registry all that well and put user-specific settings in HKEY_Local_Machine, however, so don't be surprised if you see a user preference or two in there.

Controlling 98 SE — The Registry and *.INI* Files

TABLE 15.2 continued: Location of Your Computer's Configuration Information

Subtree	Description
HHKEY_Local_Machine	Contains information about the hardware installed on the machine and the file associations and port assignments. You'll do most of your work in this subtree.
HKEY_Users	Contains both the default user profile for someone who hasn't logged in before and the profile for the current user.
HKEY_Current_Config	Points to Hkey_Local_Machine\Config, the subtree that records the current configuration of the hardware attached to the computer.
HKEY_Dyn_Data	Contains dynamic information about Plug-and-Play hardware attached to the computer. The information contained in this subtree is stored in RAM, so you don't have to reboot to update it.

Opening the Registry

If you're like me, you like to play with something when learning how to use it. At the very least, it's nice to have it in front of you. Therefore, at this point you may be saying to yourself, "This talk of the Registry is all very well, but how do I *start* the silly thing?"

By default, the Registry Editor is not included on any menus, perhaps so that idle curiosity doesn't blow away the system configuration. However, you can open the Registry in a few ways:

- Choose Start ➢ Run, and type **regedit** in the Open box of the Run dialog box.

Or,

- Open the Windows folder, and double-click the Regedit.exe file.

Or,

- You can add the Registry Editor to the Start menu. Follow these steps:
    1. Choose Start ➢ Settings ➢ Taskbar & Start Menu to open the Taskbar Properties dialog box.

2. Click the Start Menu Programs tab, and then click the Add button to open the Create Shortcut dialog box.

3. In the Command Line box, type **C:\windows\regedit.exe**. Click Next.

4. In the Select Program Folder dialog box, select Start Menu, and click Next.

5. In the Select A Title For The Program dialog box, accept the selected name or enter another name.

6. Click Finish, and then click OK.

The Registry Editor is now available from your Start menu.

Navigating in the Registry

Navigating in the Registry is pretty simple. When you open the Registry Editor, the six branches are visible. Click the one you want, and it opens into its keys. Click the key you want, and you'll see *its* keys (if the key icon has the plus sign in a box, it has subkeys) and values. Double-click the entry in the data column of a value to edit it.

The big trick in the Registry lies not in moving around, but in finding where you want to be. When you're looking for something, how do you know where to find it?

Finding things in the Registry is partially a function of logic and experience, and partially a function of the available tools. So far as the logic part goes, where would you look for configuration information about your mouse? `Hkey_Current_User` doesn't sound very likely, as the mouse drivers for a machine won't change from user to user. `Hkey_Local_Machine` is a much more likely starter, as the mouse is part of the machine *any* user will use.

Using the Find Tool

When logic won't help you, there's always the Find tool. Think of a word that relates to the configuration information you're looking for (keep it short, as the Registry Editor's style is telegraphic, to say the least) and choose Edit ➢ Find. If the first Find that you come up with doesn't work, press F3 or click Find Next, and the Registry Editor will look for the next incidence of that word for you.

Notice that the Find tool is more useful in Windows 98 SE than in Windows NT, as the Registry is organized differently. Rather than devoting a separate window to each subtree, as Windows NT does, Windows 98 SE includes every subtree in the same window so you can extend searches from subtree to subtree.

> **TIP**
> When searching for a word, start as close to the top of the Registry as possible if you're not certain which subtree you should be looking in. If the word doesn't appear in the subtree in which you started, the Registry Editor will begin searching in the next subtree on the list. If you begin the search in one of the lower subtrees and the word does not appear in that subtree or any of the ones listed after it, the Registry Editor does not go to the top of the list and begin again.

Editing the Local Registry

Editing the Registry is mostly a matter of finding what you want—once you get that far, the rest is easy. The simplest way to understand how to make changes to the Registry is to do it. In this section, we'll go through the process of changing the color of the buttons from the gray of the default Windows color scheme to blue. The process includes three main steps:

- Backing up the Registry
- Editing the configuration
- Restoring the Registry (if necessary)

One problem with the Find tool: it won't search for text in Registry entries. (It *will* search for text in Registry *keys*, however.) You can get around the problem by exporting the Registry to ASCII and then searching the ASCII file.

Backing Up the Registry

One of the better features of Windows 98 SE is that it automatically scans the Registry when booting to see if it is corrupted and creates a backup of the system files once each day. If the Registry is corrupted, Windows 98 SE will automatically restore the previous day's Registry backup. If the backup isn't available, Windows 98 SE will attempt to repair the Registry.

> **WARNING**
>
> Before making any changes directly to the Registry, back it up to a safe place (either your local drive or, for extra security, to your computer's Startup disk). If you have this backup copy, you can restore your Registry very easily if you mess up your system. (If you don't, and the corruption is bad enough, you might have to reinstall the operating system. So don't skip this step.)

There are a few ways to back up your system's Registry: SCANREG.EXE, SCANREGW.EXE, and exporting the Registry using REGEDIT.EXE. SCANREG.EXE and SCANREGW.EXE do basically the same thing. SCANREG is the DOS-based version; SCANREGW is the Windows-based version. Each has separate functions, however.

SCANREG.EXE

This tool is really easy to use if you accidentally deleted or changed important Registry settings. The easiest way to show its usefulness is to show you step-by-step how you can bring a corrupted Registry back from the dead.

Backing Up the Registry Using SCANREG

The first thing I want you to do is to change your display settings—background color, font, wallpaper—just so that you have a customized Desktop. Now we'll back up the Registry so that we have a copy that we can work with. Our aim here is to delete those settings from the Registry and then restore those settings by restoring the original Registry.

OK, have you changed your Desktop? Good. Now, we're going to back up the Registry. Choose Start ➢ Run and type **scanreg**. Click Enter, and you'll see the dialog box shown in Figure 15.8.

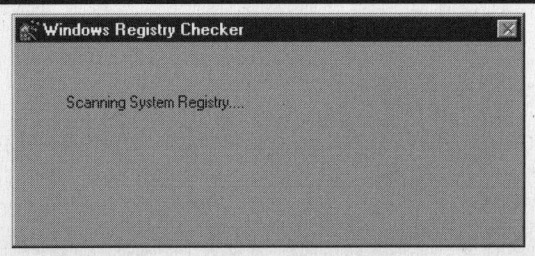

FIGURE 15.8: Scanning the Registry for errors

Controlling 98 SE — The Registry and .INI Files

Once the Registry Checker has scanned the Registry for errors, it'll tell you that the Registry has already been backed up today. Actually, the Registry gets backed up every time you reboot your machine. However, you've just made a change that you want to preserve, so click Yes, and SCANREG will back up the Registry.

The Registry will be backed up to an RB###.CAB file in your C:\WINDOWS\SYSBACKUP directory by default, where ### is the backup number. If you see a file named RBBAD.CAB, *don't use it*. It's more than likely a corrupted file. If you use it, it may cause problems later on. The maximum number of backups you can have by default is five, but you can change that by editing SCANREG.INI in your C:\WINDOWS folder.

Each backup file consists of your SYSTEM.DAT, SYSTEM.INI, USER.DAT, and USER.INI. If you like, you can also add other system files to the backup by editing SCANREG.INI.

Editing *SCANREG.INI*

Get out your favorite text editor and open SCANREG.INI. Editing this file will allow you to do a number of things:

- Skip the backup altogether and just scan the Registry for errors
- Skip the Registry automatic optimization
- Specify the maximum number of backup copies you can create
- Specify the directory path where the backups will be written
- Specify system files to be saved in addition to Registry

If you've used REGEDIT to export a copy of your Registry as a backup, you'll notice that REGEDIT can't do any of these things. While it may take a little more work at first, you have a lot more flexibility when working with SCANREG.

OK, having said that, we can now get to work. First, we'll want to change SCANREG.INI so that the Registry is scanned for errors without being backed up. To do this, change the Backup setting from 1 to 0. If it is set to 0, the backup is skipped. Setting Backup to 1 causes the backup to automatically occur every time SCANREG is run. While you should always have a backup handy in case of a catastrophe, you may want to change this setting if you're experiencing problems with your system and you want to scan the Registry for errors. You sure wouldn't want to back up the Registry if problems kept recurring, would you?

Now you can change the optimization setting. If you set Optimize to 0, automatic optimization is skipped every time you run SCANREG. Setting the value to 1 has the opposite effect. If you set this value to 0, you can always run SCANREG/OPT to optimize your Registry whenever you feel like it.

By default, the maximum number of Registry copies is set to 5, but you can change this to suit your needs. Just specify a numeric value for the `MaxBackupCopies` parameter.

As I mentioned earlier, the default Registry backup directory is located in `C:\WINDOWS\SYSBCKUP`. If you're running out of space on your system partition or you just want the backups to be located elsewhere, you can always specify another directory path using the `BackupDirectory` parameter. Make sure, however, that you designate the entire path (that is, `c:\temp\backup`).

Oh, and one other thing—you can back up system files in addition to backing up the Registry. This is a good idea just in case you're making changes to your system directories. You never know—you could accidentally delete a crucial system file. Configure this setting using the following convention:

    `Files=[dir code,]file1,file2,file3…`

Where *dir code* can be one of the values shown in Table 15.3.

TABLE 15.3: Directory Codes Used in SCANREG.INI

DIR CODE	FILE LOCATION
10	C:\WINDOWS folder
11	C:\WINDOWS\STSTEN folder
30	Boot directory (that is, C:\)
31	Boot host dir (that is, C:\)

The *file* parameters indicated above specify the files in the designated folders that you want to back up. If they don't exist in the designated directory, they won't be backed up.

Next time you run SCANREG, you may see it run differently. If you specified additional system files to be backed up, open the most recent .CAB file, and you should see them listed along with SYSTEM.DAT, SYSTEM.INI, USER.INI, and USER.DAT.

Restoring the Registry Using SCANREG

OK, now we can get to the fun stuff. Let's go and destroy your display and printer settings. Don't worry that you won't be able to see anything once you've logged on—we're just going to remove the wallpaper, background color, fonts, icons, and whatever else you put on your Desktop, as well as your printer settings, if you have any. Basically, when you reboot, you'll just see the default settings you had when you logged on for the first time.

Run REGEDIT and drill down to HKEY_LOCAL_MACHINE\Config. Right-click the 0001 subkey, and click Delete. If you're sure you want to delete the subkey, click Yes (this is your last chance to back out, so be careful).

Now you've done it—you've deleted your Desktop and printer settings, and you need to restore them. In order to do this, however, you're going to need to reboot your machine to DOS mode. At the command prompt, type **scanreg**. You'll be prompted to let the Registry Checker scan the Registry.

Once the Registry has been scanned, you'll be given the opportunity to back up the current Registry or to view one of the Registry backups. Select View and you'll see a list of .CAB files (.CAB files are compressed files that contain original Windows setup files), some of which have been started, and some of which have not. Some of them will have dates, indicating when they were last restored. You'll want to select the highest-numbered file that doesn't have a date attached to it. This will be the file containing the most recent Registry backup. Press Enter when you've selected the file you want, and SCANREG will restore your Registry to its original state.

Reboot your machine, and you will see that your display and printer settings are back to normal. Even though you only had to restore display and printer settings—which you could have easily done manually through the Display Properties dialog box and adding a new printer—it could have easily been something much worse. You could have deleted all of the sub-keys under one of the HKEY keys and rendered your Windows 98 SE installation useless. However, if you're able to restore a backed-up Registry, everything will be back to normal in a matter of minutes. Otherwise, you're starting over from scratch—installing Windows 98 SE and all your applications.

SCANREGW.EXE

This utility essentially does the same thing as SCANREG, with one exception—it won't restore your Registry. Think of it as a protected-mode version of SCANREG. Your machine uses this version to scan your Registry for errors when it boots up and defers to SCANREG when it finds an error so that it can fix the problem. You probably won't have to use this version—neither SCANREG nor SCANREGW will restore a Registry in Windows mode, and SCANREGW won't restore the Registry at all. So, if you're worried about accidentally restoring a corrupted Registry or overwriting your current Registry when you experiment with these tools, don't bother. Unless you're using SCANREG in DOS mode and actually specify that you're going to restore your Registry, you shouldn't have any problems.

Exporting a Registry with *REGEDIT.EXE*

Another way to back up your system's configuration is to export the Registry to disk or to another directory. When REGEDIT exports a Registry, it is dumping out the entire Registry in a simple ASCII format. Essentially, exporting the Registry converts USER.DAT and SYSTEM.DAT to something you can view, search, and save. Once exported, those versions of the system configuration are not available to the system until you import them. In the meantime, you're able to make all the changes that you like to the Registry information. Take a look at Figure 15.9 to see how this works.

When you export a Registry, it maintains a copy of the system configuration files with it. This copy, however, is isolated from the operating system (as represented by the ring around the exported files). Changes made to the current Registry do not affect the exported copies. Therefore, when you replace the current Registry with an exported one, you'll restore the operating system to the way it was when you exported the Registry.

To export the configuration information's front end, open the Registry Editor (choose Run from the Start button, and type **regedit.exe**). You should see a screen that looks like the one in Figure 15.10.

TIP
Almost every Windows user who's ever restored their Registry with a corrupted version of an exported file knows that eventually they'll end up with a corrupted version of Windows 98 SE that won't boot. If this happens to you, fret not—your Registry is automatically backed up when it first boots. Use the SCANREG tool mentioned earlier in this chapter to restore this version of your Registry. Yes, you'll have to start over and may even lose whatever Registry changes you made since you first started your machine, but at least you won't have to completely reinstall everything you worked so hard for.

Controlling 98 SE — The Registry and *.INI* Files

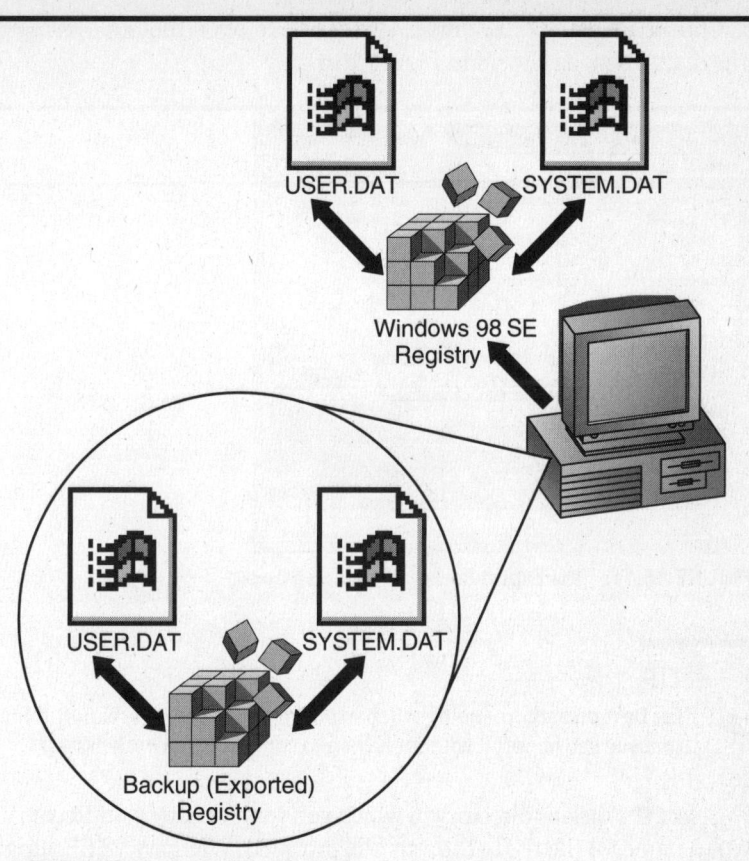

FIGURE 15.9: Exporting a Registry

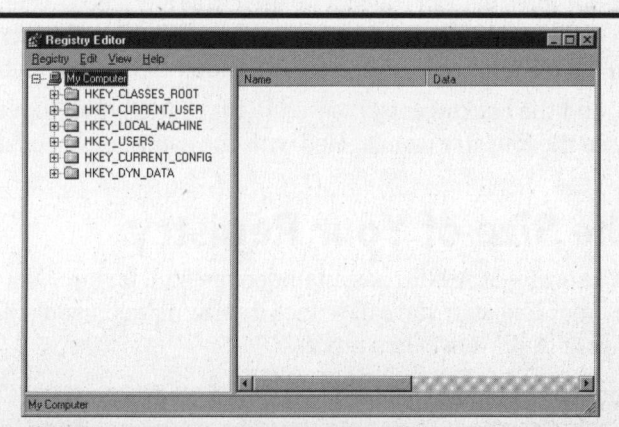

FIGURE 15.10: Opening screen of the Registry Editor

Chapter Fifteen

Choose Registry ➤ Export Registry File to open the Export Registry File dialog box, as shown in Figure 15.11.

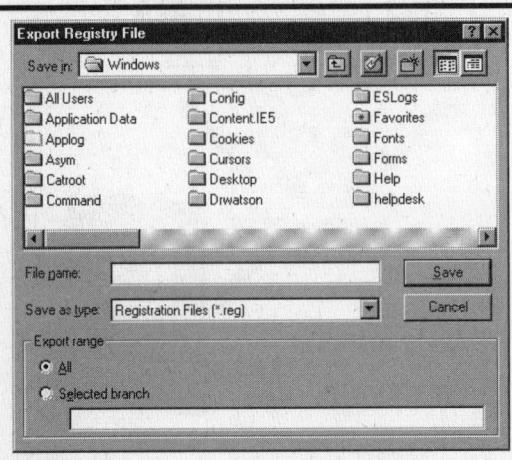

FIGURE 15.11: The Export Registry File dialog box

> **TIP**
> For best disaster planning when exporting your Registry, export it locally so that you can import it without having to connect to network drives.

Select the disk or directory to which you want to copy your Registry and type a name for the file in the text box provided. Windows 98 SE supports long filenames when running in protected mode, so this name can be longer than the eight-dot-three pattern you may be used to as a Windows user. As you can see in Figure 15.12, I named my backup copy **Working Registry for ORBITER on 7-7-99** and copied it to my C:\Windows\backup directory.

Click Save, and the backup copy is saved to that folder. If you open the folder, you'll see the Registry icon labeled with the name you specified.

Reducing the Size of Your Registry

Wouldn't you know it—SCANREG has an undocumented feature. Not only can you repair your Registry, you can reduce its size, as well, using SCANREG /OPT. Actually, it's a two-step process:

1. Reboot to DOS mode and run SCANREG /FIX.
2. Run SCANREG /OPT and reboot your machine.

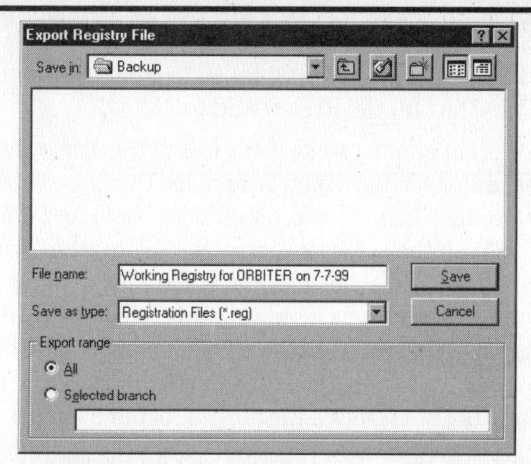

FIGURE 15.12: Export Registry File dialog box with export information

Why would I want to fix the Registry first if it's not broken? Well, you're not really fixing it but removing duplicate entries that may exist. I mean, you take your car in to the mechanic once in a while even though there's nothing wrong with it, don't you? Of course you do. Along those same lines, think of this as Registry maintenance. You're just getting rid of the junk you don't need and cleaning it up a little bit.

And I do mean little. I ran this sequence on my machine, and it decreased the size of my SYSTEM.DAT file from 2.57MB to 2.46MB. OK, so I didn't have a whole lot of stuff installed on my machine and it was recently installed, but all the same, it only turned out to be about 101K. Not only that, it *increased* the size of my USER.DAT file from 236K to 240K. Are you kidding me? 4K? So, my total Registry size was only reduced by 95K. If I'm so desperate for space that I need that extra 6K, I should probably go ahead and repartition my hard drive. Freeing up 6K on my hard drive won't cure whatever memory problems I'm having now. That's like saying cutting your hair helps you lose weight.

Still, it's not a bad thing to do every once in a while. Sure, you may not have many applications installed on your machine at one time, but if you install and uninstall programs on your computer over time, you'll see your Registry balloon up to 6–8MB in no time. Sometimes when you reinstall applications on a machine, you'll see duplicate entries appear. Every time you do this, your Registry increases in size. Having a leaner, more robust Registry will help you out in the long run. It'll help your system to run more efficiently, too.

Editing the Registry's Contents

Now that we've saved the current configuration, we can mess around with it. Run REGEDIT to start up the Registry Editor.

As I said earlier, in this experiment we're going to edit the display to change the color of the buttons in the dialog boxes. One thing you should probably know before we start doing this: You won't be able to find the individual display setting right off the bat, as Windows 98 SE uses the "Windows Standard" color scheme. The scheme contains the color settings for each item, so there's no need to have each individual item listed. However, we only want to change *one* item, not all of them. We can give it a little kick, though—and let me warn you now that it might seem redundant to go ahead and do what I'm about to do, but it serves the purpose of our example.

First, since I already know that I won't find the key for the specific item I'm looking for, I have to let Windows 98 SE create the list for me. To do so, I'll right-click anywhere on the Desktop and choose Active Desktop ➤ Customize My Desktop. Next, I'll click the Appearance tab and change the color of the dialog box button.

OK, so the color's been changed. Easy enough, right? But there was another reason I had to change the color like this: to create a key in the Registry to control the color of the dialog-box buttons. Now if I want to edit the Registry to change the color again, I can do it.

Off the top of my head, I don't know which key contains the values that relate to this information, so I've got two options: I can guess (the subtree that relates to the current user and the display key within it seem likely contenders), or I can do a search for instances of the word "color" throughout the Registry. The second method seems like less work, so I'll use it.

Position the cursor in My Computer so that the search will extend through every subtree. Choose Edit ➤ Find to open the Find dialog box, as shown in Figure 15.13.

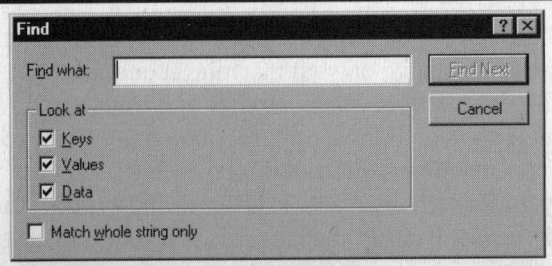

FIGURE 15.13: The Find dialog box

Controlling 98 SE — The Registry and .INI Files 419

Type **color** in the Find What text box and click Find Next. While REGEDIT is searching, a dialog box like the one in Figure 15.14 will appear.

FIGURE 15.14: Searching for color

To keep the search as broad as possible, I've instructed the Editor to look at keys, values, *and* data for the keyword, as it does by default. If I checked Match Whole String Only, REGEDIT would only find "color," but by leaving this option unchecked, matches like "ButtonColor" or "Colors" will count as hits as well. I'll keep it unchecked, as I'm not sure exactly how the word will appear.

The first hit, as you can see in Figure 15.15, doesn't look like what I need (I can't manipulate the hex accurately), so I'll click F3 to find the next "color."

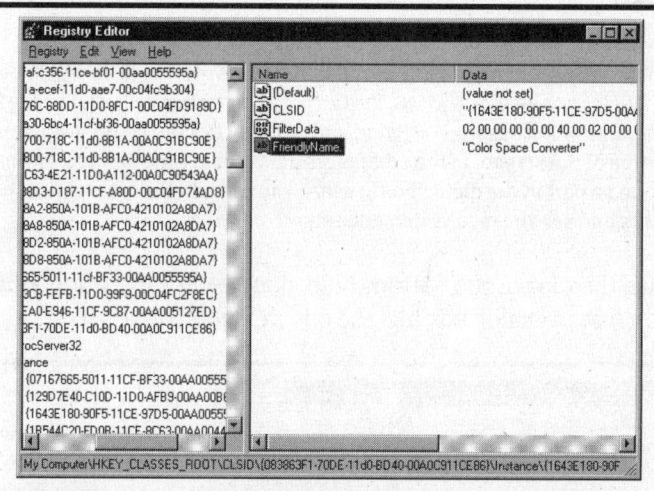

FIGURE 15.15: First result of Find action

And so it goes, until I find the one I want as in Figure 15.16.

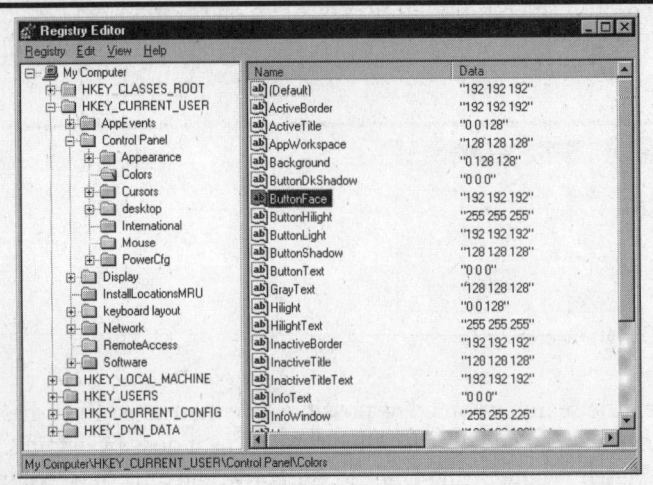

FIGURE 15.16: The section of the Registry that controls display colors

Aha! "ButtonFace" looks like the value name I need. If you've messed around with changing color values numerically, you'll know that the value 192 192 192 indicates a nice medium gray made of middling amounts of red, green, and blue.

> **NOTE**
>
> When setting color intensity, 0 is least, 255 is most; three 0s would be black, and three 255s would be white. You can get a feel for this in Paint. Choose Start ➢ Programs ➢ Accessories ➢ Paint, and double-click the colored squares at the bottom of the screen. In the Edit Colors dialog box, click Define Custom Colors to open a part of the dialog box in which you can edit the numeric values of the colors and see the results immediately.

To make the tops of the buttons blue, double-click the word "Button-Face." You'll see a dialog box like the one in Figure 15.17.

FIGURE 15.17: Editing a Registry value

Type **0 0 255** in the Value data text box to show no red and no green but full-intensity blue, and click OK. Notice that the button faces are still gray—the change has not taken effect yet.

Exit the Registry Editor and log off (you don't have to restart the computer). When the login dialog box shows up, it will be an obnoxious shade of blue.

Restoring the Registry Using *REGEDIT.EXE*

As the change you made is pretty easy to remember, you could restore the Registry (and get rid of that obnoxious blue) by searching for "Button-Face" and changing its value data back to 192 192 192. Once you logged off and back on again, the change would take effect.

> **WARNING**
> You can't reverse an importing action; once you've imported a Registry or a subtree thereof, it replaces whatever was there before. If you want to save a copy of the configuration, export it before you import the old one.

Since we're practicing for real-world changes that may not be quite so easy to reverse, however, let's do a real trial. There are two ways in which you can restore your Registry to the way it was before:

- Import the Registry from the Registry Editor
- *Or*, activate the icon of the backup in its folder

In either case, what you're doing is replacing the current configuration with the one you exported. As you recall from earlier in this chapter, when you export the Registry, it maintains a copy of what the .DAT files looked like at the time you exported. When you import that saved file, you replace the current configuration with that saved one.

To import a saved Registry, choose Registry ➤ Import Registry File, and move to the folder where you stored the backup (in my case, `C:\backup`). You'll see the name of the backup copy, as you do in Figure 15.18.

Select the name of the file, click Open, and the Registry Editor will replace the current copy of the Registry with the one you just imported. A status box like the one in Figure 15.19 will show the progress of the importing process.

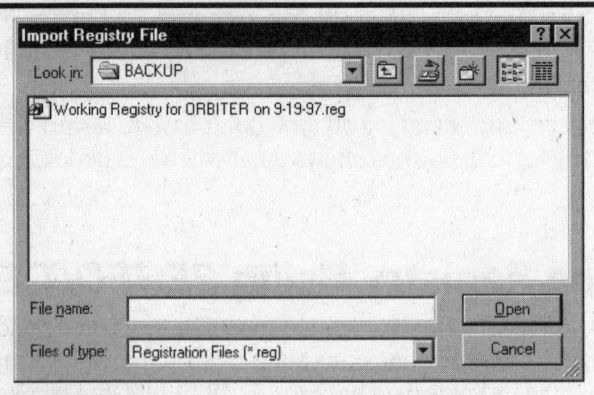

FIGURE 15.18: The Import Registry File dialog box

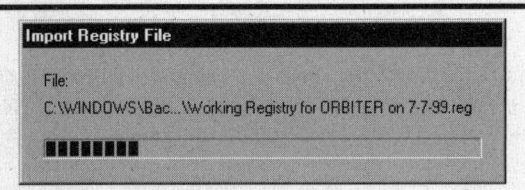

FIGURE 15.19: Importing a Registry

When the file is fully imported, a dialog box like the one in Figure 15.20 will announce the fact.

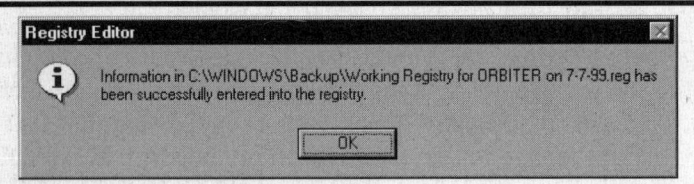

FIGURE 15.20: Import confirmed

Importing a saved Registry from its folder is even easier. Open the folder to which you exported the file (as in Figure 15.21) and double-click it.

When you activate the saved file, it imports itself into the Registry, showing the same dialog boxes that you saw with the previous approach.

Whichever method you choose, the system configuration will revert to the one in the restored Registry as soon as you log off and log back on.

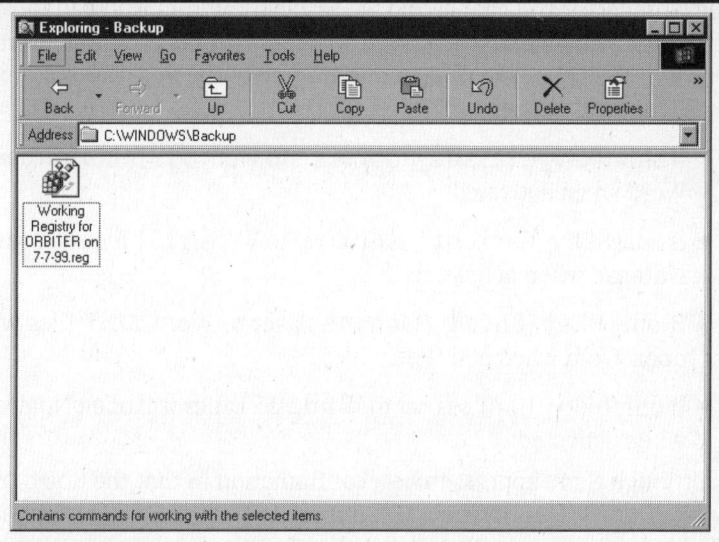

FIGURE 15.21: Folder containing exported Registry

What About Duplicate Entries?

The Registry sometimes repeats itself. For example, as we noted earlier, some of the information found in Hkey_Classes_Root also appears in Hkey_Local_Machine. If the same values appear in two different subtrees, which subtree controls?

The subtrees of the Registry are arranged in a hierarchy. If the same information appears in more than one subtree of the Registry and you manually change it in only one subtree, the effect of the change on the system depends on where that subtree falls in the hierarchy. Generally speaking, system-specific information outranks user-specific information. For example, a setting that appears in both the Local_Machine and Users subtrees will be controlled by what's in Local_Machine. Please note that this only applies to those times when you've edited the Registry directly; if you edit the system configuration from the Control Panel, the settings will be updated in every subtree in which they appear.

For example, you can set file associations through the Registry to link files with a particular extension to an application. Four subtrees of the Registry contain value data for file associations: Hkey_Classes_Root, Hkey_Current_User, Hkey_Local_Machine, and Hkey_Users. By default, all files with the extension .1ST (as in README.1ST) are linked with Notepad, so if you activate a file with that extension, you'll also open Notepad. If you change the file association from Notepad to Word, you'll open Word when you activate any file with the .1ST extension. But if you edit the file association in one subtree of the Registry at a time, here's what will happen:

- If only Hkey_Classes_Root is set to Word, .1ST files will open Word when activated.

- If only Hkey_Current_User is set to Word, .1ST files will open Notepad when activated.

- If only Hkey_Local_Machine is set to Word, .1ST files will open Word when activated.

- If only Hkey_Users is set to Word, .1ST files will open Notepad when activated.

Although there appears to be a contradiction in that the Root subtree and the Local_Machine subtree appear to control file associations independently of each other, remember that the Root subtree is really Hkey_Local_Machine\Software\Classes, so changes made to Root are changes made to that key and subkey within Local_Machine.

Preparing to Administer a Remote Computer

Why would you need to edit the Registry of a remote machine? It's handy in any of the following situations, where it's easier to fix the problem from your desk than it is to go to the ailing workstation or where you *can't* fix the problem from the local machine:

- The person using that machine played with the display settings and turned his screen entirely black.

- You want to copy the same user configuration to several machines.

- A user has connected to the wrong network drives and can't find her files.

Controlling 98 SE—The Registry and *.INI* Files

Editing the Registry of a remote computer works much the same way as editing a local one: the main difference lies in the process of connecting to the remote Registry in the first place. In this section, we'll talk about how to connect to the remote machine (and some of the potential connection glitches you may encounter) and what you can expect to see when you've connected.

Before you can edit another computer's Registry, both you and the other computer must have at least one network protocol (like NetBEUI or IPX/SPX) in common and the Remote Registry service set up. In addition, your network must use either an NT domain or a NetWare server.

To install the Remote Registry (or any other) service on a computer, insert the Windows 98 SE CD-ROM into the drive, and follow these steps:

1. Open the Control Panel and choose Network to open the Network dialog box.

2. Click the Add button, and in the Select Network Component Type dialog box, double-click Service.

3. From the Select Network Service dialog box, click the Have Disk button. When prompted, specify the path to `\Tools\Nettools\Remotreg` on the CD. You'll see a file called `REGSERV.INF` in the menu. Select it, and click OK.

4. Select Microsoft Remote Registry from the Models list and click OK; then click OK to get out of the dialog box altogether. Windows 98 SE will search the CD for all the files that it needs to set up the service.

After you exit from the Network dialog box, Windows 98 SE will tell you that you must restart for the change to take effect, but you don't have to reboot then unless you want to be able to use the Remote Registry service right away.

You'll need to install the Remote Registry service on both the administering machine and any Windows 98 SE machine to be administered.

Connecting to the Remote Computer

You must initiate a specific connection to a remote machine's Registry in order to edit it. To do so, open the Registry Editor and choose Registry ➤ Connect Network Registry to open the Connect Network Registry dialog box as shown in Figure 15.22.

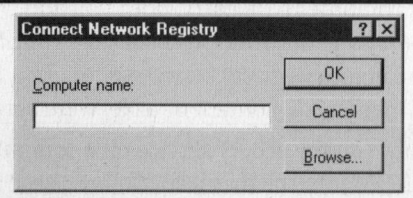

FIGURE 15.22: The Connect Network Registry dialog box

Type the name of the computer you want to administer, or, to make sure that you type it correctly and choose from the right domain, click Browse and choose a computer from the dialog box like the one in Figure 15.23. All machines connected to the network will be displayed, whether they're Windows 98 SE machines or have the Remote Registry service running.

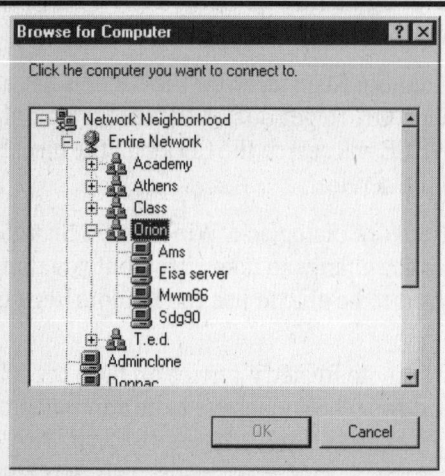

FIGURE 15.23: The Browse list for Remote Registry administration

Choose the machine to connect to (in this case, I'll choose AMS) and click OK. Click OK again at the next dialog box to connect to the Registry.

Troubleshooting a Remote Registry Connection

At this point, you should be connected successfully. If you are not, you may see a dialog box like the one in Figure 15.24. If you see this dialog box, make sure of the following things:

▶ You've connected to a machine running Windows 98 or 98 SE.

▶ The Remote Registry service is running on both machines.

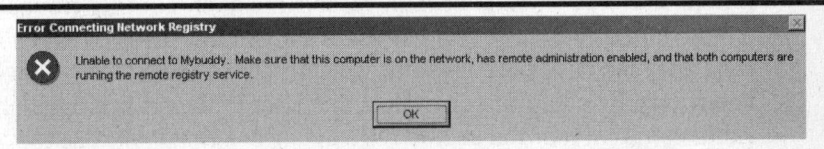

FIGURE 15.24: Unsuccessful attempt to connect to remote Registry

You might see a message telling you that you don't have permission to edit the remote Registry, as in Figure 15.25. You'll see this message if:

▶ You've logged onto a domain that doesn't have permission to administer the machine's Registry.

▶ Your account is a member of a group not permitted to administer the remote computer (by default, only Domain Administrators have this permission).

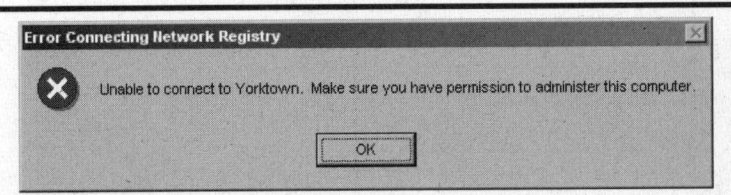

FIGURE 15.25: No permission to edit remote Registry

If you're running NT on your network and have more than one domain, you may wonder if establishing a *trust relationship* between two domains means that the trusted domain can administer machines which have permitted members of the other domain to administer them.

Nope.

No matter what the trust relationships between the two domains are, if you don't log on to the domain with explicit permission to administer the remote machine, you'll see a message like the one in Figure 15.25.

Permitting Other Groups to Administer Remote Registries

The previous section described how to set up a computer for the remote administration of its Registry by members of the network's Domain Administrators group. If, for some reason, members of other groups require this ability, the setup process is a little more involved. Open Control Panel and click the Passwords icon. You'll see three tabs: Change Passwords, Remote Administration, and User Profiles. Click the Remote Administration tab. You should see a dialog box that looks like the one in Figure 15.26.

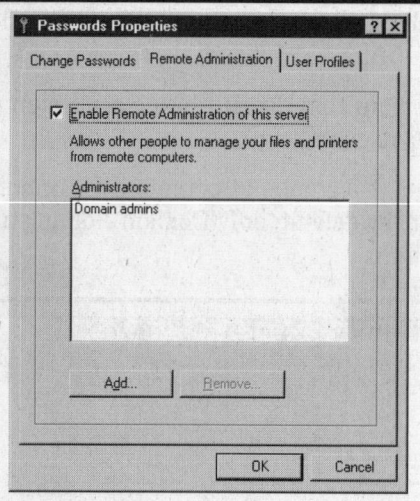

FIGURE 15.26: Setting remote administration options

In this screen, you can see the users and/or groups (by default, only the group Domain Administrators) that currently have permission to remotely administer this machine. Click the Add button to select other remote administrators. You'll see a screen that looks like Figure 15.27, with a list that includes a globe icon and various head icons.

Controlling 98 SE—The Registry and *.INI* Files

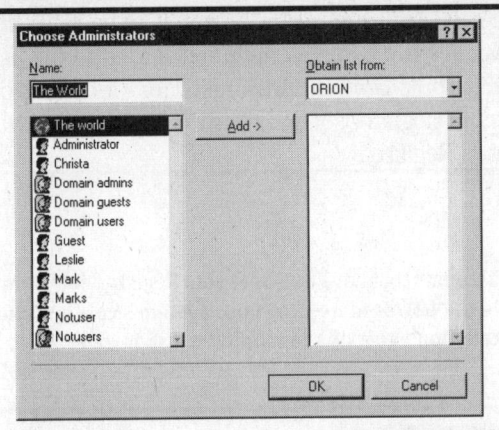

FIGURE 15.27: Adding remote administrators

Single heads are individuals; double heads are groups. The globe signifies everyone on the network. Notice that a list box in the upper right corner lets you specify the domain to draw administrators from. It's perfectly OK to have some administrators from one domain and some from another, thus eliminating the need to set up double accounts for remote administrators. Click the individuals or groups who you want to be able to administer your computer, and then click Add. If you chose your administrators from more than one domain, the administrator's domain name will appear in parentheses next to his or her name. In Figure 15.28, I've added the group Domain Administrators from Orion and the user Leslie from Orion to the list of those permitted to remotely administer my computer.

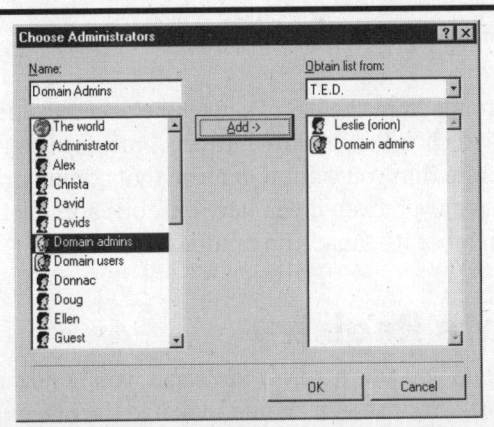

FIGURE 15.28: Administrators from two workgroups added to the list

Click OK and, as you can see in Figure 15.29, you'll be back at the initial screen, where you can see the two new members added to the list. If Leslie or any member of Orion's Domain Administrator group logs on to a machine with the Remote Registry service running, that person will be able to edit my computer's Registry.

> **WARNING**
> When choosing the accounts that have access to your Registry, don't forget that you're giving people the power to destroy your system's configuration and require you to reinstall. Don't give this capability to just anyone.

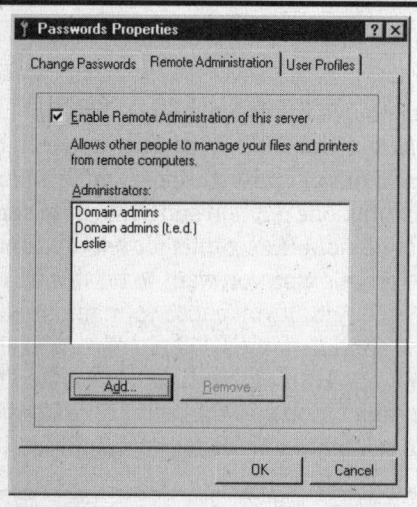

FIGURE 15.29: New list of remote administrators

To remove users or groups from the list of a machine's remote administrators, click the name and click the Remove button. A message box will appear, asking if you're sure that you want to remove that administrator; click OK to confirm the removal. Even if you have only one administrator in the list, you can still remove it—there's no minimum.

Editing the Remote Registry

If everything went well and you saw no error messages, you're now ready to edit the remote Registry. Your screen should look like the one in Figure 15.30.

Controlling 98 SE—The Registry and .*INI* Files

From here on out, the editing process is the same as it is for the local Registry. When you've finished making changes, exit the Registry Editor or choose Registry ➤ Disconnect Network Registry from the Registry menu.

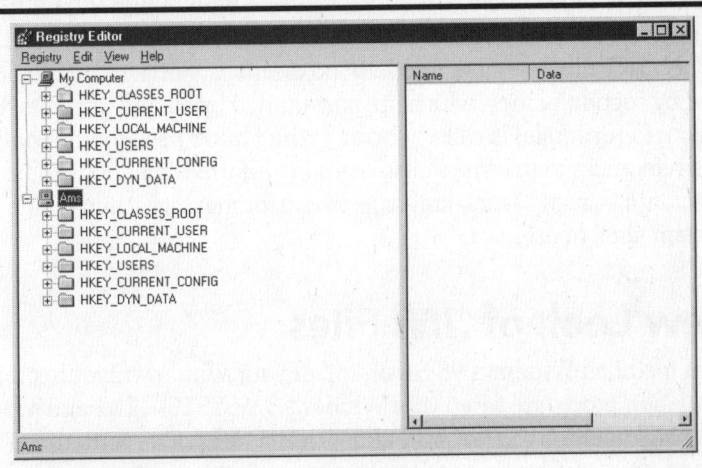

FIGURE 15.30: View of remote Registry

WIN.INI AND *SYSTEM.INI* UNDER WINDOWS 98 SE

There are lots of files in the Windows world with the extension `.INI`, for *initialization*. Excel, for example, creates and maintains a file called `EXCEL.INI` that tells Excel things like whether to start up in a maximized condition, what the previous few files accessed were, and what user options should be set. Most other applications create their own `.INI` files.

If a program creates an initialization file for itself, however, that file is for its personal use *only*—other programs don't access it. For general configuration information, Win16 applications access two more general initialization files: `WIN.INI` and `SYSTEM.INI`.

Contents of *.INI* Files

It's hard to draw a clear and distinct line between what `SYSTEM.INI` and `WIN.INI` do, as `WIN.INI` has existed since the Windows 1.0 days, and

SYSTEM.INI has only been around since version 3.0. Although it's tempting to say that SYSTEM.INI controls the hardware configuration of Windows, and WIN.INI contains user preferences and software configuration, that's not 100 percent accurate. It *is* a decent approximation, however, so use it if you like, just to get a grasp on what these two files do.

The .INI files are all divided up into *sections*. Sections are demarcated by section names, which are surrounded by square brackets. One section, for example, is called [boot]; the [boot] section not only contains references to drivers, it also contains information about some Windows fonts, screen savers, language to use for messages, and which program shell to use.

The New Look of *.INI* Files

If you installed Windows 98 SE on top of your Windows 3.*x* directory, the installation procedure saved your Windows 3.*x* SYSTEM.INI and WIN.INI under the names SYSINI.W31 and WININI.W31. The contents of the old and the new files do not match—although they're similar, the entries in the new .INI files reflect the differences between a Windows overlay on DOS and the Windows 98 SE operating system. The old configuration information was set aside in the .W31 files, and new .INI files were created from the information in the Registry.

What's different? The exact entries will vary from PC to PC, depending on your hardware and how you set up Windows, but here are some of the more important differences in each initialization file.

SYSTEM.INI versus *SYSINI.W31*

SYSTEM.INI, recall, is more or less responsible for recording hardware information. It contains configuration information for drivers, network setup, the display, the process of starting Windows, and so forth.

Thus, when you change the operating system, the display modes it supports, and the way that it does networking, it's not surprising that entries corresponding to those qualities should change also. Many of the important differences occur in the [boot] and [386enh] sections of SYSTEM.INI. For example:

- ▶ The default shell in SHELL= (the program that, among other things, provides the background to Windows) differs from Windows 3.*x*; in Windows 98 SE, it provides access to user programs with EXPLORER.EXE rather than to PROGMAN.EXE.

Controlling 98 SE—The Registry and .*INI* Files

- The protected-mode screen grabber (the program that saves the information in your DOS screens when you flip from DOS programs to Windows) is now called `VGAFULL.3GR` instead of `VGADIB.3GR`. There *is* no real-mode screen grabber (indicated in `SYSINI.W31` as `286Grabber`) in the Windows 98 SE `SYSTEM.INI`.

- Windows 3.*x* defined the display font for non-Windows applications displaying either 40 or 80 columns and 25 or fewer lines (`EGA80WOA.FON`, for example). Windows 98 SE skips these entries entirely—the display settings for DOS programs are set in their Properties dialog boxes, as discussed in Chapter 15.

- The line allowing Windows to bypass DOS and BIOS to access a Western Digital hard disk (`device=*wdctrl`) is now gone, as Windows 98 SE is its own operating system and doesn't need special statements to permit 32-bit disk access.

- Many Windows 3.*x* virtual device drivers are rolled into `VMM.VXD`, so individual statements referring to those drivers are missing from Windows 98 SE.

- The `[mci]` section, which describes how Windows handles multimedia applications that use the media control interface, has some new entries for video handling.

- `SYSTEM.INI` under Windows 98 SE contains an entirely new section devoted to networking, including entries to define how TCP/IP works.

Please note that this list doesn't include *every* difference between a Windows 3.*x* `SYSTEM.INI` and a Windows 98 SE `SYSTEM.INI`, but these are some of the more important variances. There are some other differences, in that the names of some programs have changed so the entries look different (such as the `mouse.drv=Logitech Mouse` entry changing to `mouse.drv=Logitech`), but variations like that aren't really substantial. Of course, if you change your system configuration after installing Windows 98 SE, the contents of the `.INI` file will change as well.

WIN.INI versus *WININI.W31*

`WIN.INI` more or less keeps track of the user setup and application software for Windows. It also keeps configuration information for Windows programs that don't have an `.INI` file (like Micrografx Designer). It's a much larger file than SYSTEM.INI, containing information about all of your software's fonts and OLE links.

The WIN.INI files for Windows 3.*x* and Windows 98 SE are more similar than their respective SYSTEM.INI files. The major changes are as follows:

- Some new entries relating to Windows 98 SE's video capabilities are added to the [mci extensions] section.
- Several entirely new sections have been added, relating to:
  - The Registry
  - The ATM (Adobe Type Manager, not Asynchronous Transfer Mode) workaround for printing
  - New Microsoft applications

In general, however, you don't need to worry about these settings. They're not anything that you should need to change from inside the .INI file—path settings and other such information are more easily edited from the Control Panel or by choosing Start ➢ Settings ➢ Taskbar & Start Menu.

Why Do I Have *.INI* Files?

.INI files have some built-in failings. They can only be nested in two layers (the [section] name and the entries included in the section). They can only be up to 64K in size. If you're using .INI files, backing up your system's configuration requires copying four files (both .INI files, CONFIG.SYS, and AUTOEXEC.BAT). If you've got this wonderful Registry that keeps all of your configuration files in one manageable database (and, even if the entries are cryptic, they're certainly no more cryptic than the entries in a CONFIG.SYS or SYSTEM.INI file), then why do you still *have* WIN.INI and SYSTEM.INI files?

The answer is: for backward compatibility.

Versions of Windows prior to Windows 95 relied on SYSTEM.INI and WIN.INI. These two ASCII text files control roughly the same things as SYSTEM.DAT and USER.DAT respectively, so retaining the .INI files might seem to be a waste of time. But applications written for previous versions of Windows don't know how to look in the Registry for the information that they need.

Controlling 98 SE — The Registry and .*INI* Files

Windows 98 SE is a 32-bit operating system, but Microsoft realized that it couldn't possibly make Windows 98 SE incompatible with the 16-bit applications that Windows users have been buying for years. In the interests of avoiding a riot on the front steps of the Redmond compound, Windows 98 SE was designed to accommodate both 32-bit applications written for 98 SE, which can access the Registry, and 16-bit applications, which *cannot*. Hence, you've still got WIN.INI and SYSTEM.INI files floating around your system.

If you install Windows 98 SE on top of Windows 3.*x*, then the information in WIN.INI and SYSTEM.INI is copied into the Registry during Setup. When you make changes to the Registry, either directly or via one of the graphical tools like the Control Panel, they're updated in WIN.INI and SYSTEM.INI for the use of applications not designed to work with the Registry.

> **NOTE**
> Your Windows 3.*x* .INI files (now with .W31 extensions) are not affected by changes to the system Registry.

Generally speaking, you shouldn't need to edit either WIN.INI or SYSTEM.INI directly—most of the settings that they control are accessible via the Control Panel. If you need to fine-tune an application (for example, to change the default source directory to import pictures from), you'll need to make those changes to that specific application's .INI file. You can edit or view any .INI file in Notepad.

Some Neat Registry Tips

Now that you've learned all about how the Registry works, wouldn't it be nice if you could use this knowledge in some useful way? Once you get the hang of it, it should seem pretty clear how the Registry works.

Saving Your Desktop Settings

Even though Windows 98 SE allows multiple user settings, there's still the possibility that more than one person can be using the same machine under the same user ID. You see this a lot in school libraries, where machines are set up solely for the purpose of connecting to the Internet. If users are allowed access to the Desktop and they're relatively smart individuals, they may figure out that you can remove the Desktop icons. Removing these icons would eliminate access to the Internet for a lot of beginning users.

The simplest way to avoid this problem would be to lock the Desktop settings in place. New users will be able to change the Desktop while they're logged on, but the changes won't be saved when they restart the machine.

> **WARNING**
> I can't say this enough: before you start fooling around with the Registry, make sure you've backed up your system. You really don't want to make changes you can't restore later.

First, change your Desktop to the way you want it to look (wallpaper, icons, shortcuts, and so on). In the Registry Editor, drill down to the following key:

```
HKEY_USERS\.Default\Software\Microsoft\Windows\CurrentVersion\
Policies\Explorer
```

Double-click `NoSaveSettings` and change the value from 0 to 1. Click OK, and exit the Registry Editor. The next time you reboot, your settings (and those of everyone else, for that matter) will return to their current state. If you want to change only your settings, and not anyone else's, change this key instead:

```
HKEY_CURRENT_USER\Software\Microsoft\Windows\CurrentVersion\
Policies\Explorer
```

Remove the Shut Down Option from the Start Menu

I had a friend in college who worked in a computer lab. He'd constantly complain that users would "accidentally" shut down their machines and couldn't figure out how to get them started again. Since the machines are supposed to run 24 hours a day, why can't you keep users from shutting down their machines in the first place? Well, you can. Drill down to this key:

```
HKEY_USERS\.Default\Software\Microsoft\Windows\Current Version\
Policies\Explorer
```

Now, double-click `NoClose` and change the value from 0 to 1. Once you've restarted your machine, the Shut Down option will be gone from the Start menu. Even if you type Ctrl+Alt+Del, the Shut Down option will be grayed out. Unless a user physically turns off the machine, it can't be shut down.

Preventing Windows Menus from Following Your Mouse

One of my pet peeves was that I would often click the wrong menu item if my hand suddenly flinched even slightly. Instead of logging off my machine, I'd reboot the computer instead. If you've got a sensitive mouse or notebook pointing device, this can be especially irritating. You can, however, keep this from happening by following these steps:

1. Drill down to the `HKEY_CURRENT_USER\Control Panel\Desktop` key.

2. Add a string value named `MenuShowDelay`, and specify 65534 for its value.

3. To enable this feature for all users, add this value to the `HKEY_USERS\.Default\Control Panel\Desktop` key, as well.

4. Reboot your machine in order for the change to take effect.

Zooming Windows

This can be categorized as an "ooh and ahh" feature of Windows 98 SE. I say this because it's one of those things that serves no purpose other than to impress the beginning user. It also has a rather detrimental effect on your display if you use one of the slower video cards (the title bars can flicker when windows zoom in and out). You can turn this effect off by following these steps:

1. Drill down to the `HKEY_CURRENT_USER\Control Panel\Desktop\WindowMetrics` key.

2. Add a string value named MinAnimate and specify a value of 0 if you want to turn zooming off or 1 if you want to turn it on.

3. Restart your machine in order for the change to take effect.

NOTE

If you have the AutoHide feature selected in the Taskbar Properties dialog box, disabling the zooming feature will also turn off the animated disappearing Taskbar.

Changing Your System's Shell Folders

One of the biggest mistakes I made when installing Windows 98 SE was that I installed it on a partition that had barely enough space to contain the operating system itself. Actually, I had about 50MB or so left on my partition without installing any applications. As you may know, Internet Explorer keeps a cache of all the files it has downloaded from the Internet in the Temporary Internet Files folder. It's really easy to accumulate quite a lot of data in a matter of days. In fact, in one day recently, I accumulated 18MB of Web pages and graphics in this folder. So, when I only have 50MB of space available, I soon find that my computer will grind to a halt.

Your machine, in addition to having 8MB, 16MB, or even 64MB of RAM requires additional disk space to process applications. This space, called *virtual memory*, needs to be available or else you'll receive an "out of memory" error. Going back to my example, we know that I have 50MB of disk space on my boot partition. Just running Internet Explorer will write an additional 5–10MB of data to the partition, so that 50MB will quickly dwindle down to nothing. When Windows 98 SE needs that disk space to process an application, it's no longer there. Thus, it runs out of memory.

Another way you can lose disk space is through installing applications. Some applications place files in your system's shell folders. A good example of this is the My Documents folder that many users use to save their personal files.

However, there is a way to save yourself some disk space before you panic, wipe out your hard drive, and end up having to reinstall Windows 98 SE from scratch. In the Registry you'll find a list of shell folders in the `HKEY_USERS\.Default\Software\Microsoft\Windows\CurrentVersion\Explorer\Shell Folders` key, shown in Figure 15.31.

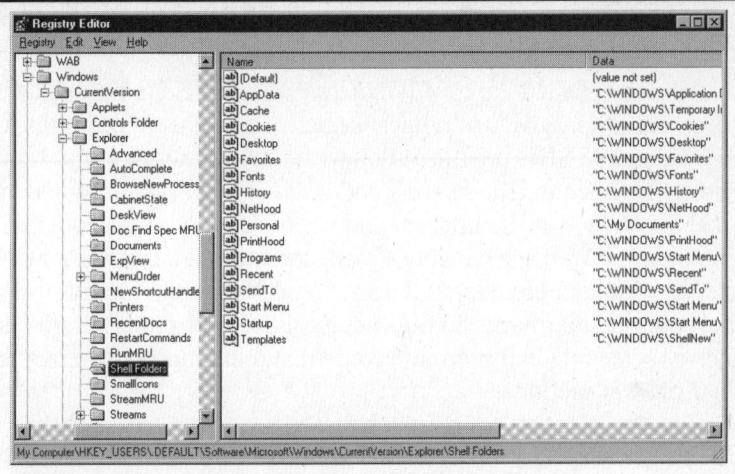

Controlling 98 SE—The Registry and .*INI* Files 439

FIGURE 15.31: System shell folders listed in the Registry

Just change the paths so that the folders reside on another partition on your machine. Copy the folders to the directory paths you named in the Registry and delete the folders from their old locations. Now, you should see quite a bit of space made available on your boot partition.

Hiding Your Machine from Your Network's Browse List

All Windows servers by default will show in your network's browse list. If you have File and Print sharing activated, your computer can be seen by others. Suppose, though, that you want to share files with others, but don't want to show your computer in the browse list. You can do this by making a change to the Registry.

Drill down to the KEY_LOCAL_MACHINE\SYSTEM\CurrentControl-Set\Services\LanManServer\Parameters key and add a REG_DWORD value named Hidden. If you don't want the computer name to show in the browse list, specify a data value of 1. Specifying a value of 0 will allow your machine name to be listed.

Next time the browse master updates the browse list, your machine will not be included.

What's Next?

You've now finished Part I of *Windows 98 Second Edition Complete*, covering Windows 98 SE itself. Because one of the most important features of Windows 98 SE is its integration with the Internet Explorer browser, Part II of this book, *The Internet and Windows 98 Second Edition*, takes an in-depth look at the Internet and the tools you've just acquired for browsing the Web, exchanging e-mail, and even building your own Web site. As an added bonus, you'll learn about Netscape Communicator, the most popular alternative to Internet Explorer, and about security issues such as screening inappropriate content and maintaining privacy for financial transactions.

PART II
THE INTERNET AND WINDOWS 98 SECOND EDITION

Chapter 16

UNDERSTANDING INTERNET AND WORLD WIDE WEB BASICS

These days the Internet seems to be everywhere. Web addresses appear on television ads and billboards. There are TV shows and magazines devoted to the Internet. And virtually every new computer program that comes out has some Internet features. With the arrival of Windows 98 and now Windows 98 Second Edition, your computer Desktop can connect you just as easily to Internet resources as it does to the files on your hard drive.

I know, you're raring to go. You want to start sending and receiving e-mail, browsing the Web, and exploring the global library of fun stuff out on the Internet. Well, I don't want to hold you back. Feel free to skip to Chapter 18, *Communicating with E-Mail*, and start right in on e-mail (or even jump to Chapter 19, *Browsing the Web with Internet Explorer*, to start messing around with the World Wide Web). However, if you're not clear on what the Net actually is, how you get access to it, and what you can do once you're there, you'll want to peruse this chapter first.

Adapted from *The Internet: No Experience Required*
by Christian Crumlish
ISBN 0-7821-2168-3   528 pages $24.99

Notice that I just used the word *Net* and not *Internet*. For the most part, the words are synonymous, although some people will use the word Net to refer to just about any aspect of the global internetworking of computers. (Check out Appendix B—a glossary of Windows, Internet, and general computer terminology—to become more familiar with Internet jargon.)

Introducing the Internet

Everybody talks about the Internet and the World Wide Web these days, but most people don't really know what the Internet is or what the differences are between the Internet and the Web. One reason for this is that how the Internet looks depends on how you come across it and what you do with it. Another reason is that everyone talks about it as if it's actually a network, like a local network in someone's office or even a large global network like CompuServe. Fact is, it's something different. A beast unto itself. The Internet is really a way for computers to communicate.

As long as a computer or a smaller network can "speak" the Internet lingo (or *protocols*, to be extra formal about it) to other machines, it's "on the Internet." Of course, the computer also needs a modem or a network connection and other hardware to make contact too. Regardless of the hardware needs, if the Internet were a language, it wouldn't be French or Farsi or Tagalog or even English. It would be Esperanto.

Having said that, I might backtrack and allow that there's nothing wrong with thinking of the Internet as if it were a single network unto itself. It certainly behaves like one in a lot of important ways. But this can be misleading. No one "owns" the Internet. No one even really runs it. And no one can turn it off.

Communicating through E-Mail or Discussion Groups

In addition to being a network of interconnected computers, the Internet is also a collection of tools and devices for communicating and storing information in a retrievable form.

Take e-mail, for example. If you work in an office with a local-area network, chances are you have an e-mail account and can communicate with people in your office by sending them messages through the company's internal system. (See Chapter 18 for an in-depth discussion of all the ins and outs of e-mail.) This is not the Internet.

Understanding Internet and World Wide Web Basics 445

Similarly, if you have an account at America Online and you send a message to someone else at AOL, you're still not using the Internet. But, if your office network has a *gateway* to the Internet, and you send e-mail to someone who does not work at your office, you are sending mail over the Internet. Likewise, if you send a message from your AOL account to someone at CompuServe or elsewhere, again you are sending messages over the Internet (see Figure 16.1).

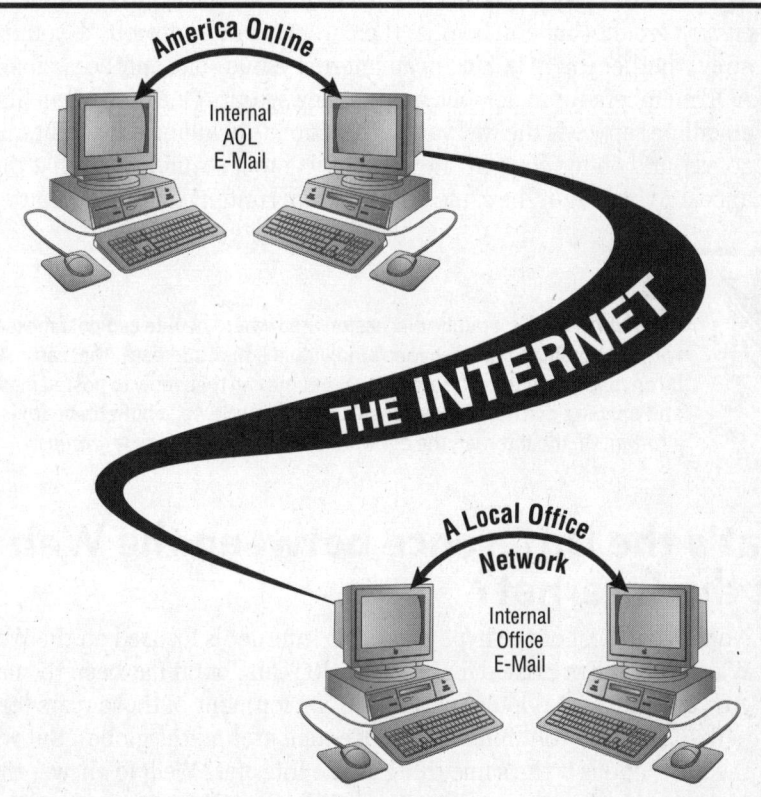

FIGURE 16.1: The Internet carries e-mail from one network to another.

> **NOTE**
> A *gateway* is a computer or the program running on it that transfers files (or e-mail messages or commands) from one network to another.

But from your point of view, the Internet is not just a collection of networks all talking to one another. A single computer can also participate in the Internet by connecting to a network or service provider that's connected to the Internet. And although the local office network I described and the big commercial online services are not themselves the Internet, they can and often do provide access through their gateways to the Internet. (I cover online services later in this chapter, in the "Cruising the Net at Home" section)

All this can be confusing to first-time Internet users (universally referred to as *newbies*). Say you have an AOL account and you join one of the *discussion groups* (bulletin boards) there. It may not be obvious to you right away whether you're talking in an internal venue—one only accessible to AOL members—or in a public Internet newsgroup. One of the benefits of an online service is the way various functions, including e-mail, Internet access, and online content, are brought together seamlessly so that they appear to be part of the same little program running on your computer.

> **NOTE**
> A *bulletin board* is a public discussion area where people can post messages—without sending them to anyone's individual e-mail address—that can be viewed by anyone who enters the area. Other people can then reply to posted messages, and ongoing discussions can ensue. On CompuServe, a bulletin board is called a *forum*. On the Internet, the equivalent areas are called *newsgroups*.

What's the Difference between the Web and the Internet?

Nowadays, most of the hype about the Internet is focused on the World Wide Web. It has existed for less than 10 years, but it has been the fastest-growing and most popular part of the Net for many of those years (except, perhaps, for the voluminous flow of e-mail around the globe). But what is the Web, and is it the same thing as the Internet? Well, to answer the second question first: yes and no. Technically, the *Web* is just part of the Internet—or, more properly, a way of getting around part of the Internet. But it's a big part, because a lot of the Internet that's not (strictly speaking) *part of* the Web can still be reached with a Web browser.

So the Web, on one level, is an *interface*. A window onto the Net. A way of getting to where you're going. Its appeal derives from three benefits:

1. It disguises the gobbledygook that passes for Internet addresses and commands. (See "Getting on the Internet" later in this chapter.)

Understanding Internet and World Wide Web Basics

2. It wraps up most of the different features of the Internet into a single interface used by Web applications.

3. It allows you to see pictures and even hear sounds or watch movies (if your computer can hack it), along with your helpings of text.

TIP
To play sounds, your computer needs a sound card and speakers and, before the release of Windows 98 SE, some kind of software (such as Microsoft Sound Recorder for Windows). To play movies, your computer needs a lot memory (or else the movies will look herky-jerky) and, before the release of Windows 98 SE, some kind of software (such as Media Player or QuickTime). Now, however, you no longer need more than one player on your PC. Windows 98 SE includes the Windows Media Player, with which you can play sounds, movies, and mixed-media files.

It helps to know a little bit about the history of the Net to understand why these three features of the Web have spurred the Internet boom. First of all, before the Web existed, doing anything beyond simple e-mailing (and even that could be difficult, depending on your type of access) used to require knowing weird Unix commands and understanding the Internet's system for numbering and naming all the computers connected to it. If you've ever wrestled with DOS and lost, you can appreciate the effort required to surmount this type of barrier.

Imagine it's 1991 and you've gotten yourself an Internet account, solved the problems of logging in with a communications program to a Unix computer somewhere out there, and mastered the Unix programs needed to send and receive e-mail, read newsgroups, download files, and so on. You'd still be looking at lots of plain text, screens and screens of words. No pictures. Well, if you were dying for pictures, you could download enormous text files that had begun their lives as pictures and then were encoded as plain text so that they could be squeezed through the text-only pipelines that constituted the Net. Next you'd have to decode the files, download them onto your PC, and then run some special program to look at them. Not quite as easy as flipping through a magazine.

The Web uses a coding method called *hypertext* to disguise the actual commands and addresses you use to navigate the Net. Instead of these commands and addresses, what you see in your *Web browser* (the program you use to travel the Web) is plain English keywords highlighted in some way. Simply click the keywords, and your browser program talks the

Internet talk, negotiates the transaction with the computer at the other end, and brings the picture, text, program, or activity you desire onto your computer screen. This is how all computer functions should work (and probably how they will work one day).

Early Unix-based Web browsers, such as Www (developed at CERN, the European particle physics laboratory where the Web was invented) and Lynx (developed at the University of Kansas), were not especially attractive to look at, but they did offer the "one-step" technique for jumping to a specific location on the Net or for downloading a file or a piece of software.

The next advance on the Web was the development of graphical Web browsers that could run on a desktop PC (or Macintosh), permitting the user to employ the familiar point-and-click techniques of other software and incorporating text formatting and graphics into the browser screen. The first program of this type was NCSA Mosaic, which was developed at the National Center for Supercomputer Applications and distributed for free.

Furthermore, the various Web browsers can more or less substitute for a plethora of little specialty programs (such as Gopher clients, newsreaders, FTP programs, and so on) that you had to assemble and set up yourself "in the old days." The browsers all have their own little idiosyncrasies, but they're still remarkably uniform and consistent compared with the maze of different programs and rules you had to work your way through just a few years ago. These days, the two most popular browsers are Netscape Navigator, shown in Figure 16.2 (which is now part of Communicator, Netscape's all-purpose network client program) and Microsoft Internet Explorer. (For information on both of these browsers, see Chapters 19 through 21.)

NOTE
"Just a few years ago" is the old days on the Internet. Changes happen so rapidly in the online world that time on the Internet is like "dog years"—something like seven years go by for each one in the real world.

The Web has made it possible for browsers to display pictures right there in the midst of text, without your having to know how to decode files. A picture's worth a lot of words, and pictures look better in newspaper articles and on TV than scads of typewritten text. So this final ingredient made the Web seem both accessible and interesting to people who

Understanding Internet and World Wide Web Basics 449

would never in a million years care to learn what a Unix "regular expression" is.

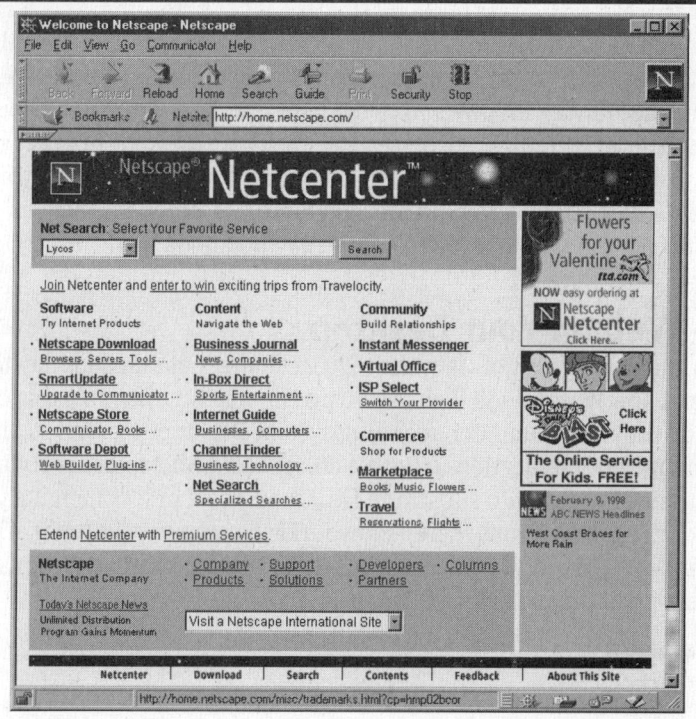

FIGURE 16.2: Netscape Navigator is a popular World Wide Web browser program.

I have tried to answer the question that heads up this section: What's the difference between the Web and the Internet? Technically the Web and the Internet are not exactly the same, but for all intents and purposes they have a lot in common. Web browsers are the must-have programs that have made the Internet what it is today.

> **NOTE**
> You can use the Internet and the Web to find new friends and uncover fun facts and interesting Web sites. Individuals and groups all over the planet have gotten together on the Internet to explore mutual interests. Environmental and political causes, pets, sports, leisure activities, the arts, and the sciences are just some of the popular topics continually updated on the Internet.

Discovering What's New on the Net

These days, the latest Internet developments are mostly being driven by the access tools. Browser makers Netscape and Microsoft are each trying to develop all-in-one solutions that make their own products the "platform" for everything you do on the Net. New companies are offering free Internet accounts with a Web-based e-mail interface. The catch? You have to keep the ad window open on the screen. There are even Internet solutions that don't require you to have a computer, such as WebTV (your TV plus a modem plus a keyboard plus a remote), or a modem, such as DirectPC (your computer plus a special satellite hook up).

The Web on Your Desktop

From the user's point of view, the biggest changes planned for day-to-day Internet and World Wide Web use are in the way Internet access is being built directly into computer operating-system Desktops (as well as directly into many new applications). Both Netscape and Microsoft are trying to turn their browsers into substitute Desktops, more or less merging your view of the Internet (out there) and your own computer (in here). The integration of Windows 98 with Internet Explorer was an ambitious step in this direction.

> **NOTE**
> The Internet has also become a great source of career information. Companies list jobs and freelance opportunities. You can research companies on the Internet and train yourself on a variety of topics that might come up in an interview. You can find business contacts and develop new ones through Internet e-mail, conferencing, and forums on particular subjects.

Netcasts Beamed onto Your Screen

The popularity of PointCast (see Figure 16.3), a program that displays news on your screen and automatically connects to the Internet for updates, has demonstrated a market for "netcasting" software (programs that "broadcast" over the Internet directly to your computer screen). This

Understanding Internet and World Wide Web Basics 451

use of the Internet is more passive, more like TV than the interactive, Web-browsing model, but it's possible to do both.

FIGURE 16.3: The PointCast Network (shown here in screen-saver mode) automatically downloads news from the Net and displays it on your computer screen.

> **NOTE**
> The type of news you can have netcasted to your Desktop ranges from sports to headline and financial news, as well as more specialized topics (science and technology, fashion, arts and entertainment) that you define and refine with your netcasting software.

Applications with Internet Features

The growth of the Internet, coupled with the advent of smaller, local, company or organization intranets running on Internet principles, has led users to expect their everyday business software to help them deal with retrieving remote documents, collaborate with colleagues over network links, and save or publish documents to Web and intranet servers. To meet this demand, software publishers are adding Internet features to their programs left and right. You can expect your next upgrade of various programs to include the ability to transfer files (open them from and save them to remote computers) and probably to create documents and reports in HTML (hypertext Web format) as well. See Chapter 22, *Creating Web Pages with FrontPage Express*, for more on how to make Web documents.

> **NOTE**
> Knowing how to use Internet features in common business applications is a great job skill, even if you don't work in a high-technology field. All kinds of companies are depending more on the Internet and the World Wide Web to find information and promote their services and products. Companies and organizations are also developing in-house intranets to store policies, manuals, and other information. Having knowledge of the Internet is certainly a big plus in today's competitive job market.

Getting on the Internet

So what exactly does it mean to be "on the Internet"? Generally, if someone asks you, "Are you on the Net?" it means something like, "Do you have an Internet e-mail address?" That is, do you have e-mail and can your e-mail account be reached over the Internet? With the popularity of the Web being what it is, another common interpretation of what it means to be on the Net is, "Do you have the ability to browse the World Wide Web?" Often these two features—Internet e-mail and Web access—go hand in hand, but not always. We're also getting to a time when being on the Internet will entail having your own home page, your own "place" on the Web where information about you is stored and where you can be found.

Cruising the Net at Work

More and more companies these days (as well as schools and other organizations) are installing internal networks and relying on e-mail as one of the ways to share information. E-mail messages are starting to replace interoffice memos, at least for some types of announcements, questions, and scheduling purposes. The logical next step for most of these organizations is to connect their internal network to the Internet through a gateway. When this happens, you may suddenly be on the Net. This doesn't mean that anything will necessarily change on your Desktop. You'll probably still use the same e-mail program and still send and receive mail within your office in the same way you always have.

> **WARNING**
> Some companies run Internet-usage monitoring programs that tell them how long employees have been using the Internet and what type of sites they are visiting. Use good judgment when you surf the Internet at work, and try to explore only those sites that have potentially important work-related information.

What will change at this point is that you'll be able to send e-mail to people on the Internet outside your office, as long as you type the right kind of Internet address. (Generally, this means adding @ and then a series of words separated by periods to the username portion of an address, but I'll explain more about addresses in "The Anatomy of an Internet Address" later in this chapter.) Likewise, people out there in the great beyond will be able to send e-mail to you as well.

Depending on the type of Internet connection your company has, e-mail may be all you get. Then again, it might also be possible for you to run a Web browser on your computer and visit Internet sites while sitting at your desk. Of course, your company will only want you to do this if it's relevant to your job, but it works the same way whether you're researching a product your company uses or reading cartoons at the Dilbert site.

> **NOTE**
> Your ability to find information on the Internet that your company needs will become a highly prized career asset, especially as more and more organizations contribute to the growth of the Internet.

Cruising the Net at Home

If you're interested in exploring the Internet as a form of entertainment or for personal communication, a work account is not really the way to do it. (An account minimally consists of a username and an e-mail Inbox; it may also provide storage space on a computer or access to a Web server.) You'll need your own personal account to really explore the Internet on your own time, without looking over your shoulder to make sure nobody's watching.

Chapter Sixteen

> **TIP**
> If your office is quite sophisticated, you may actually be able to dial into a company network from home via a modem to check your e-mail messages. Chapter 13 shows how to use Windows 98 SE features for remote access.

Your best bet is to sign up for an account from a commercial online service or a direct-access Internet service provider. What's the difference between those two choices? Well, an *online service* (such as CompuServe, America Online, Prodigy, Microsoft Network, and so on) is first and foremost a private, proprietary network, offering its own content and access to other network members, generally combined with Internet access. An *Internet Service Provider* (*ISP*) offers just access to the Internet and no proprietary content (or only very limited local information and discussion groups). Figure 16.4 illustrates this distinction.

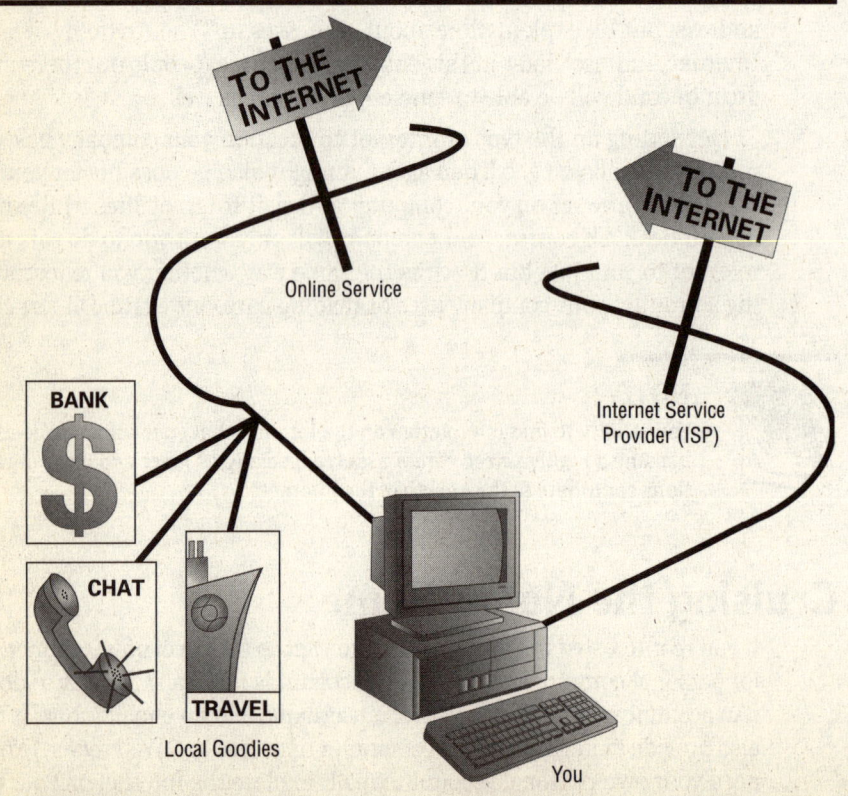

FIGURE 16.4: Online services connect you to the Internet but encourage you to explore their own offerings, whereas ISPs just connect you to the Internet and let you fend for yourself.

Understanding Internet and World Wide Web Basics 455

Online services have only recently begun offering full (or somewhat limited) Internet access. Because they are trying to do two things at once (sell you their own content and connect you to the Internet), they are usually an expensive way of exploring the Net. On the other hand, they tend to offer a single, simplified interface. I often recommend signing up for a free trail account at one of the online services if you just want to get your feet wet before plunging wholeheartedly into the Net. If you like what the Internet has to offer or if you start using the Net so much that you run up an expensive bill (after that first free month), I recommend that you switch to a direct-access ISP.

ISPs can be much cheaper than online services, especially if you can find one that offers a flat rate—a monthly charge that doesn't vary no matter how much time you spend connected to the Net. They also don't try to compete with the Internet by offering their own content and sponsors. Instead, they function as a gateway, getting you onto the Internet and letting you go wherever you want.

What Kinds of ISP Accounts Are There?

An ISP account generally includes, along with the e-mail address, storage space on a computer somewhere on the Net. You will be billed monthly, and depending on the provider, there may be a surcharge based on the amount of time you spent connected that month or the amount of space you used on their hard drive.

But how do you use an account? Well, you need a computer with a modem, and you need software that knows how to use that modem to call up (dial up) your provider and allows you to log in to your account. Fortunately, most modems come with their own software.

Your ISP will take care of all the technical details for you and will probably supply you with a setup disk and easy-to-use software for connecting to the Internet. Once you're set up, you won't have to think much about whether you have a PPP or SLIP account or any other kind of account, but I want to introduce the terminology now so you'll know what I'm talking about when I mention it again. If you want more than simply a connection to a Unix command-line and a plain-text account (and I suspect that you do), nowadays you need something called a *PPP* or *SLIP account*. (The other kind is usually called a *shell account* or sometimes a *Unix shell account*.)

A PPP (or SLIP) account lets your computer behave like it's connected directly to another computer on the Internet—when it's really connected over a phone line whenever you dial in—and it enables you to run software, such as graphical Web browsers like Microsoft Internet Explorer and Netscape Navigator, that functions in your computer's native environment (Windows) instead of forcing you to deal with plain-text programs like the text-only browsers Lynx and Unix (see Figure 16.5).

PPP-Type Internet Connection

Cool Stuff!
▶ If you want to see all kinds of cool stuff, just click...

Unix-Shell Type Internet Connection

c:> To see some cool stuff all you have to do is connect via FTP to cool.stu.com and log in as guest, then download...

FIGURE 16.5: With a PPP (or SLIP) account, your connection to the Internet is seamlessly integrated into your computer's normal environment.

WARNING
By the way, the speed of your modem—and that of the modem at the other end of the dial-up line, that is, your provider's modem—determines the speed of your Internet connection, and even the fastest modems these days are still slower than a direct network connection to the Net, such as you might enjoy at your office.

The Anatomy of an Internet Address

One of the confusing things to Internet newbies is that the word "address" is used to mean at least three different things on the Internet. The most

Understanding Internet and World Wide Web Basics

basic meaning—but the one used least often—is the name of a computer, also called a *host* or *site*, on the Internet in the form `something.something.something`. (To really use the lingo properly, you have to pronounce the periods as "dot"—you'll get used to it and it saves a lot of time over the long haul.) For example, I publish a magazine (or 'zine) on the Internet called *Enterzone*; it's stored on a machine at Vassar that is part of the American Arts and Letters Network. The address of that machine is

`ezone.org`

Reading from right to left, you first have the *domain*, `org`, which stands for (nonprofit) organization. Next you sometimes have a *subdomain*. Finally, you have the *hostname*, `ezone`, which is the name (or a name) of the specific computer the magazine is stored on.

Another type of address is an e-mail address. An e-mail address consists of a *username* (also called a *login*, a *log-on name*, a *userID*, an *account name*, and so on), followed by an at sign (@) and then an Internet address of the type just described. So, for example, say you want to send mail to me in my capacity as editor of Enterzone. You could address that e-mail message to a special username created for that job (it will stay the same even if someone else takes over in the future):

`editor@ezone.org`

The third type of address is the kind you see everywhere these days, on billboards, on TV commercials, in the newspaper, and so on—a Web address, also called an *URL* (*Uniform Resource Locator*). You'll learn more about how to read (or ignore) URLs in Chapter 19. For now, it's enough just to know what one looks like. The Web address of that magazine I told you about is

`http://ezone.org/ez`

TIP
You can leave out the `www.` portion of the address when using certain Web browsers. Some Internet addresses use the `http://` designation, but leave out the `www.` portion, so try both ways if you have difficulty getting through.

Fortunately, you often can avoid typing in Web addresses yourself and can zip around the Web just by clicking pre-established *links*. Links are highlighted words or images that, when clicked or selected, take you directly to a new document, another part of the current document, or some other type of file entirely.

NOTE

The most common domain names on the Internet are .com, a commercial organization; .edu, an educational institution; .gov, a branch of the U.S. government; .int, an international treaty organization; .mil, a branch of the U.S. military; .net, a network provider; and .org, a nonprofit organization.

USING THE NET WITH OTHER PLATFORMS

Of course, Windows 98 SE and Internet Explorer 5 integrate the Web and your computer Desktop more closely than any previous software. But if you sometimes work with other platforms, such as the Macintosh or Unix, you'll be glad to know that the Internet makes some of the seemingly important distinctions between types of computers a lot less important. The information out on the Internet, the public discussion areas, and the World Wide Web look and act more or less the same, no matter what kind of computer you use. In fact, the Web is quickly becoming a sort of universal computer platform now that certain types of programs and services are being designed to run on the Web, rather than to run on one specific type of computer.

Part of the elegance of the Internet is that much of the heavy-duty processing power and storage of large programs and dense information takes place "out there," and not on your computer. Your computer—whether it's a PC, a Mac, or a Unix workstation—becomes just a convenient beanstalk to climb up to the land of the Internet giants. You'll sometimes hear this common structure of Internet facilities referred to as *client-server* (sorry for the jargon). In this scenario, you are the client (or your computer or the program running on it is), and the information source, or World Wide Web site, or mail-handling program is the server. Servers are centralized repositories of information or specialized handlers of certain kinds of traffic. All a client has to do is connect to the right server and a wealth of goodies are within your reach, without your having to overload your machine. This is a major reason that it doesn't matter what kind of computer you prefer.

WHAT YOU CAN DO ON THE NET

I've touched on the most popular facilities on the Internet—e-mail and the World Wide Web—but I'll run down some of the other useful features.

> **NOTE**
> Some of these Internet tools are covered elsewhere in *Windows 98 Second Edition Complete*, but for others, you'll need to consult books written specifically about the Internet. Current Sybex titles in this area include *The Internet: No Experience Required* (1998), *Surfing the Internet with Netscape Communicator 4* (1997), and others.

Search Engines Once you start exploring the Web, you might get tired of its disorganization (imagine a library in which every card-carrying member worked part-time as a librarian for one of the shelves, and each micro-librarian used their own system for organizing their section) or with not knowing for sure where anything is on the Internet. Fortunately, a lot of useful *search engines* are available on the Net. A *search engine* is a program or a Web page that enables you to search an Internet site (or the entire Internet) for a specific word or words. Not as thorough as a card catalog, perhaps, but easier to use. (See Chapter 19 for more about search tools in Internet Explorer.)

Usenet For many Internet users, the first step beyond e-mail and the Web is into the Internet's sometimes loosely organized system of public message boards called *Usenet* (or simply News). Here you'll find discussion groups (known as "newsgroups") on just about any area of interest imaginable. People "post" messages expressing opinions on topics related to the group or looking for information; other people reply with their own opinions or the requested information.

Usenet has a highly evolved subculture and a set of rules for good behavior known as "Netiquette." For example, if a newsgroup provides a FAQ (answers to Frequently Asked Questions), it's good Netiquette to read the FAQ before asking the whole group your question; someone may have already answered it. A good way to get started with newsgroups is to "lurk"—to read discussions without participating. Both Internet Explorer and Netscape Navigator provide access to News, directly and through search engines. You'll also find some Usenet terminology in this book's glossary (Appendix B).

Chat If you prefer the idea of communicating with people "live" rather than posting messages and waiting for people to reply later, you'll want to know about the various chat facilities available on the Internet—particularly *IRC* (*Internet Relay Chat*). Briefly, if you're connected to another user via Chat, you can type messages back and forth. Each of you will see the other's response right away. It's like a telephone call, on your computer screen. And more than two people can participate, in conferences known as "chat rooms." A Chat program is part of Netscape Communicator, the larger suite that includes Navigator; Internet Explorer's NetMeeting tool also includes a Chat feature.

FTP The File Transfer Protocol is one of the Internet's oldest and most reliable tools for exchanging ("uploading" and "downloading") files of any kind. FTP servers (known as "hosts") can make files available to specific users (who must provide a password) or to anyone (a technique called "anonymous FTP"); for example, software companies often provide updates or demonstration versions of their products for downloading via anonymous FTP. With both Internet Explorer and Netscape Navigator you can connect to FTP sites, either by clicking links to them in some Web pages or by typing the server's URL in the browser's Address or Location field.

Building Your Own Web Page Finally, if you want to join the ranks of people with their own home pages on the Web—to create a "presence" on the Net or publicize your favorite Internet sites—Chapter 22 of this book shows you how to do that as well.

Downloading Files from the Internet

Another aspect of the Internet that you will especially enjoy is the ability to download files from a vast selection of sample applications, digital art and music, and many other offerings. Software companies promote their new products by maintaining sites where their customers can obtain samples, updates, and related information. Entertainment conglomerates supply sound and video files for movies, bands, and video games. Some organizations just collect information relevant to their interests, such as schedules of upcoming activities, databases of similar organizations, and the like.

Understanding Internet and World Wide Web Basics

> **WARNING**
> Before you attempt to access files from the Internet, you should protect your computer (or your company's network) with anti-virus software. Computers downloading Internet files are the principal point of entry for computer viruses. You'll learn more about viruses and how to defend against them in Chapter 20, *Browsing with a Sense of Security*.

The files obtained from the Internet can be quite large, so they often arrive compressed to a smaller size, and they may also be coded for protection against unauthorized use or modifications. These files have to be decompressed and decoded before you can use them. Compression-decompression software and decoding applications are readily available, both as free Internet downloads (called *freeware*) and as commercial applications that you pay for.

Many Internet users are concerned about their privacy while using the Net, especially if they are filling out forms or making purchases with credit cards over the World Wide Web. Programming geniuses have given us applications that try to protect our good credit and our privacy. Some of these efforts are even given away free on the Internet. Chapter 20 will touch on some of the privacy precautions you can take on the Internet.

Using Web Sites to Gather Information about the Internet and the Web

You can visit the Internet itself to glean more details about its history, policies, and users. Use the Web sites listed below as the starting point for a journey through various interpretations of how to use the Internet, how it evolved, and how it should be regulated. These sites all contain links to even more sites that will take you surfing farther afield in your quest for knowledge about the Web.

The Internet Society http://info.isoc.org A simple site that includes Internet history and a timeline, as well as links to other technical organizations dealing with the Web and communication in general.

Electronic Frontier Foundation http://www.eff.org A mainly civil-rights–oriented site with many pages on free speech, privacy, and policy. Also home of the (Extended) Guide to the Internet, a lengthy document containing everything you might ever want to know about the origins of the Internet.

World Wide Web Consortium http://www.w3.org
A site hosted by MIT, the European Union, and DARPA (the defense agency that developed the Internet). This site has everything from very technical and lengthy documents to press releases and policy statements.

Well, I think I've kept you waiting long enough. Are you ready for e-mail?

What's Next?

In the following chapters, Bob Cowart and other *Windows 98 Second Edition Complete* contributors will show how to connect to the Internet, use e-mail, browse the Web with Internet Explorer or with Netscape Navigator, make your Internet use more secure, build your own Web pages, and retrieve Windows software from the Web.

Chapter 17

CONNECTING TO THE INTERNET

Before you can use Internet Explorer (or any other Internet application program), you must connect your own computer to the Internet. In this chapter, you will find information about choosing an Internet Service Provider (ISP); making the connection through a modem, a LAN, or other link; and installing and configuring your system for a TCP/IP connection.

One of the most fascinating new features in Windows 98 SE is Internet Connections Sharing (ICS). This allows networked computers to share a single modem connection to the Internet. Although most business network users have been doing this with proxy-server software for quite a while, ICS makes it that much easier, especially for the growing number of home networks.

If you already have an Internet connection that supports other TCP/IP Internet client programs, you may be able to use it with Internet Explorer, Outlook Express, NetMeeting, and the other Internet tools discussed in this book. If that's the case, you can skip this chapter.

Adapted from *Mastering Windows 98 Second Edition*
by Robert Cowart; revised by Keith Underdahl
ISBN 0-7821-2618-9   928 pages $39.99

> **NOTE**
> TCP/IP is the networking software (protocol) established during the 70s that allows many different kinds of computers to interact with one another regardless of type and operating system. First debuted in 1978 for use on the ARPANET (the predecessor of the Internet), TCP/IP remains the most widely used network protocol software today, and it forms the basis of the Internet. It is not owned by any one agency or company.

What Kind of Connection?

Choosing a way to connect your computer to the Internet is a trade-off between performance and cost; more money gets you a faster link between your own system and the backbone. (Just like in the human body, the Internet's backbone forms the core high-speed communications channel on which the Internet is built.) While the difference between file transfers through a modem and a high-speed link can be dramatic, the cost of improved performance may not always be justified. For most home users and many small businesses, a dial-up telephone line and a 33.6Kbps (kilobits per second) or 56Kbps modem is still the most cost-effective choice.

If it's available in your area, you might want to consider ISDN (Integrated Services Digital Network) as an alternative to conventional POTS (Plain Old Telephone Service) lines. ISDN is more expensive and complicated to install and configure, but once it's in place, it offers substantially faster network connections. Your Internet Service Provider can tell you if ISDN service is available and explain how to order the lines and obtain the necessary interface equipment.

> **TIP**
> Microsoft offers an easy means for establishing an ISDN hookup. Go to www.microsoft.com/ and look around or search the site for "Get ISDN." You should find a page with an online Wizard that will find the nearest ISDN provider and let you order service. I used this approach to get my ISDN service, and it was pretty painless.

In a larger business, where many users can share the same link to the Internet, a connection with more bandwidth is probably a better approach. Many users can share a single high-speed connection through a LAN, so the cost per user may not be significantly greater than that of a second telephone line.

If your PC is already connected to a LAN, you should ask your network administrator or help desk about setting up an Internet account; it's likely that there's already some kind of connection in place. If you have just set up a small network in your home or office, you can use ICS to make sharing a connection easier.

As with most decisions related to data communications, the simple answer to "What kind of connection should I use?" is "The fastest that you can afford." With the drastic increase in the number of Internet users, and growing awareness of how aggravating a slow connection can be, alternatives are beginning to crop up. A wide variety of higher-speed access vendors have appeared in recent months. Cable modems that use existing cable-TV service wires, digital satellite dish systems, and new telephone-system technologies such as ADSL (Asymmetrical Digital Subscriber Line) are among the most promising. Table 17.1 lists several types of connections and speed(s) you can expect from each. The prices are in flux, obviously. Also, don't forget that hardware equipment is needed for all of these solutions. You can buy an analog modem for about $50, but some of the other solutions will cost you thousands for your hardware. Some of these solutions, such as satellite hookup, do not include the ISP costs, either. They only supply the hookup to their system, one stop short of the Internet.

TABLE 17.1: Popular Means for Connection to the Internet

TECHNOLOGY	SPEED/NOTES	SPEED RELATIVE TO 28.8K MODEM (APPROX)	TYPICAL COST
Standard 28.8Kbps–56Kbps dial-up service over standard POTS lines	28.8Kbps–33.6Kbps or so. Rarely is 56Kbps achieved due to noise on phone lines.	1x	$20/month + telephone connect charges
ISDN	56Kbps–128Kpbs	2x–4x	$20–$50/month + connect time (typically 1 cent/minute)
Satellite	Varies, typically 400Kbps, some as high as 27Mbps	8x–900x	$20/month + ISP charges
T-1	1.54Mbps	50x	$3,300/month
T-3	45Mbps	1,500x	$32,000/month

TABLE 17.1 continued: Popular Means for Connection to the Internet

Technology	Speed/Notes	Speed relative to 28.8K modem (approx)	Typical cost
Frame relay	Available in 64Kbps increments, up to 1.5Mbps	As high as 50x	$200–$500/month depending on speed
xDSL—includes ADSL, IDSL, SDHL, HDSL, VDSL, RADSL	Asymmetrical Digital Subscriber Line (ADSL) can deliver up to 8Mbps over the 750 million ordinary existing "twisted pair" phone connections on earth. Actual speed offerings of these technologies range from 1.5Mbps to as high as 60Mbps on VDSL.	50x–2000x	$75/month (128Kbps), $250/month (768Kbps) + ISP service
Cable modem, using existing TV cable systems	10Mbps maximum. In reality probably about 1.5Mbps with typical number of users. Some systems offer only 500Kbps. Most systems require separate phone line for uplink since they only *receive* data over the cable. Others are bi-directional.	50x	$40/month

> **TIP**
>
> For a good source of information on high-speed Internet connections, and the inside scoop, check www.teleport.com/~samc/cable1.html. It's *extremely* complete. Another good site is www.specialty.com/hiband/.

Now come back down to Earth for a moment and stop daydreaming about how fast your connection to the Internet *could* be. For the time being, it will probably be either 56Kbps using one of the three 56Kbps standard modem types (but you'll probably only get about 33Kbps maximum connect speed) or 128Kbps using ISDN. But I expect that a combination of ISDN, ADSL, and cable modems will dominate the market for high-speed seekers soon. Even then, good old POTS line dial-ups will continue to be very popular since they work on virtually any phone line and accounts are cheap.

However, the telcos (that's short for telephone companies) have a vested interest in stopping people from tying up phone lines with modems all day, since the telephone system was designed for relatively short-term connections and works most economically that way. ADSL is a terrific solution for delivery of data and even video, since it uses the existing phone wires (no cable wiring necessary), *and it doesn't tie them up for other uses*. What, you say? That's right, you can pick up the regular old phone and make calls while your computer stays online downloading Web pages at T-1 speeds. This is because the Internet data is carried inside a high-frequency carrier signal that rides on top of the phone lines regardless of whether low-frequency voice calls are going on.

With that background, let's get down to the job of getting your modem hooked up and maybe even getting you online.

Choosing a Service Provider

As you know, the Internet is the result of connecting many networks to one another. You can connect your own computer to the Internet by obtaining an account on one of those interconnected networks.

Several different kinds of businesses offer Internet connections, including large companies with access points in many cities, smaller local or regional ISPs, and online information services that provide TCP/IP connections to the Internet along with their own proprietary information sources. You can use popular programs such as Internet Explorer with a connection through any of these services.

When you order your account, you should request a PPP connection to the Internet. PPP is a standard type of TCP/IP connection, which any ISP should be able to supply.

The Information Superhighway version of a New Age gas station, ISPs are popping up all over the country (and all over the world, for that matter). And like long-distance telephone companies, they offer myriad service options. If you're not among the savvy, you may get snowed into using an ISP that doesn't really meet your needs. As with long-distance telephone providers, you'll find that calculating the bottom line isn't that easy. It really depends on what you are looking for. Here are some questions to ask yourself (and any potential ISP):

▶ Does the ISP provide you with an e-mail account? It should.

- Can you have multiple e-mail accounts (for family members or employees)? If so, how many?

- Do they offer 56Kbps support? If so, which format? It should match your modem.

- Will they let you create your own *domain name*? For example, I wanted the e-mail address bob@cowart.com rather than something cryptic like bobcow@ic.netcim.net. Sometimes creating your own domain name costs extra, but it gives your correspondents an easier address to remember. You can decide if it's worth it.

- Does the ISP provide you with a news account so you can interact with Internet *newsgroups*? It should, and it shouldn't restrict which newsgroups you'll have access to unless you are trying to prevent your kids from seeing "dirty" messages or pictures.

- Do you want your own Web page available to other people surfing the Net? If so, does the ISP provide online storage room for it? How many "hits" per day can they handle, in case your page becomes popular? How much storage do you get in the deal? Do you want them to create the Web page for you?

- What is the charge for connect time? Some ISPs offer unlimited usage per day. Others charge by the hour and/or have a limit on continuous connect time.

- Do they have a local (i.e., free) phone number? If not, calculate the charges. It may be cheaper to use an ISP that charges more per month if there are no phone company toll charges to connect.

- Do they have many points of presence or an 800 number you can use to call into when you are on the road?

- Do they have too much user traffic to really provide reasonable service? Ask others who use the service before signing up. This has been a major problem with some ISPs, even biggies like AOL. Smaller providers often supply faster connections. Remember that even if you can connect without a busy signal, the weakest link in the system will determine the speed at which you'll get data from the Net. Often that link is the ISP's internal LAN that connects their in-house computers together. It's hard to know how efficient the ISP really is. Best to ask someone who's using them.

▶ Are they compatible with the programs you want to use? Can you use Internet Explorer or Netscape Web browsers? Which newsgroup and mail programs are supported?

> **TIP**
> If you have access to the Web, try checking the page www.thelist.com/. You'll learn a lot about comparative pricing and features of today's ISPs, along with links to their pages for opening an account. Another good site is www.boardwatch.com/.

Using a National ISP

The greatest advantage of using a national or international ISP is that you can probably find a local dial-in telephone number in most major cities. If you want to send and receive e-mail or use other Internet services while you travel, this can be extremely important.

The disadvantage of working with a large company is that it may not be able to provide the same kind of personal service that you can get from a smaller, local business. If you must call halfway across the continent and wait 20 minutes on hold for technical support (especially if it's not a toll-free number), you should look for a different ISP.

Many large ISPs can give you free software that automatically configures your computer and sets up a new account. Even if they don't include Internet Explorer in their packages, you should be able to use some version of the program along with the application programs they do supply.

You can obtain information about Internet access accounts from the national service providers listed in Table 17.2.

Many local telephone companies and more than a few cable TV companies are also planning to offer Internet access to their subscribers. If it's available in your area, you should be able to obtain information about these services from the business office that handles your telephone or television service. In San Jose, California, a local UHF TV station is using TV broadcasting technology to deliver high-speed Internet service, for example.

TABLE 17.2: National Internet Service Providers

ISP	Phone Number	Web Address
AT&T WorldNet	1-800-288-3199	www.ipservices.att.com/splash.html
MCI WorldCom	1-800-955-6505 (for Business Use)	www.mci.com/
SPRYnet	1-800-447-2956	www.sprynet.com/
PSInet	1-800-395-1056	www.psi.net/
MindSpring	1-888-MSPRING (1-888-677-7464)	www.mindspring.net/
Earthlink Network	1-888-EARTHLINK (1-888-327-8454)	www.earthlink.com/
Concentric Networks	1-800-939-4262	www.concentric.net/
IBM Internet	1-800-722-1425	www.ibm.net/

Using a Local ISP

The big national and regional services aren't your only choice. In most American cities, smaller local service providers also offer access to the Internet.

If you can find a good local ISP, it might be your best choice. A local company may be more responsive to your particular needs and more willing to help you get through the inevitable configuration problems than a larger national operation. Equally important, reaching the technical support center is more likely to be a local telephone call. Furthermore, in some rural areas you might find that a local ISP is the only Internet service with a local dial-up number, making it your only option for avoiding long distance charges while you are online.

But, unfortunately, the Internet access business has attracted a tremendous number of entrepreneurs who are in it for the quick dollar—some local ISPs are really terrible. If they don't have enough modems to handle the demand, or if they don't have a high-capacity connection to an Internet backbone, or if they don't know how to keep their equipment and servers working properly, you'll get frequent busy signals, slow downloads, dropped lines, and unexpected downtime rather than consistently reliable service. And there's no excuse for unhelpful technical support people or endless time on hold. If a deal seems too good to be true, there's probably a good reason.

To learn about the reputations of local ISPs, ask friends and colleagues who have been using the Internet for a while. If there's a local computer user magazine, look for schedules of user group meetings where you can find people with experience using the local ISPs. If you can't get a recommendation from any of those sources, look back at the previous Tip regarding lists of ISPs on the Web (assuming you already have Web access, which I realize is sort of a Catch-22).

> **TIP**
> No matter which service you choose, wait a month or two before you print your e-mail address on business cards and letterhead. If the first ISP you try doesn't give you the service you expect, take your business someplace else.

Connecting through an Online Service

One of the welcome additions to later versions of Windows 95 has continued into Windows 98 and Windows 98 SE. It's the inclusion of easy signup software for the major information services in the United States. Evidently this was done in reaction to complaints that Microsoft Corp. was gaining unfair advantage by bundling software for their own service, The Microsoft Network. The services included are America Online, CompuServe, AT&T Worldnet, and Prodigy. Any one of these services will get you connected to the Internet, using a "name brand" so to speak.

With the exception of Worldnet, which offers little more than a standard ISP connection, these services not only get you connected to the Internet—they sell you *content* too. Content providers such as CompuServe have been around for years now (I think I signed up with them about 10 years ago, before the Internet was used by anyone except universities and government agencies). In essence, these outfits are their own isolated mini Internet, with e-mail, bulletin boards, chat groups, and so forth. They typically provide you with special software that makes the whole process of working online simpler than using the more generic software tools designed for e-mail, newsgroups, and the Web. The proprietary information content supplied on services such as AOL and Prodigy is also a bit more supervised than what is available on the Internet at large. On the other hand, you're often somewhat crippled, since you may not be able to use the latest Web browsers.

In addition to supplying their own content, all the major services such as AOL now will connect you through to the Internet, so you can use the

Web, newsgroups, and Internet mail. I'd want to use a generic ISP such as Netcom, myself, since I want to be allowed the choice of Web browser I use (Netscape, Internet Explorer, NeoPlanet, etc.) and which mail reader (Eudora, Netscape, Outlook, Pegasus Mail, and so on). Services such as AOL and CompuServe don't give you a big choice there. But if a service lets you use the latest versions of Internet Explorer or Netscape for Web browsing, and the mail program they give you is decent (has folders to organize your mail, has a decent editor, and displays or deals reasonably with attachments such as gif and jpg pictures), then go for it, especially if they make it easy to get hooked up.

Be careful, though. Generally speaking, the most expensive way to connect to the Internet has been through one of these national providers. I used to pay $6/hour to be connected to CompuServe, for example. And that amounted to a monthly bill far and away more expensive than the $19 I pay to Netcom now to get unlimited hours on the Internet. AOL and CompuServe are now keeping up with the Joneses (or down, rather) and offering $20 rates, too. Read the fine print though to see just what you *do* get for that 20 bucks. Also check the access numbers to see that you won't be paying additional hourly phone connect charges. Then choose.

> **NOTE**
> By selecting an online service provider listed in this folder (not the MSN icon), you will be establishing an account with that online service provider and not with Microsoft Corporation. Therefore, your payment will be due to the online service provider. The online service provider you select will provide you with specific payment instructions.

If you decide to select one of the online service providers listed in this folder, just click the icon for that online service provider; this will begin setting up your computer for access with that provider. Here's how:

1. Clear the Desktop by clicking the Desktop icon in the Quick Launch bar at the bottom of the screen, or by any other method.

2. Look for a folder called Online Services and open it.

3. Run the icon of the service you want to check out. A "splash" screen about the product will appear, or you'll be prompted to insert your Windows CD-ROM, or take some other action, depending on the service. You should ensure your modem is on and connected to the telephone line, since a phone call will be made to sign you up. You'll need a credit card number, too, so get that ready.

4. Once signed up, you'll see instructions about what your services will include, how to proceed, and how to connect with the Internet.

> **WARNING**
> There may be specific instructions for how to run an online service's software with Windows 98 SE. Be sure to carefully answer any questions or read relevant instructions about the operating system you are using. For example, AOL has different versions of its software for Windows 3.11 than for Windows 95 or 98/SE. Read carefully.

Getting Directly on the Internet—Finding a Local ISP

Suppose you don't want to use one of the big content providers such as AOL, CompuServe, or AT&T, and you just want onto the Internet. Then what? As you probably know, there are thousands of smaller ISPs out there in the world, especially in the United States. These are the folks that don't supply "content" like AOL and CompuServe do, but that's OK. Maybe all you want is to get onto the Internet, not join clubs on AOL. So why pay for AOL or CompuServe features you don't need, or be limited by their regulations or in some cases, censorship of the material they'll provide you? Or be limited by the types of Web browser or mail or news readers they support?

These are some reasons why many folks get directly onto the Internet via a local or even national ISP. I, for one, use Netcom, probably the nation's largest ISP. They have dial-up numbers almost everywhere in the country, which is great. I can travel and still plug in my laptop, make a local call, and get my mail. For my ISDN line, I use a different provider, called Verio, in Berkeley, California. They are only local, but it's affordable ISDN service.

So, if you've decided that you can get cheaper or better service through a generic ISP, Microsoft has made it easy to get connected to the Internet via a little Wizard called Get on the Internet. Normally you'd have to find out on your own who your local ISPs are, and call them or otherwise contact them to get signed up for service. This can be a hassle. Depending on where you live, some local newspapers or computer rags sometimes list all the ISPs in the area. (This is true here in the San Francisco Bay Area where I can find a huge chart of all the local ISPs in the *Computer Currents* magazine.)

Microsoft decided to make this process easier by providing a Web page that lists ISPs around the country.

So, how do you get connected to an ISP? It's easy. In fact, if you don't have some dial-up connections to the Internet already, and you've tried running Outlook Express or Internet Explorer, you've probably already seen the Get Connected dialog box that has been insistently trying to sign you up with an ISP.

> **TIP**
> Have your Windows 98 SE Setup CD handy. The Wizard may need to install some Windows 98 SE files in order to set up your Internet connection.

1. Click Start ➢ Programs ➢ Accessories ➢ Internet Tools ➢ Internet Connection Wizard. You'll see the Wizard.

2. You'll see the dialog box shown in Figure 17.1. Choose which kind of setup you want. Referring to the figure, the choices in order are:

    ▶ Shows you a list of ISPs and helps get you signed up with them.

    ▶ Sets up the computer for use with your current ISP account, assuming you have one.

    ▶ Set up a connection manually, or set up a connection via a LAN.

3. Click Next. You may be asked which modem you want to use. Then it will try to dial your modem and call a toll-free number that accesses the Microsoft Internet Referral Service. If you are having trouble connecting, click Help in the dialog box and this will run the Internet Connection Wizard Help with troubleshooting tips.

4. When you finally connect to the Service, the Wizard displays a list of ISPs with some facts about each. If you choose the Sign Up For A New Account option back in the first dialog box, you'll see a list similar to that shown in Figure 17.2. Since they will undoubtedly be modified from time to time, I won't try to second guess what the remote instructions will say when you read them. However, you will probably have to provide information such as your address and credit card number. Just fol-

Connecting to the Internet 477

low the instructions you find there. A phone number is usually listed for each service if you don't feel comfortable signing up using this Wizard. If you want to quit the whole shebang and sign up later, click Cancel at the bottom of the page.

FIGURE 17.1: Running the Internet Connection Wizard

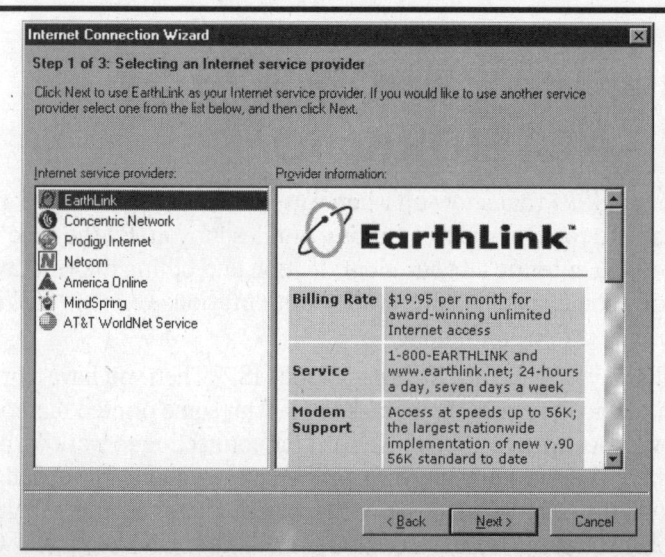

FIGURE 17.2: Typical ISP display resulting from using the Internet Connection Wizard

It's likely that you'll see the more national ISPs and information services listed here. No big surprise, I guess. It probably takes some doing to get on the Microsoft list. As I said earlier, you might have to sleuth around to find the smaller fry ISPs in your local area. If you don't want to go with one of the ISPs listed in the Microsoft Internet Referral Service, you will have to go back to the first screen of the Wizard and choose the second or third option. Contact the ISP you want to sign up with the "old-fashioned" way (i.e., call them on the phone). They should provide you with the following pieces of information to help you get your account set up in Windows:

- ▶ A phone number to use for your Internet connection
- ▶ Your *username* (might also be called *user ID* or *login name*)
- ▶ A dial-up password

Additionally, if your account includes mail service, you obtain the following information:

- ▶ Your e-mail address
- ▶ Incoming mail server type (POP3, IMAP, or HTTP) and address
- ▶ Outgoing mail server (SMTP) address
- ▶ Mail account login name and password

SETTING UP WINDOWS 98 SE DIAL-UP NETWORKING

The premium ISPs that show up when you run the Connection Wizard create ready-to-roll Dial-Up Networking profiles for you. By the time you're through entering all your identification and billing information, and clicking some buttons, all the dirty work previous versions of Windows required is done automatically.

But what if you're using a little backwoods ISP? Then you have a little more work to do. As a rule, simply ask the ISP for some printed material about how to set up your Dial-up Networking connection to work with their service. They undoubtedly have printed matter about this or can walk you through the necessary steps over the phone. There are several hairy dialog boxes you get to via the Dial-Up Networking (DUN) folder (My Computer ≻ Dial-Up Networking) and via Control Panel ≻ Network icon.

Creating a new profile is not difficult, but it's a little more complicated than simply clicking an option in the Setup Wizard. Here are the basics, just so you know what you're talking about when you do contact the ISP, or if you have the info already and want to get set up to configure a Dial-up Networking connection profile, you must complete two separate procedures: load the software and create a connection profile.

Loading the Software

If you didn't load Dial-Up Networking when you installed Windows 98 SE, you must add it before you can connect to the Internet. Follow these steps to add the software:

1. Open the Control Panel.
2. Open the Add/Remove Programs icon.
3. Click the Windows Setup tab to display the Windows Setup dialog box.
4. Select the Communications item from the Components list and click the Details button.
5. Make sure there's a check mark next to the Dial-Up Networking component, and click the OK button.
6. When you see a message instructing you to insert software disks, follow the instructions as they appear.
7. When the software has been loaded, restart the computer.
8. The Control Panel should still be open. Open the Network icon.
9. Click the Add button to display the Select Network Component Type dialog box, shown in Figure 17.3.

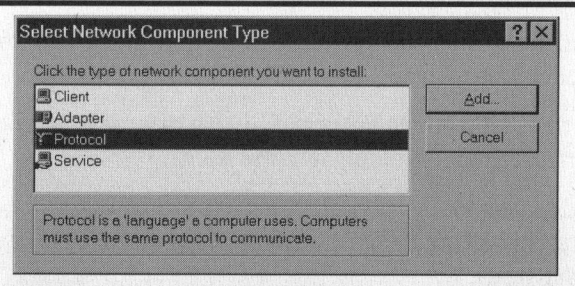

FIGURE 17.3: Use the Select Network Component Type dialog box to set up Dial-Up Networking.

10. Select Protocol in the list of component types and click the Add button.

11. Select Microsoft from the list of manufacturers and TCP/IP in the list of network protocols. Click the OK button.

12. You should see TCP/IP in the list of network components. Click the OK button to close the dialog box.

Creating a Connection Profile

Once you've added support for TCP/IP networking, you're ready to set up one or more connection profiles. Follow these steps to create a profile:

1. Start Dial-up Networking from either the My Computer window on the Desktop or the Programs ➢ Accessories ➢ Communications menu.

2. Double-click the Make New Connection icon.

3. The Make New Connection Wizard will start. The name of the computer you will dial is also the name that will identify the icon for this connection profile in the Dial-Up Networking folder. Therefore, you should use the name of your ISP as the name for this profile. If you have separate profiles for telephone numbers in different cities, include the city name as well. For example, if you use SPRYnet as your access provider, you might want to create profiles called SPRYnet Chicago and SPRYnet Boston.

4. Click the Next button to move to the next screen, and type the telephone number for your ISP's PPP access. Click Next again.

5. Click the Finish button to complete your work with the Wizard.

6. You will see a new icon in the Dial-Up Networking window. Right-click this icon and select the Properties command.

7. When the Connections Properties dialog box appears, click the Server Type tab to bring it to the front.

8. When the Server Types dialog box, shown in Figure 17.4, appears, choose the PPP option in the drop-down list of dial-up server types.

Connecting to the Internet 481

9. Make sure there are check marks next to these options:
   - Log on to network.
   - Enable software compression.
   - TCP/IP (you can turn off NetBEUI and EPX/SPX if you are only connecting to the Internet. Those are used for networking with IBM PCs running Novell and Microsoft networking protocols on a LAN).

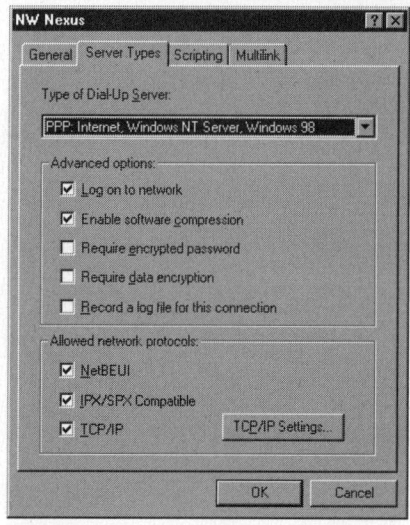

FIGURE 17.4: Use the Server Types dialog box to set up a PPP connection.

10. Click the TCP/IP Settings button.
11. Ask your ISP how to fill in this dialog box. You will probably use a Server Assigned IP Address and specific DNS addresses, but your ISP can give you the exact information you need. *This is an important step!*
12. Click the OK buttons to close all the open dialog boxes.

To confirm that you have set up the connection profile properly, turn on your modem and double-click the new icon. When the Connect To dialog box, shown in Figure 17.5, appears, type your user ID and password and click the Connect button. Your computer should place a call to the ISP and connect your system to the Internet.

If you have accounts with more than one ISP, or if you carry the same computer to different cities, you can create separate connection profiles for each ISP or each telephone number. If you aren't worried about other people using your computer to connect to your ISP, place a check mark next to the Save Password option.

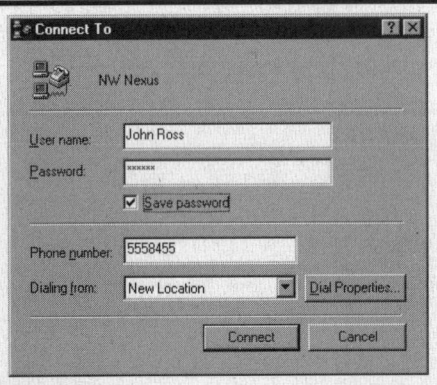

FIGURE 17.5: The Connect To dialog box shows the name and telephone number of your ISP.

Changing the Default Connection

When setup is complete, you will have a Dial-Up Networking connection profile for each of your ISPs. Internet Explorer and other Winsock-compliant or Internet-dependent programs will use the current default to connect your computer to the Internet whenever you start the programs. But what if you have several connections, and want to declare which one will be the default that Windows should use?

To change the default, follow these steps:

1. Open Control Panel and then run the Internet Properties applet.

2. When the Internet Properties dialog box appears, click the Connections tab to display the dialog box shown in Figure 17.6.

3. In the list of dial-up connections, choose the one that you want as the default and click Set Default.

Connecting to the Internet

4. Click OK to close the dialog box and close the Control Panel.

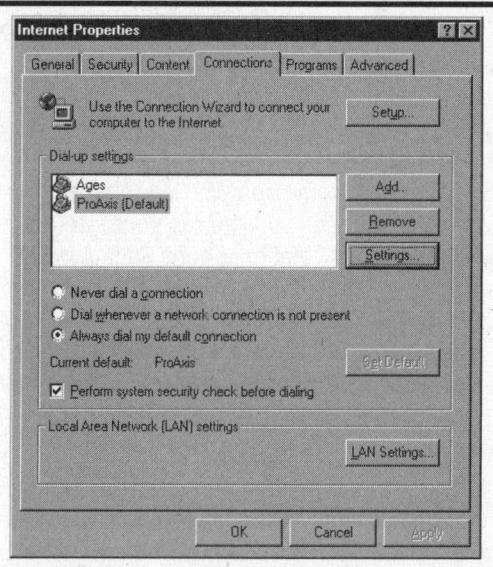

FIGURE 17.6: Use the Connection tab to change the default connection profile.

> ### TELLING INTERNET PROGRAMS NOT TO DIAL THE PHONE!
>
> Notice in Figure 17.6 that you can choose to connect via the local area network rather than by a modem. This is intended for workstations connected to a local area network running the TCP/IP protocol and which has a connection to the Internet via a router, ICS, or some other approach such as Microsoft Small Business Server, or Windows 2000 Server. But you can use this setting to your advantage, even if you've just got a lowly stand-alone computer.
>
> Here's why: It can be annoying when you open your mail program or IE or Netscape and suddenly the phone is being dialed by Windows in hopes of making life easy for you by connecting automatically to the Internet to carry out your wishes. Maybe you're on the phone already, talking to someone, and don't want your modem blasting into your ear. Or you want to ensure that if you're not home, but you've left your computer on, that your e-mail program doesn't cause Windows to dial the phone and stay online accidentally racking up connect-time charges.
>
> CONTINUED →

Chapter Seventeen

If you choose Never Dial A Connection in the dialog box in Figure 17.6, running IE, or OE, or Netscape will not run the phone dialer to try to log you on. Actually, nothing will happen except that you'll most likely eventually get an error message from your program saying a connection couldn't be made. Make your connection to the Net manually, by running the DUN profile from My Computer ➣ Dial-Up Networking. Once connected, then you can run your Internet programs without having them try to dial the phone. In fact, what I do is tell any Internet programs (i.e., Winsock-compatible programs) that they are not to bother connecting to the Internet except through the LAN. (How you do this depends on the program. Some have no settings, and rely on the default setting explained above.)

Anyway, this arrangement can give you much more flexibility. For example, when I want to connect to the Internet, I run the DUN profile for the connection I want at the time. Sometimes I want a fast connection, so I dial up with my ISDN connection. Other times I want to be on all day with minimal cost, so I use my analog Netcom connection ($19.95/month unlimited connect time). The programs I'm using don't know how the connection was made. All they know is that the TCP/IP connection to the Internet is active. As long as the little connection icon appears down on the task bar's right edge,

all popular Winsock Internet programs such as Netscape, Eudora, Pegasus Mail, Internet Explorer, WS_FTP, and so on should work fine. When it's time to get off the connection, I have to do that manually, too (or face the consequences). I double-click the little connection icon, and click Disconnect.

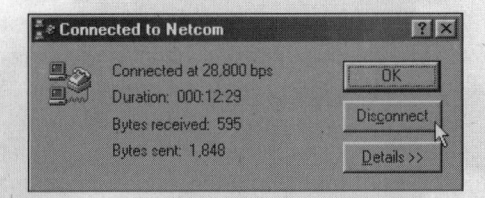

Sharing Your Internet Connection with Networked Computers

Personal computers in the home are nothing new. The relatively mature PC market—combined with remarkable price drops on new computers in recent years—means that many homes now have multiple PCs. These multi-PC owners are now seeking to create their own networks to connect all those computers together. The online news source C|NET (www.cnet.com) projects that the home networking market will grow from an expected $230 million in 1999 to $1.4 billion by 2003.

Microsoft is doing its best to keep pace with the growing home network market, and Windows 98 SE includes a number of useful tools to make networking worthwhile. Perhaps the most interesting new feature is Internet Connection Sharing (ICS), which allows computers on your home network to share a single Internet connection. This means that two or more computers can access the online world using only a single phone line and modem.

Admittedly, this kind of sharing is nothing new. Networked computers have been able to share Internet access over the network for years using third party proxy server software. The proxy server is usually set up on the network server, and workstations go online through that central connection. By incorporating ICS into Windows 98, Microsoft made the whole process far simpler. Installing ICS is no more complicated than installing any number of other Windows components, such as the TV Viewer or Desktop Themes.

> **NOTE**
> ICS can put a real strain on your modem connection, especially if more than one computer is trying to access the Internet simultaneously. As a general rule, assume that each Internet user will require 28.8Kbps worth of bandwidth. Thus, if you have two computers sharing the connection, it should be capable of 56Kbps transfer rates. With three or more computers on ICS, your best bet is to upgrade to an ISDN or DSL connection. Otherwise, you may find that even relatively simple actions like downloading e-mail or viewing a Web page is maddeningly slow, if not impossible.

Setting Up Internet Connection Sharing

Once your network is up and running, decide which computer will be used to facilitate the Internet connection. This will be called your Connection Sharing computer.

Next, make sure that the modem and Dial-Up Networking connection in your Connection Sharing computer is installed and ready. Beginning on the Sharing computer, place your Windows 98 SE CD into the drive and perform the following:

1. Run the Control Panel and open the Add/Remove Programs applet.

2. Click the Windows Setup tab to bring it to the front. Choose Internet Tools and click Details.

3. Place a check mark next to Internet Connection Sharing and click OK twice.

> **NOTE**
> If you do not have the Internet Connection Sharing option available in your Internet Tools list, you probably don't have the Second Edition of Windows 98. Double-check the documentation that came with your Windows 98 CD to make sure that it is the Second Edition, and that it includes ICS.

4. The Internet Connection Sharing Wizard begins. Click Next to begin the setup process. You will first be asked to create a Client Disk to be used when setting up ICS on the other computers on your network. Follow the instructions on screen to create the disk.

5. When you are done creating the Client Disk, click Finish to complete installation. You will be prompted to restart the computer.

6. After the computer is restarted, open the Control Panel again and launch the Internet Options applet. Bring the Connections tab to the front and click Sharing, as shown in Figure 17.7.

7. In the Internet Connection Sharing dialog, make sure there is a check mark next to Enable Internet Connection Sharing. Also check that your dial-up adapter is listed under Connect To The Internet Using, and that your correct network adapter appears at the bottom. Click OK to exit all of the dialogs.

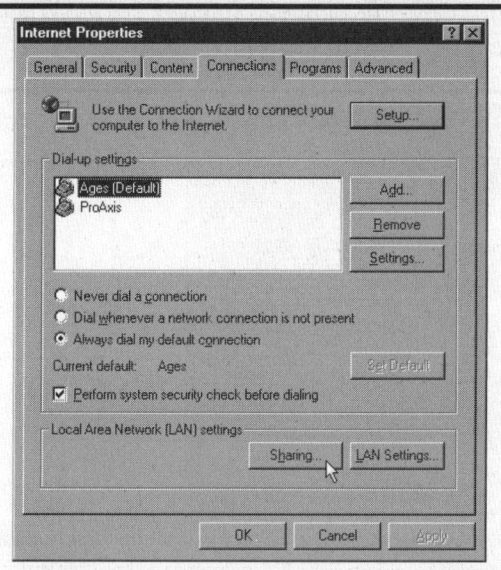

FIGURE 17.7: Click Sharing on the Connection tab to configure your Connection Sharing computer.

Now that your Connection Sharing computer is configured, you need to set up the other computers on your network to utilize the shared connection. Bring the Client disk you created in step 4 with you and perform the following:

1. Insert the client disk into the floppy drive.
2. Click Start ➤ Run... and type `a:\icsclset.exe`.
3. Click OK to open the Browser Connection Setup Wizard, and then click Next. The Wizard warns you that it is about to check—and change—the settings in the Web browser, as shown in Figure 17.8. Click Next to proceed.
4. Click Finish in the last Wizard screen.

The Wizard changes the connection setting in your browser so that it looks for an Internet connection over the LAN instead of a dial-up. If the client computer has Internet Explorer 5, you can view this change by opening the Control Panel and launching the Internet Options applet. On the Connections tab, you will see that Never Dial A Connection has been selected, as shown in Figure 17.9. This is important to note, especially if the client is a computer you plan to remove from the network periodically (such as a laptop). In this case, I recommend you choose Dial Whenever A Network Connection Is Not Present instead.

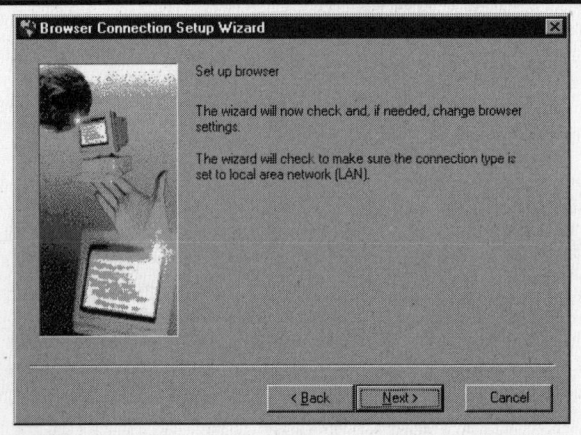

FIGURE 17.8: The Browser Connection Setup Wizard will set up your browser to access the Internet over your LAN instead of a dial-up connection.

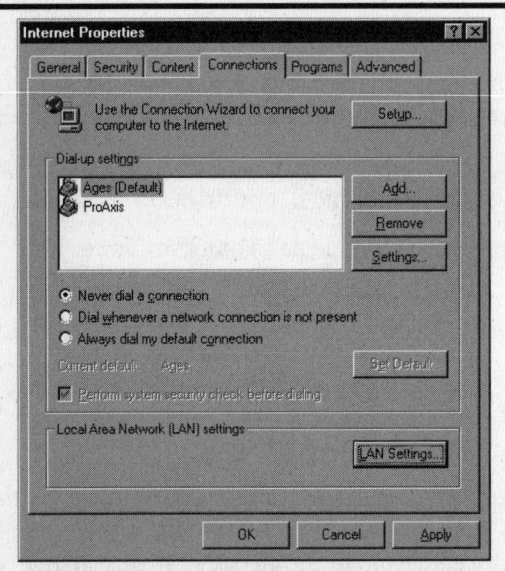

FIGURE 17.9: If the client computer is a laptop or will be removed from the network periodically, consider changing the settings in this dialog box.

WHAT'S NEXT?

One of the best parts of being connected to the Internet is the ability to connect to millions of people around the globe for nothing more than the cost of your ISP! In the next chapter, Christian Crumlish gives you all of the details of communicating with e-mail.

Chapter 18

COMMUNICATING WITH E-MAIL

This is the real stuff. The reason you're on the Net. E-mail! Instant (more or less) communication with people all over the globe. Once you can send and receive e-mail, you're wired.

When you get used to sending e-mail, you'll find that it's as useful a form of communication as the telephone, and it doesn't require the other person to drop whatever they're doing to answer your call. You can include a huge amount of specific information, and the person you sent mail to can reply in full in their own good time. And unlike the telephone, with e-mail you can write your message and edit it before you send it.

Adapted from *The Internet: No Experience Required*
by Christian Crumlish
ISBN 0-7821-2168-3   528 pages $24.99

E-mail is the lifeblood of the Internet. Daily, millions of written messages course through the wires, enabling people all over the planet to communicate in seconds. One reason for the widespread use of the Internet as the international computer network is that it's a flexible enough system to allow just about any type of computer or network to participate. Of course, this book assumes you're using a PC with Windows 98 SE and either the Outlook Express mailer that's bundled with Internet Explorer or the Messenger mailer included in the Netscape Communicator suite. But it's important to remember that e-mail programs basically do the same things.

I'll start off by explaining the most common activities associated with e-mail, the kinds of things you'll want to know how to do no matter what program you have. I'll use generic terminology in this part of the lesson, such as Inbox and Outbox, even if some specific programs use different terms for the same ideas. Focus on the concepts and the standard features, not what they're called in one program or another. Then, I'll cover specific commands and tips for the e-mail programs you're most likely to use.

> **NOTE**
> Christian Crumlish wrote *The Internet: No Experience Required* for all new Internet users, no matter what operating system and software they are using; not just for Windows 98 SE users working with Internet Explorer or Netscape Communicator. In particular, its e-mail chapters include extensive coverage of other e-mail programs that we've omitted in adapting this material for *Windows 98 Second Edition Complete*. If you have access to a Macintosh or Unix system, or a mailer such as Eudora or Pegasus, you may want to consult *The Internet: No Experience Required* for details.

E-Mail Basics

These are the things that you will do most often with e-mail:

- Run the mail program
- Send mail
- Read incoming mail
- Reply to mail
- Delete mail
- Exit the mail program

In the second half of this chapter, I'll show you some additional e-mail tricks you might find useful, such as how to forward mail and create an electronic address book.

Running an E-Mail Program

You start most e-mail programs the way you do any program, usually by double-clicking an icon or by choosing a program name from a menu (the Start menu in Windows 98 SE). If your Internet connection is not already up and running, your e-mail program may be able to start that process for you.

Your e-mail program will start and show you either the contents of your Inbox (the mailbox where your new messages arrive) or a list of all your mailboxes (in which case you'll want to open the Inbox).

NOTE
There are some new free Internet accounts (such as Hotmail and Juno.com) that offer Web-based e-mail access. The accounts are paid for by advertising you have to keep on your screen while you're connected. To find out more about them, go to http://www.hotmail.com or http://www.juno.com in your Internet browser.

In addition to an Inbox where just-arrived messages appear, you'll automatically have an Outbox in which copies of your outgoing messages can be saved (some programs will do this automatically), and you'll usually have a deleted-messages or Trash mailbox where discarded messages are held until they are completely purged.

Mailboxes generally list just the sender's name and the subject line of the message (and probably its date as well). When you double-click a message in any of your mailboxes, the message opens in a window of its own.

Sending Mail

All mail programs have a New Message or Compose E-Mail command, often located on a message menu, and they usually have a keyboard shortcut for the command as well, such as Ctrl+N for New Message. When you start a new message, your program will open a new window. Figure 18.1 shows a new message window in Outlook Express.

TIP

You can also save addresses and then select them from an address book or list of names rather than type them in directly. See "Managing an Address Book" later in this chapter for more on this.

FIGURE 18.1: A blank New Message window

Type the address of the person to whom you want to send the mail. The person's address must be in the form *username@address.domain*, where *username* is the person's identifier (the name they log in with); *address* is the identifier of the person's network or machine on the network (the address might consist of several words—the host and subdomain—separated by dots); and *domain* is the short code at the end indicating whether the address is a business (.com), a nonprofit (.org), a university (.edu), a branch of the government (.gov), a part of the military (.mil), and so on. (Some e-mail programs require special text before or after the Internet e-mail address.) Would you rather write your message ahead of time and then just paste it in when it comes time to send it? See "Writing E-Mail with Your Word Processor," later in this chapter.

By the way, all the rules just mentioned apply only to sending mail over the Internet. Generally, if you're sending mail to someone on your own network (or another member of your online service or a subscriber of your service provider), you only have to specify the username, not any of the Internet information.

Communicating with E-Mail

TIP

The easiest way to send mail to someone is to reply to mail that they've sent you. If you're not sure exactly how to form someone's e-mail address, ask them to send you some mail and then simply reply to it. That's what I always do.

One of my addresses is `xian@netcom.com` (you pronounce the "@" as "at," and the "." as "dot"). I log in as "xian," my service provider is Netcom, and Netcom is a commercial business.

Sending Mail to People on Other Networks

Many people have Internet addresses even though they are not, strictly speaking, on the Internet. Most other networks have gateways that send mail to and from the Internet. If you want to send mail to someone on another network, you'll need to know their identifier on that network and how their network address appears in Internet form. Here are examples of the most common Internet addresses:

Network	Username	Internet Address
America Online	Beebles	Beebles@aol.com
AT&T Mail	Beebles	beebles@attmail.com
CompuServe	75555,5555	75555.5555@compuserve.com
MCI Mail	555-7777	555-7777@mcimail.com
Microsoft Network	Beebles	beebles@msn.com
Prodigy	Beebles	beebles@prodigy.com

To compose and send a message, follow these steps:

1. After entering the recipient's address in the Address box, press Tab and then type a subject in the Subject box (keep it short). This will be the first thing the recipient of your mail sees.

TIP

The subject you type in the subject line should be fairly short, but should be a good description of the contents of your message. Good subject lines can help recipients categorize their mail and respond more quickly to your messages.

2. If you want to send a copy of the e-mail message to more than one recipient, you can either:

Chapter Eighteen

- Type that person's address on the Cc: line.
- Type multiple addresses in either the To or Cc line, separating each address by a comma or a semicolon. In some e-mail programs, the addresses may appear on separate lines.

> **TIP**
>
> In both Internet Explorer and Netscape Messenger, you can press Tab to jump from box to box or from area to area when filling in an address and subject. You can also just click directly in the area you want to jump to.

3. Press Tab until the insertion point jumps into the blank message area.

4. Type your message, and when you are done, send the message or add it to a *queue*, a list of outgoing messages to be sent all at once. Click the Send button, or choose File ➤ Send Message. Figure 18.2 shows a short e-mail message.

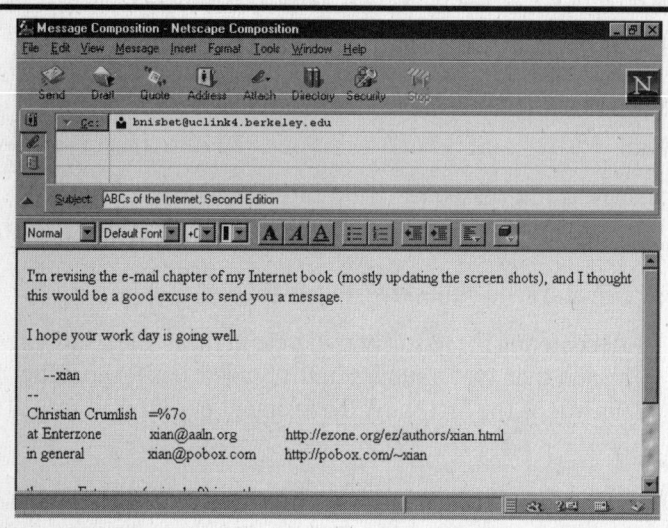

FIGURE 18.2: A short e-mail message to a friend

> **TIP**
> Both Outlook Express and Netscape Messenger can word-wrap your message, so you only have to press Enter when you want to start a new paragraph. I recommend leaving a blank line between paragraphs, to make them easier to read.

You can also filter messages, which is the same thing as sorting them according to some criteria as they come into your Inbox. The post office sorts mail according to zip code, and you can use your e-mail program to automatically sort messages according to who sent them, the subject, the date they were sent or received, or any other category that is useful to you from an organizational standpoint. And you can flag messages according to the urgency of the response needed or other priorities. These options provide you with powerful organizational tools and transform your messages into valuable records that can be filed and retrieved for later reference. See "Filtering Messages as They Come In" later in this chapter for more on message filters.

Reading Mail

Whenever I connect to the Net, the first thing I do is check my e-mail. It's like checking your mailbox when you get home, except the contents are generally more interesting—and usually don't contain bills! Some mail programs (including Outlook Express and Netscape Messenger) combine the process of sending queued messages with checking for new mail. Most also check for new mail when you first start them.

Unread (usually new) mail appears with some indicator that it's new, such as the Subject line in bold or a bullet or check mark next to the new messages. This is supposed to help you pick out the messages you haven't read yet, so you don't miss any.

Here are the steps for reading an e-mail message:

1. Open your e-mail program by double-clicking its shortcut icon or selecting it from the Start menu. By default, both Outlook Express and Netscape Messenger begin by displaying your Inbox contents automatically.

2. To view the contents of a mail message, highlight it in the Inbox window and press Enter (or double-click it). The message will appear in its own window, much like an outgoing message. Figure 18.3 shows an incoming message in Outlook Express.

3. If the message continues beyond the bottom of the window, use the scroll bar to see the next screenful.

4. After reading the message, you can close or reply to the message.

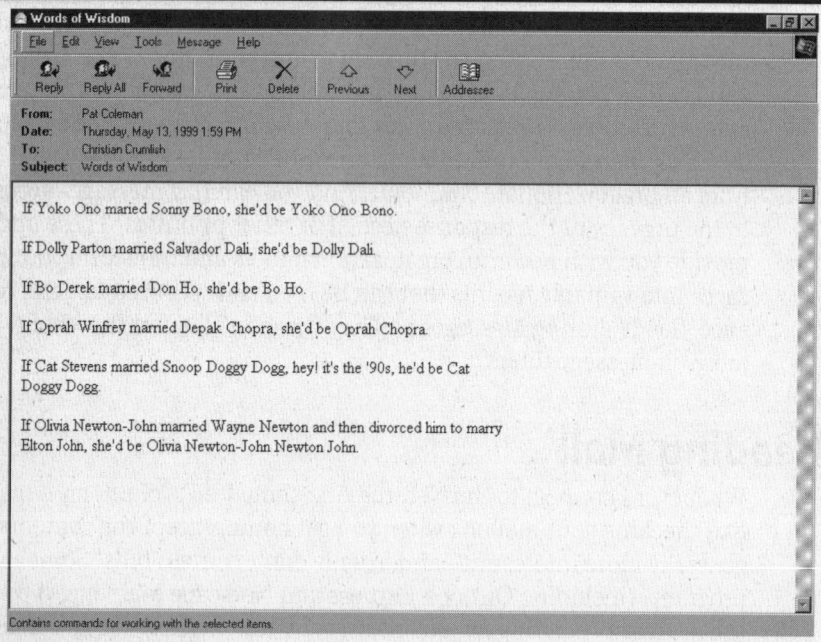

```
Words of Wisdom
File  Edit  View  Tools  Message  Help

Reply  Reply All  Forward    Print    Delete    Previous  Next    Addressee

From:    Pat Coleman
Date:    Thursday, May 13, 1999 1:59 PM
To:      Christian Crumlish
Subject: Words of Wisdom

If Yoko Ono married Sonny Bono, she'd be Yoko Ono Bono.

If Dolly Parton married Salvador Dali, she'd be Dolly Dali.

If Bo Derek married Don Ho, she'd be Bo Ho.

If Oprah Winfrey married Depak Chopra, she'd be Oprah Chopra.

If Cat Stevens married Snoop Doggy Dogg, hey! it's the '90s, he'd be Cat Doggy Dogg.

If Olivia Newton-John married Wayne Newton and then divorced him to marry Elton John, she'd be Olivia Newton-John Newton John.

Contains commands for working with the selected items.
```

FIGURE 18.3: Here's an e-mail message I received.

> **TIP**
> I keep my mail around until I've replied to it. I could save it to a mailbox (as I'll explain later in this chapter) but then I might forget about it. When my Inbox gets too cluttered, I bite the bullet and reply to mail I've been putting off, and then I delete most of it.

Replying to Mail

Both Outlook Express and Messenger offer menu options and toolbar buttons for replying to messages you've received. When you reply to an e-mail message, your new message is automatically addressed back to the sender, and you can easily quote the message you received.

Communicating with E-Mail

> **TIP**
> If you start to reply by mistake, just close the message window and don't save the reply if prompted.

To reply to an e-mail message, follow these steps:

1. Highlight the received message in the Inbox or open the message, and then click the Reply (or Reply To Author) command.

2. Your program will create a new message automatically addressed to the sender of the message you're replying to. In Messenger, you can click the Quote button to include the original message. In Outlook Express, you'll need to choose Tools ➢ Options and, in the Send tab, click Include Message in Reply.

> **TIP**
> Any Web addresses mentioned in e-mail messages to you can function as clickable links in Messenger and Outlook Express. To use these links, click the highlighted address, which will probably be underlined or depicted in a different color, such as blue. You will be transported to the Web site using that address. Outlook Express users can also add Web shortcuts as file attachments. Just click the Web icon to head for that site.

3. Sometimes, you'll want to reply to everyone who was sent a copy of the original message. Select Reply to All or a similar command to send your reply to everyone.

4. Tab to the subject line and type a new subject if the old one isn't very meaningful anymore. (People often fail to change the subject line of messages, even when the conversation has evolved onto a new topic.)

5. Add other recipients if necessary or tab your way into the message area to type your reply, and then choose the Send (or Queue) command when you are done.

TIP

E-mail tends to take on a life of its own, with people forwarding you messages from other people asking for help, information, you name it. Sometimes people send you long chains of related messages, often called *threads*. To avoid confusion when replying to a message forwarded to you, or when replying to many recipients, direct the mail program to "retain the original text," or however the command is worded, so that people reading the message will know what you are talking about and will know the history of the issue. However, if the thread starts getting too long, try to abbreviate it as described below in the "Using Proper E-Mail Netiquette" section.

Deleting Mail

If you have read a piece of mail and you're positive that you have no need to save it, you should delete it so that it doesn't clutter up your Inbox (and waste precious hard-disk storage space). To delete a message, highlight it and press Delete (or click the Delete button).

Using Proper E-Mail Netiquette

Like any social system, the Internet has evolved to the point where its users observe a variety of informal rules for interacting politely. Collectively, these rules are known as *Netiquette*, and most of them can be inferred through the application of some common sense to various social situations.

For example, it's generally not considered good manners to misquote what someone said when talking to someone else, to take their words out of context, or to repeat something that was told to you in confidence (though the media and gossips often commit such acts!). Think of e-mail as a kind of online conversation. If people send you messages containing sensitive material, don't forward them on to others without the author's permission.

If you retain only part of the original text of messages in your replies (to keep the replies from becoming too long), be sure it is not misleadingly taken out of its full context (and likely to be misinterpreted). And please do not intersperse your own comments with the retained pieces of other people's messages so that it's not clear to the recipients who wrote what.

Keep Your Messages Brief and Tactful

When you write messages to business associates and colleagues, stick to the point and be informative. Break up large blocks of text into smaller paragraphs. Reread your messages and run a spell check before sending them—this will give you a chance to minimize mistakes, fix poorly organized sentences, and reconsider bad word choices.

If you are writing to friends (or potential friends in newsgroups or chat rooms), you can relax a little more, but still hold back on anything that could be considered offensive, even if you think it's funny and you are sure that your friends will, too. Seemingly innocuous statements in spoken conversation can take on a whole new meaning when written down. Figures of speech, jokes, and your own private way of referring to situations or people seem a lot more serious when viewed in writing.

> **WARNING**
> The old adage about never saying or putting anything in writing that you would not want to see in a headline the next day applies to e-mail and the Internet. Now you also have to worry about your words appearing on someone's Web page or showing up when someone searches the Web, a chat service, or a newsgroup. Journalists search the Web for juicy opinions every day. There's no law preventing potential employers from checking you out on the Web and uncovering some embarrassing thing you wrote or posted years ago.

When replying to messages, try to minimize the amount of quoted text that you keep in your return message. Leave enough so it's clear what you're replying to (people don't always remember exactly what they wrote to you). However, as mentioned at the beginning of this section, don't send abbreviated message bits attributed to other people that could be taken out of context. Just use your good common sense!

Don't Fly off the Handle

E-mail is a notoriously volatile medium. Because it is so easy to write out a reply and send it in the heat of the moment, and because text lacks many of the nuances of face-to-face communication—the expression and body cues that add emphasis, the tones of voice that indicate joking instead of insult, and so on—it has become a matter of course for many people to dash off ill-considered replies to perceived insults and therefore to fan the flames of invective.

This Internet habit, called *flaming*, is widespread, and you will no doubt encounter it on one end or the other. All I can suggest is that you try to restrain yourself when you feel the urge to fly off the handle. (And I have discovered that apologies work wonders when people have misunderstood a friendly gibe or have mistaken sarcasm for idiocy.)

> **TIP**
> If you are the sort to flare up in an angry response, or if you find yourself getting emotional or agitated while composing a response to a message that upsets you, save your message as a draft rather than sending it right away. You can review the draft message later when you have calmed down, and you can decide then whether you want to send it, or you can send the draft to a disinterested third party and ask them if it is too harsh before you send it out.

Exiting an E-Mail Program

When you are finished sending, reading, and replying to mail, you can quit your program or leave it running to check your mail at regular intervals. You can quit Outlook Express or Messenger by selecting File ➤ Exit or File ➤ Quit.

Trying Out Microsoft Outlook Express and Netscape Messenger

Well, now you know the basic e-mail moves no matter which program you're using. In the following sections, I'll detail the specific commands for our two e-mail programs. The second half of this chapter covers some of e-mail's more interesting possibilities. Jump to chapter 19 if you're impatient to get onto the World Wide Web.

Microsoft Outlook Express

Outlook Express is an Internet standards-based e-mail and news reader you can use to access Internet e-mail and news accounts. In this section, we'll look at how to use Outlook Express Mail.

You can open Outlook Express by selecting Start ➤ Programs ➤ Outlook Express, or by clicking the miniature Launch Outlook Express icon in the QuickLaunch bar to the immediate right of the Start button.

> **NOTE**
> You'll start off in a window showing two panes. The pane on the left shows the various features of the program that are available, with your Inbox first and foremost. The pane on the right shows you the contents of your Inbox (but you can click any other folder, and Outlook Express will show its contents below). Outlook Express has a big Preview pane that shows you the contents of the highlighted message. You can turn this Preview on or off and change its appearance and location by choosing View ➢ Layout.

Here's how to create a new Outlook Express e-mail message:

1. Click the New Mail button (or press Ctrl+N) to open the New Message window.
2. Type an address and press Tab to get down to the Subject box where you can type a subject.
3. Tab down to the message area and type your message. Click the Send button. If you are accumulating messages to send in bulk, choose File ➢ Send Later, and then click the Send/Recv button in the main Outlook Express window when you are ready to send them all.

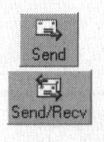

To read a message in your Inbox, just double-click its subject line. The message will appear in its own window. To reply to the message, select Reply (Ctrl+R) or Reply All (Ctrl+Shift+R). Outlook Express will supply the recipient's address. Proceed as if you were sending a new message.

To delete a message, just highlight it and click the Delete button or press the Delete key on your keyboard. The message will be moved to the Deleted Items folder until you specifically open that folder and delete its contents.

> **TIP**
> To undelete a message, open the Deleted Items folder and select the message you want to restore. Then choose Edit ➢ Move to Folder, choose the Inbox folder from the Move dialog box that appears, and click OK.

To exit Outlook Express, choose File ➢ Exit.

Netscape Messenger

Netscape Communicator 4.6 (the successor to Navigator 3 and Navigator Gold series) sports a full-featured mail program called Netscape Messenger. It's a redesigned version of Netscape Mail.

Chapter Eighteen

> **NOTE**
> You'll learn more about Netscape Communicator's Web capabilities in Chapter 21, *An Alternative to Internet Explorer: Netscape Navigator.*

Using Netscape Messenger for e-mail is a lot like using Outlook Express and many other mail programs. Here's how to create and send an e-mail message:

1. Choose File ➤ New ➤ Message or select New Message from the Message pull-down menu (you may also press Ctrl+M or click the New Message button).

2. Type an address in the To box. Press Tab and type a subject.

3. Press Tab again to enter the message area and type your message (see Figure 18.4).

4. When you're done, click the Send button.

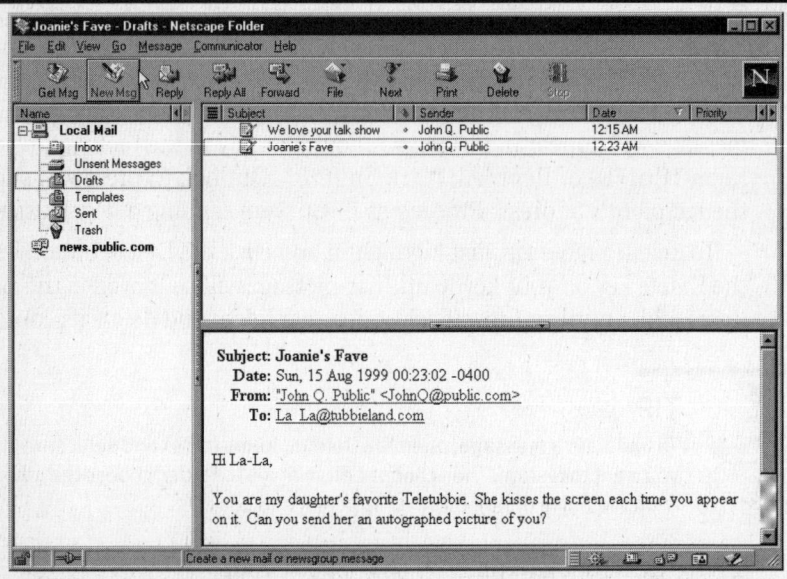

FIGURE 18.4: The Netscape Messenger window lists messages in the top pane and shows the contents of the current message in the hideable lower pane.

Communicating with E-Mail

If you receive mail while working in Netscape (the little envelope in the lower-right corner of the Netscape window will alert you), choose Window ➢ Inbox. (The first time you do this, Netscape may require you to enter your password.) Just highlight a message in the upper pane to see its contents in the lower pane.

> **TIP**
> Remember that any Web addresses mentioned in Netscape Messenger e-mail messages you receive will function as clickable links. That means when you finish reading, all you have to do is click a highlighted word to go to that Web page and start surfing. For more information on the Web, see Chapter 19, *Browsing the Web with Internet Explorer*.

Here are some other Netscape Messenger commands you will find useful:

- To reply to a message, click the Reply button, press Ctrl+R, or choose Message ➢ Reply ➢ To Sender.
- To delete a message, just highlight it and click the Delete button. Netscape will move the message to a Trash folder.
- To undelete a message, select the Trash folder in the drop-down folder list just above the top pane, select the message, and then choose Message ➢ File Message ➢ Inbox.

You can close the mail window and keep Netscape running if you want—in Windows 98 SE, click the close button in the upper-right corner—or you can quit Netscape entirely by choosing File ➢ Exit.

Using E-Mail More Effectively

Now that you've learned the essentials of sending and receiving e-mail, we'll use the rest of this chapter to look at somewhat more advanced techniques that can help to streamline your work with either Outlook Express or Netscape Messenger.

Sending Mail to More Than One Person

Sometimes you'll want to send a message to more than one recipient. You can do this in one of several ways. Both Outlook Express and Netscape

Messenger (as well as most other programs) allow you to list multiple recipients in the To line, usually separated by commas (some programs require that you use a different character, such as a semicolon, to separate addresses). Most programs also have a Cc line. As with traditional paper office memos, the Cc line in an e-mail message is for people who should receive a copy of the message, but who are not the primary recipients.

> **NOTE**
> When you reply to a message, your reply will be sent only to the person in the To line if you select the Reply To Sender option. If you select Reply To All, your reply will be sent to everyone in the Cc list as well.

Some programs also offer a Bcc line, which lets you list one or more people to receive blind copies of that message. This means that the primary (and Cc) recipients will not see the names of people receiving blind copies.

> **WARNING**
> You can typically include as many names on the Cc line as you want, but some mail servers will "choke" on a message if its headers are too long.

Sending Files via E-Mail

It sounds too good to be true. Just "attach" a file to an e-mail message, and it zips across the globe to your recipient, without having to be put on a disk and sent by mail or courier. Naturally, it's not that simple. Some files are just too big to send this way (anything close to a megabyte is probably too big). Let's start with what an attachment really is.

> **NOTE**
> Each Internet Service Provider is a little different, so you can experiment with the size of files you can send. Some services limit the size of files you may attach to messages, while others will take anything, but the transmission may become extremely slow. You can compress files to make them smaller, and you can send each file in a group of files in separate messages to keep the size low.

Attaching Files to E-Mail Messages in Outlook Express

An *attachment* is a data file, in any form, that your program will send along with your e-mail message—it could be a word processor file, a picture, a spreadsheet, or any other kind of file. In Outlook Express, use one of these options to attach files to your messages:

- ▶ Use Explorer or My Computer to open the window the file is in, click the file, and drag it into the new message window.

- ▶ Choose Insert ➢ File Attachment, and choose the file you want from the Insert Attachment dialog box that appears and then click OK. Figure 18.5 shows an attached file in an Outlook Express message. Your recipient can double-click the icon next to the filename on the Attach line to open the attached file.

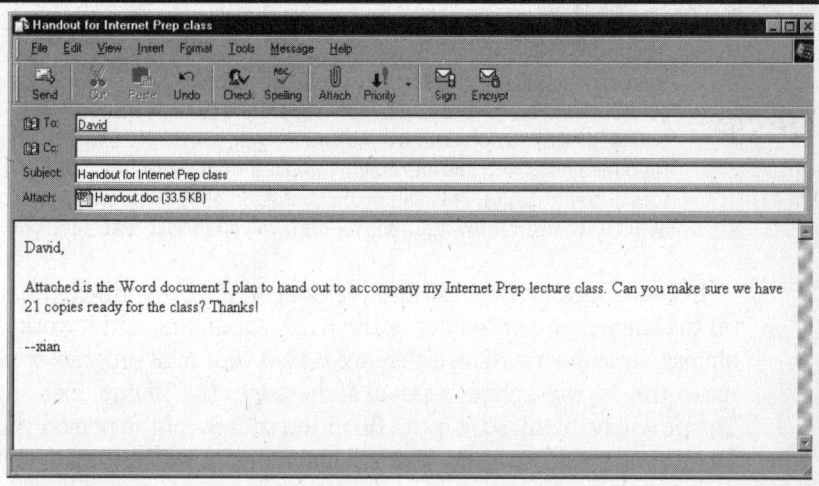

FIGURE 18.5: Outlook Express inserts an icon and the filename of the attachment on the Attach line.

Attaching Files to Messenger E-Mail

Netscape Messenger's provisions for attaching files to e-mail are quite simple. You can also attach Web page links to your messages with these commands:

1. Choose Message ➢ New Message to open the Composition window. Or click the New Message button in the Messenger toolbar or type Ctrl+M.

2. Address your message and type your message in the message body. To attach a file to the message, click the Attach button.

3. Choose File (you can also attach Web pages, among other things).

4. In the dialog box that appears, choose the file you want to send, and then click Open.

5. Click the Save button or the Send button to save a draft or send your message on its way.

Forwarding Mail to Someone Else

If someone sends you an e-mail message and you'd like to send a copy of it to someone else, most mail programs let you select a Forward command.

> **WARNING**
> Never send mail to a third party without the express permission of the original sender. Also, be sure to use a *reply separator*, such as a solid horizontal line, between all of the forwarded e-mail messages, to delineate where one person's response ends and another begins (most e-mail programs add reply separators automatically). This will avoid confusion about who wrote what and will avoid uncomfortable situations for both you and those who send you e-mail.

In both Outlook Express and Messenger, the Forward command is on the same menu or toolbar as the Reply command, and it works in almost the same way. The difference is that your mail program won't insert the original sender's e-mail address into the To line. Instead, the To line will be blank so you can fill in the address of the person you are forwarding the message to. The original message will automatically be included in the new message, often with some characters (like the standard ">" Internet e-mail quoting character) or other formatting to distinguish it from what you yourself write.

Here's how to forward e-mail messages:

1. Open your e-mail program, and either highlight or open the message you want to forward.

2. Click the Forward icon in the toolbar of your e-mail program, or use a command such as Compose ➢ Forward. A new message window will appear with the forwarded message included in the text area.

3. Enter the recipient's e-mail address on the To line and then Tab your way down to the message area.

4. Edit the message if you want, or add your own note to the beginning, perhaps explaining why you are forwarding the message.

5. Send the message as usual.

To forward a message in Outlook Express, click the Forward button. You can also choose Message ➢ Forward or press Ctrl+F and then proceed as you would with a new message.

To forward a message in Messenger, click the Forward button (or select Message ➢ Forward or press Ctrl+L). Then proceed as you would with a new message.

Enhancing Your E-Mail with HTML Formatting

Internet mail has long been an "unformatted" medium, with only a guarantee that basic text would be transmitted from site to site. Formatted messages typically lose their formatting as soon as they pass through an e-mail gateway. Some mail programs can understand or create formatting that conforms to the Internet's MIME standard, but again, not all programs recognize MIME, so the point of the formatting may be lost.

Now, some mail programs are more closely integrated with Web browsers, such as Netscape Messenger, part of the same Netscape Communicator suite that contains Netscape Navigator. Microsoft Outlook Express, which is installed as part of Windows 98 SE, works in tandem with Internet Explorer. These e-mail programs have become more Web-savvy: able to recognize Web addresses (URLs), hyperlinks, and now most HTML formatting. (HTML is the coding language used to create Web documents.)

> **WARNING**
> Don't rely too heavily on any "brand" of formatting to make your point, because you can't be sure your audience will see the pulsing, blinking green text or other effects you may add. Your careful selection of just the right font may also backfire when the message arrives, because some programs substitute basic fonts for less common fonts, resulting in poorly aligned text at the message's destination.

Both Outlook Express and Messenger also let you create messages with HTML formatting. In fact, you can compose mail messages much the same way you can Web pages, inserting images and links to pages on the Web or other Internet resources. You don't need to "know the code" either, because the software makes it as easy to add HTML formatting as it is to change font styles with your word processor. See Chapter 22 for more on HTML and Web-style formatting.

Formatting an E-Mail Message with HTML in Outlook Express

Your messages will resemble Web pages if you use Outlook Express HTML formatting to add colorful fonts and even graphics. Just the two steps here give you this capability:

1. Choose Format ➢ Rich Text (HTML). The Formatting toolbar will appear at the top of your message.

2. Select the text to be formatted and use the buttons on the Formatting toolbar to add HTML formatting, such as bold and italic, bulleted lists, alignment (center, flush left, or flush right), and text color.

Formatting an E-Mail Message with HTML in Netscape Messenger

In Messenger, you can add any HTML formatting (or insert hyperlinks or even graphic images) to your message using the convenient toolbar in the Message Compose window. (Insert links and images with the Insert Object button farthest to the right.)

Writing E-Mail with Your Word Processor

If you're more comfortable writing in a word-processing program than you are writing in your e-mail program, you can write your message there, copy it using the Copy command, and then switch to your e-mail program and paste it into a new message window.

One problem with putting word-processed text into e-mail messages is that some e-mail programs substitute special characters for apostrophes and quotation marks. If they are not correctly interpreted by the receiving program, these special characters come out as garbage characters that make your mail harder to read. Also, there are sometimes problems with line breaks, either with lines being too long or with extraneous characters (weird stuff, such as ^M or =20) appearing at the end of each line.

Here's how to copy a message from your word processor to your e-mail:

1. In your word processor, create your message. When you are done, save it as a text file. (Figure 18.6 shows a text file I created in Microsoft Word 97.)

2. Close the file and open it again to ensure that none of the special (non-text) characters are still in the file. Look for odd characters that you would not see on a standard keyboard and delete them.

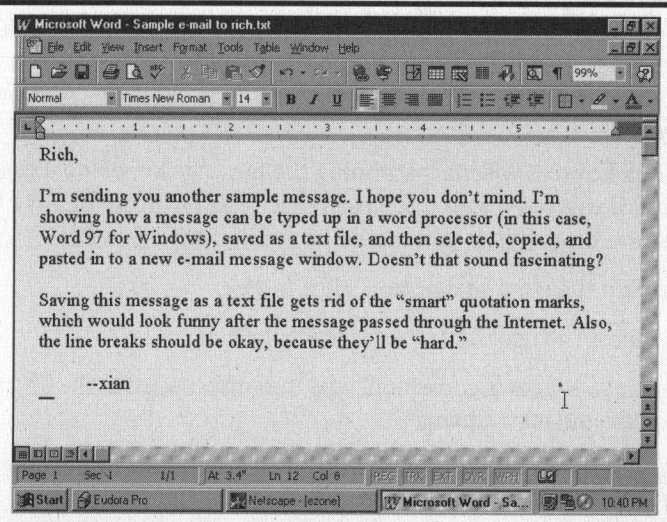

FIGURE 18.6: I created this file in Word 97. Now I'm going to save it as a text file.

3. Select the entire document and copy it (Ctrl+C in Windows programs).

4. Then switch to your e-mail program.

5. Create a new message as usual, go to the message area, and paste the text you copied (Ctrl+V).

6. The text will appear in the e-mail program as if you had typed it there.

Checking Your Spelling

Most e-mail programs now offer spell checking (so the traditional excuses for sloppily edited e-mail messages are vanishing fast!), but the specific techniques vary from program to program (as you might expect). It's a good idea to check the spelling in a message before sending it, especially if the message is long, formal, or for some business purpose.

If you write your messages ahead of time using a word-processing program, you can use your word processor's spelling checker to check the message. You may find this easier than working with two different spelling checkers.

Correcting Spelling Errors in Outlook Express

If in addition to Outlook Express, you also have Microsoft Word, Excel, or PowerPoint installed, in the Outlook Express New Message window, you can choose Tools ➢ Spelling (or press F7) to check the spelling of a message.

Outlook Express will start scanning the message for words it doesn't recognize. If you've ever used the spelling checker in Word or any other standard word processor, you should be familiar with this drill:

- To skip the word in question, click Ignore.

- To accept a suggested correction, click Change.

- To make your own correction, type the correct word in the Change To box and click Change.

- To add the word in question to the spelling checker's dictionary, click Add.

Spell Checking in Netscape Messenger

To check the spelling of your e-mail message in Netscape Messenger, choose Tools ➢ Check Spelling in the Composition window.

ATTACHING A SIGNATURE

On the Internet, it's traditional to include a short *signature* at the end of each message. An e-mail signature is a few lines of text, usually including your name, sometimes your postal (*snail mail*) address, and perhaps your e-mail address. If you are including a signature in a business message, you might want to include phone and fax numbers, and maybe the company Web page address. Many people also include quotations, jokes, gags, and so on. Signatures (also called *sig blocks, signature files, .signatures,* or *.sigs*) are a little like bumper stickers in this respect.

> **TIP**
> You can never be too careful when using company online resources, so consider adding a disclaimer to your signature block if you post to Usenet groups or mailing lists from a corporate e-mail address. The disclaimer can identify your views as solely your own and not those of the company.

Some e-mail programs do not support signature files, particularly those designed for local networks and those of some online services where signatures are less common, but many do and more are adding the feature all the time. Here's my current signature (I change it from time to time):

```
-
Christian Crumlish                http://www.pobox.com/~xian
Internet Systems Experts (SYX)    http://www.syx.com
Enterzone                         http://ezone.org/ez
```

It includes my name, the address of my home page on the Web, the name of my company and its home page address, and the name of my online magazine with its address.

> **WARNING**
> Test your signature block with various e-mail systems to see if it still looks good at the receiving end, especially if it uses unusual fonts, has a logo or other graphic, uses tabs, or is formatted in columns. Some of these features do not translate well to other programs, where monospaced fonts may be substituted for fancier proportional fonts.

I'll show you how to create your own signature when I discuss the specific programs that support them.

> **NOTE**
> Some e-mail programs let you include a graphic, such as a company logo, in your signature. For example, Microsoft Word and Outlook Express both have commands you can use to import graphics files into your signature file. Just be sure to format the signature in such a way that it looks good even for those who do not have graphics support in their e-mail setup, so that the absence of the logo or graphic will not detract from the appearance of your message. Logos are an easy way to cultivate a professional presence on the Internet.

Using E-Mail Signatures in Outlook Express

Outlook Express supports signature files. These files retain your personal or professional information and add it to your messages according to your instructions. Here are the steps for creating a standard e-mail signature:

1. Choose Tools ➣ Options, and then select the Signatures tab.
2. Click New.
3. In the Edit Signature section, Text is selected by default. Enter the text you want to use for your signature in the box. If you have already created a signature in a file, click the File button, and then either enter the filename or click Browse to locate the file.
4. Click the Add Signatures To All Outgoing Messages checkbox to put this signature at the end of new messages. (You can also prevent the signature from being added to messages you reply to or forward.)
5. Click OK.

Adding a Signature File to Messenger E-Mail

Messenger's signature file feature does not include much formatting support, but you can create basic signature files and add them to your messages with a minimum amount of fuss. Here are the steps for creating and adding a signature file:

1. First, use a text editor or word processor to create and save a text file containing the signature you want to have at the end of your e-mail messages.

2. Then, in Netscape, select Edit ➤ Preferences. Double-click the Mail & Groups item in the Category list in the Preferences dialog box.

3. Click Identity in the Mail & Groups list item, and type the full path and filename of your signature file in the Signature File box (or click the Browse button to find and select the file, and click OK).

4. When you're done, click OK.

> **TIP**
> If your signature exceeds the recommended four lines (this rubric is a widely accepted Netiquette standard, though many people violate it), Netscape will warn you, but all you have to do is click OK again to accept it.

Filing Your Messages

Even after you delete all the messages you've replied to or no longer need to leave lying around in your Inbox, your undeleted messages can start to pile up. When your Inbox gets too full, it's time to create new mailboxes to store those other messages.

> **NOTE**
> Your e-mail storage should conform to your general scheme of organization. I arrange mine alphabetically, chronologically, and/or by project, depending on the person involved. Think about the best system for yourself before you find your Inbox filled with 200 messages to sort. If your e-mail program allows you to save your own messages that you have sent to other people, you will also need to organize them before they accumulate and become unmanageable.

Different programs offer different commands for creating mailboxes and transferring messages into them, but the principles are more or less the same as those used for real-life filing. Don't create a new mailbox when an existing mailbox will suffice, but do file away as many messages as you can (even if you have to create a new mailbox to do so), to keep the number of messages in your Inbox manageable. When you find yourself scrolling up and down through screenfuls of message lists trying to find a particular message, you know that your Inbox has officially become disorganized.

TIP
You can also save your messages as text files or word processing files to move them outside the e-mail program. This way you can store them with other files related to the same topic. Choose File ➢ Save As in your message window and select a text file type. Or, select the message contents, press Ctrl+C to copy it to the Clipboard, open your word processor, paste the message into a document with Ctrl+V, and then save the new file.

Creating More Message Folders in Outlook Express

As you begin to accumulate messages, replies, and copies of original messages you sent to others, you will need additional folders to store them in for easy retrieval. Fortunately, creating new message folders isn't difficult.

In Outlook Express, it's quite easy to add new message folders to your set of personal folders:

1. Choose File ➢ New ➢ Folder (or press Ctrl+Shift+E).
2. In the Create Folder dialog box, select a folder in which you want to create the new folder, type a name for the folder, and click OK.

Once a folder is created, moving a message into it is even easier—simply click the message and drag it to the folder (in the left pane).

Creating New Folders for Filing Messenger E-Mail

Messenger also allows you to create new folders for filing messages. Here's how you do it:

1. Press Backspace to get to your Message Center (your master mail folder).
2. Select the folder in which you want the new folder to appear (or select Mail to create an upper-level folder).
3. Choose File ➢ New Folder.
4. Type a name for the new folder in the dialog box that appears and then click OK.

Filing Netscape Messenger Messages in Folders

Netscape Messenger (like the rest of the Communicator suite) has a revamped menu structure that gives toolbar buttons mini-menus of their own. This means that it really is even easier and faster to file messages in Messenger than it is in other e-mail programs, because you do not have to open a folder window or use a dialog box to find the folder where you want to put the message.

1. Highlight the message to be moved.
2. Click the File button (or choose Message ➤ File Message).
3. Choose the destination folder from the menu that pops up (subfolders appear on submenus).

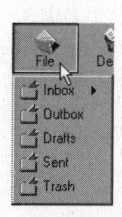

Filtering Messages as They Come In

When you start developing carpal-tunnel syndrome from "hand-filing" all your mail as it comes into your Inbox, it's time to start looking for an e-mail program with filters (called Message Rules in Outlook Express). The basic use of a filter is to recognize a type of mail, usually by one of its headers (such as who it's from, who or what mailing list it was sent to, or what it's about) and to automatically transfer it out of your Inbox and into the appropriate folder (or mailbox, depending on what your program calls it). More sophisticated filters can send automatic replies, forward mail to other recipients, perform multiple actions (such as replying and saving a message in a specific folder), and so on.

> **NOTE**
> Your e-mail filters can also be used to automatically clear the old messages out of your Inbox. Depending on what type of functionality is built into your program, you can tell the filters to delete all messages older than a certain date. Even better, some programs (including Outlook Express) allow you to automatically archive old messages in a special file that you can move to a different directory or to storage media (tape cartridges, floppies, and so on).

Setting up a filter to work usually takes just a small investment of time compared with the donkey work you save yourself from doing in the long run. Once you start relying on filters to keep your mail manageable, you'll wonder how you ever got on without them (or you'll just up and subscribe to twelve more mailing lists!).

Sorting Outlook Express Messages with Message Rules

Mail with specified text in one or more of four headers can be automatically filed in a specified folder. Follow these steps to get started setting up rules for the e-mail messages you receive. As an example, I'll set up a rule for filing all the messages from a particular person in a folder for that person.

1. Choose Tools ➢ Message Rules ➢ Mail to open the Message Rules dialog box.

2. Click New to open the New Mail Rule dialog box:

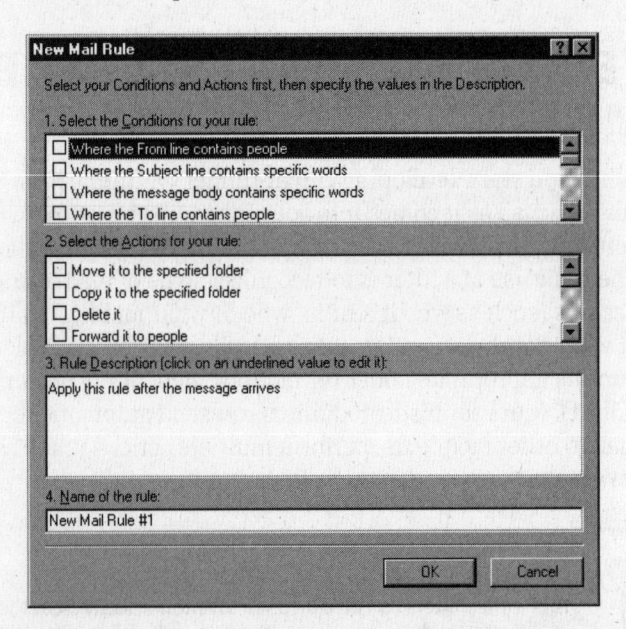

3. In the Select The Conditions For Your rule section, click the Where The From Line Contains People checkbox.

4. In the Select The Actions For Your Rule section, click the Move It To The Specified Folder checkbox.

Communicating with E-Mail

5. In the Rule Description section, click the contains people hyperlink to open the Select People dialog box:

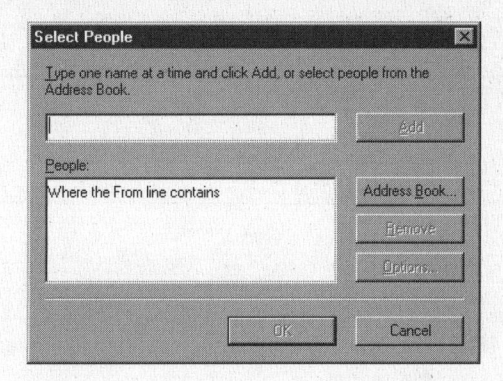

6. Type the name or select it from your Address Book, and click OK.

7. In the Rule Description section, click the specified hyperlink to open the Move dialog box.

8. Click New Folder to open the New Folder dialog box, enter a name for the folder, and click OK.

9. Click OK three more times.

Filtering Netscape Messenger E-Mail

Netscape Messenger's rules for filtering e-mail are quite specific. Most of the time you can use the existing rules provided by Netscape. If none of these rules are customized enough for you, you can construct unique rules for your own mail management needs.

Here's how you create a new filter for incoming messages:

1. Choose Edit ➢ Mail Filters.

2. Click the New button in the Mail Filters dialog box.

3. In the top half of the Filter Rules dialog box, enter a name for your filter (see Figure 18.7).

4. Choose one of the nine aspects of the message to base your filter on (such as the subject, the priority, or who's on the Cc list).

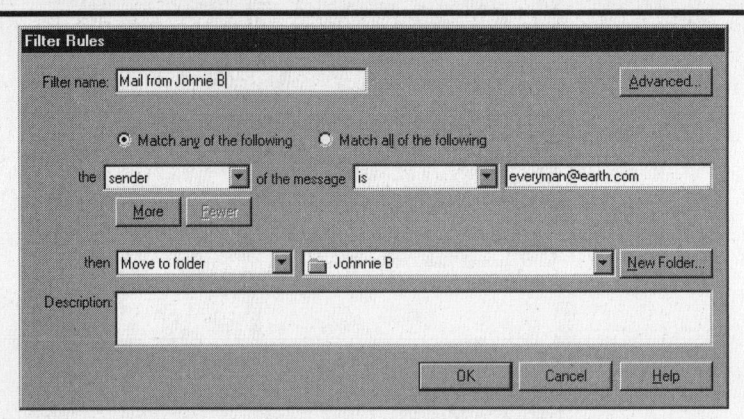

FIGURE 18.7: You can put together sophisticated filters easily with Netscape Messenger.

5. Choose one of the six comparison criteria (Contains, Doesn't Contain, Is, Isn't, Begins With, and Ends With), and then enter the text that is to be looked for or avoided in the third box.

6. Click the More button if you want to add additional criteria.

7. Below the More button, choose from six actions (usually you'll want Move to Folder—some of the instructions are more suited for discussion groups than for private e-mail), and then choose a folder (if applicable).

8. Finally, you can enter a description if you wish, and click OK.

NOTE
Netscape Messenger has no provision, as of yet, for checking mail from multiple accounts when the ISP only supports POP mail. In this instance, you can, however, have a number of User Profiles. Each profile can have a distinct e-mail address. This is very cumbersome since you have to switch profiles, but it works. If your ISP offers IMAP service, as most do, then the procedure below is simple to follow.

To check mail for multiple accounts:

1. Choose Edit ➢ Preferences ➢ Mail & Newsgroups ➢ Mail Servers.

Communicating with E-Mail 521

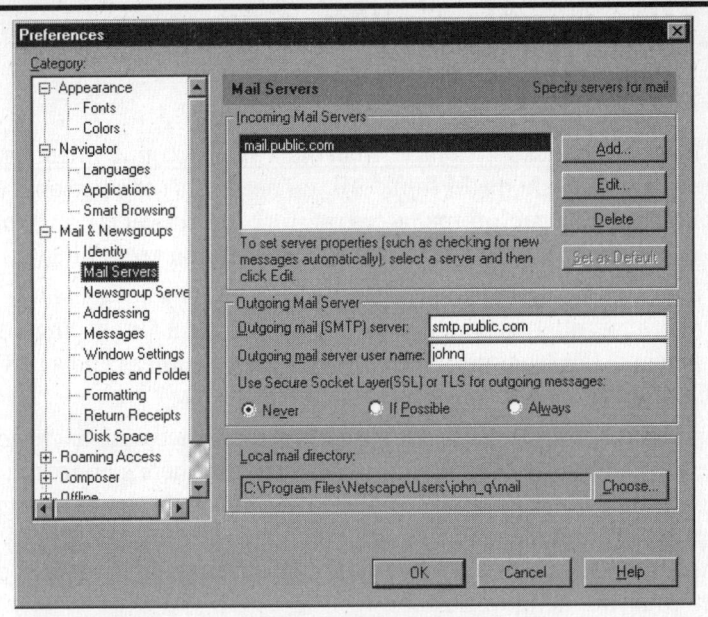

FIGURE 18.8: The Mail Servers Preference window

2. Click the Add button in the Incoming Mail Servers box.

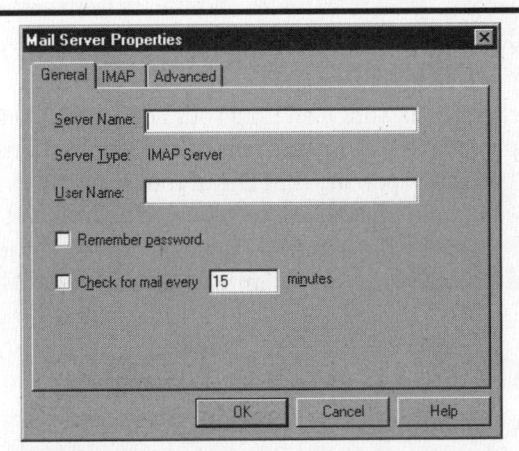

FIGURE 18.9: The Mail Servers Properties window

3. Fill in your user and account information and click OK.
4. Repeat steps 1–3 as needed for each additional e-mail account.

Dealing with E-Mail from Several Accounts

You may find yourself with more than one e-mail account. It can happen more easily than you might think. All you need is to get a personal e-mail account and then get Internet access at work (or vice versa), and voilà! You've got multiple accounts to manage. How do you keep things straight?

There are several approaches. One is to try to keep any e-mail accounts you may have totally separate. This approach is ideal for keeping work and personal life separate or for keeping a public address and a private "back channel" for friends and emergencies.

On the other hand, some people get a personal account just to get access to an existing work account, in which case there's no reason to store the mail in separate places. Then the problem becomes how to consolidate all your mail and make sure you're not missing any of it. (A related problem is how to look at your mail when at home without deleting it from your main workspace.)

Consolidating mail from multiple accounts will make sure you get all your e-mail. You can set the secondary account (or all the accounts but one) to automatically forward mail to your primary address. However, this is not always possible. Even if it is, the methods vary from system to system, and you should check with your system administrator and ask about "automatic forwarding of e-mail."

When you want to check your work mail from your home computer, you need an e-mail application that supports remote mail connections. Microsoft Outlook 97 has this capability (but only if your company is using Microsoft Exchange Server) and even allows you to quickly download just the message headers from your work account. Then you can select the specific messages you want to download, to minimize connection time.

Managing an Address Book

Once you start using e-mail regularly, you will probably find yourself typing a few addresses over and over or trying to remember some long and confusing ones. Fortunately, most e-mail programs enable you to create aliases (sometimes called nicknames) for these people. Aliases are shorter words that you type instead of the actual address. These lists of addresses and aliases are usually grouped together in something called an address book. Modeled on real-world address books, these windows or modules often have room for other vital information (such as street addresses and phone and fax numbers).

Some e-mail and groupware programs share a single address box with other applications on your computer, so your contact information is available to various programs.

When you type an alias or choose a name from an address book, your e-mail program inserts the correct address into the To line of your message (some programs can also insert an address into the Cc line).

You can also set up an alias for a list of addresses, so you can send mail to a group of people all at once. I've got an alias for a group of people to whom I send silly stuff I find on the Net (no one's complained yet) and another one for contributors to my online magazine.

> **TIP**
> When you make up an address book entry or alias for an e-mail address, keep it short—the whole point is to save yourself some typing—and try to make it memorable (although you can always look it up if you forget).

Using the Outlook Express Address Book

The Outlook Express address book is useful for keeping track of all the e-mail addresses of your friends and business associates. Here's how to update the address book with new names:

1. To add a name to your address book, click the Addresses button, and then choose New ➤ New Contact to open the Properties dialog box.

2. Enter the person's name and e-mail address information, and then click OK.

Using address book names in Outlook Express messages is even easier than adding them:

1. To send a message to someone in your address book, create a new message as usual, but instead of typing a recipient's address, click the To button to the left of the To box to open the Select Recipients dialog box.

2. Select a name from the address book list, and click the To button.

3. Click OK to copy the address to the e-mail message.

> **TIP**
> If you want to automatically put the e-mail addresses of people you reply to in your Address Book, choose Tools ➤ Options, select the Send tab, and click the Automatically Put People I Reply To In My Address Book checkbox.

Using the Netscape Messenger Address Book

You can add names to Netscape Messenger's address book by following these steps:

1. Choose Communicator ➤ Address Book from any of the Messenger windows.
2. In the Address Book window, click the New Card button.
3. Enter the name, e-mail address, and nickname, and then click OK.
4. Choose File ➤ Close to close the Address Book window.

To use the addresses in your new messages, do one of the following, depending on how good your memory is:

- In the Message Composition window, type the nickname on the To line.
- If you don't remember the nickname you made up, click the Address button, select the name, click To, and then click OK.

Finding Internet E-Mail Addresses

Because the Internet is such a large, nebulous entity, there's no single guaranteed way to find someone's e-mail address, even if you're fairly sure they have one. Still, if you're looking for an address, here are a few things you can try.

Use Search Tools on the Web

As discussed in the next chapter, Internet Explorer makes available a number of "search engines"—free services, based on the World Wide Web, that you can use to look up information. (Netscape Navigator also provides these services.) Most of them search for Web sites containing a word or phrase you specify, but some, described as "white pages," search for e-mail addresses. Two of the most common, included with both Internet Explorer and Navigator, are WhoWhere Internet Directory Service and Four11. These services are quite easy to use. You just enter a name, optionally provide other information such as location or organization, and click a Search button. The program then reports any results it finds.

Say "Send Me E-Mail"

If you're not sure how to send mail to someone but you know they're on the Net, give them a call and ask them to send you some mail. Once their mail comes through, you should have a working return address. Copy it and save it somewhere, or make an alias for it, or just keep their mail around and reply to it when you want to send them mail (try to remember to change the subject line if appropriate, not that I ever do).

TIP
The best way to collect e-mail addresses is from people directly. Many people now have their e-mail addresses on their business cards, so you can get people's addresses this way too.

Send Mail to Postmaster@

If you know someone's domain, such as the company where they work, or you know they're on one of the online services, you can try sending mail to `postmaster@address` and asking politely for the e-mail address. Internet standards require that every network assign a real person to `postmaster@address`, someone who can handle questions and complaints. So, for example, to find someone at Pipeline, you could send mail to `postmaster@pipeline.com` and ask for the person by name.

WHAT'S NEXT?

Whew! You have just completed a very thorough examination of the e-mail capabilities of two celebrated Internet programs. Now that you're an e-mail "expert," it's time to push on and master the mysteries of the World Wide Web.

Chapter 19

BROWSING THE WEB WITH INTERNET EXPLORER

As you saw in an earlier chapter, installing and configuring Windows 98 SE to connect your computer to the Internet are steps that you must complete before you can explore the World Wide Web. Once you make your connection, you're ready to start looking around. In this chapter, you'll find the information you need to use Internet Explorer to display Web pages and other Internet resources. After you spend a little time working with the program, you'll probably stop noticing the details of Internet Explorer and devote your attention to the Web pages themselves.

Adapted from *ABCs of Microsoft Internet Explorer 4*
by John Ross
ISBN 0-7821-2042-3   400 pages $19.99

Starting Internet Explorer

If you've chosen not to use the Active Desktop, you can start Internet Explorer by double-clicking the Internet Explorer icon, by choosing Start ➤ Programs ➤ Internet Explorer, or by clicking the Launch Internet Explorer Browser icon in the Quick Launch bar. If you've decided to use the Active Desktop, look in Appendix A, *Windows 98 SE Command and Feature Reference*, for information about this feature.

When Internet Explorer starts, it looks for an active connection to the Internet. If you use a modem and a telephone line to make your connection, and there isn't an active connection, Internet Explorer starts Dial-Up Networking (unless you chose not to allow Explorer to automatically dial your service provider), and dials your ISP. If you have more than one Dial-Up Networking Connection profile, Internet Explorer chooses the one you designated as the default in the Connection tab of the Internet Options dialog box.

You can use the same network connection with more than one application program at the same time. If you have other Internet tools (such as a Telnet client or an e-mail reader), you can run them along with Internet Explorer through the same network connection. This can be especially convenient when you want to use one program to download a large file while you're using another program to read your e-mail or participate in an online conference.

The Internet Explorer Screen

Figure 19.1 shows the main Internet Explorer screen, which includes these features and functions:

Title bar The title bar contains the name of the current Web page or other file on display in the Internet Explorer window, along with the familiar sizing buttons and the Close button.

Menu bar The menu bar contains a set of menus; each includes individual commands that you can use to control the way Internet Explorer works.

Toolbars The Internet Explorer toolbar has three parts: a set of standard command buttons that duplicate many of the most frequently used menu commands; an address field, the Go button, and the Links bar; and the Windows Radio bar, which you can use to listen to radio broadcasts from around the world, if your computer is set up to do so. When you move your cursor over a button, the icon changes from black and white to color. To enter a command from the toolbar or jump to a Link site, click a button. To display or hide text labels for the icons in the standard toolbar, choose View ≻ Toolbars ≻ Customize, and in the Customize Toolbar dialog box, select the option you want.

Activity indicator   The Internet Explorer symbol to the right of the toolbar is animated when Internet Explorer sends and receives data from the network.

Main window   The main portion of the Internet Explorer screen displays the text, images, and other graphic elements of the most recent Web page or other file.

> **NOTE**
> The Web pages and other data you see in Internet Explorer are copies of files located on your own computer or LAN. Internet Explorer downloads files from distant servers, but it does not maintain a live connection to the server after the download is complete.

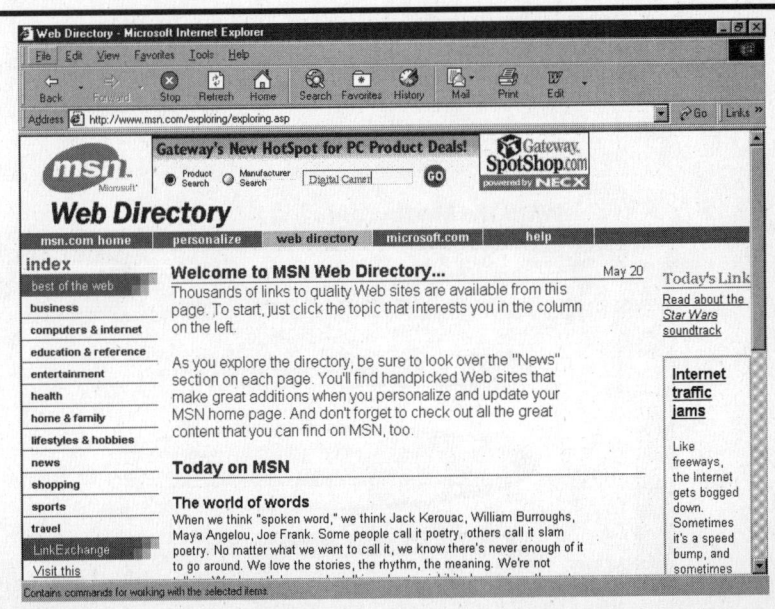

FIGURE 19.1:   The Internet Explorer screen uses many standard Windows conventions.

Chapter Nineteen

Status bar At the bottom of the Internet Explorer window, the status bar supplies additional information about the current Web site. When you move your cursor to a link, the status bar shows the destination of that link. During a file transfer, the status bar displays a bar graph that shows the progress of the transfer. If a Web page includes multiple pictures, graphic elements, audio clips, or other files, the status bar displays the name of the specific file that is currently being transferred. Some Web pages also include a special script that places a scrolling message across the status bar.

Security zone At the right side of the status bar, an icon and text identify the security zone assigned to the current Web page. You can assign Web sites to security zones by choosing Tools ➢ Internet Options and selecting the Security tab in the Internet Options dialog box.

USING THE RADIO TOOLBAR

A new feature in this version of Internet Explorer is the Radio toolbar. Windows Radio gives you direct access to radio stations throughout the United States and around the world through the Internet. To display the Radio toolbar, choose View ➢ Toolbars ➢ Radio:

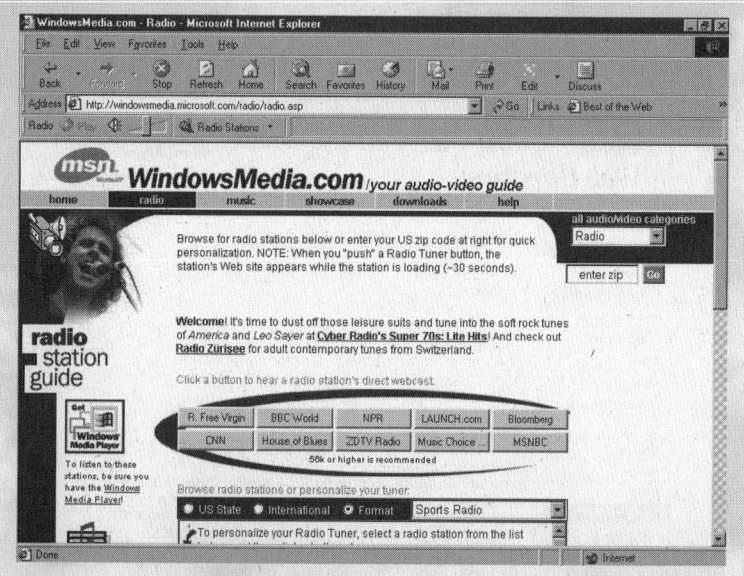

CONTINUED ➡

> To select a station, click the Radio Stations button, and choose Radio Station Guide to open the WindowsMedia.com site. Click a button to listen to a Webcast. The station's home page loads while the station is being found. To adjust the volume, move the slider on the Volume Control. To turn the radio off, click the Stop button on the Radio toolbar.
>
> The quality of your listening experience will depend on your speakers, your system, and the speed at which you are connected. An Internet access speed of at least 56Kbps is recommended.

Changing the Toolbars' Appearance

To display or hide one or more toolbars, choose View ➤ Toolbars, and check or uncheck the toolbar you want to display or hide. It's also possible to combine the menu bar and two or more of the toolbars on a single line by dragging a toolbar up or down. When more than one toolbar occupies the same line, you can view the hidden toolbar by dragging left or right.

To move the menu bar or a toolbar, follow these steps:

1. Place your cursor over the vertical bar at the left side of the section you want to move. Notice that the cursor changes to a two-headed arrow.
2. Drag the toolbar or menu bar up to merge it with the toolbar immediately above, or drag it down to place it on a separate line.

If two or three toolbars are on one line, you can open a hidden toolbar by double-clicking when the cursor is over the vertical bar.

USING AND CUSTOMIZING THE LINKS BAR

The Links bar contains links to specific Web sites. When you install Internet Explorer, all links are assigned to Microsoft sites, but you can add and remove links and even change their associated icons.

The default links are:

Best of the Web Click this link to jump to a page with links to a variety of online information sources, including financial services, telephone and address directories, home and garden information, and online reference books.

Channel Guide Click this link to jump to a page of online audio and video, including live feeds. You can also preview and download music selections from this page.

Customize Links Click this link to open a page that gives you step-by-step instructions for personalizing the Links bar.

Free HotMail Click this link to sign up for a free e-mail account.

Internet Explorer News Click this link to go to the Internet Explorer home page where you can download IE 5, order it on a CD, and get help and news about Internet Explorer features.

Internet Start Click this link to go to www.msn.com, which contains links to news, weather, personal finance, business, shopping, and entertainment sites, as well as a number of other features.

Microsoft Click this link to go to the Microsoft home page, which contains links to information about Windows and other Microsoft products and free downloads of programs, patches, and add-on software for Microsoft programs.

Product News Clicking this link also takes you to the Internet Explorer home page.

Today's Links Clicking this link also takes you to the MSN home page.

Web Gallery Click this link to jump to a collection of images, sounds, ActiveX controls, fonts, and other elements that you can download and use to create your own Web pages.

Windows Click this link to go to the Windows home page, which contains information about current and future Windows technology.

Browsing the Web with Internet Explorer

Windows Update   Click this link to get the latest product updates and support information.

All these sites are fine if you want to spend all your online time looking at stuff from Microsoft. You don't. Trust me: You will find other sites that you visit a lot more often than these.

To add a link to the Links bar, drag the icon of the Web page from the Address bar to the Links bar. You can also drag a link from any Web page to the Links bar.

To remove a link, right-click it, and choose Delete from the shortcut menu.

To rearrange the order of the items in the Links bar, simply drag an item to a new location.

To select a different icon for a link, follow these steps:

1. Right-click the link, and select Properties from the shortcut menu to open the Properties dialog box.

2. Click the Change Icon button to open the Change Icon dialog box:

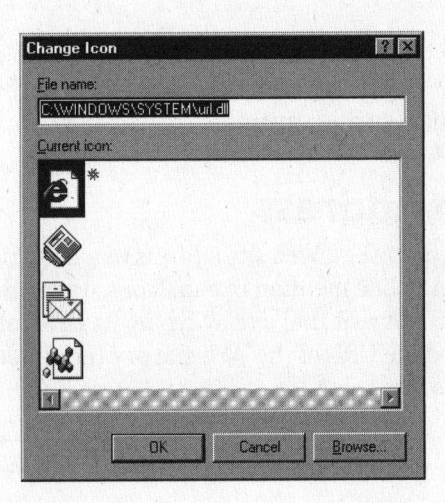

3. Select the icon you want and click OK.
4. Click OK again in the Properties dialog box.

Moving around the Web

The whole World Wide Web is built around seamless links from one place on the Internet to another. Any Web page can include links to other files that may be physically stored on the same computer or on any other computer connected to the Internet. At its center, Internet Explorer is a tool for retrieving Web pages and following those links.

You can tell Internet Explorer which Web page or file you want to see next in several ways:

- Click a link in the currently visible page.
- Type the URL of a new site in the Address bar.
- Choose a URL from a list of favorites.
- Choose a URL from a list of sites you've visited before.
- Use the Back and Forward buttons in the toolbar to return to a site you've recently seen.
- Click a link in the Links bar.
- Select a link from one of the Explorer bars.
- Double-click a shortcut to a Web site from the Windows Desktop or from the Start menu.

Typing an Address

When you discover a Web site address in a magazine article, on a TV show, in an online mention in e-mail or a newsgroup, or from some other source, you can visit that site by typing its URL into Internet Explorer. Simply type the URL of the Web site or other Internet file or service you want to see into the Address bar, and press Enter.

```
Address  Y? http://www.yahoo.com/
```

If you don't include the URL type, Internet Explorer assumes that you're trying to reach a Web page or other HTML document, and it automatically adds **http://** to the beginning of the URL. Therefore, you will reach exactly the same Web site if you type either **www.website.com** or **http://www.website.com**.

> **USING THE GO BUTTON**
>
> Instead of pressing Enter after you type a URL, a filename, the name of a program, or something to search for, you can click the Go button, which by default is located to the right of the Address bar. If you don't see the Go button, choose Tools ➢ Internet Options, select the Advanced tab, and click the Show Go Button in Address Bar checkbox.

Internet Explorer's AutoComplete feature can make it even easier to find a Web page. AutoComplete compares the address you're typing with addresses you've visited before and automatically fills in the remaining characters. For example, when you start to type **www.website.com**, AutoComplete will add the remaining **w** and the dot (.) after you type the first two **w**s. When you start typing **website.com**, AutoComplete will offer to finish it for you. However, if you have previously visited www .webster.com and www.webb.com, AutoComplete won't know which one you want this time, so it will fill in **web**. To select from a menu of possible complete addresses, click the down arrow in the Address bar.

You may want to overtype some or all of the addresses that AutoComplete offers you. To jump forward or back to the next separation character (\ \ \ . , ? or +) within an address, hold down the Ctrl key and press the left or right arrow key.

AutoScan is another timesaver, especially when you aren't sure of the exact address of a Web site. When this option is active, it will try several variations of the address until it finds one that matches an address in the Domain Name Server's database. In other words, if you type name, AutoScan will try name.com, www.name.com, name.org, www.name .org, name.edu, and www.name.edu. This won't do much good if the site's address is www.name.gov. If none of those produces anything useful, AutoScan can offer to perform a search in one of the popular Internet search engines, such as Yahoo!.

To turn AutoScan on or off, use the Advanced Options dialog box.

If you're trying to reach some other type of server, such as an FTP archive, a Telnet host, or a gopher server, you must type the full URL address, including the type designator. For example, the URL for an FTP site might be ftp://ftp.archive.edu. If you leave out the type, Internet Explorer will try to reach an http server.

You can also use the address field to open up a file located on your own computer's hard drive, on a floppy disk, on a CD-ROM, or on another computer connected to yours through a LAN. For example, to see a file called `schedule.txt` in your `c:\calendar` folder, type **c:\calendar\schedule.txt** in the address field. You don't need to worry about a URL type identifier when you load a local file into Internet Explorer, but you should remember that DOS and Windows use the backslash (\) to separate folders in a path, instead of the forward slash (/) used by most Internet servers.

Using Hot Links

Except for a handful of Web sites that specialize in spicy sausages, like `www.incrediblelink.com`, *hot links* on the Internet are places on a Web page that contain jumps to other Web pages, files, and online services. A link may be a word or a phrase in a block of text, a graphic image such as a picture of a push-button, or an image map that contains links to several URLs, depending on the exact location within the image map. Web pages with links are illustrated throughout this chapter.

When you move your cursor over a link, the cursor changes to a pointing finger, and the destination of the link appears in the status bar at the bottom of the Internet Explorer window. If the "hover" option is turned on, the link also changes color. To jump to that URL, click the link.

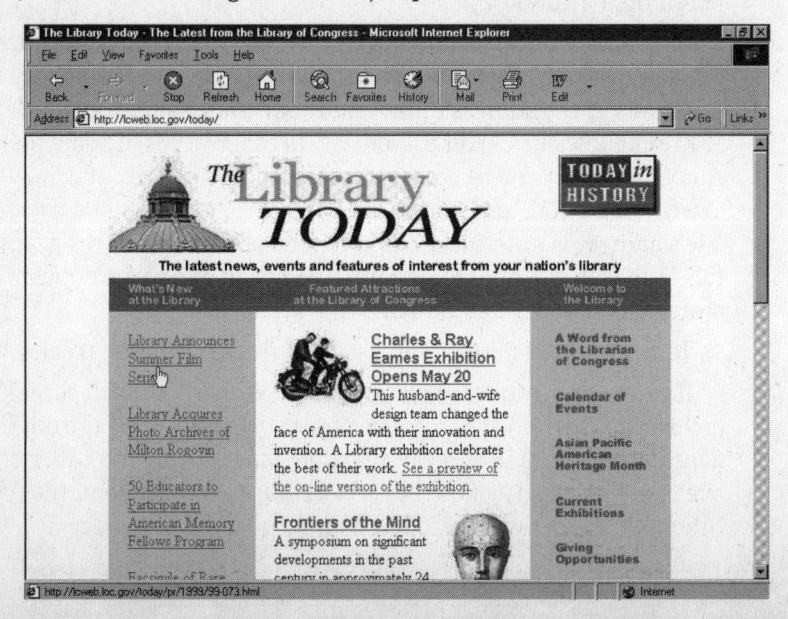

Internet Explorer displays text links in a different color from other text. If an entire picture or other image is a link to another Web site, you may see a colored border around the image.

Returning to Sites You've Recently Visited

After you view a Web page, Internet Explorer stores a copy in a temporary folder, so you can return to that page without having to wait for another download. This is very convenient, because Internet Explorer can load and display a file from your hard drive a lot more quickly than it can transfer it from a distant server. However, there are two possible drawbacks to this technique: if the original Web page has changed since the original download, you won't see the changes, *and* you're filling up your hard drive with Web pages.

Fortunately, there are ways to work around both problems. Choose Tools ≻ Internet Options, and then click the Settings button to open the Settings dialog box shown in Figure 19.2.

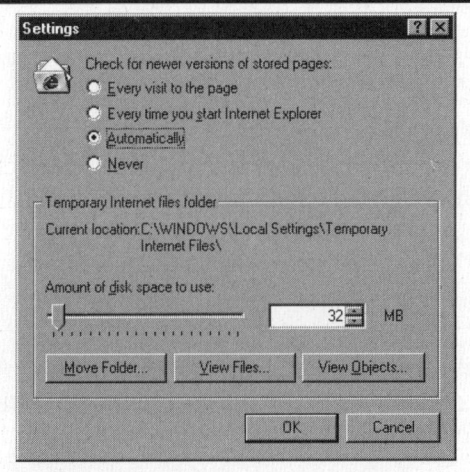

FIGURE 19.2: Use the Settings dialog box to control the way Internet Explorer handles temporary Internet files.

The Settings dialog box includes these options:

Check for Newer Versions of Stored Pages When Every Visit To The Page is active, Internet Explorer will obtain a new (and possibly updated) copy of a Web page each time you view a Web page. When Every Time You Start Internet Explorer is active, the browser will go back to the server the first time during a session that you jump to a Web page, even if there's a copy of that page in the Temporary folder. When the Automatically option is active, Internet Explorer checks for new content only when you return to a page that you viewed in an earlier session or on a previous day. When the Never option is active, Internet Explorer will always use the file in the Temporary Internet Files folder. To check for a new version of a Web page you've already seen, click the Refresh button in the command toolbar, or choose View ➤ Refresh.

Amount of Disk Space to Use   Move the slider to the left to reduce the maximum size of the Temporary Internet Files folder, or move it to the right to increase the maximum size of the folder.

Move Folder   Click the Move Folder button to change the path of the folder that contains your temporary files.

View Files   Click the View Files button to open your Temporary Internet Files folder. To view a file in a new Internet Explorer window, double-click the name of that file.

View Objects   Click View Objects to open your Downloaded Program Files folder.

To delete all of the files in your Temporary Internet Files folder, click the Delete Files button in the General tab of the Internet Options dialog box. In the Delete Files dialog box, click OK.

Explorer Bars

Explorer bars create a split-screen display in the browser window, with links to a list of Web pages that fit a specific category in the left-hand pane. Figure 19.3 shows the Internet Explorer window with an Explorer bar open.

The five types of Explorer bars are:

- Search
- Favorites
- History
- Folders
- Tip of the Day

Browsing the Web with Internet Explorer 539

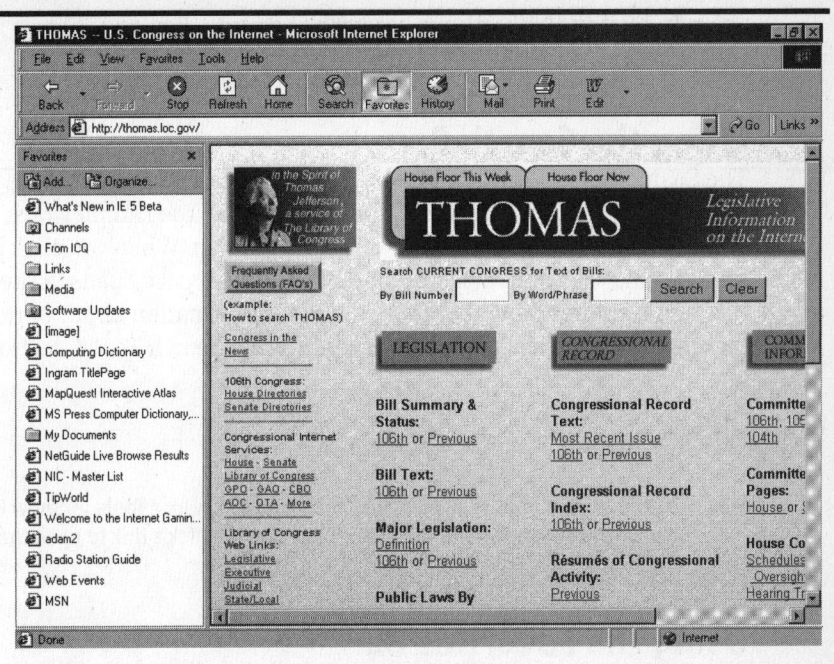

FIGURE 19.3: Explorer bars display links to Web sites and other files in a split-screen display.

To open the Search, Favorites, or History bar, you can click its icon on the toolbar or choose View ➢ Explorer Bar and select the bar from the submenu. To open the Folders or Tip of the Day bar, choose View ➢ Explorer Bar and select either item from the submenu.

When you click a link to a Web site or other file in an Explorer bar, Internet Explorer opens the target of that link in the right-hand pane, while the list of sites remains visible in the left pane. This makes it possible to move directly from one site on a list to the next, without the need to return to the Web page that contains the list. This is a major timesaver when you're trying to visit a series of sites, such as the result of a search.

Because most Web pages are designed to take up the full width of a browser window, the Explorer bars usually cut off the right side of the page. To see the full width of the page, click again on the icon button in the toolbar that you used to open the Explorer bar, or choose View ➢ Explorer Bar and click the name of the bar. Click again to reopen the Explorer bar with the same display that was visible when you hid it.

Using the Search Bar

The Search bar is a window in which you can search for a Web page, a person's address, or a business. You can also use it to run previous searches if you have saved them and to find a map. When you click a link displayed as the result of a search, the target Web page opens in the main Internet Explorer pane. For more detailed information about performing Internet searches, read the "Using Internet Search Tools" section later in this chapter.

> **TIP**
> To see a list of links related to the current page, choose Tools ≻ Show Related Links. The list appears in the Search bar. Simply click a link to go to that site.

Using the Favorites Bar

The Favorites bar contains your own list of Web pages and other files that you want to revisit more than once. Later in this chapter you'll find detailed information about creating and using Favorites.

Using the History Bar

Whenever you view a Web site, Internet Explorer adds a shortcut to that site to the History list. You can use these shortcuts to return to Web sites you've recently visited. Figure 19.4 shows the History bar.

The subfolders in the History bar are organized by date—there's a separate folder for each day of the current week and one for last week and two weeks ago. Each of those folders contains a folder for each site you visited that day or week, with links to individual pages within the site folders. If you use Web style folders to view both Web sites and local files, the History bar will also include local files.

To return to a Web page or a file listed in a History folder, click the listing for that page or file. To hide the History bar and expand the current Web page, click the Close button or click the History icon in the toolbar.

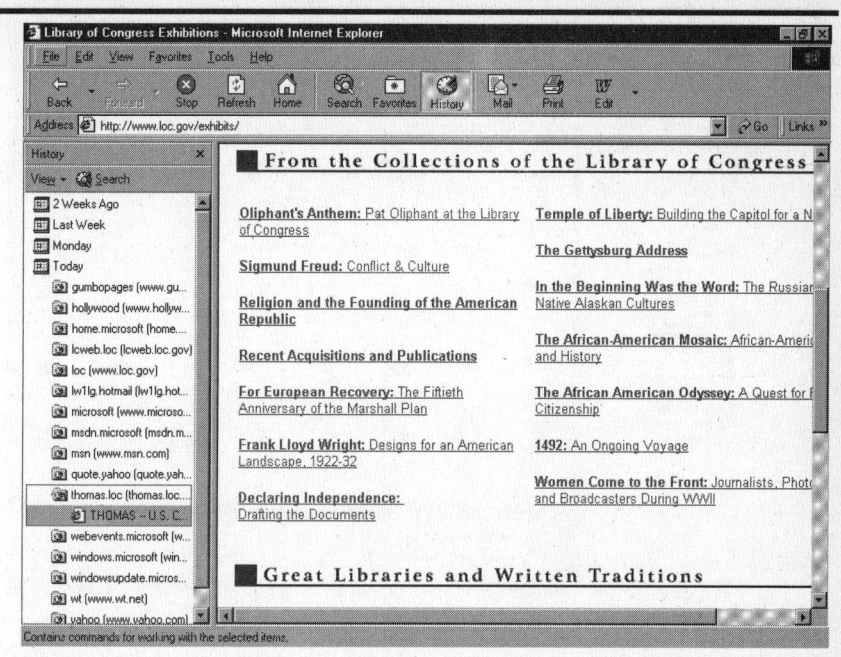

FIGURE 19.4: Use the History bar to return to a Web site you've visited before.

Using the Folders Bar

The Folders bar is essentially a Web view of Windows Explorer. Selecting a folder in the Folders bar displays the contents of the folder in the pane on the right.

Using the Tip of the Day Bar

The Tip of the Day bar is displayed at the bottom of the Internet Explorer window. You can cycle through tips by clicking Next Tip. To close the Tip of the Day bar, click its Close button. Figure 19.5 shows both the Folders bar and the Tip of the Day bar.

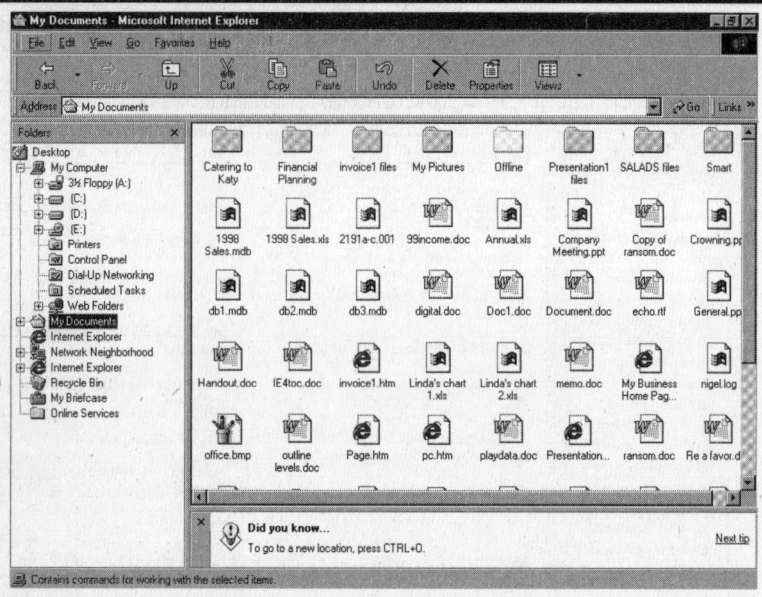

FIGURE 19.5: The Folders bar and the Tip of the Day bar

Moving Forward and Backward

In addition to the History folders, which provide a long-term record of your visits to Web sites, Internet Explorer also keeps track of the Web pages you open during the current session, and the order in which you visited those pages.

Use the Back command in the toolbar to return to the Web page from which you jumped to the current page. Use the Forward command in the toolbar to repeat the last jump you made from the current site. The Back and Forward buttons also have drop-down menus that list all the other sites you visited during the current session. To jump directly to one of those sites, select the description of that site from one of the menus. In addition, you can right-click the Back and Forward buttons and select from a list of previously visited pages.

> **TIP**
>
> The Back command is particularly useful when you try to follow a series of links, but you discover that you've reached a dead end—either a link to a site that's no longer available or a site that doesn't have any links that you want to follow. You can retrace your steps to return to a page with other links that you want to follow.

Using More Than One Window at a Time

In most cases, Internet Explorer loads the new page into the same window when you click a link or enter a URL in the Address bar. But sometimes it's convenient to keep the current page visible while you open a new page in a separate Internet Explorer window. For example, you might want to read the text in one window while you wait for the next one to load, or you might want to keep one eye on a page that automatically updates the score of the big game while you conduct other online business in a second window.

To open another copy of the current Web page in a new window, choose File ➤ New Window.

To jump to a new Web page and load it into a new window, follow these steps:

1. Right-click a link to open the shortcut menu:

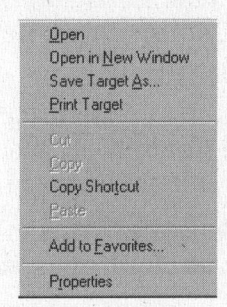

   ```
   Open
   Open in New Window
   Save Target As...
   Print Target

   Cut
   Copy
   Copy Shortcut
   Paste

   Add to Favorites...

   Properties
   ```

2. Choose Open In New Window.

The new window works exactly the same as the existing one. Once it's open, you can use the Address bar, the Favorites list, the History bar, and other navigation tools to move around the Web, while keeping an earlier page visible in the other window.

Home Pages

Every time you start Internet Explorer, the program automatically loads and displays the page that you have specified as your home page.

Home page also has another meaning: it's a page that an individual or organization uses to provide pointers to other related pages or files. For example, many people have created home pages that contain links to information about their hobbies, favorite entertainers, and other interests. Businesses frequently have home pages with links to separate pages about each of their products or divisions. See Chapter 22, *Creating Web Pages with FrontPage Express*, for information about creating this kind of home page.

Choosing a Home Page

Your home page is the first Web page you see every time you open Internet Explorer, so it's a good idea to choose a page that contains information you can actually use, rather than one that has nothing but advertisements for products and services that you may not ever want. Most people never bother to change the default page, but you may want to replace the msn.com page with one of these options:

- A home page from another online information provider, such as GNN's Whole Internet Catalog (www.gnn.com/wic/index.html) or PC/Computing's Web Map (www.zdnet.com/pccomp/java/webmap/).

- The front page of your favorite newspaper, weather, sports, or other Web site that contains information that you want to see every time you open the browser.

- Your own home page with links to your favorite sites, which you can create with an HTML editor, such as FrontPage Express.

Changing Your Home Page

To change the home page, follow these steps:

1. Open the page you want to use as your home page.
2. Choose Tools ➤ Internet Options to open the Internet Options dialog box.
3. Click the General tab, which is shown in Figure 19.6.
4. Click the Use Current button to define the current page as your home page.

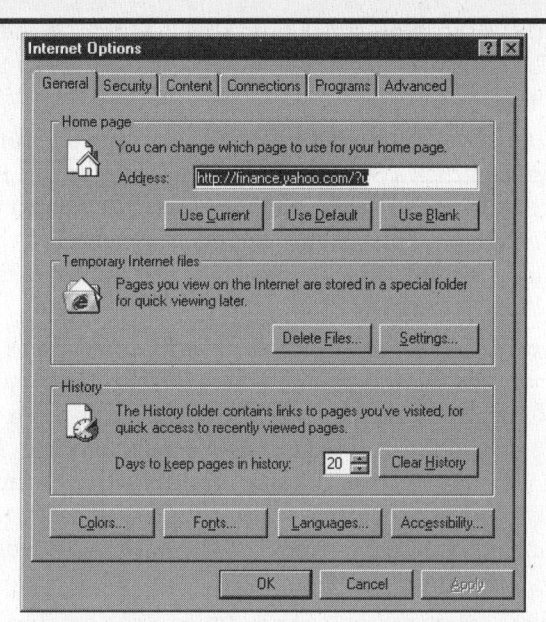

FIGURE 19.6: Use the Home Page section of this dialog box to change your home page.

To use some other page as your home page, type the URL of that page in the Address field.

Using Internet Search Tools

The World Wide Web resembles a huge library in which all the books are arranged on the shelves by size and color. You may stumble across a lot of interesting things by accident, but without a catalog to tell you exactly where to look for a specific item, the book you want is extremely difficult to find. In the library, you can search for a book by looking up the title or subject in a catalog or by asking a librarian for help. Internet search tools serve a similar purpose.

When you look for, say, a Hebrew dictionary in a library catalog, you will discover that the Dewey Decimal number is 492.43. Since the librarian places books on the shelves in numeric order, you'll find Hebrew books (492.4) between books about Balto-Slavic languages (491.8) and those about the Arabic language (492.7). Once you know where to look, that dictionary is easy to locate.

On the Internet, URLs serve the same purpose as the library's shelf numbers. And like the library catalog, the Internet's search tools can point you to the item you want to find.

Most Web search tools work in a similar manner: you type the words you want to search for and click a Search button. The search engine looks for those words in a database and displays a list of URLs that match your request, with links to each one. To examine a possible match, click the link. If that's not what you want, click the Back button to return to the list and try another item.

There are about two dozen major general-purpose Internet search tools, and a couple hundred more specialized ones. Each uses a somewhat different set of rules to conduct its search, and each will give you a different list of URLs in response to a request. Some tools search for individual pages, others will take you to entire sites, and still others search through the text of each page rather than limiting their searches to titles or keywords. Some include subjective reviews or ratings of individual sites, while others list everything they find.

As a result, the same search through several services can produce radically different results. For example, one search for the keywords "Joseph Conrad" produced 244 hits with Yahoo!, 4351 with Lycos, and about 30,000 with AltaVista. A search for "Andrew Jackson" produced 55 hits using Lycos, 231 with Open Text, and about 2000 matches with AltaVista. The exact numbers are not important, but they do illustrate the differences among search engines.

> **WARNING**
> The links that a search tool identifies are not always useful, especially when you enter more than one keyword, because some search engines include partial matches that include just one word in the search phrase. For example, a search for "Andrew Jackson" using the Magellan search engine produced 85 matching links. However, only one of the first ten had anything to do with the seventh president; the other nine were pointers to a Web page about the Jackson State University Computer Science Department, Steve Jackson Games, and singers named Alan Jackson, Michael Jackson, and Joe Jackson. See "Focusing Your Searches" later in this chapter.

If you're looking for a popular Web site, you can probably find it with almost any general-purpose search engine. But if you want everything related to a specific subject, you should perform the same search through several services.

Browsing the Web with Internet Explorer 547

Using the Search bar (shown in Figure 19.7) you can conduct a search in one pane of the browser window and follow search results in a separate pane. In other words, you don't have to return to the page that contains the results of your search, because it's visible on the side of your screen.

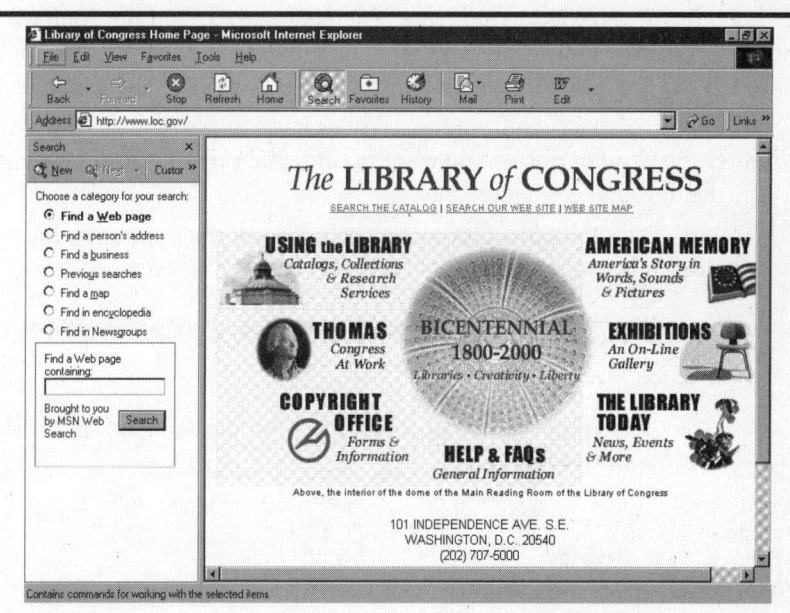

FIGURE 19.7: Using the Search bar to find information on the Internet.

To use the Search bar, follow these steps:

1. Click the Search button in the toolbar, or choose View ➢ Explorer Bar ➢ Search to open the Search bar.

> **TIP**
> If you don't see all the categories shown in Figure 19.7, click More.

2. Select a category, and then type the word or phrase you want to find in the search field.

3. Click the Search button. The predetermined search provider will return a list of links to Web sites that match your request and display the list in the Search bar.

Chapter Nineteen

4. Click the link to the first item you want to see. Internet Explorer will display that page in the main section of the browser window. To move to another item on the list in the Search bar, select the link to that item.

5. If you want to hide the Search bar and expand the main window to fill the browser, click the Search button in the toolbar. Click the Search button again to reopen the Search bar.

You can also search from the Address bar. Simply type **go**, **find**, or **?**, enter the word or phrase you want to find, and press Enter. The results are displayed in the Search bar.

To use a search provider that you select, click the Customize button in the Search bar to open the Customize Search Settings dialog box:

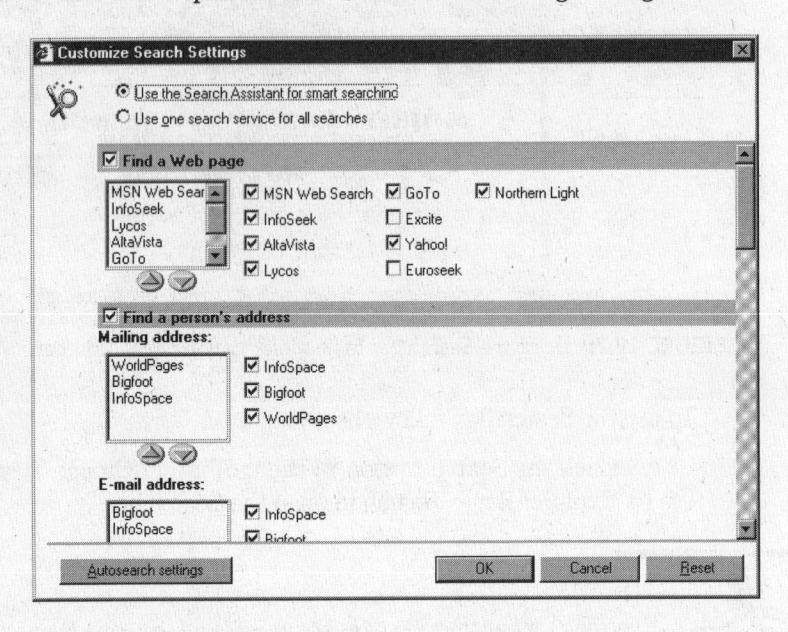

If you always want to use the same search provider, click the Choose A Default Search Provider at the bottom of the Customize Search Settings dialog box.

For more specific searches, you might want to bypass the Search bar and use a specialized directory Web page instead. A good place to start is www.search.com. At this site, you can search the Web in more than 100 different ways.

Focusing Your Searches

Each search engine handles search requests differently, especially if you include more than one word in a request. For example, if you enter **apple cider**, some search engines will list every page that includes either "apple" or "cider," but not necessarily both. When you're looking for information about fermented fruit juice, it doesn't do you much good to find thousands of sites related to Apple computers.

It's always a good idea to read the specific instructions for each search engine on the search service's Web site, but in general, you can reduce the number of irrelevant hits with the following common techniques:

- To search for a phrase rather than separate words, place quotation marks around the phrase. For example, **"apple cider"** (with the quotation marks) will limit the search to sites that contain the two words as a phrase.

- To find sites that contain more than one word or phrase, even if they're not together, place a plus sign (+) in front of each word or phrase. So a search for **+apple +cider** will find sites that include both words, even if they're separated.

- To exclude sites that contain a specific word or phrase, place a minus sign (–) in front of it. A search for **+apple +cider -recipes** will find sites that contain the words "apple" and "cider," but it will exclude pages on which the word "recipes" appears.

Returning to Favorite Web Pages

As you wander around the World Wide Web and other parts of the Internet, you will discover sites that you want to revisit later. You could write down the URL of each site on a notepad and then type it in Internet Explorer's Address bar every time you want to return to that site, but that approach is both tedious and messy. There's an easier way—you can use shortcuts that take you directly to your favorite Web sites.

In fact, there are two easy ways. You can create a list of links to your favorite pages that you can open from within Internet Explorer, or you can place shortcuts to Web sites on your Desktop or Start menu, just like shortcuts to programs and files located on your own hard drive. In the rest of this chapter, we'll talk about using both of these techniques.

Working with the Favorites List

When you come across an interesting Web page, you can save a link to that page by adding it to your list of Favorites. Later, you can return to that page by opening the list and clicking the name of the page.

For example, if you're interested in finding online versions of newspapers from all over the world, you might want to add the AJR NewsLink directory (//www.newslink.org/news.html), shown in Figure 19.8, to your list of favorites.

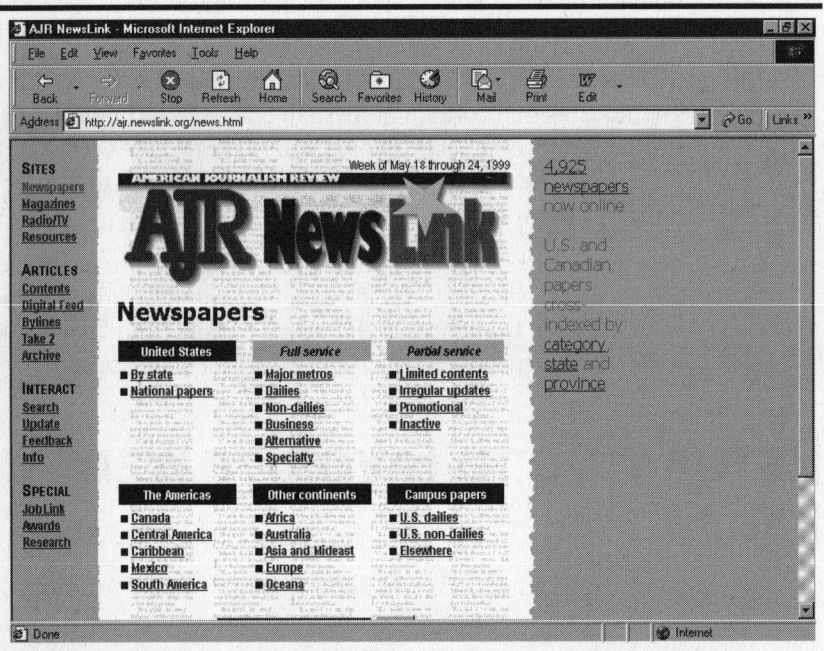

FIGURE 19.8: NewsLink offers an extensive directory of online newspapers.

NOTE

In Netscape and other Web browsers, the list of sites that you want to revisit is called a *bookmark list*. A note on a Web page that suggests you "bookmark this site" is encouraging you to add it to your Favorites list.

Favorites are not limited to Web sites. The Favorites list can also include files located on your own computer.

Viewing the Favorites List

You can open the Favorites list within Internet Explorer as either a conventional menu or a separate Favorites bar. You can also open it by choosing Start ➢ Favorites.

The Favorites Menu The Favorites menu, shown in Figure 19.9, shows submenus and links as menu commands. If your list has too many entries, the bottom of the list might run off the screen. When that happens, you can display the whole list by clicking the arrowhead at the bottom of the menu.

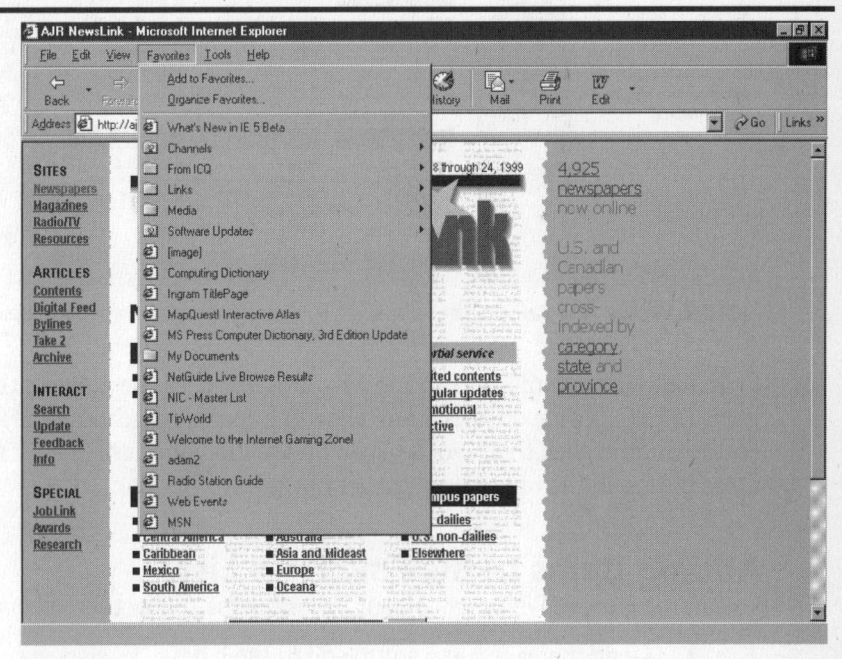

FIGURE 19.9: Use the Favorites menu on the Internet Explorer menu bar to jump to a bookmarked site.

The Favorites Bar The Favorites bar is a separate Explorer bar within the Internet Explorer window, as shown in Figure 19.10. Like the Search bar and the History bar, it can remain visible on your screen while you

552 Chapter Nineteen

jump to the pages on the list. To open the Favorites bar, either click the Favorites icon on the toolbar or choose View ≻ Explorer Bar ≻ Favorites.

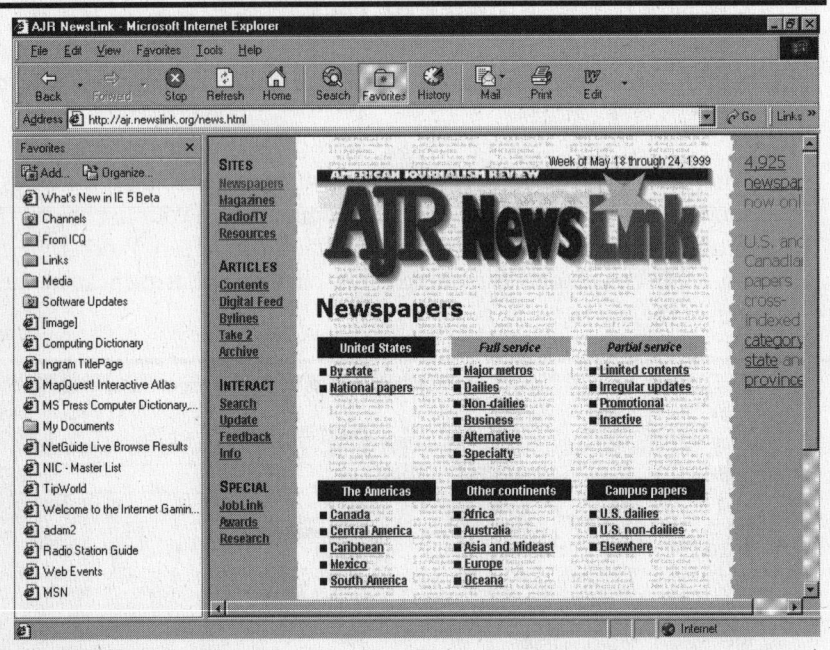

FIGURE 19.10: The Favorites bar displays your list of Favorites in a separate pane.

To jump to an item listed on the Favorites bar, click the name of that item. To hide the Favorites bar and allow the current page to fill the entire window, click the Favorites icon on the toolbar again, or click the Close button in the upper-right corner of the Favorites bar.

Adding Items to the Favorites List

To add the current Web page to your Favorites list, follow these steps:

1. Open the page you want to add to the list.
2. Choose Favorites ≻ Add To Favorites to open the Add Favorite dialog box.
3. If you want to place this page in your top-level Favorites menu, click the OK button. If you want to add it to a submenu, click

Browsing the Web with Internet Explorer 553

the Create In button and select the folder where you want this item to appear. Click the New Folder button to create a new submenu.

You can also add a link in the current page to your Favorites list by dragging and dropping the link to the Favorites icon on the toolbar, or you can right-click a link and choose the Add To Favorites command from the shortcut menu. When you use the shortcut menu to add an item to your Favorites list, the exact location determines whether you will add the current page or a link on the current page to the Favorites list:

- If your cursor is over a link when you right-click, you will add the destination of that link to your list, rather than the current page.

- If you right-click a picture or other graphic, you will add that image to the list without the rest of the current Web page.

- If the cursor is over any other part of a page, you will add the current page to your list.

Organizing Items in Your Favorites List

Internet Explorer normally arranges Favorites in alphabetic order. You can change the order in which items appear in the Favorites menu or on the Favorites bar by dragging an item to a new position in the list. You can also drag and drop items between submenus and the main Favorites menu.

TIP
Internet Explorer can open and display local files (including Windows 98 SE folders) just as easily as it downloads files from the Internet. In fact, all the pages you see in Internet Explorer are really copies that you have downloaded to your own system. Therefore, the program treats the Favorites folder (which is a subfolder located within the top-level Windows folder, although the exact location doesn't matter) just like any other Web page. You can open this folder—or any other folder on your hard drive or LAN—by typing the path in the Internet Explorer Address bar.

Choosing Favorites ➢ Organize Favorites opens the Organize Favorites dialog box, shown in Figure 19.11, which you can use to do the following:

- Add and delete files and subfolders
- Move files to subfolders

- Change the names of files
- Make files available for offline viewing

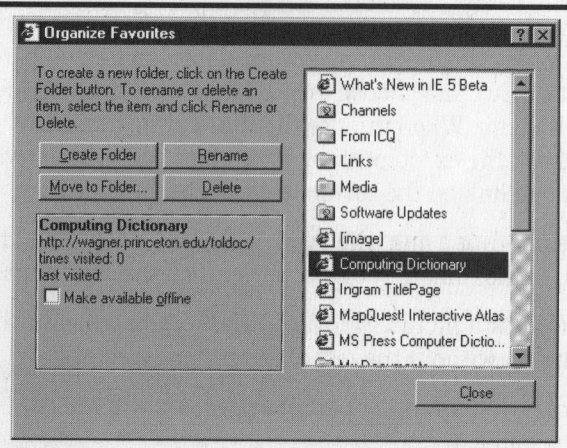

FIGURE 19.11: The Organize Favorites dialog box

Adding Other Items to Your Favorites List

The Favorites list is not limited to Web sites. It can also include shortcuts to any other program, data file, or folder on your own computer or on a computer connected to yours through a LAN. This feature can make Internet Explorer even more flexible.

Here are some of the things you might want to add to your Favorites list:

- Copies of HTML documents or text files stored on your hard drive.
- A shortcut to the Notepad program. When you want to extract text from a Web page, you can select and copy the text, open Notepad, paste the selected text, and save it as a text file.
- A shortcut to the Windows Desktop folder (`c:\windows\desktop`). If you keep shortcuts to frequently used files and programs on your Desktop, you can use the Favorites list to open them from within Internet Explorer. If you do create a shortcut to your Desktop, you should also use the Shortcut tab in the Properties dialog box to change the shortcut icon.

Creating New Subfolders

Once your list of Favorites reaches about a dozen entries, you should think about moving some of them into subfolders. If there are a few Web sites that you expect to revisit more often than others, you can leave shortcuts to those pages in the main Favorites list (or you could create links to those sites in the Links bar) and move less frequently used items to subfolders. You can organize your shortcuts in whatever way best suits your needs. for example, you can sort them:

- By topic
- In alphabetic groups (A through D, E through H, and so forth)
- In separate folders for particular types of Web sites, such as FTP archives or news summaries

Each folder listed on the Favorites bar has a folder icon. When you click the name of a folder, the files and subfolders within that folder open in the pane on the right. In the Favorites menu, folders show up as subcommands; when you move your cursor over the name of a folder, the contents appears as a submenu.

To create a new folder, follow these steps:

1. Choose Favorites ➢ Organize Favorites to open the Organize Favorites dialog box.
2. Click the Create Folder button. A new folder appears at the bottom of the list, as shown in Figure 19.12.
3. Type the name you want to assign to this folder, and press Enter.

The next time you open the Favorites list, the name of the new folder will move to the top of the list, in alphabetic order relative to other folder names. To move an item from the main list or another subfolder to a new subfolder, follow these steps:

1. Select the name of the Web page or folder you want to move.
2. Click the Move To Folder button to open the Browse For Folder dialog box.
3. Select the destination folder and click OK.

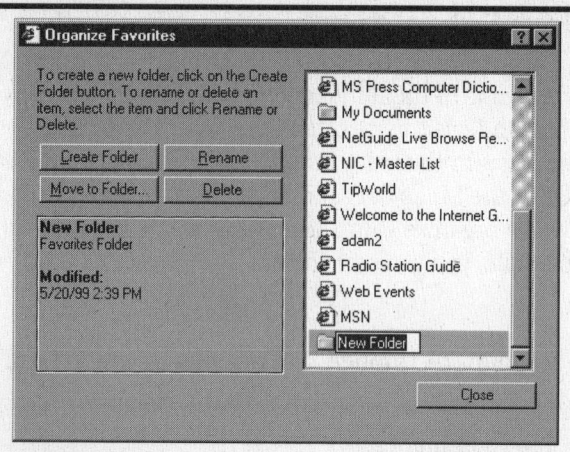

FIGURE 19.12: The new folder appears at the bottom of the list of Favorite pages.

When your list gets even larger and more complicated, you might want to consider placing subfolders within subfolders. For example, you might want to create a folder called Travel, with separate subfolders called Airlines, Trains, and Hotels. Or you may want separate subfolders for each letter within an alphabetic list.

Cleaning Out Your List

So there you are, surfing your way around the World Wide Web, finding all kinds of amusing and interesting Web sites: "Add to Favorites." Click. Here's another good one. "Add to Favorites." Click. Click. Click.

The next time you open your list of Favorites, it has dozens of items, most of whose names you don't recognize. And when you select a site, you cannot imagine why you thought it was worth saving in the first place. Did you really think that you would ever want to return to the History of Corn Flakes home page?

It's time to do some serious weeding. If you're never going to use a link, there's no good reason to keep it on your list at all. On the other hand, it's entirely reasonable to maintain a "not-so-hot list" separate from the main folder. You might want to keep this list in a subfolder or in a separate folder with a shortcut from the Favorites list. This secondary list will be just a couple of mouse clicks away, but its contents will be out of the way when you're looking for your daily news updates.

To clean up your list, follow these steps:

1. Open the Organize Favorites dialog box.
2. Select the item you want to remove, and click the Delete button, or move the item to your "not-so-hot" list.
3. If you want to keep this item on your list, consider changing the name to something that identifies it more clearly. Click the Rename button to change the description of the currently selected item.

> **TIP**
> As a rule of thumb, your top-level Favorites list should have no more than about 16–18 items in it — maybe a few more if you have a larger screen. When the list gets bigger than that, it's time to start moving things to subfolders.

Making Your Own Hot List

The Favorites list is easy to use, but it doesn't tell you much about the Web sites that are listed. If you want to give yourself more information about each link, you might want to create a local Web page with a one- or two-sentence description of your favorite sites. If you create a link to your hot list page, you can jump to the hot list with a single mouse click.

Creating a Hot List Page

The easiest way to create a quick-and-dirty HTML page (and quick and dirty is all you need for your own hot list, since you're the only person who will see it) is to use FrontPage Express, the HTML editor supplied with Internet Explorer. (You'll learn more about FrontPage Express in Chapter 22.)

When you save your HTML hot list, name the file **my list.htm**. Each item on the list includes a link to another site and a description of the information or service that's offered at that site. To jump to a site, click the link, just as you would on any other Web page.

Adding the Hot List Page to Your Favorites List

When the page is ready to use, follow these steps to add it to your Favorites list:

1. Open my list.htm.

2. Choose Favorites ➢ Add To Favorites to open the Add Favorite dialog box.

3. Change the name to **A Better Hot List**.

The next time you open your Favorites list, you should see a link to this page at or near the top of the alphabetic list of Web sites, but after all the folders. Click the link to open the page.

Viewing Web Pages Offline

At times, you may prefer to access a Web page when you are not connected to the Internet. For example, you might run across a page at work and want to read it at home at your leisure. You can save the entire page, or you can save only the text or the images. To make the current page available for offline viewing, follow these steps:

1. Open the page you want to view offline.

2. Choose Favorites ➢ Add To Favorites to open the Add Favorite dialog box.

3. Click the Make Available Offline checkbox.

4. By default, the page is saved in your Favorites folder. To save it in another folder, click Create In or New Folder.

5. Click OK.

To save a Web page on your computer, follow these steps:

1. Open the page you want to save.

2. Choose File ➢ Save As to open the Save Web Page dialog box:

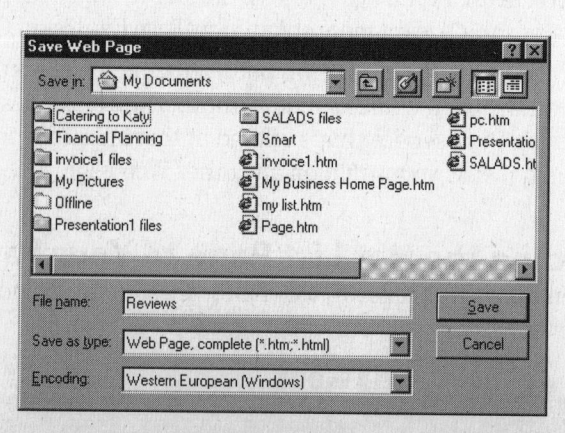

Browsing the Web with Internet Explorer

3. In the File Name box, enter a name for the page.
4. In the Save As Type box, select a file type:
   - Selecting Web Page, Complete saves all the files needed to display this page.
   - Selecting Web Archive For Email saves a snapshot of the page.
   - Selecting Web Page, HTML Only saves the information on the page but not the graphics, sounds, or other files.
   - Selecting Text File saves only the text in text format.
5. Click Save.

If you save the page as Web Page, Complete or as Web Archive For Email, you can view it offline without adding it to your Favorites list.

> **TIP**
> To save a page or a link without opening it, right-click it and choose Save Target As from the shortcut menu.

Creating and Using Web Shortcuts

You can set up shortcuts to Web pages in exactly the same way that you set up shortcuts to programs, documents, and data files located on your own hard drive. In fact, the Favorites list and the History list in Internet Explorer are really just Windows folders full of shortcuts to Web sites.

Like other shortcuts, a Web shortcut may be located on your Desktop, in any folder, or in your Start menu. When you click a shortcut to a Web site, three things happen:

- Internet Explorer starts.
- Dial-Up Networking connects your computer to the Internet.
- Internet Explorer downloads a copy of the Web page specified in the shortcut.

The benefit of using a shortcut is obvious: You can go directly to a Web page with just a couple of mouse clicks. You can create a shortcut to the current Web page, to a graphic file embedded in the current Web page, or to a link on the current page.

Creating a Shortcut to the Current Web Page

To create a shortcut to the current Web page, load the target page in Internet Explorer, and either choose File ➢ Send ➢ Shortcut To Desktop, or right-click a place on the page that is not a link or an image and choose Create Shortcut from the shortcut menu. When you create a shortcut, Internet Explorer places the shortcut icon on your Windows Desktop, as shown here. You can drag and drop the icon from the Desktop to any folder or to a floppy disk, network drive, or other destination, just like any other shortcut.

Changing a Web Shortcut Icon

Internet Explorer uses the same icon for all Web shortcuts, but it's easy to change the icon to something that's related to the contents of the target Web site.

> **TIP**
>
> You can download more extra icons than any rational person could ever want from the file archives at ftp://mjablecki.extern.ucsd.edu/archive/cica/win3/icons/ or ftp://ftp.cdrom.com/pub/cica/win3/icons/ (these are mirror sites that contain the same files). The index file contains descriptions of each of the files in this archive.

Here's the way to change icons:

1. Right-click the item whose icon you want to change.
2. Choose Properties from the shortcut menu.
3. Click the Shortcut tab.
4. Click the Change Icon button at the bottom of the dialog box to open the Change Icon dialog box, as shown in Figure 19.13.
5. Choose an alternative from the Current Icon field, or click the Browse button to find an icon in another file or folder.

6. To use the currently selected icon, click OK.
7. In the Properties dialog box, click OK.

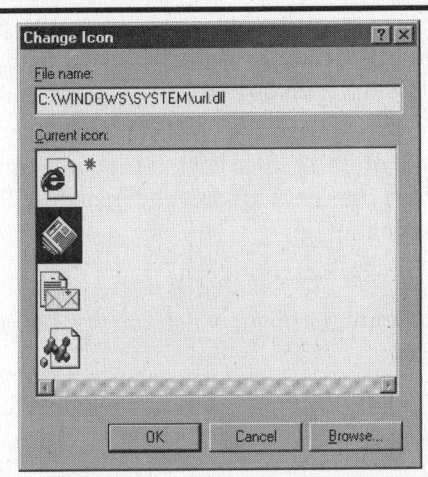

FIGURE 19.13: Use the Change Icon dialog box to assign a new icon to an item in your list of Favorites.

Creating a Web Shortcuts Folder

If you have more than three or four Web shortcuts on your Desktop, you might want to place them in a separate Web Shortcuts folder, with a shortcut to the folder on the Desktop. Follow these steps to create a new folder:

1. Move your cursor to a blank spot on your Desktop.
2. Right-click and choose New ➤ Folder from the shortcut menu. A folder icon similar to the one shown here will appear.
3. Enter **Web Shortcuts** as the new name for this folder.
4. Drag the icons for each of the Web shortcuts you want to place in this folder from the Desktop to the Web Shortcuts icon.

Unfortunately, Windows won't let you change a folder icon to something more interesting, so you're stuck with the boring old file folder.

Opening Shortcuts from the Keyboard

There's still another way to use a shortcut to start Internet Explorer and jump to a Web site. You can define a set of keystrokes as a keyboard shortcut. Keyboard shortcuts are especially convenient when you're using a word processor, spreadsheet, or other application, because you don't have to take your hands away from the keyboard.

Keyboard shortcuts are combinations of the Ctrl key, the Alt key, and almost any other key. When you press all three keys at the same time, Windows will automatically start Internet Explorer and open the Web page assigned to that combination.

To create a keyboard shortcut, follow these steps:

1. Right-click the Web shortcut icon for which you want to create a keyboard shortcut.
2. Choose Properties from the shortcut menu to open the Properties dialog box.
3. When the Properties window opens, click the Web Document tab as shown in Figure 19.14.
4. Move your cursor to the Shortcut Key field.
5. Hold down the Ctrl or Alt key and the letter or other key you want to assign to this shortcut. Even though you don't press both Ctrl and Alt, the keyboard shortcut will require both those keys. If you plan to use this shortcut with Microsoft Word, don't use Ctrl+Alt+*a number key*, because those combinations are already assigned in Word.
6. Click OK.

Sending a Shortcut to Another User

Unlike shortcuts to programs and data files located on your own system, the target addresses of Web shortcuts are universal; you can point to a URL from anywhere on the Internet. Therefore, you can embed a Web shortcut into a document or copy it to a floppy disk and send it to another user. For example, you might want to send a daily or weekly "best of the Web" bulletin to friends and customers via e-mail, with shortcuts to new or otherwise important Web sites that you want them to see. The recipients can jump to the sites you describe by clicking the

Browsing the Web with Internet Explorer 563

shortcuts within the bulletin. If you and the person receiving your messages are both using an e-mail client that can handle Rich Text Format (RTF), you can include your shortcuts in a message.

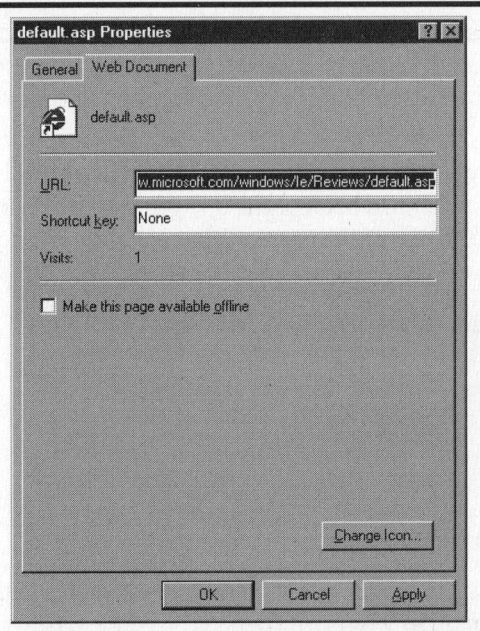

FIGURE 19.14: Use the Web Document tab to assign a keyboard shortcut.

To attach a shortcut to an existing document, follow this procedure:

1. Open the document in a word processor such as WordPad or Word.

2. Drag and drop the shortcut icon into the open word processor application window.

3. Use the formatting tools in the application program to control the placement of the icon in the document.

In general, you can treat a Web shortcut just like any other embedded object in a Windows application program. If you haven't worked with embedded objects before, consult the manual and online help for your application.

Changing the Default Browser: A Warning

If Internet Explorer is your only Web browser, you can skip this section. But if you have both Internet Explorer and Netscape Navigator or some other browser loaded on your computer, only one program at a time can be your default browser.

When you open a browser that is not your current default, it will display a message like the one shown below, asking if you want to change the default. As you read the rest of this section, you will understand why you should always make the current browser the default.

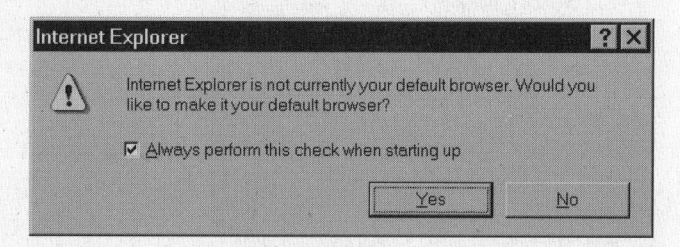

![Internet Explorer dialog box: "Internet Explorer is not currently your default browser. Would you like to make it your default browser?" with checkbox "Always perform this check when starting up" and Yes/No buttons]

The default browser is the program that Windows associates with .HTM and .HTML files. In other words, the default program is the one that starts when you use a shortcut to a Web page. Just because you used Internet Explorer to create a shortcut doesn't mean Internet Explorer will automatically start when you select that shortcut—if that other browser is your default. To make things even more confusing, Windows uses the default browser to open Web sites in the Internet Explorer Favorites and History folders.

If the current browser is not the default when you start it, things can get extremely messy. If Internet Explorer is not the default, it will open the default browser when you try to jump to a new Web site. If you open the Favorites folder, you will see an icon for the current default browser next to each item. And in general, things won't always work the way you expect them to work.

The only way to avoid this confusion is to answer "Yes" whenever a browser asks if you want to make that program the default. Even if that browser is not your favorite, you should still make it the default, at least for the moment. This is really not a big deal because it's so easy to change defaults. Using a non-default browser is just not worth the trouble.

What's Next?

In the next chapter, *Browsing with a Sense of Security*, Gene Weisskopf and Pat Coleman discuss the security concerns that face every Internet user—maintaining privacy online, avoiding or restricting access to inappropriate Web content, securing financial transactions, and keeping viruses out of the computer. They also show how to use the tools that Internet Explorer provides in these areas.

Chapter 20

BROWSING WITH A SENSE OF SECURITY

As we spend more of our daily lives on the Internet, we confront and must resolve new issues. One that has quickly become important is security, which we'll discuss in this chapter. Internet Explorer provides many features for ensuring that our time online is private when needed, free of inappropriate Web content, secure when we are making financial or confidential transactions, and safe from viruses or other malevolent programs.

Adapted from *Mastering Microsoft Internet Explorer 4*
by Gene Weisskopf and Pat Coleman
ISBN 0-7821-2133-0   960 pages $44.99

Guarding Your Privacy on the Web

Sitting at a keyboard and browsing the Web in your own home gives a wonderful *illusion* of privacy. However, every bit of information you send or receive over the Internet passes through multiple computer servers and networks. Unlike our public phone system, the Internet was designed as an open, accessible system, and privacy was not a foundation of the architecture.

That lack of privacy is still one of the best features of the Internet. The coalition of Internet networks throughout the world can expand with ease, and new computers can hook into the Internet without seeking approval from any one company or government. From our perspective as users, we can simply enter a URL, and Internet Explorer fetches whatever it finds there. The password is "Welcome," and we're all invited. Whether you're visiting Web sites, sending e-mail, or participating in online chat sessions or newsgroups, you're taking advantage of the built-in openness of the Internet.

Privacy becomes an issue, however, when you're no longer just viewing Web pages or sharing information with your peers on the Internet. What would you think if a business were collecting information about how much time you spend browsing the Web, the places you visit, and what you purchase? What if your government were tracking your spending habits via your online financial transactions or surreptitiously monitoring what you say in a newsgroup?

> **NOTE**
> This lack of privacy is why Internet Explorer displays a notice when you are about to send information over the Internet, such as when you click the Submit button in a form you have filled out. If that form contains your credit card number or other confidential information, you may not want to send it if you are not currently connected to a secure server, as discussed later in this chapter. Once you understand the reason for this notification message, you can disable it by clearing a checkbox.

Many of the potential security issues on the Internet are no different from the ones we already deal with. For example, how do you feel about talking on a telephone in a public place with people standing nearby? Or giving your credit card to a waiter in a crowded restaurant, and watching as the waiter disappears into the back room with it? Or taking cash from an ATM machine on a public street? You need to familiarize yourself with the issues and take precautions where pertinent, but learn to accept the others as minor sources of potential, but usually rare, problems.

Internet Explorer can maintain the security and privacy of your online sessions by allowing you to:

- Store your passwords securely on your own computer and offer them automatically when requested by a Web site, so you don't have to remember them.
- Limit how cookies collect information about you for a server.
- Control your personal information with the Profile Assistant, and send some or all of it when a server requests it.
- Keep financial transactions secure and reliable with Microsoft Wallet.
- Prevent Internet Explorer from opening Web sites that you may find offensive for yourself or for those in your care.
- Assign Web sites to security zones, in which all sites have the same set of restrictions.
- Connect to secure Web sites that encrypt all data transfers between you and the server, making them virtually impossible to decipher by anyone else.
- Limit the extent to which ActiveX and Java programs are allowed to run on your computer.
- Verify the validity of Web sites, and identify yourself to others, with certificates.

Staying Secure with Passwords

People used passwords to protect their private resources long before computers came along. Remember "Open, Sesame"? With the advent of computerized transactions, passwords have become an essential part of our daily routine. Have you ever counted how many different passwords you use? Can you even remember all the places where you've been issued a password?

When you work on the Internet, you end up collecting a large number of passwords. Some will be for high-security sites such as your online bank or stockbroker, where the password plays a critical role in your online security. Other passwords will simply identify you as a registered user with rights to access a site, such as for many online newspapers.

Most Web sites give you the option of having them remember your password, just as Windows' Dial-Up Networking allows you to do. Once a site remembers your password, you don't have to enter it each time you visit the site. You may still be prompted with a dialog box, but your user name and password will already be filled in (the password will be displayed as asterisks), so you can simply press Enter or click OK.

Some passwords are stored in your password file (with the PWL file name extension) in your Windows folder, where they are encrypted and safe from prying eyes. Most Web sites store your password in their cookie files on your computer; in most cases the password portion of the file is encrypted.

You can develop several habits to ensure that your privacy (and perhaps your money) is protected to the fullest extent possible:

- Don't use a real word when you create a password. It is best to mix letters and numbers, and punctuation characters, too, when they are allowed by the server. Doing so makes it much more difficult for someone to crack your password.

- Use a minimum of six characters; the more you use, the more secure the password.

- Avoid the obvious passwords, such as your birthday or Social Security number.

- Change your password every month or two at sites that contain crucial personal or financial information. You can be more relaxed about changing other passwords, but it's still a good idea to do so every now and then.

- When changing a password, don't recycle an old password.

- Resist the temptation to keep a list of all your passwords in an easily accessible file on your computer.

Although you'd find it quite convenient to have a file for looking up a password, it would be equally convenient for someone who was surreptitiously using your computer, either in your office or in their getaway car. A simple alternative is to keep a list of your passwords in a password-protected file, which most word processors allow you to do. You'd then have to memorize just one password. (But please, don't name that file My Passwords.)

Saying "No Thank You" to Cookies

A server at a Web site can have Internet Explorer (or Netscape Navigator) create a *cookie*, which is a file on your hard disk that contains information the server will need when you visit that site. For example, the Web sites that allow you to create customized pages usually store your preferences in cookies. When you return to one of those sites, the server will ask for its cookie file and set up your personal page appropriately.

When you are purchasing items at a Web site, you might put the items you want to buy into a virtual "shopping basket" until you're finished. That shopping basket is actually a cookie file on your computer that contains a list of the items you've selected to purchase. When you're finished shopping, the server uses that file to calculate your charges and draw up your bill.

It's easy to see how the cookie concept could be rife with security problems—another computer is creating files on your computer about your activity while you browse that site. In reality, however, cookies are typically used for mundane purposes. Because they are simple data files, they cannot "look" at your hard disk and report back to the server or run other programs on your computer.

But the potential for gathering personal information and sending it back to a server is the real issue. Although a server can't use a cookie to discover and store truly private information, such as your name, address, credit card number, and so on, would you still feel comfortable knowing that a market research company is collecting a list of all the pages you've visited at a site? Worse, we have no idea what type of data, or how much of it, is being collected while we're visiting a Web site.

To adjust the settings for cookies, follow these steps:

1. Choose Tools ➤ Internet Options.

2. Click the Security tab, and then click Custom Level to open the Security Settings dialog box:

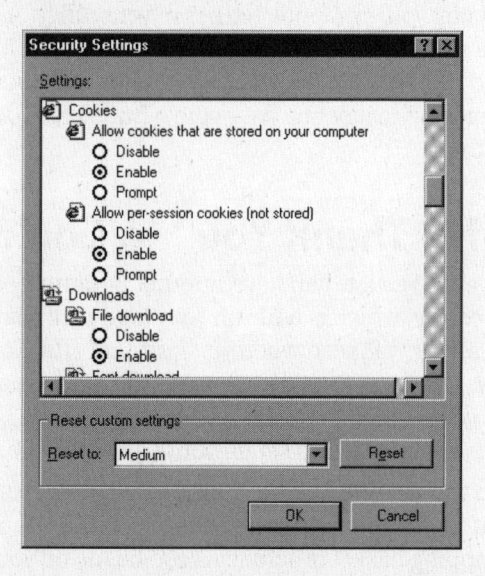

3. Scroll down to the Cookies section in the Settings area, select how you want Internet Explorer to handle cookies, and click OK.

4. Click OK again.

You can choose to allow cookies to be stored, to be notified when a server wants to create a cookie, or to disallow all use of cookies (which would truncate your Web experience quite a bit). A new solution to the cookie conundrum is discussed in the next section.

Retaining Your Privacy with the Profile Assistant

Most of us understand that Web sites are much more valuable when they're allowed to know something about our preferences and who we are. But we would like to have a little control over just how well Web sites can get to know us! That's why Microsoft worked with the industry to develop a standard for Internet Explorer and other browsers that allows us to restrict "unverifiable transactions," such as when a server reads a cookie on our computer or creates one there.

When a server wants to transfer personal information between it and our computers, the Open Profiling Standard (OPS) allows us to choose whether to send any of that data. This not only lets us know what type of information the server is requesting, but also lets us control the process. Here's how OPS works:

▶ Each user of Internet Explorer can use the Profile Assistant to create a personal profile, which is a file that contains commonly used personal information, such as name, address, telephone number, e-mail address, and so on.

▶ When you visit a Web site and the server asks you for information from your profile, you can decide whether to give it all, some, or none of that information.

▶ When a server exchanges information with your profile, the transaction can be done through a secure (encrypted) connection (as discussed later in this chapter), so that your information will remain private during its travels over the Internet.

▶ The information in your profile need only appear in that one place to be available to any Web site that asks you for it, instead of being spread among many cookie files for different sites. If you move and get a new address, you can update your profile accordingly, and any Web site you visit will be able to access the most current information (if you choose to give it).

▶ While you're browsing a site, the server might want to store new information in your profile and will have to ask you for permission to do so. This is the type of data that would otherwise have ended up in yet another cookie file.

▶ Whenever you return to that site, the information the server stored in your profile will be available, but only with your permission. Once you get to know a Web site, you can tell Internet Explorer that this site no longer needs permission to access your Personal Profile.

Handling personal information is more sensible with personal profiles than with cookies. As we use the Web more and more, these issues will only grow in importance, so it's critical to establish a means for handling them now. Your profile is designed to be flexible. Although you set it up with a core of basic information, new types of information can be stored there as the industry adopts new standards.

Chapter Twenty

To create your personal profile, follow these steps:

1. Choose Tools ➢ Internet Options and select the Content tab.

2. In the group of options labeled Personal Information, click the My Profile button. This opens the Address Book–Choose Profile dialog box.

3. Click the Create A New Entry In The Address Book To Represent Your Profile option, and click OK to open the Main Identity Properties dialog box, shown in Figure 20.1. If this dialog box looks familiar, you must be using the Windows Address book, as they share the same tabs and fields.

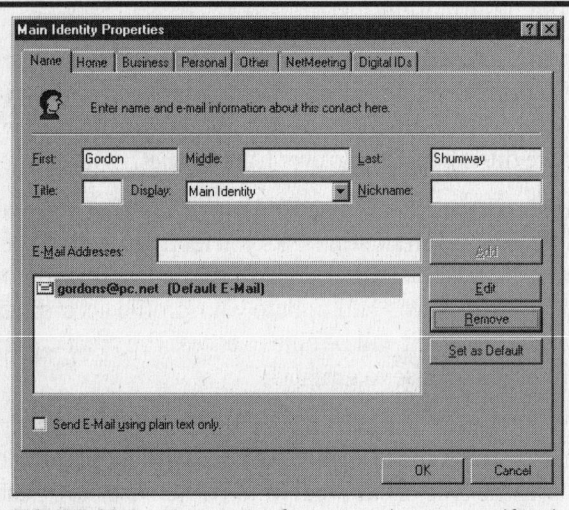

FIGURE 20.1: You enter information about yourself in the Main Identity Properties dialog box.

4. Enter your information in the relevant fields. If you don't have a cell phone, for example, just leave that field blank (you can press Tab or Shift+Tab to move between fields).

> **NOTE**
> Keep in mind that filling in *any* of this information is optional. Its only purpose is to make your travels on the Web easier, more enriching, and more secure. You may want to limit the amount of data you include at first, until you see a pattern to how it is used by the Web sites you visit.

5. When you've filled in all the relevant fields, or at least those you want to fill in at this time, click OK, and then click OK again in the Internet Options dialog box.

Once you've created your profile, it will be available to any server that requests that information—with your permission, of course. When a server at a Web site makes that request, you'll be shown its URL for identification purposes, the type of information it is requesting, and how the information will be used. After you've visited sites that ask to tap into your profile, you'll begin to appreciate the security the profile provides, as well as the welcome relief from having to enter your name, e-mail address, mailing address, and so on for the wide variety of sites that request that information.

WORKING WITH IDENTITIES

In Windows 98 SE, identities are a new feature of Outlook Express and other identity-aware applications. You can create an identity for each person who uses the application. For example, if several family members use Outlook Express, each can create an identity and use it to access personal e-mail and contacts. Once you create multiple identities, you can switch identities without closing the application or disconnecting from the Internet.

To create an identity, in Outlook Express, follow these steps:

1. Choose File ➣ Identities ➣ New Identity to open the New Identity dialog box.

2. Enter a name for the new identity (and a password, if you want), and click OK.

3. Click Close in the Manage Identities dialog box.

To switch to a different identity, choose File ➣ Switch Identity, select the identity in the Switch Identities dialog box, and click OK.

To remove or modify an identity, choose File ➣ Identities ➣ Manage Identities, and make your changes using the Manage Identities dialog box.

Keeping Transactions Secure with Microsoft Wallet

Along with the Profile Assistant, Internet Explorer offers Microsoft Wallet as a convenient and secure way for you to manage your credit card or other payment information (debit cards, ATM cards, and so on) and transmit it privately to Web sites. By storing that information on your computer, you avoid having to type it every time you make a purchase online. Of course, you can only take advantage of Wallet at those sites where the server has been configured to accommodate it.

Once you set up Wallet with your relevant information, you can shop at a Wallet-enabled Web site and have that information just a click away. When you're ready to purchase items and you've gone to the page where you usually enter your credit card information, the site's server asks Internet Explorer to display your information to you. All you have to do is click the credit card you want to use, and the relevant information from it will be sent to the server over a secure connection.

> **NOTE**
> Microsoft Wallet is not installed when you install Windows 98 SE. However, the first time you attempt to access Wallet, you will be asked if you want to download it. Click Yes to do so (of course, you must be connected to the Internet).

To set up Wallet on your Internet Explorer, choose Tools ➤ Internet Options and select the Content tab. In the Personal Information group of options, click Wallet to open the Microsoft Wallet dialog box, as shown in Figure 20.2.

The Microsoft Wallet dialog box has three tabs—Payments, Addresses, and Receipts:

- ▶ Payments stores the pertinent information for any credit cards you will use for online transactions. The information you enter is password-protected.

- ▶ Addresses stores the mail and e-mail addresses and phone numbers that you'll want to be able to send over the Internet.

- ▶ Receipts store electronic copies of receipts for online purchases. They are protected by a password you create.

Browsing with a Sense of Security 577

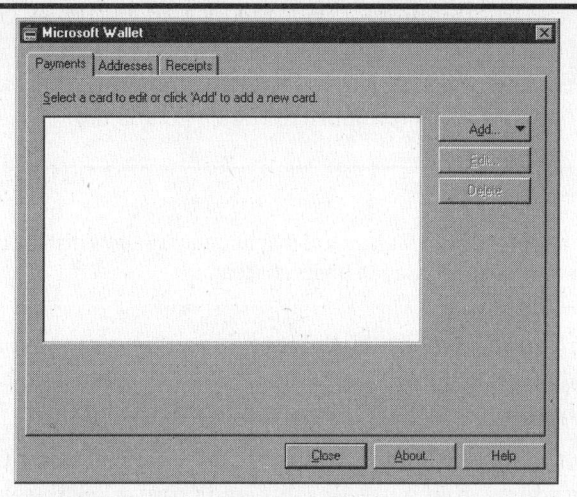

FIGURE 20.2: Use Microsoft Wallet to store information about yourself that you want to make available when purchasing over the Internet.

Entering Credit Card Information

To enter information about your payment transaction cards, follow these steps:

1. Click the Payments tab, click Add, and then click the menu item that corresponds to the credit card for which you want to enter information to open the Add A New Credit Card dialog box.

2. Click Next to open the Credit Card Information dialog box:

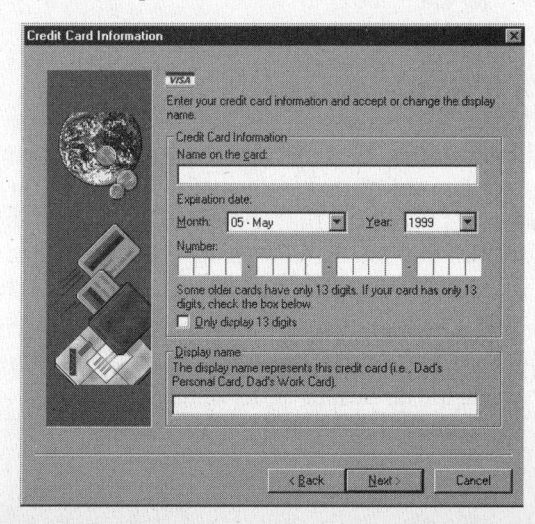

3. Enter the information for your credit card exactly as you would when you're making a purchase over the phone or on the Web. You can enter a friendly name in the Display Name field, one that you'll recognize in the Payments tab.

> **NOTE**
> If you have an older Visa or MasterCard that has only 13 digits instead of 16, be sure to select the Only Display 13 Digits checkbox.

4. When you're finished, click Next. If you have entered an invalid credit number or expiration date, or if the date has already passed, you will be prompted to fix the problem.

5. In the Credit Card Billing Address dialog box, you select the billing address that is used for this credit card. Click the New Address button to open the Add A New Address dialog box.

6. When you've completed the billing address for this card, click OK and then click Next.

7. Finally, you'll be asked to enter a password that will be needed to send this credit card information over the Internet or to revise the information on your computer. Enter the password in both the Password field and the Confirm Password field, and click the Finish button. The new credit card will appear in the list in the Payments tab of the Microsoft Wallet dialog box.

Entering Addresses

The addresses you enter in Microsoft Wallet will be available for sending to a site that supports Wallet and requests that type of information. For example, when you're making a purchase online, you can select a shipping address from those that are in Wallet. That's much faster than typing it yourself and much more accurate than trying to remember the ZIP code for your company's branch office in another state.

To enter a new address or revise an existing one, click the Addresses tab, and then click Add to open the Add A New Address dialog box, as shown in Figure 20.3. This is the same dialog box you use to enter address information for a credit card.

FIGURE 20.3: Enter a new address or revise an existing one in this dialog box.

> **NOTE**
> The names and addresses you enter here will also be placed in your Windows Address Book. Note that if you delete a name from the Address Book, it will also be deleted from Wallet. On the other hand, you can delete a name from Wallet and the name will remain in the Address Book until you delete it there.

Enter the necessary information for each field, or click the Address Book button and select a name from your Address Book.

You define an address either as home or business by clicking the appropriate button near the middle of the dialog box. The one you choose will determine where the address will appear in this person's entry in the Address Book—either on the Home or the Business tab. You also enter a friendly, easy-to-identify name for this address, which will appear in the list in the Addresses tab of the Microsoft Wallet dialog box.

When you're finished, click OK to save this name and address. You can then create another name by clicking the Add button, or click Close to return to the Internet Options dialog box.

Figure 20.4 shows an address that has already been entered. To delete an address, select it and click Delete; to revise its information, select it and click Edit.

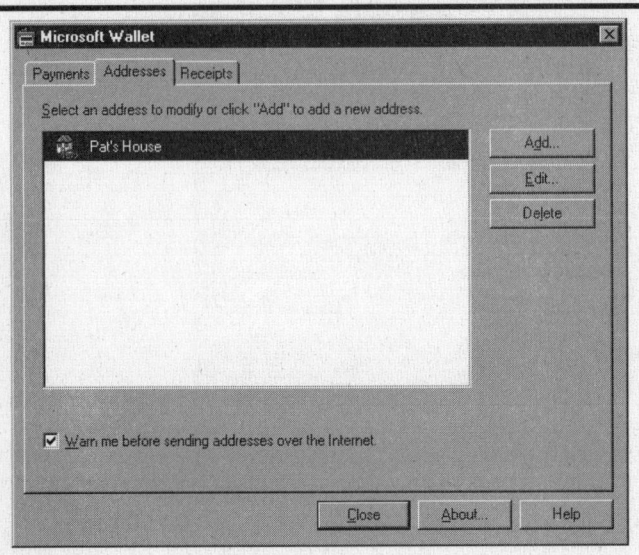

FIGURE 20.4: Each address is represented by a friendly name in the Addresses tab of Microsoft Wallet.

Storing Receipts

If you make a purchase from an Internet merchant who accepts payment from Microsoft Wallet, the merchant can supply an electronic receipt for your purchase. The merchant will notify you if this is the case.

Before the receipt can be stored on your computer, you must supply your receipt password. To do so, click the Receipts tab in the Microsoft Wallet dialog box, and enter and then confirm a password.

Filtering Sites with the Content Advisor

The free-flowing wealth of information on the Internet brings with it the need to filter out content that may not be appropriate. This is especially true for parents who are concerned about what their children might encounter on the Internet. It's also true for employers, teachers, librarians, and anyone else who wants to regulate the use of their computers. Of course, deciding what material is appropriate and who has the authority to block that type of content is the overwhelming question of the day. Are we being appropriately protective or acting like sinister Thought Police? The issue is definitely food for thought, and the answer will vary depending on whom you ask.

Avoiding www.offensive

Before you can view a Web page in Internet Explorer, you must specifically ask for that page from its server. It's important to remember this, as it means that objectionable Web sites can't come looking for you. You don't need to worry about nefarious Web pages lurking about your computer, just waiting to pop up when you least expect them. In order to be offended, you have to go to them. Nevertheless, it's possible to reach these sites by accident.

We once queried a search site on the Web, which returned a long list of links that the site thought relevant to the keywords we had entered. While quickly sampling some of those result links, we hit one that contained what is euphemistically called "adult material." We were certainly surprised and wondered how in the world this search site thought we were looking for this type of content.

The answer is simple enough: Search engines search and index the entire Web, without regard to content. The keywords we had used for the query happened to return the adult site near the top of the list. We're still not sure which keywords did the trick, but it really doesn't matter. There are probably thousands of everyday words that will rank some lascivious sites near the top of the list.

You can reduce the chances of this sort of close encounter if you:

▶ Read a link and its description before you click.

▶ Use Internet Explorer's Content Advisor to help filter out pages whose ratings don't meet your standards.

▶ Block individual objectionable sites that may not be rated by assigning them to the Restricted zone of sites (choose Tools ➢ Internet Options and select the Security tab). This is discussed later in this chapter.

▶ Be prepared to click the Stop or Back button when a site is being opened if that site seems to come from the wrong side of the ethical tracks.

If you exercise a little caution, you may rarely run into objectionable content on the Web. When you need to enforce some restrictions, however, you can limit the type of content that Internet Explorer will open, as discussed in the next section.

The Content Advisor

Should the responsibility fall into your lap, you can use Internet Explorer's Content Advisor to block Web pages whose content ratings exceed the limits you set. This system relies on Web authors to include a content rating in their pages, but as you'll see in the following discussion, it's to their own benefit to do so.

By default, Internet Explorer lets you set limits based on the Big Four issues that affect literature, art, movies, television, and advertising:

▶ Language

▶ Nudity

▶ Sex

▶ Violence

The Content Advisor is a powerful tool for parents who are concerned about their children's travels in the vast reaches of the Web. You can specify acceptable levels for each of the four categories, and Internet Explorer will not open pages that have content ratings that exceed those levels. Because you must have a password to set up or change the acceptance rules in Internet Explorer, you're assured that your standards will be upheld no matter who is using the computer.

> **NOTE**
> The Content Advisor performs some of the functions that are found in several "net watching" software products, such as Cyber Patrol, Cybersitter, and Net Nanny. If you want more control over how Internet Explorer is used on your computer, you can visit the Web sites for these products and others, which are listed in the Yahoo category "Business: Companies: Computers: Software: Internet: Blocking and Filtering: Titles."

Internet Explorer makes use of the rating system pioneered by the Recreational Software Advisory Council, or RSAC. That system has been tuned to Internet content and goes by the acronym RSACi. It is based on the World Wide Web Consortium's (W3C) Platform for Internet Content Selection, or PICS.

The PICS standard was developed by the computer software industry to enable Web authors to include a standardized rating in their pages and to enable Web browsers to block inappropriate pages based on those ratings. When Internet Explorer begins to open a page, it first reads any PICS rating codes that it finds in the HTML code. If the PICS rating exceeds the limits set in the Content Provider, Internet Explorer will display a message explaining why it cannot open the page, as described a little later in this chapter. You can read more about how the PICS standard works at

www.w3.org/pub/WWW/PICS/

Other ratings systems based on the PICS standard are also available. A parent or other Web overseer can choose the rating systems that best fit their own way of judging the appropriateness of Web content. As you'll see a little later, a Web author can assign multiple ratings to a page, and you can add multiple rating systems to the Content Advisor in Internet Explorer, allowing you to make use of those that work best for you.

Cooperation between Web-Page Authors, Rating Systems, and Parents

Now that you understand the concept behind the Content Advisor, you may notice that there's a weak link in the chain. Internet Explorer can only judge the content of a Web page when the page's author has included the necessary HTML code that defines the various levels of smut, violence, profanity and the like. That may sound as workable as the proverbial lead balloon, but it can actually work quite well when authors are truly interested in their pages being seen by those who want to see them.

Another way a parent can filter undesirable Web content in Internet Explorer is with the help of a third-party reviewing service, which is a company that acts like a rating system by reviewing and vouching for the appropriateness of Web sites. For example, the Cyber Patrol filtering software from Microsystems Software, Inc., at www.microsys.com offers parents two lists of rated sites. One is called the CyberNOT List, which contains sites that would be inappropriate for children. The CyberYES List contains sites that parents don't need to worry about. When a parent chooses to use the CyberNOT List, their children can visit any site on the Web *except* those in the list. When they use the CyberYES list, only the sites on that list can be visited.

As you can see, parents can control the type of sites their children visit on the Web in many ways. If Internet Explorer's filtering capabilities don't go far enough, you can look into buying one of the many third-party content-filtering software packages.

Determining the Ratings for Pages You Author

The RSACi rating standard, along with several others, helps authors rank their pages via an online questionnaire and checklist that asks the author very specific questions about the content of the Web page or site in question.

> **TIP**
> Even if you think the pages you've authored are quite innocuous, it can still be a good idea to include content ratings in them. A browser that uses a content filter such as the Content Advisor will by default block any pages that aren't rated. It's the only way the filters can do their job, and your pages would be blocked if they didn't include a rating.

When an author completes the questionnaire at the RASCi site, for example, the site displays the RSACi ranking, or score, for the page in question. It also displays the necessary PICS code (in HTML) that the author can include in the page's header to establish its ranking.

If you'd like to rank Web pages you've authored or a site you manage, or if you simply want to learn more about these ratings systems, you can visit the RSAC home page at www.rsac.org.

Enabling the Content Advisor

By default, the Content Advisor is disabled in Internet Explorer, and is therefore *not* filtering pages, and Internet Explorer will open *any* Web page you or another user requests.

Browsing with a Sense of Security

The first time you enable the Content Advisor in Internet Explorer, you'll be asked to create a supervisor's password. Thereafter, you or anyone else who wants to enable or disable the Content Advisor or change any of its settings must supply the password. Once you create the password, it's up to you to decide who else should have it.

> **NOTE**
> You can change the password at any time by clicking the Change Password button, which you'll find on the General tab of the Content Advisor dialog box.

To access the Content Advisor in Internet Explorer, choose Tools ≻ Internet Options and select the Content tab. The group of options labeled Content Advisor contains two buttons (shown below). When you first access the Ratings options, the button on the left is labeled Enable. The Content Advisor is inactive until you click this button.

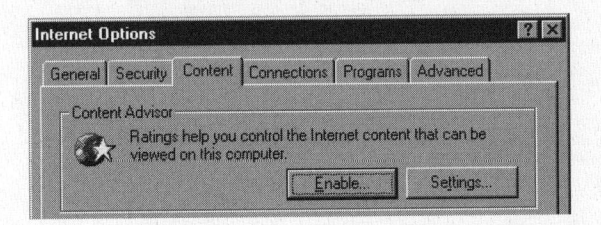

Here's how to sign yourself up as a content supervisor and the keeper of the password, prior to setting up any content-rating criteria. Remember, this procedure assumes that no one has yet created a password for the Content Advisor.

1. Choose Tools ≻ Internet Options and select the Content tab, where you'll see the Content Advisor buttons, as shown above.

2. Click the Enable button to open the Create Supervisor Password dialog box. Because this is the first time, you'll need to create a password before you can set any ratings.

3. Enter the password you want to use, and then click OK.

4. You'll see a message telling you that the Content Advisor is enabled, and when you click OK, you'll be returned to the Internet Options dialog box.

Chapter Twenty

5. To see where you define the ratings, click the Settings button, enter your password, and click OK.

6. This opens the Content Advisor dialog box; its Ratings tab is shown in Figure 20.5.

7. You can click OK at this point to close the dialog box and return to the Internet Options dialog box.

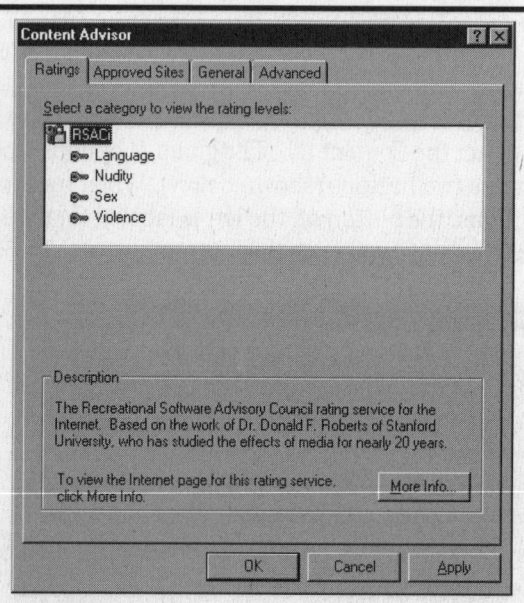

FIGURE 20.5: You can apply ratings to various types of Web content with the Content Advisor.

Notice that the first Ratings button is now labeled Disable, indicating that the Content Advisor is now actively filtering Web pages that you open. When you want to turn off its filtering, click the Disable button and enter your password.

If you enable the Content Advisor without changing any of its settings, it will check the RASCi rating (its default rating system) for each page you open. It will also use its default filtering criteria, which are the strictest possible. In the next section, you'll see how to relax or fine-tune those criteria.

> **WARNING**
>
> Before you consider the job finished, you might want to make sure that the "Users can see sites that have no rating" option, which you'll find on the General tab in the Content Advisor dialog box, is disabled (deselected). Internet Explorer will then block (not open) any pages that have no PICS rating. Unfortunately, this means a lot of the Web will be inaccessible, but it ensures that your content filtering will work as you want it to. Then be sure to read the section named "What to Do When a Page Is Disallowed" a little later in this chapter.

Setting the Ratings Criteria in the Content Advisor

You can change the filter settings for the Content Advisor whether the Advisor is enabled or disabled, but you'll need the supervisor password to do so.

1. Choose Tools ➢ Internet Options and select the Content tab.
2. Click the Settings button in the Content Advisor options.
3. Enter the supervisor password and click OK. This opens the Content Advisor dialog box at the Ratings tab. The Category list displays all the rating systems and their various filtering categories that are currently installed in Internet Explorer. In Figure 20.5, only the RSACi system is available, with its four categories of Language, Nudity, Sex, and Violence.
4. To read a short description of a rating system, select its name in the list. For example, in Figure 20.5, the RSACi rating system name was selected, and you can see a description of it in the lower portion of the dialog box.
5. To adjust the filtering effects, select a category in the list, which displays a slider bar in the center of the dialog box. By default, each category will be set to level 0, which creates the most restrictive filter possible for that category. Any page you try to open in Internet Explorer that has a RASCi PICS rating for that category that is higher than 0 will be disallowed by the Content Advisor.
6. Move the slider to the right to relax the filtering effect for this category. The stops on the slider bar are numbered, and a

short description of the current selection appears in the lower portion of the dialog box.

7. Continue to select categories and set their rating levels. Remember, once you have enabled the Content Advisor, *all* the categories in the list will be applied when Internet Explorer checks the content rating of a Web page.

8. To see what happens when a page is disallowed, set the Nudity category to a level of 2 or less.

9. When you are finished, click OK to return to the Internet Options dialog box.

10. To test your settings, as we'll do in the next section, remember to enable the Content Advisor; otherwise, your filter settings will have no effect. Click OK to close the Internet Options dialog box and return to Internet Explorer.

What to Do When a Page Is Disallowed

When you have enabled the Content Advisor, it will check the PICS rating for each Web page that you or anyone else opens in Internet Explorer. If the page exceeds the rating levels you have specified, Internet Explorer will display a dialog box alerting you to the problem. You can experiment with the Content Advisor by going to www.playboy.com. This is the home on the Web for *Playboy Magazine*, which is well known for its gauzy journeys into the uncharted and boundless seas of sex, nudity, and language. The Web site maintains PICS ratings for all its pages using both the RASCi and SafeSurf rating systems, so this is a great place to see how the Content Advisor works.

When you go to the Playboy Web site, the Content Advisor will read the PICS ratings for the home page and compare it with the settings in your Content Advisor. Unless you have increased those settings a great deal, the page will be disallowed, and you'll see the dialog box shown in Figure 20.6. It lists all the categories that exceed the content rating levels in the Content Advisor.

In this example, the dialog box offers four options:

▶ Click the Cancel button to close the dialog box and not open the page. This is the option that a child would need to choose.

Browsing with a Sense of Security 589

▶ Click Always Allow This Web Site To Be Viewed, Always Allow This Web Page To Be Viewed, or Allow Viewing Only This Time, and then enter the supervisor password. This allows you to make exceptions when you're around to do so and lets you keep the Advisor enabled while you go to a site that you don't want your kids to visit.

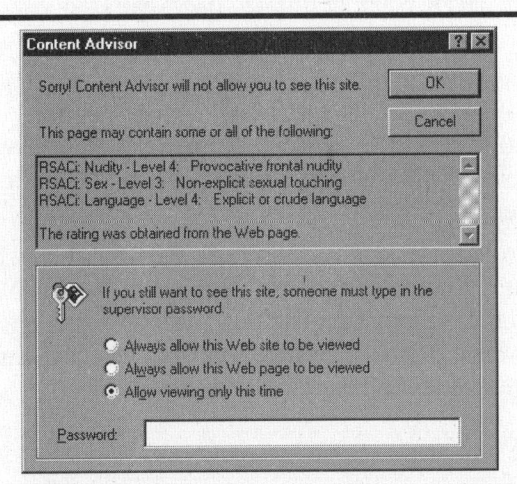

FIGURE 20.6: When any of the PICS ratings for a page exceeds the settings in the Content Advisor, Internet Explorer will not be allowed to open the page.

You can choose to disable the password field so that the options other than Cancel are not displayed. In Internet Explorer, choose Tools ➢ Internet Options, select the Content tab, click the Settings button, enter your password, and then choose the General tab. There you can deselect the "Supervisor can type a password to allow users to view restricted content" option. If you have kept your password away from prying eyes, you can safely leave this option enabled.

The Content Advisor may disallow a page for several other reasons, even if that page would be quite acceptable to you:

▶ The rating in the page includes an optional expiration date, and that date has expired.

- The page includes PICS codes from a rating system that you do not have installed in the Content Advisor (see the next section about installing other systems).
- The page has no PICS rating.

This last possibility is an important one, because you, as the Content Advisor supervisor, can decide whether unrated pages can be opened in Internet Explorer.

As mentioned earlier, when in doubt, it's safer to block unrated pages by deselecting the "Users can see sites that have no rating" option. Although this will vastly restrict the amount of browsing that can be done in Internet Explorer, it will ensure that only pages that meet your rating levels will be seen.

You might choose to select this option and relax the restriction when you're going to be around to supervise the children you're responsible for (and to keep an eye on the computer screen too). But when you're not going to be around to watch over your charges, you should enable this option again so that the Content Advisor will have its full effect.

WARNING
At this time only a small percentage of all the pages on the Web include a PICS rating, although that fraction is sure to grow as the Web matures. For now, no matter how restrictive you make the Content Advisor, it will only be effective with that small number of rated pages.

Adding Another Rating System

The Content Advisor in Internet Explorer comes equipped with the RASCi content-rating system, but there are other page-rating systems in use on the Web. When the Content Advisor is enabled and you attempt to open a page that uses a rating system that you do not have installed, the page will be blocked. You'll see a message similar to the one shown in Figure 20.7. Notice that the message includes the URL of the site where you can learn about this rating system. You can also download its rating vocabulary file from that site, which you should do if you want the Content Advisor to accept or reject pages that use this system.

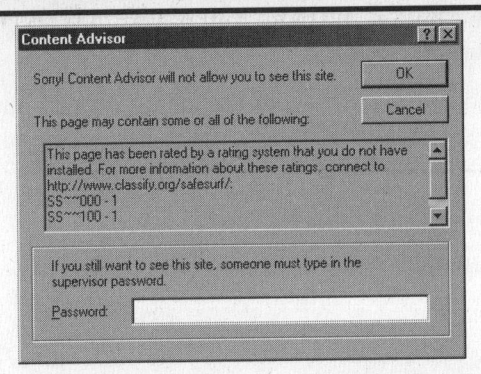

FIGURE 20.7: The Content Advisor will block a page that includes a PICS rating that you do not have installed.

> **NOTE**
> You can have more than one rating system installed, and each has its own criteria for content filtering. If a page uses just one PICS rating system that you have installed, your others will be ignored. If a page uses more than one system that you have installed, however, the settings in each will be used to determine whether the page is acceptable.

Anyone can download a rating file, but you'll need the content supervisor password to install it in Internet Explorer. Here's how to install the new rating system:

1. In Internet Explorer, go to the site listed in the dialog box in Figure 20.7: `www.classify.org/safesurf/`.

2. Here you can see a description of the categories used by this system (the SafeSurf system in this case). To download its rating file, click the link that downloads the SafeSurf Ratings file, which is named `SafeSurf.rat`. (All rating vocabulary files have the file name extension .RAT.)

3. Once you have downloaded the file, you can move it to your Windows\System folder, which is the default location where the Content Advisor looks for these files.

4. In Internet Explorer, choose Tools ➤ Internet Options and select the Content tab.

5. Click the Settings button and enter your password to access the Content Advisor dialog box.

6. Select the General tab and then click the Rating Systems button. This displays the Rating Systems dialog box, where you can see all the rating files that are currently installed:

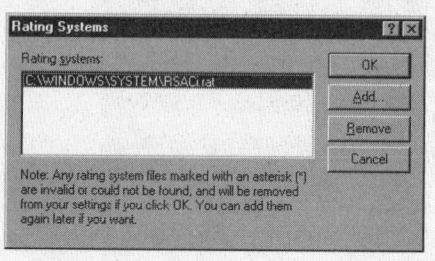

```
Rating Systems                                    ? X
Rating systems:
C:\WINDOWS\SYSTEM\RSACi.rat          [   OK   ]
                                      [  Add...  ]
                                      [ Remove ]
                                      [ Cancel ]
Note: Any rating system files marked with an asterisk (*)
are invalid or could not be found, and will be removed
from your settings if you click OK. You can add them
again later if you want.
```

7. Click the Add button to add a new system. In the file-selection dialog box that is displayed, select the `SafeSurf.rat` file that you previously downloaded and stored in your Windows\System folder, and then click the Open button.

8. You'll see the name of the new file in the Rating Systems dialog box; click OK to continue.

9. Back in the Content Advisor dialog box, choose the Ratings tab. You'll see that the Category list now includes the categories for the new rating system.

10. You'll need to set the rating criteria for each new category, as explained earlier in this chapter.

11. When you're finished, click OK to close the Content Advisor dialog box.

Setting and fine-tuning the rating levels for the categories in multiple rating systems can become a maintenance chore. If you find that you're really relying on the Content Advisor, you might want to look into purchasing separate filtering software for Internet Explorer.

Assigning Trust through Security Zones

One of the problems with life on the ever-evolving Internet is that it's a lot like a young man or woman moving from life on the farm to life in the big city—the pace is maddening, and it's hard to know whom (or what) to trust.

We've already looked at how you can use Internet Explorer's Content Advisor to filter out potentially objectionable material. Now we'll look at how you can limit the amount of interaction a Web server has with Internet Explorer and your computer. The main issue is how Internet Explorer handles downloaded *active content* (programs), or *dynamic content* as it is also called. Dynamic content refers to programs that are downloaded by Internet Explorer from the server when you open a page. You'll commonly encounter two types of programs: ActiveX controls and Java applets.

The main concern with any unknown program that you run on your computer is that the program might be malicious, such as a computer virus. As you'll read a little later, Internet Explorer can notify you when a page contains active content and let you decide whether to accept it.

The problem with this is that more and more sites are using more and more active content to bring their pages to life. This means that not only will you be inundated with announcements from Internet Explorer about incoming programs, but you'll also be left scratching your head and wondering which sites are safe and which are questionable. In other words, you're not about to inspect the source code of every program a site wants to send you! Instead, you simply want to know if this site is trustworthy. That's where the security zones of Internet Explorer come into play.

Dividing the Web into Security Zones

Internet Explorer lets you divide the Web into *security zones*. Each zone has its own set of security restrictions that determine how to handle active content, download files, run other applications on your computer, and more. There are four predefined zones:

Zone	Security	Description
Internet	Medium	All Web sites, except those URLs that you assign to other zones or are on your local intranet
Local Intranet	Medium	Sites that you access through your own private network; the URLs are defined by your system administrator

Chapter Twenty

Zone	Security	Description
Trusted Sites	Low	Sites you are familiar with and trust to a high degree
Restricted Sites	High	Sites you visit but do not trust

When you first install Internet Explorer, all sites are assigned to the Internet zone. As you browse the Web and become familiar with a site you frequent, you can assign that site to any of the other three zones. This will apply the zone's security settings to that site. If you look on the right side of Internet Explorer's status bar, you'll see the zone to which the current page is assigned.

The three security levels—Low, Medium, and High—provide a simple way to apply a group of restrictions to a zone without having to adjust each individual setting. You can, however, choose the Custom security level for a zone and fine-tune each of the security options. Setting the security level is discussed in the next section.

To change the security level for a zone or to assign sites to a zone, choose Tools ➤ Internet Options and select the Security tab, which is shown in Figure 20.8.

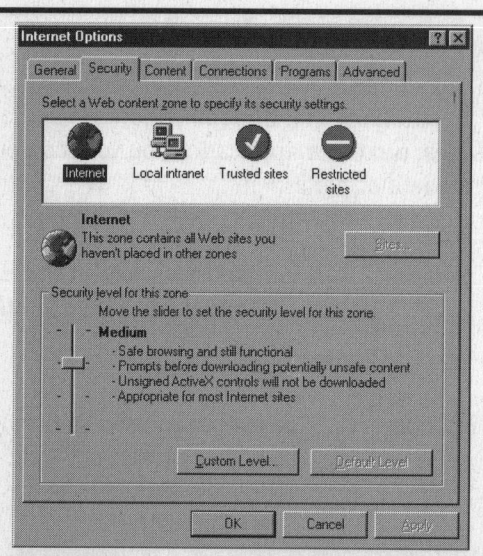

FIGURE 20.8: In the Security tab, you assign sites to a security zone or adjust the security restrictions for a zone.

Changing the Security Level for a Zone

You can change the overall security setting for any of the four zones. For example, you might loosen the restrictions on the Local Intranet zone by setting it to Low so that few restrictions would apply to sites in that zone. In Figure 20.8, you would select the Local Intranet icon and then move the slider bar to Low. When you click OK, the security level for all sites assigned to that zone would now be Low.

It is unlikely that you would ever want to relax the security level for the Internet zone, as the Medium setting offers a good balance of protection without overly restricting your freedom to browse.

When you have specific reasons for changing the security level of any of the zones, you can choose to set each individual security option, instead of relaxing or tightening the entire collection of options. In the Security tab in the Internet Options dialog box, select the zone you want, and then click the Custom Level button to open the Security Settings dialog box, shown in Figure 20.9. As you can see, most of the options offer three choices: Disable, Enable, and Prompt. For the Medium security level, most of the options are set either to Enable or Prompt so that either a task will happen automatically when needed, or you will be prompted and allowed to choose whether to proceed with that task.

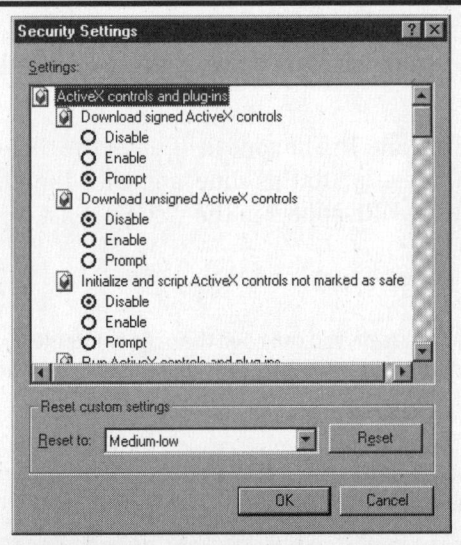

FIGURE 20.9: You can adjust each of the security settings in the Security Settings dialog box.

> **WARNING**
> Avoid changing these individual settings unless you know exactly which settings you want to change and why you want to do so. On the other hand, looking over this list of options is a good way to familiarize yourself with the security issues that confront you each time you browse the Web.

When you've made changes to the security options, you can always return to one of the three security levels by choosing Low, Medium, Medium-Low, or High from the Reset to drop-down menu near the bottom of the dialog box.

Assigning a Site to a Zone

As mentioned earlier, *all* Web sites are initially assigned to the Internet zone, which by default has a security level of Medium. You can assign an individual site either to the Trusted Sites or Restricted Sites zone, which will give that site either a Low or High security level, respectively (or whatever level is currently assigned to the zone). Here's how to assign a site to a zone:

1. In the Security tab of the Internet Options dialog box, select either the Trusted Sites or Restricted Sites zone.

2. Click the Sites button to open a dialog box similar to the one shown in Figure 20.10, which is for assigning a site to the Trusted Sites zone.

3. In the Add This Web Site To The zone field, enter the URL of the site you want to assign to this zone, and click the Add button. You'll see the URL appear in the Web Sites list.

> **TIP**
> Instead of typing the URL yourself, you can open the page in Internet Explorer, select its URL in the Address bar, and then copy and paste it into the zone-assignment dialog box.

4. You can continue to add other URLs, each of which will appear in the list of sites for this zone.

5. When you're finished, click OK to return to the Security tab in the Internet Options dialog box.

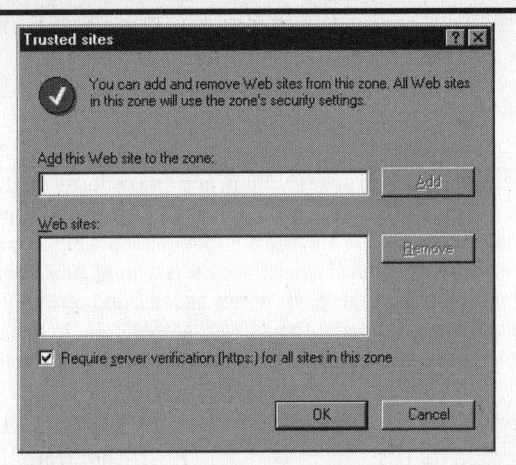

FIGURE 20.10: You can assign URLs either to the Trusted Sites or Restricted Sites security zone.

You can assign individual pages to a zone, but you can also assign entire sites by using the asterisk wildcard in the URL. For example, `*://sample.com` would assign all protocols for this site, such as HTTP and FTP, to the same zone.

ENCRYPTING TRANSFERS OVER A SECURE CONNECTION

The Internet is fast becoming a vital means for conducting our daily business, and security looms large in that context. Again, any data you send or receive on the Internet can be viewed at numerous points along the route it travels.

Internet Explorer can provide you with a great deal of online security when you connect to a Web site that uses data encryption when exchanging data with you. As you might think, encrypted data is encoded when sent and will be meaningless to anyone except the recipient.

Internet Explorer supports three encrypting protocols on the Web: Secure Sockets Layer (SSL, the most widely used one), Private Communications Technology (PCT), and Transport Layer Security (TLS). When you connect to a secure Web site that uses one of these protocols, the server first sends a *certificate* to Internet Explorer that guarantees that the site is both secure and authentic. In other words, this site is what it says it is, and not an impostor.

> **WARNING**
> There are no absolutes in the field of encryption, and any code, no matter how sophisticated, can eventually be broken when there's a large and concerted effort. However, the amount of time and the number of people and computers required to do so can be astronomical when the code is a tough one. Therefore, code breaking is not something that can be done casually, and certainly not by an amateur cracker who has tapped into a server. At this point in history, we can consider the encryption technologies used on the Web safe and reliable.

You may first notice that you're connecting to a secure Web site that uses the SSL protocol when its URL begin with HTTPS, rather than HTTP. Whether you notice or not, Internet Explorer will use the security protocol automatically; there's nothing for you to do. However, it is important to know when you're connected securely and when you're not so that you don't send any sensitive information over an unsecure connection.

> **WARNING**
> By default, when you open a page in Internet Explorer, it is cached (saved) in your Temporary Internet Files folder. To keep your connection to secure sites completely private, you should choose Tools ≻ Internet Options and select the Advanced tab. In the Security group of options, select either Do Not Save Encrypted Pages To Disk or Empty Temporary Internet Files Folder When Browser Is Closed. Any secure pages you open will no longer be stored in the cache.

> **ABOUT SSL SECURITY**
> A computer works a lot harder when it has to encrypt data it sends or decrypt data it receives. That's why secure connections are usually reserved only for those pages that contain sensitive information. For example, you might spend hours browsing unsecure pages at an online shopping site, but when you click the button to purchase the items you've selected, the page in which you enter your credit card information will be a secure one. Out of dozens of pages on that site, only one secure page might be needed to protect your finances.
>
> CONTINUED ➝

The same is true when you access a site for which you need a password. Only the page that actually prompts you for your name and password may be a secure one, while the other pages that follow will be unsecure.

Until mid-1997, a special export license was required when a company in the United States or Canada wanted to export any software that utilized security features stronger than what is known as 64-bit encryption (the more bits, or pieces of information, the stronger the encryption). Anything greater than that was considered a potential threat to national security if not regulated closely.

That's why the standard Internet Explorer software and other browsers did not use encryption stronger than 64-bit (in fact, the default encryption in Internet Explorer 3 was 40-bit). There was a stronger version of Internet Explorer available that used 128-bit encryption, which any citizen of the United States or Canada could use as long as they filled out a form asserting their citizenship.

But that changed in 1997, when the export laws were relaxed, so that we may soon find that the off-the-shelf version (or off-the-Net) of Internet Explorer has 128-bit encryption built in (as of this writing, it's still a separate version). This is an extremely tough level of security that has been used by banks and other financial institutions, so Internet Explorer now can offer you an extremely high level of safety when it comes to transferring encrypted data.

That's why Internet Explorer displays a Security Alert message when you are about to open a secure site. It's a notice, not a warning, that your connection is going to be secure, and any information you send or receive will be safe from prying eyes on the Internet.

Other than the Security Alert, the only difference you'll notice when you're connected to a secure site is the small padlock security icon on the status bar. When you see that icon, you'll know that any data you receive or send will be encrypted and secure from prying eyes. If you point to the padlock, you'll see a ToolTip that shows the type of security currently in effect.

When you leave a secure site for an unsecure one, you'll see another Security Alert message. This time it advises you that the connection is going to be an open, unsecure one and that any data you send or receive is no longer safe from scrutiny by others. When you are no longer connected securely, the padlock icon on the status bar will no longer be displayed.

Verifying Identity with Certificates

One of the most difficult security issues on the Internet is that of identities. How do we know that a Web site is really what it claims to be—that the company or organization whose name appears in the heading actually maintains the site—or that its active content is safe to download? For that matter, how do we prove to a Web site that we are who we claim to be?

Internet Explorer can help you deal with identities through the use of certificates, which are electronic assertions that guarantee the identity of a Web site, a downloaded program, or a person. These certificates of authenticity are issued by independent companies acting as third parties in the relationship between clients and servers. When using Internet Explorer, you'll encounter three types of certificates:

Publisher certificates authenticate active content or other programs that are downloaded and run by Internet Explorer.

Site certificates authenticate a secure Web site, so you can exchange personal or other private information with the site, knowing it is the real McCoy.

Personal certificates authenticate you as a client and guarantee your identity to Web sites that request the certificate.

You're most likely to encounter publisher certificates as you open pages that include active content.

> **WARNING**
> Certificates add a substantial layer of security when browsing the Web, but they are only effective when they are actually implemented for a program, Web site, or person. Even then, they are not a fail-safe system. If you have any doubts about the veracity of a certificate or the object it claims to identify, stop and take the time to track down the owner or issuer of that certificate.

Software Publisher Certificates

We've all learned that people can create malicious software, which we often refer to as viruses (the software, not their creators). A potentially easy way to find malicious software is by downloading active content from the Web. Do we really feel comfortable downloading and running programs from any Web site that we visit?

To help avoid this problem and protect our computers, Microsoft introduced Authenticode technology. No, this isn't a new technology for miraculously detecting and eliminating viruses, but it goes a long way toward providing that same level of protection.

> **NOTE**
> Many of the popular antivirus programs can screen downloaded programs as they come to Internet Explorer. You can check out the Web sites of the publishers of these programs from the following category at Yahoo: Business and Economy: Companies: Computers: Software: System Utilities: Utilities: Virus Protection.

When you buy software from a store, you probably don't even think about viruses or other malicious problems because you're familiar with the company and its reputation, and the software has been safely shrink-wrapped by that company before it was shipped out.

With the Internet, however, you really don't know where software comes from. An IP address isn't a physical address, so you can't even trace it to its country of origin. When you surf the Web and connect to a site that wants to send you active content with the page you requested, you simply don't know who's attempting to install that new program on your computer. This situation is bursting with potential hazards.

The solution proposed by Microsoft is to create *electronic packaging* for programs such as ActiveX controls (a popular form of active content), which is sometimes called a *digital signature*. This is an excellent method of molding the software manufacturer's identity onto the program itself and lets you know who is ultimately responsible for the software.

Downloading a Certified Program

In a typical case, when you open a page that contains active content, such as an ActiveX control, Internet Explorer downloads that control but does not install or run it. That's because the default security setting for Web sites in the Internet security zone asks you if you want to download and install the active content.

> **NOTE**
> If a downloaded program has no certificate, Internet Explorer may reject it without even notifying you. Or, if your security settings for this page are relaxed, it may let you decide whether to download it. You'll read about certificate security settings in the next section.

The Security Warning message asks whether you want to install and run the downloaded program and shows you the name of the publisher and of the certificate provider. You have several choices:

Yes accepts the downloaded program. Internet Explorer will install it on your system and run it. If it's an ActiveX control, it will remain on your computer and may be used by this page or any other page that needs it in the future.

No rejects the program; Internet Explorer will not install or run it. Note that the page that sent you this program may be effectively "dead" without it, but it's your choice.

More Info displays a page from Internet Explorer's help system that explains certificates for downloaded software.

Company name displays the certificate properties for the publisher of this program.

Always trust software from always accepts the downloaded program. If you feel comfortable accepting programs from this publisher in the future, select this option. Thereafter, you won't be prompted when Internet Explorer downloads active content published by this company. You can view a list of publishers you've identified as trusted by clicking the Publishers button on the Content tab of the Internet Options dialog box. You can remove one from the list by selecting it and clicking the Remove button.

You might choose to reject the active content because you don't know the company that published the program or simply because you're not interested in what that program will do.

> **NOTE**
> Downloaded ActiveX controls are stored by default in Windows\Downloaded Program Files. You can open that folder in the Internet Options dialog box by clicking the Settings button on the General tab, and then clicking the View Objects button. You'll see which controls are installed on your system. You can view the properties of a control to see what other programs or objects use it, and you can delete any control that you no longer want.

Setting Certificate Security Options

The download scenario you just read is typical, but the actual course of events depends on the security settings in Internet Explorer and the security zone to which you have assigned this page.

By default, all Web pages fall into the security zone called Internet in Internet Explorer, until you specifically assign a site either to the Trusted Sites or Restricted Sites zone. Each zone has its own group of security settings, which by default are grouped into four categories: Low, Medium, Medium-Low, and High. By default, Internet Explorer handles active content in the following ways for each level of security:

Low The program is assumed to come from a trusted publisher because it comes from a trusted site, and is automatically downloaded, installed, and run without your being prompted.

Medium-Low This is the same as the Medium level, but you are not asked whether to download or run the program. Appropriate for the Local Intranet security zone.

Medium You are allowed to choose whether to download and run the program, as described in the example in the previous section.

High The program is rejected without your being prompted, because no downloading of active content is allowed from pages given a High security setting.

You can see the actual security options that come into play by opening the Internet Options dialog box (choose Tools ➢ Internet Options) and choosing the Security tab. Then click the Custom Level button to open the Security Settings dialog box.

The first group of options in the Security Settings dialog box is ActiveX Controls And Plugins. Each option has three choices—Disable,

Enable, and Prompt, which coincide with the security settings discussed above. For example, when a zone's security level is Medium, the Download Signed ActiveX Controls option will be set to Prompt, while the option Download Unsigned ActiveX Controls will be set to Disable.

Of course, you can set the security level for any zone to Custom and adjust any of these options. But the initial settings should be appropriate for most users.

Site Certificates

A certificate can also be issued to a secure Web site to authenticate its identity when you log on to that site. In fact, a certificate is required for sites that use the SSL security protocol. This ensures that when you log on to your bank's Web site, for example, you're not actually connecting to a counterfeit site that is just itching to get your password.

When you connect to a secure Web site, Internet Explorer will verify the IP address stored in the certificate, and check that the certificate's date has not expired. If this information is not valid, Internet Explorer can warn of the potential problem. If everything is correct, you'll connect to the site without a hitch.

You can view a list of the Web site certificate providers that Internet Explorer recognizes. Choose Tools ➢ Internet Options, select the Content tab, and click the Certificates button in the group of options labeled Certificates. To view the properties of a certificate provider, select it in the list and click the View button. To remove a provider, select it and click the Remove button.

Personal Certificates

Even though you know quite well who you are, your identity is not easy to prove when you're trying to connect to a Web site somewhere out on the Internet. One way of providing that proof is through a personal certificate that guarantees your identity. In fact, in order to send encrypted e-mail with Outlook Express, you'll first have to obtain a personal certificate.

One of the more well-known certificate providers that issues personal certificates is VeriSign, Inc. You can apply for a certificate at `digitalid .verisign.com/ms_client.htm`. Although there's usually an annual fee involved with getting any certificate, VeriSign has been offering a free trial, Class 1 personal certificate for quite some time. You can use this type of certificate to send and receive secure e-mail through

Outlook Express, and you won't need a password to log on to Web sites that support personal certificates.

Like all certificates, a personal certificate has an expiration date and must be renewed in order to remain valid.

What's Next?

In the next chapter, *An Alternative to Internet Explorer: Netscape Navigator*, you'll learn about the most popular alternative to Internet Explorer. You can then decide which browser best meets your needs.

Chapter 21

AN ALTERNATIVE TO INTERNET EXPLORER: NETSCAPE NAVIGATOR

Although Internet Explorer is closely integrated into Windows 98 SE, Netscape Navigator is such a popular alternative that *Windows 98 Second Edition Complete* wouldn't live up to its name without a look at what you can do with this browser. In this chapter, you'll learn how to start Navigator, how to open and save Web documents, and how to switch between documents and other hypermedia (sound and video, for example) via hot links. You'll also get a good look at navigating through *frames*, which are like window panes within a document.

Adapted from *Surfing the Internet With Netscape Communicator 4* by Daniel A. Tauber and Brenda Kienan with J. Tarin Powers
ISBN 0-7821-2055-5   496 pages $24.99

Chapter Twenty-One

> **NOTE**
> This chapter assumes you already have an Internet connection and have installed Netscape on your PC. Once you're connected to an Internet Service Provider, you can use Internet Explorer to download Navigator (or the whole Communicator suite) from one of Netscape's dedicated FTP sites, `ftp2.netscape.com` through `ftp8.netscape.com`. On the Netscape FTP site, first select the `pub` directory and then follow the links to the version of Communicator or Navigator you want. By the time you read this, a Windows 98 SE version should be available for downloading. If you have an earlier version of Navigator, check the Netscape Web site for information about upgrading.

Launching Netscape Navigator

Launching Netscape Navigator is easy. Once you have the software installed and set up, you'll have a Netscape Communicator icon on your Desktop, and you'll have a new item in your Programs menu named Netscape Communicator. To start Navigator, follow these steps:

1. Start your Internet connection. How you do this depends on the sort of Internet service you have.

2. Now start up Navigator. You can do this in one of two ways:

   ▶ Double-click the Desktop's Netscape Communicator icon, shown here. (Navigator will launch by default.)

   or

   ▶ From the Windows 98 SE Start menu, select Programs ➤ Netscape Communicator ➤ Netscape Navigator. Either way, Netscape Navigator, the central component of Communicator, will open.

> **NOTE**
> Depending on your connection speed, the traffic level of the Internet, and how fast-acting the server that holds the Web page is, it may take more than a few seconds for the entire thing to load. In current Net parlance, that's known as *cometizing*—named for what the N icon does while you wait (and wait, and wait...).

An Alternative to Internet Explorer: Netscape Navigator

SLIP AND PPP: THE COMMUNICATOR CONNECTION

Before you can start using Communicator, you must start the connection software that you use to access the Internet. This may seem a bit more complicated than starting many other programs, but it's really no big deal.

Here's how it works: You start your connection software—by default, Windows 98 SE Dial-Up Networking—which then connects your computer to the Internet. This software "introduces" Communicator to the Internet; it is a vital link in your Internet connection. (At one time, this could be accomplished only through special SLIP/PPP software, but Windows 98 SE includes newer technologies that accomplish the same purpose.) Your connection software and your provider will then pass back and forth the TCP/IP packets that make it possible for you to run Communicator (which is on your machine). Voilà—your machine is accepted as a little network hooked into the bigger, more exciting network called the Internet, and you're on your way! If all goes well (and it surely will), the Netscape Navigator window will open, and the Netscape icon in the window's upper-right corner will become animated. This tells you that Navigator is transferring data, which will appear in a few seconds in the form of a Web page. Whenever Navigator is "working" (downloading a document, searching, and so on), the Netscape icon is animated. It stops when the action has been completed.

When you first start Netscape Navigator, you'll see the Welcome To Netscape home page, with its sleek, colorful graphics. The home page is where you begin, where Navigator first lands you on your Internet voyage. Think of it as one of many ports of entry into the Web. The Web, you'll recall, doesn't just go from here to there—it's a *web*. It doesn't really matter where you start, because everything's interconnected.

You can return to the start-up home page (the one you see when you start a Netscape Navigator session) at any time simply by clicking the Home icon on the Navigator Navigation toolbar.

> **TIP**
> You can always return to Netscape's own home page, no matter what else you've chosen as your start-up home page, just by clicking the N icon in the upper-right corner of the Netscape Navigator window.

If you followed the steps just presented and have Navigator running now, try clicking the Search button in the Navigation toolbar. This brief exercise will test your Internet connection. The N icon should become animated, and in a few seconds Netscape's Search page should appear. Now try clicking the Back button. The N icon will again become animated, and Netscape's home page will reappear.

What You See: The Navigator Interface

Let's look at the parts of the Navigator window. The interface shows the Document View window. Figure 21.1 shows you what's what.

> **NOTE**
> Via the View menu, you can display or hide any of the toolbars, including the Navigation toolbar, the Location toolbar, and the Personal toolbar. Or you can click the blue arrow buttons at the left of any toolbar to collapse it (and expand it again later). You may want to hide this stuff if you want the page display area to be larger.

Title bar   In the title bar, you can see the name of the page you are currently viewing.

Menu bar   The menu bar in Navigator is similar to menu bars in other Windows applications: It provides you with drop-down menus. When you move the mouse to the menu and click a selection, choices appear.

Navigation toolbar   The Navigation toolbar performs some common actions. It's like other Windows toolbars in that all you have to do is click the button for the specified action to occur. (If you point at a tool for a few seconds, a ToolTip will appear, telling you what the tool does. The ToolTip is simply a text box that displays the name of the tool to which you are pointing.) Let's quickly go over the Navigator toolbar buttons.

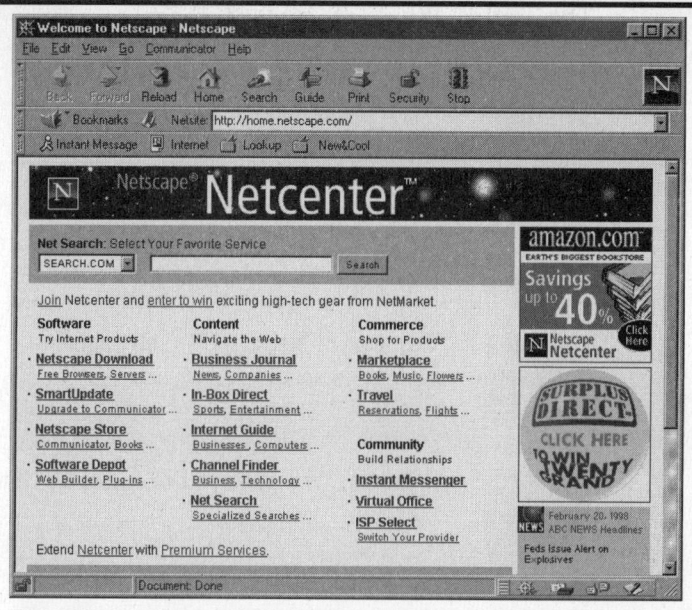

An Alternative to Internet Explorer: Netscape Navigator 611

FIGURE 21.1: Here's the Navigator window, followed by a list of its parts so you can see what's what.

The Tool	What You Do with It
Back	Jump back to the previous page in your History list (that is, the page you were viewing just prior to the current page).
Forward	Jump forward to the next page in your History List. (If you're on the last item in the History list, this button is dimmed—it looks grayed out.)
Reload	Refresh the document in the page display area.
Home	Return to the start-up home page.

The Tool	What You Do with It
 Search	Visit Netscape's Net Search page.
 Images	When you have turned off image auto-loading, use this button to see images in the current Web page.
 Guide	Visit one of Netscape's Web pages.
 Print	Print the Web page you're currently viewing.
 Security	If this button is not grayed out, you can click it to find out about the security of the current Web page.
 Stop	When a page is loading, click Stop to cancel the process of loading an incoming document.

> **TIP**
>
> Images load automatically unless you tell Navigator to do otherwise. If you have a slow Internet connection and prefer to decide whether to view pictures on a Web page, you can turn off image auto-loading. To toggle image auto-loading from Navigator's menu bar, select Edit ➢ Preferences ➢ Advanced. A check mark will appear next to Automatically Load Images when auto-loading is turned on. When auto-loading is turned off, the Images button appears on Navigator's Navigation toolbar. You can click this button to load images on a selected Web page.

An Alternative to Internet Explorer: Netscape Navigator 613

> **NOTE**
> Security is a topic of great concern to many users who want to protect their personal information—such as credit card numbers and bank records—from theft. Netscape Communicator has encryption and security features that make it the preferred Web client for accessing all types of commercial Web servers. Check out the "A Few Quick Words on Security" sidebar in this chapter for more on Communicator's security features. Or look at Netscape's Web Security Solutions page, at home.netscape.com/info/security-doc.html. Chapter 20, *Browsing with a Sense of Security*, covers Internet Explorer's security tools.

Location Toolbar   On the left is a blue folder icon you can click to access bookmarks (shortcuts to favorite sites; you create one by selecting Bookmarks ➤ Add Bookmark while viewing a page). The rest of this toolbar is occupied by the Location text box, where you'll find the *URL* (the Uniform Resource Locator) of the current document. We'll get to a discussion of URLs a little later in this chapter.

> **TIP**
> Here's a sneaky trick: Click the arrow on the far-right end of the Location text box, and any URLs you typed into the box recently will pop up. Select any one of them to visit that site again. Even neater than that: If you're in the habit of typing URLs directly into the Location text box, you'll be pleased to see a type-ahead feature there: Type the first several characters of an oft-used URL, and Navigator will guess the rest for you.

Personal Toolbar   Below the Location toolbar is a toolbar that you can customize by dragging and dropping URLs into it using the page icon.

Page Display Area   This is the main portion of the screen—it's where you'll see what you came to the Web to see.

Status Bar   The status bar is at the bottom of the screen. As you move the cursor about the viewing area and come across links, the cursor changes into the shape of a hand with one finger pointing, and the status bar displays the URL for the link you're pointing to. When content is being transferred to your machine, you'll see numbers in the status bar indicating the progress of the transfer.

Scroll Bars These are just like regular Windows scroll bars: They appear on the side of the viewing area, and possibly at the bottom, when the page is too big to fit in the window. Click the scroll bars to bring into view whatever's off-screen.

Component Bar Netscape Communicator includes a task bar with which you can open Navigator (the browser), Messenger's Inbox (the e-mail program), Collabra (the newsgroup reader), or Composer (the HTML editor). This component bar can be *docked,* meaning that it appears at the bottom of the Navigator window as part of the status bar; or it can *float,* meaning that it appears as a tiny window with buttons that launch the various Netscape components.

To make the component bar float (see Figure 21.2) when it's currently docked on the Navigator status bar, click the gray bars at the left side of the component bar. Once it floats, you can drag it to wherever you'd like it to live for the time being. To dock the component bar, click the little N icon on the floating component bar. Alternatively, you can use the Navigator menu bar and select Communicator ➢ Show Component Bar to float the component bar, or Communicator ➢ Dock Component Bar to anchor the component bar to the Navigator window's status bar.

FIGURE 21.2: Communicator's floating component bar lets you open Communicator programs while you work.

Opening Your First Document

You actually opened your first document when you started Navigator and the home page appeared. But let's dig around a little further and see what else we can do.

> **TIP**
> The Netscape Assistance area, online documentation for Netscape Communicator, is at home.netscape.com/assist/.

Following Hot Links

Moving around the World Wide Web is a snap, thanks to hyperlinks. It's as easy as a mouse-click on the link—each link points to some other piece of the Internet, just as Windows 9x shortcuts point to something on your hard drive.

As we've said before, hypertext is nonlinear. (That means you don't have to follow a straight path from point A to point Z, but rather you can skip around from one place to another to another, back to the first, round to a fourth, and so on.) Hypertext is hypertext because it has links—*hot links*, they're often called—to other sources of information. You follow these links through a document, or from document to document, document to image, or perhaps from server to server, in any way you like as you navigate the Web. (You can think of hypertext as both the text and the links—it's the navigational means by which you traverse the Web.) The great thing about the Web is that you don't have to know whether the information you're looking at is in Paris, France, or Paris, Texas—all you need to do is follow a link.

> **NOTE**
> If you do want information about a link before you click it, just check the status bar at the bottom of your screen. There you'll see a URL for anything from another site to a sound or video file, to an e-mail address. For example, if you drag your mouse over the linked word *Webmaster* on any given Web page, you might see the URL for the Webmaster's home page, an e-mail address provided by the Webmaster for feedback, or the URL for a Help page about the site you're viewing. Read on, and we'll tell you more about URLs later in this chapter.

How can you tell what is hypertext in a document? Words that are hyperlinks will usually be in a special color and underlined. On Netscape's home page, the special color is blue. A Webmaster (or producer) can choose any color at all to designate links, but in most cases the chosen color will be different from the color chosen for "ordinary" text. The words that stand out on a page are generally the links.

Images can also be links. Sometimes an image will have a border of color around it to designate it as a link, but in any case, the cursor will almost always turn into a pointing hand when you drag it over part of a Web page that is linked to something else.

Just as both text and images on a Web page can be hyperlinks, these hyperlinks can lead you to many different kinds of information. A link could lead you through a single document, off to a different Web page, across the world to a page on a different server, or to an FTP server, Gopher site, newsgroup, or e-mail address. Links can also lead you to images, sounds, movies, and multimedia files.

TO CLICK OR NOT TO CLICK?

When you click a link on the Web, it may take a few seconds to access the information you requested. Don't click again; let Navigator do its job. Every time you click a link, Navigator cancels the last order you gave it and starts a new one. So if you click the same link four or five times, Navigator has to start all over again each time.

If we slowed this whole business down and showed you its underpinnings, you'd see that when you click a hyperlink, Navigator contacts the machine (or machines) on the Internet that you told it to call. Then the dance between software and servers does one of these things:

- ▶ It gets and displays the document that the link specifies.
- ▶ It goes to another location in the current document.
- ▶ It gets a file, such as an image or a sound file, and through the use of a plug-in or an external viewer or player (another piece of software on your PC) displays the image or plays the sound.

An Alternative to Internet Explorer: Netscape Navigator

- It gives you access to another Internet service, such as Gopher, FTP, Telnet, and so on.

If you still have the Netscape home page open now, click a few links. Don't be shy—just click anything that looks interesting. You'll soon see why they call it the Web. Try jumping back and forth a couple of times, too, by clicking those tools on the Navigation bar. When you've had enough, simply click the Home button or the N icon to get back to the Welcome To Netscape home page.

> **NOTE**
> When you look at a document that has a link to something you've already seen, the color of that link changes. These are called *visited links*, and this is Navigator's way of letting you know you've been to that place before.

Opening a Document Using Its URL

Sometimes you're going to want to go straight for the jugular—you know where the document is, and you just want to see it without starting on a home page and skipping through a lot of hot links. Maybe your pal just sent you the URL for the Exploratorium, a really wonderful interactive science museum in San Francisco.

To open a document using its URL, follow these steps:

1. From the Navigator menu bar, select File ≻ Open Page, or press Ctrl+O. The Open Page dialog box will appear.

2. In the Open Page dialog box (see Figure 21.3), type the URL of interest (in our example, www.exploratorium.edu).

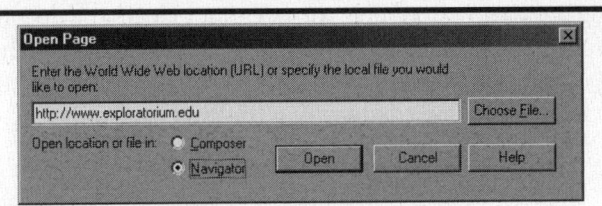

FIGURE 21.3: The Open Page dialog box

TIP

If you need a refresher on URLs, see Chapter 16, *Understanding Internet and World Wide Web Basics*, for a complete explanation. Always keep in mind that, unlike e-mail addresses, URLs are case-sensitive—capitalization matters! This is because lots of Web servers are Unix machines; in Unix, filenames in uppercase letters are not considered the same as filenames in lowercase letters. All the punctuation marks you see in some URLs are significant too—one misplaced hyphen, period, or tilde (~) will trip up the whole works. So if you're typing in a complex URL, look at it closely as you type. You can copy URLs from e-mail or other documents and paste them directly into either the Open Page dialog box or the Location text box.

3. Click Open, and Navigator will find the document for this URL and display it on your screen.

TIP

You can also jump quickly to a document by typing or pasting its URL directly into Navigator's Location text box, if you have the Location toolbar displayed. And you don't even have to type **http://** every time you want to type in a URL. You can start with the next bit of the URL instead. Navigator assumes that the URLs you ask for are HTTP URLs (Web pages) unless you tell it otherwise. In fact, you can often type just one word. For example, typing **Ford** and pressing Enter will get you straight into that car maker's site.

The Web is very big. And it changes all the time. From time to time you might have difficulty locating or accessing content. The original may have been removed by its owner, the machine that holds the content may be unavailable or overworked when you try to access it, or the network path between your machine and the server might be down. If Navigator has been trying for a while to access a document without success, it will display a dialog box saying that it just plain cannot locate the document. (See "Error Messages Demystified" later in this chapter for the dish on error messages and what to do about them.) To go back to the document that was on-screen before you tried making the jump, just click OK.

An Alternative to Internet Explorer: Netscape Navigator 619

TIP

If you're waiting for a page to arrive, and you want to look at something else (another page, for example) while you're waiting, select File ≻ New Navigator Window from Navigator's menu bar. A second Navigator window will open, and you can use it to look at something other than what you were trying for in the first window. You can then use Alt+Tab or the Communicator menu to switch back and forth between the two open windows. Now who said attention spans are getting shorter?

A FEW QUICK WORDS ON SECURITY

Keeping the data that passes across the Internet safe and secure is an issue that bigwigs in both business and government are discussing now, and one that will soon become relevant even to the casual user.

You've probably noticed a lot of talk in newspapers and magazines and on TV about commercial ventures on the Web—merchants and malls all setting up shop and taking your credit card order, or banks offering home services through their sites. You can even use the Web to buy and sell stocks. If this data (your credit card number, your bank balance and access code, or your stock portfolio) is not safe, it can be read by some eavesdropper lurking in an electronic shadow. Well, you can surely see the concern!

Fortunately, the designers of Netscape Communicator had this issue in mind when they developed the software. Netscape Navigator was the first Web browser to allow secured transactions to take place (between your computer running Navigator and a Web server running Netscape's Netsite Commerce Server). In practical terms, this means that when you, running Navigator at home, connect to a home page on a special server that was purchased from Netscape Communications, the data sent back and forth can be secure from prying "eyes."

By now you may have noticed the little blue lock icon on Navigator's command toolbar. Usually, if you click the security lock, a Netscape window will pop up and tell you that "There Is No Security Info for This Page." If, however, you are connected to a secure page—one where such eavesdropping is not possible because the data is encrypted before it is transferred and decrypted upon arrival—clicking the lock will open a similar window, but one that's filled with reassuring data that offers copious detail about the relative security of the Web page.

CONTINUED ➡

> Netscape Communicator (and therefore Navigator 4) offers even more sophisticated security with the addition of certificates to its features. Certificates are meant to prove your identity to Web servers through a system of verification. Look for this technology to become an increasingly important security feature as Web producers upgrade their sites to take advantage of new versions of Netscape's server software using certificates.
>
> You can find out more about security by selecting Help ➤ On Security from the Navigator menu bar. To get a directory of sites using Netsite Commerce Servers and other Netscape software, visit Netscape's Customer Showcase at home.netscape.com/home/netscape-galleria.html. To find out more about the current document on your screen, select View ➤ Page Info from Navigator's menu bar.

Changing the Size and Color of Displayed Text

If you've been working along with this chapter, you'll notice that text appears on your screen in different sizes. Usually, the text that makes up the substance of the page—the *body text*—is about the size you'd expect, while the title of the page is larger.

Changing Fonts and Type Sizes

Some folks are annoyed by gigantic titles all over the page that necessitate scrolling around a lot, while others can deal with big headlines in order to make the main text of the page larger and easier to read. Whichever you prefer, you can change the font and size of displayed text in Navigator.

Here's how you do it:

1. From Navigator's menu bar, select Edit ➤ Preferences. The Preferences dialog box will appear.

An Alternative to Internet Explorer: Netscape Navigator

2. In the Category column along the left of the Preferences dialog box, double-click Appearance (or click the plus sign next to that word). The Preferences dialog box will be updated to reflect your choice.

3. Indented below the word *Appearance,* you'll see the word *Fonts.* Click that word and, once again, the Preferences dialog box will change to reflect your last click.

4. Now, in the Fonts And Encodings area, you can set either a variable-width or a fixed font. Just click the menu boxes for either the font face or the font size to choose any font and size available on your machine.

5. When you're finished making your selections, click OK to return to the Navigator window.

The variable-width or proportional font is the one used for most of the text—body, head, and lists. The fixed font is the one used for preformatted text, which is a rarely used HTML element, but it also happens to be the font that appears when you type stuff in to the forms that some pages offer; for example, when responding to surveys.

NOTE
Leave the Preferences dialog box's "encoding" set to Western. Western is the proper setting for English and most European languages. Note, too, that while other choices are apparent in this dialog box, they aren't really available unless you have a version of Windows that's been localized to a specific language or country. Leave this stuff alone unless you know what to do with it.

TIP
As a shortcut, you can change font sizes without opening the Preferences dialog box at all. From Navigator's menu bar, select View ➤ Increase Font or View ➤ Decrease Font, depending on what you want to accomplish.

How does changing one font size change the style of more than one kind of text on a single page? Good question. Basically, Navigator displays different sizes of text (the title, headings, body text, and so on) in comparison to one "measure"—the basic font size. Navigator will display the title so-and-so many times larger than this base measure, and so forth. It is the base measure that you are changing in the procedure we just described.

> **TIP**
> A good rule of thumb is to select the font you find the most readable as your Proportional Font. A font such as Times New Roman or Bookman Old Style would be a sensible choice. For the Fixed Font, which is generally supposed to resemble a computer code look, Courier New or some other "typewriter" font will work well. A size of 12 or 14 for both fonts will make text readable on almost any screen.

Changing Colors

In Navigator, you have the option of changing the color of text. To do so, follow these steps:

1. From Navigator's menu bar, select Edit ➤ Preferences. The Preferences dialog box will appear.

2. If the word *Colors* is not already visible in the Category column along the left of the Preferences dialog box, double-click Appearance (or click the plus sign next to that word). The Preferences dialog box will be updated to reflect your choice.

3. Indented below the word *Appearance,* you'll see the word *Colors.* Click that word, and the Preferences dialog box will show Navigator's true colors (see Figure 21.4).

4. To make your upcoming color choices override any other settings, select the checkbox Always Use My Colors, Overriding Document. To allow the settings that exist in a given document to override the color choices you are about to make, deselect this checkbox.

5. As you can see in Figure 21.4, you can set the color for Text, Background, Unvisited Links, or Visited Links. Click any of these buttons to adjust the color choice for that option. The Color dialog box will appear.

6. In this dialog box, you can select any of a number of predefined colors by clicking one in the Basic Colors area, or you can define a custom color by clicking the Define Custom Colors button. You can also choose here to use the default Windows color scheme.

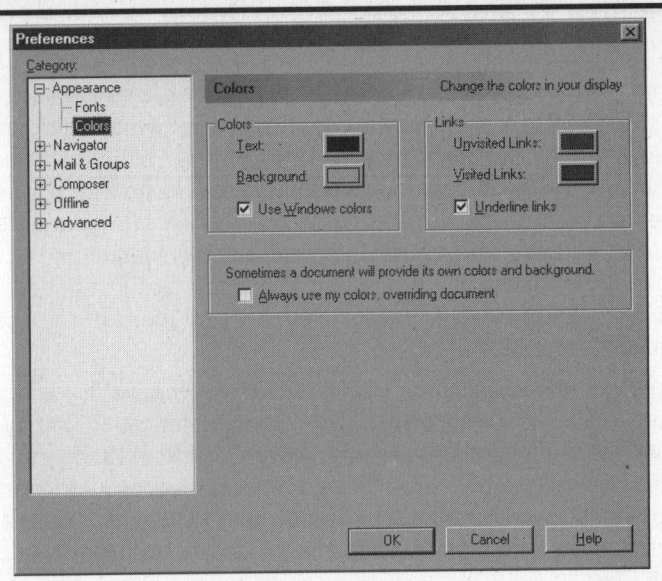

An Alternative to Internet Explorer: Netscape Navigator

FIGURE 21.4: The Preferences dialog box displaying color information

7. Click OK to close the Color dialog box. The Preferences dialog box will reappear, with the color(s) you've chosen appearing in place of the default Netscape colors that were there before.

8. You can repeat steps 4–6 for all four elements (text, background, unvisited links, and visited links), if you like.

9. When you are done specifying Navigator's colors, click OK. The Preferences dialog box will close, and you will once again see the Netscape window.

The changes you've made will take place immediately. If you don't like the results, you can always go back and repeat the whole color-changing process, selecting something new and different.

GUESTBOOKS, SURVEYS, AND FORMS—GEE WHIZ!

When you see a box on a Web page that lets you type stuff in it, that's often what's called a *form*. Forms are used by Web site producers to let users participate in Internet surveys, order merchandise, "sign" guestbooks, and give feedback, among other fun

CONTINUED ➡

things. The purpose of a form is usually obvious, as is the way you use it. You'll type some words in a text box, then perhaps click a few radio buttons and checkboxes, and finally press a button at the bottom of the page that whisks that information on its way. You may be invited at some sites to fill in a guestbook with your name, e-mail address, and a message to tell the Webmaster and other Web users what you think about the Web page you just visited. Or you may be asked to fill out a survey or registration form as a prerequisite to seeing the rest of a site.

This process is usually quick, simple, and free. However, if you're not sure exactly who might be receiving personal information, and if you don't want your e-mail box cluttered with junk from strangers, you may want to think twice about filling out every survey or questionnaire you run across. Watch for sites that do not sell their mailing lists—they usually tell you as much, and they usually stick to their word.

SAVING STUFF TO YOUR LOCAL MACHINE

Let's say you've been skipping around the Internet and looking at a lot of stuff, and you've found something really nifty you want to hold on to.

Saving takes up valuable disk space. This means you don't want to save *everything*. You do want to save things you want to keep for reference or access quickly in the future. For alternatives to saving, see Chapter 4's discussions of bookmarks and Internet shortcuts.

You can save a document to your local hard drive in three ways. We'll get to those in a second; first, a word or two on naming files in general and hypertext files in particular.

WHICH BROWSER SHOULD I USE?

If you're running Navigator with Windows 98 SE, you have the option of viewing any Web page with either Navigator or Internet Explorer. Generally both of these browsers can handle any kind of Web content, including fancy things such as special colors and the use of

CONTINUED ➡

An Alternative to Internet Explorer: Netscape Navigator

> columns, frames, and tables, as well as audio and animation. Older Web browsers might not be able to display that stuff as it was intended to appear, and so you will occasionally see messages like "Use Netscape for best viewing" or "Netscape not required." A few pages, including some (not surprisingly) on the Microsoft Web site, seem to work only with Internet Explorer. In any case, if you have problems viewing a site with one of your browsers, you can always try the other one.

Saving Stuff You Can See

Saving documents and images to your hard drive can be a good idea if you want to look at them later without paying for connect time. You can also use your store of saved documents as a library to jog ideas in constructing your own home page—this may be an easier process if the page is on your hard drive. See Chapter 22, *Creating Web Pages with FrontPage Express*, for more on creating your own Web pages.

Saving Web Pages

Here's how to save the page you are viewing at the moment to your hard disk:

1. From the Navigator menu bar, select File ➤ Save As. The Save As dialog box will appear (see Figure 21.5). This is much like a Save As dialog box you'd see in any other Windows application.

2. In the File Name text box, type a filename. Navigator will usually assign either .htm or .html as the extension automatically—these are the extensions for hypertext files. (If you want to be sure the program is assigning one of those extensions, just take a look at the bottom of the dialog box, where the Save As Type drop-down list appears.)

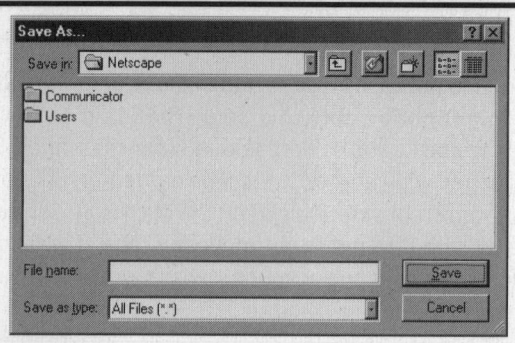

FIGURE 21.5: The Save As dialog box

> **NOTE**
> Some files on the Web don't end in .html or .htm—they end in trailing slashes, as in www.webpage.com/ (rather than www.webpage.com/home.htm), or they end in some sort of goop given them by a CGI or other interactive script. Generally, Navigator rolls with the punches and gives the file a name ending in .html, but you may want to double-check your filenames before you save them anyway.

> **TIP**
> If you want to save just the page's text, and not the HTML format, you can select Plain Text as the file type.

3. Pull down the Save In list by clicking its down arrow. From the list, select the drive to which you want to save the file. Below the Save In drop-down list, the contents of the drive you selected will appear as a list of folders and icons.

4. In that list, double-click the directory into which you want to save the file.

> **NOTE**
> If you want to place the file in a subdirectory (within a directory), first double-click the directory that contains that subdirectory so you can see it. For sub-subdirectories, repeat this process as needed until you find the target subdirectory.

An Alternative to Internet Explorer: Netscape Navigator

5. Click the Save As dialog box's Save button.

Perhaps this is obvious, but you won't see the document you've saved on-screen when you save it. You'll know it's been saved when you check the Directory list and see the filename there.

Saving Images

You might want to save one special image to your hard drive instead of a whole Web page. What for? Well, you can use that image as desktop wallpaper for your computer, send it as a map to a friend who's coming to town, or print it to hang over your desk at work. If the image is clip art (or otherwise in the public domain), you can also use it on your own home page. (See Chapter 22 for more on creating Web documents.)

Saving an image to your hard drive is easy. Just do this:

1. Using your right mouse button, click the image of interest. A pop-up menu will appear asking you what you want to do.

> **NOTE**
> Your other choices from this menu include viewing the image on a separate page, or if the image is a link, creating a Bookmark or Internet Shortcut to the page it's pointing to. See "Pop-Up Menus and You," later in this chapter, for more on how to use your handy right-mouse-button tool.

2. From the pop-up menu, select Save Image As. The Save As dialog box will appear.

3. Now follow steps 2 through 5 in the "Saving Web Pages" procedure just shown. Navigator will automatically detect and choose the correct file format (usually either GIF or JPEG) for the image.

4. To verify that the save was successful, you can use Windows Explorer to look in the directory to which you just saved the file. You should see the file listed.

Saving Stuff That's Not in View

Let's say the page you are viewing at the moment includes a link to something (maybe to a sound or to an image) that you want to save to disk to check out later. You can save the stuff at the other end of the link without first having to travel that link. Just follow these steps:

1. Pointing to the link that goes to the stuff you want to save, click the right mouse button. A pop-up menu will appear.
2. From the menu, select Save Link As. The Save As dialog box will appear.
3. Now follow steps 2 through 5 in the section titled "Saving Web Pages," earlier in this chapter.

To verify that the save was successful, you can use Windows Explorer to look in the directory to which you just saved the file. You should see the file listed.

NOTE
When you save an HTML document to your hard drive, what you get is the HTML code and the text—not the images. When you load the page later into Navigator, the images won't be there. This is because HTML documents tell Navigator where to find images, but they don't actually contain any pictures. An image in a Web page is really a link to a picture located on the Internet—but Navigator loads the pictures onto the page instead of just linking to them.

Viewing Documents You've Saved

You can view a document you've saved to your local hard drive by selecting File ➢ Open Page from Navigator's menu bar.

TIP
You don't have to be running your Internet connection to use Navigator to look at files on your computer.

The Open Page dialog box will appear; to open a file on your local drive, click Choose File, and the standard Open dialog box will appear. Again, this is a standard Windows dialog box. Select and open the HTML file of interest by double-clicking it. Once you're back at the Open Page dialog box, click the Open button to display the file in the Navigator window.

An Alternative to Internet Explorer: Netscape Navigator

By the way, saving a file and then viewing it this way is a lot faster than accessing and viewing it when it's somewhere else in the world; the drawback is that if the owner of the document has made changes to it, you won't know about them. A really cool aspect of this, though, is that when you view a document that's been saved to your local machine, the links have been saved with it, and you can simply click those links and start up your Web travels again—assuming you're dialed in for the clicking part.

POP-UP MENUS AND YOU

Netscape Navigator offers a lot of handy shortcuts that are no further away than your right mouse button. The available shortcuts change depending on where you point your cursor when you click. Try these:

- Point at some white space or non-linked text and click the right mouse button. A pop-up menu will appear offering options for going back or forward and for adding a bookmark or Internet shortcut for the page you're currently viewing, among other things.

- Point your mouse at a link and click with your right mouse button. A pop-up menu will appear offering options to copy the link's URL to the Clipboard, to add a bookmark or an Internet shortcut, to save the document behind the link to your hard drive, to open the link in Netscape Communicator's HTML Editor, or to open the link in a new window instead of the one the link is in.

- Point at an image and click with the right mouse button. A pop-up menu will appear offering options for saving the image to your hard drive, copying the image's URL, or viewing the image in a separate window.

JUMPING BACK AND FORTH WHILE VIEWING A DOCUMENT

The Back and Forward buttons on the toolbar provide a convenient way to jump back and forth among the hot links you've followed. This is because Navigator tracks the documents you visit in a History list. The Back and Forward buttons actually let you travel through the History list.

If you have Navigator running, try clicking the Back button to jump backward along the links you just followed, and then try clicking Forward to jump forward.

> **TIP**
>
> In addition to going back and forward one page at a time, try clicking the Back button and holding down the left mouse button for a second or two. A small pop-up menu will appear, listing the last five pages you've visited. You can do the same thing with the Forward button; the menu will list the next five pages in your History list.

There is an end to this—if you jump back to the first document you viewed in a session, or forward to the last one, you reach the end of the History list. The Back or Forward button, depending on which end of the history you reach, will be grayed out. (You can, as always, create more history—click another hypertext link to explore further.)

> **NOTHING'S SHOWING UP! WHAT TO DO?**
>
> Sometimes the N icon will be animated, its comets flying along, and either nothing shows up, or the text arrives sans any images. What's going on?
>
> When a Web server is busy, overloaded, or just plain slow, you'll get the text and basic HTML from it first and the images last. Images are a lot bigger (file-size-wise) than text, so they take longer to load. You can try any of these ways to address this:
>
> **Stop**   Click the Stop button. Often, the images that were trying to load are mostly there, and hitting Stop will say, "Hey images! Hurry up and load!" Many times, they will.
>
> **Reload**   If that doesn't work, click the Reload button. In fact, if a Web page ever looks funny or incomplete in some way, try reloading it.
>
> **View Image**   If a single image hasn't shown up, but the rest of them have, click the right mouse button over the placeholder (that funny-looking picture that represents an image that should be there, but isn't). When the pop-up menu appears, select View Image. Navigator will then try to retrieve that single image and load it onto the page you're viewing.
>
> CONTINUED →

An Alternative to Internet Explorer: Netscape Navigator

> **Give up**   Sometimes Webmasters goof up, and sometimes, particularly if the Web server you're trying to access is halfway around the world, the connection is just too danged slow. Oh well. If you really want to see that picture of Joe Namath as a baby, try your luck again some other time.

> **NOTE**
> At the bottom of many documents, you'll find a hot link that says something like *Go Back*. If you click this link, you won't necessarily go back to where you came from; instead, you'll visit the page that the Webmaster assumed you just came from (usually another page at the same site). If you want to go back to where you were before, click the Back button on the Navigator toolbar.

Getting Around in Frames

Frames are popping up all over, ever since they became a design option in version 2 of Netscape Navigator. Frames appear on a Web page looking like a bunch of panes within the larger viewing area window; these "panes in the window" each hold some piece of the larger whole. Like everything else in life, frames are good when used purposefully, and not so good when they're used gratuitously. In Figure 21.6, you can see News of the Day, a Web page that uses frames to enhance the organization of the page by offering a navigation frame on the left and a larger frame in which various news sources appear on the right.

Having too many frames in a Web site is like putting too many bows on a dress—too much. Frames are best used when no other option will do. To be fair, many sites use frames quite well—one of the most practical applications of frames are pages that offer a table of contents in one of the frames. That index stays put (in some form or other) the whole time you're navigating the rest of the site.

Chapter Twenty-One

> **NOTE**
> Many frames-based sites are quite apparent—there are solid lines of one sort or another, and maybe even scroll bars, that make it clear that the Navigator viewing area is being divided into little window panes. Recently, however, it's become possible to create a site that uses *borderless frames*—the usual, obvious gray lines and bars that divide the window are invisible. You may not even notice that a site uses frames until you start navigating through it and notice that only part of the page is changing while you click.

Whatever their purpose in a Web site, each individual frame has its own URL. They also can have their own scroll bars, various background colors, images, text, Java or JavaScript elements—anything, in short, that a non-frame Web page can have.

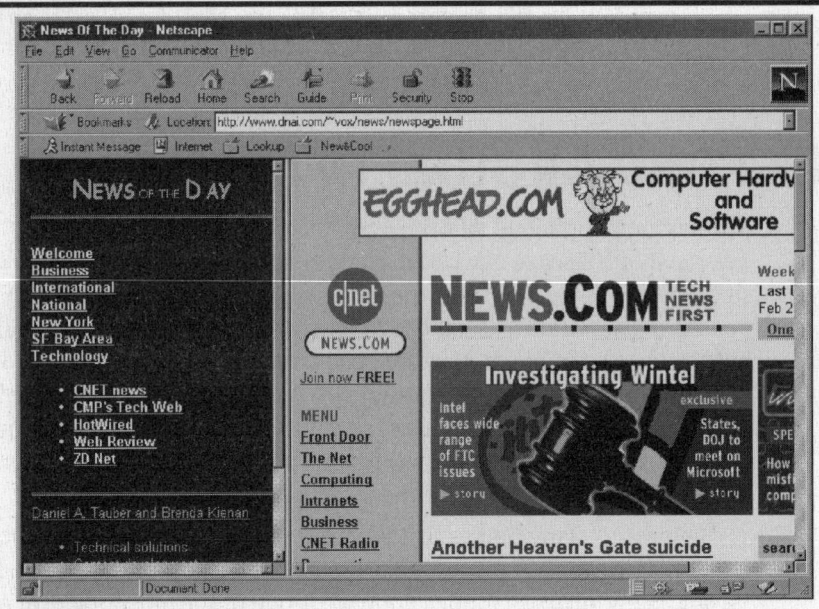

FIGURE 21.6: The News of the Day page uses frames to enhance the navigation of its contents.

When you click a link in one frame, often another frame on the page will change to reflect that click. That means you can easily get lost trying to find some information that was in a frame you saw five clicks ago.

An Alternative to Internet Explorer: Netscape Navigator

Still, using frames, you can easily get back to where you once belonged. The easiest way is to use the Back button; in Navigator 4, the Back button sends you back one frame at a time until you reach the beginning of a framed-up site. You can also use the right mouse button to navigate backward; click, and when the handy pop-up menu appears, select Back. You'll navigate backward one frame at a time.

> **NOTE**
> You can bookmark a document or a frame; this is much like putting a bookmark in a book in the sense that it helps you find where you've been without having to retrace your steps.

Caching and Reloading

Navigator stores the pages you visit in what's called the *cache* (pronounced "cash"). A cache is just a chunk of storage—it can be RAM or the disk drive—on your computer that's been set aside as a temporary storage place. Your PC stores parts of the programs that you're running in its cache to make them run faster. Similarly, Navigator caches the Web pages you look at, so when you go back and forth between pages, you don't have to access the Internet anew every single time you look at the same page. Instead, your machine accesses the copy of the page that's in the cache. As you continue to visit new sites on the Web, old stuff in the cache is flushed out, and the newer stuff you visit in your travels is added.

> **NOTE**
> Navigator actually maintains two caches of documents—one in your computer's memory that goes away when you end your Netscape session, and another on disk that it uses between sessions. When you access a Web page, Navigator first checks to see if you have a current copy of the page either in the memory cache or in the disk cache. If a copy of the current page is located in either of these places, that copy is displayed instead of a fresh copy, relieving Navigator of the slow process of downloading the page from the Internet anew. (This is also true of images, sounds, video—in short, anything on the Net you access via Navigator.)

When you click around from page to page, you may not be seeing the most current version of a Web page; you may instead be seeing the cached version. This can be a drag if the page changes a lot and you want the fresher version. Certain pages, like weather maps, newsfeeds, and live camera links, for example, change minute by minute, and you want the freshest view of them. If you ever doubt that you're seeing the most current version of a page, just click the Reload button and the page will appear from scratch, rather than from the cache.

Specifying How Often to Check the Cache

You can specify how you want Navigator to approach this matter by checking the cache Every Time, Once per Session, or Never settings in the Network Preferences dialog box. The default is Once per Session. It's best not to mess with this unless you have some compelling reason and know what you're up to, because it'll slow down other operations. But here are the details:

1. From Navigator's menu bar, select Edit ➢ Preferences. The Preferences dialog box will appear.

2. In the Category area of the Preferences dialog box, double-click the word *Advanced*. The Preferences dialog box will change to reflect this choice, and some other options should become visible.

3. Click the word *Cache*, and the Preferences dialog box will be updated once again (see Figure 21.7).

4. Locate the label marked "Document in cache is compared to document on network." Below the label you'll see three radio buttons, one for each option:

    Once per Session Navigator will go looking for each page once (the first time you access this particular Web page in this particular session). This is the default setting, and it's the best for most of your usual activities.

    Every Time Navigator will not look at your disk cache and will always retrieve from the Internet instead of locally. This setting is good when you're viewing lots of pages that change frequently, and especially if you're on a high-speed line.

    Never Navigator will always go for the copy in your disk cache unless it becomes unavailable (or unless you click the Reload button). Choose this when you're not dialed in to the Net, and you want to look at pages in the cache.

An Alternative to Internet Explorer: Netscape Navigator 635

Click the button of choice. Then click OK to close the dialog box. Navigator will hereafter comply with your choice.

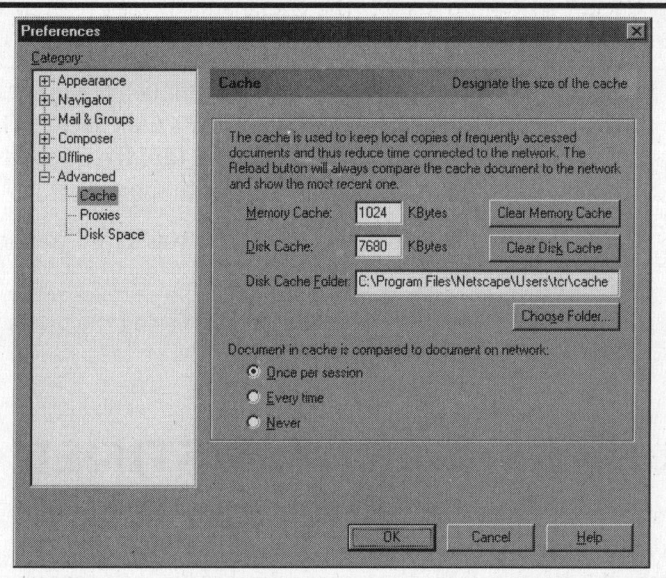

FIGURE 21.7: The Preferences dialog box displaying information about the cache

Increasing the Size of Your Disk Cache

As a default, Communicator sets the disk cache at 7680KB unless it picked up your Preferences from a previous version of Navigator. This is a good minimum, but you may want to increase it, depending on how much disk space you want to dedicate to Net surfing. The more disk space you allocate to Navigator's cache, the more stuff it will hold.

> **WARNING**
>
> It makes a lot less sense to increase the size of the memory cache than to increase the size of the disk cache. The other programs you're running, including Windows 98, need all the memory they can get. Don't shortchange Windows for the sake of Navigator or other applications that rely on Windows.

To increase your disk cache, follow this simple procedure:

1. Follow steps 1–3 in the "Specifying How Often to Check the Cache" section to display the Cache area of the Preferences dialog box, as seen in Figure 21.7.

2. In the Disk Cache text box, type the number of kilobytes (KB) you want to reserve for Navigator's disk cache. The default is 7680KB (or 7.7MB); 20000KB (20MB) is a better choice if you have that much disk space to spare.

3. Click OK. The dialog box will close, and you'll find yourself in the familiar Navigator window.

From this moment forward, you should find accessing the pages you visit most often a lot faster than it was before.

Error Messages Demystified

The Internet works really well most of the time, but both computers and humans are fallible, and sometimes you'll click a link or enter a URL and get an unhappy message from Netscape instead of the Web page you wanted. See Table 21.1 for a listing of error messages and what they mean.

A few general tips:

- Most errors aren't permanent. If you get an error, try a few minutes, hours, or even days later, and the page you want will usually come back.

- You're more likely to get Busy or Connection Refused messages during peak hours, like lunchtime and right after the workday ends. Try accessing busy pages during off-peak hours.

- Good Webmasters do routine maintenance on Web pages fairly often, and this can increase the chances of certain parts of a server being off-limits. If you try accessing the site a day or two later, you'll usually be able to access the page you want, or you'll be given a pointer that says the site has moved.

- If a page disappears inexplicably or permanently, check your favorite search engine to see if it can locate an alternate address for the page.

An Alternative to Internet Explorer: Netscape Navigator 637

▶ There are probably lots of other error messages you could get, and a good rule of thumb is to try the page again later, especially if you know you've been there before, or to check the spelling and format of the URL.

> **NOTE**
> As always, when in doubt, click Reload and see what happens.

TABLE 21.1: Navigator Error Messages We Know and Love

Error Message	What It Means	What To Do
Too Many Users	This Web site may restrict the number of accesses allowed per day or per hour.	Try again later.
A Network Error Occurred. Unable to Connect to Server	Either the host is busy, the URL is spelled wrong, or something else is funny.	Make sure you actually put the forward slashes in after `http:`. If that doesn't work, just try again later.
Broken Pipe	Something went wrong en route and some data got lost	Click the Reload button, or try again later.
Connection Refused	The line is "busy," and this is the Web's busy signal.	Try again later.
Document Contains No Data	The Web page you tried to link to is there, but there's nothing on it.	Forget about it. Whoever pointed you there made a mistake.
The Location (URL) Is Not Recognized	You asked for a type of URL that doesn't exist.	Look for typos in the URL you entered, especially the `http://` part.
The Server Does Not Have a DNS entry.	This server doesn't exist right now, at least not the way you spelled it.	Check your spelling of the domain name. If it's spelled correctly, try again later.
Netscape Is Out of Memory	Boy, you've been looking at a lot of huge Web pages today!	Quit Navigator, and then launch it again.
403 Forbidden	The part of the Web server you're trying to access is off limits right now.	Try it again tomorrow or next week. If that doesn't work, forget about it. Someone doesn't want any visitors.

TABLE 21.1 continued: Navigator Error Messages We Know and Love

Error Message	What It Means	What To Do
Please Enter Username and Password	If you don't have an account on this server, it won't let you in.	Try visiting the site's home page to see if they require you to complete a registration process.
404 Not Found	The page you tried to link to may be gone forever, or there may be a typo in the URL you entered	Try it again tomorrow or next week. If that doesn't work, the thing's probably gone.

Printing a Document or a Single Frame

To print a Web document, you must first have it open. Then, follow the usual printing procedure:

1. From the Navigator menu bar, select File ➤ Print. The Print dialog box will appear.
2. Fiddle with the dialog box to specify what you want exactly, and click OK.

The whole document will pop out of your printer. Note, however, that the document probably will not be a single page long (unless it's a very brief home page, for example). This, of course, is because Web pages do not have the same physical boundaries as paper pages. So a single Web page may be several paper pages long.

TIP
It may be helpful to print out a page at less than 100 percent scale. If your printer dialog box has options for printing a page at 75 percent of its normal size (or some other likely ratio), give that a try.

Also, perhaps obviously, if you want to print other pages linked within a single site, you'll have to go to those pages and print them separately.

An Alternative to Internet Explorer: Netscape Navigator

(Of course, you can't click a printed-out Web page. But you already knew that, right?)

With frames, the matter gets a little stickier. You can't print out an entire Web page full of frames, because each pane in the window is technically a distinct document. To select the frame you want to print, again with the page (with frames) open:

1. Click some blank space within the frame, and that frame will appear highlighted.

NOTE
To see how this works, try clicking from frame to frame in a site that uses frames. Try News of the Day, which is located at www.dnai.com/~vox/news. You can see how each individual frame gets highlighted as you go from frame to frame. Keep in mind, though, that the highlight may not be apparent in sites that use borderless frames.

2. From Navigator's menu bar, select File ➢ Print Frame. The Print dialog box will appear.
3. Fiddle with the dialog box to specify what you want, and click OK.

TIP
To make sure you're printing the frame you want, you can select File ➢ Print Preview from Navigator's menu bar before you print. A window will appear showing you what you're printing, how many pages long it is, and other nifty things about the page. To exit Print Preview and return to the Navigator window, click Close from Print Preview's toolbar. To go ahead and print, click the Print Frame button.

The frame you selected will pop out of your printer. Now, the thing to remember is that it's one frame that you've printed, and a whole Web page can be made up of several frames. If you want to print an entire Web page with all its frames, you'll unfortunately have to print each frame individually.

Quitting Netscape Navigator

You can quit Navigator any ol' time—even when the N icon is animated. To leave Navigator, simply do the following:

1. If the N icon is animated, click the Stop button on the toolbar. This will cancel whatever Navigator is trying to do at the moment. (If the N icon is not animated, skip this step.)

2. To actually quit the program, click the Control button in the upper-left corner of the screen, or select File ➢ Exit from the menu bar. The Windows Desktop will reappear.

3. Remember, even if you aren't running Navigator, you are still connected to your Internet service provider, and you must break this connection, using whatever techniques are appropriate. (Check with your Internet Service Provider to find out about that.)

> **WARNING**
> If you have more than one Navigator window open, or another Communicator component running, such as Messenger, you can exit all Netscape windows at once by selecting File ➢ Exit from any Communicator menu bar. A dialog box will appear asking if you wish to close all windows and exit Netscape Communicator. Click Yes to close all the windows. Click No to continue Communicator.

What's Next?

For many Internauts, the next logical step beyond browsing the Web is building one's own site. Individuals, organizations, and businesses of all sizes are taking advantage of easy-to-use Web authoring tools to publish their messages to the world. One of the best authoring tools for new Webmasters is bundled with Internet Explorer and Windows 98 SE—FrontPage Express. In the next chapter, Gene Weisskopf and Pat Coleman guide you through the process of building your own site.

Chapter 22

CREATING WEB PAGES WITH FRONTPAGE EXPRESS

The common language for creating content on the Web is the Hypertext Markup Language, or HTML. You can use any text editor, such as Notepad, to create a Web page in HTML, but the job is greatly simplified if you use a dedicated HTML editor that displays your page as it will appear in a browser. FrontPage Express, a worthy HTML editor, is part of the Internet Explorer suite of applications, and it can make the job of creating Web pages as simple as creating documents in your word processor. The more you learn about HTML, the more you'll appreciate that simplicity. With FrontPage, anyone can create Web pages that include a variety of HTML features.

Adapted from *Mastering Microsoft Internet Explorer 4*
by Gene Weisskopf and Pat Coleman
ISBN 0-7821-2133-0   960 pages $44.99

> **NOTE**
> FrontPage Express is the slightly trimmed down HTML editor component included with Windows 98 SE. FrontPage 98, the full-blown version, has even more advanced features, and if you're planning to create Web pages and put together Web sites, it could be a worthy addition to your software arsenal. Any mention in this chapter of the full-featured product will include the "98" to differentiate it from FrontPage Express.

Starting Out in FrontPage Express

No matter how complicated HTML coding can look, if you think of FrontPage in the same way that you do your word processor, you'll be up to speed in no time. The only difference is that when you save a file in FrontPage, the result is a pure HTML file in plain text, ready to be opened in a Web browser.

Starting FrontPage

You can start FrontPage from the Start menu, as you would any other program; choose Start ➤ Programs ➤ Internet Explorer ➤ FrontPage Express. The program opens in its own Window with a new blank document, ready for you to get to work.

When you install FrontPage, it becomes the default editor for HTML files. When you right-click a Web page in Windows Explorer and choose Edit, that document opens in FrontPage.

> **NOTE**
> If you install some other HTML-enabled program after FrontPage is installed, that program might then become the one associated with editing HTML documents. You can change the association back to FrontPage for the file type Internet Document (HTML) by going to the File Types tab in the Options dialog box in Windows Explorer.

When you're viewing a page in Internet Explorer, you can choose View ➤ Source to open the underlying HTML code in Notepad. When FrontPage is installed, you can choose Edit ➤ Page or click the Edit button on the toolbar to open the current page for editing in FrontPage.

Creating Web Pages with FrontPage Express   645

As you create Web pages in FrontPage, be sure to save your work regularly, as you would in your word processor. (You'll read about file operations later in this chapter.) When you're finished with FrontPage, you can close it by choosing File ➣ Exit.

Navigating in FrontPage

FrontPage looks much like a typical WYSIWYG word processor, where "what you see is what you get." In this case, what you see in FrontPage is what the rest of the world will see when they view this page in their Web browsers. Figure 22.1 shows FrontPage with an open document.

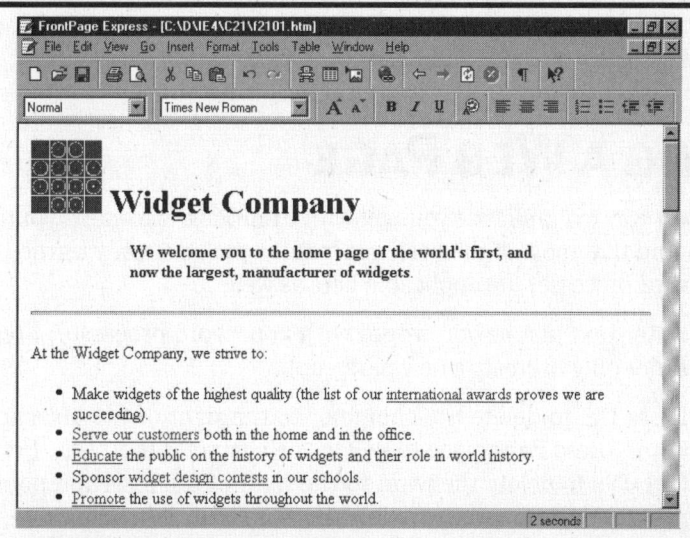

FIGURE 22.1: You create Web pages in FrontPage in a WYSIWYG environment.

Let's take a quick look at some of the features you'll find when you're creating Web pages in FrontPage:

- ▶ At the top of the screen is the title bar, where you'll see the current page's HTML title (if you opened that page via a Web server) or the filename (if you opened the page from your local disk).

- ▶ Beneath the title bar are the menu, the Standard toolbar, and the Format toolbar. When you're creating an HTML form page, you can also display a Forms toolbar. You can turn on or off the display of a toolbar by selecting it from the View menu, and you can move a toolbar simply by dragging it to a new location.

- At the bottom of the screen is the status bar, which behaves much like the status bar in Internet Explorer. For example, the left side of the status bar displays a description of the currently selected command on the menu, and it displays the target address of a hyperlink when you point to a link in the page.

- The document (Web page) that you're editing appears in the window beneath the toolbars. You can open multiple documents (pages) and switch between them in the standard ways, such as by selecting a document name from the Window menu or by pressing Ctrl+F6.

- The horizontal and vertical scroll bars offer one way to scroll through your document; you can also use the expected keyboard keys, such as PgUp and PgDn.

Editing a Web Page

The best way to familiarize yourself with FrontPage is to start typing. You'll find that most of the basic procedures you've already learned in your word processor are applicable here as well:

- Enter text just as you would with your word processor; press Enter only to create a new paragraph.

- Press Del to delete the character to the right of the insertion point; press Backspace to delete the character to its left. Press Ctrl+Del to delete the word to the right of the insertion point; press Ctrl+Backspace to delete the word to its left.

- Press Ctrl+Home to go to the top of the document, and press Ctrl+End to go to the bottom.

- Using the standard Windows commands, you can change the size of the active document's window, minimize it to an icon, or maximize it so it's as large as possible (like the document you saw in Figure 22.1).

- Select text or graphic images by dragging over them with your mouse or by pressing the Shift key while you use a keyboard arrow key to select the material.

- Once you select a portion of the document, you can invoke a command from the menu or toolbar to act on that material. For example, choose Edit ➤ Cut or click that button on the toolbar to remove the selection from the document and place it in the Clipboard.

- You can transfer text or images between FrontPage and other programs in the usual ways, such as with Edit ➤ Copy in FrontPage and then with Edit ➤ Paste in the other program.

- Choose Edit ➤ Undo (Ctrl+Z) or click that button on the toolbar to undo your most recent action in the document. You can "undo an undo" by choosing Edit ➤ Redo or by clicking that button.

- To change the properties of an object in a page, such as selected text or a horizontal line, select the object and choose Edit ➤ Object Properties (such as Font Properties when you have selected text) or press Alt+Enter. You can also right-click the object and choose Object Properties from the shortcut menu.

Inserting Line Breaks and Special Characters

In most browsers, a paragraph in an HTML Web page (designated by the <P> tag) has a blank line above and below it, which may not always be appropriate for the format you want. For example, a name and address will appear on multiple lines, but you won't want extra paragraph spaces between them.

Use the Insert ➤ Break command, and the text that follows will appear on a new line without starting a new paragraph. This saves the new line from having to appear with a blank line above and below it. Another advantage of using the line break is that any paragraph formatting continues on the new line, whereas it won't if you create a new paragraph (you can read about formatting text and paragraphs later in this chapter).

FrontPage also offers a way for you to insert characters into your document that you cannot normally enter from the keyboard, such as the degree symbol (°), the copyright symbol (©), and the trademark symbol (™).

Place the insertion point where you want the character or characters to appear, and choose Insert ➤ Symbol. In the Symbol dialog box, click the character you want, and then click the Insert button to place it in the document. You can continue to insert characters as needed; click the Close button when you're finished.

> **TIP**
>
> Some symbols require special encoding in HTML in order to be displayed in a browser; FrontPage will do this for you. For example, the HTML code for the trademark symbol is &trade. In fact, a few characters you can type from the keyboard must be specially encoded because they have special meaning within HTML code. Such is the case with the ampersand, which precedes a variety of character codes in HTML. When you type an ampersand in FrontPage, it actually enters the special code &amp. Likewise, the less-than and greater-than symbols are part of HTML tags. When you enter those characters in a page, FrontPage encodes them as &lt and > this way, the browser software that eventually displays your page will interpret them as characters and not tags.

Finding and Replacing Text

You can use the Edit ➢ Find command to find all occurrences of text you specify in the current page. In the Find dialog box, enter the characters you want to find. You can also choose to find those characters only when they are a complete word or when the case exactly matches what you entered. You can also choose to search up or down the page, starting from the insertion point.

To begin the search, choose the Find Next button. The first occurrence of the specified text is selected in the page. At this point you can:

- Choose Find Next to find the next occurrence.
- Click Cancel to close the Find dialog box.
- Click within the page so that you can continue to work in it, perhaps to edit the text that was found. The Find dialog box remains open.

You can only search for text that is displayed in FrontPage, which means you can't search for HTML tags or other encoded characters that are hidden behind the scene. For example, you might want to search for a URL that is targeted in a link somewhere in the page. To do that, open the current page in WordPad or another text editor, where you'll see the HTML code itself. Now when you search, you'll be looking through everything that's in the file, including any URLs referenced in a link.

For the Edit ➢ Replace command, you specify the text to search for as well as the text with which to replace it. If you leave the Replace With field empty, the text that is found will effectively be deleted.

Adding Comments

You can add comments in a page with the Insert ➤ Comment command. A comment can be used to explain an area in the page, serve as a reminder to you or another author, or provide a more detailed explanation of a task that needs to be completed. The text you enter is displayed in FrontPage, but not when the page is viewed in a browser, because the text is enclosed in the HTML comment tags:

```
<!- This text is a comment. ->
```

Actually, FrontPage adds a bit more to the comment tag, so that the previous comment would actually look like this in FrontPage:

```
<!- webbot bot="PurpleText" preview="This text is a comment."
->
```

In case you're wondering, the WebBot is a FrontPage tool for adding nonstandard HTML features to a page. In this case, the WebBot tells FrontPage not only to display the comment text, but to display it in purple. Again, in Internet Explorer this comment would not be shown at all.

Seeing the HTML Source Code

When you want to see the HTML code on which the current page is based, choose View ➤ HTML. A window will open that displays the actual HTML code for your page, the same code that will be saved to disk when you save your page.

Figure 22.2 shows the View or Edit HTML window for the page that was displayed in Figure 22.1. Use caution when you make changes to the HTML code, as they will be reflected in the page when you return to the Editor. If you accidentally delete one of the angle brackets for an HTML tag, you'll immediately see the result in the Editor.

If you're just viewing the code and do not want to make any changes to it, you can close the window by clicking the Cancel button or pressing Esc (a good way to negate any accidental changes you might have made). If you make changes to the code and want to keep them, click the OK button to close the window.

> **NOTE**
> Although the Editor's menus are not active while you are in the HTML window, you can still cut or copy text to or paste text from the Clipboard—just use the standard shortcut keys for those commands (they are shown on the FrontPage menu).

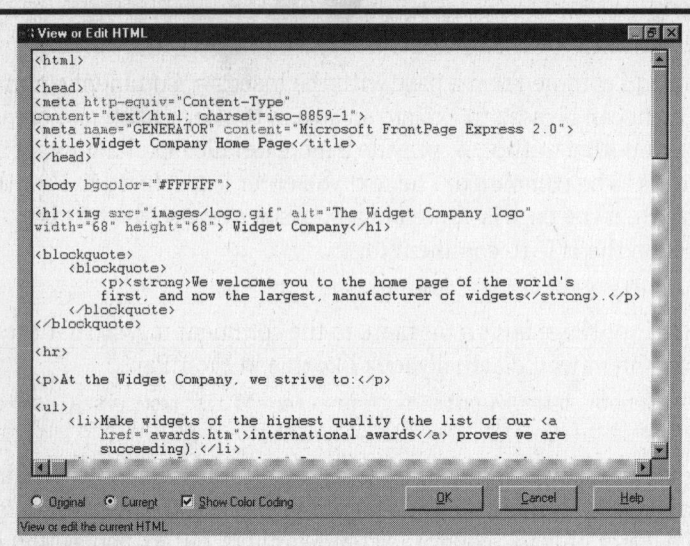

FIGURE 22.2: Choose View ➤ HTML to view or edit the underlying HTML code for a page.

The HTML window also helps you interpret the code by color-coding it:

▶ The text you have entered is in black.

▶ HTML tags are in purple.

▶ The attribute or argument names within tags are in red.

▶ The actual attributes that you have entered (via the formatting or other choices you make in FrontPage) are in blue.

The colors help make sense of the code as you scroll through it, and viewing the code is always a good exercise that will help you get a feel for the ins and outs of HTML.

Previewing Your Work in Internet Explorer

The ultimate destination for your work in FrontPage is a browser, possibly any browser on the planet if you post your work to the World Wide Web. Keep in mind that a lot of variables affect the way your page appears in a browser, and it's important that you preview your work outside FrontPage and inside Internet Explorer regularly as you're building the page.

Creating Web Pages with FrontPage Express 651

> **NOTE**
> If you are creating pages for the Web, consider previewing your work in several browsers and on different computers as well. Try viewing the page at different screen resolutions (640×480 or 800×600) and at different color depths (256 colors or 16 million colors). You need to keep your page design somewhat flexible to accommodate the various combinations of computer hardware and software that may visit your site.

While you're working in FrontPage, open the current page in Internet Explorer to view it there, such as with the File ➢ Open command. If your page includes any animated GIF images, scrolling marquees, or active content such as ActiveX controls or Java applets, you'll see them go into action inside Internet Explorer.

You can switch back to FrontPage to continue working on the page. Whenever you want to preview the file, just save it, switch to Internet Explorer, click the Refresh button on the toolbar or press F5, and there it will be.

Printing Your Work

You can print the current page in the same way that you print a document in your word processor (or just about any other Windows program, for that matter). Of course, the need to do so may arise only rarely, because a page is meant to reside on a Web site and be viewed by a browser. Nonetheless, you may want to print pages in order to edit them for correctness outside the computer or to show them to others who may not have access to a computer.

Choose File ➢ Print to display the standard Print dialog box, in which you can specify the number of copies to print, the range of pages to print, and the printer to which the job should be sent.

> **NOTE**
> As in Internet Explorer, the document you view in FrontPage is not literally divided into pages. After all, it's formatted not to be printed, but to be viewed in a browser. If you want to print just a few pages of a large document, first choose File ➢ Print Preview to view on-screen what would be printed. This will also show you the pages and their numbers so that you can make a note of the pages you want to print.

Before you print, you can modify the page layout via the File ➤ Page Setup command; its dialog box is shown here. You can specify the margins for the printout, as well as the text that should appear in the header and footer on each page.

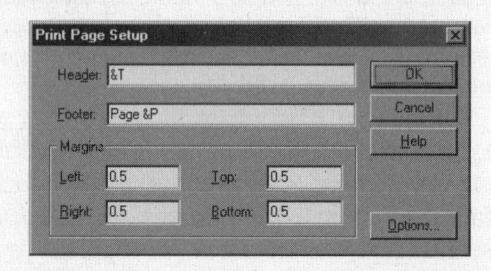

You can include two special codes in the header and footer, each of which begins with the ampersand (&). Use &T to display the page's title (this is the same title you specify with the File ➤ Page Properties command); use &P to display the page number in the printout.

> **NOTE**
> Unlike your word processor, the settings in the Page Setup dialog box affect all the pages (files) you print within FrontPage, and they remain in effect until you change them.

Before you print a page, take a few seconds to preview on the screen what your printout will look like on paper by choosing File ➤ Print Preview or by clicking the Print Preview button on the toolbar. The preview screen displays the page as it would appear when printed on paper. You can use the buttons on the toolbar to navigate through the page. When you're satisfied that you're ready to print, click the Print button. Click Close to return to your document in FrontPage.

Creating New Pages and Saving Your Work

FrontPage offers you a variety of ways to work with Web pages, whether they're from your local disk or directly from your Web site. You'll find that its templates and Wizards give you a real boost when creating new pages. If you want to bring in non-HTML files from other sources, you can import a variety of file types.

Creating a New Page

To create a new page, choose File ➢ New (Ctrl+N). This displays the New Page dialog box (shown in Figure 22.3), which lists the available templates and Wizards that you can use to create a new page (a Wizard includes that word in its name).

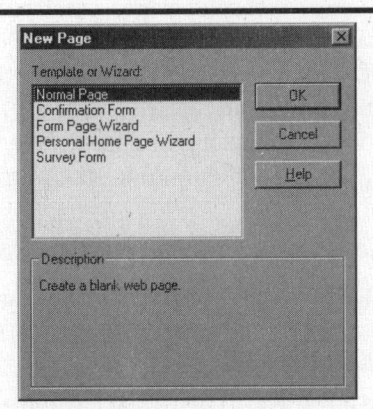

FIGURE 22.3: The New Page dialog box

Creating a Page from a Template

A *template* is simply a ready-made page that you can use as a starting point for a new page. A template makes it easier to get a page going and also provides a consistent look when you create several pages from the same template.

If you choose the template named Normal in the New Page dialog box, you'll create a new, blank page that's basically the same page you see when you start FrontPage. Use this when you want to start a new page from scratch. You can also create a new page based on the Normal template by clicking the New button on the FrontPage toolbar.

You'll find several other templates in the New Page dialog box, including Confirmation Form and Survey Form, which let you create form pages without having to start from scratch.

> **NOTE**
>
> The Confirmation and Survey templates include FrontPage WebBots that will work only on a Web site where the server has the FrontPage Server Extensions installed. These add-ons for servers are available for free from the Microsoft Web site, and allow a server to interact with the pages you create using FrontPage WebBots. Some WebBots require no server interaction and can be used in any pages you create.

At first glance, each template looks like a completed page, with titles, sections, bulleted lists, names, and dates. At second glance, you'll see that some of the text consists of instructional comments that help you fill in your own information on the page. Other text is generic, such as a title that simply says Company Name, and you should replace it with your own text. Be sure to read the comments for tips on using the page, and be sure to delete any information in the page that is not relevant to your purposes.

Creating a Page with a Wizard

A Wizard helps you create a new page by asking you a series of questions about the content or layout of the page. It then builds the page based on your responses, and you get to work on the result.

For example, the Personal Home Page Wizard helps you customize a home page for your own use. The number of steps in this Wizard depends on the choices you make in the first step. There can be well over a dozen steps in all, each of which lets you fine-tune the page to your own needs. When you choose this Wizard from the New Page dialog box, you'll see the first dialog box of the Personal Home Page Wizard, as shown in Figure 22.4. You can select the main sections for your personal home page, which will appear as main headings, with relevant information beneath each one.

As you proceed through the steps of this Wizard, you'll specify a URL for the page you're creating if it's going to a Web site, or you'll specify a filename if it's staying on your local disk. You can make many choices for each of the categories you chose in the first step. When you finally click the Finish button, the page appears in FrontPage, containing the sections and information you specified. You are now free to modify the page as you would any other page.

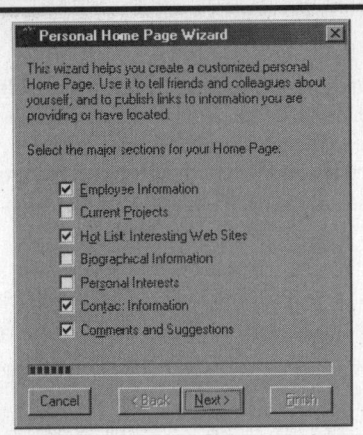

FIGURE 22.4: The first step of the Personal Home Page Wizard

Opening an Existing Page

To open an existing Web page or another type of file, choose File ➢ Open (Ctrl+O), or click the Open button on the toolbar. This displays the Open File dialog box, from which you can open a file from your local disk, or open a page from a Web site by supplying the URL. Instead of using the Open command, you can select a name of a recently opened file from the bottom of the File menu.

To open a page from disk, select the From File radio button and enter the path and filename in that field. If you don't know the path and filename, click the Browse button.

To open a page by specifying its URL, select the From Location radio button and enter the URL in that field. Using this method, you can open any page from any Web site to which you have access, just as you do in Internet Explorer. Once the page is open, you are free to save it to your local disk or another Web site.

Free, that is, within the constraints of upright behavior and copyright law. But this is a handy way to bring a page from one Web site into FrontPage, where you can revise it as necessary and then save it to a different location.

> **TIP**
>
> You can navigate through the hyperlinks in your Web pages from inside FrontPage—hold down the Ctrl key and click the link. When multiple pages are open in the Editor, you can switch between them in the usual ways, such as by pressing Ctrl+F6. You can also use the Back and Forward buttons on the toolbar to move from one page to another, just as you do in Internet Explorer. In this case, the pages must already be open.

You can open many types of files besides standard HTML Web pages. FrontPage will convert an incoming file from its native format into an equivalent-looking HTML file. You can then save it as an HTML Web page in the usual way.

To make it easier to find a file, and to see the types of files that FrontPage can convert, use the Browse button and look at the Files of Type drop-down menu in the Open File dialog box. When you choose one of the file types on the list, only files with the appropriate filename extension for that type, such as .doc or .xls, are displayed in the dialog box.

You will find a wide variety of file types in the list, including several versions of Microsoft Word, Excel, and Works and also WordPerfect. The more generic Rich Text Format (.rtf) and plain text (.txt) file types are also on the list.

> **TIP**
>
> If you can't open a certain file type in FrontPage, you may be able to save that file in HTML format in the program that created the file. You could then open the HTML file directly into FrontPage.

If the incoming file contains any graphic images, FrontPage will attempt to place them in the document where they belong. Because images are always separate files from the pages in which they appear, you will be asked if you also want to save the images as separate files when you later save this document as an HTML page (see the next section). By saving the images, you are making them available the next time you open this page, either in FrontPage or in a browser on your Web site.

You can bring another file into the current page by choosing Insert ➤ File. The contents of the other file appears at the insertion point's position within the page. Choose Insert ➤ Image or Insert ➤ Video to display an image or video file in your page.

Saving Your Work

When you have opened an existing page, you can save it back to its original location under the same filename by choosing File ➤ Save (Ctrl+S) or by clicking the Save button on the toolbar. The page is saved immediately, and you can continue with your work.

When you are working on a new page that you have not yet named, choosing File ➤ Save displays the Save As dialog box. This is the same dialog box you will see when you choose File ➤ Save As to save an existing page under a new name or to a different location.

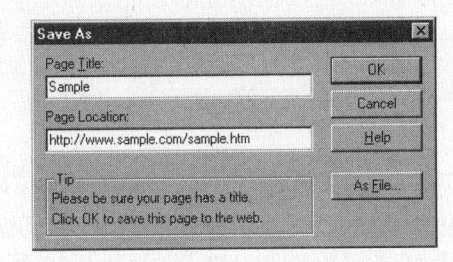

If you have not yet done so, enter a page title; you can also specify a page title at any time in the Page Properties dialog box, which you'll read about later in this chapter. In the Page Location field, you can enter the URL where you want to store the page and then click OK. With the help of the Web Publishing Wizard, the file will be saved at the location you specified. To save the page as a file on your local disk, click the As File button and enter a path and filename for the file.

If you added one or more graphic images to this page from an outside source (such as from the Web or by copying the image from another program), you will be asked if you want to save those images when you save the page. In the dialog box shown here, you can enter a new name for the image file if you choose, and then click the Yes or Yes To All button if there is more than one image. If you don't want to save the image, click the No button.

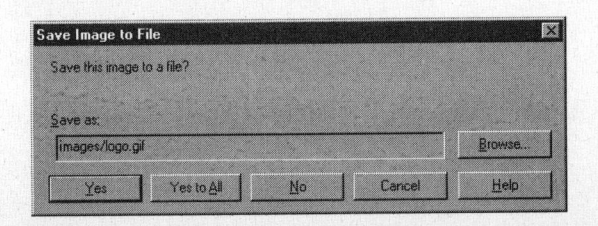

Adding Structure to a Page

HTML offers several elements for creating structure or hierarchy within a page, including horizontal lines, headings, and bulleted or numbered lists. These features can make your Web page more attractive and easier for someone to browse.

> **TIP**
> Tables offer another way to organize a page, into columns and rows. To begin creating a table, place the cursor where you want the table to appear and choose Tables ➢ Insert Table. This displays a dialog box where you can define the size and look of the table. A toolbar button is also available but offers less control in defining the table.

Separating Sections with a Horizontal Line

You can use the Insert ➢ Horizontal Line command to do just that—place a horizontal line in the page. The line is built on the HTML tag <HR> and is often referred to as a horizontal rule. By default, the line spans the entire width of the page in FrontPage or in a browser. It is a simple but effective way to delineate one section from another.

Changing the Look of a Line

To modify the look of a horizontal line in FrontPage, open its Properties dialog box (shown here) by right-clicking the line and choosing Horizontal Line Properties from the shortcut menu.

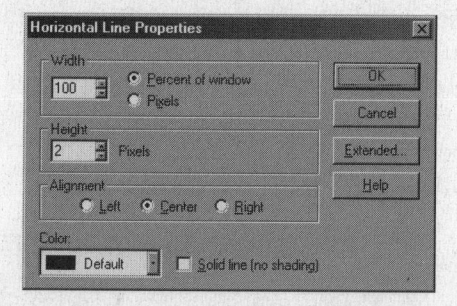

You can change the width, height, alignment, and color of the line:

Width The width of a default line is 100 percent of the width of the window in which it is displayed. Change the percentage to 50 for a line that is half the width of the window. Choose Pixels to specify an exact width for the line, no matter how wide the window may be. If the resulting line is longer than the width of the window, you'll have to scroll to the right in Internet Explorer to see the rest of the line.

Height The default height (thickness) of the line is 2 pixels; increase or decrease the height as needed.

Alignment If you specify a width for the line other than 100 percent, you can choose to align the line to the left or right side of the window, or you can center it within the window.

Color Select a color for the line. You can also choose to display the line with a shadow effect or as a solid line.

When you have modified several of these attributes, the HTML tag will reflect your choices, such as

    <HR ALIGN="left" WIDTH="50%" COLOR="#FF0000">

for a red line that is left-aligned, with a width that is 50 percent of the width of the current window.

INSERTING YOUR OWN ATTRIBUTES FOR AN HTML TAG

The changes you make to the properties of a horizontal line appear as attributes in the HTML tag that creates the line. You're not limited to the options that FrontPage offers, however. If there are other accepted attributes for a tag that FrontPage doesn't provide, you can include new attributes at any time. FrontPage will ignore those it doesn't recognize, but they will be in the page when a browser later views it.

Look for a button labeled "Extended" in the properties or options dialog box for a component in the page, such as a horizontal line, a hyperlink, a marquee, and selected text (Paragraph Properties).

Click that button to open the Extended Attributes dialog box, where you can click the Add button to create a new attribute. You enter the name of the attribute in the Name field and the value of that attribute in the Value field. For example, to create the alignment attribute shown earlier for the horizontal line, you'd enter **align** as the name and **left** as the value. Click OK, and the attribute is added to the list in the Extended Attributes dialog box. You can repeat this process for other attributes, each of which would appear within the tag.

Using Images of Lines

Another way to create a dividing line in a page, which you'll find on many Web sites, is with a linear graphic image. An image can add multiple colors, patterns, or a picture to a page to liven it up. (Working with other kinds of images is discussed in the next chapter.)

NOTE
One small disadvantage of using a graphic image is that it takes time to download. But most line image files are quite small, and if you reuse that image as a horizontal line elsewhere in the page or in the Web site, the browser only needs to download it once.

One easy way to find suitable line images for your pages is to visit the Microsoft Web Gallery at www.microsoft.com/gallery/. You'll find a variety of multimedia components here, including images that can serve as lines (called *rules* at the site, as in *horizontal rule*). You just click one of the names in the list to display that image, then right-click the image, choose Save Picture As from the shortcut menu, and save the image to your local disk. (You'll read more about this great resource and others later in this chapter.)

You can then choose the Insert ➢ Image command in FrontPage to bring that image into a Web page. Several examples of images from Microsoft's gallery that can serve as horizontal dividing lines are shown here.

TIP
Besides Microsoft's Web Gallery, dozens of other sites offer graphic images suitable for Web pages (lots of them are free, too). You can read about these resources and others later in this chapter in "Getting the Picture."

Creating Headings to Subdivide a Page

There are six HTML heading tags, <H1> through <H6>, which you can use to create six levels of headings in a page. The look of each heading depends on the browser in which it is displayed, but what you see in FrontPage is exactly what you'll see in Internet Explorer.

To create a heading for an existing paragraph, click within that text, and then choose one of the six headings from the Change Style drop-down menu on the Format toolbar. You can also select a heading from the list of paragraph styles with the Format ➢ Paragraph command.

To create a new heading before typing any text, move the insertion point to a blank line, choose the heading style you want, and then start typing. When you end the paragraph by pressing Enter, the heading style will not be applied to the next line.

You can align a heading at the left or right side of the window, or you can center it. You can choose the alignment (left is the default) in the Paragraph Properties dialog box, or you can simply click one of the three alignment buttons on the toolbar. The HTML tag for a right-aligned heading looks like this:

    <H1 ALIGN="right">This is the Heading Text</H1>

Organizing Data with Bulleted and Numbered Lists

You can create several types of lists in HTML, such as the ordered, or numbered, list with the <OL> tag, and the unordered, or bulleted, list with the <UL> tag. It's easy to create these types of lists in FrontPage—just click a button and the job is done. To change existing paragraphs in a page into a bulleted list, simply select them all, such as by dragging over them with your mouse, and then click the Bulleted List button on the Format toolbar (or select Bulleted List from the Change Style drop-down menu on the Format toolbar). The process is the same for a numbered list.

> **NOTE**
> To create a new list, click the appropriate list button and type the first item in the list. Press Enter to create the next item in the list, and so on. When you're finished, press Enter twice or press Ctrl+Enter to end the list and return to the normal paragraph formatting.

While the text in this example is still selected, you can click the Numbered List button on the Format toolbar to change the paragraphs to that type of list. You can switch back and forth between the two list styles at any time.

The four items in the left column are shown as they would appear as a bulleted list (center) and as a numbered list (right).

Table of Contents	Table of Contents	Table of Contents
International awards	• International awards	1. International awards
Corporate history	• Corporate history	2. Corporate history
Public education	• Public education	3. Public education
Widget hotline	• Widget hotline	4. Widget hotline

You can nest one list with another so that the second is a subordinate of the first. This allows you to create outlines or tables of contents with indented subheadings. Shown here is the bulleted list from the previous example, this time with a second list nested within it:

Table of Contents

- International awards
- Corporate history
- Public education
    - Kidz Widget Magazine
    - Public television Widget Night
    - Widgets at Home pamphlet
- Widget hotline

NOTE
Although FrontPage displays a different type of bullet in the nested list, not every browser will bother to do so.

Here is how you would create the nested list shown above:

1. At the end of the Public Education line, press Enter to create a new item in the primary list.
2. With the insertion point still on the new line, click the Increase Indent button on the Format toolbar:

Creating Web Pages with FrontPage Express   663

3. Now click the Bulleted List button to turn this new line into an item in a bulleted list (you could make it a numbered list by clicking the Numbered List button).

4. Enter the text for this line and then press Enter, which will create the next item in this nested bulleted list.

5. Continue to create new items until you're finished with the nested list. Then simply move the insertion point to another location in the page or click the Decrease Indent button twice to create a new bullet in the primary list.

> **NOTE**
> You can change the look of a bulleted or numbered list by selecting the list (or only some of the items in it) and choosing Format ➢ Bullets And Numbering or by right-clicking the list and choosing List Properties from the shortcut menu. Then select the list style in the List Properties dialog box.

Formatting Pages

This section deals with the way things look on a page and the way a page looks behind the text and images it displays. You'll learn how to change the formatting of text, paragraphs, and the page itself.

The first thing to remember about formatting your pages in HTML is that it is the *browser* that ultimately determines how your pages are displayed. You can play with page formatting all you want, but once it's out on your Web site, all your design work and artistry may be lost on an older browser that can't support the features you've included. With that said, you are reasonably safe formatting your pages in FrontPage because most of its features are mainstream and part of the HTML specification.

Setting Character Properties

Most of the formatting you can apply to characters in a page—text—is found in the Font dialog box, shown in Figure 22.5. To display it, choose Format ➢ Font or right-click selected text and choose Font Properties from the shortcut menu. The properties, or attributes, that are associated with text include the familiar ones such as bold, italic, underline, subscript, and superscript. You can apply some of these from their buttons on the Format toolbar.

> **TIP**
>
> You can return selected text to its default style (for that paragraph) by choosing Format ➤ Remove Formatting or by pressing Ctrl+Spacebar. This is a quick way to eliminate any changes you've applied to that text, such as a font, font size, or font style.

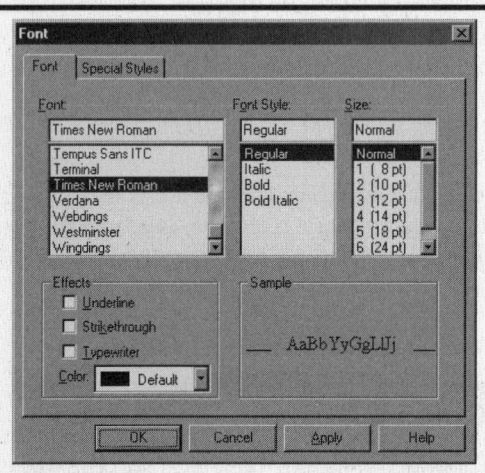

FIGURE 22.5: Choose Format ➤ Font to change the look of selected text with the options in the Font dialog box.

The Font dialog box shown in Figure 22.5 displays the default settings for text in FrontPage. Because we haven't applied any special formatting to the selected text, a browser will display the text in its own default style.

Incidentally, Internet Explorer uses a 12-point Times New Roman font as its default, the same as FrontPage (as shown in the Font dialog box). Nonetheless, you can change that default font in Internet Explorer, as well as the screen magnification (making all fonts larger or smaller than their actual size). What you create in FrontPage may often be displayed quite differently in a browser.

Changing the Font

In the Font dialog box, you can select a specific font from the list of all the fonts available to Windows on your computer. You can also choose a font from the Change Font list on the Format toolbar. Again, keep your eye on the Sample pane in the dialog box to see the effect of your font changes.

The font you choose will appear in the FACE attribute for the <FONT> tag in the HTML code, such as

```
<FONT FACE="Arial">This is not the default font.</FONT>
```

Now comes the big caveat. Any font you apply must also be available to the browser that opens this page from your Web site. If the font you choose isn't on the browser's computer, the browser will display the text in its default font. The result may or may not be to your liking, but those are the breaks when you're publishing on the Web! To play it safe, stay away from the more obscure fonts that other computers aren't likely to have.

When you become more experienced and confident as an HTML author, you can use the View ➢ HTML command and then include multiple font names in the FACE attribute. If a browser doesn't have the first font, it will try the second, and so on until it finds one it does have. Otherwise, it will use its default font. Here's how the previous code looks with alternative fonts included:

```
<FONT FACE="Arial,Helvetica,Humana">This is…</FONT>
```

Changing the Font Style

The choices in the Font Style list give you the expected options of Bold, Italic, and Bold Italic (you can also press Ctrl+B and Ctrl+I as shortcuts for those styles). The Regular choice removes any bold or italic formatting from the selected text. You can also use the Bold and Italic buttons on the Format toolbar to turn those text styles on or off for the selected text.

Changing the Font Size

To change the size of the font, select one of the seven sizes from the Size list. The other choice, Normal, specifies no size so that a browser will use its default font size, whatever that might be.

You can also change the font size from the Format toolbar with either the Increase Text Size or the Decrease Text Size button. Click a button once to change to the next size.

The choices in the Size list range from 1 through 7. A point size is shown in parentheses next to each of those numbers, but use that only as a guide. The font-size choices are HTML-related, and each number represents a *relative* font size that is either bigger or smaller than the default font that a browser is using. Size 3 is assumed to be the default size in any HTML page. If you choose a size bigger than that, the browser will display that text in a font larger than its default font. The resulting HTML code will look like this:

```
<FONT SIZE="5">
```

which displays the text two sizes larger than the default text in a browser. Obviously, specifying a smaller number gives a smaller font.

Setting Paragraph Properties

You can apply a variety of styles that affect entire paragraphs, not just some text within a paragraph. You've already seen some of them, such as the heading tags <H1> through <H6> and the list tags which separate each item in the list into a separate paragraph.

First, select the paragraphs whose style you want to change. To change only the current paragraph, you don't need to select anything; the format will automatically apply to the entire paragraph. Access the paragraph styles either in the Change Style list on the Format toolbar or via the Format ➤ Paragraph command:

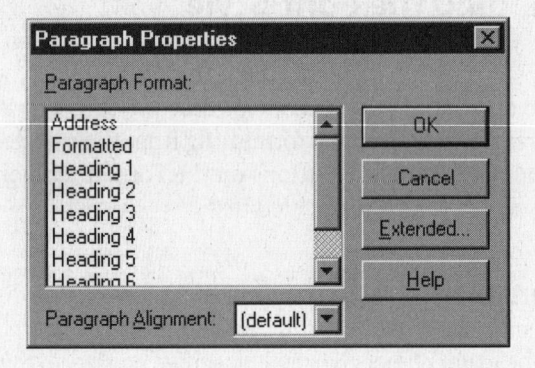

The opening and closing tags for each of these styles surround entire paragraphs. In fact, by definition these tags create paragraphs, so you may not see the regular paragraph tag, <P>, when these paragraph-related format tags are present.

> **NOTE**
> The Normal style is a special case that removes any paragraph formatting and resets the paragraph to its default style.

Creating Web Pages with FrontPage Express

When you create a new paragraph, you can choose whether it should have the same formatting as the preceding paragraph:

- ▶ To begin a paragraph in the same style as the current paragraph, position the insertion point just after the last character in the paragraph and press Enter.

- ▶ To split a paragraph in two and retain the formatting of the original paragraph for both, position the insertion point where you want the split and press Enter.

- ▶ To create a new paragraph after the last paragraph in the page that uses the default style, move to the last line of the paragraph and press ↓ to create a new line and a new paragraph.

The Address style is represented by italicized text in Internet Explorer and most other browsers. It is typically used for paragraphs that contain an address or other contact information, such as an e-mail address or a URL.

> **NOTE**
> You can include text formatting, such as <STRONG> or <EM>, within a paragraph format, such as <H3> or <PRE>. However, only one *paragraph* format can be applied to a paragraph.

The Formatted paragraph style in FrontPage is particularly useful. It uses the <PRE> tag (for *preformatted*). Internet Explorer and other browsers display text in this style in a monospace (fixed-width) font; each character takes up exactly the same amount of space. It is the one instance in HTML when multiple spaces or hard returns are displayed exactly as they appear in the code. You can use the Formatted style to align text in columns or with indentions, and the characters will fall exactly where you expect them. The HTML table obviates some of the need for the Formatted style, but the style is still quite practical and easy to apply when you need to align text.

By default, paragraphs are aligned along the left side of the window, both in FrontPage and Internet Explorer. You can change the alignment of the current paragraph or the selected paragraphs by clicking the appropriate button on the Format toolbar:

You can also choose an alignment from the drop-down menu in the Paragraph Properties dialog box.

You can indent the current paragraph or selected paragraphs from both the left and the right with the Increase Indent button on the Format toolbar. Click the button multiple times to increase the amount of indention. Click the Decrease Indent button to remove indention one level at a time.

Setting Page Properties

A Web page has its own set of properties that you can access by choosing File ➤ Page Properties or by right-clicking anywhere on the page and choosing Page Properties from the shortcut menu. The Page Properties dialog box has four tabs: General, Background, Margins, and Custom.

Changing the Title and Other General Options

In the General tab of the Page Properties dialog box, shown in Figure 22.6, you can view or revise the title for the current page. You usually create a title the first time you save a page. You'll find the <TITLE> tag appearing within the <HEAD> tag near the top of the page's HTML code. You should make the title descriptive of the page, not only for readers of the page, but also because it is often used by Web searching and indexing sites to name your page.

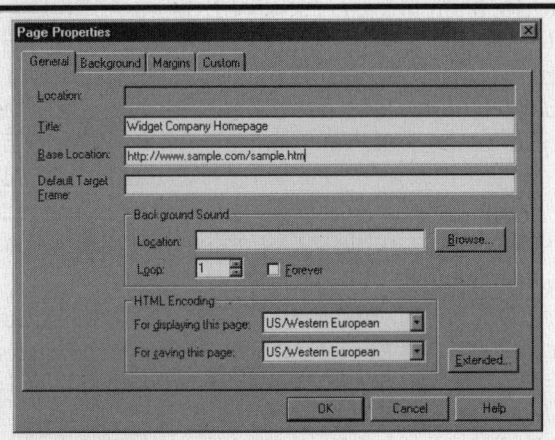

FIGURE 22.6: The General tab of the Page Properties dialog box

Creating Web Pages with FrontPage Express

The Location field shows the page's complete URL or filename. To change a page's name or location, either choose the File ➢ Save As command or rename or move the source file.

You can specify the name of a sound file in the Background Sound options, such as a WAV or MIDI file, that Internet Explorer will play when it opens this page. By default, the sound file is played once, as specified in the Loop field in the Page Properties dialog box; you can increase the number if you want to play the file more than once. Select the Forever checkbox to have the sound play continuously while this page is open in a browser.

> **WARNING**
>
> Visitors to your page may enjoy hearing a short, welcoming sound, but they may be annoyed when that sound plays over and over. Use discretion with the background sound; probably you should never use the Forever option.

Changing the Background Color

Use the options in the Background tab of the Page Properties dialog box (shown here) to set the look of the page's background. You can also access these settings via the Format ➢ Background command. You can specify either a color or an image file that a browser will display as a page's background. These settings are attributes of the page's <BODY> tag.

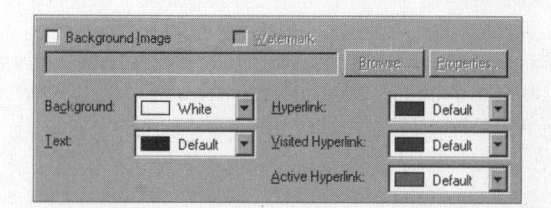

The default setting for the page's background color is white. The setting for text is called Default, in that no color is specified. In other words, a browser will be told to display this page with a white background, but to use its own default color for the text.

You have three options for specifying the colors of hyperlinks. They are all set to Default so that no specific color is specified (the color shown next to each one is the default color in Internet Explorer). It's generally best to leave them this way, unless they conflict with the page's background color;

using your own colors may make it difficult for a reader of this page to recognize text as links.

Specifying a Background Image

You can specify an image file that will serve as the page's background instead of a color. Select the Background Image option in the Background tab and enter the filename of the image, or click the Browse button to select an image.

A browser normally tiles a small image to fill the background completely, so you need not specify a large image. In fact, the smaller the image file, the faster it will load into a browser. Many visitors to a Web site will simply skip over a page if it takes too long to load.

Another aspect of the image file is how well it serves as a background. For example, dropping a stunning M.C. Escher picture into the back of a page of text may make the page almost jump out of the screen at you, but it may also make the text mostly unreadable. You'll find that most background images in use are small and textured, and can be easily tiled together into a seamless background. They provide a muted and comfortable backdrop that will not dominate the page.

Again, you'll find plenty of suitable background images at the Microsoft Web Gallery.

> **NOTE**
> When a background image is tiled to fill a page, Internet Explorer scrolls the background as you scroll the page. If you choose the Watermark option in the Background tab, Internet Explorer leaves the background image stationary while you scroll the page.

Setting Page Margins

You can use the options on the Margins tab of the Page Properties dialog box to specify a top or left margin for the page. By default, they are set to zero so that no margins are specified. You define the margin in pixels, so the actual width of the blank area at the top or left side of the page in a browser depends on the screen resolution for that computer. For this reason and because not all browsers support the MARGINS attribute for the <BODY> tag, avoid setting margins for your pages.

Creating Meta Page Information

You can use the <META> tag to include information in a page that can be read by the server that sends out that page or by the browser that receives it. When included in a page, the <META> tag normally appears within the page's <HEAD> tag. You'll find that this tag is used in many ways. For example, the following tag (shown on two lines) tells the browser to use the Japanese character set:

```
<META HTTP-EQUIV="Content-type"
CONTENT="text/html; charset=x-sjis">
```

Other <META> tags could include a description and keywords to be used by search spiders that come to your site, or rating information so that a browser such as Internet Explorer can determine if the page meets its rating criteria (see Chapter 20 for more about site ratings).

You can create these types of page-definition tags in FrontPage via the Custom tab in the Page Properties dialog box. You can add, modify, or remove what FrontPage refers to as *variables*, which appear within the <META> tag for a page. Creating a variable is much like creating an extended attribute for an HTML tag, as discussed earlier in this chapter.

By default, FrontPage creates two variables for a page. The single system variable tells a browser or server what type of document this is and the character set to use for it. The user variable simply lets the world know which program generated this page.

To create a description that a search engine could use, go to the Custom tab and click the Add button next to the User Variables list. In the dialog box (shown here), enter the attribute **Description** in the Name field and the text that you want to describe the page in the Value field. Click OK, and you'll see this new variable in the list.

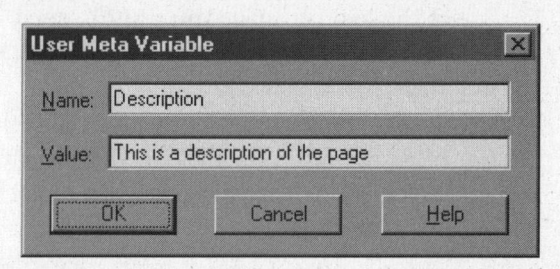

When you click OK to return to the page, choose View ➤ HTML and look for your new tag near the top of the page. It will look something like this:

```
<META NAME="description" CONTENT="This is a description of the page">
```

Any system variables you create will appear as part of the `HTTP-EQUIV` attribute for the `<META>` tag.

Creating Links

You can make a hyperlink in a Web page from either a graphic image or text (which will be displayed in a different color and underlined); click the hyperlink in Internet Explorer to open the link's target resource. You can easily create a document that links to several other documents anywhere on the Web. A hyperlink always contains at least two components:

- The text or image you click to open the link's target file
- The URL of that file (which can be a relative reference or an absolute one)

FrontPage makes it easy to create links because you see the clickable link in the WYSIWYG editing environment, and you create the link in a straightforward dialog box where it's easy to specify the URL of the target.

Creating a New Hyperlink

You can create a link from either text or an image in several ways, but here's the most common way:

1. Select the text or image you want to serve as a hyperlink (either click an image or use the Shift+drag method you would use to select text).

2. Choose Edit ➤ Hyperlink (Ctrl+K) or click the Create or Edit Hyperlink button on the toolbar. This displays the Create Hyperlink dialog box, where you specify the target file of the link in one of its three tabs:

    Open Pages Select the target from a list of all the pages currently open in FrontPage.

Word Wide Web Choose the type of hyperlink to create—such as HTTP, Mailto, or FTP—and then enter the URL of the target.

New Page Enter a page title and a URL to create a new Web page in FrontPage that will serve as the target for the link.

3. When you are finished defining the hyperlink, click the OK button.

If the hyperlink is textual, the selected text is now underlined and displayed in blue. You can edit the text that serves as the link just as you would edit any other text in the page. When you move your mouse over the text or image hyperlink, you'll see the URL of the target displayed on the left side of the status bar.

> **NOTE**
> A *frameset* is one page that displays multiple pages, each in its own frame or window. When the link you're defining will be in a page in a frameset, you can use the Target Frame option to specify the name of the frame in which the target should be displayed.

Creating a Link Automatically

Once you understand how links work, you can take advantage of these other methods to create links:

- Type the URL of the target file (it must begin with a valid protocol, such as HTTP) and press the spacebar; FrontPage automatically defines that text as a link to the URL. You can then revise the text so that it no longer looks like a URL, but the target URL would remain.

- Drag the icon in the Address toolbar in Internet Explorer into your document in FrontPage to create a link to that page. The title of the page will appear as the text of the link, and its URL will be the target.

- Drag a hyperlink from a page in Internet Explorer into your document in FrontPage to create the same link.

- Drag an Internet shortcut (a URL file) into your document in FrontPage to create a link to that URL. For example, choose Favorites ➢ Organize Favorites in Internet Explorer and drag a link from the dialog box.

Linking to a Bookmark

A *bookmark* is simply the FrontPage name for a specific, named location within one page that can serve as the target for a link (you'll read about creating bookmarks a little later in this chapter). You'll also hear the term *destination* or *named target* to describe this HTML feature. When you define a hyperlink by targeting a page listed on the Open Pages tab in the Create Hyperlink dialog box, you can include a bookmark from the page in the URL by selecting it from the Bookmarks drop-down menu.

> **NOTE**
> To create a link to a bookmark in the current page (the page in which you're creating the link), just select that page in the Open Pages tab, and then choose a bookmark from the drop-down menu.

For example, suppose you create a link to a page named GUIDE.HTM that's open in FrontPage, and you select the bookmark in that page named Section 1.0. In HTML, a reference to a bookmark name is preceded by a pound sign (#), so the complete reference for this link is

```
guide.htm#Section 1.0
```

When a reader later clicks the text or the image for this link in a browser, the page GUIDE.HTM will open, and the browser will display the bookmark named Section 1.0 at the top of the screen.

Revising and Deleting a Hyperlink

You can change the text of a hyperlink (the text you click to activate the link) simply by editing it as you would any other text. As long as the text you revise is still underlined, you'll know it's still a link.

You can also change the image for an image hyperlink. Simply right-click the image and choose Image Properties from the shortcut menu. In the Image Properties dialog box, specify the new image in the Image Source field.

To modify the target URL of a hyperlink, select the image (click it) or position the insertion point anywhere within the link text (you need not select any of the text), and choose Edit ➤ Hyperlink or click the Create or Edit Hyperlink button on the toolbar.

You can delete a link from a page in several ways:

- Delete the image or all of the text for the link, and the link to the target file (but not the actual file, of course) will be deleted as well. Keep that in mind when you're simply revising the text of a link, and be careful not to accidentally delete all the text (if you do, remember Undo).

- To delete a link without deleting the link text or link image from the page, select the link image or position the insertion point anywhere within the link text, and then choose Edit ➢ Unlink.

- To remove the link definition from just some of the link text, select that text and choose Edit ➢ Unlink.

- When you're working in the Create Link or Edit Link dialog box, click the Clear button to delete the link definition.

Working with Bookmarks

Creating a bookmark is essentially naming a location in the page so you can then refer to that location by that name in the target of a link. Here's how to do it:

1. Move the insertion point to the line where you want to create the new name.

2. Although you can create a name there without selecting any text, it's a good idea to select the text you want the name to define. That way, if you add more text to the paragraph, the bookmark will still be attached to the text you selected.

3. Choose Edit ➢ Bookmark, which displays the Bookmark dialog box (shown here).

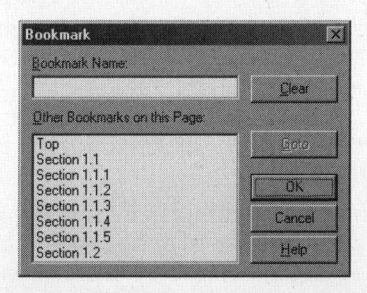

4. Enter the text for the new name in the Bookmark Name field. If you selected some text before invoking the command, you'll find that text already in the field, which you can revise as necessary.

5. When you're finished, click OK.

> **NOTE**
> The name you create for a bookmark should clearly describe the location you're naming so that you or another author can easily find it in the list of bookmarks when you are creating a hyperlink to its page. Try to keep your bookmarks reasonably short, perhaps just a word or two in most cases (spaces are allowed).

The HTML tag for a bookmark is the NAME attribute of the anchor tag. If you selected the text Section 1.2 Production Cycles and then created the bookmark name Section 1.2, here's how the code would look:

```
<A NAME="Section 1.2">Section 1.2 Production Cycles</A>
```

In FrontPage, any text within the opening and closing anchor tags will be underlined with a dashed blue line, as long as the View ➤ Format Marks command is enabled. You can also click the Show/Hide button to toggle this command on or off. Internet Explorer, however, does not indicate any bookmarks within a page (nor does any other browser); it simply uses them as reference points when they are included in hyperlinks.

Within FrontPage, you can jump to any bookmark in a page by selecting it in the Bookmark dialog box (Edit ➤ Bookmark) and clicking the Goto button. If you want to remove this bookmark name (but not the text it defines), click the Clear button.

To revise the name of a bookmark, click anywhere within the text defined as the bookmark, or use the Goto command to get there. In the Bookmark dialog box, you should see the name of that bookmark in the Bookmark Name field. Edit the name as needed, and, when you're done, click the OK button.

> **WARNING**
> If the current page is part of a Web site, changing a bookmark name would affect any links that reference it—those links would no longer target the bookmark. This type of operation requires a little planning and note taking.

WORKING WITH IMAGES

Most images you'll encounter on the Web are either GIF or JPEG files. Both file types compress the image to shrink the file size and, therefore, the time required to download the image. The GIF format can handle images with as many as 256 colors (8-bit). The JPEG format, on the other hand, can handle true-color images (24-bit), making it better suited for photographs or other richly colored images. FrontPage can display either type of image in a page, and you can import many other types of images, but FrontPage will translate them into either the GIF or the JPEG format.

Getting the Picture

Even if you aren't an artist, you can add interesting and lively pictures to your Web pages in lots of ways. Some may already be at your fingertips, and others are just waiting for you to access them.

The first thing to remember is that you can right-click any image in any Web page you're viewing in Internet Explorer and choose Save Picture As to save that picture to your local disk. Instant art—although common courtesy and copyright laws usually dictate that you aren't allowed to borrow someone else's work if you plan to use it for commercial purposes.

> **NOTE**
> You might want to create an archive of useful images on your own disk so that you can reuse them in the future. You could follow the lead of many Web sites that supply images by placing them in relevant folders, such as Buttons, Lines, Backgrounds, Photographs, and the like. When you're collecting GIF and JPEG images, there's no need to fuss with compressing these files to save disk space, because those file formats are already compressed about as small as they can be.

You may already have thousands of pictures scattered among the disks and CDs you own. Many software packages, including the major office suites, come with a collection of clip art. You'll generally want to use only GIF and JPEG images in your Web pages, but you can convert other image types in many ways, such as by inserting them into a FrontPage document and saving them to disk.

The Web is burgeoning with an ever-growing number of sources of great drawings, clip art, photographs, animations, and so on. You can even keep your credit card safely ensconced in your wallet, because many of these images are free. The first place to visit is the Microsoft Web

Gallery, where you'll find a great collection of images that you can use as buttons, icons, page backgrounds, lines, and more. Another site is Andy's Art Attack at www.andyart.com where you can find loads of art for your Web pages. Then pay a visit to the Yahoo category `Computers and Internet: Graphics` for a long list of sites you might want to visit.

Don't forget that you can use a scanner to create an image from any drawings or photographs you have, and inexpensive video capture devices are available, as well. When the output from your scanning will be displayed on the screen at a modest resolution, just about any scanner will do. This is especially true when you consider that a small file size is the ultimate goal for any art you include in a Web page, because that file must be downloaded (often at modem speeds) to be viewed.

Creating an Inline Image

Inline images are those displayed as part of a page, without requiring the user to click a link. Because HTML pages are always just plain text, an inline image is actually stored as a separate image file, which is then opened and displayed along with the page in a browser. Of course, you can also specify an image file as the target of a hyperlink, so a browser will open and display only that image when you activate its hyperlink. To bring an image file into a page:

1. Position the insertion point where you want the image to appear (although you can move the image later).

2. Choose Insert ≻ Image to open the Image dialog box. (To insert a video clip, choose Insert ≻ Video.)

3. Enter the name and location of an image file, either a location on disk or a URL. You can click the Browse button to select a file from disk in a standard Windows files dialog box. To display only files of a certain type, such as Bitmap (`BMP`) or TIFF (`TIF`), select that type from the Files of Type drop-down menu.

4. When you click OK to close the Image dialog box, the image you selected is inserted into the page.

> **NOTE**
> When you insert an animated GIF image into your document, it will appear to be static. You won't see its animations until you open the page and image in Internet Explorer.

In addition to using the Insert ➤ Image command, you can bring an image into a page in the usual Windows way. Select the image in another program and choose Edit ➤ Copy, then switch to FrontPage and choose Edit ➤ Paste. You can also drag an image from another program into FrontPage, assuming that both programs are visible on the screen at the same time.

In Internet Explorer, you can also save the image to disk by right-clicking the image and choosing Save Picture As. In FrontPage, you can then choose Insert ➤ Image to bring that image into your document.

> **NOTE**
> As we mentioned earlier in this chapter, when you save a page that contains new images that are not available locally, you will be asked if you want to save the images to disk. This ensures that you have a local copy of each image always available, and it lets you make changes to those images without affecting their source files.

The HTML code FrontPage uses for an image in a page includes the name of the image (ARROW.GIF in this case) and its size, such as

```
<IMG SRC="images/arrow.gif" WIDTH="40" HEIGHT="38">
```

In the next section, you'll read about adjusting the look of an inline image.

Setting Image Properties

When you click an image to select it, you'll see selection handles appear at each corner and in the middle of each side. You can move the selected image by dragging it, or you can change its size by dragging any of its selection handles (you'll read about changing image sizes later in the chapter).

You can also choose Edit ➤ Image Properties or right-click the image and choose Image Properties from the shortcut menu, to display the Image Properties dialog box, shown in Figure 22.7. In the General tab, you can specify a different source file for the image. All the other settings will now apply to the new image. The alternative is to delete the image and start over (select the image and choose Edit ➢ Clear or press Del).

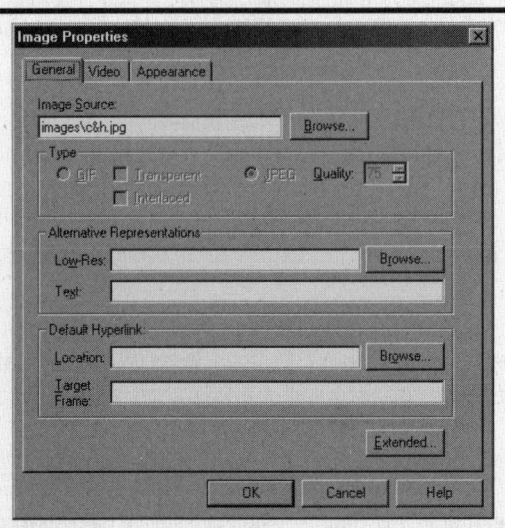

FIGURE 22.7: You can adjust the settings for an image in the Image Properties dialog box.

Choosing the Image Type

If the image you inserted into the page is a GIF or JPEG file, that option will already be selected in the Type group of options in the Image Properties dialog box. If the image is any other type of file, choose either the GIF or the JPEG option, which is how the image will be saved when you save this page.

With the GIF option, you can also choose to make the image Interlaced. When the image is displayed in a browser, it will seem to fill its allotted space faster, sort of "coming into focus," instead of appearing line by line from the top down. Of course, you'll only notice this effect when the image file is fairly large and it takes more than a second or two to download and display.

When you select the JPEG option, the image is saved in that format when you save the page. You can specify the amount of compression to apply when the image is saved by adjusting the value in the Quality field—the higher the number, the lower the compression, so lower the Quality setting if you want to shrink the file size.

Specifying an Alternative to the Image

The Image Properties dialog box lets you specify two alternatives to an image. If the image is large and will take some time to download to a browser, you can specify a second, smaller image (smaller in file size) in the Low-Res option (low resolution). Internet Explorer will download and display this image first, so the person viewing the page can see the image relatively quickly, even if it is a low-resolution version of the larger, primary image.

The second alternative is the Text option. Any text you enter here will be available to browsers to display, such as when the image is not available or when the browser is not accepting images. In Internet Explorer, you'll see this text in a ToolTip when the mouse pointer is over the image.

The Default Hyperlink option is relevant only when the image is being used as an image map. It allows you to define the target that will be opened when a viewer clicks outside a defined hotspot in the image map.

> **TIP**
> If you need to create image maps, you'll probably want to get a copy of FrontPage 98 or a similar full-featured Web publishing package.

Specifying Image Alignment

If you place an inline image within the text of a paragraph, it appears in that same position in Internet Explorer. For example, the following code

```
<P>This text is before the image<IMG
SRC="images\rightarrow.gif"> and this text is after it.</P>
```

would look something like this in Internet Explorer:

This text is before the image ➡ and this text is after it.

The bottom of the image is aligned with the baseline of the text. If you were to type more text to the left of the image, that text would then appear to the left of the image in Internet Explorer. You can change alignment and size of an image with the options in the Appearance tab in the Image Properties dialog box:

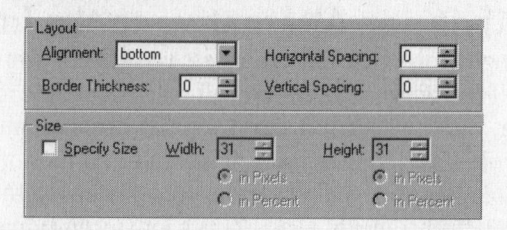

If you choose Right for the Alignment option, the image will now align with the right side of the window in Internet Explorer and look something like this:

This text is before the image and this text is after it.

Of course, if you maximized the Internet Explorer window, there could be a lot of blank space between this short line of text and the image to its right.

In the Horizontal Spacing option, you can specify the amount of space (in pixels) between the image and any text, image, or window edge to its left or right. The Vertical Spacing option determines the amount of space above or below the image. Finally, to enclose the image in a border, specify its thickness (in pixels) in the Border Thickness field. The default is zero, so no border is displayed.

Specifying Image Size

By default, an image is displayed in its actual size, so an image that is 200×200 pixels will take up that amount of room on the screen. You can change the size of an image in two ways.

The easiest but less precise way is simply to select the image in the page and then drag one of its selection handles to expand or contract the image. If you drag a corner handle, the image's width and height will both be changed and the image's original proportions will be maintained. If you drag a handle from the center of one of the sides, you can shrink or enlarge just one dimension of the image.

Creating Web Pages with FrontPage Express

The more precise way to change the size of an image is with the Size options on the Appearance tab in the Image Properties dialog box:

1. Select the Specify Size checkbox, enabling the sizing options to its right.

2. Choose how to define the image's width and height. To specify an exact size, select the In Pixels checkbox. To size the image in relation to the window in which it is displayed, choose In Percent.

3. Enter a number in the Width and Height fields. If you have chosen In Percent, the largest number you can enter is 100.

When you change the size of an image, you are also changing the way it looks. If you stretch an image in only one dimension, the image may end up looking silly. If you enlarge an image to three or four times its original size, it may end up looking "grainy."

Some examples of changing an image's size are shown below. The image on the left is its original size, 40 pixels wide by 38 pixels tall. The size of the second image has been doubled in both directions (80×76 pixels); the graininess is one effect of that enlargement. The width of the third image and the height of the fourth image have been doubled, and you can see the "fun-house mirror" effect taking hold.

What's Next?

This chapter has given you a wide-ranging tour of many of the everyday features you'll use in FrontPage Express. It's a great program that makes the perfect complement to Internet Explorer. In the next chapter, *Finding and Downloading Windows Software Online*, we'll conclude our discussion of Windows 98 SE's Internet features with a look at searching the Web, downloading files, and shopping online.

Chapter 23

FINDING AND DOWNLOADING WINDOWS SOFTWARE ONLINE

Once you've had the chance to explore the Web a bit, you may start wondering how you're ever going to *find* anything there. As easy as it is to follow tangents and get lost wandering from interesting site to interesting site, there's no clear path through the Web and no obvious way to find a destination if you don't know its address.

That's not a problem as long as you're content to browse and surf. But for most users, it doesn't take long before we are looking for something in particular. It might be information—job opportunities in Vancouver, for example, or the natural history of the bluebelly lizard, or pictures from Mars—or it might be software. Suppose you've heard that there's a demo version of a great new program available for downloading from the Web. It's free, for 30 days. You know the name of the program, approximately, but not the software publisher. And, of course, you didn't get the URL. Or maybe, after reading about hardware upgrading

Adapted from *The Internet: No Experience Required*
by Christian Crumlish
ISBN 0-7821-2168-3   528 pages $24.99

earlier in this book, you've decided to see if there's a new driver for your printer or video adapter. In any of these cases, you've got some Web-searching to do.

Fortunately, various clever individuals and companies have set up sites to help you find information on the Web. Although there's no single, definitive location for searching, there are, in fact, quite a few ways to search the Web (and more coming on line all the time), and the Net is changing so rapidly that any central listing of sites presented in a book would be out of date almost before it was published. Still, the process of "mapping the Net" is going on all the time, and the work in progress is usually useful enough to help you find what you're looking for.

Because there's no single, definitive way to search the Web, it's sometimes best to try several different approaches. This chapter introduces you to a few different ways to search (by subject, keyword, date, or language) and different search tools, such as AltaVista and Yahoo!.

Later, you'll see how to download (save) files from the Web to your own computer and how to buy stuff online.

What's New with Searching?

With Microsoft Internet Explorer, you can type search terms directly into the address box and get results back from your default search page (which you can change if you prefer a different place to search from). As the Net continues to grow exponentially and becomes more complicated along the way (as if it weren't chaotic and confusing enough!), you can be sure that new, sophisticated search mechanisms will appear on the market, helping you zero in on the information or resources you need.

Searching the Web

Most of the search tools on the Web offer two models for finding specific information. One model is that of a directory, organized by topic and subtopic, something like a yellow pages phone book. The other model is that of a searchable index, where you enter a keyword to search for, and the search page gives you a list of suggested sites that seem to match what you're searching for. You'll see an example of each approach.

Searching through a Directory

One of the best directories on the Web is the Yahoo! site. To see it for yourself, type http://www.yahoo.com into the address box at the top of your Web browser. Figure 23.1 shows how Yahoo! looks as I'm writing this. Remember, most Web sites update their design and layout from time to time, so the site may look slightly different to you today.

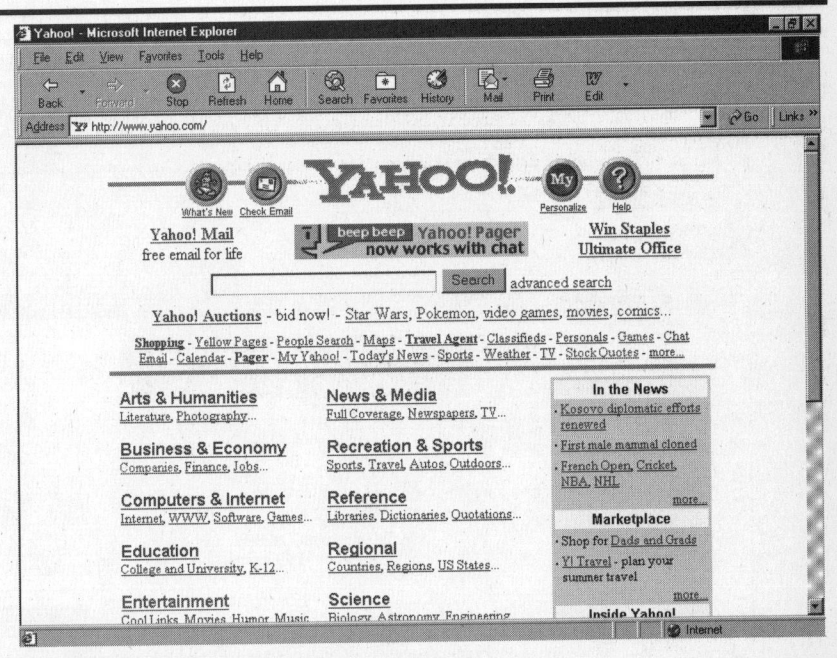

FIGURE 23.1: The popular Yahoo! directory site

> **TIP**
> Make a Favorites listing in Internet Explorer (or bookmark in Navigator) for Yahoo!, as discussed in Chapter 19, *Browsing the Web with Internet Explorer*, (or 21, *An Alternative to Internet Explorer: Netscape Navigator*), so you can come back here easily any time you want to start looking around.

Searching by Topic

Yahoo! is organized hierarchically, which means that you can start with a general topic area and then narrow to more specific topics as you go.

Some of the major subtopics are listed under each topic as well, so you can skip one step, if you like.

Let's say you're interested in finding some Windows programs on the Internet. You could start by choosing the Computers and Internet link on Yahoo!'s main search page.

This will take you to Yahoo!'s Computers and Internet page (see Figure 23.2).

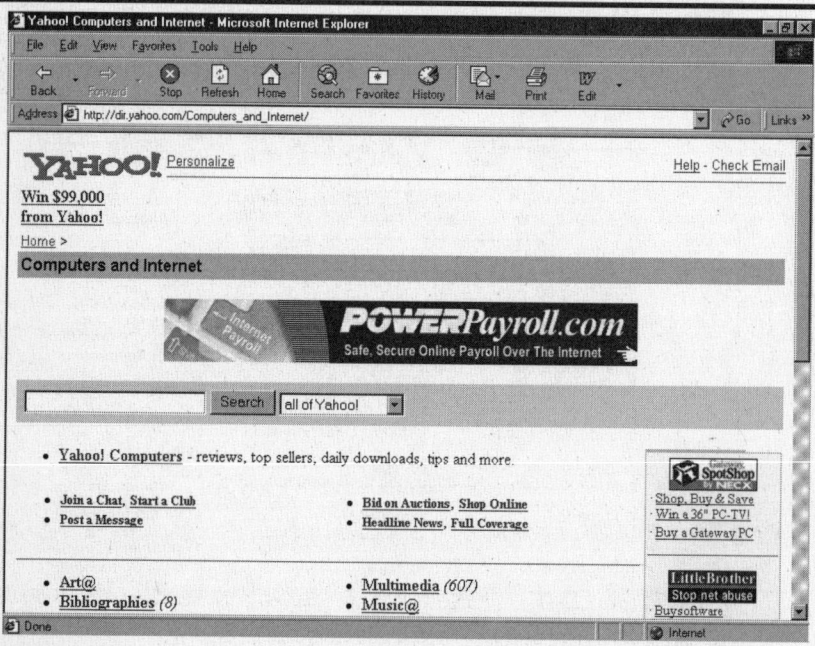

FIGURE 23.2: You can get to the Computers and Internet page by clicking the Computers and Internet link in Yahoo!'s main search page.

If you scroll down the page, you'll see that one of the sub-subtopics is Software. (An @ sign after a listing means that topic appears in several different places in Yahoo!'s listings—this means you can reach topics of interest by more than one route, without having to read the minds of the people who set up the site.) Click Software to go to the list of pages on that subject (see Figure 23.3).

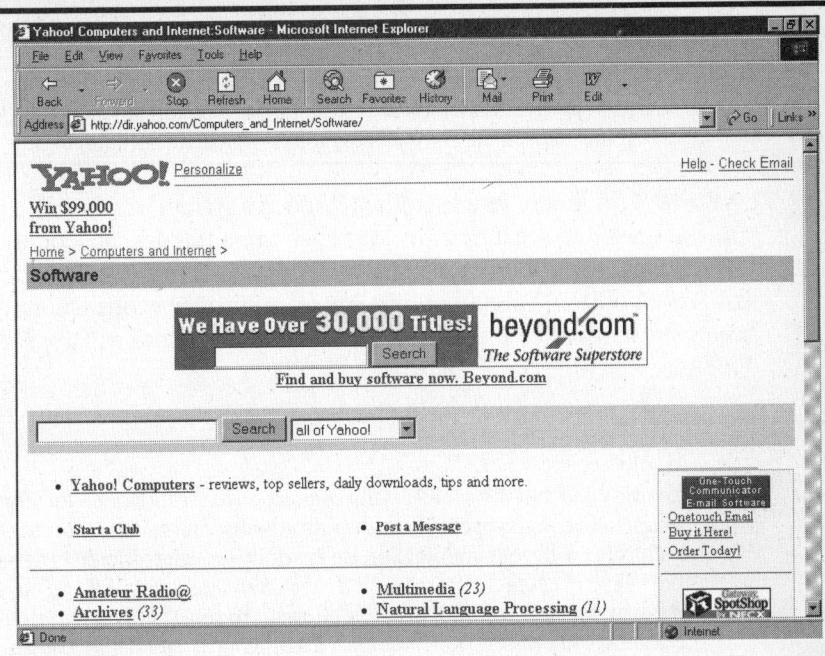

Finding and Downloading Windows Software Online 689

FIGURE 23.3: The Computers and Internet: Software page at Yahoo!

> **TIP**
> Remember to use the Back button if you want to return to a previous topic in Yahoo!'s hierarchies.

Needless to say, there's plenty on this page that sounds interesting. If you'd like to look for general-purpose Windows programs, simply click the link to Shareware and then click Microsoft Windows. From here, you'll be able to access sites that offer tens of thousands of Windows programs.

Searching by Keyword

Of course, it's not always easy to guess where a page or topic might be listed in an organized structure such as Yahoo!'s. Fortunately, the site also includes a search feature at the top of each page.

To perform a search, type a word (or a few words, to make the search more specific) in the box near the top of the page, and then click the Search button.

> **TIP**
>
> If you perform your search from any of the pages besides the home page, you have the choice of searching the entire Yahoo! directory (Search All of Yahoo!) or just the items in the current category (Search Just This Category).

So, let's say you're interested in a Windows system monitoring program and want to see if there are any such programs available on the Net. Type the phrase **Windows system monitor** into the search box and click the Search button. Yahoo! quickly returns a list of categories relating in some way or another to your keywords (in fact, the word will appear in bold type in a blurb for each category).

> **NOTE**
>
> Keep in mind that the speed of your connection to the Internet—for most home and small-business users, that's the rate at which your computer's modem communicates with your Internet Service Provider—is what ultimately determines the speed of category searches and other Web interactions. If you have a fast modem, be sure your ISP account allows it to run at full speed; there is no advantage in owning a 56K modem if it's running at 33K. A direct network connection to the Internet, typically found in larger organizations, is much faster than a modem connection, and delays are unlikely in search operations.

Note that there are some programs listed, but there are many extraneous entries listed too because each of those pages contains the words **Windows** and **system** and **monitor**. To search for an exact phrase, simply enclose your phrase in quotes. The **"Windows system monitor"** search turns up only the programs you're looking for, as shown in Figure 23.4.

From there, all you have to do is start clicking the most promising looking files or sites.

Searching with a Search Engine

Now that you know how to search the contents of a directory hierarchically, it's easy to perform a search of the entire Net. Most search engines allow you to enter specific, even complicated, search queries, much like ones you would submit to a database program. Fortunately, for your everyday searches you shouldn't need those advanced features. Instead, a single keyword—or a couple, for a narrower search (such as *Windows screen saver* or *Windows animated cursors*)—will usually do the job.

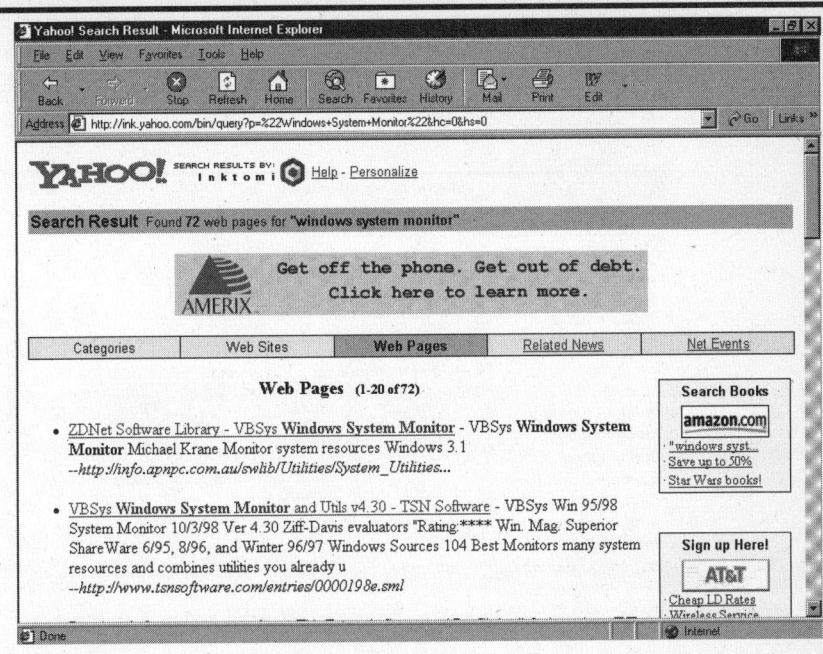

Finding and Downloading Windows Software Online 691

FIGURE 23.4: Some of the Windows system monitoring-related pages listed as the result of a Yahoo! search

One of the more popular search engines is AltaVista at `http://www.altavista.com` (see Figure 23.5).

> **TIP**
> Make a Favorites listing (or bookmark) for the AltaVista site as well.

As with the search feature in Yahoo!, just type a keyword (or several words) into the box and click the Search button. AltaVista will return a list of sites, ranked in order of their likeliness to match your keywords (this is especially useful when you've entered more than one word). Figure 23.6 shows the results of an AltaVista search on the phrase *Windows screen saver*.

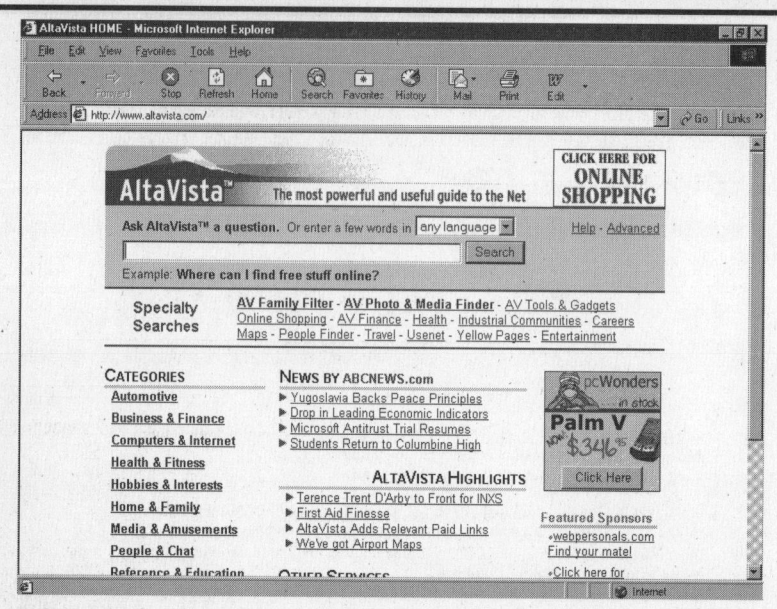

FIGURE 23.5: The AltaVista search engine is powerful and easy to use.

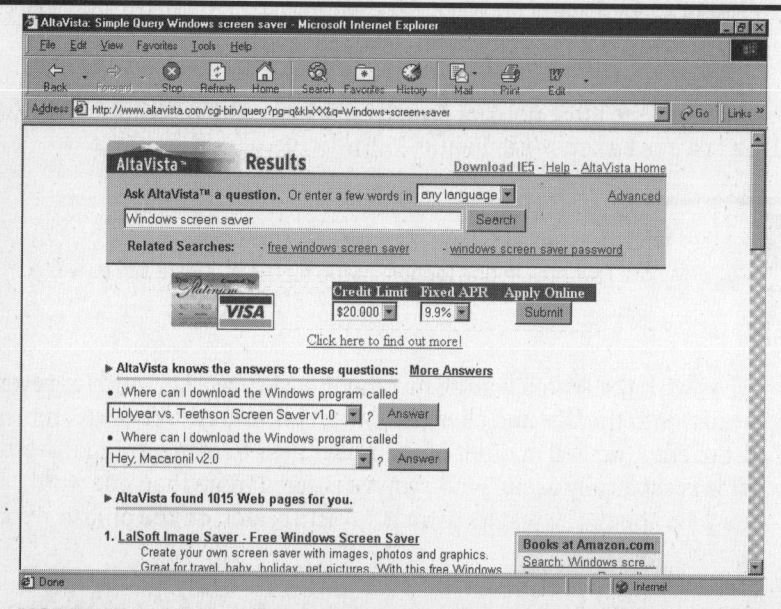

FIGURE 23.6: Web sites turned up by AltaVista in a search using the phrase *Windows screen saver*

Finding and Downloading Windows Software Online 693

Click any of the hyperlinked listings to visit the listed site.

Unlike Yahoo!, the AltaVista search engine displays the same 1015 sites that best match the search terms *Windows screen saver*, regardless of whether you include the quotation marks. The most relevant sites are listed first. In addition, you can pose a question in any of several languages or click the Advanced button to narrow the search to certain dates or enter a Boolean expression.

Refining Your Search

Sometimes your first attempt to search for a topic will fail. You won't find what you're looking for, or you'll get so many results that you won't have time to review them all. When this happens, you need to refine your search. If you're getting no results or too few, you'll have to come up with an alternate search term that's more general than whatever you tried at first.

If you're getting too many results, you can try to narrow your search. At any search site (or directory), you can enter more than one keyword to get results containing any one of the words you enter. This broadens the search, though, instead of narrowing it. To limit the pages you find to those that match more than one word, you need to require that *each* word match, not just *any*. At most search pages, you do this by preceding each required keyword with a plus sign, but check the help or hints section of the search engine you prefer to see what options are available to you there.

> **NOTE**
> At some search sites, you can also narrow your search by date (type in a very recent range to get only the sites that were updated a short time ago), by language (English is a good place to start), or by stringing together search words with the *logical operator* "AND" (*screen saver AND fish*, for example, will match sites that have both of these phrases). In addition to AltaVista, HotBot (at www.hotbot.com) offers this capability.

Visiting a Central Search Page

Most of the popular Web browsers have a shortcut to one or more directory or search pages built into the program.

In Microsoft Internet Explorer, click Search and then click the Customize button to open the Customize Search Settings dialog box, as shown in Figure 23.7. You can then specify to always use only one search service, or you can accept the default option, which is to use the Search Assistant.

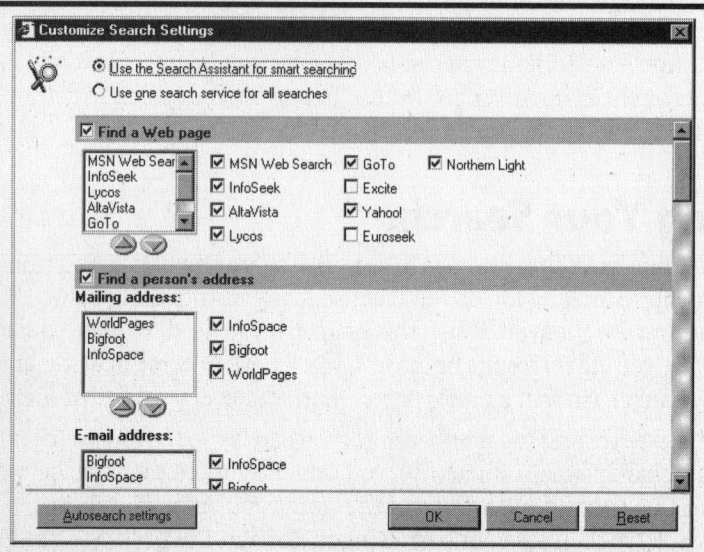

FIGURE 23.7: Using the Internet Explorer Search Assistant

In the Customize Search Settings dialog box, you can specify search services and what to search for, including the following:

- A Web page
- A person's mailing address
- An e-mail address
- A business
- A category
- An address on a map
- A place name on a map
- A term in an encyclopedia, a dictionary, or a thesaurus
- A picture
- Information in a newsgroup

TIP
In Windows 98 SE, choose Start ➤ Find ➤ On The Internet to open the Search bar in Internet Explorer.

Some Search Addresses

Here are the Web addresses of some other good directories and search pages:

Resource	Web Address
Excite	http://www.excite.com
Infoseek	http://infoseek.go.com
Lycos	http://www.lycos.com
Magellan	http://magellan.excite.com

Downloading and Decompressing Files

Sometimes when you search the Net you're looking for information, but often you're looking for files to download from the Internet to your computer. For example, a lot of software is available either for free or as *shareware* (meaning you're expected to pay for it after evaluating it, if you decide to keep using it). Also, a lot of programs, especially Internet-related software programs, are updated from time to time, with newer versions being available for downloading from the Net.

NOTE
Coming soon are programs that can update themselves whenever the developer adds a new feature. This may lead to more programs being sold on a subscription basis instead of as a one-time license. There are already programs, such as online service interfaces, that you can upgrade by choosing commands within the program itself.

Once you start using Internet software (such as Web browsers, news readers, mail programs, and so on), you have to get used to the idea that if you want to have the latest version of the program, you occasionally have to check the software manufacturer's Web site to download the latest update.

Regardless of your reason for downloading a file, the procedure with most Web browsers is much the same. It generally involves finding your way to the appropriate site, working your way through a few links, and ultimately clicking a link that connects directly to the file in question. When you do this, your browser will realize that you've requested something that can't be displayed in a browser window, and it will offer to download or even try to run the file for you.

> **TIP**
>
> The file you're downloading may be a compressed file. See "Compression Programs" later in this chapter for tips on how to "unsquish" files.

Figure 23.8 shows the dialog box that Internet Explorer displays when you click a link to download a file.

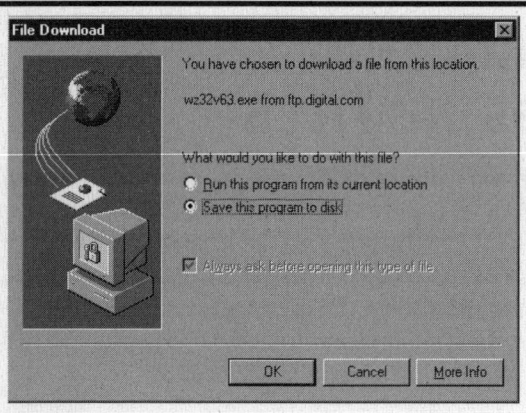

FIGURE 23.8: Internet Explorer gives you choices when you download a file.

Be sure to select Save This Program To Disk. After you click OK, the Save As dialog box appears; here you should select a folder where you want to save the file. Usually a Temp folder is best, since most of the time you'll be unpacking a compressed file or running an installation program to actually set up the software you're downloading.

Finding and Downloading Windows Software Online 697

TIP
If you need to create a Temp folder, just switch to Windows Explorer. Once you're ready, click the browser's icon in the Taskbar to resume downloading.

Your browser will then download the file, showing you its progress either in a special dialog box or in the bottom-right corner of the browser window.

WARNING
Be careful when downloading files from the Internet. Only take files from reputable sources. If you download a file from some unofficial archive, it could easily contain a virus or other software designed to damage your computer. If you're downloading from a well-established company site, though, you usually have nothing to worry about.

DOWNLOADING AND VIRUS PROTECTION

Viruses are prankish computer programs written by renegade programmers to play tricks on your files and your system. Most viruses enter your system from files downloaded from the Internet, although some viruses can be picked up from contaminated files sent to you via e-mail or on a floppy disk or other storage media. (You cannot "infect" your system with a virus simply by reading an e-mail message; but you can do so by running an infected executable file attached to a message.)

An entire software industry has sprung up to deliver products to protect computers, programs, and company networks from viruses. These programs can scan files for viruses, remove the viruses, and notify you if you are about to download a file containing a virus. Antivirus software is often bundled with new computers; if you already have such a program, you'll probably see its "splash" screen as part of the startup sequence.

If you don't have an antivirus program yet, you can download one from the Internet. You can use the search tools described earlier to find a site. In Yahoo!, for example, try the following sequence of categories: Business and Economy: Companies: Computers: Software: System Utilities: Utilities: Virus Protection.

CONTINUED ➞

> Once you have an antivirus program, get in the habit of using it. With a virus scanner installed, you can simply right-click an executable file in Windows Explorer, and Scan for Viruses will appear as one of the context-menu options.
>
> See Chapter 20, *Browsing with a Sense of Security*, to learn about related security features in Internet Explorer.

COMPRESSION PROGRAMS

Files archived for downloading are usually stored in a compressed format. Each of the major platforms (Windows, Macintosh, and Unix) has its own compression standards. Fortunately, files intended for a specific platform are invariably compressed in a format favored on that platform. Compressed Windows (or DOS) files usually end in `.zip`, `.arc`, or `.lhz`, with `.zip` being by far the most common. If you're a Windows user, get yourself an up-to-date copy of WinZip (and pay for it—it's shareware and a bargain at the price). It "speaks" all the major PC compression formats and is easy to use. Compressed files that end in .exe are self-extracting. Just double-click the icon when it's finished downloading.

Downloading WinZip

If you do happen to download a file ending in .zip instead of .exe, you have obtained a zip *archive*, or a file that contains many other files in compressed format. You need to unzip this archive with the WinZip program (or another unzipping program) before you can use the files inside it. The following steps will take you through the process to download WinZip:

1. Open your browser and log on to your Internet service. In the browser Address window, type **http://www.winzip.com**. WinZip's home page (sponsored by WinZip's owner, Niko Mak Computing, Inc.) is shown in Figure 23.9.

Finding and Downloading Windows Software Online

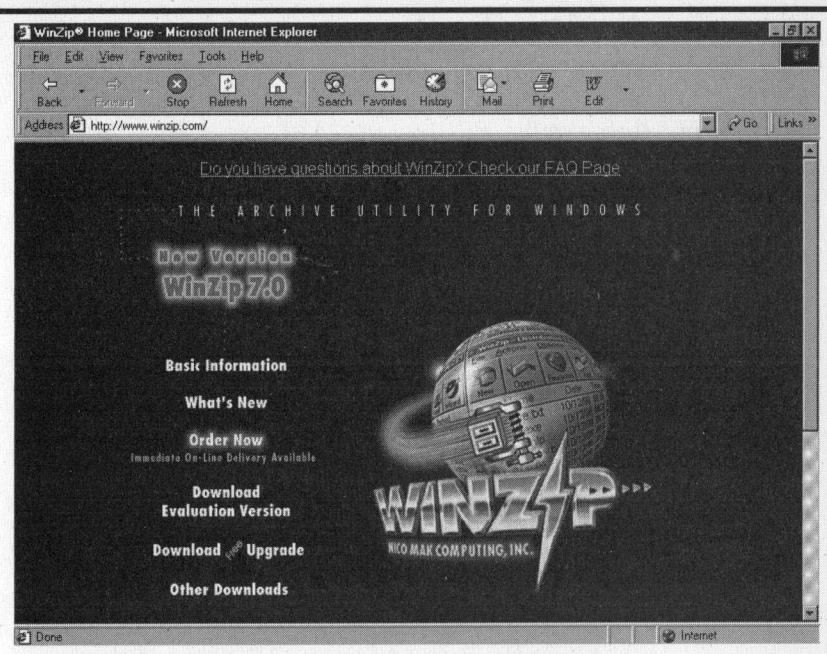

FIGURE 23.9: Download an evaluation copy of WinZip from `http://www.winzip.com` by clicking Download Evaluation Version and then choosing the correct version of the program.

2. Click Download Evaluation Version. Instruct your browser where on your hard drive you want the file downloaded.

3. When the file is finished downloading, you will have WinZip in an `.exe` (self-extracting) archive called `winzip70.exe` or something similar, depending on which version you downloaded.

4. Exit from your Web browser and disconnect from the Internet.

> **NOTE**
> WinZip is a shareware program. It's OK to evaluate it for 30 days, but after that, you should pay Niko Mak Computing for an official copy. The WinZip Web site has information on online ordering of an official copy at `http://www.winzip.com`.

Using the WinZip Program

After you download WinZip and exit from your browser, use My Computer or Explorer to open the folder you downloaded WinZip into. When you find the `.exe` file, such as `winzip70.exe`, follow these directions:

1. Double-click `winzip70.exe` to begin installing WinZip. Then click the Setup button in the WinZip Setup dialog box. In the second WinZip Setup box, type in a different directory name in the Install To text box if you prefer something other than `C:\Program Files\WinZip`, and then click OK.

2. You will see the first WinZip Setup screen, extolling the virtues of WinZip. Click Next when you are finished reading.

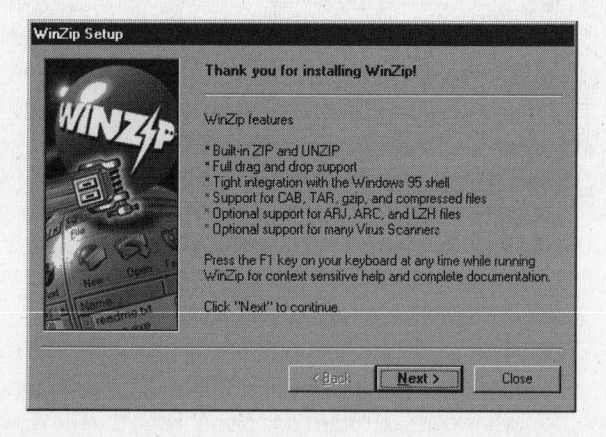

3. Click View License Agreement in the License Agreement And Warranty Disclaimer dialog box. You can print out the agreement or just read it on the screen. Click Close when you are finished and click Yes if you agree to the agreement's terms.

4. In the second WinZip Setup screen, you have two choices:

    ▶ Select Start with the WinZip Wizard option if you are new to this program and would like to be guided through its basic features.

    ▶ Select the Start with WinZip Classic to use all of WinZip's features with less wizard help.

Finding and Downloading Windows Software Online

5. Click Next, and in the next screen, click Next so that the Wizard searches for and adds folders to include in the Favorite Zip Folders folder.

6. In the Favorite Zip Folders dialog box, click OK to add the folders that the Wizard found. (You can remove these folders at any time.)

7. The setup is complete, and you can click Next to start the program or Close to exit from Setup.

It's easy to switch back and forth between the WinZip Wizard, which guides you through the entire zipping process, and WinZip Classic, which just brings up the standard program. If you selected Start with the WinZip Wizard during the installation, you will be greeted by the Wizard screen shown here each time you start the program.

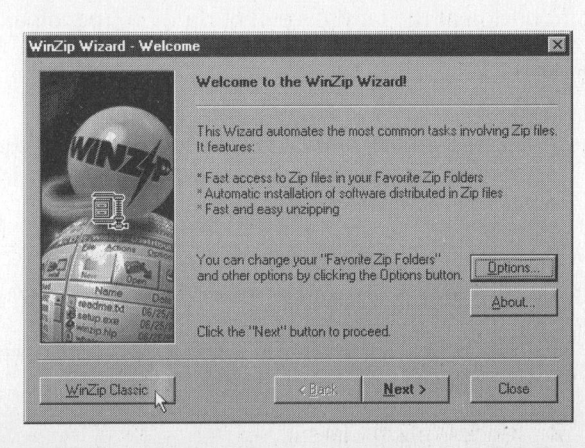

Click the Options button to specify how your zip folders will be handled, or select Next to proceed with the Wizard, which will assist you in unzipping archives and installing programs from zipped archives you may have already downloaded, such as the antivirus programs discussed earlier. You can also click the WinZip Classic button in the WinZip Wizard to close the Wizard and proceed with the basic program, shown next.

> **NOTE**
> Click Close to hide the WinZip Tip Of The Day dialog box.

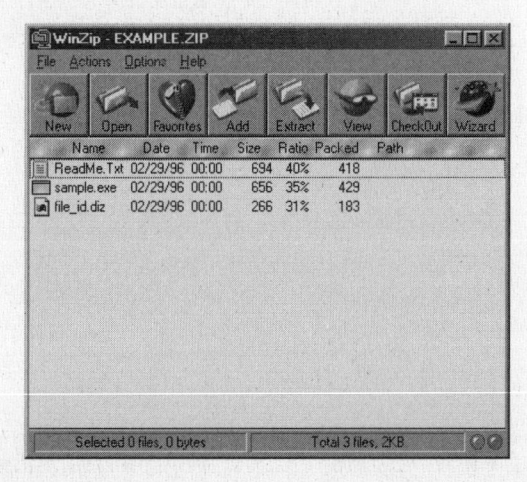

WinZip's interface is simple, and you can learn more about it by using the WinZip Wizard or by selecting Help ➤ Brief Tutorial or Help ➤ Hints And Tips. You can activate the WinZip Wizard at any time by clicking the Wizard button at the far right end of the WinZip toolbar.

> **TIP**
> If you use the WinZip Wizard to open your archive and extract files, it will also activate the Setup program if there happens to be one in the zip archive you obtained or downloaded.

To open a zip archive and unzip, or *extract*, the files inside of it, follow these steps in WinZip Classic:

1. Double-click the WinZip Desktop shortcut, or choose Start ➤ WinZip.
2. Click WinZip Classic.

Finding and Downloading Windows Software Online 703

3. Click the Open button in the WinZip Classic toolbar, or select File ➤ Open Archive.

4. Browse through your hard drive in the Open Archive dialog box until you find the zip archive, and then highlight it and click the Open button.

5. Highlight all the files in the archive by clicking the top one and then pointing to the last file and shift-clicking it. Then click the Extract button or choose Actions ➤ Extract.

6. Browse through your folders in the Extract dialog box to specify where the unzipped files should be placed, and then click Extract.

7. Choose File ➤ Close Archive, and then choose File ➤ Exit to leave WinZip.

Shareware.com

A good "one-stop-shopping" place to go to download the latest version of software available free on the Net is C|NET's Shareware.com site (see Figure 23.10).

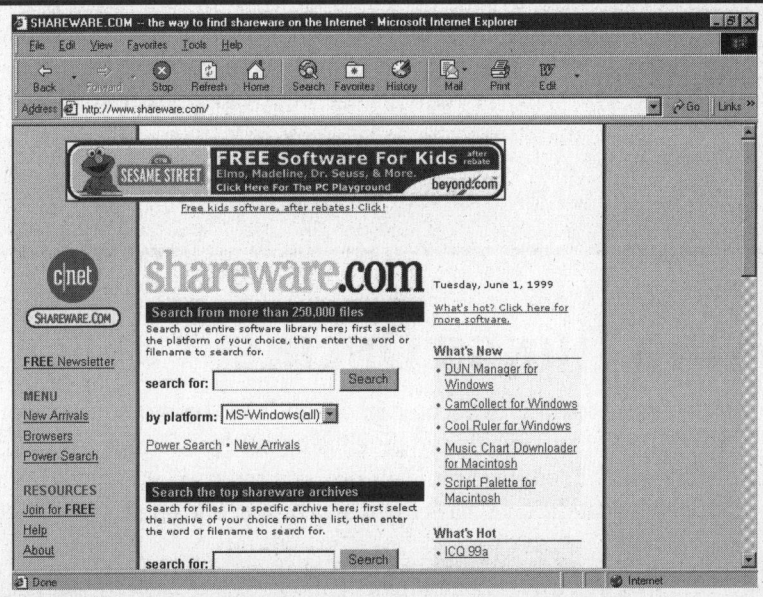

FIGURE 23.10: Finding software is a breeze at Shareware.com.

The Shareware.com site will offer automatic links to recent arrivals and popular downloads, but you can search for any program by name. Just type the name (or part of it) in the search box, specify Windows as your operating system, and click the Search button. Shareware.com result pages contain links to various files (including duplicates at different sites) matching your search terms. Click a filename to download a file.

> ### HOW SHAREWARE WORKS
>
> Shareware is software that's distributed for free (sometimes in a limited or *lite* format) on a trial basis. If you like the software and want to continue to use it beyond its trial period, it is your responsibility to register and pay for it. Sometimes you will gain access to additional features (or prevent the program from expiring entirely), printed documentation, or technical support.
>
> Software distributed absolutely free is called *freeware*. Although the software is given away, the programmer retains all rights to it and does not put it into the public domain. In practice, this usually means that other programmers are expressly forbidden to incorporate the freeware into for-profit software of their own, unless they have written permission. Programmers who make freeware either derive personal satisfaction from the adoption and use of their handiwork, or they benefit financially from the reputation that accrues to the developer of a popular program. Software that periodically reminds you to register is often called "nagware."
>
> A good shareware site for owners of Windows computers is http://www.tucows.com (the name is an acronym for The Ultimate Collection of Winsock Software).

Buying Things Online

As electronic commerce becomes more and more commonplace, you may find yourself searching for and purchasing products online. Although software can be sent electronically over the Internet, other purchases are "fulfilled" in traditional ways (by mail, courier, and so on), much like catalog sales.

Perhaps the biggest remaining bugaboo holding back the inevitable tide of online commerce is the question of security. How can you safely transmit something delicate like your credit-card information over an open, public network such as the Internet? There are several different answers to this question, but no single universal model yet for online credit purchases.

> **TIP**
> See Chapter 20 for a complete discussion of Web security issues and Internet Explorer's tools for dealing with them.

One way to look at it is to compare it to handing your credit card to a waiter without worrying that someone in the kitchen might jot down your number and expiration date. The difference is that data transmitted over the Internet could lie around on drives and backup disks indefinitely, and individuals so inclined could probably hunt for likely information long after the fact.

Some online businesses have invested in secure Web servers that, when coupled with savvy Web browsers, initiate an encrypted "secure" connection, thereby preserving the secrecy of your private information. For that matter, most browsers will inform you *any* time you send information on a form to an unsecure server, just in case the information in the form might be sensitive.

Other companies skirt the entire issue for now, offering alternative verification methods using 800 numbers or the like. This is an adequate approach for the time being, because it relies on more dependable existing methods of checking credit-card info, but it takes away a good deal of the convenience of shopping online by adding those extra steps. Another approach some businesses take is to have you set up an account (and choose from various payment methods) the first time you make a purchase.

> **WARNING**
> Just as a general matter of common sense, do not send private information, such as credit-card numbers via regular, unencrypted e-mail, and be suspicious of any messages you receive suggesting that you do so. Beware of official-looking Web pages that turn out to be fronts for people who just want your credit card number for their own nefarious purposes.

In addition to the matter of security, you may also have legitimate concerns about your privacy. Of course, these issues are not limited to the Internet. Any time you use a credit card or automatic-teller (debit) card you are leaving an electronic "paper trail" tracking your spending habits. The issue is similar on the Net. Beyond the basic transaction information any store would naturally expect to track, some online businesses will also request or require that you fill out a questionnaire before completing your purchase. Your answers on such a form will become part of a customer database that may then find its way into the hands of other businesses.

If you're concerned about limiting your exposure when spending money on the Net, refuse to fill out such questionnaires whenever possible and refuse to be put on mailing lists or to have your registration information "made available" to other entities, again, whenever possible.

Having addressed all the potential negatives of online shopping, I'd like to avoid giving too negative or scary an impression. I've bought a number of real-world objects and services online and have not had a problem yet.

At most "store" sites, such as Columbia House CD-ROM (`http://www.columbiahouse.com`; see Figure 23.11), you can search or browse your way to the merchandise you want and then add it to a shopping basket (essentially a list of items you wish to buy), to be "rung up" all at once when you're finished shopping. You repeat this process as often as you wish, and then proceed to an Order page or area where you can buy the items you selected.

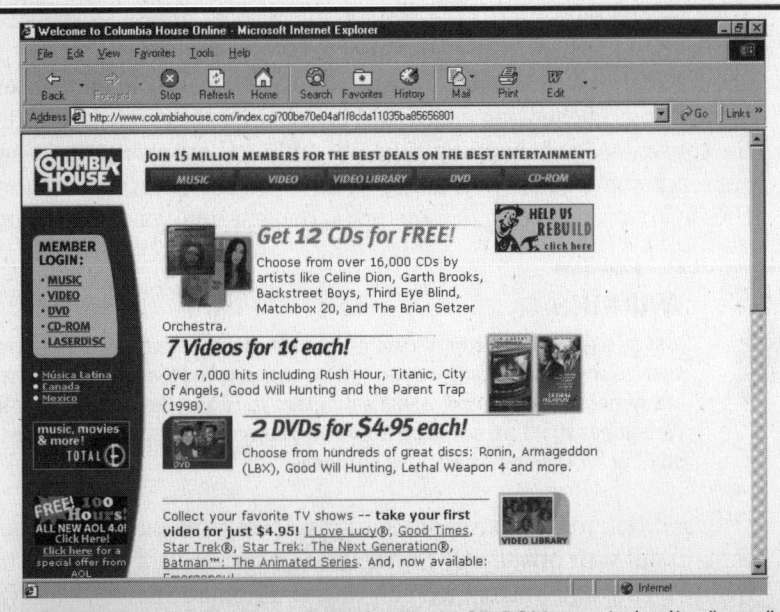

FIGURE 23.11: Browsing at Columbia House CD-ROM, a typical online "store" site

What's Next

With this chapter, we've now completed our look at the Windows 98 SE Internet features and at Windows 98 SE itself. Part III, *Your PC and Hardware*, offers an in-depth look at maintaining and upgrading the hardware side of your computer system.

PART III
Your PC and Hardware

Chapter 24

A Buyer's Guide to PCs

If you're the kind of person who fixes your own or someone else's PC then you're likely to be the kind of person who's often looking to the next PC, the latest-and-greatest machine. Perhaps your palms itch when you see that someone else owns a dual processor Pentium III system, when all you can afford is a Pentium. You eye 18GB hard drives the way some teenage boys eye Corvettes.

Or maybe you're not that way. Maybe your computer is just a tool for you, a platform upon which to get some work done. But you've found that your current platform just isn't fast enough to support today's software: Windows 98 SE requires a Pentium with at least 32MB of RAM in order to be useful. And you need to know how to either upgrade your existing machines or buy new ones that won't offer as much trouble when it's time to upgrade again in a year or two.

Adapted from *The Complete PC Upgrade & Maintenance Guide* by Mark Minasi
ISBN 0-7821-2606-5   1664 pages $49.99

It's a good time to upgrade; with prices these days, everybody can own some of the fastest PCs on the planet. Buyers with tons of money don't have much advantage over the rest of us currently. (Unless, of course, you've *got* to have a 550MHz Pentium III-based system with the digital, active matrix, flat panel screen and 18GB drive.)

But *which* one to buy? Well, I'm not going to tell you *that*: there are zillions of honest vendors out there who deserve your money. I'd just like to give you some advice on how to make sure that your vendor is one of the good ones.

I tell my clients that when they're going to buy a PC, they should consider four things: compatibility, upgradability (I know, it's not a word), serviceability, and price/performance.

Because I'm concerned about those things, I recommend that people avoid many of the big names in the PC business and buy a *generic* computer, rather than a *proprietary* computer.

Parts of a Generic PC

Now, I've discussed this before, but before I go any further, let me remind you about what I mean when I say "generic" and "proprietary." *Generic* refers to machines designed like the IBM AT, even if the machine is built around a Pentium. Generic machines are PCs consisting of a few separate industry standard parts. Those parts include:

Standard Case If you buy a computer with an unusually shaped case, as you'd see in the "slimline" PCs or the micro towers, then you'll find that all of the boards inside the computer may be unusually shaped as well. That means that you probably won't be able to easily locate affordable replacement parts, should you need them. It also means that you can't put an industry-standard ("generic") power supply in your system. That's undesirable because there are some very nice power supply alternatives these days, such as super-quiet fans or power supplies with built-in battery backup.

ATX Case This is a newer case style, which actually rotates the processor and expansion slots 90 degrees inside the case, giving room to add more cards. A side-mounted fan on the power supply does a better job of cooling the system than the standard version. But the most visible difference is the double-height aperture in the back where the keyboard, mouse, and ports are located; these ports are all piled on top of one another. A standard motherboard will not fit in an ATX case, and vice versa.

Motherboard   The largest circuit board in the case, the motherboard holds the CPU, memory, and expansion slots. On that motherboard there should be *eight* expansion slots, rather than the three that you find on some computers these days, so that you can add expansion boards to your PC now and in the future. Three slots just aren't enough.

I/O   This used to be a separate entity, now it is built in to most motherboards. It's good to get a motherboard with two EIDE controllers. EIDE controllers allow your hard drives to talk to the CPU, and two of them let you have up to four hard drives or CD-ROMs. The parallel port resides here as well; get one that is ECP/EPP so that you can connect to a nice, fast printer. There should be a PS/2 port for your mouse so that you don't need to waste a perfectly good serial port. Speaking of which, serial ports and floppy drive connectors are considered I/O as well; not much to concern yourself with here, but just be sure you have the standard setup of one floppy controller and two communication (COM) ports.

Video Adapter Board   This is the component that allows the PC to display images on the monitor. It will probably be a so-called "super" VGA board. VGA is Video Graphics Array, a common video standard. I'll recommend VGA accelerators a bit later.

That's just a generic overview. I'll zoom in on particular features you should be looking for in a few pages.

Problems with Proprietary PCs

How is one of these generic PCs different from a proprietary PC? Well, you find all of the same functions in a proprietary PC, but you find all of them on a single circuit board, a kind of "workaholic" motherboard. The big problem with proprietary computers is that you can't upgrade them easily, nor can you fix them for a reasonable price. Proprietary computer motherboards are typically shaped differently from each other and from generic motherboards, making it impossible for you to replace an old or damaged proprietary motherboard with anything but another motherboard of the exact same make and model. As motherboards of that particular make and model are only available from that particular vendor (by definition, since the motherboard is proprietary), it may be expensive or impossible to get a replacement. Likewise, it's almost certainly impossible to get an upgrade.

For more specific problems with proprietary designs, let's return to my four criteria.

Compatibility is at stake because if the vendor did anything wrong, For example, if the company chose a mildly incompatible video chip, as AT&T did for some of their systems, you must either throw away the computer or hope that the designer was farsighted enough to allow you to disable the built-in video function so you can go out and spend more money on a separate video board.

Upgradability is a concern because not all boards are built alike. Take, for example, the Compaq Deskpro systems. Although they work very well, they are difficult to upgrade the motherboards especially, because they are not a standard shape. You must buy new motherboards from Compaq, as opposed to running to your local vendor and picking up a newer, faster one when it comes out.

Serviceability is a problem for reasons touched on above. A generic design like a Gateway 2000 is a safe buy in many ways, not the least of which is that even if Gateway goes bankrupt tomorrow, the entire machine is composed of generic parts that can be bought at *thousands* of clone houses around the country. And this isn't brain surgery; you can break down and rebuild a PC in about 30 minutes, leaving it better than when you started.

And what about *price/performance*? First of all, notice that I put this last. That's because compared to what computers used to cost, *any* PC is a bargain, even if you pay list price for one made by IBM. In regard to the proprietary computers, in theory, a single-board design can be faster and cheaper for many reasons. You don't see that in actual fact because single-board designs tend to be embraced by the big-name companies that need to pay for four-page color spreads in *Byte* and *PC Magazine*.

You don't need to buy a big name to get big performance, reliability, or flexibility. Look in your local paper's business section for the names of companies near you that sell generic PCs. It couldn't hurt if the company offers service through a national service company like Wang or TRW. Then choose that fire-breathing 500 MHz Pentium III you've been eyeing and put it to work for you and smile, knowing that you've bought the security of easy upgrades and independence from any single vendor.

Choosing a Market Niche

Where will you buy your PC? People in some companies are only allowed to buy from IBM or Compaq; others put machines together from parts. Computer dealers basically fall into three categories.

First Tier IBM and Compaq. The *definitions* of compatibility. The systems that these companies pump out are top of the line. It used to be that you could not upgrade them short of an act of Congress, but now they are much easier to work with; you can plop any old generic card in them. However, particularly with low-end systems, not all cards will work as well as you'd like them to. But they are quite easy to get serviced in the event of a problem, since just about every computer store in existence has technicians certified by one or more of these companies. The real drawback here is cost; they work well, but they cost quite a bit more than the other two tiers.

Second Tier Dell, Gateway 2000, and Micron. While the majority of these companies have seen the wisdom of generic architecture, some of them still use proprietary parts. You will find good price/performance with these companies, but there are some drawbacks. Both Micron and Gateway, for example, decided to experiment on me with some new motherboards that didn't work at all. Getting them to admit and then fix their mistakes was a hassle, but they did make it all better eventually, although it took longer than I would have liked. The moral of the story is this: don't let vendors experiment on you; ask for name brand parts if they are using a generic architecture.

Third Tier Also known as "box shovers" or "Three Guys and a Goat PCs." This group gets a scary reputation that's really not deserved. Yes, some of them are sleazy, deceptive, and unreliable, but then those are adjectives that have been aptly applied to some of the *big* names in the business, too. On the positive side, these companies are always aware of the fact that every sale is a significant portion of their total business, and they'll do just about anything to get a multi-machine contract with a large company or government client. You usually needn't worry about shoddy parts, as they're putting together pieces made by fairly big U.S., Taiwanese, Korean, and Japanese vendors. If you look at the sum total of all third-tier vendors, you'll see that between them they use only about three or four suppliers for any given part (drives, motherboards, controllers, etc.). That means that if you really look at the companies that are *supplying* those parts—Micronics, DTK, AMI, Chips & Technologies, Adaptec, and G2—you'll see that they're pretty large and reliable companies. The absolute best part about these machines is that they're the simplest to upgrade and maintain. And service is usually easier and faster, often at your own worksite (which beats having to pack up your machine and trust shipping services not to wreck it completely). They also have the best price/performance in the group, and compatibility is usually as good as the second-tier machines. Your only real concern with such vendors is the need for a warranty *in writing*. If you have no warranty and your machine breaks, then you have no machine, just a large, beige paperweight.

Choosing PC Parts

In the process of choosing a PC, I look at what it's made of in order to decide if it's the kind of machine that I'm looking for. Let's look at the important parts of a PC and summarize what you should consider when buying a PC.

CPU

If you're buying today, consider the Pentium III. Pentium III chips are coming down in price and are quite fast. Most games written today are, in fact, written to take advantage of the Pentium CPU. If you go any lower than Pentium II (say Pentium Pro), look for MMX (Multimedia Extensions) as well, since a good number of programs are written to take advantage of it. MMX (which is built into the Pentium II and III) is actually just a set of extra commands in the CPU itself that allows it to process multimedia functions, like video and sound, faster. Make sure to get at least one fan with this too; Pentiums run a little warm and will not function for long without one.

The fact of the matter today is that CPUs are leveling out in speed. To explain: a 386 was twice as fast as a 286 at the same speed, thus a 386/20 was twice as fast as a 286/20. Same difference between the 386 and 486, and the Pentium and 486 again. Yet what about the difference between the Pentium II and the Pentium? Between the Pentium II and Pentium Xeon, or how about the Celeron? They are a little faster in clock speed only; the real difference is in the way these processors handle their work—Xeon, for example, gives access to more memory than a Pentium II, but it is not twice as fast. What's *not* getting faster, however, are the peripherals. CPUs today are hundreds of times faster than XT-level CPUs; modern peripherals, however, are only dozens of times faster than XT-era peripherals. Take the money you're saving by not buying the latest and greatest CPU and spend that on a faster bus and faster peripherals. (There are exceptions; some processes are very CPU-intensive and will benefit from a faster processor.)

Additionally, there is a lot of evidence that Pentium architecture chips require some kind of special cooling hardware for the CPU itself. That includes heat sinks and fans mounted on the CPU, much like the faster 486 chips required. If you get a CPU with a built-in heat sink, this may not be a problem for you, so check with the vendor when you buy.

"Upgradable" PCs

What about modular "upgradable" PCs? The idea *sounds* good, but the upgrades are proprietary and can be quite expensive. Generic PCs are the original "upgradable" PCs.

Bus

You need a fast bus to drive fast peripherals. You want a *smart* bus so that your system works with Plug and Play and so that you can set up new boards easily. There's really only one smart and fast bus: PCI.

Unfortunately, most PCI implementations sport only three or four PCI slots and supplement with EISA slots. Most new boards also include an AGP slot, which is currently reserved for high-speed video. Which brings me to my next bus requirement: Plug and Play. Make absolutely sure that your new machine will support Plug and Play as implemented by Windows 98 SE; I say "as implemented by Windows 98 SE" because a good number of vendors have a kind of loose interpretation of what Plug and Play means. The simplest hard-and-fast test is "Does it work with Windows 98 SE?"

Not every board you plug into your system needs to be a PCI board, although that is preferable. You should be pretty sure, however, that the following adapters are PCI:

- SCSI host adapter
- Any LAN cards
- Any video capture or sound capture hardware

RAM

Remember this simple mathematical equation to help you buy the right amount of RAM: More = Better. Today's operating systems like RAM (especially so with NT). Get a system with at least 32MB of RAM. Be certain to get enough cache memory as well. Cache memory is used by the processor to access frequently used pieces of data and can speed up your system. It is fairly standard to find 256K of cache on the board already; you may want to consider upgrading that to 512K or even 1MB since Windows operating systems use this much cache quite well.

ROM BIOS

This is an important part of compatibility. Buy from one of the big three—Phoenix, Award, or AMI. That way, it's easy to get upgrades. Nice BIOS features include:

- User-definable drive types
- Bus speeds that can be set in the setup
- Processor cache enable/disable

Motherboard/System Board

This board contains the above items. If you're buying from a first- or second-tier company, you'll end up with their board. From a third-tier place, look for motherboards from Acer, Micronics, DTK, Mylex, ASUS, and FIC.

Disk Drives

You're probably going to end up buying EIDE-type drives mainly because they're so amazingly cheap, fast, and reliable. Just back the silly things up *regularly*, because there's only a limited array of repair options open to you.

Floppy Disks

I've seen too many problems with Mitsubishi drives to recommend them; TEACs seem the most trouble-free. I would recommend getting an Iomega Zip or Jaz drive also, if you need a lot of data storage space. Don't bother with the 2.88MB floppies; nobody else uses them.

Video Board

Get an AGP bit-blitting video accelerator board to support modern graphical operating systems. Any accelerator based on the S3 chip set will be easy to support, as S3 drivers are common for any operating system. Alternatively, look at one of the two market leaders: either an accelerator card from Diamond, or one from ATI.

Video Monitor

Buy a monitor based on the resolution at which you'll use it. If you're doing regular old VGA (with a resolution of 640 dots across the screen by 480 dots down the screen), buy a 15-inch fixed frequency VGA monitor; it'll cost around $120. For the super VGA 800×600 resolution, get a 15-inch multisyncing monitor that can handle that resolution. For 1024×768, buy a monitor that's at least 17 inches diagonally. And *do not* buy interlaced 1024×768: sure it's cheaper, but the lawsuits from your employees going blind will be expensive. Buy non-interlaced. And only worry about it at 1024×768: nobody I know of tries to interlace 640×480 or 800×600. My favorite for a 17-inch monitor is the Viewsonic 17G.

Mice

Although I hate to put more money in Microsoft's pocket, any of the Microsoft mouses (meese, mice?) seem the best of all the ones I've worked with. But $30 for a mouse? Arggh. If you have that PS/2 port I mentioned earlier, then don't forget to make the little guy a PS/2 mouse instead of serial.

Printers

Although laser printers used to be the standard for high-quality output, today's ink jet printers are excellent. In fact some like the Lexmark 7000 series printers, actually support up to 1200×1200 dpi. Additionally, these printers can produce photo-quality color. And ink jet printers are usually only a couple hundred dollars, while color laser printers can cost upwards of thousands of dollars.

Serial Ports

Look for serial ports based on the 16550 UART chip. It's built for multi-tasking.

Parallel Ports

Make sure that your parallel ports are Enhanced Parallel Ports, or ECP/EPP interfaces. They're faster and bi-directional. Bi-directional parallel ports are essential for modern printers, which send status information back to the PC over those ports.

Universal Serial Bus (USB)

How many things do you currently have attached to your computer? A modem, monitor, sound card, etc.? Eventually, on a standard system, you'll run out of room for more additions. USB is designed to solve this problem—you can have up to 127 devices attached to a USB port. Not only that, you can simply plug in the device and forget it, no messy configurations, or even reboots. When you get a system, look into one with USB ports on the motherboard, since so many people are coming out with compatible add-ons.

From Whom Should You Buy?

When I ask this question, I don't mean whether you should buy from Dell, IBM, or Jeff and Akbar's House of Clones; instead, I mean, "Should you buy direct from the manufacturer, via mail order, or at a store?"

Well, if you're a really large company, then it probably makes sense to go straight to Compaq or whomever and negotiate a specific deal. But if you're a hobbyist or a SOHO (small office/home office) shop, then you'll have to examine your strategies.

You can probably buy cheapest from mail order. *But* if you do that, then returning defective merchandise involves shipping things around, getting RMA (Return Merchandise Authorization) numbers, etc. That can be a hassle.

Going to a big computer retailer is just a fast way to waste money, so I'm not intending to shove you into the arms of Computerland or the like. But there are many small businesses whose main line of work is to sell computer parts, software, supplies, and systems at a reasonable price. These local vendors often offer prices that aren't much more expensive than mail order. (Besides, the nice thing about local stores is that I like my vendors within choking distance....) And patronizing your local PC store means that when you need that disk drive on Saturday, you need only run down the street to get it, rather than waiting a week for it to ship.

That's not to say that mail order doesn't make sense. Mail order firms are more likely to have the latest and greatest software and hardware. Their prices will, again, sometimes be lower than the local store's. They may even know more about the product than a local vendor might. But take it from a veteran, there are a few things to be sure of:

- ▶ First, use a credit card. It's your first line of defense when mail order companies get nasty. If you didn't get what you wanted, then just box it up, ship it back, and cancel the charge. Years ago, Dell used to charge a 15 percent "restocking fee." (They may still, but I refuse to do business with them, so I wouldn't know.) They sent me a hard disk that had clearly been dropped. When it worked, it registered seek times in the hundreds of milliseconds, despite what their ad promised. They tried to convince me that the drive was just what I wanted, but I knew better and sent it back. They tried to charge me a restocking fee, so I just complained to Citibank, and Dell backed off.

- ▶ Second, find out whom you're talking to. If the person responds, "operator 22" (I suppose his friends call him "22"), ask to speak with a supervisor. You're about to give this guy your name, address, phone, and credit card number, and he won't even tell you who he is? Write the name down. Also get a confirmation number or order number.

- ▶ Third, only buy the product if it's in stock. Back-ordered things can take months to arrive, and by the time they do, you'll be charged the older (and higher) price. Get the salesperson to check that it can ship today. If not, don't place the order.

- ▶ Ship it overnight or second day. By default, mail order companies use UPS ground, which can take anywhere from one week to a millennium to arrive. Second day is usually only a few dollars more, and then you can get a guaranteed delivery date out of the salesperson.

- ▶ Once you have the product, keep the carton that it came in for 30 days. That way, if a problem arises, it's easy to ship it back. And if you do have to ship something back, then by all means insure it.

- ▶ Another new way of buying computers is over the Internet. Many computer manufacturers will sell directly from their Web sites. Some of those that do are Compaq, Dell, and Gateway. What's nice about these sites is that you can custom-design your own system right online choosing your CPU, memory, video display, and so on. Once ordered (usually with a credit card) the company builds your system to order and ships it to you within days.

Just follow those rules, and you'll have some great luck getting things through the mail.

What's Next?

In the next chapter, Mark Minasi offers valuable guidance on preventive maintenance—simple things you can do to keep your computer hardware running smoothly and to protect it from physical hazards ranging from dust and static electricity to flooding. Everyone should read Chapter 25, *Avoiding Service: Preventive Maintenance*; even old pros may find new tips there.

Chapter 25

Avoiding Service: Preventive Maintenance

The most effective way to cut down your repair bills is by good, preventive maintenance. There are things in the PC environment—some external, some created in ignorance by you through inattention—that can drastically shorten your PC's life.

Now, some of the things that affect your PC's life are commonsense things; I don't really imagine that I've got to tell you not to spill soft drinks (or, for that matter, *hard* drinks) into the keyboard. But there are other PC gremlin sources that aren't quite so obvious; so, obvious or not, we'll get to all the environmental hazards in this chapter. A few factors can endanger your PC's health:

- Excessive heat
- Dust
- Magnetism
- Stray electromagnetism
- Power surges, incorrect line voltage, and power outages
- Water and corrosive agents

Adapted from *The Complete PC Upgrade & Maintenance Guide* by Mark Minasi
ISBN 0-7821-2606-5 1664 pages $49.99

Heat and Thermal Shock

Every electronic device carries within it the seeds of its own destruction. More than half of the power given to chips is wasted as heat—but heat destroys chips. One of an electronic designer's main concerns is to see that an electronic device can dissipate heat as quickly as it can generate it. If it cannot, heat slowly builds up until the device fails.

There are several ways you can help control your PC's heat problem:

- Install an adequate fan in the power supply or add an auxiliary fan.
- Install a heat sink.
- Adjust your box design for better ventilation.
- Run the PC in a safe temperature range.

Removing Heat with a Fan

In general, laptops don't require a fan, because enough heat dissipates from the main circuit board all by itself. But most desktop and tower PCs will surely fail without a fan.

When designing a fan, engineers must trade off noise for cooling power. Years ago, power supplies were quite expensive, running in the $300 range for the cheapest power supply, so great care was exercised in choosing the right fan for protection. Nowadays, power supplies cost under $25, and I doubt that most engineers at PC companies could even tell you what kind of fan is sitting in their machines, any more than they could tell you who makes the case screws.

Now, that's a terrible shame, because the $3 fan that's sitting in most PC power supplies is a vital part. If it dies, your PC will cook itself in just a few hours.

And they *do* die.

The more stuff that's in your PC, the hotter it runs. The things that make PCs hot inside include:

- Chips, memory chips, and CPUs in particular, because they have the greatest number of transistors inside them.
- Drive motors in hard disks, floppies, and CD-ROMs. Some CD-ROMs run quite warm, like the Plexor 4-Plex models. Large hard disks run *extremely* hot. I've seen an old Maxtor 660MB ESDI

drive run so hot that it almost burned my fingers; I've seen the same thing more recently on my 1.7GB Fujitsu drive. Newer drives in the 3 1/2" half-height or third-height format run much cooler. Some circuit boards can run quite hot, depending on how well (or how poorly) they're designed.

Truthfully, heat buildup inside a PC is much less of a problem than it was in the mid-1980s. In those days, every drive was a full-height drive, and every computer had 640K of memory built up from 90 separate 64K chips. Add one of those early hot 8087 coprocessors, and it was common to find the inside of a PC running 30 degrees F (16 degrees C) warmer inside its box than outside in the room.

Removing Heat with a Heat Sink

For years, electronic designers have had to struggle with hot components on circuit boards. Sometimes a fan just isn't enough, so they need more help cooling an infernal chip. They do it with a *heat sink*. A heat sink is a small piece of metal, usually aluminum, with fins on it. The heat sink is glued or clamped to the hot chip. The metal conducts heat well, and the fins increase the surface area of the heat sink. The more area on the heat sink, the more heat that can be conducted off to the air and thereby removed from the PC.

The standard Pentium II and Xeon processor packages have a heat sink and a fan integrated with the chip. The idea is that the heat sink pulls the heat off and the fan disperses it. The Celeron doesn't come with a heat sink, but that doesn't mean that it's not a good idea to think about putting one on a hot chip. You can find heat sinks in electronics supply catalogs. Adding a fan can really increase the heat sink's ability to cool its chip. I've noticed that many modern motherboards have connections to power a couple of auxiliary fans, and you can buy fans that attach to those connections from PC clone parts places (look in the back of *Computer Shopper* for them).

Good and Bad Box Designs

It's frustrating how totally unaware of heat problems many computer manufacturers are. The first tower computer I purchased was from a company named ACMA, and they put together an impressive machine. There were two fans in the case—a very nice touch—as well as a CPU fan. I've got to say that they spoiled me. A later (1994) purchase, from an outfit called

Systems Dynamics Group, was somewhat less enjoyable. The back of the PC chassis had room for two fans, but there was only one fan in the system. There's nothing intrinsically wrong with that, except that the cutout for the second fan—which is right next to the first fan—was left empty. The result was that the fan just sucked in air from the cutout a few inches away from it, and blew it back out. Made the fan happy, I suppose, but didn't do much for the CPU.

I noticed this pointless ventilation system pretty quickly, so I took some tape and covered up the extraneous cutout. Within seconds, the air being pumped out the back of the Pentium got 10 degrees warmer. If I'd left the extra cutout uncovered, then the only ventilation that my Pentium system would have gotten was just the simple convection from the heated boards and drives. Even at that, however, the Pentium system—which included a 1GB drive, 80MB of RAM, a CD-ROM, video capture board, video board, SCSI host adapter, and Ethernet card—only ran 10 degrees hotter inside the box than outside the box.

Things could have been a bit worse if the case was like some I've seen, with the fan *on the bottom of the tower*! This is not too common, fortunately, but it's worth asking so you can avoid it when purchasing a PC. This setup puts the circuit boards on the top of the tower, and the fan on the bottom. I have no idea who designed this case, but it's nice to know that the banjo player kid from *Deliverance* finally has someone to look down upon. The point I'm making here is, take a minute and look at the airflow in the box. Of course, even if you have a good box, you can still run into heat problems.

Dead Fans

Years ago (around 1995), I installed Freelance Graphics on my system. Pulling the first floppy out of my A drive, I noticed that the floppy was warm. My memory flashed back to 1982, when something similar had happened—so I knew what was going on. My system's fan had died.

Fortunately, I found the problem early and shut down the computer. I had to travel to Europe for a few weeks to teach classes and consult, but I figured, no problem—I'll just leave the computer off.

Unfortunately, while I was gone, one of my employees helpfully started up the computer—reasoning that I always leave my computers on all the time, so what the hey? So, despite the "do not turn it on" sign I'd left on it, the computer merrily melted itself down while I lectured in Amsterdam.

By the time I returned, the hard disk had self-destructed, as had the Ethernet card in it.

It's actually pretty amazing what *didn't* die in the system. The CPU (a 50MHz 486DX) ran for a couple of years afterward (until it became too slow to be of value) and the Adaptec 1742 SCSI host adapter is still in service in an old server.

Heat Sensor Devices

Now, I could have avoided this problem altogether with a 110 Twinalert from a company called PC Power and Cooling, Inc. They're a name to know when you're buying power supplies. The 110 Twinalert is a circuit board about the size of a business card that plugs into a floppy power connector. When the PC's internal temperature gets to 110 degrees F, it starts making an annoying squealing noise. At 118 degrees F, it just shuts the computer down. The device is under $50, and every network server should have one.

While I'm on the subject of PC Power and Cooling, I should mention that this company also makes an interesting variety of power products for the PC, including power supplies with very quiet fans, power supplies with built-in battery backup, and high-quality PC cases. I use their stuff when I want to increase the odds that my PC will be running when I need it.

My introduction to PC Power and Cooling came with a hot 386. When I say "hot," I mean that this PC ran 25 degrees warmer inside than the temperature outside. PC Power and Cooling sells the Turbo Cool, a power supply that claimed at the time to cool your PC by 35 to 40 degrees (all Fahrenheit). Now, obviously, my 386 could not be cooled by 35 degrees, because it is only 25 degrees over ambient—the best that a fan can do is to lower the temperature inside the machine to the surrounding temperature. However, buying PC Power and Cooling's Turbo Cool cooled my machine from 25 degrees over ambient to only *four* degrees over ambient. You can find PC Power and Cooling's address in Appendix C, *Vendors Guide*.

Safe Temperature Ranges for PCs

Electronic components have a temperature range within which they are built to work. IBM suggests that the PC, for instance, is built to work in the range of 60 to 85 degrees F. This is because the circuit boards can run as hot as 125 degrees, but a typical machine may be as much as 40 degrees hotter *inside* than outside. And 125 minus 40 yields 85 degrees, the suggested maximum temperature.

Obviously, if you have a good fan, the acceptable range of room temperatures expands considerably. If you had a really good fan, the inside of the machine would be close to the same temperature as the outside. You don't want the inside of the PC to get any hotter than 110 degrees—hard disks can fail at that point, although, again, circuit boards can function in higher temperatures than that.

Since the temperature inside the PC is the ambient temperature plus some constant, there are two ways to cool the inside of the PC—either lower the constant with a good fan or lower the ambient temperature. Keep the room cooler and the PC will be cooler.

Heat also aids the corrosion process. Corrosion is a chemical process, and inside a computer, corrosion can roughly *double* in speed when the temperature of the process is raised by 10 degrees C (about 18 degrees F). Chips slowly deteriorate, the hotter the faster.

How do you measure temperature and temperature changes in your PC? Simple—get a *digital temperature probe*. Radio Shack markets one for around $30. Or you can buy one from Edmund Scientific Corp., whose address is listed in Appendix C.

The easy way to use the probe is to tape it over the exit vents by the fan's power supply. An indoor/outdoor switch lets you quickly view the PC's inside temperature and the ambient temperature.

Duty Cycles

We said before that a device should get rid of heat as quickly as it creates it. Not every device is that good, however. Devices are said to have a *duty cycle*. This number—expressed as a percentage—is the proportion of the time that a device can work without burning up. For example, a powerful motor may have a 50 percent duty cycle. This means that it should be active only 50 percent of the time. A starter motor on a car, for example, must produce a tremendous amount of power. Powerful motors are expensive to produce, so instead, cars use a motor that can produce a lot of power for a very short time. If you crank the engine on your car for several minutes at a stretch, then you will likely damage or destroy the car's starter motor. Floppy disk drive motors are a similar example: run a floppy motor continuously and you'll likely burn out the motor. *Hard* disk motors, on the other hand, run continuously and must be designed with a 100 percent duty cycle.

Duty cycle is used to describe active versus inactive time for many kinds of devices, although this definition could be misleading, since it implies that all devices can be continually active without problems. Not all devices are designed to be active all of the time. Some desktop laser printers, for example, will not run well if they are required to print continuously.

Thermal Shock

Because a PC is warmer inside than outside, changes in room temperature can become multiplied inside a PC.

This problem leads to a hazard called *thermal shock*. Thermal shock comes from subjecting components to rapid and large changes in temperature. It can disable your computer due to expansion/contraction damage. The most common scenario for thermal shock occurs when the PC is turned on Monday morning after a winter's weekend. Many commercial buildings turn the temperature down to 55 degrees over the weekend: your office may contain some of that residual chill early Monday morning. Inside the PC, though, it may still be 55. Then you turn the machine on. Within 30 minutes some PCs can warm up to 120 degrees. This rapid, 65-degree rise in temperature brings on thermal shock.

This is an argument for leaving the PC on 24 hours a day, seven days a week. (We'll see some more reasons to do this soon.) The temperature inside the PC will be better regulated. By the way, you can't leave portable PCs on all the time, but you should be extra careful with portables to avoid thermal shock. If your laptop has been sitting in the trunk on a cold February day, be sure to give it some time to warm up before trying to use it. And give it some time in a *dry* place, or water vapor will condense on the cold disk platters. Water on the disk platters is a surefire way to reduce your drive's life.

Sunbeams

Another heat effect is caused by sunbeams. Direct sunlight isn't a good thing for electronic equipment. A warm sunbeam feels nice for a few minutes, but sit in one for an hour and you'll understand why PCs don't like them. Direct sunlight is also, of course, terrible for floppy disks. Find a shadowy area, or use drapes.

Dealing with Dust

Dust is everywhere. It consists of tiny sand granules, fossil skeletons of minuscule creatures that lived millions of years ago, dead skin, paper particles, and tiny crustaceans called dust mites that live off the other pieces. Dust is responsible for several evils.

First, it sticks to the circuit boards inside your computer. As dust builds up, an entire board can become coated with a fine insulating sheath. That would be fine if the dust was insulating your house, but thermal insulation is definitely a bad thing for computers. You seek, as we have seen, to minimize impediments to thermal radiation from your computer components. To combat this, remove dust from inside the computer and from circuit boards periodically. A good period between cleaning is a year in a house and six months in an office. A simpler approach is to use the "while I'm at it" algorithm—when you need to disassemble the machine for some other reason, clean the insides while you're at it. A tool that can assist you is a can of compressed air. Just as effective for the case and inside support assemblies is a dust-free cloth wetted with a little water and ammonia (just a few drops). Don't use the cloth on circuit boards—get a can of compressed air and blow the dust off.

Actually, *compressed air* isn't actually compressed air, but some kind of compressed gas. Take a second look when you buy this stuff: a lot of it is Freon or some other chlorinated fluorocarbon (CFC), which enlarges the hole in the ozone layer. Rather than using one of these, choose one of the "ozone-friendly" alternatives, such as the one marketed by Chemtronics.

This should be obvious, but when you blow dust off boards, be aware of where it is going: if you can, have the vacuum cleaner nearby, or take the board to another area, then you'll have better luck. *Please* don't hold the board over the PC's chassis and blow off the dust with compressed air—all it does is move the dust, not *remove* the dust.

The second dust evil is that dust can clog spaces, like:

- ▶ The air intake area to your power supply or hard disk
- ▶ The space between the floppy disk drive head and the disk

To combat the floppy drive problem, some manufacturers offer a floppy dust cover that you put in place when the machine is turned off. The sad part of this is that you really need the cover when the machine is on. CRT displays have an unintended, unexpected, unpleasant, and unavoidable side effect—they attract dust. Turn your screen on, and all of the dust in the area drops everything (what would dust particles drop, I wonder?) and heads straight for the display. Some of the particles get sidetracked and end up in the floppy drives. Some vendors say that the way to cut down on dust in floppy drives is to close the drive doors. This is wrong because the door *isn't* dust-tight.

One place that creates and collects paper dust is, of course, the printer. Printers should be vacuumed or blown out periodically, *away* from the computer (remember, dust goes somewhere when blown away).

By the way, another fertile source of dust is ash particles. Most of us don't burn things indoors, *unless* we are smokers. If you smoke, fine: just don't do it near the computer. Years ago, I ran across a study by the U.S. Government Occupation Safety and Hazard Administration (OSHA), which estimated that smoke at a computer workstation cuts the computer's life by 40 percent. That's $1200 on a $3000 workstation. (Alas, I saw that back in 1985, and didn't note the information in detail—I wish I had!—so I can't cite the particular study.)

MAGNETISM

Magnets—both the permanent and electromagnetic type—can cause permanent loss of data on hard or floppy disks. Most often, the magnetism found in an office environment is produced by electric motors and electromagnets. A commonly overlooked electromagnet is the one in phones that ring using a real bell (not common these days). The clapper is forced against the bell (or buzzer, if the phone has one of those) in the phone by powering an electromagnet. If you absent-mindedly put such a phone on top of a stack of floppy disks, and the phone rings, you will probably have unrecoverable data errors on at least the top one.

Don't think you have magnets around? How about:

- ▶ Magnets to put notes on a file cabinet
- ▶ A paper clip holder with a magnet
- ▶ A word processing copy stand with a magnetic clip
- ▶ A magnetic screw extractor

Another source of magnetism is, believe it or not, a CRT. I have seen disk drives refuse to function because they were situated inches from a CRT. X-ray machines in airports similarly produce some magnetism, although there is some controversy here. Some folks say, "Don't run floppies through the X-ray—walk them through." Others say the X-ray is okay, but the metal detector zaps floppies. Some people claim to have been burned at both. Personally, I walk through an average of three to four metal detectors per week carrying 3.5-inch floppy disks, and have never (knock wood) had a problem. My laptops have been through X-ray machines everywhere, and I've never lost a byte on the hard disk because of it.

Airport metal detectors should be sufficiently gentle for floppies. Magnetism is measured in a unit called *gauss*. Metal detectors *in the U.S.* (notice the emphasis) emit far less gauss than that necessary to affect disks. I'm not sure about Canada and Europe, but I notice that the fillings in my teeth seem to set off the metal detectors in the Ottawa airport.

What about preventive maintenance? For starters, get a phone with a ringer that is not a real bell, to minimize the chance of erasing data inadvertently. Another large source of magnetism is the motor in a printer—generally, it is not shielded (the motors on the drives don't produce very much magnetism, in case you're wondering).

Do you (or someone who you assist) work in a word processing pool? Many word processors (the people kind, not the machine kind) use a copy stand that consists of a flexible metal arm and a magnet. The magnet holds the copy to be typed on the metal arm. The arm can sit right in front of the operator's face, so that he or she can easily type the copy.

The problem arises when it's time to change the copy. I watched a word processing operator remove the magnet (so as to change the copy), and slap the magnet on the side of the computer. It really made perfect sense—the case was steel, and held the magnet in a place that was easy to access. The only bad part of the whole operation was that the hard disk on that particular PC chassis was mounted on the extreme right-hand side of the case, right next to the magnet. You can start to see why I hate magnets.... A few years ago, I was a keynote speaker at a conference held in San Antonio, next to the Alamo. As part of the "thank you" package that the conference organizers put together, we speakers got a refrigerator magnet in the shape of the Alamo. After almost placing my wallet (with my credit cards in it) on the magnet, almost laying demonstration floppies that I'd gotten at the conference on it, and almost storing the Alamo magnet in my laptop case (you know, next to the laptop's hard disk and any floppies that I had in the case), I finally gave up and threw the magnet away before I had a chance to *really* do some damage.

Oh, and by the way, *speakers* have magnets in them. Years ago, a friend purchased a home entertainment system: a VCR, a stereo, and some monster speakers. That's when I noticed that he had stacked his videotapes on top of the speakers. I almost didn't have the heart to tell him, but I eventually advised him that his videos were history—and, sad to say, they *were*. Modern multimedia PCs all have speakers that claim to have shielded magnets; but I've got a Sony woofer/satellite speaker system that makes my monitor's image get wobbly when I put the speakers too near the monitor. No matter what the manual says, I think I'll just keep the floppies away from there.

My advice is to go on an anti-magnet crusade. Magnets near magnetic media are disasters waiting to happen.

A sad story: a large government agency's data center bought a handheld magnetic bulk floppy eraser. (I'm not sure why—they weren't a secret shop, and thus did not have the need.) The PC expert in the shop tested it on a few junk floppies, then turned it off and didn't think about it. The next day, he remembered that he had left it on top of a plastic floppy file drawer. This meant that the eraser, even though turned off, was about an inch from the top of the floppies. He spent the next day testing each of the floppies, one by one. Most were dead. They got rid of the bulk eraser. I'm not sure what they did with the PC expert.

Stray Electromagnetism

Stray electromagnetism can cause problems for your PC and, in particular, for your network. Here, I'm just referring to any electromagnetism that you don't want. It comes in several varieties.

- Radiated *electromagnetic interference* (*EMI*)
- Power noise and interruptions
- *Electrostatic discharge* (*ESD*)—static electricity

Electromagnetic Interference

EMI is caused when electromagnetism is radiated or conducted somewhere that we don't want it to be. I discuss two common types—crosstalk and RFI—in the next two sections.

Crosstalk

When two wires are physically close to each other, they can transmit interference between themselves called *crosstalk*. We're not talking about short circuits here: the insulation can be completely intact. The problem is that the interfering wire contains electronic pulses. Electronic pulses produce magnetic fields as a side effect. The wire being interfered with is touched or crossed by the magnetic fields. Magnetic fields crossing or touching a wire produce electronic pulses as a side effect. (Nature is, unfortunately, amazingly symmetrical at times like this.) The electronic pulses created in the second wire are faint copies of the pulses (the signal) from the first wire. These pulses interfere with the signal that we're trying to send on the second wire.

Crosstalk is not really a problem when applied to power lines, although I have heard of cases where the alternating current in power lines creates a hum on a communications line through crosstalk. The larger worry is when bundles of wires are stored in close quarters, and the wires are data cables.

There are five solutions to crosstalk:

- ▶ Move the wires farther apart (not always feasible).

- ▶ Use twisted pair cable (varying the number of twists reduces crosstalk).

- ▶ Use shielded cable (the shield reduces crosstalk—don't even think of running ribbon cables for distances over six feet).

- ▶ Use fiber optic cable—it's not electromagnetic, it's photonic (is that a great word, or what? It means that they use light instead of electricity to transmit data), so there's no crosstalk.

- ▶ Don't run cables over fluorescent lights. The lights are noise emitters.

I once helped troubleshoot a network that had been installed in a classroom. The contractor had run the wires through the ceiling, but the network seemed to not work. (Ever notice how often the words "network" and "not work" end up in the same sentence? A Russian friend calls them "nyetworks.") I pushed aside the ceiling tiles and found that the cable installer had saved himself some time and money by foregoing cable trays, instead wrapping the cables around the occasional fluorescent lamp. So, on a hunch, I said to the people that I was working with,

"Start the network up again," and I turned off the lights. Sure enough, it worked.

Radio Frequency Interference

Radio Frequency Interference (*RFI*) is high-frequency (10kHz) radiation. It's a bad thing for computer communications. Sources are:

- High-speed digital circuits, like the ones in your computer
- Nearby radio sources
- Cordless telephones
- Keyboards
- Power-line intercoms (intercoms that use the power line's 60Hz as the carrier wave)
- Motors

Worse yet, your PC can be a *source* of RFI. If this happens, the FCC police come to your place of business and take your PC away. (Well, not really. But they *will* fine you.)

RFI is bad because it can interfere with high-speed digital circuits. Your computer is composed of digital circuits. RFI can seem sinister because it seems to come and go mysteriously. Like all noise, it is an unwanted signal. How would we go about receiving a *wanted* RF signal? Simple—construct an antenna. Suppose we want to receive a signal of a given frequency? We design an antenna of a particular length. (Basically, the best length is one quarter of the wavelength. A 30-meter wavelength is best picked up by a 7.5-meter antenna. But it's not important that you know that—to learn more about it, pick up an amateur radio book.) Now suppose there is some kind of RFI floating around. We're safe as long as we can't receive it. But suppose the computer is connected to the printer with a cable that, through bad luck, happens to be the correct length to receive that RFI? The result: printer gremlins. Fortunately, the answer is simple: shorten the cable.

Electric motors are common RFI-producing culprits. I recently saw a workstation in Washington where the operator had put an electric fan (to cool *herself*, not the workstation) on top of the workstation. When the fan was on, it warped the top of the CRT's image slightly. Electric can openers, hair dryers, electric razors, electric pencil sharpeners, and printers are candidates. Sometimes it's hard to determine whether the device is messing up the PC simply by feeding back noise onto the power line or whether it is troubling the PC with RFI. The answer either way is to put the devices on separate power lines.

Your PC also *emits* RFI, which can impair the functioning of other PCs, televisions, and various sensitive pieces of equipment. By law, a desktop computer cannot be sold unless it meets "Class B" specifications. The FCC requires that a device 3 meters from the PC must receive no more than the RFI shown in Table 25.1.

TABLE 25.1: Permissible RF Output (FCC Class B Specification)

FREQUENCY	MAXIMUM FIELD STRENGTH (MICROVOLTS/METER)
30–88MHz	100
89–216MHz	150
217–1000MHz	200

RFI became an issue with personal computers when the PC came out because IBM had shielded its PC line and sought to make life a little tougher on the clonemakers. By pushing the FCC to get tough on PCs, IBM had a bit of a jump on the market. Unfortunately, getting Class B certification isn't that hard, and just about every PC qualifies these days: clonemakers now say that their machines are "FCC Class B Certified." This has caused the reverse of IBM's original intent, because the FCC certification seems a mark of legitimacy. In reality, FCC certification is not a measure of good design, quality components, or compatibility; it just means that the equipment doesn't produce excessive amounts of electromagnetic interference.

Protecting your PC from the devices around it and protecting the devices from your PC are done in the same way. If the PC doesn't leak RFI, then it's less likely to pick up any stray RFI in the area. Any holes in the case provide entry/exit points. Use the brackets that come with the machine to plug any unused expansion slots. To prevent unplanned air circulation paths, it is also a good idea to plug unused expansion slots. Ensure that the case fits together snugly and correctly. If the case includes cutouts for interface connectors, find plates to cover the cutouts or simply use metal tape.

A simple AM radio can be used to monitor RFI field strength. A portable radio is ideal, because it has light headphones and a small enough enclosure to allow fairly local signal strength monitoring. A cheap model is best—you don't want sophisticated noise filtering. Tune it to an area of the dial as far as possible from a strong station. Lower frequencies seem to work best. You'll hear the various devices produce noises. I first noticed these noises when working ages ago on a clone computer with an XT motherboard, a composite monitor, an external hard disk, and a two-drive external Bernoulli box. The quietest part of the system was the PC: the hard disk screamed and buzzed, the Bernoulli made low frequency eggbeater-like sounds, and the monitor produced a fairly pure and relatively loud tone.

The PC sounded different, depending on what it was doing. When I typed, I heard a machine-gun–like sound. When I asked for a text search, the fairly regular search made a "dee-dee-dee" sound. It's kind of fun (okay, I guess I don't get out much), and you might pop the top on your system and do a little "radio astronomy" on it.

I've also used the radio in a number of other ways. Once, I received a new motherboard, a 486 that I was going to use to upgrade a 286 system. I installed it, and nothing happened. No beeps, no blinking cursor, nothing but the fan. So I removed the motherboard and placed it on a cardboard box (no electrical short fears with a cardboard box). Then I placed a power supply next to it, plugged in the P8/P9 connectors, and powered up. I ran the radio over the motherboard and got no response, just a constant hum. Placing the radio right over the CPU got nothing. I reasoned that what I was hearing was just the clock circuit. I felt even more certain of my guess when I noticed that the CPU had been inserted backwards into its socket. One dead motherboard, back to the manufacturer.

Power Noise

Your wall socket is a source of lots of problems. They basically fall into these three categories:

- ▶ Overvoltage and undervoltage
- ▶ No voltage at all—a power blackout
- ▶ Transients—spikes and surges

Right now, however, let's look at the fourth kind of power noise, the one that *you* cause: *power-up power surges*.

In the process of discussing how to fix this, I'll have to weigh in on The Great PC Power Switch Debate.

Leave Your Machines On 24 Hours a Day

I'd like to discuss one power-related item here: user-induced power surges. What user-induced power surges, you say? Simple: every time you turn on an electrical device, you get a power surge through it. Some of the greatest stresses that electrical devices receive are when they are turned on or turned off. When do light bulbs burn out? Think about it—they generally burn out when you first turn them on or off. One study showed that when a device is first turned on, it draws as much as four to six times its normal power for less than one second. (This phenomenon is called *inrush current* in the literature. I found this bit of information on page 27 of *Computer Electric Power Requirements* by Mark Waller, published by Sams in 1987.) For that brief time, your PC may be pulling 600 to 900 watts—not a prescription for long PC life.

The answer? Leave your PCs on 24 hours a day, seven days a week. We've done it at my company for years. Turn the monitor off, or turn the screen intensity down, or use one of those annoying automatic screen savers so the monitor doesn't get an image burned into it. Turn the printer off also. Leaving the machines on also regulates temperature and reduces a phenomenon called chip creep.

What? You're still not convinced? I know, it seems non-intuitive—most people react that way. But it really does make sense. First of all, consider the things that you keep on all the time, like these:

- *Local area network (LAN)* servers usually run all the time.
- Digital clocks, which obviously run continuously, incorporate some of the same digital technology as microcomputers, and they're pretty reliable.
- Calculators—I've seen accountants with calculators that are on all the time.
- Mainframes, minis, and your phone PBX never go off.
- TVs (part of the TV is powered up all the time so that it can "warm up" instantly, unlike older sets).
- Thermostats—the temperature-regulating device in your home or business is a circuit that works all the time.

Avoiding Service: Preventative Maintenance

Most of the things that I just named are some of the most reliable, never-think-about-them devices that you work with.

In addition to the things I've already said, consider the hard disk. All disks incorporate a motor to spin them at high speeds (depending upon the drive, they may spin at speeds ranging from 3600 to 10,000 rpm). You know from real life that it's a lot harder to get something moving than it is to keep it moving. (Ever push a car?) The cost, then, of turning hard disk motors on and off is that sometimes they just won't be able to get started.

For example, back in 1984 I bought my first hard disk, an external 32MB drive. It cost $929, and while it's dead and buried now, for years I was loathe to stop using it, because nine hundred bucks is a lot of money. For a long time I kept it attached to a server and constantly running. This illustrates the don't-turn-it-off point of view. The drive required a "jump-start" when it was turned off overnight: if the thing didn't want to work, we just removed it from the system, took off the hard disk's circuit board to expose the motor, and gave the motor a spin. After a couple of spins, we reassembled it, and it would start up fine. (No, I didn't put anything important on it, but it was a great demonstration tool. And it kept data just fine.)

Here's the point: as long as we didn't turn the system off, the hard drive worked quite well, at least as well as old 32MB hard drives work. This applies to hard disks in general, and in fact to anything with a motor. Yes, the motor's life is shortened when continuously on, but even then the expected life of the motor is beyond the reasonable life of a hard disk.

Leaving your computer on all the time heads off thermal shock, which is yet another reason to leave it on. Machines should never be power cycled quickly. I've seen people fry their power supplies by turning their computers on and off several times in a 30-second period "to clear problems" and end up creating bigger problems.

A final word of caution. Leaving the machine on all the time is a good idea only if:

- ▶ Your machine is cooled adequately. If your machine is 100 degrees inside when the room is 70 degrees, it'll overheat when the room goes to 90 degrees on summer weekends when the building management turns off the cooling in your building. Make sure your machine has a good enough fan to handle higher temperatures.

- ▶ You have adequate surge protection. Actually, you shouldn't run the machine at all unless you have adequate surge protection.

- You have fairly reliable power. If you lose power three times a week, there's no point in leaving the machines on all the time—the power company is turning them off and on for you. Even worse, the power just after a power outage is noise-filled.

Before moving on, let's take a quick peek at the other kinds of power problems.

Transients

A *transient* is any brief change in power that doesn't repeat itself. It can be an undervoltage or an overvoltage. Sags (momentary undervoltage) and surges (momentary overvoltage) are transients. Being brief, the transient may be of a high enough frequency that it slips right past the protective capacitors in your power supply and punches holes in your chips. (No, they're not holes you can see, at least not without some very good equipment.) Transients have a cumulative effect—the first 100 may do nothing. Eventually, however, enough chickens come home to roost that your machine decides, one day, to go on vacation. (You might say that if enough chickens come home to roost, the machine "buys the farm.") Permanently.

Overvoltage

You have an *overvoltage* condition when you get more than the rated voltage for a period of greater than 2.5 seconds. Such a voltage measurement is done as a moving average over several seconds.

Chronic overvoltage is just as bad for your system as transient overvoltage: the chips can fail as a result of it.

Undervoltage

Summer in much of the country means air conditioners are running full blast, and the power company is working feverishly to meet the power demands that they bring. Sometimes it can't meet the full needs, however, so it announces a reduction in voltage called a *brownout*.

Brownouts are bad for large motors, like the ones you'd find in a compressor for refrigeration. Brownouts make your TV screen look shrunken, and they confuse power supplies. A power supply tries to provide continuous power to the PC. Power equals voltage times current. If the voltage drops and you want constant power, what do you do? Simple: draw more current. But drawing more current through a given conductor heats up the conductor. The power supply and the chips get hot, and may overheat.

Surge protectors can't help you here. A power conditioner can—it uses a transformer to compensate for the sagging voltage.

Electrostatic Discharge

ESD—or, as you probably know it, *static electricity*—is annoyingly familiar to anyone who has lived through a winter indoors. The air is very dry (winter and forced hot-air ducts bring relative humidity to around 20 percent in my house, for example) and is an excellent insulator. You build up a static charge and keep it (until you touch something like a metal doorknob—or much worse, your computer). On the other hand, in the summer, when relative humidity can be close to 100 percent (until 1998 I lived in a suburb of Washington, D.C., a city built over a swamp), you build up static charges also, but they leak away quickly due to the humidity of the air. Skin resistance also has a lot to do with dissipating charges. The resistance of your skin can be as little as 1,000 ohms when wet and 500,000 ohms when dry. (This fun fact is courtesy of Jearl Walker's *Flying Circus of Physics*, published by John Wiley in 1977.)

You know how static electricity is built up. Static can damage chips if it creates a charge of 200 volts or more. If a static discharge is sufficient for the average person to notice it, it is at least 2,000 volts.

Scuffing across a shag rug in February can build up 50,000 volts. This is an electron "debt" which must be paid. The next metal item you touch (metal gives up electrons easily) pays the debt with an electric shock. If it's 50,000 volts, why doesn't it electrocute you when you touch the metal? Simple, the amperage (which is the volume of electricity) is tiny. This is because even though the voltage is high, the resistance is up in the millions of ohms and 50,000 volts divided by millions of ohms is a tiny amount of current. (As my physics professor used to tell us, "Twinkle, twinkle, little star; power equals I squared R." And people say physics is dull.) Different materials generate more or less static. Many people think that certain materials are static-prone, while others are not. As it turns out, materials have a triboelectric value. Two materials rubbed together will generate static in direct proportion to how far apart their triboelectric values are.

Some common materials, in order of their triboelectric values, are:

- Air
- Human skin
- Asbestos
- Rabbit fur
- Glass
- Human hair
- Nylon
- Wool
- Fur
- Lead
- Silk
- Aluminum
- Paper
- Cotton
- Steel wool
- Hard rubber
- Nickel and copper
- Brass and silver
- Gold and platinum
- Acetate and rayon
- Polyester
- Polyurethane
- Polyvinyl
- Chloride
- Silicon
- Teflon

Once an item is charged, the voltage potential between it and another object is proportional to the distance between it and the other item on the table. For instance, suppose I charge a glass rod with a cotton cloth. The glass will attract things below it on this list, like paper, but will attract more strongly things listed below paper.

Why does static damage PC components? The chips that largely comprise circuit boards are devices that can be damaged by high voltage, even if at low current. The two most common families of chips are CMOS (Complementary Metal Oxide Semiconductor chips, which include NMOS (Negative Metal Oxide Semiconductor), PMOS (Positive Metal Oxide Semiconductor) and an assortment of newer devices that seem to appear on an almost daily basis, and TTL (Transistor-Transistor Logic) chips. TTLs are an older family. TTLs are faster–switching chips—so potentially faster chips (memories, CPUs, and such) could be designed with TTL. Ah, but TTL has a fatal flaw: it draws a lot of power. TTL chips need much more electricity than CMOS chips, so they create more heat, and so, while fast TTL CPUs could be constructed, CPUs are tough because densely packed TTLs produce so much heat that they would destroy themselves. One common family of TTL chips has ID numbers starting

Avoiding Service: Preventative Maintenance

with 74, as in 7400, 7446, 74LS128, and the like. Actually, the LS in the middle of the ID means it is a variant on TTL called Low power Schottky, hence the LS.

CPUs and memories are generally CMOS chips. CMOS has a lower theoretical maximum speed, but it runs on a lot less power. Sadly, they are also more subject to static electricity damage. TTL chips can withstand considerably more static electricity than CMOS chips.

Even if static doesn't destroy a chip, it can shorten its life. Static is, then, something to be avoided if possible. Another effect occurs when the static is discharged. When the fat blue spark jumps from your finger to the doorknob, a small electromagnetic pulse (EMP) is created. This isn't too good for chips, either. (It's the thing you've heard about that could cause a single nuclear explosion to destroy every computer in the country, except a lot smaller.) The easiest way I get rid of my static is to discharge the static buildup on something metal that is not the computer's case. A metal desk or table leg is good.

For your business, however, you may want something a trifle more automatic. The options are:

- Raise the humidity with a humidifier (evaporative, not ultrasonic—ultrasonic creates dust).
- Raise the humidity with plants, or perhaps an aquarium.
- Install static-free carpet.
- Put anti-static "touch me" mats under the PCs.
- Make your own anti-static spray (see below).

From the point of view of comfort, I recommend the first option strongly. Your employees don't feel dried-out, and the static problem disappears. Raise humidity to just 50 percent and the problem will go away.

You can make inexpensive, homemade anti-static spray. Just get a spray pump bottle and put about an inch of fabric softener in it. Fill it the rest of the way with water, shake it well, and you've got a spray for your carpets to reduce static. Just spritz it on the rug, and the rug will smell nice, and everyone will know that you've been busy. (I hear you asking, "How long does it last?" Don't worry, you'll know.)

In a similar vein, a person from a temporary services agency once told me that they tell their word processing operators to put a sheet of Bounce under the keyboard to reduce static. While this may make the area smell nice, it will have no effect on static around the computer.

Technicians who must work with semiconductors all of the time use a ground strap to minimize ESD. The idea with a ground strap is that you never create a spark—and therefore EMP—because you've always got a nice ground connection that's draining off your charges. A good ground strap is an elastic wristband with a metal plate built into it to provide good electrical connection, attached to a wire with an alligator clip. You put the clip on something grounded—the power supply case is the most common place—and put the strap around your wrist. As you're connected to a ground, you continuously drain off your charges. A resistor in the ground strap slows down the discharge process a bit (from a microsecond to a few milliseconds), so you don't end up with one of the dangerous sparks that we've discussed before. If you do a lot of board work in a dry place, ground straps are essential. Several Silicon Valley defense-contracting firms have a policy of firing employees for not wearing their ESD wrist straps when working on high tech equipment such as satellites and military equipment.

When you must handle electronic components, take these precautions:

▶ Get an anti-static strap.

▶ Reduce the amount of static that you transfer to a chip with a ground strap, or remember the high-tech equivalent of knocking wood—touch unpainted metal periodically. One member of my staff has suggested handling chips only while naked on a wooden floor. While this might be entertaining to some of the staff, it would not, unfortunately, prevent static charges from building up, since on a very dry day, even the movement of your hair can build up a charge.

▶ Get an anti-static strap. They're cheap.

▶ Don't handle components in areas having high static potential. For example, avoid carpets unless they are anti-static or in high humidity environments. Don't wear an acrylic sweater when changing chips. Get leather-soled shoes. If your work environment allows it, you can really avoid static by removing your shoes and socks.

▶ Don't handle chips any more than is necessary. If you don't touch them, you won't hurt them.

- Use anti-static protective tubes and bags to transport and store chips.
- If possible, pick up components by their bodies. Don't touch the pins any more than necessary.
- Have I mentioned yet that you should have an anti-static strap and use an anti-static mat?

Use the proper precautions, and your PC won't get a big "charge" out of being touched by you.

Avoiding Water and Liquids

Water is an easy hazard to detect and avoid. You don't need any sophisticated detection devices. Shielding is unnecessary—you just keep the computer away from water.

Water and liquids are introduced into a computer system in one of several ways:

- Operator spills
- Leaks
- Flooding

Spills generally threaten the keyboard. One remedy—the one recommended by every article and book I've ever read on maintenance—is to forbid liquids near the computer. In most shops, this is unrealistic. Some people use clear flexible plastic covers on the keyboard, kind of like what Burger King uses on their cash registers. They've got normal cash registers, but they have a plastic skin over the keys that allows the user to spill "special sauce" all over the keyboard without harming it. Use the plastic covers, and they can just hose down the keyboard. (Just kidding.) With one of these keyboard "skins," you might say that you can "practice safe typing."

SafeSkin is offered by Merritt Computer Products in Dallas. (Their address is listed in Appendix C.) They offer versions for the various odd keyboards in the PC world.

A similar disaster, flooding, sometimes occurs. Don't assume that flooded components are destroyed components. Disassemble the computer and clean the boards by cleaning the contacts and edge connectors.

You can buy connector cleaner fluids, or some people use a hard white artist's eraser—do not use pencil erasers! (A Texas Instruments study showed that they contain acids that do more harm than good to connectors.) Blow out crevices with compressed air. (And if you do disassemble, clean, dry, and reassemble your computer, and then find that it works, write the manufacturer a letter; they might put your face in an advertisement.)

Avoid floods by thinking ahead. Don't store any electrical devices directly on the floor; they'll be damaged when the floor is cleaned. Generally, flooding indoors is under six inches. Be aware of flooding from improper roofing; when installing PCs, don't put one in directly under the suspicious stain on the ceiling. ("Oh, that—it was fixed two years ago. No problem now.")

Corrosion

Liquids (and gases) can accelerate corrosion of PCs and PC components. Corrosive agents include:

- Salt sweat in skin oils
- Water
- Airborne sulfuric acid, salt spray, and carbonic acid

Your fear here is not that the PC will fall away to rust; the largest problem that corrosion causes is oxidation of circuit contacts. When a device's connector becomes oxidized, it doesn't conduct as well, and so the device does not function, or—worse—malfunctions sporadically. Salt in sweat can do this, so be careful when handling circuit boards; don't touch edge connectors unless you have to. This is why some firms advertise that they use gold edge connectors; gold is resistant to corrosion.

You don't believe that you have detectable traces of finger oils? Try this simple experiment. Pour a glass of soda or beer into a very clean glass—preferably a plastic cup that has never been used before. There will be a noticeable "head" on the drink. (Diet soda seems particularly fizzy.) Now put your finger into the center of the head, just for a second. The head will rapidly dissolve, because the oils damage the surface tension required to support the head. It's the quickest way to eliminate a large head so you can pour a larger glass of beer. Or you could try buying a nice new 20-inch color computer monitor and see how many of your colleagues fail to understand that it is not a touch-screen device. You will end up with numerous thick, oily smudge marks on your monitor that are very visible and annoying when a dark background is displayed on it.

Carbonated liquids include carbonic acid, and coffee and tea contain tannic acids. The sugar in soda is eaten by bacteria that leave behind conductive excrement—like hiring some germs to put new traces on your circuit board. Generally, try to be very careful with drinks around computers.

Don't forget cleaning fluids. Be careful with that window cleaner that you're using to keep the display clean. If your PC is on a pedestal on the floor, and the floor is mopped each day, some of the mopping liquid gets into the PC. Cleaning fluids are very corrosive.

You can clean edge connectors with either hard white erasers (remember, don't use the pink erasers—they're acidic!) or connector cleaner products. One of the best-known vendors of these products is Texwipe.

Making the Environment "PC Friendly"

Let's sum up what we've seen in this chapter. Protect your PC by doing the following:

- Check power considerations:
    - No heating elements (Mr. Coffee, portable heaters) in the same outlet as a PC
    - No large electric motors (refrigerators, air conditioners) on the same line as the PC
    - Some kind of power noise protection
- Check temperature ranges:
    - Maximum 110 degrees F (43 degrees C)
    - Minimum 65 degrees F (18 degrees C)

The minimum temperature can actually be considerably lower, as long as the computer remains *on* all of the time.

- Prevent dust buildup—you can buy (from PC Power and Cooling) power supplies with a filtered fan that suck air in through the *back* rather than the usual approach of pulling it in through the front.

- Make sure there isn't a vibration source like an impact printer on the same table as the hard disk.
- Make sure you're familiar with or (if you're a support person) teach your users about:
    - Leaving the machines on all the time
    - Keeping cables screwed in and out of the way
    - Basic "don't do this" things in DOS, like formatting the hard disk
- Protect against static electricity.

What's Next?

Now that Mark Minasi has shown you how to protect your computer hardware against the most common environmental hazards, the next two chapters will show you how to install RAM and multimedia devices.

Chapter 26

Installing Random Access Memory

Random Access Memory (RAM) is part of the engine that runs your computer. While advertisements and sales pitches place a large emphasis on CPU speed, touting the clock speed of the central processing unit in the same manner that car dealers wax rapturous about raw horsepower, the amount of RAM in your computer is often more important than the processor type and clock speed.

The amount of RAM in your computer is something like the road on which you drive your car. A larger engine may allow your car to go faster, but if the only road you're permitted to drive on is your driveway, you can't go very fast—a driveway just doesn't give you any room to build up speed. In the case of your computer, a faster or more advanced CPU may do things faster—but without memory, your "engine" is limited in its performance by a lack of space in which to run.

Chapter written by Ben Ezzell exclusively for *PC Complete*
ISBN 0-7821-2422-4   1040 pages $19.99

In brief, both your CPU and your available memory determine how well your computer is going to work and how fast it will work. Of the two, a slow CPU with sufficient memory will generally outperform a fast CPU with limited memory.

One advantage of this relationship between CPU and memory is that you can add memory to your computer quickly, simply, and (nowadays) without much cost. In fact, adding more memory is not only the least expensive upgrade you can make, it's also the most important in terms of performance.

How Much Memory Is Enough?

In the "good old days"—back when DOS was the standard operating system—the amount of memory in your computer was less critical. And, in the very early days, when PCs were first being introduced, computers were commonly sold with a grandiose 16KB (that's kilobytes, not megabytes) of memory and with the capability of upgrading to a whopping total of 48 or, sometimes, 56KB or 64KB. At the time, memory was expensive—very expensive.

As PCs began to be popular and MS-DOS took its place as the preeminent operating system in the market, an arbitrary and badly chosen upper limit for memory was set at 640KB, with the addresses above the 640KB limit reserved for the system video and for other system processes.

Very early on, a mere 640 kilobytes proved to be very constricting. Applications running under DOS simply could not—i.e., were not permitted to—reach memory addresses above the 640KB limit. The arbitrary limit was enforced by the structure of DOS itself as well as by the address structures permitted for applications executing under DOS.

> **NOTE**
> The 640KB limitation was set by a young computer entrepreneur who was quite satisfied that 640 kilobytes of memory were more than adequate to satisfy anyone's requirements. Of course, the entrepreneur in question was one Bill Gates, and the segment:offset addressing schema that resulted remained an industry bottleneck for years, even as prices for RAM chips dropped and memory requirements rose, both quite sharply.

Installing Random Access Memory

To address the unfortunate limitations built into DOS, two methods of accessing and using memory beyond the 640KB limit were developed. Known as XMS (eXtended Memory System) and EMS (Enhanced Memory System) respectively, these methods were supported by a variety of utilities to allow applications to have access to physical memory above the 1 megabyte (1MB) address point.

Today DOS is simply a historical relic—to the regret of very few, if any, computer users—and virtually all users have moved to more advanced operating systems, with the Windows 95/98/NT operating systems dominating the market. At the same time, even the most basic computer sold today is provided with a minimum of 16MB of RAM memory—approximately 1,000 times as much as was supplied with the earliest PCs.

While Microsoft has made varying claims about the minimum amount of memory that various versions of its operating systems need in order to function correctly, the minimums stated have always been just that: bare minimums with which a specific version of Windows will—however poorly—function. To be more specific, the accepted definition of "minimum configuration" for a graphical operating system (such as Windows) is the smallest amount of memory that will allow the OS to handle all of the system's advanced graphical tasks and to run one or two typical applications at the same time without performance suffering badly.

With Windows 3.*x*, for example, the minimum requirement was for 4MB of RAM, which was a major jump from the 640K minimum expected under DOS. As I said, however, this 4MB requirement was a minimum; by adding another 4MB to bring the system up to 8MB performance was greatly enhanced.

Although Windows 3.*x* was not an operating system in the true sense, it ran on top of DOS and was subject to the limitations imposed by DOS, including the limitation that it did not have true access to memory beyond 640KB. To get around the 640KB limitation, Windows 3.*x* could be enhanced by the appropriate installation of EMS/XMS memory drivers, such as Quarterdeck's QEMM (Quarterdeck Extended Memory Manager).

The first operating system that really could address memory directly without using block-swapping memory drivers was OS/2 (way back in 1989 and thus predating Windows 3, which originally came out in 1990), which did not operate on top of DOS and was not subject to the same memory limitations.

> **NOTE**
> Despite the fact that OS/2 was originally a joint project between Microsoft and IBM, the popularity of the operating system was limited because it required more memory (at a time when memory was expensive) as well as more-advanced CPUs than average users felt they could afford.

In the Microsoft world, it was not until the introduction of Windows NT (version 3.1, released in 1992) that the 640K limit was finally left behind. Windows NT was a true operating system: it did not require DOS. However, it did need more memory than was required by Windows 3.0; like Windows 3.1, Windows NT also benefited from more powerful (faster) CPUs.

Windows NT expected a minimum of 16MB of RAM but benefited from larger amounts. Because both memory and advanced CPUs were still relatively expensive, Windows NT did not become popular with the average user and, instead, was adopted primarily in corporate and research environments where cost was less important than speed and power.

For the average user, then, the 640K barrier—however it may have been masked by Windows 3.*x*—did not vanish until the introduction of Windows 95. Even though Windows 95 (appearing, of course, in 1995) still contained 16-bit code for backward compatibility to run DOS and Windows 3.*x* applications, it was a true operating system and was thus independent of the structural limitations of DOS.

Windows 95 was billed as requiring a minimum of 8MB of RAM. (Actually, Microsoft claimed that Windows 95 *could* run in 4MB of RAM, a fact that was proved by several demos, but they didn't recommend it. For one thing, on 4MB it "ran" in the same sense that a tortoise "runs.")

Windows 95 was introduced at a time when memory chips were relatively inexpensive (compared to when Windows 3.*x* was first available), so installing 8MB in a computer was not a financial strain, and at the time, units were commonly being sold with 16MB standard. For advanced users—particularly those working with video or with large amounts of complex data—upgrades to 32MB were more than helpful, providing significant improvements in performance.

With the introduction of Windows 98, the newest Windows OS, the bar has been raised again, with a minimum requirement of 16MB. As usual, a more realistic configuration would have 32MB; advanced users with complex requirements may well want to install 64 or 128MB—or even more.

Installing Random Access Memory 757

> **NOTE**
> Claims have been made for running Windows 98 under 12MB of RAM, but given today's prices and SIMM configurations, you may as well stick with a minimum of 16MB.

TABLE 26.1: Operating System RAM Requirements

Operating System	Minimum	Realistic	Advanced Users
Windows 3.x	4MB	8MB	n/a
Windows 95	8MB	16MB	32MB
Windows 98	16MB	32MB	64/128MB
Windows NT	16MB	64MB	128/256MB

Windows Swap Files

Windows uses a mechanism called a *Windows swap file* to extend the amount of RAM available for executed applications. A swap file is a file on the hard drive that is managed as if it were an extension of the system RAM, and is used by the operating system to store data that is not immediately required.

> **NOTE**
> OS/2, Linux, and other operating systems also use swap files in a similar fashion, and for the same reasons.

When Windows needs more memory than is physically available, such as for spooling a large print job or for many other purposes, Windows *swaps* some part of the data from active RAM to the swap file, freeing RAM for more important uses. This is a background process that is happening all the time while you are working, and it's handled transparently, without requiring your attention and without requiring any special provisions by the applications being executed.

In effect, even if a computer has only 16MB of RAM, Windows can still attempt to use much more memory by treating a part of the hard drive as a special-purpose file that functions like (emulates) a larger block of RAM.

The downside of using a swap file is simple: transferring and retrieving data from this "virtual" memory—i.e., the swap file on the hard drive—is labor intensive, and it is slower than accessing data that is located in physical RAM (active memory). Windows optimizes this process by swapping elements out of memory on the basis of use—that is, sending less-recently used material to the swap file in preference to frequently or recently used data.

The big advantage of having a large amount of RAM (active memory) is that Windows will only resort to the swap file when the active memory is filled (or is about to be filled).

RAM versus Hard Drives

Partially because the hard drive (swap file) is used as an extension of RAM memory, users sometimes become confused about the difference between RAM and disk memory. While a large hard drive allows you to store a great many applications and data files, the size of the hard drive has nothing to do with the system performance (other than giving you some place in which to create your swap file) and is not a replacement for RAM memory.

How Much Memory Is Installed?

Before you run out and buy more memory for your computer, take this simple first step: find out how much memory you have installed already.

Although there is no "memory gauge" on the front of your computer, there is a memory test performed every time you power up (i.e., boot or reboot) your computer. The memory test is commonly identified by the BIOS (not by the operating system) as part of the POST (Power-On Self Test)—and its report may look something like this:

```
Memory Test: 65536K OK
```

This particular reading is rather easy to miss because, commonly, it goes by so fast that you don't really have time to see it unless you are looking for it. The length of time the report appears on-screen is dependent on the BIOS settings and the CPU speed.

There are, however, several other ways to check your system to determine the amount of memory installed. One of the easiest is from a DOS prompt (assuming you're running Windows 95 or 98, choose MS-DOS Prompt from the Start menu). Once the DOS window opens—see Figure 26.1—simply type MEM at the prompt; the Memory utility will test the system memory and report on the amount of memory installed.

Installing Random Access Memory

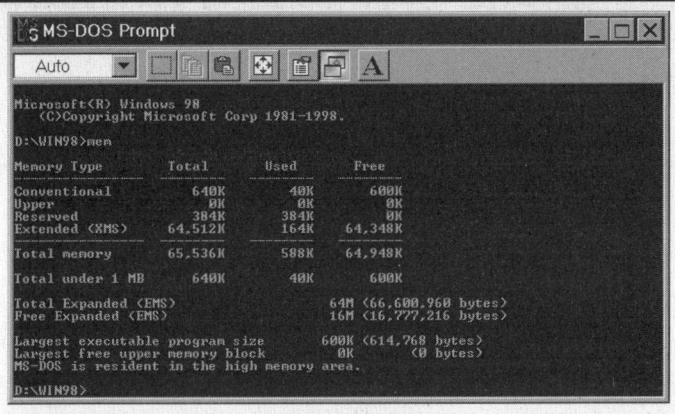

FIGURE 26.1: Using the DOS MEM utility

As you can see, the Mem utility is reporting memory as though the old DOS 640KB limits were still relevant and reports the bulk of the memory available as XMS memory (see the Totals column), while the real total is the sum of the Conventional, Reserved, and XMS memory.

> **NOTE**
> Under Windows 95/98/NT, the distinctions between Conventional, Reserved, and XMS memory really no longer exist or apply.

A second method of checking system memory is to open the Control Panel (from the Start menu, select Settings ➢ Control Panel). From the Control Panel, select the System (System Properties) utility and then choose the Performance tab—see Figure 26.2.

Alternatively, you may right-click the My Computer icon on the Desktop and then select Properties from that right-click menu to display the System Properties utility, which offers a few ways of seeing your computer's configuration.

In Figure 26.2 the Performance status reports the system memory as 64.0MB of RAM, without any obsolete references to Conventional, Reserved, or XMS memory settings.

From this utility's Performance tab, the Virtual Memory button also allows management of the Windows swap file, as shown in Figure 26.3.

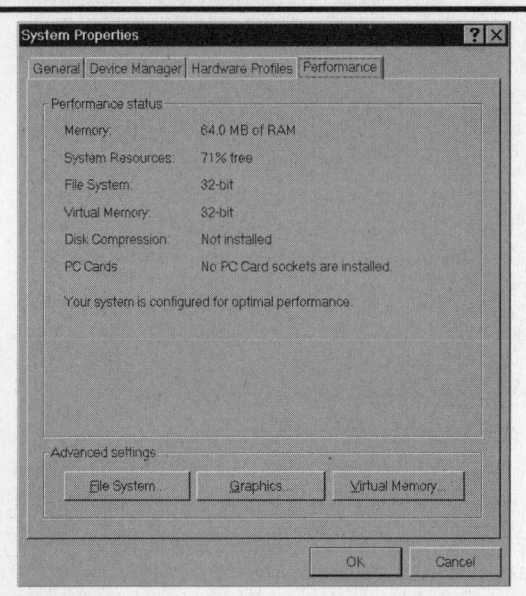

FIGURE 26.2: The System utility showing installed memory

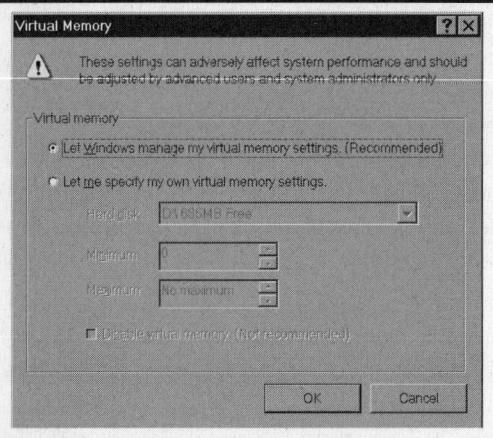

FIGURE 26.3: Virtual Memory settings

With rare exceptions, the optimum choice for managing virtual memory (the swap file) is to allow Windows to handle virtual memory. If necessary, however, you may specify which physical or logical drive to use for the swap file, and you may specify a minimum and a maximum size for the swap file.

A final option with the System Properties utility allows the virtual memory (swap file) to be disabled entirely.

Installing Random Access Memory

> **WARNING**
> Disabling virtual memory is not recommended, because selecting this option will have adverse effects on system performance, and may even cause the system to hang or crash.

Once you know how much memory is installed in your system and have decided to add memory, the next step is to determine what type of memory your system uses.

Types of Memory Modules

Simply walking into your neighborhood computer store (or office supply store, or contacting an Internet supplier) and buying more memory is not appropriate. Before buying memory, you need to know what kind of memory chips your computer uses and you also need to decide what kind of memory to upgrade with.

> **TIP**
> If you are using a portable or laptop computer, your options may be further limited by what memory upgrades the computer will accept and even whether there is space in the portable to add more memory. For portable or laptop computers, you should contact the manufacturer or consult a reliable computer shop/technician.

Computer memory comes in a variety of configurations, as described by such factors as packaging, speed, and type.

Memory Packaging

In the early days of PCs, memory was purchased as "DIP chips." DIP was shorthand for Dual-Inline Pins, which referred to the two rows of pins that protruded from opposite sides of the chip package and bent down to plug into a DIP socket.

Today, instead of installing individual chips, you add to the main memory in most computers by installing *package* chips, where more than one chip is mounted on a SIMM (Single Inline Memory Module) or DIMM (Dual Inline Memory Module). Identifying the type of package you have or need is discussed further later in this section.

Packaging details are only one consideration, however.

Memory Speed

A second consideration is speed. There are actually two considerations here. First, memory speed is not the same as the CPU speed. For one thing, it is measured in *nanoseconds* (abbreviated *ns*), and the smaller the number, the faster the memory—i.e., a 50ns chip is faster than a 70ns chip. Compare that to the speeds you typically see for CPUs, where it's a case of the higher the number, the faster the processor: 300MHz (megahertz) is definitely faster than 166MHz.

> **NOTE**
> The numerical readout on the front of many computers is indicating the CPU speed, not the memory speed. (Actually, please note, however, that the speed indicated may or may not bear any relationship to the actual CPU speed.)

The second consideration when it comes to memory speed is whether you plan to mix your speeds. On the one hand, slower memory chips can be installed as additions to faster chips in a computer, but your computer will then treat *all* of your memory as though it were *all* rated at the slower speed. On the other hand, you should avoid installing chips that are faster than the computer is rated to use (the computer mainboard, that is).

To determine the memory speed supported by the computer, refer to the documentation for your computer. Specifically, refer to the documentation for the computer's mainboard, which should tell you what type of memory is required, what packaging (module type) is used, and what memory speed is supported.

Memory Blocks

Computer memory is installed in blocks. Normally, the computer mainboard will have four sockets for memory packages. Commonly two of these will be used when the computer is manufactured, leaving two slots (sockets) open for memory expansion.

Therefore, if you want to add 16MB of memory to the existing memory, you would want to buy two 8MB modules, installing one in each of the two open sockets.

If there are no open sockets for memory, you may need to remove existing modules and replace them with larger capacity modules. Your computer mainboard documentation should also tell you whether you must replace/upgrade memory modules in pairs only or whether single memory modules may be installed.

Memory Types

Two principal types of RAM are in use: DRAM (dynamic RAM) and SRAM (static RAM), but these also occur in a number of variations, each with different characteristics:

DRAM   Dynamic Random Access Memory is both the most common and the cheapest type of memory chip, but it is also the slowest type of memory. DRAM consists of capacitors that store individual bits (1s and 0s) of data. The capacitors hold a charge only for a brief period—milliseconds, actually—and must be continually refreshed to maintain the data; hence these are termed dynamic RAM. DRAM chips comprise the bulk of the memory used in computers and are found in both low-cost SIMMs and DIMMs.

SRAM   Static Random Access Memory chips consist of banks of transistors that do not need to be refreshed and are roughly four times faster than DRAM memory. In general, SRAM chips are also larger than other types of memory, and are commonly used only in some of the more specialized memory requirements in a computer, such as Pipelined Burst or Synchronous Cache memory where speed is at a premium.

EDO RAM   Extended Data Out Random Access Memory is the fastest memory because EDO RAM can read and write data from different locations at the same time. EDO RAM is faster than DRAM, speeding memory performance by as much as 40 percent, but is effective only up to bus speeds of 66MHz, while modern CPUs are commonly operated at much higher speeds.

FP Mode DRAM   Fast Page Mode DRAM is very similar to EDO RAM but uses a different access mode, with random page access speeds below 30MHz—much slower than the bus speed. To compensate for this discrepancy, DRAM manufacturers use a RAM cache as a bridge between slow memory and faster CPUs.

SDRAM   Synchronous Dynamic RAM (also called PC-100 RAM) is faster than EDO RAM; it handles bus speeds up to 100MHz, but it's also more expensive. SDRAM is synchronized with the system clock; i.e., it runs at the CPU's speed.

Sync SRAM Synchronous burst SRAM, like SDRAM, is also synchronized with the system clock, making it faster than the Async SRAM commonly used in L2 caches.

PB SRAM Pipeline Burst SRAM uses pipelining to collect data requests, which are executed as a burst on a nearly instantaneous basis. PB SRAM is designed to work at bus speeds above 75MHz; it is a major component in Pentium II and later systems.

ECCDRAM Error Correcting Circuit DRAM; in wide usage in servers these days.

VRAM Video Random Access Memory is used on video cards. VRAM is similar to DRAM but has two ports to increase access speeds. One port is used to read VRAM contents to constantly update the display while the second port is used to write changes to the display data. The combination significantly increases video performance, as well as reducing the load on the CPU. Adding additional video memory allows your computer to support higher screen resolutions and higher color resolutions and improves system performance by making it easier (faster) to create images on the screen.

When upgrading system RAM, the same type of memory modules *must* be used. What this means is that if your computer presently uses DRAM modules, you can only add additional DRAM modules; you cannot change to EDO RAM or SRAM. The reason is simple: the circuits on the mainboard do not support other types of memory and may be damaged or may fail to operate if you try to force the issue.

In some cases, particularly with newer mainboards, more than one type of memory may be supported, and sockets may be provided for different types of modules. Always refer to the documentation for your computer mainboard to determine which module types are supported. (Actually, these types of boards are rare, and are typically provided for specialty purposes only. You will find few vendors willing to deal in these types of boards and few people who will need them.)

> **TIP**
> Chips known as *Parity RAM* chips included an extra bit for every byte (eight bits) of memory; the extra bit was used to verify the data during use. While Parity memory was common in early computers, RAM has been greatly improved since the first computers and the parity bit is no longer required. Parity RAM is now difficult to find and is not necessary for contemporary machines.

SIMM and DIMM Memory Sockets

While DIP chips are still manufactured, most of us are not expected to work with them individually. They are awkward to install, and even harder to remove without inflicting damage; they also occupy unacceptable amounts of valuable board space. Today, instead of expecting users and administrators to install chips individually, the chipmakers install (package) the DIPs in modules that are small strips of phenolytic board (circuit board) with etched traces leading to contacts along the side. The person installing the memory merely has to hold the board along the edges that don't have the contacts (i.e., please don't touch the contacts), and slip it into the memory socket in such a way as to align the board's connectors with the socket's connectors. Typical individual modules may include anywhere from three to nine DIP chips.

SIMM Modules

The first modular memory package introduced was the SIMM or Single Inline Memory Module, which held a single row of chips soldered to one side of a narrow circuit board with contacts on one edge that is inserted in a socket. SIMMs may also come with chips installed on both sides and come in several varieties: 30-pin, 72-pin, and 168-pin designs.

The 30-pin SIMMs are commonly found on older computers, while the 72-pin SIMMs are used with newer mainboards. The 168-pin design is usually reserved for the newer DIMM design (described in the next section).

A SIMM module is installed (see Figure 26.5) by holding the SIMM at an angle (approximately 45 degrees) to slip easily into the socket. One end of the SIMM has a hole matching a pin in the socket holder, a notch in one end of the board at the end of the row of contacts, and an offset notch near the center (see Figure 26.4). The SIMM can be installed one way only, and the hole and notches are designed to ensure that the module is installed correctly.

> **WARNING**
>
> Never *force* a SIMM into the socket!

The SIMM module should seat in the socket without force. Once the module is seated at an angle, hold the module down in the socket and tilt it back until the clips at each end of the socket snap into position.

30-pin SIMM

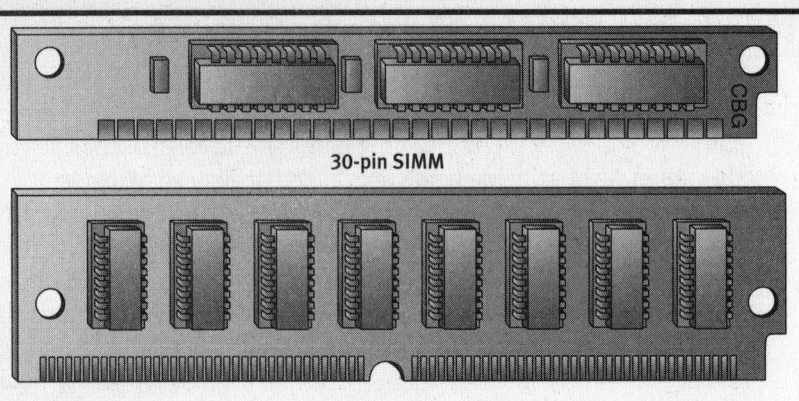

72-pin SIMM

FIGURE 26.4: Single and double-sided SIMMs

To remove a SIMM module, the clips at each end of the socket must be released—by pulling both of them gently outward, away from the module—allowing the module to tilt out. Once the module is tilted, it can easily be lifted free from the socket.

DIMM Modules

DIMM Modules—Dual Inline Memory Modules—are similar to SIMMs and are installed in the same fashion. The two big differences are that DIMMs are thicker, with chips stacked to provide more memory per module; and that DIMMs commonly use a 168-pin socket rather than a 30- or 72-pin socket. Like SIMMs, DIMMs may have chips on only one side or they may have them on both sides.

All DIMM modules have two notches, one near the center and one near one of the ends, along the contact edge (see Figures 26.6 and 26.7).

The DIMM sockets on the mainboard have a couple of "keys" (precisely positioned nubs) corresponding to precisely positioned notches along the module's contact edge to ensure that the socket will only accept, for the first key, a DIMM module with the correct voltage requirements (either 5.0V or 3.3V) and, for the other key, the proper type of DRAM (RFU, Buffered, or Unbuffered). The notch keys shown in Figure 26.7 are for an unbuffered 3.3V module.

Installing Random Access Memory 767

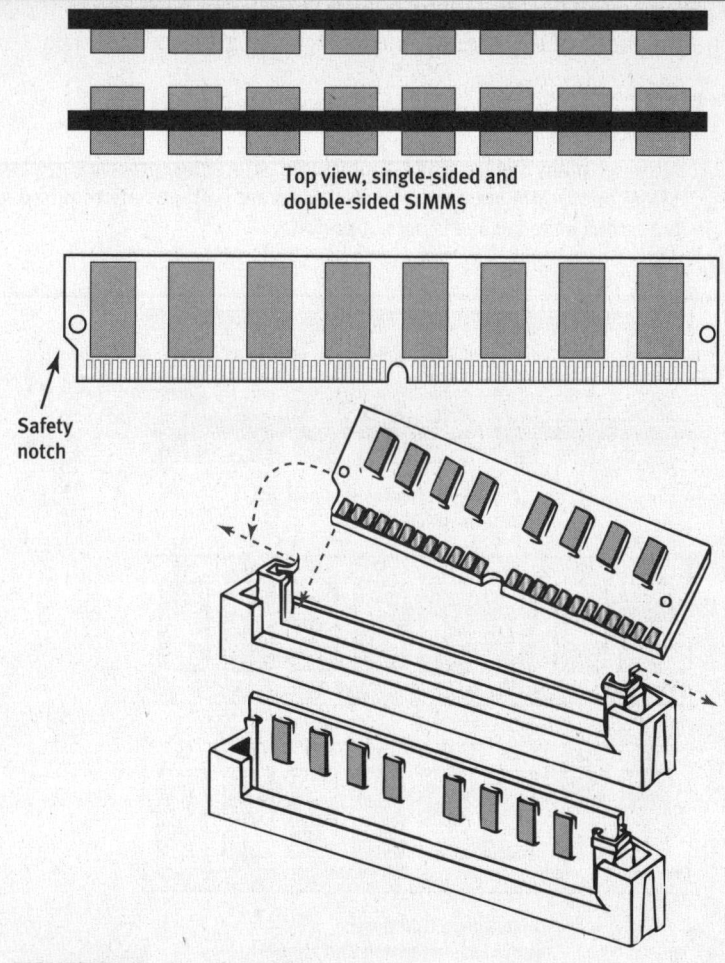

Top view, single-sided and double-sided SIMMs

Safety notch

FIGURE 26.5: Installing a SIMM module

> **NOTE**
> Refer to the manual for your mainboard to determine the exact parameters required before purchasing DIMM modules. Attempting a match merely from visual characteristics is not likely to be correct.

The DIMM module should seat in the socket without having to be forced, by inserting the module directly into the socket at a 90-degree angle. Once the module is seated, the clips at each end engage the module and hold it in position.

768 Chapter Twenty-Six

To remove a DIMM module, release the clips at each end of the socket by pulling both of them gently outward, away from the module.

> **WARNING**
> Although many mainboards manufactured before 1997 provide sockets for both SIMM and DIMM memory modules, different voltages are required for each type; thus mixed usage is *not* supported.

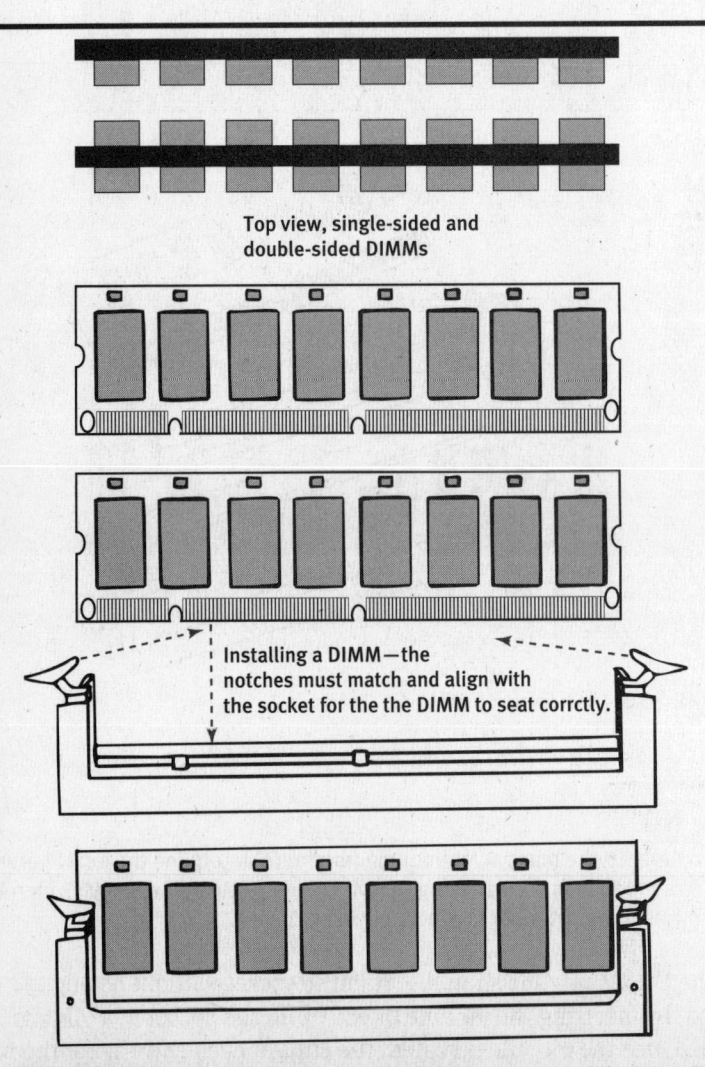

Top view, single-sided and double-sided DIMMs

Installing a DIMM—the notches must match and align with the socket for the the DIMM to seat corrctly.

FIGURE 26.6: Dual Inline Memory Modules (DIMM)

For purposes of simplicity, the following instructions refer only to the SIMM configuration, but computers using DIMM modules can be treated in exactly the same fashion.

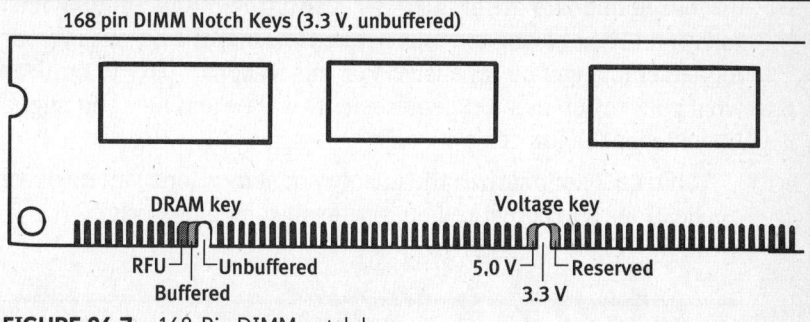

FIGURE 26.7: 168-Pin DIMM notch keys

Using Older Memory Modules in Newer Machines

Older memory modules such as 30-pin SIMMs can be installed in newer mainboards where only 72-pin sockets are provided, by using a module adapter. Module adapters are inexpensive and provide four or eight 30-pin sockets on an extended board with a 72-pin connector on the side.

There are a few factors to consider before using an adapter:

▶ Memory is cheap today, and it may actually be more practical to buy new memory using 72-pin SIMM or 168-pin DIMM modules than to reuse older memory.

▶ Some 30-to-72-pin adapters may physically conflict with installing conventional modules. Some adapters are made extra wide in order to have the adapter sockets positioned above the area where the conventional SIMMs are installed.

▶ Some companies will accept older 30-pin memory modules as trade-in against 72-pin packages, or they will remount 30-pin packages as 72-pin packages for a nominal fee.

In any case, consider the economics first before deciding whether to replace or reuse existing memory. But also plan ahead to decide what your memory requirements will be both today and six months in the future, as discussed below.

Planning Memory Requirements

While memory is probably the cheapest and most effective upgrade you can perform on your computer, the slots where memory can be installed on your mainboard are limited. Because of this, simply adding memory today and then having to replace it in a few months because you need more memory can be expensive. For this reason, it pays to think about what your future memory requirements will be and how you might upgrade for the future.

Table 26.2 summarizes the memory demands for a variety of common applications and activities being performed on a modern PC (i.e., running Windows 95, 98, or 98 SE).

TABLE 26.2: RAM requirements for optimal operation on a typical Windows 95/98/98 SE machine

Applications and Use	Min	Max
Light use of word processing, e-mail, database. Not more than one or two applications open at a time.	16MB	24MB
Medium use of word processing, e-mail, fax, communications, spreadsheets, business graphics, database. Not more than one or two applications open at a time.	24MB	32MB
Number crunching with spreadsheets, accounting software. Not more than one or two applications open at a time.	32MB	48MB
Heavy number crunching, spreadsheets, statistical applications, large databases. Commonly three or more applications open at a time.	48MB	64MB
Page layout, light illustration/graphics; also application development using most compilers. Commonly not more than one or two applications open at a time.	64MB	96MB
Medium illustration/graphics, including photo editing, extensive presentation software, font packages, multimedia. Commonly three or more applications open at one time.	96MB	128MB
Power users, heavy graphics editing, developers with complex compiler packages. Commonly with multiple applications open at any time.	128MB	256MB

The requirements listed in Table 26.2 are optimums, not minimums, for the different types of usage, and virtually all of the categories can be operated using less memory than specified.

Sources

Where you buy memory and where you get the best price is always an open question. Once you know the type and size of modules needed, a variety of Internet search agents can give you comparative prices from a variety of mail-order sources.

What you should be considering, however, is the reliability of the source. Paying a dollar or two more to a reliable dealer can save you a whole lot of dollars later. Sometimes memory goes bad. Sometimes you may be wrong about what kind you needed. Sometimes a mistake can be made by the supplier. Dealing with someone you know—and someone who can guarantee quality—is the real economy.

Also, most reputable dealers will have a means for testing memory modules, so ask for the modules to be tested before leaving the store. This in itself can save headaches.

INSTALLATION

Installing RAM is probably the easiest upgrade you can perform on your computer. Installing memory can take 10 minutes or less and can make even a slow computer perform much better.

> **NOTE**
> RAM memory is the highway your computer CPU runs on!

The more memory in your computer, the less time the system needs to spend swapping data into and out of the Windows swap file, and the faster the CPU can work.

In actual fact, it will probably take you longer to learn the terminology and to research what type of memory your computer uses than it will to actually install the memory.

Static Electricity—IMPORTANT!

Before you touch anything inside the computer and before handling parts for installation, you should make absolutely sure that you have discharged your static electricity. If you do not, even a small static charge—one that you do not even notice—can permanently damage computer components.

> **WARNING**
> Always unplug your computer before installing any components. While voltages inside the computer are too low to harm you (or to even notice), they are plenty strong enough to damage the tiny electronic components! Never install or remove components while the computer is powered up or plugged in!

A static charge can be produced by a variety of circumstances: walking across a carpeted floor, sliding across a fabric seat cushion, wearing the kind of fabric that generates static charges easily merely from the act of walking (as your trouser legs brush against each other), touching the TV, etc. All of these and others can cause static buildup, and especially in a dry environment.

Guarding against static is simple:

- After sitting down but before you reach for those memory chips or the card you're about to install, reach out and ground yourself by opening the computer case and touching the metal frame inside the computer.

Do this before you touch any component inside or outside the computer.

Alternatively, you can buy a grounding strap at any electronic supply store or Radio Shack. The strap attaches by one end to your wrist, usually with a Velcro strap. A coiled wire attached to the strap has a clip on the other end. Once the clip is attached to the chassis of the computer, you are grounded and any static charge is equalized.

> **TIP**
> Grounding is not required during normal usage. Only while working with electronic components.

Opening the Computer

Obviously, the first step to adding memory to your computer is going to be opening the computer for access. You've probably done this before, as you needed to open the computer simply to determine what type of module is required and how much space—i.e., what open slots—you have available.

The procedure outlined in this section is for desktop computers made by what we used to call "clone" manufacturers, who all followed more or less standard equipment designs. If you have a portable or laptop computer, the designs vary tremendously, and the following instructions may only apply in part.

> **NOTE**
> If you are upgrading a portable or laptop computer, you *must* refer to the manual for the laptop for instructions. The locations, types, and methods of access vary greatly from one brand to another and from one model to another. If you are in doubt, consult a qualified computer technician for assistance.

Before doing anything, begin by closing all open programs and the performing a normal shutdown. Then turn the computer off.

Next (and this is where the portable/laptop instructions probably begin to differ from the instructions for a desktop machine), slide the computer out and disconnect the cables from the back. Pay attention to which cables are connected where, and if you are not familiar with the cabling, make notes or draw yourself a diagram. This can save you a lot of trouble later.

And be sure to unplug the power cord from the computer. This will insure that the computer is not left powered on and that it is not accidentally powered up during installation or examination.

> **WARNING**
> Having the power on while removing or installing modules or cards can result in serious damage both to the items being installed or removed and to the computer as a whole!

Now you are ready to open the case. Some computers allow the case to be removed or opened by simply pinching a tab, lifting a lever, or turning one or two knurl nuts, but most require removing anywhere from two to six screws.

If you must remove screws, these are commonly Phillips screws or may also have hex heads. Do not remove any screws holding the power supply (near the computer's fan and electrical power connector) or ports, all of which are found on the rear of the machine. The screws holding the case in place are along the sides and are visibly anchoring the metal shell to the rear of the frame. See Figure 26.8.

774   Chapter Twenty-Six

Once the screws have been removed, the outer case should be free to be removed by sliding it back (or forward in some cases). In many cases, it may be necessary to lift the back of the case to disengage a lip that interlocks with the front and side panels.

Again, before touching anything inside, ground yourself to the metal frame to discharge any static electricity.

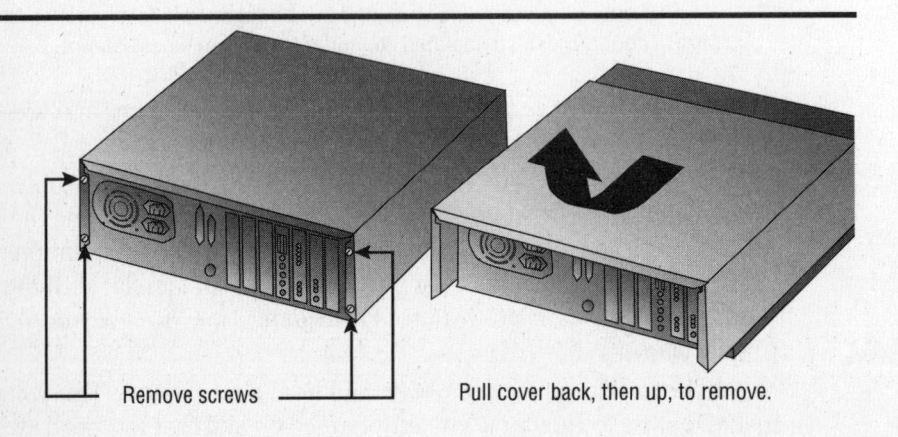

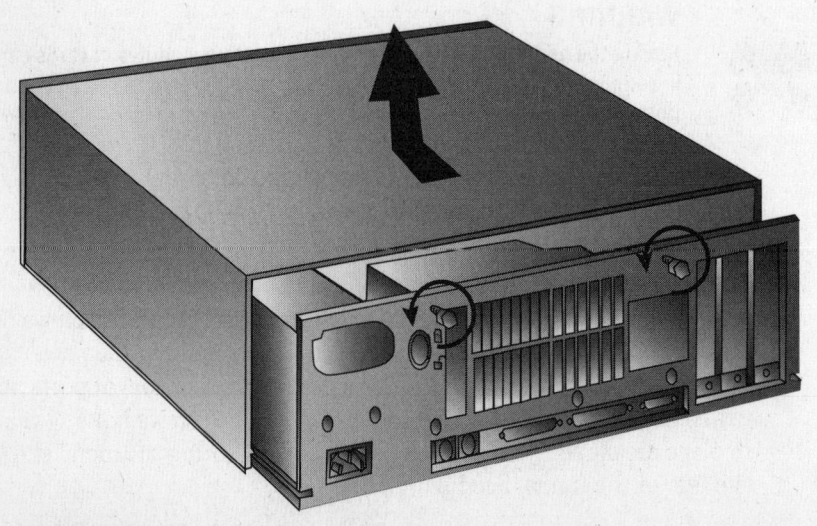

FIGURE 26.8: Removing the computer case

Installing Random Access Memory

Locating the Memory Sockets

The RAM memory modules and sockets can be located several places inside the computer. The manual for your computer's mainboard should have a diagram showing the placement and location of the sockets and other principal components (see Figure 26.9). Even without the diagram, however, these sockets are usually easily identified.

Looking at the mainboard from the front, the SIMM sockets are usually on the far right of the board and may be located to the rear or further forward toward the front. Also, some manufacturers place the SIMM sockets at the front left of the mainboard.

Where both SIMM and DIMM sockets are provided, they are normally next to each other with a bank of four SIMM sockets and two DIMM sockets.

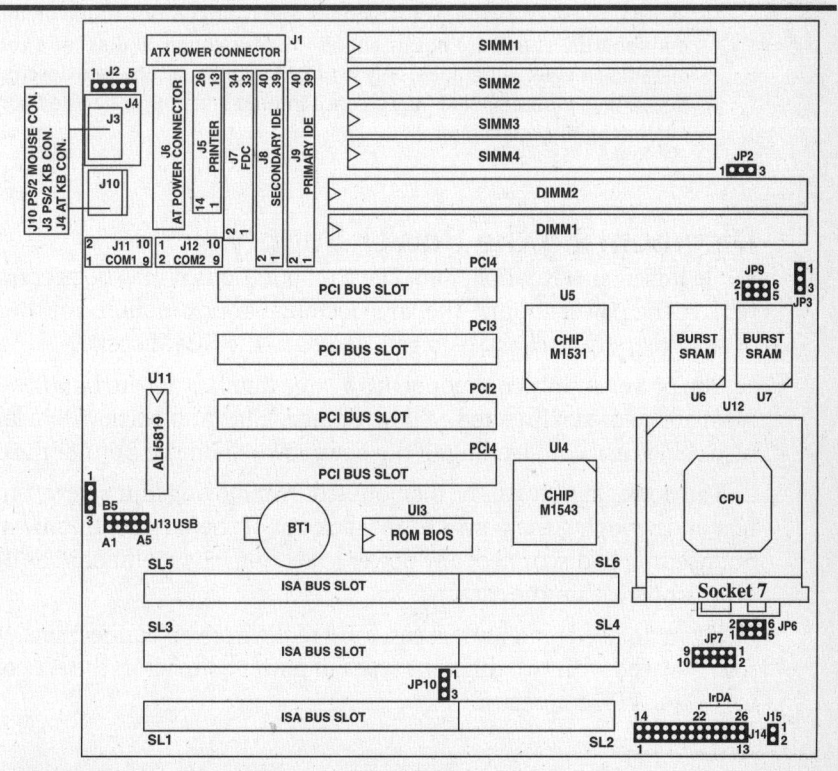

FIGURE 26.9: A typical mainboard layout diagram

In some cases, particularly for SIMMs at the right rear, there may be cables covering the area and making access difficult. Therefore, it may be necessary to unplug one or more cables before adding or removing memory modules. Read through the following subsections to see if any of these apply to your situation.

> **NOTE**
> Once you have determined which type of socket your computer uses (30- or 72-pin SIMM, or 168-pin DIMM) and whether or not you have free sockets to install additional memory, and once you have cleared the access to the memory sockets, you may proceed to the sections titled "Is Space Available?" and "Adding Memory," later in this chapter.

> **TIP**
> The instructions contained in this and the following sections are very detailed in order to cover a variety of situations and configuration found on different mainboards. These are not intended to scare you or to dissuade you from installing memory upgrades, only to provide a full and complete description of the various problems that may be encountered and how to handle them without damaging your computer.

Dismounting the Power Supply

While it is a rare situation, for some configurations it may be necessary to remove the power supply—the large rectangular box mounted at the top or right rear of the chassis—to gain access to the SIMM sockets.

The power supply commonly has a large number of wire bundles—most are colored white, red, yellow, orange, blue, and black with a larger black electrical cord leading to the power switch on the front of the case.

The power supply can be dismounted by removing four screws on the rear and swinging the power supply box out of the way, commonly without needing to disconnect any power leads from the mainboard or from other units within the case.

If you do need—in extreme cases—to remove power connections, you may be faced with two different types of power connector: the AT connector or the ATX connector.

> **NOTE**
> Some newer mainboards—such as the one illustrated—may have both the AT and ATX connectors present but will use only the one set matching the enclosure's power supply.

Installing Random Access Memory

The AT Power Connector The AT power connector is the most common and is found on all older mainboards. It consists of two plugs usually at the rear of the mainboard. The two side-by-side plugs comprising the AT power connector can be pulled straight up—*gently*—until they catch. The plugs are then tilted—again, *gently*—about 45 degrees to disengage the keys (protruding plastic tabs) along one side from the locking strip.

Notice that the two black wires, one on each plug, are in the center. When the AT power connector is reinstalled, the plugs must be placed with the black wire to the center and the keys against the arresting strip. Tilt the plug at 45 degrees to engage the keys with the arresting strip, bring the plug back to the upright position, and—*without force*—slide the plug down over the pins, as shown in Figure 26.10.

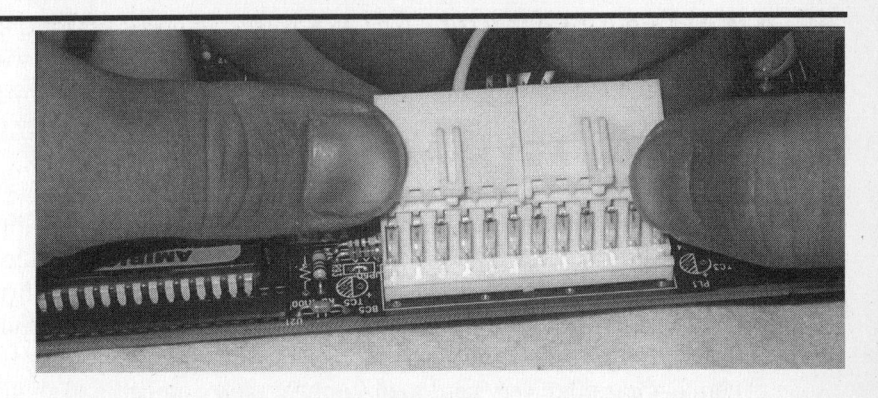

FIGURE 26.10: AT power connectors

Each AT connector has five wires and connects to five pins. Be sure that the connectors are not misaligned and that they are correctly in place with the two black wires side by side in the center. Do not apply power until you have checked all plugs and connections.

> **WARNING**
>
> Never force any connector of any kind to fit into a socket! Connectors in computers are "keyed" by shape or by type so that they can only be installed easily one way. Forcing a connector into a socket usually means that the connector is not aligned correctly or is not the correct connector for that socket. *Forcing incorrect connections can and will seriously damage your computer.*

The ATX Power Connector   The ATX power connection is for the newest ATX enclosures and is used primarily (but not exclusively) with Pentium II mainboards using the Slot 1 design. Unlike the AT power connectors, the ATX connector has two rows of pins and can only be installed one way.

Other Power Connectors   Other connectors from the power supply go to your floppy drive, hard drive(s), CD-ROM drive(s) and, often, to a cooling fan attached to the CPU. These can all be disconnected by firmly grasping the white plastic shell—do not ever pull on the wires—and pulling the plug straight out. Some of these plugs may be pretty tight. This type of connector is often very hard to disconnect (and connect) and should be disconnected only if absolutely necessary.

Notice that these plugs have two beveled corners and the sockets where they are mounted also have beveled corners. These permit the plugs to be inserted in the sockets only one way. While they are tight, they will go in or come out without the use of excessive force.

Another type of power plug in use is a smaller, rectangular plug that commonly connects to the floppy drive only (see Figure 26.11). This plug has keys—those protruding plastic tabs—along one side that slide together with the plastic mounting on the unit. Again, be sure the plug is inserted correctly and do not force the plug to go in if it is not a smooth fit. This type of plug is very easy to remove and install without force.

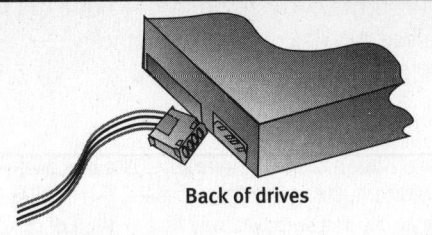

FIGURE 26.11: Small 12V/5V power plug for 3.5" drives

Removing Ribbon Cable Connectors

The mainboard on a newer computer or a plug-in board on older computers will have several (as many as six or more) gray ribbon cables connecting to the floppy drive, to one or more hard drives, to one or more CD-ROM drives, and to the parallel and serial port connectors on the back plate of the chassis.

> **TIP**
> The newest Slot 1 mainboards for the Pentium II have the serial and parallel ports permanently mounted at the rear of the board and do not have cables or connectors for these ports.

On newer systems, all of these ribbon cables are connected to the mainboard. On older systems, they may be connected to two or more plug-in boards or some combination of both.

Usually there's enough slack in the cables to permit you to move them around to get at what's behind or underneath them. In some cases, however, they may be so much in the way when you're trying to reach the SIMM sockets that they require removal.

Before removing any flat ribbon cables, please take note that each of these cables—even though they are different widths—has a marked stripe on one side. This is important! You need to remember which end of the connector connects to the color-coded edge of the cable. Fortunately, each flat ribbon cable carries some indication along one side or edge to make it easy to keep track of which side is which, and, commonly, there will also be a small number 1 (or possibly only a dot) on the mainboard next to the end of the socket where the marked end of the cable belongs. However, the only way this "mating" is helpful is if both of those features are actually present and visible. It will save you a lot of neck craning and eyestrain if you simply write down the correspondences (along the lines of "red edge to right side") before you disconnect the cable.

> **TIP**
>
> For rainbow (i.e., multicolor) ribbon cables, the marker is a black wire with a brown wire immediately next to it. For gray ribbon cables, the marker is commonly a red or black stripe along one side but may be any type of continuous marking.

If it is necessary to remove one or more of these ribbon cables for access, mark the cables as you remove them. Each connector should have a label on the mainboard—such as 'J9', 'J10', 'J11', etc.—to identify the cable. Using a piece of tape or a marker, mark the cable with the same identifier.

Look at the connectors on the mainboard. Each is a double row of pins and may or may not be surrounded by a plastic shell outlining the connector.

If the connector has a shell, this will make it easier to align and replace the plug and may, as well, have a slot on one side at the center to accept a matching key on the plug on the ribbon cable.

If the connector does not have a shell, be very careful replacing the plug to be sure that both rows of pins are mated and that the plug is not off to one end or the other. Also be very careful that no pins are bent or tilted. And as before, let me repeat: *do not force the connection!*

Finally, the marked side of the ribbon cable must be replaced with the same alignment—corresponding to the mark or number '1' on the mainboard—that it had when it was removed.

Motherboard/Daughterboard Combinations Some computer manufacturers—including Compaq, Hewlett-Packard, Packard Bell, and Dell—use a motherboard/daughterboard design where the motherboard (mainboard) has a special connector along one side that mounts the daughterboard at a right angle. In turn, the daughterboard provides mounting slots for multiple plug-in cards.

Depending on the configuration, it may be necessary to remove the plug-in boards or even the daughterboard to gain access to the SIMM sockets. Fortunately, removing cards is as simple as gently rocking them back and forth (front to back, that is; not side to side!) along the connecting edge until they can slip straight out of the socket.

Installing Random Access Memory

> **NOTE**
> While this may sound like a bad joke, there have been reports of individuals who have used silicon sealant to "protect" card connections and have sealed cards into their slots. DON'T DO THIS! Others have used solvent or cleaners (such as Windex) to remove dust and dirt, while some people have reportedly even gone a step further and sprayed lubricants, such as WD-40, all over the insides of their computers (and sometimes opening their hard drives to lubricate the interiors)! Again, don't do this either. Since any of these practices—sealants, cleaners, or lubricants—can produce serious and detrimental results, never attempt to add anything other than an actual computer component to the inside of your computer.

Is Space Available?

If you find the SIMM sockets in your system (Figure 26.12) but there are no modules installed, this means that the computer was hardwired by the manufacturer with a small amount of memory on the mainboard. In this case, consult the manufacturer's manual to determine what type of memory is required and what module configurations are accepted.

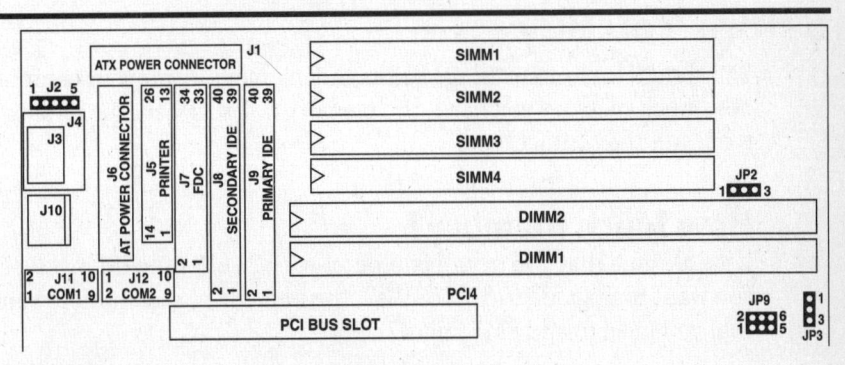

FIGURE 26.12: 72-pin SIMM and 168-pin DIMM sockets

More often than discovering that there are no modules whatsoever, you may find your SIMM (or DIMM) sockets but discover that there are no empty sockets. This does not mean that you cannot upgrade your computer, only that you will need to remove some of the existing modules to replace them with modules with a higher capacity.

Before you blithely set about doing just this, take note of this important fact: Many computers require memory modules to be installed as pairs, using two sockets at a time with modules with the same capacity in each. In this situation, the four SIMM connectors commonly consist of two *banks* of memory and are identified as bank 0 and bank 1.

> **TIP**
> Configurations vary, so a bank of memory may consist of one socket, two sockets, or even four sockets. Consult your computer mainboard's documentation for details.

Alternately, if there are DIMM sockets present, the two DIMM sockets may be identified as bank 0 and bank 1 respectively while the pairs of SIMM sockets are identified as bank 2 and bank 3.

> **WARNING**
> When a computer requires a two-socket bank but only one socket has SIMMs installed, or if there are two but the SIMMs are mismatched, the computer may fail to boot or may report an error during the POST (Power-On Self Test).

Before You Buy

You should know four things before buying memory for your computer: how much memory you need, the memory access speed, the memory type, and the contact type.

How Much Memory?

Let's assume that you have a computer with 24MB of RAM installed and you want to upgrade to 32MB. Well, the immediate assumption would be that you need to add 8MB, right?

The immediate assumption, however, is not necessarily the right one.

First, because you have 24MB installed, this probably means that you have two 8MB SIMMs and two 4MB SIMMs with all four slots filled. Therefore, you're going to remove the two 4MB SIMMs to make room for additional memory.

Second, now that you've decided that you need 16MB—instead of only 8MB—you're going to go out and buy a single 16MB module?

Well, the answer is "no" again simply because the system will probably work better if you buy two new 8MB modules rather than a single 16MB module. Remember, a lot of boards require memory in full banks and even those that don't require this may still work better using paired modules by supporting interleaving.

Now, what about later? Are you going to find yourself needing more memory? And will you—six months from now—be pulling the 8MB SIMMs to replace them with 16s?

If this appears even likely, why not simply install two 16MB SIMMs now and bring the system up to 48MB. Then, later, if you do need more memory, you can replace the remaining 8MB modules to go from 48MB to 64MB.

Remember, the dealer may be willing to offer you a trade-in on the old memory or you may know someone who could use them. And memory is cheap—why be stingy in the short run and waste money in the long run?

Memory Access Speed

Okay, maybe you can't find the manual for the mainboard but you still need to know what access speed is required. To find out, you can remove one of the existing SIMMs and read the label on the chips. On one side of the chip, there should be a series of characters followed by a dash and a number. That number is the chip's access speed. This may be a two-digit number (such as 60, 70, 80) or a single digit (such as 6, 7, 8)—either of which means essentially the same thing: i.e., a 6 or a 60 identifies a 60ns access speed.

EDO, Non-EDO, or Other

This consideration applies primarily to Pentium-based (or equivalent) computers where EDO chips are used to provide faster operations between the memory and the CPU. EDO chips can be used in non-EDO computers without any problems.

However, the converse is not acceptable: placing non-EDO RAM in an EDO system may result in the computer not booting. Alternately, if it does boot, the computer may operate more slowly than if the proper EDO chips were used.

Many of the newer computer mainboards may support multiple types of chips. My own, as an example, accepts DRAM, EDO RAM, or FP Mode DRAM using either 72-pin SIMM or 168-pin DIMM modules (but not both). If there is a question, the best way to find out is—as before—by referring to the manual for your mainboard, or asking a knowledgeable technician.

Contact Types: Tin or Gold

The fourth item is the type of contacts used in the SIMM or DIMM sockets. These may be either tin or gold, with the higher-end systems using gold contacts of course. Ideally, the modules you install should have matching metals to prevent deterioration of the contacts due to mismatched metals. This particular information is not commonly found in your mainboard manual, but a strong flashlight should tell you if the contacts in the socket are tin (a silver color) or gold.

Adding New Memory

Okay, you've purchased new memory modules and you're ready to install them. To do so, follow these steps:

1. The modules were shipped or supplied to you in an anti-static plastic bag or wrapping. This is a plastic that contains embedded carbon particles—which are conductive—and which prevent a static buildup or static charge from damaging the chips on the modules. Do not remove the modules from the protective enclosure and toss them around, drop them in your pocket, or carry them around unwrapped.

> **TIP**
> Leave the computer modules in their protective wrapping until you are ready to install them!

2. After disconnecting the computer and opening the case—as described previously—ground yourself by touching the metal chassis or by connecting the ground strap. See Figure 26.13.

3. If you are removing memory modules to make space for new modules, place the old modules in the same protective wrapping or, temporarily, lay them on a grounded metal surface—such as the power supply case. But be sure to place them in a protective wrapping before you finish.

4. Remove the new module(s) from the protective wrappings. Hold the modules by the edges and do be careful not to touch the metallic contacts.

Installing Random Access Memory 785

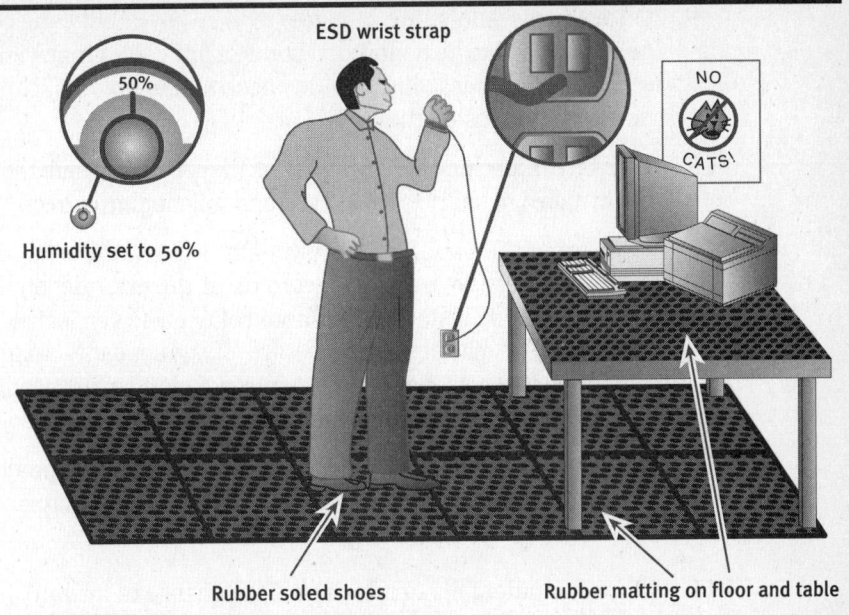

ESD wrist strap

Humidity set to 50%

Rubber soled shoes

Rubber matting on floor and table

FIGURE 26.13: A static-free environment

5. Identify the notched end of the module and the hole matching the pin on the locking post. Fit the module into the socket at a 45-degree angle for a SIMM module or a 90-degree angle for a DIMM module.

6. Seat the module with gentle pressure, then lift to bring the module upright. The module should snap into position solidly with two clips, one at each end, holding the module in the upright position.

7. Both ends of the module should be the same height and neither end of the module should give under gentle pressure.

8. If the module does not appear to be seated correctly, release the end clips—if necessary—and try to reseat the module.

WARNING

Do not, under *any* circumstances, attempt to force a fit. Investigate the possibilities that you've either tried to insert the module incorrectly or have the wrong sort of module. If nothing seems wrong other than the fit, return the module for another one to see if it makes any difference (and take advantage of the dealer's expertise at the same time by asking for advice).

9. Once the module(s) are in place, replace any other components that had to be removed, reconnect any cables that were removed for access, and double check all alignments, connections, and installations.

10. Turn on the machine (before replacing the cover) to ensure that the installed memory is recognized and functioning correctly.

    ▶ During the boot POST (Power-On Self Test), the BIOS may report an error. The wording of the error depends on the BIOS installed, but should offer on-screen instructions. The reason for the message—if one appears—is simply that the system has recognized a change but needs to update the system configuration accordingly.

    ▶ Most newer systems will recognize the change, update the system settings automatically, and may or may not issue a warning message.

11. If the computer fails to reboot or if the change in memory is not recognized, shut down the computer, remove the newly installed modules and carefully go back over the checklist to ensure that you have the appropriate memory module types.

12. If this does not identify a problem, try to reinstall and reseat each of the modules following the preceding steps. If this still does not resolve the problem, seek technical assistance from a trusted computer store or dealer.

Success!

In most cases, you should be able to install or upgrade your computer memory without any particular problems. This is a very simple process and should take much less time than it has taken for you to read through this chapter (even if you are a speed reader). And, once it's done, you should find that your applications run faster and more efficiently while overall performance should be visibly improved.

And—please don't dislocate your shoulder doing so—you can give yourself a well-earned pat on the back.

What's Next?

Now that you've done the hardest part of adding memory to your computer—i.e., now that you've read about all the varieties and concerns that might affect your particular configuration—you should feel confident about trying it for yourself. Once you have more memory, of course, your machine should zip along so much better than before that you'll start wondering why you don't just add a few higher-level applications and gizmos while you're at it.

What you do next is entirely up to you. If you've decided to add any of the hardware upgrades covered here, the Vendors Guide (Appendix C) would be a logical next step. If you haven't yet read earlier coverage of Windows 98 SE's support for multimedia and other hardware, you might want to go back to Chapters 9 and 10 now. Or dip into the following Command and Feature Reference (Appendix A) or the Windows 98 SE User's Glossary (Appendix B). Finally, you might decide to just put this book down and start exploring Windows 98 SE on your own. Happy Computing!

Part IV
Windows 98 Second Edition User's Reference

Appendix A

Windows 98 SE Command and Feature Reference

Adapted from *Windows 98 Second Edition Instant /Reference*
by Peter Dyson
ISBN 0-7821-2616-2   320 pages $14.99

Active Desktop

In Windows 98 SE, you can use a conventional Windows interface similar to that in earlier versions of Windows, or you can use the Active Desktop. The Active Desktop brings the world of the Web right to the Windows 98 SE Desktop, allowing you to replace the static Windows wallpaper with a fully configurable, full-screen Web page. The Active Desktop can contain other Web pages, dynamic HTML; even Java components such as stock tickers and ActiveX controls, and you can add these elements to the Taskbar or to a folder.

> **NOTE**
> You can combine the Active Desktop and Internet Explorer's subscription capabilities to create your own personal push-content client, displaying data on your Desktop from whatever sources interest you. For example, you can display a continuously updating stock ticker or sports results right on your Desktop; assuming of course that you have continuous Internet access.

To set up your Active Desktop, choose Start ➤ Settings ➤ Active Desktop, and you will see three options: View As Web Page, Customize My Desktop, and Update Now. You can also right-click the Desktop and select Active Desktop from the menu.

View As Web Page

Turns on the Active Desktop interface. Selecting this option a second time removes the checkmark and turns the Active Desktop off again.

Customize My Desktop

Opens the Display Properties dialog box. You can also right-click the Desktop and select Properties, or if you prefer, choose Start ➤ Settings ➤ Control Panel and select the Display icon. The Display Properties dialog box contains six tabs, but we are only concerned with the following two:

Background Lets you choose an HTML document or a picture to use as your Desktop background. In the Wallpaper box, select the background you want to use, or click Pattern to choose or modify the background pattern. You can also click the Browse button to locate a file or to go directly to a Web site to find the HTML document you are interested in using as a background. To cover your entire Desktop with a small wallpaper image, select Tile from the Display box, or choose Center if you prefer to see the image centered. Click the Apply button to see the effect of your changes before you exit the Display Properties dialog box, or click OK to accept the changes and close the dialog box.

Web Lets you select and organize Active Desktop elements. At the top of the tab, you will see a representation of your Desktop, indicating the location of any Active Desktop elements. These same elements are listed in the box below. To add a new element such as a stock ticker or a weather map, click New to open the New Active Desktop Item dialog box. If you want to browse through Microsoft's Active Desktop Gallery on Microsoft's Web site for a component to add, click Yes. To select a different Web site, click No, and then enter the address or URL for the Web site, or click the Browse button to locate it. Be sure that the View My Active Desktop As A Web Page box is checked if you want your Desktop to look like a Web page.

> **NOTE**
> You can also right-click any link on a Web page, drag it to your Desktop, and then click Create Active Desktop Item Here.

Update Now

Updates the Desktop contents right now to display any changes you have made.

ADD NEW HARDWARE

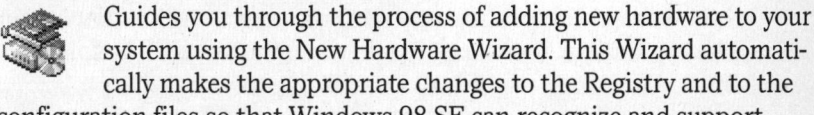

Guides you through the process of adding new hardware to your system using the New Hardware Wizard. This Wizard automatically makes the appropriate changes to the Registry and to the configuration files so that Windows 98 SE can recognize and support your new hardware. Be sure you have installed or connected your new hardware before you go any further.

Add/Remove Programs

Installs or uninstalls individual elements of the Windows 98 SE operating system itself or certain application programs.

Installing or removing application or system software components in this way enables Windows 98 SE to modify all the appropriate system and configuration files automatically so that the information in them stays current and correct.

To start Add/Remove Programs, choose Start ➤ Settings ➤ Control Panel, and then click the Add/Remove Programs icon to open the Add/Remove Programs Properties dialog box. This dialog box contains four tabs if you are connected to a local area network; otherwise, it contains three tabs.

Install/Uninstall Tab

To install a new program using the Add/Remove Programs applet, follow these steps:

1. Select the Install/Uninstall tab if it isn't already selected, and then click the Install button.

2. Put the application program CD or floppy disk in the appropriate drive, and click the Next button to display a setup or install message, describing the program to be installed.

3. To continue with the installation process, click the Finish button. To make any changes, click Back and repeat the procedure.

To uninstall a program previously installed under Windows 98 SE, you must follow a different process. The programs that have uninstall capability (not all of them do) will be listed in the display box of the Install/Uninstall tab. Click the program you want to uninstall, and then click the Add/Remove button. You may see a warning message about removing the application. You will be to told when the uninstall is finished.

Windows 98 SE Command and Feature Reference 795

> **NOTE**
> Once you remove an application using Add/Remove Programs, you will have to reinstall it from the original program disks or CD if you decide to use it again.

Windows Setup Tab

Some components of the Windows 98 SE operating system are optional, and you can install or uninstall them as you wish; the Windows Clipboard Viewer is an example. Select the Windows Setup tab to display a list of such components with checkboxes on the left. If the box has a checkmark in it, the component is currently installed. If the checkbox is gray, only some elements of that component are installed; to see what is included in a component, click the Details button. Follow these steps to add a Windows 98 SE component:

1. Click the appropriate checkbox.
2. If the component consists of several elements, click the Details button to display a list of them, and check the boxes you want to install.
3. Click OK to display the Windows Setup tab.
4. Click the Apply button, and then click OK.

To remove a Windows 98 SE component from your system, follow these steps:

1. Click the Details button to see a complete list of the individual elements in the component you want to uninstall.
2. Clear the check mark from the checkboxes of the elements you want to uninstall, and then click OK to open the Windows Setup tab.
3. Click the Apply button, and then click OK.

Startup Disk Tab

A startup disk is a floppy disk with which you can start, or "boot," your computer if something happens to your hard drive. When you originally installed Windows 98 SE, you were asked if you wanted to create a startup disk. If you didn't do it at that time or if the disk you created then is not usable, you can create one now. Simply insert a disk with at least 1.2MB capacity in the appropriate drive, click Create Disk, and follow the instructions on the screen.

Network Install Tab

In some cases, you can also install a program directly from a network using the Network Install tab. If the Network Install tab is not present in the Add/Remove Programs Properties dialog box, this feature may not have been enabled on your computer or on your network; see your system administrator for more details.

If the Install/Uninstall tab is selected, your system is currently connected to the network, and you can click Install followed by Next to find the setup program for your network.

If the Network Install tab is selected, follow the instructions on the screen.

Address Book

Manages your e-mail addresses, as well as your voice, fax, modem, and cellular phone numbers. Once you enter an e-mail address in your Address Book, you can select it from a list rather than type it in every time. To open the Address Book, choose Start ➤ Programs ➤ Internet Explorer ➤ Address Book, or click the Address Book icon on the Outlook Express toolbar.

Importing an Existing Address Book

Address Book can import information from an existing address book in any of the following formats:

- Windows Address Book
- Microsoft Exchange Personal Address Book
- Microsoft Internet Mail for Windows 3.1 Address Book
- Netscape Address Book
- Netscape Communicator Address Book
- Eudora Pro or Lite Address Book

- Lightweight Directory Access Protocol (LDAP)
- Comma-separated text file

To import information from one of these address books, follow these steps:

1. Choose Start ➤ Programs ➤ Internet Explorer ➤ Address Book, or click the Address Book icon on the Outlook Express toolbar.
2. Choose File ➤ Import ➤ Address Book to open the Address Book Import Tool dialog box.
3. Select the file you want to import, and click Import.

Creating a New Address Book Entry

To add a new entry to your Address Book, click the New Contact button on the Address Book toolbar or choose File ➤ New Contact to open the Properties dialog box. This dialog box has six tabs:

Personal Lets you enter personal information including the person's first, middle, and last names, a nickname, and an e-mail address. If the person has more than one e-mail address, click Add and continue entering addresses.

Home Allows you to enter additional information about this contact; enter as much or as little information as makes sense here.

Business Allows you to enter business-related information; again, enter as much or as little information as makes sense.

Other Offers a chance to store additional information about this contact as a set of text notes.

NetMeeting Lets you enter NetMeeting information such as a person's conferencing e-mail address and server name. If NetMeeting is not installed on your system, this tab will be called Conferencing.

Digital IDs Allows you to specify a digital certificate for use with an e-mail address.

Setting Up a New Group

You can create groups of e-mail addresses to make it easy to send a message to all the members of the group. You can group people any way you like—by job title, musical taste, or sports team allegiance. When you want to send e-mail to everyone in the group, simply use the group name instead of selecting each e-mail address individually. To begin creating a new group, click the New Group icon on the Address Book toolbar or choose File ➤ New Group to open the Group Properties dialog box.

Address Toolbar

Shows the location of the page currently displayed in the main window; this may be a URL on the Internet or an intranet, or it may be a file or folder stored on your hard disk.

To go to another page, click the arrow at the right end of the Address toolbar to select the appropriate entry, or simply type a new location. When you start to type an address that you have previously entered, the Auto-Complete feature recognizes the address and completes the entry for you.

The Address toolbar is available in most Windows 98 SE applications, including the Explorer, Internet Explorer, My Computer, the Control Panel, and others.

Backup

Creates an archive copy of one or more files and folders on your hard disk and then restores them to your hard disk in the event of a disk or controller failure or some other unforeseen event.

Browse

The Browse button is available in many common dialog boxes when you have to choose or enter a file name, find a folder, or specify a Web address or URL. Clicking the Browse button or the Find File button opens the Browse dialog box.

You can look through folders on any disk on any shared computer on the network to find the file you want. When you find the file, folder, computer, or Web site, double-click it to open, import, or enter it in a text box.

CD Player

Allows you to play audio compact discs on your CD-ROM drive. Choose Start ➤ Programs ➤ Accessories ➤ Multimedia ➤ CD Player to open the CD Player dialog box.

> **NOTE**
> See Chapter 9 to learn more about using CD Player.

Chat

See NetMeeting

Clipboard

A temporary storage place for data. You can use the Cut and Copy commands as well as the Windows screen capture commands to place data on the Clipboard. The Paste command then copies the data from the Clipboard to a receiving document, perhaps in another application. You cannot edit the Clipboard contents; however, you can view and save the information stored in the Clipboard by using the Clipboard Viewer, or you can paste the contents of the Clipboard into Notepad.

> **WARNING**
> The Clipboard only holds one piece of information at a time, so cutting or copying onto the Clipboard overwrites any existing contents.

Closing Windows

Closing an application program window terminates the operations of that program. In Windows 98 SE, you can close windows in a number of ways.

- Click the Close button in the upper-right corner of the program title bar.

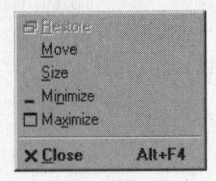

```
Restore
Move
Size
Minimize
Maximize
X Close    Alt+F4
```

- Choose Control ➤ Close (identified by the icon to the left of the program name in the title bar) or simply double-click the Control Menu icon.

- Choose File ➤ Close or File ➤ Exit within the application.

- If the application is minimized on the Taskbar, right-click the application's icon and choose Close or press Alt+F4.

CONNECTION WIZARD

Walks you through the steps of setting up your Internet connection. All you need is an account with an ISP (Internet Service Provider), and you're all set. You can start the Connection Wizard in several ways:

- Choose Start ➤ Programs ➤ Internet Explorer ➤ Connection Wizard.

- From the Windows 98 SE Help system, choose the Using the Internet Connection Wizard topic.

- Choose Start ➤ Settings ➤ Control Panel ➤ Internet to open the Internet Properties dialog box, and then select the Connection tab and click the Connect button.

- In Internet Explorer, choose View ➤ Internet Options to open the Internet Options dialog box, and then select the Connection tab and click the Connect button.

No matter which method you use, you first see the Welcome screen; click the Next button to continue. The Setup Options dialog box gives you three choices:

- Open a new account with an ISP. Select the first option if you do not have an account. The Wizard takes you through the steps of finding an ISP and starting an account and sets up the dial-up link for you.

- Establish a connection to an existing Internet account. Select the second option to set up a connection to your existing Internet account or to revise the settings for your current account.

- Make no change to your existing account. If you choose this option and click the Next button, the Wizard closes because there is nothing for it to do.

Creating a New Connection to the Internet

To create a new dial-up connection to the Internet, start the Connection Wizard, click Next at the Welcome screen, and then follow these steps:

1. In the Setup Options dialog box, choose the first option to select an ISP and set up a new Internet account, and then click Next.

2. The Connection Wizard now begins the automatic part of the setup by loading programs from your original Windows 98 SE CD. You may be asked to restart your computer; the Wizard will resume automatically. Be sure you complete all the steps; otherwise, the Wizard may not be able to set up your connection properly.

3. If you have a modem, the Wizard attempts to locate an ISP in your area and sets up the appropriate Dial-Up Networking software on your system. Follow the prompts on the screen to complete the setup.

Modifying an Existing Connection to the Internet

You can modify your existing Internet account settings at any time. Start the Connection Wizard, click Next at the Welcome screen, and then follow these steps:

1. In the Setup Options dialog box, select the second option to set up a new connection to an existing Internet account.

2. Choose the method you use to connect to the Internet, either by phone line or through your local area network, and click Next.

3. In the Dial-Up Connection dialog box, check the Use An Existing Dial-Up Connection box, select the connection from the list box, and click the Next button.

4. You'll then be asked if you want to modify the settings for this connection. Click Yes, and then click Next to open the Phone Number dialog box where you can enter the phone number to dial to make the connection.

5. In the next dialog box, enter your username and password information, and click Next.

6. In the Advanced settings dialog box you are asked if you want to change any of the advanced settings for this connection, such as connection type, logon script filename, and IP address. You should only change these settings when your ISP or system administrator tells you to and provides the new information to use. Click Next.

7. You'll then be asked if you want to set up an Internet e-mail account; click Yes and then Next to specify whether you want to use an existing account or create a new one. If you opt to continue using an existing account, you will be asked to confirm your e-mail account settings; if you establish a new account, you will have to enter this information from scratch. Click Next.

8. Next, you'll be asked if you want to set up an Internet news account; follow the instructions on the screen.

9. Finally, click the Finish button to complete the configuration and close the Wizard.

CONTROL PANEL

Provides a way to establish settings and defaults for all sorts of important Windows features. To access the Control Panel, choose Start ➢ Settings ➢ Control Panel.

Windows 98 SE Command and Feature Reference

If you are using the conventional Windows interface, you will see a window that looks like this:

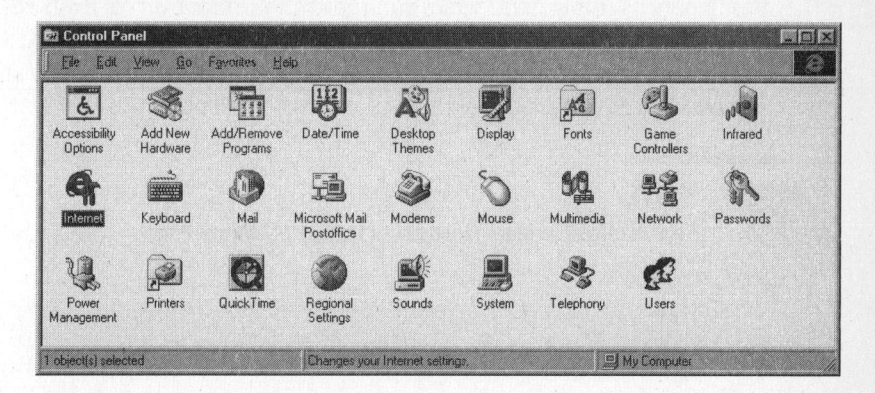

To open an applet, double-click it, or click once on its icon to select it and then choose File ➢ Open.

If you are using the Active Desktop and you have View As Web Page turned on, you will see a much different Control Panel:

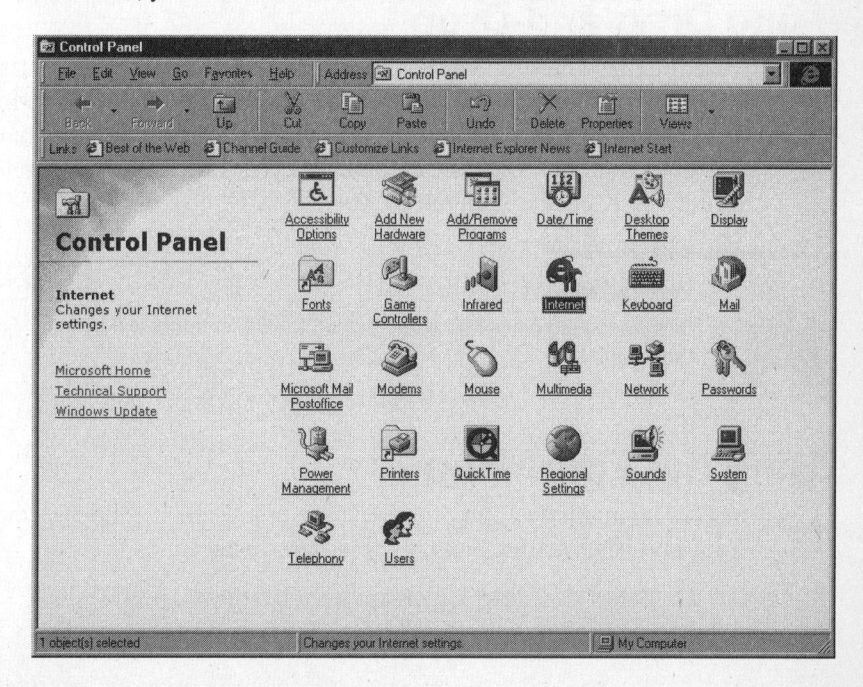

The Control Panel now looks and works like a Web page displayed in a browser. All the names of the applets are underlined, and the mouse pointer turns into a hand when you move the cursor over an icon. You will also see a short description of what each Control Panel applet does on the left side of the window. More important, it now takes only a single mouse-click to open an applet.

> **NOTE**
> See Chapter 7 to learn more about using the Control Panel.

Copying Files and Folders

When you copy a file or a folder, you duplicate it in another location and leave the original in place. In Windows, you can copy files and folders in three ways. Let's take a look.

Using Drag-and-Drop

To use the drag-and-drop method, both the source and the destination folders must be open on the Desktop. Press and hold the Ctrl key while holding down the left mouse button, and drag the file or folder from one location to another. When the file or folder is in the correct place, release the mouse button and then release the Ctrl key.

> **WARNING**
> Be sure to hold down Ctrl. If you do not, the file or folder will be moved rather than copied.

Using the Edit Menu

The Edit menu in My Computer, Explorer, or any folder window provides a Copy and Paste feature. Follow these steps to use it:

1. Select the file or folder you want to copy.
2. Choose Edit ➤ Copy.

3. Find the destination file or folder and open it.
4. Choose Edit ➢ Paste.

You will see the name of the file in the destination folder.

> **TIP**
> You can select multiple files or folders to be copied by holding down Ctrl and clicking them. If the files are contiguous, you can also use Shift to select files.

Using the Right Mouse Button

Right-clicking a file or a folder opens a pop-up menu that you can use to perform a number of functions, including copying. To copy using the right mouse button, follow these steps:

1. Locate the file or folder you want to copy, and right-click to open the pop-up menu. Select Copy.
2. Open the destination folder, click the right mouse button, and select Paste.

You will see the name of the file in the destination folder.

Creating New Folders

Sooner or later you will want to add a new folder to a disk or to another folder, and you can do so in Explorer. Follow these steps:

1. In Explorer, select the disk or folder in which you want to place a new folder.
2. Choose File ➢ New ➢ Folder. A new folder is added to the disk or the folder you indicated with the name "New Folder" highlighted.
3. Type a new folder name, something that will act as a reminder as to the files it contains, and press Enter.

You can also right-click in the blank part of the Windows Explorer file pane to open a pop-up menu from which you can choose New ➢ Folder.

Appendix A

> **TIP**
> If you would rather bypass Explorer altogether, you can create a new folder on the Desktop by clicking My Documents and then choosing File ➤ New ➤ Folder. Give the folder a new name, and then drag it to the Desktop.

Date/Time

The clock that appears in the right corner of the Taskbar displays the system clock, which not only tells you the time, but also indicates the time and date associated with any files you create or modify. At any time, you can place the mouse pointer on the time in the Taskbar to display the complete date. To vary the format of the date and time displayed in the Taskbar, select the Regional Settings applet in the Control Panel.

To set the clock, follow these steps:

1. Double-click the time in the Taskbar, or choose Start ➤ Settings ➤ Control Panel ➤ Date/Time to open the Date/Time Properties dialog box.

2. Select the Date & Time tab to set the day, month, year, or current time.

3. To change the time, either drag across the numbers you want to change beneath the clock and type the new time, or highlight the numbers and click the up and down arrows to increase or decrease the values.

4. To change the date, click the drop-down arrow to select the month, use the up and down arrows to change the year, and click the appropriate day of the month.

Deleting Files and Folders

You can delete a file or a folder in several ways. First, select the file or folder you want in My Computer or Windows Explorer, and then do one of the following:

▶ Choose File ➤ Delete. After you confirm that you want to delete the file or folder, Windows sends it to the Recycle Bin.

- Press the Delete key on the keyboard and verify that you want to delete the selected file or folder; Windows then sends it to the Recycle Bin.

- Right-click the file or folder to open the pop-up menu. Select Delete and then verify that you want to delete the selected file or folder. Off it goes to the Recycle Bin.

- Position the My Computer or Explorer window so that you can also see the Recycle Bin on the Desktop; then simply drag the selected file or folder to the Recycle Bin.

NOTE
If you accidentally delete a file or folder, you can choose Edit ➢ Undo Delete or retrieve the file or folder manually from the Recycle Bin. You cannot retrieve a deleted file or folder if the Recycle Bin has been emptied since your last deletion.

TIP
To delete a file without placing it in the Recycle Bin, select the file and then press Shift+Delete. You cannot recover the file if you do this. You will be asked to confirm the deletion.

Desktop

What you see on the screen when you first open Windows. If you are not using any of the Web-like features of the Active Desktop, you see the conventional Windows Desktop. Initially, it contains a set of icons arranged on the left, plus the Taskbar with the Start button across the bottom. As you work with Windows and load application programs, other objects such as dialog boxes and messages boxes are placed on the Desktop.

You can also change the appearance of the Desktop by right-clicking it and selecting Properties. This allows you to change display properties for the Desktop background and screen savers. You can also change the monitor type, as well as font types, sizes, and colors for objects on the screen.

Disk Cleanup

A quick and convenient way to make more space available on your hard disk. Choose Start ➤ Programs ➤ Accessories ➤ System Tools ➤ Disk Cleanup to open the Disk Cleanup dialog box.

Alternatively, you can open Explorer or My Computer, right-click the disk you want to work with, and then choose Properties from the pop-up menu. On the General tab, click the Disk Cleanup button.

> **NOTE**
> See Chapter 11 to learn more about using Disk Cleanup.

Disk Space

To find out how much disk space a file or folder occupies, select it (hold down the Ctrl key to select more than one) in My Computer or Explorer. The window's status bar will display the number of objects selected and the amount of disk space they occupy.

Alternately, you can choose File ➤ Properties or right-click a file or folder and select Properties. The General tab displays the amount of disk space or, in the case of a folder, its size plus the number of files or other folders it contains.

To see how much disk space remains on the entire disk, select the disk name in My Computer or Explorer and then choose File ➤ Properties or right-click and choose Properties. The Properties dialog box displays both the amount of used and the amount of free space. The status bar of My Computer also displays the free space and capacity of a disk drive.

Display

Controls how the objects on your screen—patterns, colors, fonts, sizes, and other elements—look. Choose Start ➤ Settings ➤ Control Panel ➤ Display (or simply right-click the Desktop and select properties) to open the Display Properties dialog box. It has six tabs: Background, Screen Saver, Appearance, Effects, Web, and Settings.

> **NOTE**
> See Chapter 7 to learn about setting and modifying display properties.

Documents

Choosing Start ➢ Documents displays a list of all the documents you have created or edited recently. If you select a document from the list, Windows opens the document in the appropriate application, making this a quick way to continue working on an interrupted project.

Windows maintains this list of documents and preserves it between Windows sessions even if you shut down and restart your computer. The last 15 documents are preserved in this list, but some of them may look more like applications or folders than documents.

To clear the list of documents and start the list over, choose Start ➢ Settings ➢ Taskbar & Start Menu. Select the Start Menu Programs tab and click the Clear button. Once you do this, only one entry will remain in the list, the shortcut to the My Documents folder.

Drag and Drop

You can use drag and drop to move, copy, activate, or dispose of files and folders on the Desktop and in many accessory and application windows. Place the mouse pointer on a file, press the left button, and drag the file or folder to another disk or folder. Position the pointer over the destination and release the mouse button. The result depends on the file or folder being dragged and the destination:

- ▶ Dragging a file or folder to another folder on the same disk moves it (hold down the Ctrl key if you want to copy the file or folder).

- ▶ Dragging a file or folder to another disk copies it.

- ▶ Dragging a file to a shortcut printer icon on the Desktop prints the document.

- ▶ Dragging a file or folder to the Recycle Bin disposes of it.

Entertainment

Menu used to access the Windows multimedia applications. Choose Start ➤ Programs ➤ Accessories ➤ Entertainment. This menu includes CD Player, Media Player, Sound Recorder, TV Viewer, and others.

Explorer

Windows Explorer (to use its full name) is *the* place to go when working with files and folders in Windows 98 SE. Explorer lets you look at your disks, folders, and files, in a variety of ways and helps you perform such tasks as copying, moving, renaming, and deleting files and folders, formatting floppy disks, and so on.

Explorer Menus

To access Explorer, choose Start ➤ Programs ➤ Windows Explorer, or right-click the Start button and choose Explore. You may want to create a shortcut for it on the Desktop or in the Start menu itself since it is used so often.

The Explorer menus give you access to all common functions. However, for some menu selections to work, you may first have to select an appropriate object in the main Explorer window, and the type of object you select determines the available options. You may, therefore, not see all these options on any given menu, and you may see some options not listed here. You will also find similar menus in My Computer, the Recycle Bin, and Network Neighborhood.

File Menu

Displays basic file-management options. It allows you to do the following:

- Open a folder or file
- Explore the contents of a selected computer, disk, or folder
- Print a file or get a Quick View of the contents of a file (not shown on the menu unless it is available)
- Set parameters for sharing a folder with other users

- Send a file to a floppy disk, to an e-mail or fax correspondent (using Windows Messaging), to My Briefcase, or to another destination
- Create a new folder or a shortcut
- Make a shortcut to a file or folder
- Delete or rename a file or folder
- Display a file's properties
- Close a file or a folder

If you are working with the Printers folder, you will also see options to Capture Printer Port and to End Capture.

Edit Menu

Allows you to work with the contents of a folder or file. It allows you to do the following:

- Cut, copy, and paste folders or files
- Paste a shortcut within a folder
- Select all files and folders
- Select all files except those already selected, which become deselected

View Menu

Allows you to change the window to include or exclude the toolbars, Status bar, and Explorer bar. You can choose how the files and folders are displayed:

- As a Web page
- With large icons or small icons
- In a list
- With details, describing the size and type of a file and the date modified

You can arrange icons by name, type of file or folder, size, or date created or last modified. You can also arrange icons into columns and rows. Refresh redisplays your screen. Folder Options lets you set defaults for how information is displayed in the main Explorer window, and Customize This Folder lets you change the appearance of the folder.

Go Menu
Lets you go back, forward, or up one level and gives fast access to certain Web sites and other Windows elements such as Mail, News, My Computer, Address Book, and Internet Call.

Favorites Menu
The Favorites menu is divided into two parts. You use the first part to manage your favorite Web sites with Add to Favorites and Organize Favorites, as well as those Web sites to which you subscribe with Manage Subscriptions and Update All Subscriptions. You use the second part for fast access to groups of Web sites with Channels, Links, and Software Updates.

Tools Menu
Gives you quick access to Find so that you can find Files or Folders, Computer, On the Internet, or People. You can also map a networked drive and disconnect a networked drive.

Help Menu
Provides access to the Windows Help system.

> **TIP**
> Some functions available from the Explorer menus are also available as buttons on the toolbar.

Explorer Toolbar
The following buttons are available on the standard Explorer toolbar:

- **Back** Displays the item you last displayed. Click the small down arrow just to the right of this button to see a list of all the items you have displayed in this Explorer session and click an item to go to it directly.

- **Forward** Displays the item you were viewing before you went back to the current item. Click the small down arrow just to the right of this button to display a list of items. Click an item to go to it directly.

Windows 98 SE Command and Feature Reference

Up   Moves up the directory tree in the left Explorer window, changing the contents displayed in the right window as it goes.

Cut   Moves the selected items to the Clipboard.

Copy   Duplicates selected items, placing their content on the Clipboard.

Paste   Transfers the contents of the Clipboard to a file or folder. A destination folder must already exist and must be selected.

Undo   Cancels the previous action. The label changes depending on what you did last—for example, Undo Delete or Undo Copy.

Delete   Places the selected file or folder in the Recycle Bin.

Properties   Opens the Properties dialog box for the selected disk, file, or folder.

Views   Changes the way information is displayed in the right-hand Explorer window. Click the small down arrow just to the right of this button to display a menu you can use to select the various displays. Alternatively, each time you click the Views button, the display cycles through these four views:

> **Large Icons**   Displays larger-sized icons representing the contents of the selected folder or disk.
>
> **Small Icons**   Displays smaller-sized icons in a horizontal, columnar list representing the contents of the selected folder or disk.
>
> **List**   Displays the contents as small icons, except in a vertical rather than horizontal orientation.
>
> **Details**   Displays the contents in a detailed list with additional information about the file size, file type, and modification date.

The Explorer also contains two other toolbars:

> **Address**   Displays the location of the item currently displayed by the Explorer. The arrow at the right end of the Address toolbar opens a drop-down list of items; select one to open it.

Links Displays a set of hyperlinks to various parts of Microsoft's Web site; you can also access these links from the Links selection in the Favorites menu.

You will also see a single status line across the bottom of the main Explorer window; it displays messages about your actions and lists information on disk storage space, including the number of items in a folder and the occupied and free disk space.

Explorer Window

When you run the Explorer, all items that make up your computer are listed in the left pane. Some objects have a plus sign (+) next to them, indicating that the object contains other objects that are not currently visible. To display the contents of such an item in the right pane, click the item, not the plus sign.

When you click the plus sign associated with an object, you display all the subelements, usually folders, in the left window, where they become part of the overall tree structure. The plus sign becomes a minus sign (–) if an object's contents are expanded. This tree structure is a graphical representation of how the files and folders on your system are related; the name of each folder appears just after its icon.

Customizing a Folder

Choose View ➤ Customize This Folder to open the Customize This Folder Wizard with these options:

Create or Edit an HTML Document Lets you create an HTML (Hypertext Markup Language) document in three steps:

1. Open the editor and create the HTML document.
2. Save the document.
3. Close the editor.

Choose a Background Picture Lets you select a picture that will be displayed as wallpaper when you open this folder.

Remove Customization Lets you return this folder to its original look and feel.

Selecting a Drive and Choosing a File or a Folder

When you open the Explorer, all the disks and folders available on your computer are displayed in the left pane. The right pane displays the contents of the disk or folder you selected on the left. Follow these steps to find a file or a folder:

1. Scroll up and down using the left scroll bar. On the left, you can see all the disks on your computer, plus those that are shared on your network, and all the folders within each disk. On the right, you will see all the folders and files within the selected disk or folder.

2. If the drive you want is not visible, you may have to expand the My Computer icon by clicking its plus sign. Normally, you will be able to see a floppy disk and at least one hard disk.

3. Click a disk or folder in the left pane to display its contents in the right pane; when a folder is selected, its icon changes from a closed folder to an open one.

4. Once you find the file or folder you want, open it and get to work.

Favorites

Contains selections you can use to track your favorite Web sites. You can open your favorite Web sites from many places within Windows 98 SE. You can choose Start ➤ Favorites, or you can use the Favorites menu in Windows Explorer, My Computer, Internet Explorer, Network Neighborhood, and Control Panel; even the Recycle Bin has a Favorites menu.

Add to Favorites

Choose Favorites ➤ Add To Favorites to bookmark a Web site so that you can find it again quickly and easily. Once you place the address, or URL, for the site in this list, you can revisit the site simply by selecting it from the Favorites menu; the result is the same as if you had typed the whole

URL into the Address toolbar and pressed Enter. You can also display your Favorites menu from the Explorer Bar; choose View ➤ Explorer Bar ➤ Favorites.

Organize Favorites

Choose Favorites ➤ Organize Favorites to group your Web sites into an arrangement that makes sense to you; a single long list is certainly not the most efficient organization.

Subscribing to a Web Site

In addition to visiting Web sites in the normal way with Internet Explorer, you can also subscribe to a Web site. A subscription is a mechanism that Internet Explorer uses to check for new or updated content on a Web site without your involvement.

Fax

Sends and receives faxes between computers or fax machines. You can send a fax in several ways:

- Drag a text or graphics file to the Microsoft Fax icon in the Printers folder.
- Right-click an icon and select the Send To Fax Recipient command.
- Select Microsoft Fax as the printer in any application program.
- Use Windows Messaging.
- Choose Start ➤ Programs ➤ Accessories ➤ Fax ➤ Compose New Fax.

No matter which of these techniques you use, the Compose New Fax Wizard will guide you through creating and sending a fax. Once you have a suitable profile set up under Start ➤ Programs ➤ Windows Messaging, the rest is a breeze.

> **TIP**
> To install Fax, you must have Exchange, Windows Messaging, or Outlook already installed on your system.

Compose New Fax

Follow these steps to compose a new fax message:

1. Open the Compose New Fax dialog box using one of the techniques discussed earlier.

2. If you are using a laptop (and therefore may not always be calling from the same location), click Dialing Properties and review the methods used to dial an outside line. If you are not using a portable computer, you can click I'm Not Using A Portable Computer, So Don't Show This To Me Again. Click Next.

3. Complete the information on the person to whom you want to send the fax. Type a name, country, fax number, and a recipient list, if applicable.

4. Select whether to send a cover page and its type. Click Options to open the Send Options For This Message dialog box.

5. Specify the following settings for this fax:

    Time to Send Specifies when the fax will actually be transmitted. Choose from As Soon As Possible, Discount Rates (click Set to specify the times when discount rates take effect), or a Specific Time (which you set using the up and down arrows).

    Message Format Specifies whether the recipient can edit the fax message. You can send a message that is Editable, If Possible (the fax will be sent in the binary editable format; the recipient must also have Microsoft Fax to be able to edit the fax), Editable Only (Microsoft Fax will try to send the fax as binary files and will refuse to send the message if the receiving system cannot accept that format), or Not Editable (the fax is sent as a bitmap).

Paper Establishes the paper specifications, including size, orientation (landscape or portrait), and image quality—choose from Draft (200×100dpi), Fine (200×200dpi), 300dpi, or Best Available.

Cover Page Confirms your choice of cover page.

Dialing Specifies how fax numbers are dialed, how many times you want to retry a busy or unavailable number, and the waiting period between such retries. Click Dialing Properties to set the default location you normally dial from, the dialing prefix, and credit card information. Click Toll Prefixes to identify phone-number prefixes that are inside your default area code but which require you to use the area code.

Security Specifies the security method to use with this fax. You can choose from None, Key-Encrypted (which uses a public-key encryption technique), and Password-Protected (the recipient must enter the same password you used when creating the fax to read the message).

6. When you have made your selections, click OK to return to the Compose New Fax dialog box. Click Next.

7. Type the subject of the fax, and in the Note box, type the contents of your fax message. Check the checkbox if you want the Note contents to be part of the cover page. Click Next.

8. If you want to send a file with this fax, click Add File to open the Open A File To Attach dialog box. Locate the file, and then click Open. The name will appear in the Files To Send text box. Click Next.

9. Your fax is now complete, and all you have to do to send it is click the Finish button. You will see two icons in the notification area of the Taskbar for the fax and dialing actions.

Request a Fax

You can also use Fax to call a remote computer, information service, or fax machine to retrieve a specific document; and you can retrieve all the documents available. Once the call is complete, the documents are placed in your Inbox. Follow these steps:

1. Choose Start ➢ Programs ➢ Accessories ➢ Fax ➢ Request A Fax to open the Request A Fax dialog box.

2. To retrieve all faxes stored at the remote site, click Retrieve Whatever Is Available. To retrieve one particular document, click Retrieve A Specific Document, and then type the name of the document and its password (if there is one) in the two boxes in the lower part of the dialog box. Click Next.

3. Type the name of the person to whom the retrieved fax will be routed in the To box. To retrieve a name from the Address Book, click that button, select a name, and then click Add. Verify the country, and type the fax number. Click Next.

4. To specify when you want to call, select from As Soon As Possible, When Phone Rates Are Discounted, or A Specific Time. Click Next.

5. Click Finish to complete the request.

TIP
To review the list of faxes scheduled to be sent, open Inbox and choose Tools ➤ Microsoft Fax Tools ➤ Show Outgoing Faxes to open the Outgoing Faxes dialog box. You'll see the sender, subject, size, recipients, and time to send.

FIND

Windows 98 SE adds several powerful items to the Find menu, which now includes options for finding files and folders, a computer, information on the Internet, or people. Choose Start ➤ Find and select an option, or choose Tools ➤ Find in Explorer.

Find Files or Folders

To find a file or folder, you can either use My Computer or Explorer to scan the disks yourself, or you can use the Find command to have Windows 98 SE conduct the search for you. To use the Find command, choose Start ➤ Find ➤ Files Or Folders, or in Explorer, choose Tools ➤ Find ➤ Files Or Folders.

In the Find: All Files dialog box, you will see three tabs: Name & Location, Date Modified, and Advanced.

Name & Location Tab
Contains the following options:

Named Displays the name of the file or folder for which you're searching. Click the down arrow to display a list of your most recent searches.

Containing Text Lets you specify any text that you want to locate.

Look In Tells Windows to search a specific path for the file or folder. Click the down arrow to display a list of the disks and folders on your computer.

Browse Lets you look through the available disks and folders to find the one you want.

Include Subfolders Searches sublevels of folders as well as the level you specified.

Date Tab
Contains the following options:

All Files Searches all files in the specified path for the desired file or folder.

Find All Files Restricts the search to files created, last accessed, or modified between two specified dates, during the previous number of months, or during the previous number of days.

Advanced Tab
Contains the following options:

Of Type Searches for a specific type of file. Click the down arrow to display a list of registered types.

Size Is Restricts the search for files to At Least or At Most (selected by the first down arrow) the number of kilobytes specified (typed or entered using the arrow keys).

Enter the Find specifications you want, and then select one of the following buttons:

Find Now   Starts the search.

Stop   Ends the search.

New Search   Allows you to enter new search criteria.

To save a search, including its parameters, choose File ➢ Save Search. To save the results of a search, choose Options ➢ Save Results. To make a search case-sensitive, choose Options ➢ Case Sensitive.

Find a Computer

To locate a computer on your network using the Find command in either the Start menu or Explorer, follow these steps:

1. Chose Start ➢ Find ➢ Computer, or in Explorer, choose Tools ➢ Find ➢ Computer to open the Find Computer dialog box.

2. Enter the computer name or select it from a list of previous searches by clicking the Named down arrow.

3. Click Find Now to activate the search. Stop terminates the search, and New Search allows you to enter the criteria for a new computer search.

Find on the Internet

The Find menu's On the Internet option uses Internet Explorer to connect to the Web site at home.microsoft.com/search/search.asp. This site gives you access to some of the most powerful and popular search engines on the Internet, including Infoseek, AOL NetFind, Lycos, Excite, and Yahoo.

You can also use one of the other sites in the categories of General Search, Guides, White Pages, Newsgroups, Chat Guides, Specialty, or International. If you can't find what you are looking for using one of these search engines, what you are looking for doesn't want to be found.

Find People

The Find menu's People option lets you searches public LDAP (Lightweight Directory Access Protocol) directories on the Internet such as Bigfoot (www.bigfoot.com), Four11 (www.four11.com), and WhoWhere? (www.whowhere.com) for particular information. Here are the steps:

1. Choose Start ➢ Find ➢ People, or in Explorer, choose Tools ➢ Find ➢ People to open the Find People dialog box.

2. In the Look In list, select the name of the directory service you want to use.

3. Type the information on the person you are looking for, usually just the first name followed by the last name, and then click Find Now.

The results of a search may vary depending on which of the services you use, but you will normally see a long list of names with different e-mail addresses. It is then up to you to decide which of those names is actually the person you want to contact.

Folder Options

In Explorer, choose View ➢ Folder Options (or Start ➢ Settings ➢ Folder Options) to open the Folder Options dialog box, in which you specify how your folders will look and work. The Folder Options dialog box contains three tabs: General, View, and File Types. When you open the Folder Options dialog box in My Computer, Network Neighborhood, and the Recycle Bin, you will see two tabs: General and View.

General Tab

Defines how the following system-wide settings work on your computer:

Web Style Specifies that your folders work with a single click just like the Web. Icon names will be underlined, and the normal arrow-shaped mouse pointer will turn into a hand as it passes over the icon.

Classic Style Specifies that your folders behave in the traditional Windows way. Click once to select an item; double-click to open or run an item.

Custom, Based on Settings You Choose Specifies that you want to choose your own configuration. Click the Settings button to set these preferences.

View Tab

Controls advanced settings for files and folders. The Folder Views box contains two options you can use to make all the folders on your system look and work in the same way:

Like Current Folder Uses the current settings in effect in the View menu (except for the toolbar settings) on all folders on your computer.

Reset All Folders Uses the original View menu settings in effect when the program was first installed.

The Advanced Settings box contains a set of checkboxes for certain display options, such as how to treat hidden files, whether file attributes are shown in the Details view, and so on. Click the Restore Defaults button to put everything back into its original state.

File Types Tab

Displays all the file types currently registered with Windows; this is how Windows knows which program to use to open specific data files. When you select a file type in the list, the File Type Details box displays a short summary of which filename extension belongs to that type, its MIME content type, and the name of the program used to open it.

To change or delete one of the existing types, select it in the Registered File Types box, and then choose Edit or Remove. Click the New Type button to register a new file type with Windows. Here are the steps:

1. Click the New Type button to open the Add New File Type dialog box.

2. In the Description Of Type field, enter a short text description along the lines of the other entries used, such as Active Streaming File Format.

3. Type the filename extension in the Associated Extension field.

4. Select an existing MIME Content_Type from the drop-down list, or enter a new MIME type.

5. Click the New button, and in the Actions field, enter the operation you want to perform; common operations are Open (to open the file) and Print. Then, in the Application Used To Perform Action field, enter the full path and file name of the application you want to associate with this file type. Click OK when you are done.

6. Click OK to return to the File Types tab in the Folder options dialog box.

FONTS

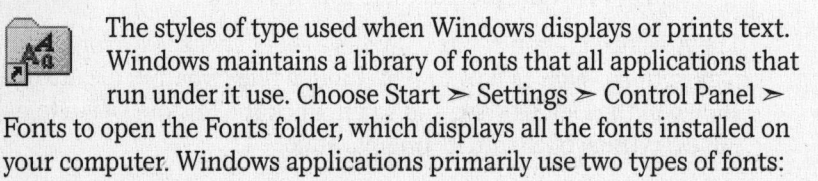

The styles of type used when Windows displays or prints text. Windows maintains a library of fonts that all applications that run under it use. Choose Start ➢ Settings ➢ Control Panel ➢ Fonts to open the Fonts folder, which displays all the fonts installed on your computer. Windows applications primarily use two types of fonts:

- TrueType fonts (represented by a pair of *T*s in the icon)
- Adobe fonts (represented by an *A* in the icon), which are bitmapped or vector fonts

The View menu of the Fonts folder offers two unique and quite useful views for fonts: List Fonts By Similarity, which groups fonts that are reasonably alike; and View ➢ Hide Variations, which hides bold, italics, and other variant forms of a typeface.

Fonts Used in Windows 98 SE

The defaults for the size and type of fonts used in the Windows 98 SE windows and dialog boxes are set in the Display Properties dialog box. You can vary the font and size for text objects and in menus, message boxes, and title bars.

Right-click the Desktop and choose Properties from the pop-up menu to open the Display Properties dialog box, or choose Start ➢ Settings ➢ Control Panel ➢ Display. You use the Appearance and Settings tabs to control the size of fonts on the screen and the size and typeface of fonts for selected objects on the screen.

Adding a New Font to Your Computer

If you have acquired some new fonts, you can add them to those that come with Windows 98 SE by following these steps:

1. Choose Start ➤ Settings ➤ Control Panel ➤ Fonts to open the Fonts folder.

2. Choose File ➤ Install New Font to open the Add Fonts dialog box.

3. Select the drive and then select the folder that contains the new font.

4. Click the font you want to add. Hold down the Ctrl key and then click to select more than one font.

Displaying and Printing Font Samples

Once you have collected a large number of fonts, remembering what each one looks like can be difficult. Fortunately, the Windows 98 SE Font Viewer can help. To use it, follow these steps:

1. Open the Font folder.

2. Select any icon in the folder to open that font in the Font Viewer. Open additional Font Viewer windows if you want to compare two or more fonts.

3. To print an example of the font, click the Print button in the Font Viewer; alternatively, right-click the font in the Font folder and select Print from the pop-up menu.

Formatting Disks

Unless you purchase formatted disks, you must format a floppy disk before you can use it the first time. Formatting a new disk places information on the disk that Windows needs to be able to read and write files and folders to and from the disk. Formatting a used disk erases all the original information it contained and turns it into a blank disk, so be sure that you are formatting the right disk.

> **NOTE**
> See Chapter 5 for instructions on formatting a floppy disk.

FrontPage Express

A quick-and-easy Web-page editor you can use to create or customize your own Web pages without having to learn the details of Hypertext Markup Language (HTML). You can edit Web-page elements by selecting them in the main FrontPage Express window and then using a toolbar button or menu selection to apply formatting and alignment.

> **NOTE**
> See Chapter 22 for instructions on using FrontPage Express.

Games

Windows 98 SE includes four games: FreeCell, Hearts, Minesweeper, and that addictive time-waster, Solitaire. You can play Hearts over the network with other players. To get to the games, choose Start ➤ Programs ➤ Accessories ➤ Games, and then click the game you want to play. If you get stuck, click Help for instructions on how to play.

Help

Windows 98 SE contains an extensive help system that provides you with online assistance at almost any time. You can use the main Windows 98 SE Help System to gain access to a huge amount of information, you can use Windows 98 SE Troubleshooters to diagnose and isolate a problem relating to specific hardware or software, and you can use Web Help to connect directly to Microsoft's Web site to look for program updates.

Windows Help System

Choose Start ➤ Help to open the main Windows 98 SE Help System dialog box, which has three tabs:

Contents Lists the main categories in the Help system itself and a general overview of Windows 98 SE.

Index Lists all the subjects in the Help system in one giant alphabetic list. Type the first few letters of the word you're looking for in the text box at the top of this tab, and the list box will automatically scroll to the subject closest in spelling to what you have typed. Or you can scroll to it yourself by using the scroll bars on the right of the display box. When you get to the subject you want, select it and click Display.

Search Allows you to find specific words or phrases contained within a Help topic. To do this, Windows 98 SE must create a database containing words used throughout the Help system. When you click the Search tab for the first time, the Search Setup Wizard creates this database. You can then use the Search tab to find the specific word or phrase you want.

When a Windows 98 SE Help topic is displayed, you may see a link icon. Click it to open the specific application, dialog box, or other element under discussion. When you close the application, you return to the same place in the Help system.

Using the Built-in Troubleshooters

Windows 98 SE extends the usual concepts of the Help system to include a set of built-in technical support troubleshooters you can use to help diagnose and isolate certain problems. There are two ways to find the right Troubleshooter and start it running on your system:

- ▶ You can choose Start ➤ Help to open the Windows 98 SE Help System. Select the Contents tab, select the Troubleshooting topic, and then open Windows 98 SE Troubleshooters. Choose the appropriate Troubleshooter from the list and follow the directions on the screen.

- ▶ Alternatively, you can start a Troubleshooter directly from a page of Help information. As you read through the information the page contains, you will come across a link to a Troubleshooter; click the link to start the Troubleshooter.

Once the Troubleshooter starts, click the Hide button on the Help toolbar to close the left pane. Be sure to follow all the steps the Troubleshooter suggests.

Troubleshooters are available for problems encountered with networking, printing, startup and shutdown, hardware such as modems, and procedures such as dial-up networking and connecting to the Microsoft Network.

Getting Web Help

Click the Web Help button on the Help System toolbar to connect to a Microsoft site to look for updated versions of programs and device drivers. You then select what you want to install; perhaps more important, you can also uninstall a program or a device driver that is causing you problems.

Help in a Dialog Box

Context-sensitive Help is also available in certain dialog boxes and on some property sheets in Windows 98 SE. You may see a Help button on a dialog box; click it to see information specific to that dialog box.

Other dialog boxes and many of the Windows 98 SE property sheets have a Help button in the upper-right corner (look for the button with a question mark on it) next to the Close button. Click this Help button and the question mark jumps onto the cursor; move the cursor to the entry on the property sheet that you want help with and click again. A small window containing the help text opens; click the mouse to close this window when you are done.

INSTALLING APPLICATIONS

You can install applications from floppy disks and CD-ROMs using the Add/Remove Programs applet in the Windows 98 SE Control Panel. You can also choose Start ➤ Run to invoke an individual Install or Setup program.

Internet

In Windows 98 SE, you can view or change the configuration options relating to the Internet in two ways:

- Via your connection to the Internet
- In Internet Explorer

To open the Internet Options dialog box, choose Start ➢ Connections ➢ Control Panel ➢ Internet, or open Internet Explorer and choose View ➢ Internet Options. The Internet Options dialog box has six tabs.

General Tab

The General tab contains these groups of settings:

Home Page   Lets you choose which Web page opens each time you connect to the Internet. The home page is the first Web page you see when you start Internet Explorer.

Temporary Internet Files   Lets you manage those Web pages that are stored on your hard disk for fast offline access.

History   Contains a list of the links you have visited so that you can return to them quickly and easily. You can specify the number of days you want to keep pages in the History folder.

Colors   Lets you choose which colors are used as background, links, and text on those Web pages for which the original author did not specify colors. By default, the Use Windows Colors option is selected.

Fonts   Lets you specify the font style and text size to use on those Web pages for which the original author did not make a specification.

Languages   Lets you choose the character set to use on those Web pages that offer content in more than one language.

Accessibility   Lets you choose how certain information is displayed in Internet Explorer, including font styles, colors, and text size. You can also specify that your own style sheet is used.

Security Tab

Lets you specify the overall security level for each of four zones. Each zone has its own default security restrictions that tell Internet Explorer how to manage dynamic Web-page content such as ActiveX controls and Java applets. The zones are:

Local Intranet   Sites you can access on your corporate intranet; security is set to medium.

Trusted Sites   Web sites you have a high degree of confidence will not send you potentially damaging content; security is set to low.

Internet   Sites you visit that are not in one of the other categories; security is set to medium.

Restricted Sites   Sites that you visit but do not trust; security is set to high.

To change the current security level of a zone, select it from the list box, and then click the new security level you want to use:

High   Excludes any content capable of damaging your system. This is the most secure setting.

Medium   Opens a warning dialog box in Internet Explorer before running ActiveX or Java applets on your system. This is a moderately-secure setting that is good for everyday use.

Low   Does not issue any warning but runs the ActiveX or Java applet automatically. This is the least secure setting.

Custom   Lets you create your own security settings. To look at or change these advanced settings, click the Settings button to open the Security Setting dialog box. You can individually configure how you want to manage certain categories, such as ActiveX controls and plug-ins, Java applets, scripting, file and font downloads, and user authentication.

Content Tab

Contains settings you can use to restrict access to sites and specify how you want to manage digital certificates:

Content Adviser   Lets you control access to certain sites on the Internet and is particularly useful if children have access to the computer. Click Settings to establish a password, and then click OK to open the Content Advisor dialog box. Use the tabs in this dialog box to establish the level of content you will allow users to view:

> **Ratings**   Lets you use a set of ratings developed by the Recreational Software Advisory Council (RSAC) for language, nudity, sex, and violence. Select one of these categories, and then adjust the slider to specify the level of content you will allow.
>
> **General**   Specifies whether people using this computer can view material that has not been rated; users may see some objectionable material if the Web site has not used the RSAC rating system.
>
> **Advanced**   Lets you look at or modify the list of organizations providing ratings services.

Certificates   Lets you manage digital certificates used with certain client authentication servers. Click Personal to view the personal digital certificates installed on this system, click Authorities to list the security certificates installed on your system, or click Publishers to designate a particular software publisher as a trustworthy publisher. This means that Windows 98 SE applications can download, install, and use software from these agencies without asking for your permission first.

Personal Information   Lets you look at or change your own personal profile; this information is sent to any Web sites that request information when you visit their site. Click Edit Profile to review the current information. Click Reset Sharing to clear the list of sites you previously allowed to access your personal information without asking your permission first. Microsoft Wallet gives you a secure place to store credit card and other information you might need for Internet shopping.

Connection Tab

Allows you to specify how your system connects to the Internet:

Connection   Lets you specify whether your system will connect to the Internet via your corporate network or by modem. Click the Connect button to run the Connection Wizard and set up a connection to an Internet Service Provider (ISP). If you use a modem, click the Settings button to open the Dial-Up Settings dialog box where you can specify all aspects of the phone connection to your ISP.

Proxy Server   Lets you access the Internet via a proxy server system connected to your corporate intranet. A proxy server is a security system designed to monitor and control the flow of information between your intranet and the Internet.

Automatic Configuration   Lets your network system administrator configure your copy of Internet Explorer automatically.

Programs Tab

Lets you set your default program choices for e-mail, newsgroup reader, and so on and specify whether Internet Explorer should check to see if it is configured as the default browser:

Messaging   Lets you choose which application programs are used for mail, news, and Internet calls.

Personal Information   Lets you choose which application programs are used for calendar functions and for your contact list.

Finally, you can specify that Internet Explorer check to see if it is configured as the default browser on your system each time it starts running.

Advanced Tab

Lets you look at or change a number of settings that control much of Internet Explorer's behavior, including accessibility, browsing, multimedia, security, the Java environment, printing and searching, and the Internet Explorer toolbar and how HTTP 1.1 settings are interpreted.

Changes you make here stay in effect until you change them again, until you download an automatic configuration file, or until you click the Restore Defaults button, which returns the settings on the Advanced tab to their original values.

Internet Explorer

The application that displays Web pages from the Internet or from your corporate intranet. In many ways, Internet Explorer resembles Windows Explorer; it is a *viewer* that presents information in a structured way. Internet Explorer is an easy-to-use program that hides a large part of the complexity of the Internet and Internet operations.

Help Menu

Gives you access to the Internet Explorer Help system through Contents And Index, lets you check for a newer version of Internet Explorer available through Product Updates, guides you through an online tutorial with Web Tutorial, and helps locate information on technical problems with Online Support.

When you choose Help ➢ Microsoft On The Web, the items on the submenu are actually links to different parts of the Microsoft Web site, including:

Free Stuff   Locates Internet Explorer program updates, free stuff, and add-on programs.

Get Faster Internet Access   Displays information about ISDN (Integrated Services Digital Network) service.

Frequently Asked Questions   Answers the most commonly asked questions about Internet Explorer.

Internet Start Page   Opens your home page.

Send Feedback   Lets you send your opinions right to Microsoft.

Best of the Web   Opens Microsoft's Exploring page, which contains a variety of links to useful and interesting sites. This is equivalent to clicking the Best of the Web button on the Internet Explorer Links toolbar.

Search the Web   Opens the same Web site as choosing Go ➢ Search The Web.

Microsoft Home Page   Opens Microsoft's Web site.

Configuring Internet Explorer

To view or set the many configuration options for Internet Explorer, choose View ➢ Internet Options to open the Internet Options dialog box. Or you can choose Start ➢ Connections ➢ Control Panel ➢ Internet. The Internet Options dialog box has six tabs. For a complete discussion of all the settings on these tabs, see the Internet entry earlier in this appendix.

Browsing Offline

You can browse the Web with Internet Explorer without being connected to the Internet. This is because many of the files that you open while browsing the Web are stored in the Temporary Internet Files folder on your hard disk. Choose File ➢ Work Offline, and Internet Explorer will not attempt to connect to the Internet when you select a resource, but will display the copy in the Temporary Internet Files folder instead. To go back to online browsing, choose File ➢ Work Offline a second time.

Speeding Up Internet Explorer

The text component of a Web page downloads quickly, but some of the other common elements, such as graphics, sound files, and animation clips, can take quite a long time to download.

Of course, there is nothing you can do to change the way a Web site is constructed, but you can stop certain types of files from being downloaded to Internet Explorer. You can essentially tell Internet Explorer to ignore all graphics files or all video clips and just collect the text. Here are the steps:

1. In Control Panel, click Internet, or choose View ➢ Internet Options within Internet Explorer to open the Internet Options dialog box.
2. Select the Advanced tab.
3. Scroll down the list box until you see the Multimedia settings, all of which are selected by default.
4. Deselect all the items you want to exclude from the Web pages you download to your system.
5. Click OK to close the Internet Options dialog box.

Remember that these options stay in effect for all subsequent Internet Explorer sessions until you turn them back on.

Keyboard

The Keyboard applet in the Control Panel allows you to set several important defaults for keyboard properties, such as the language displayed and at what speed a key must be pressed to be recognized as a repeat key.

To look at or change the keyboard properties, choose Start ➤ Settings ➤ Control Panel ➤ Keyboard to open the Keyboard Properties dialog box. It has two tabs: Speed and Language. The Speed tab contains the following options:

Repeat Delay Sets the length of time you must hold down a key before the repeat feature kicks in.

Repeat Rate Sets the speed at which a character is repeated while a key is held down.

Click Here and Hold Down a Key to Test Repeat Rate Tests the repeat delay and repeat rate speeds that you have chosen.

Cursor Blink Rate Sets the rate at which the cursor blinks, making the cursor easier to spot in some instances.

The Language tab contains the following options:

Language and Layout Displays the language and keyboard layout loaded into memory when the computer is first started. Double-click the highlighted language or layout to open the Language Properties dialog box and select another keyboard layout.

Add Adds a language and keyboard layout to those loaded into memory when the computer is booted.

Properties Allows you to change the keyboard layout default.

Remove Deletes the selected language and keyboard layout. It will no longer be loaded into memory when you boot the computer.

Set As Default with More Than One Language Installed Makes the currently selected language and keyboard layout the default to be used when the computer is started.

Switch Languages   Switches between two or more language and layout settings, as listed above. Click the key combination you want to use to switch the default.

Enable Indicator on Taskbar   Displays a language on the right of the Taskbar. Click this indicator to open a dialog box in which you can switch language defaults quickly.

Log Off

Windows 98 SE maintains a set of user profiles, each containing a different username, password, Desktop preferences, and accessibility options. When you log on to Windows 98 SE, your profile ensures that your Desktop settings—including elements such as your own desktop icons, background image, and other settings—are automatically available to you.

Windows 98 SE contains an option you can use to log off and log on again as another user quickly and easily. Click the Start button, and then click Log Off *Username*. In the Log Off Windows dialog box, click Yes. This closes all your programs, disconnects your system from the network, and prepares the system for use by other users.

Log On

When you log on to Windows 98 SE and are prompted to enter your username and password, your user profile is loaded to ensure that your Desktop settings—including elements such as your own desktop icons, background image, and other settings—are automatically available to you.

Unfortunately, you can also press the Esc key to bypass this logon screen and completely circumvent all aspects of Windows logon security. This makes Windows 98 SE a particularly unsecure system.

If you are connected to a local area network and Windows 98 SE is configured for that network, you will also be prompted to enter your network password.

Maximize/Minimize Buttons

Allows you to change the size of an application window.

The Maximize button is in the upper-right corner of an application window, and when you click it, the window expands to full-screen size. Once the window has expanded, the Maximize button changes to the Restore button, which you can then use to shrink the window back to its original starting size.

You can also place the mouse pointer on the window border, and when the two-headed arrow appears, drag the border in the direction in which you want to change its size.

Use the Minimize button to place an open application on the Taskbar; click the Taskbar icon when you are ready to work with the application again.

Media Player

Allows you to play multimedia files, such as video, animation, and sound clips, depending on the hardware installed on your computer system.

NOTE
See Chapter 9 for more information about using Media Player.

Modems

Allows you to look at or change the settings Windows uses with your modem. Choose Start ≻ Settings ≻ Control Panel ≻ Modems to open the Modem Properties dialog box.

NOTE
See Chapter 10 for instructions on working with modem properties.

Mouse

Changes your mouse settings. Choose Start ➤ Settings ➤ Control Panel ➤ Mouse to open the Mouse Properties dialog box, which contains three tabs. If you make changes to the settings in any of these tabs, click the Apply button to make sure your changes are implemented and then click OK.

Buttons Tab

Sets the mouse button configuration and speed with these options:

Button Configuration   Allows you to switch functions from the default right-handed use of the mouse buttons to left-handed.

Double-Click Speed   Allows you to set and then test the speed at which a double-click is recognized.

Pointers Tab

Allows you to change the appearance of the mouse pointer. For example, you can change the pointer used to indicate that Windows is busy from an hourglass to a symbol or caricature of your choice.

The Scheme box contains the list of pointer schemes available in Windows. By selecting one, you'll see the set of pointers in the scheme displayed in the box below. You can create additional schemes by replacing the individual pointers.

Motion Tab

Controls the pointer speed and the presence of a pointer trail, which makes the mouse pointer much easier to see on LCD screens. If you select a pointer trail, you can also choose whether it is a long or a short trail.

Moving Files and Folders

In Windows, you can move files and folders in three ways:

- By dragging and dropping
- By choosing Edit ➤ Cut and Edit ➤ Paste

▶ By clicking the right mouse button

When you move a file or folder, you move the original to another location—no duplicate is made.

Using Drag-and-Drop

To use drag-and-drop, both the source and the destination folders must be visible, for example, in Explorer or on the Desktop. Hold down the left mouse button and drag the file or folder from one location to the other. When the file or folder reaches the correct destination folder, release the mouse button. The source and destination folders must be on the same drive. If you drag a file or a folder to a different drive, it will be copied rather than moved. If you want to move a file or folder to a different drive, you must drag using the right mouse button.

Using the Edit Menu

The Edit menu in My Computer, Explorer, or any folder window provides a Cut and Paste feature. Here are the steps to follow:

1. Select the file or folder you want to move.
2. Choose Edit ➢ Cut, or click the Cut button on the toolbar.
3. Find the destination file or folder and open it.
4. Choose Edit ➢ Paste, or click the Paste button on the toolbar.

TIP
You can select multiple contiguous files or folders to move by holding down Shift and clicking the first and last file or folder. To select noncontiguous files or folders, hold down Ctrl and click the files or folders your want.

Using the Right Mouse Button

Right-clicking a file or folder opens the pop-up menu, which you can use to perform a variety of functions, including moving. Follow these steps:

1. Right-click the file or folder you want to move and select Cut from the pop-up menu.

2. Open the destination folder, right-click, and then select Paste.

> **TIP**
> If you drag a folder or a file with the right mouse button, a pop-up menu opens when you release the button, allowing you to copy the object, move it, or create a shortcut.

Moving and Arranging Icons

In Windows, you can arrange icons using any of several methods. In Explorer, Control Panel, and many other windows, you can move or arrange icons using the selections in the View menu:

Large Icons   Displays the files and folders as larger-sized icons.

Small Icons   Displays the files and folders as smaller-sized icons.

List   Displays small icons alongside the names of the files and folders.

Details   Displays files and folders in the List style and adds columns for the size of file, date last modified, and type of file. To sort entries within these columns, simply click the column heading. Click once for an ascending sort (A to Z and 0 to 9); click a second time for a descending sort.

Line Up Icons   Rearranges icons into straight vertical and horizontal lines.

> **TIP**
> To rearrange icons on the Desktop, simply drag them to their new location. To tidy up the Desktop quickly, right-click an area of free space, and choose Arrange Icons.

By clicking the Views button on the Explorer toolbar, you can cycle the display through the four presentations of Large Icons, Small Icons, List, and Details; each time you click the button, the display changes to the next format.

Multimedia

Establishes the default settings for multimedia devices connected to your computer; its contents depend on which multimedia devices you have installed.

Choose Start ➤ Settings ➤ Control Panel ➤ Multimedia to open the Multimedia Properties dialog box, containing tabs appropriate to the hardware installed on your computer. You might see the following tabs:

Audio   Sets playback and recording controls.

Video   Specifies the size of the video playback window.

MIDI   Sets Musical Instruments Digital Interface controls and adds new instruments.

CD Music   Sets the drive letter and headphone volume defaults.

Devices   Lists the multimedia hardware connected to your computer and allows you to set or change properties for any of the hardware listed. Select the hardware component you want to configure, and then click Properties to open the related dialog box.

> **NOTE**
> See Chapter 9 to learn more about multimedia in Windows 98 SE.

My Computer

One of the file-management tools available with Windows. You can use My Computer to locate folders, files, and disks or printers on your computer or on mapped drives on other computers connected to the network.

My Computer Folder

Click the My Computer icon on the Desktop to open the My Computer folder, showing an icon for each drive and drive-level folder on your computer. Click an icon to display the contents of one of these folders or drives in a separate window.

Finding a File or Folder with My Computer

When you open My Computer, the My Computer folder displays all the disks and folders on your computer. Follow these steps to find the file or folder you want:

1. Click the down arrow at the end of the Address toolbar to find the device or folder you want. You will see all the shared disks on your network, important folders such as Control Panel, Printers, and Dial-Up Networking, and other Windows elements, such as Internet Explorer, Network Neighborhood, Recycle Bin, and My Briefcase.

2. Click a disk or a folder to see its contents in the window.

3. Once you find the file or folder (which may be several levels down), click it to open it.

MY DOCUMENTS

A Desktop folder that provides a convenient place to store graphics, documents, or any other files you might want to access quickly. When you save a file in programs such as Paint or WordPad, the file is automatically saved in My Documents unless you specify a different destination folder.

To specify a different destination folder, right-click My Documents and select Properties. Type the name of the new folder in the Target field and click OK. Changing to a different folder does not move existing files stored in My Documents.

NAMING DISKS

You can give a hard or a floppy disk a name that can be a maximum of 11 characters. To name or rename a disk, follow these steps:

1. Open My Computer or Explorer.

2. Right-click the disk you want to name, and select Properties to open the Properties dialog box.

3. Select the General tab, and type the name you want to use for this disk in the Label field. Click OK.

Naming Files and Folders

The first time you save a file using the Save or Save As command, you are asked to provide a name for the file. When you create a new folder, it is always called New Folder until you change the name. Names for files and folders can contain a maximum of 255 characters, including spaces, but cannot contain any of these special characters: /,\,?,:,*,",<,>, or |.

You can rename both files and folders in Explorer or My Computer. Follow these steps:

1. Open Explorer or My Computer and find the file or folder you want to rename.

2. Click the name once, pause, and then click it again. A box will enclose the name, and the name will be selected. If you move the mouse inside the box, the pointer will become an I-beam.

3. Type the new name or edit the existing name and press Enter.

NetMeeting

A conferencing application that allows people working in different locations to collaborate simultaneously on the same project, sharing Microsoft applications to edit documents. NetMeeting also supports audio and video conferencing over the Internet (as long as you have the appropriate hardware such as a video camera or microphone attached to your computer system), as well as a file-transfer function.

Choose Start ➤ Programs ➤ Internet Explorer ➤ Microsoft NetMeeting to open NetMeeting.

Online Services

Allows you to access several popular online services such as AOL and the Microsoft Network. Before you can use any of these services, you must first register with it. You can do this using the items in the Online Services menu; each item connects you to a specific service. You can also use the Online Services folder on the Desktop.

Before you start, connect your modem to the phone line, and close any other open applications.

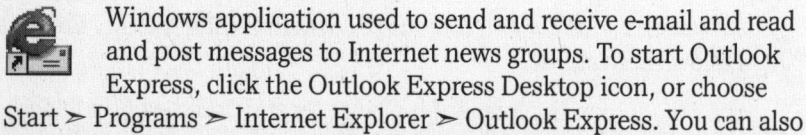

Outlook Express

Windows application used to send and receive e-mail and read and post messages to Internet news groups. To start Outlook Express, click the Outlook Express Desktop icon, or choose Start ➤ Programs ➤ Internet Explorer ➤ Outlook Express. You can also click the Launch Outlook Express button on the Quick Launch toolbar, or use the Mail menu from within Internet Explorer.

Chapter 18 shows how to use Outlook Express for basic operations such as sending and receiving e-mail, as well as managing address books and mail folders. Following are additional highlights.

Reading the News

Outlook Express is also a newsreader that you can use to access the thousands of specific-subject newsgroups on the Internet.

> **WARNING**
> Anything goes in many of these Internet newsgroups. There is absolutely no censorship, and if you are easily offended (and even if you are not), you might want to stay with the more mainstream Web pages.

In the same way that you set up an e-mail account with an ISP, you must also set up a newsgroup account, complete with password, before you can use Outlook Express as a newsreader.

Configuring Outlook Express

Configuration options for Outlook Express are quite extensive. You can customize the toolbar and add buttons for the tasks you perform most often, and you can define the rules you want Outlook Express to follow when you are creating, sending, and receiving e-mail. Choose Tools ➤ Options to open the Options dialog box. It has the following tabs:

General Contains general-purpose settings for Outlook Express.

Send Specifies the format for sending mail and articles to newsgroups, as well as several other mail-related options, such as whether to include the text of the original message in any reply.

Read Specifies options used when displaying articles from newsgroups.

Security Establishes security zones and specifies how Outlook Express manages digital certificates (also known as digital IDs).

Dial Up Specifies the options used when connecting to your ISP by dial-up connection.

Advanced Specifies options only of interest to system administrators.

You can also choose View ➤ Layout to open the Layout Properties dialog box. Click Customize Toolbar to add or remove buttons from the Outlook Express toolbar. To return the toolbar to its original layout, click Customize Toolbar again, and then click Reset followed by Close in the Customize Toolbar dialog box.

PAINT

A program with which you can create lines and shapes, with or without color, and place text within graphics. You can also use it to create backgrounds for the Desktop. Choose Start ➤ Programs ➤ Accessories ➤ Paint to open the main Paint window.

Paint Toolbar

Provides tools for drawing and working with color and text. Below the toolbar is an area containing optional choices depending on the type of tool you chose. For example, if you choose the Brush tool, a selection of brush edges is displayed. If you choose Magnifier, a selection of magnifying strengths is displayed. At the bottom of the main window, the Color Palette displays a series of colored squares.

The toolbox contains the following buttons for drawing lines and shapes and for working with color:

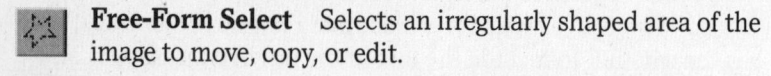

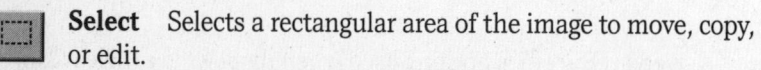

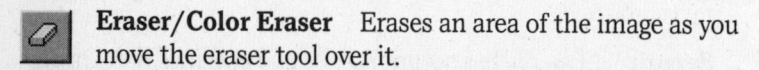

Free-Form Select Selects an irregularly shaped area of the image to move, copy, or edit.

Select Selects a rectangular area of the image to move, copy, or edit.

Eraser/Color Eraser Erases an area of the image as you move the eraser tool over it.

Fill with Color Fills an enclosed area with the currently selected color.

Pick Color Selects the color of any object you click. It is for use with the tool that you chose immediately before you selected Pick Color.

Magnifier Enlarges the selected area.

Pencil Draws a free-hand line one pixel wide.

Brush Draws lines of different shapes and widths.

Airbrush Draws using an airbrush of the selected size.

Text Inserts text onto the drawing. Click Text, click the color you want for the text, and then drag a text box to the location where you want to insert the text. In the font window that appears, click the font, size, and style (Bold, Italic, Underline) you want. Click inside the text box, and begin typing your text.

Line Draws a straight line. After dragging the tool to create a line segment, click once to anchor the line before continuing in a different direction, or click twice to end the line.

Curve   Draws a curved line where one segment ends and another begins. After dragging the tool to create a line segment, click once to anchor the line before continuing. To create a curve, click anywhere on the line and then drag it. Click twice to end the line.

Rectangle   Creates a rectangle. Select the fill style from the toolbar below the main Paint window.

Polygon   Creates a polygon, or figure consisting of straight lines connecting at any angle. After dragging the first line segment, release the mouse, place the pointer where the second line segment is to end, click the mouse button, and repeat until the drawing is complete. Click twice to end the drawing.

Ellipse   Draws an ellipse. Select the fill style from the Color Palette below the main Paint window.

Rounded Rectangle   Creates a rectangle with curved corners. Select the fill style from the Color Palette below the main Paint window.

When you create an image in Paint, first select the tool, then select the tool shape, if applicable, and then click the color you want to use from the Color Palette at the bottom of the Paint window. The currently active color is displayed in the top square on the left of the palette. To change the background color, click Pick Color, and then click the color you want. The next image you create will use the new background color.

Paint Menus

Contain many of the standard Windows options. In addition, you can set a saved paint File to be used as wallpaper, zoom in various ways, flip or rotate an image, invert its colors, define custom colors, and set various image attributes.

Passwords

Allows you to specify a logon password. Windows maintains a set of user profiles, each containing a different username, password, Desktop preferences, and accessibility options. When you log on to Windows, your profile ensures that your Desktop settings, including elements such as your own Desktop icons, background image, and other settings, are automatically available to you.

Enabling User Profiles

To enable user profiles, follow these steps:

1. Choose Start ➤ Settings ➤ Control Panel ➤ Passwords to open the Passwords Properties dialog box.

2. Select Users can customize their preferences and Desktop settings.

3. In the User Profile Settings box; you can select one option or both:

   ▶ Include Desktop icons and Network Neighborhood content in user settings.

   ▶ Include Start menu and Program groups in user settings.

4. You'll have to use Shut Down to restart your computer for these changes to be applied.

Specifying a Password

When you start Windows 98 SE for the first time, you are prompted to enter a username and password and then to confirm that password. If you are connected to a network, you may also be asked to enter a network password. On all subsequent startups, this series of dialog boxes will be slightly different. You will only be asked to enter the password; you will not have to confirm it.

Changing a Password

To change a password, follow these steps:

> **NOTE**
> You must know the current password in order to change it.

1. Choose Start ➤ Settings ➤ Control Panel ➤ Passwords to open the Passwords Properties dialog box.

2. Select the Change Passwords tab, and then click the Change Windows Password button to open the Change Windows Password dialog box.

3. Type the old password (asterisks will appear as you type), and enter the new password; you will have to retype the new password to confirm it. Click OK to close the Change Windows Password dialog box.

4. Click OK to close the Passwords Properties dialog box and finalize your new password. Next time you log on to Windows, remember to use your new password.

In addition to your logon password, you can establish a password for the following resources:

Dial-Up Connections   To change passwords, click My Computer, click the Dial-Up Networking icon, and select Connections ➤ Dial-Up Server. Click Allow Caller Access to enable the Change Password button.

Disks   To set and change passwords, right-click the disk in the Explorer window and select Sharing from the pop-up menu.

Folders   To change the password or sharing status, open Explorer or My Computer, select the folder, choose File ➤ Properties, and then click the Sharing tab.

Printers   To change the password or sharing status, open the Printers folder from either Explorer, My Computer, or Control Panel. Right-click the printer and select Sharing from the pop-up menu.

Network Administration   Set password access to shared devices from the Access Control tab in the Network applet in the Control Panel.

Screen Savers   You can use a password to prevent others from gaining access to your files when a screen saver is active. To change a password, choose Start ➤ Settings ➤ Control Panel ➤ Display to open the Display Properties dialog box. Select the Screen Saver tab and click Password Protected, and then click the Change button.

Shared Resources To change the password or sharing status, open Explorer or My Computer, select the resource, choose File ➤ Properties to open the Properties dialog box, and select the Sharing tab. If the resource is shared, you can change the password. You can also change the sharing status from the Access Control tab in the Network applet in the Control Panel.

Click the Change Other Passwords button in the Passwords Properties dialog box to work with these other passwords.

Allowing Remote Administration

You can specify whether a system administrator can create shared folders and shared printers on your computer, and see the usernames of anyone who connects to them by using the options on the Remote Administration tab in the Passwords Properties dialog box.

Paste Command

Copies the contents of the Clipboard into the current document. It is available from the Edit menu and some pop-up menus that are displayed when you right-click a file or a folder.

Plug and Play

A Windows feature that automatically detects hardware installed in your computer system. Today, most hardware is specifically designed with Plug and Play in mind. You just install the hardware, and Windows takes care of the details, loading the appropriate device drivers and other related software automatically.

Plug and Play adapters contain configuration information stored in permanent memory on the board, including vendor information, serial number, and other configuration data. The Plug-and-Play hardware allows each adapter to be isolated, one at a time, until Windows identifies all the cards installed in your computer. Once this task is complete, Windows can load and configure the appropriate device drivers. After installing a new Plug-and-Play adapter in your computer system, Windows will often ask you to restart the system. This is so the new device drivers can be loaded into the correct part of system memory.

Printers

Manages all functions related to printers and printing. From here you can add a new printer, check on a job in the print queue, change the active printer, or modify a printer's properties.

> **NOTE**
> See Chapter 8 for a complete discussion of printers and printing in Windows 98 SE.

Programs

Lists the programs available in Windows, either as stand-alone applications or as collections of applications located in submenus or program groups. Any selection that has an arrow pointer to the right of the name is not a single program but a program group. Choosing one of these groups opens another menu listing the items in the group.

Follow these steps to start a program from the Programs menu:

1. Choose Start ➢ Programs to display the current list of program groups.

2. Select a program group to display a list of the programs it contains.

3. Click an application name to start it.

Adding a New Submenu to the Programs Menu

Most Windows programs are added to the Programs menu automatically as they are installed—you are generally asked to verify in which folder or program group any new program should be placed—and the Setup program takes care of the rest. However, you can create a new submenu manually if you wish. Follow these steps:

1. Right-click the Start button and choose Open to open the Start Menu folder.

2. Select the Programs folder, and then choose File ≻ New ≻ Folder. This creates an empty folder in the Program group with the name New Folder.

3. Enter the name you want to use for the submenu as the name of this new folder, press Enter, and then open the folder you just created.

4. Choose File ≻ New ≻ Shortcut to start the Create Shortcut Wizard, which guides you through the process of adding applications to your new folder.

5. Enter the path and file name for the application in the Command Line box, or click the Browse button to locate the file.

6. Type a shortcut name for the program and click Finish.

The next time you open the Programs menu, you will see the entry you just created, and when you select that entry, you will see the list of items that it contains.

Properties

Characteristics of something in Windows—a computer, a peripheral such as a printer or modem, a file, or a folder—are displayed in the Properties dialog box. The properties for any item depend on what it is. To open any Properties dialog box, follow these steps:

1. Select the item in the Explorer.

2. Choose File ≻ Properties.

You can also open the Properties dialog box by right-clicking an object and then selecting Properties from the pop-up menu.

Recycle Bin

A folder that stores deleted files until they are finally removed from your hard disk. The Recycle Bin is represented on the Desktop by a wastebasket icon. Files are copied to the Recycle Bin both directly and indirectly; you can simply drag a file there, or you can send a file to the Recycle Bin by choosing Delete from a pop-up menu. When you empty the Recycle Bin, the files it contains are permanently removed from your hard disk; once you empty the bin, anything it contained is gone for good.

> **TIP**
> If the Recycle Bin contains deleted files, you will see paper protruding from the top of the wastebasket icon.

> **NOTE**
> See Chapter 5 for instructions on using the Recycle Bin.

REGIONAL SETTINGS

Sets the system-wide defaults for country (and therefore language), number, currency, time, and date formatting. If you are using English in the United States, you will probably never need Regional Settings; if you want to use a different language, this is the place to start. Choose Start ➤ Settings ➤ Control Panel ➤ Regional Settings to open the Regional Settings Properties dialog box.

Regional Tab

On the Regional Settings tab, click the down arrow and select a language and a country.

Number Tab

Sets the defaults for how positive and negative numbers are displayed, the number of decimal places, the separator between groups of numbers, and so on. This tab contains the following options:

Decimal Symbol Establishes which symbol will be used as a decimal point. The default in the United States is a period.

No. of Digits after Decimal Specifies how many numbers will be placed to the right of the decimal point. The default is 2.

Digit Grouping Symbol Determines the symbol that will group digits into a larger number, such as the comma in 999,999. The default is a comma.

No. of Digits in Group Specifies how many numbers will be grouped together into larger numbers. The default is 3, as in 9,999,999.

Negative Sign Symbol Establishes which symbol is used to show a negative number. The default is a minus sign.

Negative Number Format Establishes how a negative number will be displayed. The default is to display the negative sign in front of the number, such as −24.5.

Display Leading Zeroes Determines whether a zero is shown in front of a decimal number. The default is yes, as in 0.952.

Measurement System Determines whether the system of measurement will be U.S. or metric. The default is U.S.

List Separator Specifies which symbol will separate items in a list or series. The default is a comma.

If you make any changes in this tab, click Apply and then OK.

Currency Tab

Determines the format for displaying currency. For example, you might want to vary the number of decimal points or the presentation of negative numbers. This tab contains the following options:

Currency Symbol Displays the symbol of the currency, such as the dollar sign.

Position of Currency Symbol Shows where the currency symbol is displayed in the number—usually in front of a number.

Negative Number Format Specifies how negative numbers are displayed.

Decimal Symbol Determines which symbol separates the whole from the fractional parts of a number, such as a period or a comma.

No. of Digits after Decimal Specifies how many digits are shown by default after the decimal—usually two.

Digit Grouping Symbol Shows which symbol—usually a comma—separates the number groups, such as thousands, millions, and so on.

Number of Digits in Group Specifies how many digits determine a number group, such as 3 for thousands, millions, and so on.

Click Apply and then OK to put any changes you make into effect.

Time Tab

Establishes the default formatting for the time. The Time tab has the following options:

Time Style Determines how the time will be formatted.

Time Separator Determines which symbol separates the hours from the minutes and seconds; the default is a colon.

AM Symbol Specifies the default for the morning symbol.

PM Symbol Specifies the default for the afternoon symbol.

Click Apply and then OK to activate any changes you make.

Date Tab

Establishes the default formatting for the date. The Date tab has the following options:

Calendar Type Displays the types of calendars that you can choose from.

Short Date Style Lists the formats available for displaying the date.

Date Separator Lists the symbols that can be used to separate the month, day, and year.

Long Date Style Lists the formats available for displaying a formal date notation.

Click Apply and then OK to activate any changes you make.

RESTORE

Restores an archive copy of one or more files and folders to your hard disk after a disk or controller failure or some other unforeseen event. To start the Windows 98 SE backup and restore program, choose Start ➢ Programs ➢ Accessories ➢ System Tools ➢ Backup. The first time you start the program, a dialog box welcomes you to Microsoft Backup and leads directly into the Restore Wizard.

Using the Restore Wizard

Using the Restore Wizard is a quick and easy way to learn about restoring backups; it gets you going quickly with a minimum of technical knowledge. Check Restore Backed up Files, and then click OK in this opening dialog box to start the Wizard. If you would rather not use the Wizard, click Close; you can always restart it from the toolbar inside the Backup program if you change your mind.

The Wizard walks you through the following sequence of dialog boxes. Click the Next button when you have made your choice to advance to the next dialog box; click Back to retrace your steps, and click Cancel if you change your mind about using the Wizard.

> **Restore From** Specify the type and location of the backup you want to restore.
>
> **Select Backup Sets** Select a backup set for the restore.
>
> **What to Restore** You can restore all files and folders in the backup set, or you can restore selected files and folders.
>
> **Where to Restore** Specify the target of the restore; most of the time selecting Original Location to put the file back where it came from makes the most sense.
>
> **How to Restore** Specify whether existing files on your hard disk should be overwritten during the restore.

Click the Start button to begin the restore; a small progress indicator tracks the restore as it proceeds.

Using the Restore Tab

Using the Restore tab in the Backup program involves essentially the same tasks that the Restore Wizard does for you—selecting the files, deciding where to put them, and specifying how the restore should actually be made.

Run

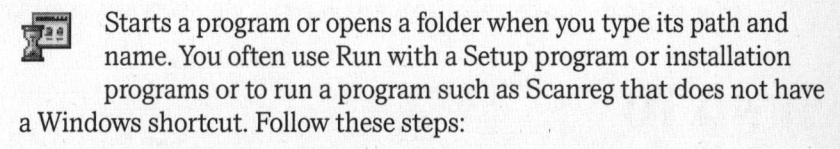

> **NOTE**
> A check mark in a gray checkbox means that only some of the files in a folder have been selected. A check mark in a white box means that all files in a folder have been selected.

Starts a program or opens a folder when you type its path and name. You often use Run with a Setup program or installation programs or to run a program such as Scanreg that does not have a Windows shortcut. Follow these steps:

1. Choose Start ➤ Run to open the Run dialog box.

2. If you have run this program recently, you may find its name already entered in the Open list box. Click the down arrow, select it by name, and then click OK.

3. If you have not run this program recently or if the Open box is blank, type the full path and program name, such as **C:*Folder\\Program***.

4. If you are not sure of the path or program name, click Browse to find and select the program. Then click OK to load and run the program.

ScanDisk

Checks a disk for certain common errors. Once ScanDisk detects these errors, it can fix them and recover any data in corrupted areas. Windows 98 SE runs ScanDisk automatically if the operating system is shut down improperly, as might happen during a power outage.

Choose Start ➤ Programs ➤ Accessories ➤ System Tools ➤ ScanDisk to open the ScanDisk dialog box.

> **NOTE**
> See Chapter 11 for instructions on using ScanDisk.

Screen Saver

Displays an image on the screen after a fixed period of inactivity. The screen saver hides the normal information displayed by the application you are using and replaces it with another image.

You can change or select a screen saver using the Display applet in the Control Panel. You can set the speed, shape, density, and color of the screen saver, and you can set a password to get back to your work and other settings. You can also use certain active channels as screen savers.

Send To

Sends items to common destinations, such as floppy disk drives, a fax, an e-mail, or My Briefcase. You can send a file quickly to a destination by following these steps:

1. Right-click the file or folder to open the pop-up menu.
2. Select Send To.
3. Click the appropriate destination.

Settings

Choose Start ➤ Settings to access all the Windows 98 SE configuration tools, including the Control Panel, Printers, Taskbar & Start Menu, Folder Options, and the Active Desktop controls.

Shortcuts

Quick ways to open an application or access a disk, file, folder, printer, or computer without going to its permanent location using Windows Explorer. Shortcuts are useful for applications that you use frequently; when you access a shortcut, the file, folder, printer, computer, or program is opened for you. You can create a shortcut using the File menu, pop-up menus, or drag-and-copy.

> **NOTE**
> See Chapter 4 for complete instructions on creating and using shortcuts.

Shut Down

The procedure for closing Windows. You must always follow the Shut Down procedure before turning your computer off or restarting your system; if you don't, you run the risk of losing data. Follow these steps to shut down:

1. When you are ready to turn off your computer, choose Start ➤ Shut Down to open the Shut Down Windows dialog box. It contains the following options:

    Shut Down Prepares the computer to be turned off.

    Restart Prepares the computer for shut down and then automatically starts it again.

    Restart in MS-DOS Mode Closes Windows and restarts the computer in MS-DOS mode.

2. Select the option you want, and then click OK.

3. Respond to any other questions that Windows displays, such as whether it is OK to disconnect network users.

When Windows 98 SE has finished saving data to your hard disk, it displays a final message telling you that it is now safe to turn off your computer.

Sounds

Assigns sounds to certain system events, such as warning dialog boxes, and to more common events such as opening or closing windows or receiving an e-mail message. Choose Start ➤ Settings ➤ Control Panel ➤ Sounds to open the Sounds Properties dialog box.

> **NOTE**
> See Chapter 9 for instructions on assigning sounds and working with sound schemes.

Start

Start — The primary way to access files, folders, and programs on your computer. Initially, the Start button is on the bottom left of your screen at the left end of the Taskbar. Click Start to display the Start menu. Some of the options on this menu are standard with Windows 98 SE, but you can add others to give you fast access to your favorite applications.

The Start menu contains the following options:

Shut Down   Prepares the computer to be shut down or restarted.

Log Off   Logs off the system quickly so that you can log back on with a different user profile or so that another user can log on.

Run   Opens the Run dialog box so that you can run a program or open a folder by typing its path and name.

Help   Opens the extensive Windows 98 SE Help system.

Find   Searches for a file, folder, device, or computer. You can also search the Internet and look for personal contact information.

Settings   Accesses the Control Panel, Printers, Taskbar & Start Menu, Folder Options, and Active Desktop controls so that you can configure the way Windows operates.

Documents   Gives you access to the last 15 documents you opened.

Favorites   Gives you access to Channels, Links, and Software Updates.

Programs   Gives you access to the program groups and files on your computer.

Windows Update   Automatically connects to the Microsoft Web site to check for updates to the Windows 98 SE operating system.

> **TIP**
> To add a program or a shortcut to the Start menu, simply drag its icon to the Start button.

Startup

An application that is activated automatically each time you start Windows. If you use certain applications frequently and do not want the bother of starting them manually every time you start Windows, simply put them in your Startup folder. Follow these steps:

1. Choose Start ➤ Settings ➤ Taskbar & Start Menu to open the Taskbar Properties dialog box.
2. Select the Start Menu Programs tab.
3. Click Add, and type the name of the path to the program you want, or click Browse to find it. Click Next.
4. Find the StartUp folder in the list of Start Menu folders, and select it. Click Next.
5. If you don't like the default, type the shortcut name that you want to appear in the StartUp folder, and click Finish.
6. If you are prompted to choose an icon, click one, and then click Finish.
7. To verify that the program you selected is now in the StartUp menu, choose Start ➤ Programs ➤ StartUp.

The next time you start Windows 98 SE, the program you just added to the StartUp folder will be automatically loaded.

Taskbar

Launches programs and is the primary tool for switching from one application to another. The Taskbar contains several types of icons:

- The Start button at the left end of the Taskbar is responsible for launching applications, opening documents, and adjusting settings.
- The Quick Launch toolbar contains buttons you can use to do the following:
    - Open Internet Explorer
    - Open Outlook Express
    - Open TV Viewer
    - Bring the Desktop to the front
    - View channels
- Any shortcut buttons to the right of the Quick Launch toolbar represent the applications currently active in memory or open folders. You can use these icons to switch between the running applications.
- The system clock at the right end of the Taskbar displays the current time.

The Taskbar may also show other icons from time to time, indicating that an e-mail message is waiting, that you are printing a document, or the battery condition on a laptop computer.

Switching with the Taskbar

When you open a new application, the Taskbar gets another button, and by clicking that button, you can switch to the new application or folder.

Switching with Alt+Tab

You can also use the Alt+Tab key combination to switch between running applications. Press and hold down the Alt key and press the Tab key once to open a dialog box that contains an icon for each application running on your system. Each time you press the Tab key, the outline box moves one icon to the right until it wraps all the way round and reappears on the left side of the box. This outline box indicates the application that will run when you release the Alt key.

Taskbar & Start Menu

The Taskbar is the main way that you switch from one application to another in Windows 98 SE. The default Taskbar contains two types of buttons: the Start button, and any number of shortcut buttons for the applications currently active in memory.

To change how the Taskbar looks and works, choose Start ➢ Settings ➢ Taskbar & Start Menu to open the Taskbar Properties dialog box. You can also choose a toolbar from a set of default toolbars and add it to your Taskbar; you can even create your own custom toolbar.

> **TIP**
> You don't have to leave the Windows Taskbar at the bottom of the screen; you can place it along any of the four edges. To move it, simply drag it to its new location.

Modifying the Taskbar Display

The Taskbar is usually at the bottom of the screen and is always displayed on top of other windows so that you can get to it quickly and easily. To change how the Taskbar is displayed, follow these steps:

1. Choose Start ➢ Settings ➢ Taskbar & Start Menu to open the Taskbar Properties dialog box. You can also simply right-click an empty spot on the Taskbar and select Properties from the pop-up menu.

2. Place a check mark in the box next to the options you want:

   Always on Top   Forces the Taskbar to remain on top of other windows, ensuring that it is always visible to you.

   Auto Hide   Displays the Taskbar as a small thin line on the bottom of the screen. To also display the thin line when a full-screen window is displayed, select both Always On Top and Auto Hide.

   Show Small Icons in Start Menu   Displays a small Start menu with smaller icons.

   Show Clock   Displays the time in the left of the Taskbar. By double-clicking the clock, you can reset the time or date.

3. Click Apply to make the changes final, and then click OK.

Adding Toolbars

Windows 98 SE includes a default set of toolbars that you can add to your Taskbar if you wish:

Address   Allows you to open an Internet address without first opening Internet Explorer.

Links   Contains a set of Internet addresses.

Desktop   Contains all your Desktop icons. Because this toolbar is longer than the screen is wide, you can use the small arrows to see the other icons.

Quick Launch   Contains buttons you can use to do the following:

- ▶ Open Internet Explorer
- ▶ Open Outlook Express
- ▶ Open TV Viewer
- ▶ Bring the Desktop to the front
- ▶ View channels

To add one of these toolbars to your Taskbar, right-click an empty spot on the Taskbar, choose Toolbars from the pop-up menu, and then select the toolbar you want to add to your Taskbar.

> **TIP**
> You can also add your own shortcut to the Quick Launch toolbar. Open My Computer or Explorer, select the application you want to add, and drag it to the Quick Launch part of the Windows Taskbar. You will see that program's icon appear next to the other icons on the Quick Launch toolbar. To remove an icon from the Quick Launch toolbar, right-click it and choose Delete.

Creating a Custom Toolbar

If the default set of toolbars don't meet your needs, you can always create your own. Follow these steps:

1. Right-click an empty part of the Taskbar to open the pop-up menu.

2. Choose Toolbars ➤ New Toolbar to open the New Toolbar dialog box.

3. Select a folder from the list or type an Internet address that you want to appear as a toolbar.

Another way to build a custom toolbar is to create a new folder, add all your favorite shortcuts to it, and then choose Toolbars ➤ New Toolbar to turn it into a toolbar.

Task Scheduler

A program you can use to run selected applications at specific times—daily, weekly or even monthly—without any input from you or involvement on your part. The Task Scheduler starts running in the background every time you start Windows 98 SE; it just sits there until it is time to run one of your selected tasks, and then it moves into action.

> **NOTE**
> See Chapter 11 for instructions about using Task Scheduler.

Undeleting Files

When you delete a file or a folder, it is stored in the Recycle Bin, but until you actually empty the Recycle Bin, you can still retrieve any files you deleted. To recover a file from the Recycle Bin and return it to its original location, follow these steps:

1. Click the Recycle Bin on the Desktop.

2. Select the file or files you want to restore.

3. Right-click and choose Restore, or choose File ➤ Restore.

If you have chosen to display the contents of the Recycle Bin as a Web page, you can also click Restore All to return multiple files to their original locations.

> **TIP**
> To select multiple files, hold down Ctrl while you click.

UNINSTALLING APPLICATIONS

The Uninstall program removes all traces that an application was ever installed. It removes all references to the program from the Windows directories and subdirectories and from the Windows Registry.

The Uninstall feature is found in the Add/Remove Program Properties dialog box. Follow these steps to uninstall a program:

1. Choose Start ➢ Settings ➢ Control Panel ➢ Add/Remove Programs to open the Add/Remove Programs Properties dialog box.
2. If necessary, select the Install/Uninstall tab.
3. Select the software you want to remove from the list and click Add/Remove.

USERS

Windows 98 SE maintains a set of user profiles each containing a different username, password, Desktop preferences, and accessibility options. When you log on to Windows 98 SE, your profile ensures that your Desktop settings—including elements such as your own Desktop icons, background image, and other settings—are automatically available to you.

To set up a new user profile, follow these steps:

1. Choose Start ➢ Settings ➢ Control Panel ➢ Users to open the Enable Multi-User Settings dialog box.
2. Click the Next button.
3. In the Add User dialog box, enter your username and click Next.

Windows 98 SE Command and Feature Reference 867

4. In the Enter New Password dialog box, type your password. Type it again in the Confirm Password field and click Next.

5. In the Personalized Items Settings dialog box, select the items from the list that you want to personalize, and then choose whether you want to create copies of these items or create new items in order to save hard-disk space. Click the Next button.

6. Click the Finish button to complete the creation of this new user profile and to close the Wizard.

Volume Control

An accessory you can use to control the volume of your sound card and speakers. If you have more than one multimedia capability installed, for example, MIDI or Wave-handling capability, you can control the volume and balance for each device separately. Follow these steps to access the Volume Control:

1. Choose Start ➤ Programs ➤ Accessories ➤ Entertainment ➤ Volume Control to open the Volume Control dialog box. It contains separate features to balance volume for the devices on your computer. Depending on the hardware installed on your computer, the following features may or may not appear:

   Volume Control   Controls volume and balance for sounds coming out of your computer. This is the "master" control.

   Line-In   Controls the volume and balance for an external device that feeds sound into your computer, such as audio tape or an FM tuner.

   Wave Out   Controls the volume and balance for playing .wav files as they come into the computer.

   MIDI   Controls the volume and balance for incoming sounds from MIDI files.

   Audio-CD   Controls the volume and balance for CD-ROM audio files as they come into the computer.

   Microphone   Controls the volume and balance for sound coming in via a microphone.

2. To control the volume of the components, move the vertical slider labeled Volume up or down to increase or decrease volume.

3. To control the balance between two speakers, move the horizontal slider labeled Balance to the left or right to move the emphasis to the left or right speaker.

4. Click Mute All or Mute to silence all components' or one component's contribution to the sound.

Varying the Recording Volume

To vary the volume and balance when you are recording, follow these steps:

1. From the Volume Control dialog box, choose Options ➢ Properties to open the Properties dialog box.

2. Select Recording to display a list of devices that apply to the recording task.

3. If it is not already checked, click the checkbox to select the device you want.

4. Click OK to open the Recording Control dialog box for the selected device.

5. Move the Balance and Volume sliders to adjust the volume and balance of the sound.

WELCOME TO WINDOWS

Opens an interactive guide to Windows 98 SE. Choose Start ➢ Programs ➢ Accessories ➢ System Tools ➢ Welcome To Windows. The Welcome screen contains the following options:

Register Now Runs the Windows 98 Registration Wizard so that you can register your copy of Windows 98 SE. In the Welcome screen, click Next to proceed with online registration, or click Register Later if you don't want to register right now.

Discover Windows 98 Starts a three-part Windows 98 tutorial consisting of Computing Essentials, Windows 98 Overview, and What's New.

Tune Up Your Computer   Runs Windows Tune-Up on your system.

Release Notes   Opens WordPad on the Windows 98 Release Notes file. You should check the information in this file as it may contain late-breaking information that didn't make it into the Windows Help system.

What's This?

`What's This?`   Provides context-sensitive help in some dialog boxes. If you right-click an item in a dialog box, a small menu opens containing the single selection What's This?. Click What's This? to display help text for that specific item.

Other dialog boxes have a Help button in the upper-right corner (look for the button with a question mark on it) next to the Close button. When you click this Help button, the question mark jumps onto the cursor; move the cursor to the entry on the dialog box that you want help with and click again. A small window containing the help text opens; click the mouse to close this window when you are done.

Windows Tune-Up

Optimizes your system for best performance. The Windows Tune-Up Wizard can help make your programs run faster, free up precious hard-disk space, and optimize system performance.

The Wizard actually does its work by running three other Windows system utilities—Disk Defragmenter, ScanDisk, and Disk Cleanup—in concert with Task Scheduler, which controls when the other utilities run on your system. To run Windows Tune-Up, follow these steps:

1. Choose Start ≻ Programs ≻ Accessories ≻ System Tools ≻ Windows Tune-Up to start the Windows Tune-Up Wizard. The Wizard welcome screen gives you two choices:

   Express   Uses the most common optimization settings.

   Custom   Allows you to select the tune-up settings.

2. Choose Express and click Next.

3. The next screen lets you schedule when the Tune-Up Wizard will run on your system. Select a time when your computer will be switched on but you won't be using it, such as in the middle of the night, very early in the morning, or during your lunch break.

4. In the final screen, you will see a list of the optimizations that the Wizard plans to execute on your system. Check the box at the bottom of the screen to run these optimizations when the Wizard closes.

5. Click Finish to close the Wizard.

If you choose Custom in the Wizard welcome screen, you can also specify in more detail how Disk Defragmenter, ScanDisk, and Disk Cleanup will operate on your system.

Windows Update

Connects to the Windows Update Web site and keeps your system up-to-date by automatically downloading new device drivers and Windows system updates as they are needed. Choose Start ➢ Windows Update, or choose Start ➢ Settings ➢ Windows Update. Internet Explorer opens and connects to the Web site. The Wizard scans your system looking for items that could be updated. It makes a list of any new device drivers or system patches that you need and then downloads and installs the files for any items you want to update.

You will also find current information on using Windows 98 SE on the Windows Update Web site as well as a set of answers to frequently asked questions about Windows. Simply follow the instructions on the screen.

Appendix B

Windows 98 SE User's Glossary

. . . .

Adapted from *PC User's Essential Accessible Pocket Dictionary* by Peter Dyson
(ISBN 0-7821-1684-1   240 pages $14.99)

And from *The Internet Dictionary* by Christian Crumlish
(ISBN 0-7821-1675-2   656 pages $14.99)

32-bit computer Any computer that deals with information 32 bits at a time. This description can be applied to:

- The *word* size of the *microprocessor* used in the computer. A 32-bit computer works with 4 bytes at a time.
- The width of the computer's data *bus*. A 32-bit data bus has 32 separate data lines.

A: In DOS and Windows, the identifier used for the first floppy disk drive. Unless instructed differently in the ROM-BIOS settings, the operating system always checks drive A: for startup (or *bootstrap*) instructions before checking the hard disk, drive C:.

access 1. A connection to the Internet; 2. A type of Internet connection (network access, dial-up access, etc.); 3. The degree of ability to perform certain activities or read privileged information.

access provider An institution providing Internet access, such as a commercial service provider, a university, or an employer. *See also* **online service**.

account A form of access to a computer or network for a specific username and password, usually with a home directory, an e-mail inbox, and a set of access privileges. Accounts are usually kept for administrative or security reasons, although in communications and online services, accounts are used to identify subscribers for billing purposes.

active window In an operating system or application program capable of displaying multiple windows on the screen at the same time, the active window is the window that contains the cursor. If a window is active, its title bar changes color to differentiate it from all the inactive windows. Only one window can be active at a time. *See also* **cascade, graphical user interface, tile**.

address 1. The precise location in memory or on disk where a piece of information is stored. Every byte in memory and every sector on a disk have a unique address; 2. A unique identifier for a computer or site on the Internet—this can be a numeric IP address (logical address) or a textual domain-name address (physical address); 3. A fully specified e-mail address (of the form `username@host.domain`).

Address bar A text box in Internet Explorer and Windows Explorer in which you can enter a URL, a path name to a local file, or a term or phrase on which to search.

Address Book An application that stores contact information, including e-mail addresses, Web site

URLs, physical addresses, business and personal data, conferencing setup, and associated digital IDs.

alias 1. An abbreviation for an e-mail address stored in a mail program, allowing the user to type or select a shorter alias instead of the full address; 2. An alternate name for an Internet address.

alt. A hierarchy of newsgroups in the Usenet mold but outside Usenet proper, devoted to "alternative" topics. These newsgroups were originally created to avoid the rigorous process required to create a normal Usenet newsgroup.

analog-to-digital converter Abbreviated ADC or A-D converter. A device that converts continuously varying *analog* signals into discrete *digital* signals or numbers. Once analog signals have been converted into digital form, they can be processed, analyzed, stored, displayed, and transmitted by computer. *See also* **digital-to-analog converter**.

anchor An HTML tag that indicates a hypertext link or the destination of such a link.

anonymous FTP The most common use of FTP, the Internet File Transfer Protocol. FTP sites that allow anonymous FTP don't require a password for access—you only have to log in as *anonymous* and enter your e-mail address as a password (for their records).

applet A small *application* program, limited in scope to a single small but useful task. A calculator program or a card game might be called an applet.

application Abbreviated as "app." A computer program designed to perform a specific task, such as accounting, scientific analysis, word processing, or desktop publishing.

application key Also called the "right-click key." The key marked with a menu symbol on 104-key enhanced keyboards; it is used in some Windows 95/98/98 SE applications to display the shortcut menu that is displayed by right-clicking in the same context.

application window A window that contains the work area and menu bar for a running application program. An application window may contain one or more document windows within it.

archive 1. On the *Internet*, a site containing a collection of files available via *anonymous FTP*; 2. A collection of related files all stored under one filename; the files may also have been compressed to save hard-disk space.

article An e-mail message posted to one of the Usenet newsgroups, accessible by anyone with a newsreader and a connection to the Internet.

ASCII The abbreviation for *American Standard Code for Information Interchange*. (Pronounced "as-kee.") ASCII is a standard character set that's been adopted by most computer systems around the world (usually extended for non-Western alphabets and for diacriticals).

asynchronous transmission In communications, a method of transmission that uses start and stop bits to coordinate the flow of data so that the time intervals between individual characters do not have to be equal. Parity may also be used to check the accuracy of the data received. *See also* **synchronous transmission**.

at symbol (@) The character that separates the account name and the domain name in an Internet e-mail address.

attach To send a document along with an e-mail message.

attribute 1. A file attribute is a characteristic that indicates whether the file is a read-only file, a hidden file, or a system file or whether the files has changed in some way since it was last backed up; 2. A screen attribute controls a character's background and foreground colors, as well as other characteristics such as underline, reverse video, or blinking; 3. In a database, the name or the structure of a field is considered an attribute of a record.

authentication Verification of the identity of the sender of a message.

backbone A large, fast network connecting other networks. backbone providers include UUNET, MCI WorldCom, and PSINet.

backslash The character that separates portions of a URL.

backup An up-to-date copy of a file or files that you can use to reload your hard disk in case of an accident. It is an insurance against disk failure affecting the hundreds or possibly thousands of files you might have on your system hard disk or on your local area network hard disk.

backward-compatible Fully compatible with earlier versions of the same application program or computer system.

baud rate In communications equipment, a measurement of the number of state changes (from 0 to 1 or vice-versa) per second on an *asynchronous* communications channel. Baud rate is often mistakenly assumed to correspond to the number of bits transmitted per second, but because in today's high-speed digital communications systems one state change can be made to represent more than 1 data bit, baud rate and bits per second are not always the same. *See also* **asynchronous transmission**.

BBS The abbreviation for *bulletin board system*. A computer system, equipped with one or more modems, acting as a message-passing system or centralized information source, usually for a particular special interest group (SIG). Bulletin board systems are often established by software vendors and by PC user groups. *See also* **online service**.

BIOS The acronym for *basic input/output system* (pronounced "bye-os"). In the PC, a set of instructions, stored in read-only memory (ROM), that let your computer's hardware and operating system communicate with application programs and peripheral devices such as hard disks, printers and video adapters.

bit A contraction of *BInary digiT*. A bit is the basic unit of information in the binary numbering system, representing either 0 (for off) or 1 (for on). Bits can be grouped to make up larger storage units, the most common being the 8-bit *byte*. A byte can represent all kinds of information including the letters of the alphabet, the numbers 0 through 9, and common punctuation symbols.

bits per second Abbreviated bps. The number of binary digits, or bits, transmitted every second during a data transfer. A measurement of the speed of operation of equipment such as a computer's data bus or a modem connecting a computer to a transmission line.

blind carbon copy Abbreviated Bcc. When you send a copy of a message to a Bcc recipient, neither the primary recipient nor the carbon copy recipients know that the Bcc recipient has also been sent the message.

bookmark In Web browsers, a reference to a page to which you might want to return later.

bounce E-mail that fails to reach its destination and returns to the sender is said to have bounced.

browse 1. To look for a file or folder on your local hard drive or a local area network; 2. To skim an information resource on the Net, such as USENET, gopherspace, or the Web.

browser A client program used to explore Internet resources. *See also* **Web browser**.

bug A logical or programming error in hardware or software that causes a malfunction of some sort.

button 1. A dialog-box element that lets the user select an option. In addition to application-specific buttons, almost all dialog boxes contain a Cancel button that allows you to abort the current operation, as well as the OK button, used to confirm a selection; 2. One of the keys on a mouse. *See also* **dialog box**.

byte A contraction of *BinarY digiT Eight*. A group of 8 bits that in computer storage terms usually holds a single character, such as a number, a letter, or other symbol. Because bytes represent a very small amount of storage, they are usually grouped into *kilobytes* (1,024 bytes), *megabytes* (1,048,576 bytes), or even *gigabytes* (1,073,741,824 bytes) for convenience when describing hard disk capacity or computer memory size.

cable modem A modem that sends and receives signals through a coaxial cable that is connected to a cable-television system, rather than being connected through telephone lines. Cable modems are much faster than conventional modems and more expensive.

cache (Pronounced "cash.") A special area of memory, managed by a *cache controller*, that improves performance by storing the contents of frequently accessed memory locations and their addresses. When the processor references a memory address, the cache checks to see if it holds that address. If it does, the information is passed directly to the processor; if not, a normal memory access takes place.

cache memory (Pronounced "cash memory.") A relatively small section of very fast memory (often *static RAM*) reserved for the temporary storage of the data or instructions likely to be needed next by the processor.

cascade In a windowed environment, the arrangement of several overlapping windows so that their title bars are always visible. The windows appear to be stacked, one behind the other. *See also* **tile**.

cascading menu A menu selection that leads to one or more further menus; usually indicated by a right-pointing triangle.

case-insensitive Not distinguishing between upper- and lowercase characters. In a case-insensitive search, *Internet*, *internet*, and *INTERNET* all match the same key word. The DOS operating system underlying Windows 98 SE is case-insensitive, as are e-mail addresses.

case-sensitive Distinguishing between upper- and lowercase characters. To a case-sensitive program, *Peter*, *PETER*, *peter*, and *PeTeR* all mean different things.

cc: A list of additional recipients for an e-mail message listed in the header of the message (from *carbon copy*, a carryover from office-memo shorthand). Most e-mail programs enable the sender to add addresses to the cc: list.

CD-ROM The abbreviation for *Compact Disc/Read-Only Memory*, a format for storing data on compact discs.

CD-ROM Extended Architecture Abbreviated *CD-ROM/XA*. An extension to the CD-ROM format, developed by Microsoft, Phillips, and Sony, that allows for the storage of audio and visual information on compact disc so that you can play the audio at the same time you view the visual data.

central processing unit Abbreviated *CPU*. The computing and control part of the computer. The Intel Pentium is a CPU.

channel 1. A special Web site that uses push technologies to deliver information to the client software. (*See also* **Dynamic HTML**.); 2. Any connecting path that carries information from a sending device to a receiving device. A channel may refer to a physical medium, such as *coaxial cable*, or to a specific frequency within a larger channel; 3. An IRC (Internet Relay Chat) topic area. *See also* **Internet Relay Chat**.

character A letter, number, space, punctuation mark, or symbol—any piece of information that can be stored in one byte.

checkbox In Windows dialog boxes, a small square box you toggle on or off to make nonexclusive choices.

circuit A communications channel or path between two devices capable of carrying electrical current. Also used to describe a set of components connected together to perform a specific task.

circuit board A computer card holding printed circuits.

Clipboard An area of memory reserved by Windows for temporary storage of text or graphics being transferred within the same file, between files in the same application program, or between applications. Material placed on the Clipboard remains there until it is replaced by another selection or until the computer is turned off or restarted. *See also* **cut, Dynamic Data Exchange**.

clock An electronic circuit that generates regularly spaced timing pulses at speeds of up to millions of cycles per second. These pulses are used to synchronize the flow of information through the computer's internal communications channels. *See also* **clock speed**.

clock speed Also known as *clock rate*. The internal speed of a computer or processor, normally expressed in MHz. The faster the clock speed, the faster the computer will perform a specific operation, assuming the other components in the system, such as disk drives, can keep up with the increased speed.

close 1. To remove a file from memory and return it to disk (with or without saving any changes), at the same time removing its window from the screen; 2. To terminate an application program in an orderly fashion and remove its window from the screen; 3. To remove any window from the screen; also, to remove a dialog box from the screen.

.com The Internet domain dedicated to commercial entities, generally in the United States.

command line Any interface between the user and the command processor that allows the user to enter commands from the keyboard for execution by the operating system. In Windows, the DOS command line is accessible via Start ➢ Programs ➢ MS-DOS Prompt.

command prompt A character or group of characters on the screen that lets you know that the operating system is available and ready to receive input.

commercial access provider A service provider that charges for access to the Internet, as opposed to employers, universities, and free-nets, which provide access for free. Commonly referred to as an Internet Service Provider, or ISP.

common carrier A communications company, such as AT&T, MCI WorldCom, or ITT, that provides telecommunication services to the general public.

compatibility The extent to which a given piece of hardware or software conforms to an accepted standard, regardless of the original manufacturer.

compressed file A file that has been processed by a special utility program so that it occupies as little hard-disk space as possible. When the file is needed, the same program decompresses the file back into its original form so that it can be read by the computer.

computer system Any complete collection of hardware, software, and peripherals, designed to work together. In the PC world, a computer system comprises at least the following: a system unit that houses hard and floppy disk drives, memory, the motherboard, and any required expansion boards; a keyboard; a mouse; and a monitor.

connect time The amount of time a user spends connected to a service provider. Many providers charge a fee based on connect time. Others charge a flat-rate.

context menu *See* **shortcut menu**.

Control Panel In Windows, a program that contains applets you can use to control your computer's settings, including the configuration of the mouse, the display, sounds, and the keyboard.

cookie On the World Wide Web, a small text file stored by the server on the system running the browser or client software and that the server can retrieve during a future session. A cookie can contain information as basic as an identification number to count visits from a single person or as detailed as a complete user profile.

copy To duplicate part of a document and reproduce it elsewhere. The material copied can range from a single character to pages of text and graphics. A copy operation leaves the original in place and unchanged. *See also* **Clipboard, cut, cut-and-paste**.

corrupted Term used to describe a damaged file, block of data, or communication.

Ctrl+Alt+Del A three-key combination used in IBM-compatible computers to restart or reboot the machine and reload the operating system. By pressing Ctrl+Alt+Del, you initiate a warm boot, which restarts the computer without going through the power-on self test normally run if the computer goes through a cold boot when power is first applied.

cursor A special character on a display screen that indicates where the next character will appear when it is typed. The cursor can take many shapes, depending on the current operation, and may also change shape as it moves to different parts of the screen. In Windows, a vertical I-beam cursor indicates the point at which text or graphics will be inserted.

cut To remove a marked portion of a document into a temporary storage area such as the *Clipboard*. This material can then be pasted from the Clipboard into a different place in the original document or even into an entirely different document. *See also* **cut-and-paste**.

cut-and-paste To remove a marked portion of a document into temporary storage (such as the *Clipboard*) and then insert it either into a different document or into a new place in the original document. Cut-and-paste allows compatible application programs to share text and graphics. *See also* **cut**.

cyberspace A descriptive term for the virtual geography of the online world. This term first appeared in print in William Gibson's novel *Neuromancer,* published in 1984. The book describes the online world of computers and the elements of society that use these computers.

data Information in a form suitable for processing by a computer, such as the digital representation of text, numbers, graphic images, or sounds.

default A standard setting, used in the absence of any user-specified alternative.

default action Any action performed when you press Enter in response to a dialog box without first changing anything; usually chosen because it is the action you would most likely want in any given circumstance.

delete To remove a file from a disk, or to remove an item of information from a file. You can delete files using operating system commands or directly from within an application program. *See also* **file recovery, undelete program**.

deselect The process of removing the highlighting from one or more choices or options. *See also* **select**.

desktop Broadly speaking, any on-screen version of a work area that represents the top of a desk and that contains icons and menus. As the user works, they open files, put them away, move items around, and perform other day-to-day tasks. When capitalized, refers to the Windows 95, 98, 98 SE, or NT Desktop.

device A general term used to describe any computer peripheral or hardware element that can send or receive data. For example, modems, printers, serial ports, disk drives, and monitors are all referred to as devices. Some devices may require special software, known as a *device driver*, to control or manage them.

device driver A small program that allows a computer to communicate with and control a *device*. Each operating system contains a standard set of device drivers for the keyboard, the monitor, and so on, but if specialized *peripherals* are added, the user will probably have to add the appropriate device driver so that the operating system knows how to manage the device.

diagnostic program A program that tests computer hardware and *peripherals* for correct operation.

dialog box A special window that elicits a response from the user. A dialog box always opens when the user chooses a menu item that is followed by an ellipsis; that is, when more information is needed from the user before the program can continue. A dialog box can contain several elements, including text boxes, list boxes, checkboxes, command buttons, and drop-down list boxes, depending on the purpose of the dialog box, but it does not have to contain all these elements at the same time.

dial-up account An Internet account on a host machine that the user must dial up with a modem to use.

Dial-Up Networking Abbreviated *DUN*. The feature of Windows that allows you to connect to another computer via the telephone line if both your computer and the other computer have a modem installed.

digital-to-analog converter Abbreviated *DAC* or *D-A converter*. A device that converts discrete digital information into a continuously varying *analog* signal. Many of today's sound boards can sample and play back at up to 44.1kHz using a 16-bit digital-to-analog converter that produces spectacular stereo sound. Compact disc players use a digital-to-analog converter to convert the digital signals read from the disc to the analog signal that you hear as music. *See also* **analog-to-digital converter**.

digital signature An electronic signature that you can attach to an e-mail message or a news post. A digital signature verifies the authenticity of the sender and certifies that the message or post has not been altered since the signature was attached.

dimmed command Also known as a *grayed command*. A command that is not currently available is displayed in light gray rather than the usual black.

directory In a hierarchical file system, a convenient way of organizing and grouping files and other directories on a disk. The beginning directory is known as the root directory from which all other directories must branch; directories inside another directory are often called subdirectories. In Windows 95, 98, and 98 SE, directories are called folders. *See also* **folder**.

disable To turn off a function or prevent something from happening. In a graphical user interface, disabled menu commands are often shown in gray to indicate that they are not available. *See also* **dimmed command, enable**.

disk drive A peripheral storage device that reads and writes magnetic or optical disks. When more than one disk drive is installed on a computer, the operating system assigns each drive a unique name—for example A: and C: in DOS and Windows.

DNS Abbreviation for Domain Name Service; sometimes referred to as Domain Naming System. A collection of distributed databases that maintain the correlations between domain name addresses and numeric IP addresses, for example, the domain name address `ruby.ora.com` gets resolved into the numeric Internet address `134.65.87.3`, and vice versa. DNS allows human beings to use the Internet without remembering long lists of numbers.

domain The general category to which a computer on the Internet belongs. The most common high-level domains are:

- `.com`: a commercial organization
- `.edu`: an educational establishment
- `.gov`: a branch of the U.S. government
- `.int`: an international organization
- `.mil`: a branch of the U.S. military
- `.net`: a network
- `.org`: a nonprofit organization

Most countries also have unique domains named after their international abbreviation. For example, `.uk` for the United Kingdom and `.ca` for Canada. *See also* **DNS, domain name, e-mail address**.

domain name The easy-to-understand name given to an Internet host computer, as opposed to the numeric IP address. *See also* **DNS**.

DOS The acronym for *Disk Operating System,* an operating system originally developed by Microsoft for the IBM PC.

DOS prompt A visual confirmation that the DOS operating system is ready to receive input from the keyboard. The default prompt includes the current drive letter followed by a greater-than symbol; for example, C>. Even in Windows 98 SE, the DOS prompt can be the most efficient way to perform some operations, particularly those in which wildcard characters can represent large groups of files or folders. *See also* **command line, command prompt**.

dot The separator character for domain names, newsgroup names, and other Unix-oriented files. Dots should only be used to separate hierarchical levels in newsgroup names, not to split compound names. In DOS and Windows, the character that separates a filename from an extension, for example, `text.doc`.

double-click To press and release the mouse button rapidly, twice in quick succession, without moving the mouse. Double-clicking is used to select an object as well as to initiate an action. For example, if you double-click a program icon, you select that program and also start the application running.

download   To transfer a file over a modem from a remote computer to a desktop computer. (Technically, to transfer a file from a larger computer to a smaller computer.)

drag   To move a selected object using the mouse. The user places the mouse cursor on the selected object and holds down the mouse button while moving the mouse to the new location. When the mouse button is released, the object is inserted.

drag-and-drop   To move a selected object onto another object with the mouse to initiate a process. For example, if you drag a document icon and then drop it onto a word processor's icon, the program will run and the document will open.

drop-down list box   A dialog box element that helps the user choose one item from a list of possible alternatives.

drop-down menu   A vertical menu that you pull down from a set of menu names arranged in a menu bar across the top of the screen or the top of the window. To make a selection from a drop-down menu, you click the item with the mouse or use the cursor-movement keys to position the highlight over the item and press Enter, or type a special key combination.

dump   To send the contents of a file (or other data) to a device or another file in order to print, display, or store the data.

Dynamic Data Exchange   Abbreviated *DDE*. A method of communication between programs available in Windows and other environments. When two (or more) programs that both support dynamic data exchange are running at the same time, they can exchange *data* and commands by means of "conversations." A DDE conversation is a two-way connection between two application programs, used to transmit data by each program alternately. DDE has largely been superseded by a more complex but more capable mechanism known as Object Linking and Embedding (OLE).

Dynamic HTML   Abbreviated *DHTML*. A more recent version of the Hypertext Markup Language. It facilitates greater control over the placement of objects on a Web page and the use of layering and style sheets.

dynamic RAM   Abbreviated *DRAM* (pronounced "dee-ram"). A common type of computer memory that uses capacitors and transistors storing electrical charges to represent memory states. These capacitors lose their electrical charge and so need to be refreshed every millisecond, during which time they cannot be read by the processor.

edit To change the contents of a file.

electronic commerce Using the Internet to buy and sell goods and services. Although this use of the Internet initially developed at a slower pace than some others, these days you can shop for a car, trade stocks, bank, place an auction bid, and purchase a great many items online—from wine to software to wedding gifts.

e-mail Also *email*, short for *electronic mail*, one of the most popular features of networks, online services, and the Internet in general. The term *e-mail* is used to describe both the overall process and the messages carried electronically from computer to computer.

e-mail address 1. An Internet mail address in the form `username@host.domain`; 2. The username portion of a mail account on a network.

enable To turn on a function or allow something to happen. When a function is enabled, it is available. In a graphical user interface, enabled menu commands are often shown in black type to indicate that they are available. *See also* **disable**.

environment Also called *operating environment*, a front end for an operating system. A set of tools and a consistent "look and feel" that allow the user to interact with the computer. Windows is an environment that runs on top of the MS-DOS operating system.

error message A message from the program or the operating system, informing the user of a condition that requires some human intervention to resolve.

Eudora An e-mail program for Windows or the Macintosh that can use the Post Office Protocol and function as an offline mail reader. You can download Eudora from `www.eudora.com`.

event-driven program Any program designed to react to a keystroke or a mouse click, rather than forcing a user to go through traditional menu selections and on-screen prompts. Microsoft Windows and the Macintosh operating system both use this design approach.

expand 1. To show all the subfolders in a folder in Windows Explorer; 2. To decompress a *compressed file*.

expandability The ability of a system to accommodate expansion. In hardware, this may include the addition of memory, more or larger disk drives, and new adapters. In software, it may include the ability of a network to add users, nodes, or connections to other networks.

export To transfer a file from one system or program to another.

Extensible Markup Language Abbreviated *XML*. A markup language for creating Web pages that lets you describe the content in terms of the information it represents.

extension The portion of a filename after the last dot, often used to indicate the type of file. DOS extensions have a three-character maximum length.

extranet A technology that corporate intranets can use to communicate and collaborate. Security safeguards allow only limited access for specific purposes.

FAQ (Pronounced "fack.") An abbreviation for frequently asked question, either a commonly asked question or a list of such questions. Online sites often provide FAQs in order not to have to continually answer the same questions.

Favorites list A list of sites or files that you want to be able to return to easily. In some systems, adding an item to the Favorites list is known as bookmarking the item.

fax modem An adapter that fits into a PC expansion slot and provides many of the capabilities of a full-sized fax machine, but at a fraction of the cost.

56K Used to describe a telephone circuit with a 64Kbps bandwidth that uses 8K for signaling and the remaining 56K for traffic. Also refers to the fastest available analog modems, of which there are two distinctive technologies: x2 and K56Flex.

file A named collection of data stored on disk, appearing to the user as a single entity. A file can contain a program or part of a program, can be a data file, or can contain a user-created document.

file format The structure in a file that defines the way information is stored in the file and how the file appears on the screen or on the printer.

filename The name of a file on a disk used so that both you and the operating system can find the file again. Every file in a folder must have a unique name, but files in different folders can share the same name.

file recovery The process of recovering deleted or damaged files from a disk. In many operating systems, a deleted file still exists on disk until the space it occupies is overwritten with something else.

file system In an operating system, the structure by which files are organized, stored, and named.

filter 1. Any command that reads an input, processes or transforms that information, and writes the result out to a designated output device; 2. In e-mail, a program that allows certain messages to reach the user while eliminating other messages.

firewall A hardware or software device that allows those on a network to access the Internet but prevents access from outsiders.

flame An insulting e-mail or Usenet post. Flames are often ill-considered knee-jerk expressions of anger, but they can also be cruelly detailed and intended for the amusement of the general audience at the expense of the "flamee."

floppy disk A flat, round, magnetically coated, plastic disk enclosed in a protective jacket. Data is written on to the floppy disk by the disk drive's read/write heads as the disk rotates inside the jacket.

folder In Windows 95, 98, and 98 SE, a collection of programs and files stored on disk, symbolized by a graphical icon representing a file folder. A folder can contain other folders, in which case they are said to be nested. In DOS and earlier Windows versions, a directory was the equivalent of a folder, and a subdirectory was the equivalent of a subfolder. *See also* **directory**.

foreground In an operating system, a process that runs in the foreground is running at a higher level of priority than a background task.

forum A feature of online services and bulletin boards that allows subscribers to post messages for others to read and to reply to messages posted by other users.

forward To send received e-mail along to another address, either manually or automatically.

freeware A form of software distribution in which the author retains copyright of the software, but makes the program available to others at no cost. Freeware is often distributed on the Internet, on bulletin boards, or through user groups. The program may not be resold or distributed by others for profit. *See also* **public-domain software, shareware**.

FTP Abbreviation for *File Transfer Protocol,* the standard TCP/IP protocol for transferring files over the Internet, across any platform.

FTP server A computer serving files from an FTP archive.

FTP site A host on the Internet containing archives and set up for File Transfer Protocol.

fully qualified domain name Abbreviated *FQDN*. The complete domain name that identifies a specific computer (or host network, at the very least) on the Internet, including a host name, a subdomain name, and a domain name. Also called *domain name address*.

gigabyte (Pronounced "gig-a-bite.") Strictly speaking, a gigabyte is one billion bytes; however, bytes are most often counted in powers of 2, and so a gigabyte becomes 2^{30}, or 1,073,741,824 bytes.

gopher A client/server application that allows you to browse huge amounts of information by performing FTP transfers, remote logins, and so on, presenting everything to the end-user in the form of menus. With the explosion of easy-to-access information on the Web, gopher has lost some of its appeal for users.

graphical user interface Abbreviated GUI (pronounced "gooey"). A graphics-based user interface like that used in Windows 98 SE, previous Windows versions, and the Macintosh, which allows users to select files, programs, or commands by pointing to pictorial representations on the screen rather than by typing long, complex commands from a *command prompt*. Application programs execute in windows, using a consistent set of drop-down menus, dialog boxes, and other graphical elements such as scroll bars and icons.

hacker In the programming community, where the term originated, *hacker* describes a person who pursues knowledge about computer systems for its own sake—someone willing to "hack through" the steps of putting together a working program. More recently, in popular culture at large, it has come to mean a person who breaks into other people's computers with malicious intent (what programmers call a *cracker*).

hard disk drive A storage device that uses a set of rotating, magnetically coated disks called *platters* to store data or programs. In everyday use, the terms *hard disk*, *hard disk drive*, and *hard drive* are all used interchangeably, because the disk and the drive mechanism are a single unit.

header 1. One or more lines at the top of a page in a printed document; 2. The rows of information at the top of an e-mail message that include who the message is from, who it's to, when it was sent, and what it's about; 3. Information preceding the data in a packet, specifying the addresses of the source and the destination as well as error-checking information.

hertz Abbreviated Hz. A unit of frequency measurement; 1 hertz equals one cycle per second.

high-level format The process of preparing a floppy disk or a hard disk partition for use by the operating system.

history 1. A list of a user's recent actions or commands; 2. A list of the gopher menus a user has passed through; 3. A list of the hypertext links a Web browser has followed.

hit 1. A connection made to a Web server (*See also* **impression**); 2. A successful match in a database search. (In some searches, you can specify a maximum number of hits.)

home page On the World Wide Web, an initial starting page. A home page may have information about a single person, a specific subject, or a corporation and is a convenient jumping-off point to other pages or resources. *See also* **browser, HTML, URL**.

host The central or controlling computer in a networked or distributed processing environment, providing services that other computers or terminals can access via the network. Computers connected to the Internet are also described as hosts and can be accessed using FTP, Telnet, gopher, or a World Wide Web browser.

hotlist A list of frequent Internet destinations, or sites, arranged on a menu, such as a list of Web pages.

HTML The abbreviation for *Hypertext Markup Language*, the language used to create Web pages. It consists of regular text and tags that tell the browser what to do when a link is activated. It is a subset of SGML (Standard Generalized Markup Language). *See also* **SGML, Dynamic HTML**.

HTTP The abbreviation for *Hypertext Transport Protocol*. The Internet protocol that defines how a Web server responds to requests for files, made via anchors and URLs.

hyperlink A hypertext link or a hypermedia link.

hypermedia An extension of the concept of hypertext to include pictures, sounds, movies, and so on, along with text and links to other documents.

hypertext Text that contains links to other text documents, allowing the reader to skip around and read the documents in various order.

IAB Abbreviation for *Internet Architecture Board*. The coordinating committee for management of the Internet.

IBM-compatible computer Originally, any personal computer compatible with the IBM line of personal computers. Now it is becoming more common to use the term "Wintel computer" to describe any PC that runs Windows and DOS and is based on one of the *Intel* family of chips.

icon A small screen image representing a specific element that the user can manipulate in some way. You select the icon by clicking a mouse or other pointing device. An icon may represent an application program, a document, embedded and linked objects, a hard disk drive, or several programs collected together in a group icon. *See also* **graphical user interface**.

identities A new feature in Outlook Express and other identities-aware programs that you can use to establish multiple views of mail and contacts.

impression A Web server's record of a browser's visit to a single page of a Web site. (The term is used to distinguish from a hit, in that a single impression may register as several hits—one on the HTML document, one for each graphic on the page, and so on.)

inbox Also *in box, in-box*. A file in which an e-mail program stores incoming messages.

infection The presence of a computer *virus*.

initialization files In Microsoft Windows, files with the filename extension .ini that contain information about an individual Windows configuration. Windows and certain application programs use the settings stored in these files. *See also* **SYSTEM.INI, WIN.INI**.

inline graphic An illustration on a Web page (as opposed to a linked graphic). Can be either a GIF or JPEG graphic file, the two formats native to the World Wide Web.

input/output Abbreviated I/O. The transfer of data between the computer and its peripheral devices, disk drives, terminals, and printers.

install To configure and prepare hardware or software for operation. Many application packages have their own install programs, programs that copy all the required files from the original distribution floppy disks or CD into appropriate folders on your hard disk and then help you to configure the program to your own operating requirements. Microsoft Windows programs are usually installed by a program called SETUP.

internal modem A modem that plugs into the expansion bus of a personal computer.

Internet An international network of networks that are linked using the TCP/IP protocols.

Internet Connection Sharing A new feature of Windows 98 SE that allows multiple PCs on a network to share an Internet connection without using a separate proxy server.

Internet Explorer Microsoft's Web browser, which is integrated into Windows 98 SE.

Internet Protocol (IP) The protocol that handles routing of datagrams from one Internet host to another. It works along with the Transmission Control Protocol (TCP) to ensure that data is transmitted accurately across the Internet. *See also* **TCP/IP**.

Internet Relay Chat Abbreviated IRC. A network of servers that allows people from all over the world to communicate in real time.

Internet Service Provider (ISP) A company or enterprise that provides Internet access.

InterNIC Short for the Internet Network Information Center, a cooperative effort of the National Science Foundation, AT&T, and Network Solutions, Inc. It registers domain names and assigns IP addresses for use on the Internet. For more information, see www.internic.net.

intranet A private network that uses the standard Internet protocols.

intruder An unauthorized user of a computer system, usually a person with malicious intent. *See also* **firewall, hacker**.

IP address Also called a *dotted quad*, the numeric Internet Protocol address that uniquely identifies each computer on the Internet, made up of four numbers separated by dots.

ISDN The abbreviation for *Integrated Services Digital Network*. A worldwide digital communications network emerging from existing telephone services, intended to replace all current systems with a completely digital transmission system.

Java A programming language for making software that can be run on any type of computer over an Internet connection.

JavaScript A scripting language developed by Netscape Communications Corp. to add dynamic (interactive) capabilities to Web pages.

Kbps An abbreviation for *kilobits per second,* a measurement of transmission speed (such as modem speed or network speed).

kill 1. To delete a post (mark it as having been read); 2. To delete posts automatically, using a kill file; 3. To stop a process; 4. To erase a file.

Window's 98 SE User's Glossary

kill file   Also a *killfile*, a file containing search instructions for automatically killing or autoselecting Usenet posts. Sometimes called a bozo filter, a kill file can be used to screen out annoying posters and avoid uninteresting threads.

kilobit   Abbreviated Kb or Kbit. It equals 1,024 *bits* (binary digits). *See also* **megabit**.

kilobyte   Abbreviated K, KB, or Kbyte. It equals 1,024 *bytes*. *See also* **megabyte, gigabyte, terabyte**.

laptop computer   A small portable computer light enough to carry comfortably, with a flat screen and keyboard that fold together. Laptop computers are battery-operated, often have a thin, backlit or sidelit LCD display screen, and some models can even mate with a docking station to perform as a full-sized desktop system back at the office. Advances in battery technology allow laptop computers to run for many hours between charges.

launch   To start an application program running, usually by double-clicking its icon with the mouse.

line length   The number of characters that fit on a line—fixed on some systems, changeable on others. The standard line length on the Internet is 80 characters; e-mail or Usenet posts produced with software using longer line lengths will wrap irregularly and appear awkward to users with 80-character lines.

link   In a hypertext document, an element (a word, phrase, graphic, or video clip) that is connected to another element in the same or a different hypertext document. *See also* **hypertext**.

link rot   Slang to describe an out-of-date link on a Web page. The link points to a page or site that no longer exists or that has moved and is no longer accessible when a visitor clicks the link.

list box   A dialog box element that helps the user make one choice from a list of possible alternatives.

listserver   An automatic mailing system on the Internet. Rather than sending e-mail on a particular topic to a long list of people, you send it instead to a special e-mail address, where a program automatically distributes the e-mail to all the people who subscribe to the mailing list. *See also* **newsgroup, Usenet**.

local   Said of a computer to which a user is connected directly or of a device (such as a printer) or process under the user's direct control, as contrasted with remote hosts, devices, and processes.

locked file A file that you can open and read, but not write to, delete, or change in any way.

login Also known as *logon*. To establish a connection to a computer system or online service before using it. Many systems require the entry of an identification number or a password before the system can be accessed. See also **logout, password**.

login script A small program or *macro* that executes the same set of instructions every time a user logs in to a computer system. A communications script may send the user-identification information to an online service each time a subscriber dials up the service. See also **script**.

logout Also known as *logoff*. To relinquish a session and sign off a computer system by sending a terminating message. The computer may respond with its own message, indicating the resources consumed during the session or the period between login and logout. Logging out is not the same as shutting down or turning off the computer. See also **login**.

long filename Any filename that goes beyond the DOS "8.3" file-naming convention of eight characters before a period and three more optional characters forming the filename extension. Windows 95, 98, 98 SE and several other operating systems are not limited to the 8.3 naming convention; these systems can all manage long filenames, even those containing spaces, more than one period, and mixed upper- and lowercase letters.

lurk To read a mailing list or newsgroup without posting to it. Every new user should lurk for a while before posting to get a feel for what the group is all about and how others in the group behave.

mailbox A file, folder, or area of hard disk space used to store e-mail messages.

mailing list A discussion group, commonly referred to on the Internet simply as a *list*, consisting of people with a common interest, all of whom receive all the mail sent, or posted, to the list. Mailing lists are often more specialized than Usenet newsgroups. Lists can be moderated or unmoderated. See also **moderated**.

MAPI The acronym for *Microsoft Application Program Interface*. An API used to add messaging capabilities to any Microsoft Windows application. MAPI handles the details of message storage and forwarding and directory services.

maximize To increase a window to its maximum size. To maximize a window, click the mouse on the Maximize button in the upper-right corner of the window, or choose the Maximize command from the Control menu. *See also* **minimize**.

MBONE The *multicast backbone*, an experimental, high-speed virtual network that can send packets simultaneously to a large number of Internet sites, suitable for audio and visual transmission.

megabit Abbreviated Mbit. Usually 1,048,576 binary digits or bits of data. Often used as equivalent to 1 million bits. *See also* **bit, megabits per second**.

megabits per second Abbreviated Mbps. A measurement of the amount of information moving across a network or communications link in one second, measured in multiples of 1,048,576 bits.

megabyte Abbreviated *MB*. Usually 1,048,576 bytes. Megabytes are a common way of representing computer memory or hard-disk capacity.

megahertz Abbreviated MHz. One million cycles per second. A processor's clock speed is often expressed in MHz. The original IBM PC operated an 8088 running at 4.77MHz; today's Pentium III processor is available in a range of clock speeds, initially from 450MHz to 500MHz versions.

memory The primary random access memory (RAM) installed in the computer. The operating system copies application programs from disk into memory, where all program execution and data processing takes place; results are written back out to disk again. The amount of memory installed in the computer can determine the size and number of programs that it can run, as well as the size of the largest data file.

memory cache An area of high-speed memory on the processor that stores commonly used code or data obtained from slower memory, replacing the need to access the system's main memory to fetch instructions. The Intel 82385 cache controller chip was used with fast static RAM on some systems to increase performance, but today's processors include cache management functions on the main processor. The Pentium II contains two separate 16K caches, one each for data and instructions.

memory chip A chip that holds data or program instructions. A memory chip may hold its contents temporarily, as in the case of RAM, or permanently, as in the case of ROM.

memory map The organization and allocation of memory in a computer. A memory map indicates the amount of memory used by the operating system and the amount remaining for use by applications.

menu A list of the commands or options available in the program displayed on the screen. A menu item is selected by typing a letter or number corresponding to the item, by clicking it with the mouse, or by highlighting it and pressing Enter. *See also* **drop-down menu**.

menu bar A row of drop-down menu names, usually displayed in a line across the top of the screen or window, just below the title bar.

microprocessor Also called simply "processor." A CPU on a single chip. The first microprocessor was developed by Intel in 1969. The microprocessors most often used in PCs are the Motorola PowerPC RISC series used in the Apple Macintosh computers, and the Intel Pentium family used in IBM and IBM-compatible computers.

Microsoft Network Abbreviated *MSN*. An online service from Microsoft, access to which comes built-in with Windows 98 SE.

millisecond Abbreviated ms or msec. A unit of measurement equal to one thousandth of a second. In computing, hard disk and CD-ROM drive access times are often described in terms of milliseconds; the higher the number, the slower the disk system.

MIME Acronym for *Multipurpose Internet Mail Extensions*, a protocol that allows e-mail to contain simple text plus color pictures, video, sound, and binary data. Both the sender and the receiver need MIME-aware mail programs to use it.

minimize To reduce the active window to an icon. To minimize a window, the user clicks on the Minimize button in the top right corner of the window or chooses the Minimize command from the Control menu.

mirror site An archive site containing an exact copy of the files at another site.

modem Short for *mo*dulator/*dem*odulator, a device that connects your computer to a phone jack and, through the phone lines, to another modem and computer. It transmits data by converting the computer's digital signal into the telephone's analog carrier signal, and vice versa.

moderated Term used to describe lists and newsgroups whose posts must pass muster with a moderator before appearing.

moderator The volunteer who decides which submissions to a moderated list or newsgroup will be posted.

modulation In communications, the process used by a modem to add the digital signal onto the carrier signal so that the signal can be transmitted over a telephone line. The frequency, amplitude, or phase of a signal may be modulated to represent a digital or analog signal. *See also* **modem**.

Mosaic The first graphical Web browser, developed by National Center for Supercomputing Applications. It greatly popularized the Web in its first few years, and by extension the Internet, as it made the multimedia capabilities of the Net accessible via mouse-clicks.

Mozilla A slang name for the Netscape Navigator Web browser.

MS-DOS Acronym for *Microsoft Disk Operating System* (pronounced "emm-ess-dos"). MS-DOS, like other operating systems, allocates system resources such as hard and floppy disks, the monitor, and the printer to the applications programs that need them. MS-DOS, or simply DOS, is the operating system underlying Windows.

multimedia A computer technology that displays information using a combination of full-motion video, animation, sound, graphics, and text with a high degree of user interaction. *See also* **hypermedia, hypertext**.

multitasking The simultaneous execution of two or more programs in one computer. Windows 98 SE multitasks natively, unlike Windows 3.*x*.

navigate Computer jargon meaning to get around a program, find commands, move through a document, or hunt around the Internet.

.net An Internet domain, corresponding to constituent networks.

Net Also *net* and *'net*, often used as an abbreviation for the Internet or for Usenet; really a more general term for the lump sum of interconnected computers on the planet.

net address An Internet address. Can fall under any of the common Internet address types (i.e., HTTP, FTP, NNTP, or *username@subdomain.domain*).

Netiquette Accepted proper behavior on the Internet, especially in regard to e-mail and Usenet. Violate Netiquette at your peril. Although the Internet and Usenet are effectively anarchies, they still have strong social cultures, and most of the rules and regulations of the Net are enforced by peer pressure. *See also* **lurk**.

NetMeeting The conferencing application that is included with Windows 98 SE. You can use NetMeeting to chat in real time, share applications and documents, and participate in audio and video conferencing if you have the appropriate hardware.

netnews Also *net news*, another name for Usenet.

network address 1. The unique name of a node on a network; 2. An e-mail address.

network news A synonym for Usenet.

Network News Transfer Protocol Abbreviated NNTP. The protocol used to distribute Usenet newsgroups.

newsfeed The packet of news articles passed along from one computer to the next on Usenet.

newsgroup A Usenet discussion group.

newsreader A program used to read Usenet articles and usually also to save, respond to, and post followups to articles, as well as to post new articles.

offline A mode of Internet Explorer that does not connect to the Internet. Also describes the state of a printer or other peripheral that is not currently in ready mode and is therefore unavailable for use. *See also* **online**.

offline reader An application that lets you read postings to Usenet newsgroups without having to stay connected to the Internet.

online 1. Most broadly, describes any capability available directly on a computer, as in "online help system," or any work done on a computer instead of by more traditional means; 2. Describes a peripheral such as a printer or modem when it is directly connected to a computer and ready to operate; 3. In communications, describes a computer connected to another, remote, computer over a network or a modem link; especially, currently connected to the Internet.

online community Also *virtual community*, a group of people with shared interests who meet, communicate, and interact via a network, BBS, Internet discussion group, or any other form of electronic common space. Online communities have many of the properties of real-world communities. *See also* **BBS**.

online service A company that maintains a proprietary network and provides e-mail, forums, chats, games, databases of information, downloadable files, and information services (stocks, airlines, and so on), such as America Online, CompuServe, Delphi, eWorld, GEnie, Prodigy, Microsoft Network, and so on. *See also* **Internet Service Provider**.

operating environment A front end for an operating system. A set of tools and a consistent look and feel that allow the user to interact with the computer. For instance, Microsoft Windows is an operating environment that runs on top of the MS-DOS operating system.

operating system Abbreviated OS. The software responsible for allocating system resources, including memory, processor time, disk space, and peripheral devices such as printers, modems, and the monitor. All application programs use the operating system to gain access to these system resources as they are needed. The operating system is the first program loaded into the computer as it boots, and it remains in memory at all times thereafter.

option button Also known as a *radio button*. A small round button used to make an exclusive choice in a dialog box where only one option can be in effect at a time, like baud rate, or to choose between an ascending or a descending sort, for example.

.org An Internet domain corresponding to (nonprofit) organizations.

Outlook Express The e-mail program that is included with Windows 98 SE. You can also use Outlook Express to read and post to newsgroups.

packet Any block of data sent over a network. Each packet contains information about the sender and the receiver and error-control information, in addition to the actual message. Packets may be fixed- or variable-length, and they will be reassembled if necessary when they reach their destination.

partition A portion of a hard disk that the operating system treats as if it were a separate drive. Very large hard drives can be partitioned into smaller, logical drives for more efficient use of space. Partitioning a drive that is smaller than 4 gigabytes in original size is not recommended.

password A secret code used to restrict access to an account, a channel, a file, and so on only to authorized users who know the code.

path The complete description of the location of a file or folder in the file system. The path consists of all the folder names that must be accessed to get to a specific file.

Pentium A 32-bit microprocessor introduced by Intel in 1993. After losing a courtroom battle to maintain control of the *x*86 designation, Intel named this member of its family the Pentium rather than the 80586 or the 586. The Pentium represents the continuing evolution of the 80486 family of microprocessors and adds several notable features, including 16K instruction code and data caches, built-in floating-point processor and memory management unit, as well as a superscalar design and dual pipelining that allow the Pentium to execute more than one instruction per clock cycle.

The Pentium is available in a whole range of models (Pentium, Mobile Pentium, Pentium Pro, Pentium II, and Pentium III) and clock speeds (from 133MHz all the way up to 500MHz). The Pentium III is equivalent to an astonishing 9.5 million *transistors*.

peripheral   Any hardware device attached to and controlled by a computer, such as a monitor, keyboard, hard-disk, floppy-disk, and CD-ROM drives, printer, mouse, tape drive, and joystick.

Plug and Play   Abbreviated PnP. A standard from Compaq, Microsoft, Intel, and Phoenix that defines automatic techniques designed to make PC configuration simple and straightforward.

PnP adapters contain configuration information stored in nonvolatile memory, which includes vendor information and serial number and checksum information. The PnP chipset allows each adapter to be isolated, one at a time, until all cards have been properly identified by the operating system.

point of presence   Abbreviated POP. A local phone number connected to a modem connected to the network of a service provider, to enable users to log in to the network without paying long distance charges.

Point-to-Point Protocol   Abbreviated PPP. A TCP/IP protocol, similar to SLIP, for transmitting IP datagrams over serial lines such as phone lines. With PPP, PC users can connect to the Internet and still function in their native environment (instead of having to deal with a character-based UNIX environment).

pop-up menu   A menu displayed next to the element with which it is associated. A pop-up menu is usually only displayed on request; in other words, it is only displayed when you specifically ask for it.

port   1. A physical connection, such as a serial port or a parallel port; 2. To move a program or operating system from one hardware platform to another; 3. A number used to identify a specific Internet application (location).

portal   A Web site that may have originally functioned as a search service but that now includes numerous other features such as free e-mail, chat, news services, stock updates, weather reports, real estate listings, yellow pages, people finders, movie listings, message boards, shopping, and even the tools to create your own Web pages.

post An individual article or e-mail message sent to a Usenet newsgroup or to a mailing list, rather than to a specific individual. Post can also refer to the process of sending the article to the newsgroup.

Post Office Protocol Abbreviated POP. A protocol that specifies how a personal computer can connect to a mail server on the Internet and download e-mail.

program A sequence of instructions that a computer can execute. Synonymous with software.

prompt Also *command-line prompt*, a string of text that a character-based operating system displays on the screen to tell a user that it is ready to accept input (such as a command or the name of a program to run).

Properties dialog box Summary information about a file or program, displayed by selecting Properties from the object's shortcut menu.

proprietary software Software developed in-house by a particular business or government agency and never made available commercially to the outside world. See also **public-domain software, shareware**.

protocol In networking and communications, the specification that defines the procedures to follow when transmitting and receiving data. Protocols define the format, timing, sequence, and error checking systems used.

proxy server A security measure that enables users behind a firewall to browse the Web (visited resources are actually downloaded by the intervening proxy server and then viewed internally from there) without exposing the contents of the intranet to public scrutiny. A proxy server may render some Web services inaccessible to the user.

public-domain software Software that is freely distributed to anyone who wants to use, copy, or distribute it. See also **proprietary software, shareware**.

push A method of distributing information over the Web, by which updates are (scheduled and then) automatically sent to the user's screen or window, as if the content were being "broadcast" to a receiver (hence the synonymous terms *Netcast* and *Webcast*).

quit To exit the current application program in an orderly way and return control to the operating system.

quoting To include a relevant portion of someone else's article or e-mail message when posting a follow-up to a Usenet newsgroup article or in another e-mail message. It is considered poor Netiquette to quote more of the original post than is absolutely necessary to make your point.

RAM The acronym for *random access memory*. The main system memory in a computer, used for the operating system, application programs, and data. *See also* **dynamic RAM, static RAM**.

RAM chip A semiconductor storage device, either dynamic RAM or static RAM.

random access Describes the ability of a storage device to go directly to the required memory address without having to read from the beginning every time data is requested.

read To copy program or data files from a floppy or a hard disk into computer memory; to run the program or process the data in some way. The computer may also read your commands and data input from the keyboard. *See also* **write**.

readme file A text file placed on a set of distribution disks by the manufacturer at the last minute that may contain important information not contained in the program manuals or online help system. Users should always look for a readme file when installing a new program on a system; it may contain information pertinent to their specific configuration. The filename may vary slightly; READ.ME, README.TXT, and README.DOC are all used. Readme files do not contain any formatting commands, so the user can look at them using any word processor.

read-only Term used to describe a file that can be read but not altered.

real time Also *realtime*, the time used for synchronous communication, in which both participants must be available (as in a telephone conversation). Also, taking place at the present time, live, not delayed or recorded.

reboot To restart the computer and reload the operating system, usually after a crash.

rec. A Usenet hierarchy devoted to recreation.

remote access The process of accessing another computer's resources, such as files or printers. Dial-up accounts and Telnet are both forms of remote access.

reply 1. A message sent in response to a previous message or post; 2. An e-mail command that takes the return path from the current message and makes that address the recipient of a new message, possibly quoting the previous message as well.

restore To return a window to its original size after it has been maximized. To restore a window, the user clicks on the Restore button in the top right corner of the window or chooses the Restore command from the Control menu. *See also* **maximize, minimize**.

ROM The acronym for *read-only memory*. A semiconductor-based memory system that stores information permanently and does not lose its contents when power is switched off. ROMs are used for firmware such as the BIOS in the PC. In some portable computers, the application programs and even the operating system are stored in ROM.

run-time version A special, limited-capability release of software bundled with a single product that allows that product to run, but does not support any of the other applications capable of running in that same environment. In other words, the run-time version provides some but not all the features of the full product.

save To transfer information from the computer's memory to a more permanent storage medium such as a hard disk.

screen-saver program A utility program that blanks the computer screen after a period of inactivity. In the past, displaying one image on the screen for a long period of time could burn in a ghost image on the screen, which is not the case with today's monitors.

script A small program or macro invoked at a particular time. For example, a login script may execute the same specific set of instructions every time a user logs onto a computer system. A communications script may send the user-identification information to an online service each time a subscriber dials up the service.

scroll To move a window up, down, left, or right, in order to see information that was previously out of sight. *See also* **scroll bar, scroll box**.

scroll bar A vertical or horizontal bar at the right or across the bottom of a window that is too small to show all the necessary information at the same time. At each end of the scroll bar, small arrows indicate the scrolling direction.

scroll box A small movable box located on one of the scroll bars. The scroll box indicates the user's relative position in the data shown in the window, and the user can drag the scroll box along the scroll bar to display a different part of the document. This is usually faster than repeatedly clicking the arrows at the ends of the scroll bars.

SCSI (Pronounced "scuzzy.") Stands for *Small Computer System Interface*, a standard for connecting personal computers to some peripheral devices, including CD-ROM drives and external hard drives.

search engine Database software, usually fronted by a Web site for searching the Internet, the Web, or some other computer domain, such as AltaVista (at `http://altavista.com`). Most search engines feature, at a minimum, a text box for typing key words and a Search (or Go or Do it Now! or whatever) button.

search string One or more characters to be matched in a search operation.

select The act of choosing a menu item or highlighting an option. When you make a selection, you expect a specific action to result. *See also* **deselect**.

session 1. The time during which a program is running on either a local or a remote computer; 2. A DOS or Windows program run as a separate protected task under certain multitasking operating systems, such as OS/2 and Windows NT; 3. In communications, the name for the active connection between a mainframe terminal (or a personal computer emulating a terminal), and the computer itself. Many different transactions or message exchanges may take place during a single session. *See also* **thread**.

SGML Abbreviation for *Standard Generalized Markup Language*. A standard (ISO 8879) for defining the structure and managing the contents of any digital document. HTML, used in many World Wide Web documents on the Internet, is a part of SGML. *See also* **HTML**.

shareware A form of software distribution that makes copyrighted programs freely available on a trial basis; if you like the program and use it, you are expected to register your copy and send a small fee to the program's creator.

shortcut In Windows 95, 98, and 98 SE, an icon you can place on the Desktop for quick access to a file, program, or other resource.

shortcut key Any key or key combination that you can press to carry out a command or an action. Some menu commands list shortcut keys immediately to the right of the menu item, and these keystrokes can be used directly from the keyboard, instead of first opening the menu and then choosing that command.

shortcut menu The menu displayed in Windows 95/98/98 SE and many applications when the user right-clicks; the options offered depend on the application context—what you are doing at the time. Sometimes referred to as a context menu.

signature file   A short text file that is automatically added to the end of any e-mail message or Usenet post. A signature file usually contains the sender's name (or alias) and e-mail address, and some people like to add pithy quotes. Netiquette dictates that a signature file should always be short, between one and five lines; anything longer will invite flames.

single in-line memory module   Abbreviated SIMM. Individual RAM chips are soldered or surface mounted onto small narrow circuit boards called *carrier modules,* which can be plugged into sockets on the motherboard. These carrier modules are simple to install and occupy less space than conventional memory modules.

SLIP   Acronym for *Serial Line Internet Protocol.* A communications protocol used over serial lines or dial-up connections to connect a PC to the Internet. SLIP is slowly being replaced by PPP (Point-to-Point Protocol).

smiley   Also known as *emoticon.* A group of text characters used in e-mail and Usenet posts to indicate humor or other emotions. Turn a smiley on its side to read it. Hundreds of smileys are in common use, and new ones appear all the time. Two favorites are :-) for smiling, and ;-) to indicate winking or flirting.

snail mail   Internet slang for mail sent via the U.S. Postal Service, so called for its relative slowness compared with electronic mail.

sneakernet   An informal method of file sharing in which a user copies files onto a floppy disk and then carries the disk to a co-worker to use in a computer in the next office.

spam   To post (or *robopost*) huge amounts of material to Usenet, or to post one article to huge numbers of inappropriate groups. (The term comes from the commercial meat product Spam and the Monty Python routine in which rowdy Vikings in a diner chant "Spam, Spam, Spam, Spam, Spam, Spam, Spam, Spam, wonderful Spam, marvelous Spam," and so on, *ad nauseam.*)

stand-alone   Describes a system designed to meet specific individual needs and that does not rely on or assume the presence of any other components to complete the assigned task.

standard disclaimer   A notice attached to the end of a Usenet or mailing list post, usually to the effect that the user is not speaking in an official capacity for the user's employer or access provider.

static RAM Abbreviated SRAM (pronounced "ess-ram"). A type of computer memory that retains its contents as long as power is applied; it does not need constant refreshment like dynamic RAM chips. A static RAM chip can only store about one-fourth of the information that a dynamic RAM chip of the same complexity can hold.

streaming Term used to describe a media format that enables a player program to begin playing back or displaying the media content quite soon after the data starts flowing (in a *stream*) from the server (as opposed to formats that require that the browser download an entire, possibly huge, file before playing anything).

subfolder A folder within another folder.

submenu A menu invoked by selecting from a previous menu.

subscribe To join a mailing list or start reading a newsgroup.

surf To browse Internet resources. When users surf, they take tangents whenever they feel like it. Sometimes known as *net surfing*.

synchronous transmission In communications, a transmission method that uses a clock signal to regulate data flow. Synchronous transmissions do not use start and stop bits. *See also* **asynchronous transmission**.

sysop Abbreviation for *system operator* (pronounced "siss-op"). The manager of a multiuser computer system or a bulletin board.

system 1. A program that supervises a computer and coordinates all its functions, also called an operating system; 2. An entire computer taken together with all its devices; 3. A large program.

system date The date and time as maintained by the computer's internal clock. You should always make sure that the system clock is accurate, because the operating system notes the time that files were created; this can be important if you are trying to find the most recent version of a document or spreadsheet.

SYSTEM.INI In Microsoft Windows, an initialization file that contains information on your hardware and the internal Windows operating environment. *See also* **WIN.INI**.

system time The time and date maintained by the internal clock inside the computer.

T1 A long-distance, point-to-point 1.544Mbps communications channel that can be used for both digitized voice and data transmission; T1 lines are usually divided into 24 channels, each transmitting at 64Kbps. *See also* **backbone, T3**.

T3 A long-distance point-to-point 44.736Mbps communications service that can provide up to 28 T1 channels. A T3 channel can carry 672 voice conversations and is usually available over fiber-optic cable.

task Any independent running program, and the set of system resources that it uses. A task may be an operating system process or a part of an application program. *See also* **multitasking**.

TCP Abbreviation for *Transmission Control Protocol*. The connection-oriented, Transport-level protocol used in the TCP/IP suite of communications protocols. *See also* **Internet Protocol (IP)**.

TCP/IP The abbreviation for *Transmission Control Protocol/Internet Protocol*. A set of computer-to-computer communications protocols first developed for the Defense Advanced Research Projects Agency (DARPA) in the late 1970s. The set of TCP/IP protocols encompass media access, packet transport, session communications, file transfer, e-mail, and terminal emulation. *See also* **FTP, IP, TCP, Telnet**.

Telnet That part of the TCP/IP suite of protocols used for remote login and terminal emulation; also the name of the program used to connect to Internet host systems. Originally a Unix utility, Telnet is available these days for almost all popular operating systems. You will find that most versions of Telnet are character-based applications, although some contain the text inside a windowed system. *See also* **FTP**.

terabyte Abbreviated *TB*. In computing, usually 2^{40}, or 1,099,511,627,776, bytes. A terabyte is equivalent to 1,000 gigabytes, and usually refers to extremely large hard-disk capacities.

text box A dialog box element that accepts text as input. Sometimes a text box will already contain a default entry that you can accept or edit; at other times it will be empty, ready to receive your input.

text editor Software used to work with ASCII text files, which contain none of the formatting information used by word processors. WordPad is the built-in, simple word processor supplied with Windows 98 SE; it does insert formatting, but it can export a text file in ASCII-only format.

text file A file that consists of text characters without any formatting information. Also known as an ASCII file, a text file can be read by any word processor. The *readme file*, containing late-breaking news about an application, is always a text file.

thread A connected set of postings to a Usenet newsgroup or to an online forum. Many newsreaders present postings as threads rather than in strict chronological sequence. *See also* **session**.

throughput A measure of the rate of data transmitted, expressed as bits per second.

tile To arrange all the open windows so that they do not overlap. To make sure that all the open windows will fit, some of them will have their position and size changed. *See also* **cascade**.

time out 1. To fail, as a network process, because the remote server or computer has not responded in time; 2. To close a connection after waiting too long for acknowledgment.

title bar A thin horizontal bar across the top of a window that contains the name of the window, as well as the Maximize and Minimize buttons. An application window's title bar will also contain the name of the file or document you are working on.

toggle A command or selection that is alternately turned on and off again each time you select it. If the command or item is selected, an X or check mark is shown in the check box or next to the menu command; if the item is not selected, this visual indicator is missing.

toolbar A convenient feature that represents commonly used commands in the form of icons or command buttons in a row across the screen.

undelete To recover an accidentally deleted file. *See also* **file recovery**.

undelete program A utility program that recovers deleted or damaged files from a disk. A file can be deleted accidentally or can become inaccessible when part of the file's control information is lost. *See also* **backup, file recovery**.

unmoderated Used to describe lists and newsgroups whose posts are not vetted by a moderator.

unread Newsgroup articles that the user has not yet read or has marked as such. Unread articles will show up again the next time the user returns to the newsgroup.

unsubscribe 1. To remove one's name from a mailing list; 2. To remove the name of a newsgroup from the list of subscribed groups.

upgrade 1. The process of installing a newer and more powerful version; for example, to upgrade to a newer and more capable version of a software package or to upgrade from your current hard disk to one that is twice the size. In the case of hardware, an upgrade is often called an upgrade kit; 2. A new and more powerful version of an existing system, either hardware or software, is also known as an upgrade.

upload To transfer a file over a modem from a desktop computer to a remote computer.

URL (Pronounced "you-are-ell.") Abbreviation for *uniform resource locator*, a Web address. It consists of a protocol, a host name, a port (optional), a directory (optional), and a filename (optional). In the URL `http://enterzone.berkeley.edu/enterzone.html`, the protocol is HTTP, the host name is `enterzone.berkeley.edu`, and the filename is `enterzone.html`. URLs can be used to address other Internet resources besides Web pages, such as FTP sites, gopher servers, Telnet addresses, and so on.

Usenet 1. From *User's Network* and often written USENET, the collection of computers and networks that share news articles. Usenet is not the Internet (though it overlaps pretty well). It's sometimes called the world's largest electronic bulletin board; 2. The newsgroups in the traditional newsgroup hierarchies. *See also* **newsgroup**.

Usenet newsgroups The individual discussion groups within Usenet. Newsgroups contain articles posted by other Internet and Usenet subscribers; very few of them contain actual hard news. Most newsgroups are concerned with a single subject; there are tens of thousands of newsgroups from which to choose.

user interface That part of a program with which the user interacts. When a program responds only to typed commands, it is said to have a *command-line interface*. A program that receives commands through the use of menus is said to be *menu driven*. A program that presents the elements of the user interface on the screen using regular letters and numbers is called a *character-based interface*, and a program that uses graphical elements with a mouse—such as Windows 98 SE—is said to have a *graphical user interface*.

username A login; the name a user logs in with. Also, the first part of an Internet e-mail address (up to the @). Choose your username well. In many ways it is more important (on the Internet) than your real name. It's the name people see most often.

version number A method of identifying a particular software or hardware release. The version number is assigned by the software developer and often includes numbers before and after a decimal point; the higher the number, the more recent the release.

videodisc An optical disk used for storing video images and sound. A videodisc player can play back the contents of the videodisc on a computer or onto a standard television set. One videodisc can contain up to 55,000 still images, or up to two hours worth of full-frame video. *See also* **CD-ROM**.

video RAM Abbreviated *VRAM* (pronounced "vee-ram.") Special-purpose RAM with two data paths for access, rather than just one as in conventional RAM. These two paths let a VRAM board manage two functions at once—refreshing the display and communicating with the processor. VRAM doesn't require the system to complete one function before starting the other, so it allows faster operation for the whole video system.

virtual Said of something that exists only in software, not physically.

virus A program that deliberately does damage to the computer it's on. Viruses are often hidden inside an apparently benign program.

Visual Basic A popular Basic language compiler from Microsoft, available for Windows. The language has been continually improved and now is often used for fast, vertical application development. Visual Basic also manages the creation of the user interface automatically, including menus, dialog boxes, and other interface elements; the Windows version also supports DDE (a precursor to OLE), OLE, and OLE2. There are also subsets of Visual Basic for Applications (VBA) and for ActiveX (VB Control Creation Edition).

WAIS Abbreviation for *Wide Area Information Service* (pronounced "ways"). A service used to access text databases or libraries on the Internet. *See also* **gopher**.

wallpaper In Microsoft Windows, the graphical pattern on the Desktop used as a backdrop for windows, icons, and dialog boxes.

Web browser A World Wide Web client application that lets you look at hypertext documents and follow links to other HTML documents on the Web. When you find something that interests you as you browse through a hypertext document, you can click your mouse on that object, and the system automatically takes care of accessing the Internet host that holds the document you requested; you don't need to know the IP address, the name of the host system, or any other details. *See also* **URL**.

Web page   An HTML document on the World Wide Web, usually containing links to other resources on the Web, often on other Web servers entirely. Surfing the Web consists of following links from page to page.

Web server   An application that stores Web pages and associated files, databases, and scripts and serves up the pages to Web browsers, using HTTP.

Web site   A site on the Internet that hosts a Web server.

WebTV for Windows   If you have a TV tuner card, you can use WebTV for Windows to receive standard and interactive television broadcasts. You can also receive Internet content and data delivered over broadcast networks.

window   A rectangular portion of the screen that acts as a viewing area for application programs. Windows can be tiled or cascaded and can be individually moved and sized on the screen. Some programs can open multiple document windows inside their application window to display several word processing or spreadsheet data files at the same time.

Windows application   Any *application* program that runs within the *Microsoft Windows environment* and cannot run without Windows. All Windows applications follow certain conventions in their arrangement of menus, the use and style of *dialog boxes*, as well as keyboard and mouse use.

Windows key   Either of two keys on the 104-key enhanced keyboard, marked with the Windows logo, that allow the user to display the Start menu.

Windows NT   A 32-bit multitasking portable operating system developed by Microsoft and first released in 1993.

Windows 3.x   Refers to versions 3.0 and 3.1; the first widely used editions of the Windows graphical user interface. Unlike Windows 95, 98, 98 SE, and NT, versions 3.*x* were 16-bit systems that could not use long filenames and did not support true multitasking.

Windows Radio   A new feature in Windows 98 SE that provides access to radio stations around the world. When you turn it on in Windows Explorer or Internet Explorer, you'll see a new toolbar and a guide with links to stations. For the best listening, you'll need 56Kbps or faster Internet access.

WIN.INI In Microsoft Windows, an initialization file that contains information to help customize your copy of Windows. When Windows starts, the contents of `WIN.INI` are read from the hard disk into memory so that they are immediately available. `WIN.INI` contains sections that define the use of colors, fonts, country-specific information, the Desktop, and many other settings. *See also* **SYSTEM.INI**.

Wizard 1. A technique used by some applications to guide the inexperienced or infrequent user through a complex set of steps by asking questions about the current process. A Wizard may also be called an expert in some applications; 2. On the Internet, someone who really understands how a piece of hardware or software works and is willing to help newcomers ("newbies").

World Wide Web Also called the *Web*, *WWW*, *W3*, and *w3*. An interlinked collection of hypertext documents (Web pages) residing on Web servers and other documents, menus, and databases, available via URLs (uniform resource locators). Web documents are marked for formatting and linking with HTML (Hypertext Markup Language), and Web servers use HTTP (Hypertext Transport Protocol) to deliver Web pages. The Web was invented as an online documentation resource by physicists at the CERN European Particle Physics Laboratory in Switzerland.

Zip drive A popular removable storage device from Iomega Corporation, capable of storing 100MB on relatively cheap, portable, 3.5-inch disks.

Appendix C

VENDORS GUIDE

The vendor listing that follows is divided into the following categories:

- ▶ Manufacturers of Computers, Peripherals, and Components
- ▶ Data Recovery Vendors
- ▶ Memory Vendors
- ▶ Storage Device Vendors
- ▶ Miscellaneous Computer Products Vendors
- ▶ Older PC Repair and Exchange
- ▶ Computer Recycling Centers

Adapted from *The Complete PC Upgrade & Maintenance Guide* by Mark Minasi
ISBN 0-7821-2606-5   1664 pages $49.99

Wherever possible, I have included non-800 numbers, as I recognize that non-American readers cannot use 800 numbers.

Products, prices, and addresses change, so you may find some vendors listed here no longer exist or cannot be reached given the information below. I am not endorsing these particular vendors, but merely providing the information as a useful resource to you, the reader.

Manufacturers of Computers, Peripherals, and Components

The following are names, addresses, and phone numbers of various manufacturers of computers, peripherals, and components:

3Com Corporation

5400 Bayfront Plaza
Santa Clara, CA 95052-8145
(800) 638-3266, (408) 326-5000
http://www.3com.com

3DTV Corporation

1863 Pioneer Parkway East #303
Springfield, OR 97477
voicemail/fax (415) 680-1678
http://www.3dmagic.com

Hardware and software for 3D (stereoscopic) video, computer graphics, and virtual reality

4Q Technologies

14425 Don Julian Road
City of Industry, CA 91746
(626) 333-6688
http://www.4qtech.com

Speakers

A4 Tech Corporation

20256 Apseo Robles
Walnut, CA 91789
(909) 468-0071
http://www.a4tech.com

Scanners

ABS Computer Technologies, Inc.

9997 Rose Hills Road
Whittier, CA 90601
(800) 876-8088
fax (562) 695-8923
http://www.buyabs.com

Abstract R&D, Inc.

120 Village Sq., Suite 37
Orinda, CA 94563
(510) 253-9588

Palmtop PCs

Acecad, Inc.

791 Foam St.
Monterey, CA 93940
voice (831) 655-1900
fax (831) 655-1919
http://www.acecad.com

Acecat III mouse replacement

Acer America Corporation
2641 Orchard Parkway
San Jose, CA 95134
(800) 733-2237
fax (408) 922-2933
http://www.acer.com

Acer Sertek Inc.
128 S. Woolfe Rd.
Sunnyvale, CA 94086
(408) 733-3174
http://www.ussertek.com

CD-ROMs, MPEG cards, sound cards

ACL/Staticide
1960 E. Devon Avenue
Elk Grove Village, IL 60007
(800) 782-8420
http://www.aclstaticide.com

Anti-static equipment & cleaning kits

ACT-RX Technology Corporation
10F, 525, Chung Cheng Road
Hsin Tien, Taipei, Taiwan ROC
(886) 2-218-8000Booth I9025

CPU coolers

Action Electronics Co., Ltd.
198, Chung Yuan Road
Chung Li, Taiwan, ROC
(886) 3-4515494

Axion monitors

Action Well Development Ltd.
Rm. 1101, 1103 and 4 Star Center
443-451 Castle Peak Road
Kwai Chung, NT, Hong Kong
(852) 2422-0010

Fax modems, sound products, controller and VGA cards, and computer cases

ActionTec Electronics, Inc.
760 N. Mary Avenue
Sunnyvale, CA 94086
technical support (408) 752-7714
main (408) 752-7700
fax (408) 541-9003
http://www.actiontec.com

PC card (PCMCIA) products

Actown Corporation
8F, 527, Chung Cheng Road
Hsin Tien, Taipei, Taiwan ROC
(886) 2-2184612Booth S2050E

Opto-electronic products, including handheld scanners, flatbeds, and sheet-fed scanners

Adaptec, Inc.
691 S. Milpitas Boulevard
Milpitas, CA 95035
(800) 934-2766, (408) 945-8600
http://www.adaptec.com

Addonics Technologies
48434 Milmont Drive
Fremont, CA 94538
(510) 438-6530, (800) 787-8580
http://www.addonics.com

Addtronics Enterprise Co.

No. 66, Chen-Teh Road
Taipei, Taiwan ROC
(886) 2-5591122

An integrated computer case manufacturer

ADI Systems, Inc.

2115 Ringwood Avenue
San Jose, CA 95131
(800) 228-0530, (408) 944-0100
fax (408) 944-0300
http://www.adiusa.com

Multi-scanning color monitors

Adobe Systems Inc.

345 Park Avenue
San Jose, California 95110-2704
(408) 536-6000
(800) 833-6687
fax (408) 537-6000
http://www.adobe.com

ADPI (Analog and Digital Peripherals, Inc.)

P.O. Box 499
Troy, OH 45373
(937) 339-2241
(800) 758-1041
http://www.adpi.com

Backup devices

Advanced Digital Systems

13909 Bettencourt Street
Cerritos, CA 90703
(800) 888-5244
http://www.adstech.com

Multimedia specialty audio/video hardware

Advanced Gravis Computer Technology Ltd.

World Headquarters
2855 Campus Drive
San Mateo, CA 94403
(650) 572-2700, (800) 535-4242
fax (610) 231-1022
http://www.gravis.com

PC game interfaces

Advanced Integration Research, Inc.

2188 Del Franco Street
San Jose, CA 95131
(408) 428-0800
http://www.airwebs.com

Manufacturer of 486 and Pentium system boards based on ISA, EISA, PCI, and VL-bus architectures

Advanced Matrix Technology, Inc.

747 Calle Plano
Camarillo, CA 93012-8598
(805) 388-5799

Dot matrix, laser, and inkjet printers and plotters

Advantage Memory

25A Technology Drive, building 2

Irvine, CA 92718
(800) 266-0488
http://www.advantagememory.com

Agfa (Bayer Corporation)
200 Ballardvale Street
Wilmington, MA 01887
(508) 658-5600
http://www.agfa.com

Scanners, film recorders, color management software, digital cameras

Ahead Systems, Inc.
44244 Fremont Boulevard
Fremont, CA 94538
(510) 623-0900

3D multimedia surround-sound, accelerator, and 3D stereo vision products

AITech International Corporation
47971 Fremont Boulevard
Fremont, CA 94538
(510) 226-8960
http://www.aitech.com

Multimedia and desktop video products

Aiwa America, Inc.
800 Corporate Drive
Mahwah, NJ 07430
(800) 920-2673
http://www.aiwa.com

Tape backup products

Alaris, Inc.
47338 Fremont Boulevard
Fremont, CA 94538
(510) 770-5700
http://www.alaris.com

Graphics acceleration and scalable full-motion video playback products

Alfa Infotech Co.
46600 Landing Pky.
Fremont, CA 94538
(510) 252-9300

Multimedia and communication products

ALi (Acer Laboratories, Inc.)
4701 Patrick Henry Drive, Suite 2101
Santa Clara, CA 95054
(408) 764-0644

ICs for personal computers and embedded systems

Alpha & Omega Computer
101 S. Kraemer Boulevard, Suite 116
Placentia, CA 92670
(714) 577-7688

486/Pentium CPU coolers

Alphacom Enterprise, Inc.
1407 Englewood Street
Philadelphia, PA 19111
(215) 722-6133

Joysticks, mice, trackballs, CPU cooling fans with built-in heat sink, and removable hard disk drive kits

ALPS
3553 N. First Street
San Jose, CA 95134
(408) 432-6000
http://www.alpsusa.com

GlidePoint input devices, drive products

AMCC (Applied Micro Circuits Corporation)
6195 Lusk Boulevard
San Diego, CA 92121
(800) 755-2622
http://www.amcc.com

AMD (Advanced Micro Devices)
One AMD Place
P.O. Box 3453
Sunnyvale, CA 94088
(800) 538-8450, (408) 732-2400
http://www.amd.com

CPUs

American Cover, Inc.
102 W. 12200 S
Draper, UT 84092
(801) 553-0600

Computer accessory products

AMI (American Megatrends, Inc.)
6145F Northbelt Parkway
Norcross, GA 30071
(770) 246-8600
sales (800) 828-9264
fax (770) 246-8791
http://www.ami.com

Motherboards and AMIDiag software

Amptron International, Inc.
1239 Etcher Ave.
City of Industry, CA 91748
(626) 912-5789
http://www.amptron.com

System boards

Amrel Technology, Inc.
11801 Goldring Road
Arcadia, CA 91006
(800) 882-6735
http://www.amrel.com

Modular notebook computers

AMS, Inc.
12881 Ramona Boulevard
Irwindale, CA 91706
(800) 886-2671

Ana Precision Co., Ltd.
Suite 694, Kumjung-Dong, Kunp'O-shi
Kyunggi-Do, 435-050, Korea
(0343) 53-0813

Inkjet and dot matrix printers

Angia Communications
441 East Bay Boulevard
Provo, UT 84606
(800) 877-9159
fax (801) 373-9847

PCMCIA fax modem

AOC International
311 Sinclair Frontage Road
Milpitas, CA 95035
(408) 956-1070

Visual display products

APC (American Power Conversion)
132 Fairgrounds Road
West Kingdom, RI 02892
(800) 800-4APC, (401) 789-5735
fax (401) 789-3710
http://www.apcc.com

UPSs, phone line surge protectors

Apex Data, Inc. /SMART Modular Technologies, Inc.
4305 Cushing Parkway
Fremont, CA 94538
(800) 841-APEX
tech support (510) 249-1605
fax (510) 249-1600
tech support fax (510) 249-1604
e-mail: sales@smartm.com
support@smartm.com
BBS (510) 249-1601 (8 data bits, 1 stop bit, and no parity)
http://www.apexdata.com

Apple Computer, Inc.
One Infinite Loop
Cupertino, CA 95014
(408) 996-1010
http://www.apple.com

APS Technologies
6131 Deramus, Suite 4967
Kansas City, MO 64120
(800) 235-2753, (816) 483-1600
fax (816) 483-3077

Arcada Software
Seagate Software
920 Disc Drive
Scotts Valley, CA 95067
(408) 438-6550
fax (408) 438-7612
http://www.arcada.com

Data protection and storage management software products

Archtek America Corporation
18549 Gale Avenue
City of Industry, CA 91748-1338
(818) 912-9800
http://www.archtek.com

Voice/data communications and network products

Arco Computer Products, Inc.
2750 N. 29th Avenue, Suite 316
Hollywood, FL 33020
(305) 925-2688
http://www.arcoide.com

IDE busless, slotless, operating system-independent mirroring adapter

Arkenstone, Inc.
1390 Borregas Avenue
Sunnyvale, CA 94089
(800) 444-4443
http://www.arkenstone.org

Products to aid individuals who are blind, visually impaired, or learning disabled to better access written information

Artek (Asicom, Inc.)
46716 Fremont Boulevard
Fremont, CA 94538
(510) 354-0900

High-end PC subsystems

Artisoft, Inc.
2202 N. Forbes Boulevard
Tucson, AZ 85745
(520) 670-7100
http://www.artisoft.com

Networking products suited to small businesses and workgroups

ArtMedia
2772 Calle del Mundo
Santa Clara, CA 95050
(408) 980-8988
http://www.artmedia.com

ASK LCD, Inc.
100 West Forest Ave, Suite E
Englewood, NJ 07631
(201) 541-2424
tech support (888) 307-2561
fax (201) 541-2391
http://www.asklcd.com

LCD presentation products

Ask Technology Ltd.
Unit 1, 4/F., Henley Ind. Ctr.,
9-15 Bute Street
Mongkok, Kowloon, Hong Kong
(852) 2398-3223

System boards, VGA cards, and sound cards

Askey Communications USA
162 Atlantic Street
Pomona, CA 91768
http://www.askey.com

PCMCIA, external, and internal modem cards and pocket models

Asolid Computer Supply, Inc.
(Biostar Manufacture Group)
4044 Clipper Court
Fremont, CA 94538
(510) 226-6678

Motherboards

Aspen Systems Inc.
4026 Youngfield Street
Wheat Ridge, CO 80033-3862
(303) 431-4606

RISC systems

Aspen Technologies
400 Rogers Street
Princeton, WV 24740
(304) 425-1111

Internal, external, and PCMCIA fax modems

Assmann Data Products
1849 W. Drake Drive, Suite 101
Tempe, AZ 85283
(877) ASSMANN (1-877-277-6266)
fax (602) 897-7255
http://www.usa-assmann.com

Ergonomic mice

AST Computer
AST Research, Inc.
16225 Alton Parkway
Irvine, CA 92618
or
P.O. Box 57005
Irvine, CA 92619-7005
(949) 727-4141
tech support (800) 727-1278
http://www.ast.com

ATI Technologies
33 Commerce Valley Drive East
Thornhill, Ontario, Canada L3T 7N6
tech support (905) 882-2626
tech support fax (905) 882-0546
faxback (905) 882-2600 (press #2)
CompuServe: GO ATITECH
http://www.atitech.com

Graphics accelerators

Atlantic Technology
343 Vanderbilt Avenue
Norwood, MA 02062
(617) 762-6300

Speakers

ATronics International, Inc.
44700-B Industrial Drive
Fremont, CA 94538-6431
(510) 656-8400
fax (510) 656-8560
http://www.ati1.com/

Advanced external storage products

ATTO Technology, Inc.
40 Hazelwood Drive, Suite 106
Amherst, NY 14228
(716) 691-1999

VantagePCI-Multi Channel SCSI accelerator card

AuraVision Corporation
47865 Fremont Boulevard
Fremont, CA 94538
(510) 252-6800
http://www.auravision.com

Multimedia IC devices

Autumn Technologies
11705 69th Way N
Largo, FL 34643
(800) 837-8551

Test Bed Pro, a commercial PC testing, assembly, and repair workbench

AVerMedia, Inc.
47923A Warm Springs Boulevard
Fremont, CA 94538
(510) 770-9899
http://www.aver.com

PC-Video multimedia hardware

AVM Technology, Inc.
9774 S. 700 East
Sandy, UT 84070
(801) 571-0967

Professional MIDI wavetable modules

Avnet Technology Co., Ltd.
6F-1, No. 102, Sung Lung Road
Taipei, Taiwan ROC
(886) 2-7607603

Audio-visual network card

Award Software International
777 E. Middlefield Road
Mountain View, CA 94043
(650) 237-6800
fax (650) 968-0274
http://www.award.com

Desktop plug-and-play BIOS for 486, 586, Pentium, and P6-based PC platforms

Axonix Corporation
844 S. 200 East
Salt Lake City, UT 84111
(801) 521-9797

CD-ROMs

Axxon Computer Corporation
3979 Tecumseh Road E
Windsor, ON N8W 1J5, Canada
(519) 974-0163
http://www.softio.com/

Jumperless I/O cards

Aztech Labs, Inc.
45645 Northport Loop East
Fremont, CA 94538
(510) 623-8988
fax (510) 623-8989
BBS (510) 623-8933
tech support (510) 623-9037
tech support fax (510) 353-4327
http://www.aztechlabs.com
http://www.aztechca.com
ftp://ftp.aimnet.com/pub/users/aztech

CD-ROM drives

Belkin Components
501 West Walnut Street
Compton, CA 90220
(310) 898-1100
(800) 2-BELKIN (223-5546)
fax (310) 898-1111
http://www.belkin.com

Standard and custom computer cables, printer sharing devices, surge protectors, and LAN cabling-related products

Benwin Inc.
345 Cloverleaf Drive, Suite B
Baldwin Park, CA 91706
(818) 336-8779

Multimedia products, specializing in speakers

Best Data Products
21800 Nordhoff Street
Chatsworth, CA 91311
(818) 773-9600

Best Power
General Signal
P.O. Box 280
Necedah, WI 54646
(800) 356-5794
http://www.bestpower.com

UPSs and shutdown software

BIS Technology
13111 Brooks Drive, Suite A
Baldwin Park, CA 91706
(818) 856-5800

High-speed voice/fax/data modems

Boca Research
1377 Clint Moore Road
Boca Raton, FL 33478
(407) 997-6227
fax (407) 994-5848
http://www.bocaresearch.com

Borland International
100 Borland Way
Scotts Valley, CA 95066
(408) 431-1000
http://www.borland.com

Products and services for software developers

Bose Corporation
The Mountain
Framingham, MA 01701
(800) 999-2673 (1-800-WWW-BOSE)
http://www.bose.com

Brooks Power Systems, Inc.
1400 Adams Road
Bensalem, PA 19020
(800) 523-1551

Power Systems' SurgeStopper surge and noise suppressors

Brother International Corporation
100 Somerset Corporate Boulevard
Bridgewater, NJ 08807-0911
(908) 704-1700
fax (908) 704-8235
http://www.brother.com

Multi-function products and laser printers

BRYSiS Data, Inc.
17431 Gale Ave.
City of Industry, CA 91748
(818) 810-0355

Touch screen monitors

BSF Components Inc.
420 Third Street
Oakland, CA 94607
(510) 893-8822

Molded and assembled computer cables

C-Cube Microsystems
1778 McCarthy Boulevard
Milpitas, CA 95035
(408) 944-6361
http://www.c-cube.com

MPEG and JPEG decoders and encoders for personal computers

California PC Products
205 Apollo Way
Hollister, CA 95023
(408) 638-9460

Computer chassis and power supplies

Calluna Technology Ltd.
1 Blackwood Road
Eastfield, Glenrothes
Fife KY7 4NP, Scotland, UK
(44) 1592-630-810

PC card hard disk drives

Canon Computer Systems
2995 Redhill Avenue
Costa Mesa, CA 92626
(800) 848-4123, (714) 438-3000
http://www.ccsi.canon.com

Canon U.S.A., Inc.
One Canon Plaza
Lake Success, NY 11042-1113
(516) 488-6700

Bubblejet CJ10 desktop color copier, scanner, and printer

Canopus
2010 N. First Street, Suite 510
San Jose, CA 95131
(408) 467-4000

High-performance multimedia products for PCs

Cardinal Technologies, Inc.
1827 Freedom Road
Lancaster, PA 17601
(770) 840-2157
tech support (770) 840-2157
http://www.cardtech.com

Fax modems

Casco Products, Inc.
3850 River Ridge Drive
Cedar Rapids, IA 52402
(800) 793-6960
fax (319) 393-6895
http://www.casco.com

LightLink infrared, cordless keyboard

CD Technology, Inc.
766 San Aleso Avenue
Sunnyvale, CA 94086
(408) 752-8500

CD-ROMs

Centon Electronics, Inc.
20 Morgan
Irvine, CA 92718
(714) 855-9111
http://www.centon.com

Manufacturer of memory upgrades for desktops, workstations, laptops, notebooks, portables, and printers

Cerwin-Vega, Inc.
555 E. Easy Street
Simi Valley, CA 93065
(805) 584-9332

Digital audio-quality multimedia speaker systems

CH Products
970 Park Center Drive
Vista, CA 92083
(619) 598-2518
http://www.chproducts.com

Joysticks, F-16 sticks, throttles, rudder pedals, flight yokes, trackballs, and gamecards

Chaintech Computer U.S., Inc.
12880 Lakeland Road
Santa Fe Springs, CA 90670
(310) 906-1698

Mainboards, VGA cards, multi I/O cards, SCSI interfaces, and sound cards

Chaplet Systems USA, Inc.
252 N. Wolfe Road
Sunnyvale, CA 94086
(408) 732-7950

Notebook computers

Chartered Electronics Industries
210A Twin Dolphin Drive
Redwood City, CA 94065
(415) 591-6717

PC PrimeTimeTV add-on board

Chase Advanced Technologies
500 Main Street
Deep River, CT 06417
(203) 526-2400

Computer peripheral products

Cheer Electronics (USA)
9740 N. Seymour
Kansas City, MO 64153
(816) 891-0050

Monitors

Cherry Electrical Products
3600 Sunset Avenue
Waukegan, IL 60087
(708) 662-9200

PC/POS keyboards, low-cost 101-key data entry keyboards

Chinon America, Inc.
615 Hawaii Avenue
Torrance, CA 90503
(310) 533-0274

Digital cameras, CD-ROM drives

Cirque Corporation

433 W. Lawndale Drive
Salt Lake City, UT 84115
(800) 454-3375, (801) 467-1100
http://www.cirque.com

GlidePoint trackpad

Cirrus Logic, Inc.

3100 W. Warren Avenue
Fremont, CA 94538
(510) 623-8300
http://www.cirrus.com

Citizen America Corporation

831 South Douglas Street, Suite 121
P.O. Box 1021
El Segundo, CA 90245-1021
(310) 643-9825
fax (310) 725-0969
http://www.citizen-america.com/

Printiva 600C near-photo-quality color printer

Clary Corporation

1960 S. Walker Avenue
Monrovia, CA 91016
(800) 442-5279
http://www.clary.com/onguard/

UPSs

CMD Technology, Inc.

One Vanderbilt
Irvine, CA 92718
(714) 454-0800
http://www.cmd.com

SCSI RAID and PC host adapters

Colorgraphic

5980 Peachtree Road
Atlanta, GA 30341
(770) 455-3921

COM2001 Corporation

4350 La Jolla Village Dr., Suite 930
San Diego, CA 92122
(619) 638-2001
http://www.com2001.com

Video and audio conferencing software

ComByte, Inc.

4424 Innovation Drive
Fort Collins, CO 80525
(970) 229-0660

Doubleplay dual-mode drive, reads and writes both floppy disks and minicartridge tapes

Comdial Corp.

1180 Seminole Trail
Charlottesville, VA 22906-7266
(800) 347-1432, (804) 978-2200
faxback (800) COMDIAL
http://www.comdial.com

PC and telephone interfaces

Command Software Systems

1061 E. Indiantown Road, Suite 500
Jupiter, FL 33477
(800) 423-9147
http://commandcom.com

F-Prot Professional anti-virus software

Compaq Computer Corporation
P.O. Box 692000
Houston, TX 77269
(800) 345-1518, (281) 370-0670
product information (800) 345-1518
http://www.compaq.com

Computer Connections America
19A Crosby Drive
Bedford, MA 01730
(617) 271-0444

Peripheral equipment for backup and data storage

Computer Fun
8250 Valdosta Avenue
San Diego, CA 92126-2130
e-mail: garyo@computerfun.com
http://www.computerfun.com/

Manufacturer of mouse pads & computer toys

Connectix Corporation
2655 Campus Drive
San Mateo, CA 94403
(800) 950-5880, (415) 571-5100
fax (415) 571-5195
http://www.connectix.com

QuickCam video camera

Conner Peripherals, Inc.
1650 Sunflower Avenue
Costa Mesa, CA 92626
(800) 4-CONNER
http://www.conner.com

Copam Dynamic Systems, Inc.
46560 Fremont Boulevard, Suite 409
Fremont, CA 94538
(510) 770-0149

CPU cooling kits and memory-related components

Copper Leaf Technology
2233 Paragon Drive
San Jose, CA 95131
(408) 452-9288

Motherboards

Cornerstone Imaging, Inc.
1710 Fortune Drive
San Jose, CA 95131
(408) 435-8900
http://www.corimage.com

Creative Labs, Inc.
1901 McCarthy Boulevard
Milpitas, CA 95035
(800) 998-1000, (408) 428-6660
fax (408) 428-6631
http://www.creaf.com

Creatix Polymedia, L.P.
3945 Freedom Cir., Suite 670
Santa Clara, CA 95054
(408) 654-9300
http://www.creatix.com

Multimedia products, high-speed modems, and PCMCIA cards

Crystal Semiconductor
3100 W. Warren Avenue
Fremont, CA 94538
(510) 623-8300

CTX International, Inc.
748 Epperson Dr.
City of Industry, CA 91748
(626) 839-0500
customer service (800) 888-2012
fax (626) 810-6703
http://www.ctxintl.com

Monitors

CyberMax Computer, Inc.
133 North 5th Street
Allentown, PA 18102
(800) 443-9868, (610) 770-1808
from Canada (800) 695-4991
http://www.cybmax.com

Cyrix Corporation
P.O. Box 853923
Richardson, TX 75085-3923
(800) 462-9749, (800) 340-7971
e-mail: tech_support@cyrix.com
BBS: (214) 968-8610
http://www.cyrix.com

Daewoo Electronics
120 Chubb Ave.
Lyndhurst, NJ 07071
(201) 460-2000
http://www.daewoo.com

Monitors

DarkHorse Systems, Inc.
Tanisys Technology
12201 Technology Blvd., Suite 130
Austin, Texas 78727-6101
(512) 335-4440, (800) 533-1744
fax (512) 257-5310
http://www.tanisys.com

Memory test systems

Data Depot, Inc.
1710 Drew Street, Suite 1
Clearwater, FL 34615
(813) 446-3402

PC diagnostic test products, including hardware and software products

DataLux Corp.
155 Aviation Dr.
Winchester, VA 22602
(800) DATALUX, (703) 662-1500
fax (540) 662-1682
faxback (540) 662-1675
e-mail: info@datalux.com
http://www.datalux.com

Space-saving PC hardware

Datasonix Corporation
5700 Flatiron Pky.
Boulder, CO 80301
(303) 545-9500

Portable gigabyte storage devices

Dell Computer Corporation
Dell Computer Corporation
One Dell Way

Round Rock, TX 78682
(888) 560-2384
http://www.dell.com

Delrina Corporation

Symantec Corp.
175 West Broadway
Eugene, OR 97401
(541) 334-6054 (outside the U.S. and Canada)
(800) 268-6082
fax (541) 984-8020
http://www.delrina.com

PC fax, communications, and electronic forms software

Delta Products Corporation

3225 Laurelview Ct.
Fremont, CA 94538
(510) 770-0660

Video display products

Deltec

2727 Kurtz Street
San Diego, CA 92110
(619) 291-4211
http://www.deltecpower.com

Uninterruptible power systems and power management software

Denon Electronics

222 New Road
Parsippany, NJ 07054
(201) 575-7810

CD-ROM jukebox that houses 200 discs

DFI (Diamond Flower, Inc.)

Exide Electronics
8609 Six Forks Road
Raleigh, NC 27615
(800) 554-3448, (919) 872-3020
fax (800) 75-EXIDE
http://www.exide.com

Motherboards, video cards, notebooks, desktop systems, and multimedia components

DiagSoft, Inc.

5615 Scotts Valley Drive, Suite 140
Scotts Valley, CA 95066
(408) 438-8247

Diagnostic software

Diamond Multimedia Systems, Inc.

2880 Junction Avenue
San Jose, CA 95134-1922
(408) 325-7000
customer service (800) 468-5846
fax (408) 325-7070
http://www.diamondmm.com

Digital Equipment Corporation (DEC)

20555 State Hwy 249
Houston, TX 77070
(281) 370-0670
http://www.compaq.com

PCs, servers, and workstations for 32- and 64-bit computing

DPT-Distributed Processing Technology

140 Candace Drive
Maitland, FL 32751
(407) 830-5522
http://www.dpt.com

SmartCache SCSI host adapters

DTC Data Technology, Inc.

1515 Centre Pointe Drive
Milpitas, CA 95035
(408) 942-4000
technical support (408) 262-7700
fax (408) 942-4027
faxback (408) 942-4005
BBS (408) 942-4010
http://www.datatechnology.com

Drives and SCSI devices

DTK Computer, Inc.

770 Epperson Drive
City of Industry, CA 91748
(818) 810-0098

Pentium-based systems

Edek Technologies, Inc.

Div. of Elite Computer, Taiwan
1212 John Reed Ct.
City of Industry, CA 91745
(818) 855-5700

Manufacturer and distributor of computer mainboard and VGA card products

ELSA, Inc.

2041 Mission College Boulevard
Suite 165
Santa Clara, CA 95054
(408) 565-9669

2D and 3D graphics accelerators and ISDN products

Enhance Memory Products, Inc.

18730 Oxnard Street, Suite 201
Tarzana, CA 91356
(818) 343-3066

Memory systems

Ensoniq

155 Great Valley Parkway
Malvern, PA 19355
(610) 647-3930
http://www.ensoniq.com

EPS Technologies

10069 Dakota Avenue
Jefferson, SD 57038
(800) 447-0921, (800) 526-4258,
(605) 966-5586
fax (605) 966-5482
http://www.epstech.com

Epson America, Inc.

20770 Madrona Avenue
Torrance, CA 90509
(800) 463-7766, (310) 782-0770
http://www.epson.com

ESS Technology, Inc.

46107 Landing Pky.
Fremont, CA 94538
(510) 226-1088

ES689 Wavetable Music Synthesizer, ES938 3D Audio Effects Processor

Evergreen Technologies, Inc.
915 N.W. 8th Street
Corvallis, OR 97330
(503) 757-0934
http://www.evertech.com

CPU upgrades for 386- and 486-based computers

Exabyte Corporation
1685 38th St.
Boulder, CO 80301
(800) 445-7736, (303) 417-7511, (303) 417-7792
fax (303) 417-7890
EXAFAX (fax-on-demand system)
(201)946-0091
support@exabyte.com
http://www.exabyte.com

EXP Computer, Inc.
141 Eileen Way
Syosset, NY 11791
(516) 496-3703

Memory and PCMCIA products for notebooks and palmtops

Expert Computer International, Inc.
129 166th St.
Cerritos, CA 90703
(310) 407-1740

Generic and name-brand VGA cards in DRAM/VRAM ISA, VL-bus, and PCI configurations

Fast Electronic U.S., Inc.
393 Vintage Park Drive
Foster City, CA 94404
(415) 345-3400

FPS60 video compression board for multi-media production

Focus Computer Products, Inc.
35 Pond Park Road
Hingham, MA 02043
(617) 741-5008

Anti-glare glass screen filters, anti-radiation glass screen filters, wrap-around screen filters, cleaning products for screen filters

Focus Electronic Corporation
21078 Commerce Pointe Drive
Walnut, CA 91789
(909) 468-5533

Signature Series keyboards

Formosa USA, Inc.
9400 Lurline Avenue, Suite B
Chatsworth, CA 91311
(818) 407-4956

MPEG decoding cards, video capture boards, TV tuners, video conference products, 16-bit sound cards, wavetable modules

Fujitsu Personal Systems, Inc.
5200 Patrick Henry Drive
Santa Clara, CA 95054
(408) 982-9500

Fujitsu Computer Products of America

2904 Orchard Parkway
San Jose, CA 95134
(408) 432-6333
http://www.fujitsu.com
http://www.fcpa.com

Peripherals including hard disk drives, optical disk drives, tape drives, laser and dot matrix printers, document imaging scanners

Fujitsu Microelectronics, Inc.

3545 N. First Street
San Jose, CA 95134
(408) 922-9000
tech support (800) 626-4686
http://www.fujitsu.com

Memory cards, LAN cards, multimedia, and communications cards

Gateway2000

610 Gateway Dive
N. Sioux City, SD 57049-2000
(888) 888-0244, (605) 232-2000
from Canada (800) 846-3609
fax (605) 232-2023
faxback (800) 846-4526
http://www.gw2k.com

GVC Technologies

376 Lafayette Road
Sparta, NJ 07871
(800) 289-4821

Modems

Hayes Microcomputer Products, Inc.

P.O. Box 105203
Atlanta, GA 30348-5203
(800) 377-4377, (770) 840-9200
fax (770) 441-1213
http://www.hayes.com

Modems

HEI

1495 Steiger Lake Lane
P.O. Box 5000, Victoria, MN 55386
(612) 443-2500

Fast Point light pens

Hercules Computer Technology, Inc.

3839 Spinnaker Court
Fremont, CA 94538
(800) 323-0601, (510) 623-6030,
(510) 623-6050
fax (510) 623-1112
tech support fax (510) 490-6745
faxback (800) 711-HERC (800-711-4372)
e-mail: support@hercules.com
CompuServe: GO HERCULES, 71333,2532
BBS (510) 623-7449
http://www.hercules.com

Hewlett-Packard

Personal Information Products Group
5301 Stevens Creek Boulevard
Santa Clara, CA 95052
(800) 762-0900
http://www.hp.com

Hewlett-Packard Co.

Information Storage Group
800 S. Taft Avenue
Loveland, CO 80537
(970) 679-6000
http://www.hp.com

HP Colorado tape products, HP DAT tape products, and HP optical products, disk drives, and disk array systems

Hewlett-Packard Co.

North American Hardcopy Marketing
16399 W. Bernardo Drive
San Diego, CA 92127
(800) 752-0990
customer information
center (800) 752-0900
http://www.hp.com

Printers

Hilgraeve, Inc.

111 Conant Avenue, Suite A
Monroe, MI 48161
(313) 243-0576
http://www.hilgraeve.com

32-bit communications software, including HyperTerminal

Hitachi America, Ltd.

50 Prospect Avenue
Tarrytown, NY 10591-4698
(800) HITACHI, (914) 332-5800
fax (914) 332-5555
http://www.hitachi.com

http://www.internetworking.hitachi.com

Computer peripherals and components, including storage products

HTP International

1620 South Lewis Street
Anaheim, CA 92805
(714) 937-9300

Hyundai Electronics America

1955 Lundy Avenue
San Jose, CA 95131
(408) 232-8000
fax (408) 232-8146
http://www.hea.com

Components including memory devices for DRAM, SRAM

I/OMagic Corporation

6B Autry
Irvine, CA 92618
(949) 727-7466
customer support (949) 597-2462
fax (949) 727-7467
customer support fax (949) 380-0696
http://www.iomagic.com

IBM PC Co.

One Orchard Road
Armonk, NY 10504
(800) 772-2227, (914) 766-1900
fax (800) 426-4323
http://www.ibm.com
http://www.pc.ibm.com

Iiyama North America, Inc.
650 Louis Drive, Suite 120
Warminster, PA 18974
(215) 957-6543
http://www.iiyama.com

Integrated Technology Express, Inc.
1557 Centre Pointe Drive
Milpitas, CA 95035
(408) 934-7330

PC core logic chip sets, I/O peripheral chips, and custom ASIC design services on x86 and PowerPC architectures

Intel Corporation
2200 Mission College Boulevard
Santa Clara, CA 95052
(408) 765-8080
customer service (800) 321-4044
fax (408) 765-9904
http://www.intel.com

Interact Accessories, Inc.
(formerly STD Entertainment)
10945 McCormick Road
Hunt Valley, MD 21031
(410) 785-5661

Multimedia gaming products such as joysticks, control pads, game cards, speakers, woofers, mice, storage cases, and cleaning kits

Iomega Corporation
1821 West Iomega Way
Roy, UT 84067
(800) MY-STUFF, (801) 778-3010
http://www.iomega.com

IPC Peripherals
48041 Fremont Boulevard
Fremont, CA 94538
(510) 354-0800

Sound cards, 24 and 32 speed CD-ROM drives, three- and seven-disc changers, PCMCIA sound and Ethernet cards, audio/fax/modem telephony products, and multimedia upgrade kits

IPC Technologies, Inc.
Austin Computer Services, Inc.
10300 Metric Boulevard
Austin, TX 78758
(512) 339-3500
http://www.ipctech.com

J-Mark Computer Corporation
13111 Brooks Drive, Suite A
Baldwin Park, CA 91706
(818) 856-5800
http://www.j-mark.com

Motherboards, fax modems, SVGA cards, PCMCIA devices, and network cards for notebooks and PCs

Jazz Speakers
1217 John Reed Ct.
Industry, CA 91745
(818) 336-2689

JBL Consumer Products, Inc.
Harmon Consumer Group
80 Crossways Pk. W
Woodbury, NY 11797
(516) 496-3400, (800) 336-4JBL
www.jbl.com

Multimedia speakers, both satellites and subwoofers

Joss Technology Ltd.
No. 20, Lane 84, San Min Road
Hsin Tien City
Taipei Hsien, Taiwan ROC
(886) 2-9102050

Motherboards, 4MB/16MB 72-pin SIMM modules

JVC Information Products of America
#2 JVC Road
Tuscaloosa, AL 35405
(205) 556-7111
authorized service centers
(800) 537-5722
http://www.jvc.com
http://www.jvcdiscusa.com

CD-ROM products and software

KeySonic Technology, Inc.
A Div. of Powercom America
1040A S. Melrose Street
Placentia, CA 92670-7119
(714) 632-8887

MPEG video and audio decoding cards

Kinesis Corporation
22121 17th Avenue SE, Suite 107
Bothell, WA 98021-7404
(206) 402-8100
fax (206) 402-8181
http://www.kinesis-ergo.com/

Ergonomic keyboards

Kingston Technology Corporation
17600 Newhope Street
Fountain Valley, CA 92708
(800) 435-0640, (714) 435-2639
fax (714) 424-3939
http://www.kingston.com

Konica Business Machines U.S.A., Inc.
500 Day Hill Road
Windsor, CT 06095
(203) 683-2222
http://www.konica.com

Multifunctional printers

Koss Corporation
4129 N. Port Washington Boulevard
Milwaukee, WI 53212
(800) USA-KOSS, (414) 964-5000
http://www.koss.com

Stereo audio accessories for computers

Labtec Enterprises, Inc.
3801 109th Ave., Suite J
Vancouver, WA 98682
(360) 896-2000
http://www.labtec.com

Lava Computer Mfg., Inc.
LSMI Division
28A Dansk Ct.
Rexdale, ON M9W 5V8, Canada
(800) 241-5282

High-speed I/O boards

Leverage International, Inc.
46704 Fremont Boulevard
Fremont, CA 94538
(510) 657-6750

Memory modules and other semiconductor products for IBM, Compaq, PC compatibles and other computers

Lexmark International, Inc.
2275 Research Boulevard
Rockville, MD 20850
(301) 212-5900
(800) LEXMARK or (800) 539-6275
http://www.lexmark.com

LG Electronics
1000 Sylvan Avenue
Englewood Cliffs, NJ 95131
(201) 816-2000

Goldstar monitors

Liberty Systems, Inc.
375 Saratoga Avenue, Suite A
San Jose, CA 95129
(408) 983-1127

CD-ROMs, hard drives, backup devices

Lion Optics Corporation (Likom Sdn BhD)
1751 McCarthy Blvd.
Milpitas, CA 95035
(408) 954-8089
http://www.likom.com.my/

CD-ROM drive products

Logicode Technology, Inc.
1380 Flynn Road
Camarillo, CA 93012
(800) 735-6442, (805) 388-9000

Logitech, Inc.
6505 Kaiser Drive
Fremont, CA 94555
(510) 795-8500
http://www.logitech.com

Pointing devices

MAG InnoVision Co., Inc
2801 South Yale Street
Santa Ana, CA 92704
(800) 827-3998, (714) 751-2008
fax (714) 751-5522
http://www.maginnovision.com

Monitors

Magnavox
Philips Consumer Electronics Co.
One Philips Drive
Knoxville, Tennessee 37914-1810
(800) 531-0039, (423) 521-4316
http://www.philipsmagnavox.com

Matrox Graphics, Inc.
1025 St-Regis Boulevard
Dorval, Quebec, Canada H9P 2T4
(514) 969-6320
http://www.matrox.com

Video boards

Maxell Corporation of America
Multi-Media Division
22-08 Rt. 208
Fair Lawn, NJ 07410
(800) 533-2836
http://www.maxell.com

Data storage media

Maxi-Switch
2901 East Elvira Road
Tucson, AZ 85706
(520) 294-5450

Keyboards

Maximus Computers
710 East Cypress Avenue, Unit-A
Monrovia, CA 91016
(800) 888-6294, (818) 305-5925
fax (818) 357-9140
http://www.maximuspc.com

MaxTech Corporation
400 Commons Way
Rockaway, NJ 07866
(800) 9-FORMAX
fax (201) 586-3308
http://www.maxcorp.com

Maxtor Corporation
510 Cottonwood Dr.
Milpitas, CA 95135
(800) 2-MAXTOR, (408) 432-1700
fax (408) 922-2050
tech support fax (303) 678-2260
http://www.maxtor.com

McAfee Associates
2710 Walsh Avenue
Santa Clara, CA
(408) 988-3832
tech support (972) 278-6100
http://www.mcafee.com/

VirusScan anti-virus software

Media Vision
47900 Bayside Pky.
Fremont, CA 94538
(510) 770-8600
http://www.mediavis.com

Semiconductor products, audio products

Mediatrix Peripherals, Inc.
4229 Garlock Street
Sherbrooke, PQ J1L 2C8, Canada
(819) 829-8749
fax (819) 829-5100
http://www.mediatrix.com

Audiotrix Pro 16-bit sound board

Megahertz Corporation
3COM Corporation
Great America Site
5400 Bayfront Plaza
Santa Clara, CA 95052
(408) 326-5000
fax (408) 326-5001
http://www.megahertz.com

Memory Card Technology
10235 S. 51st Street, Suite 180
Phoenix, Arizona 85044
(602) 785-7800
fax (602) 785-7500
http://www.memory-card-technology.com/

Memory upgrades and PCMCIA products

Micro 2000, Inc.
1100 E. Broadway, Suite 301
Glendale, CA 91205
(818) 547-0125
tech support (800) 864-8008
http://www.micro2000.com

Universal Diagnostics Toolkit

Micro Accessories, Inc.
Blue Earth Research, Inc.
1416 N. Riverfront Drive
Mankato, MN 56001-3253
(507) 387-4001
fax (507) 387-4008
http://www.blueearthresearch.com/macess.html

Computer interface cables and terminators

Micro Solutions
132 West Lincoln Hwy
DeKalb, IL 60115
(815) 754-4500
sales (800) 890-7227
fax (815) 756-4986
faxback (815) 754-4600
BBS (815) 756-9100
http://www.micro-solutions.com

MicroClean, Inc.
2050 S. Tenth Street
San Jose, CA 95112
(408) 995-5062
http://www.microclean.com

Computer care cleaning products

MicroData Corp.
3001 Exec. Dr.
Clearwater, FL 34622
(813) 573-5900

PC diagnostic hardware and software products for technicians, system integrators, and computer service professionals

Microlabs
204 Lost Canyon Court
Richardson, TX 75080
(214) 234-5842

Micron Electronics, Inc.
8000 S. Federal Way
P.O. Box 6
Boise, ID 83707-0006
(208) 368-4000
tech support (888) FIX-MYPC or (888) 349-6972
sales (800) 9-MICRON
fax (208) 368-4435
http://www.micron.com

Computer systems, WinBook notebook computers

Micronics Computers
221 Warren Avenue
Fremont, CA 94539
(510) 651-2300, (800) 577-0977
http://www.randomc.com/~dperr/micronics/microntac.htm

Orchid series graphics accelerators

Microsoft Corporation
One Microsoft Way
Redmond, WA 98052-6399
(206) 882-8080, (800) 426-9400
http://www.microsoft.com

MicroStar International
45500 North Point Loop West
Fremont, CA 94538
(510) 623-8818
http://www.msicomputer.com

PC-based mainboards, Ethernet cards, and video accelerators

Microtek Lab, Inc.
3715 Doolittle Drive
Redondo Beach, CA 90278
(800) 654-4160, (310) 297-5000
tech support (310) 297-5100
fax (310) 297-5050
BBS (310) 297-5102
AutoTech faxback (310) 297-5101
CompuServe: GO GRAPHSUP, library 6
http://www.mteklab.com

Mindflight Technology, Inc.
4-608 Weber Street North
Waterloo, Ontario N2V 1K4
(519) 746-8483
fax (519) 746-3317
http://www.mindflight.com

Portable data products that connect to a PC parallel port or a SCSI port

Minolta Corporation
101 Williams Drive
Ramsey, NJ 07446
(201) 825-4000
http://www.minolta.com

Graphics-specific input and output devices

Miro Computer Products, Inc.

Pinnacle Systems, Inc.
280 N. Bernardo Avenue
Mountain View, CA 94043
(650) 526-1600
fax (650) 526-1601
faxback (650) 237-1973
http://www.miro.com

Multimedia products

Mita Copystar America, Inc.

225 Sand Road
P.O. Box 40008
Fairfield, NJ 07004-0008
(800) ABC-MITA, (201) 808-8444
tech support (800) 652-6482
fax (201) 882-4415

Multifunctional printers

Mitsuba Corporation

1925 Wright Avenue
Laverne, CA 91750
(800) 648-7822
tech support (888) 999-2186
http://www.mitsuba.com

Custom file servers, PCs, and notebooks

Mitsubishi Consumer Electronics America, Inc.

Americas Corporate Office
Washington, D.C. Office
1150 Connecticut Avenue, N.W.
Suite 1010
Washington, D.C. 20036, U.S.A.
(202) 223-3424
fax: (202) 775-0116
http://www.mitsubishielectric-usa.com/

Mitsumi Electronics Corporation

6210 N. Beltline Road, Suite 170
Irving, TX 75063
(800) 648-7864, (800) 801-7927,
(214) 550-7300
BBS (415) 691-4469
http://www.mitsumi.com

Keyboards, mice, floppy disk drives, and CD-ROM drives

Motorola ISG

5000 Bradford Dr.
Huntsville, AL 35805
(205) 430-8000
faxback (800) 221-4380
outside of North America
(205) 430-8894
http://www.mot.com/mims/isg/

Modems

Motorola PCMCIA Products Division

50 East Commerce Drive
Shaumburg, IL 60173
(800) 4A-PCMCIA
http://www.mot.com

MP Computer Parts Supply Co., Ltd.

150 Commercial Street
Sunnyvale, CA 94086
(408) 738-3388

Cables, switches, connectors, computer accessories, and data communication accessories

MTC America, Inc.
2500 Westchester Avenue, Suite 110
Purchase, NY 10577
(800) MTC-CDRS

Mitsui Gold CD-R device

Multi-Tech Systems, Inc.
2205 Woodale Drive
Mounds View, MN 55112
(800) 328-9717
tech support (800) 972-2439
fax (612) 785-9874
http://www.multitech.com

Multiwave Technology, Inc.
15318 Valley Boulevard
City of Industry, CA 91746
(800) 234-3358, (800) 587-1730,
(818) 330-7030
fax (818) 333-4609
http://www.mwave.com

Mustek, Inc.
121 Waterworks Way, # 100
Irvine, CA 92618
(949) 788-3600
fax (949) 788-3670
http://www.mustek.com

Scanners

Nanao USA Corporation
EIZO NANAO Technologies, Inc.
5710 Warland Drive
Cypress, CA 90630
(562) 431-5011
fax (562) 431-4811
http://www.nanao.com

Monitors

National Semiconductor
Personal Systems Division
2900 Semiconductor Drive
Santa Clara, CA 95052
(408) 721-5000
http://www.nsc.com

Silicon products and systems for personal computers and peripherals

NCE Storage Solutions
9717 Pacific Heights Blvd.
San Diego, CA 92121
(619) 658-9720, (800) 767-2587
fax (619) 658-9733
Web: http://www.ncegroup.com

Emerald System backup devices

NCR Corp.
1700 South Patterson Blvd.
Dayton, OH 45479
(937) 445-5000
fax (937) 445-4184
http://www.ncr.com

NEC Technologies, Inc.
1414 Massachusetts Avenue
Boxborough, MA 01719
(508) 264-8000, (800) 338-9549
pre-sales information (800) 632-4636
http://www.nec.com

New Media Corporation
One Technology Park, building A
Irvine, CA 92718
(714) 453-0100, (800) CARDS-4-U
fax (714) 453-0114
http://www.newmediacorp.com

NewCom, Inc.
31166 Via Colinas
Westlake Village, CA 91362
(818) 597-3200
fax (818) 597-3211
http://www.newcominc.com/

Internal and external fax modems, high-fidelity stereo sound cards, and multimedia kits

Nokia Display Products
1505 Bridgeway Boulevard
Sausalito, CA 94965
(800) 396-6541, (415) 331-0322
http://www.nokia.com

Nokia Mobile Phones
Corporate Communications
6000 Connection Drive
Irving, Texas 75039
(972) 894-4573
fax (972) 894-4831
http://www.nokia.com

NSA/Hitachi
100 Lowder Brook Drive
Westwood, MA 02090
(800) 441-4832, (617) 461-8300
tech support (800) 536-6721
http://www.nsa_hitachi.com/

Number Nine Computer Corporation
18 Hartwell Avenue
Lexington, MA 02173
(781) 869-7214, (800) GET-NINE
fax (781) 869-7222
http://www.nine.com

Ocean Information Systems Inc. (Octek)
688 Arrow Grand Circle,
Covina, CA 91722
(818) 339-8888
fax (818) 859-7668
http://www.ocean-usa.com/ocean
http://www.oceanhk.com

PC computer systems, motherboards, cases, power supplies, multimedia products, and peripherals

Okidata Corporation
532 Fellowship Road
Mt. Laurel, NJ 08054
(609) 235-2600
(800) OKIDATA or (800) 654-8326
http://www.okidata.com

Olivetti Office USA

765 US Highway 202
Bridgewater, NJ 08807
(908) 526-8200
http://www.olivettilexicon.com/
http://www.olivetti.com/

Orchestra MultiSystems, Inc.

12300 Edison Way
Garden Grove, CA 92841
(800) 237-9988, (714) 891-3861
fax (714) 891-2661
http://www.orchestra.com

Orchid Technology

221 Warren Avenue
Fremont, CA 94539
(800) 577-0977, (510) 651-2300,
(510) 661-3000
fax (510) 651-6692
Fax-on-demand (510) 661-3199
BBS (510) 651-6837
CompuServe: GO ORCHID
http://www.orchid.com

Orevox USA Corporation

248 N. Puente Avenue
P.O. Box 2655
City of Industry, CA 91746
information (626) 333-6803
orders (800) 237-0700
fax (626) 336-3748
www.dynavox.com

Computer cases and multimedia speakers

Pacom Data, Inc.

1257 B Tasman Drive
Sunnyvale, CA 94089
(408) 752-1590

Monitors and multimedia products

Padix Co. Ltd.

Rockfire
18F-3, No. 75, Sec. 1, Hsin Tai Wu Road
Hsih-Chih, Taipei, Taiwan ROC
(886) 2-6981478

PC-compatible game controllers and joysticks

Panasonic Communications & Systems Co.

Two Panasonic Way
Secaucus, NJ 07094
(787) 750-4300, (800) 742-8086
fax (787) 768-2910
http://www.panasonic.com

Pantex Computer, Inc.

10301 Harwin Drive
Houston, TX 77036
(713) 988-1688, (888) PANTEX-1
fax (713) 988-2838
http://pantexcom.com/

Motherboards, bare-bones systems

Pathlight Technology, Inc.
Nine Brown Road
Ithaca, NY 14850
(800) 334-4812, (607) 266-4000
fax (607) 266-4010
http://www.pathlight.com

Storage I/O and networking interface technologies and products

PC Cables and Parts
One-Up Computer
2331 NE 50th Court
Lighthouse Point, FL 33064
(954) 418-0817
fax (954) 418-0835
http://www.pccables.com

PC Concepts, Inc.
10318 Norris Avenue
Pacoima, CA 91331
(800) 735-6071

Computer accessories including color-coded cables, manual and auto data switches, printer network devices, surge protectors, and multimedia products

PC Power & Cooling, Inc.
5995 Avenida Encinas
Carlsbad, CA 92008
(619) 931-5200

CPU cooler for Intel's P6 processor

PCMCIA (Personal Computer Memory Card Int'l. Association)
4529 Lillian Ct.
La Canada, CA 91011
(408) 433-2273

Pengo Computer Accessories
16018-C Adelante Street
Irwindale, CA 91702
(888) PENGO99, (626) 815-9885
fax (626) 815-9964
http://www.pengo.com/

Floppy disks, dust covers, keyboard drawers, disk file boxes, tool kits, and various workstation accessories

Phillips Consumer Electronics Co.
One Phillips Drive
Knoxville, TN 37914
(423) 521-4316, (800) 531-0039
http://www.philipsmagnavox.com

Phoenix Technologies, Ltd.
411 East Plumeria
San Jose, CA 95134
(408) 570-1000
fax (408) 570-1001
http://www.ptltd.com

PhoenixBIOS for desktops, Note-BIOS for notebook computers, and PhoenixPICO for handheld and embedded systems

Pioneer New Media Technologies, Inc.
Multimedia & Mass Storage
2265 E. 220th Street
Long Beach, CA 90810
(310) 952-2111, (800) 527-3766
fax (310) 952-2990

http://www.pioneerusa.com

CD-ROM and CD-R products for multimedia and mass storage applications

Pionex Technologies, Inc.
Three Riverview Dr.
Somerset, NJ 08873
(732) 764-5680
fax (732) 563-2661
http://www.phoenix.com

Pixie Technologies
46771 Fremont Boulevard
Fremont, CA 94538
(510) 440-9721
fax (510) 440-9356
http://www.pixie.com

Monitors

PKWare, Inc.
9025 N. Deerwood Drive
Brown Deer, WI 53223
(414) 354-8699
http://www.pkware.com

PKZIP compression utilities

Play, Inc.
2890 Kilgore Road
Rancho Cordova, CA 95670-6133
(916) 851-0800, (800) 306-PLAY
fax (916) 851-0801
http://www.play.com

Snappy Video Snapshot software

Plextor USA
4255 Burton Drive
Santa Clara, CA 95054
(800) 886-3935, (408) 980-1838
http://www.plextor.com

CD-ROM drives

Portrait Display Labs
5117 Johnson Drive
Pleasanton, CA 94588
(510) 227-2700
fax (925) 227-2705
http://www.portrait.com

Monitors

Powercom America, Inc.
1040A S. Melrose Street
Placentia, CA 92670-7119
(714) 632-8889
fax (714) 632-8868
http://www.powercom-usa.com/

Modems and UPSs

PowerQuest Corporation
1083 North State Street
Orem, UT 84057
(800) 379-2566
http://www.powerquest.com

Manufacturer of Partition Magic, software utility for creating and managing disk partitions

Practical Peripherals
P.O. Box 921789
Norcross, Georgia 30092-7789
(770) 840-9966
http://www.practinet.com

Princeton Graphic Systems

2801 South Yale Street
Santa Ana, CA 92704
(800) 747-6249, (714) 751-8405
fax (714) 751-5736
http://www.prgr.com

Monitors

Procom Technology

2181 Dupont Drive
Irvine, CA 92715
(714) 852-1000, (800) 800-8600
fax (714) 852-1221
http://www.procom.com

Hard drives, backup devices

Professional Technologies

21038 Commerce Pointe Drive
Walnut, CA 91789
(800) 949-5018, (909) 468-3730
fax (909) 468-1372

Computer systems

ProLink Computer

15336 East Valley Blvd.
City of Industry, CA 91746
(626) 369-3883, (800) 686-8110
fax (626) 369-4883
http://www.prolink-usa.com/

QLogic Corporation

3545 Harbor Blvd.
Costa Mesa, CA 92626
(714) 438-2200, (800) 662-4471
fax (714) 668-5008
http://www.qlc.com

Quadrant International, Inc.

269 Great Valley Parkway
Malvern, PA 19355
(800) 700-0362
tech support (610) 251-9999
fax (610) 695-2592
e-mail: qi-tech@quadrant.com
http://www.quadrant.com

Video editing and capture products

Quantex Microsystems, Inc.

400B Pierce Street
Somerset, NJ 08873
(800) 864-9022
fax (732) 563-9262
http://www.quantex.com

Quantum Corporation

500 McCarthy Boulevard
Milpitas, CA 95053
(800) 624-5545, (408) 894-4000
fax (408) 894-5217
http://www.quantum.com

Quarterdeck Select

13160 Mindanao Way
Marina del Rey, CA 90292-9705
(800) 225-8148
fax (813) 523-2331
http://www.quarterdeck.com

Troubleshooting tools

Quatech, Inc.
662 Wolf Ledges Pky.
Akron, OH 44311
(330) 434-3154, (800) 553-1170
fax (330) 434-1409
http://www.quatech.com

Communication, data acquisition, industrial I/O, and PCMCIA products

QuickPath Systems, Inc.
46723 Fremont Boulevard
Fremont, CA 94538
(800) 995-8828, (510) 440-7288
fax (510) 440-7289
e-mail: qpinfo@quickpath.com
http://www.quickpath.com/

QuickShot Technology, Inc.
QuickShot Technology, Inc.
950 Yosemite Drive
Milpitas, CA
(408) 263-4163
fax (408) 263-4005
http://www.quickshot.com

QVS, Inc.
2731 Crimson Canyon Drive
Las Vegas, NV 89128
(800) 344-3371

Computer cables, computer electronic products

Regal Electronics, Inc.
4251 Burton Drive
Santa Clara, CA 95054
(408) 988-2288, (800) 882-8086
fax (408) 988-2797, (800) 345-2831
http://www.regalusa.com/

Plug-and-play CD-ROM changers and multimedia speakers

Relisys (Teco)
320 S. Milpitas Boulevard
Milpitas, CA 95035
(408) 945-9000
http://www.relisys.com

Video monitors, scanners, and multi-functional facsimile products

Repay Trading, Inc.
3345 Wilshire Boulevard, Suite 901
Los Angeles, CA 90010
(213) 385-2580

CD-ROMs and CD-R drives

Reveal Computer Products, Inc.
CNM Corp
(900) 225-3000
http://www.reveal.com/

Rockwell Telecommunications
Multimedia Communications Division
4311 Jamboree Road
Newport Beach, CA 92658
(714) 833-4600, (800) 854-8099
fax (714) 221-6375
http://www.nb.rockwell.com

Modems

Roland Corporation U.S.
Desktop Media Production
7200 Dominion Cir.
Los Angeles, CA 90040
(213) 685-5141
http://www.rolandus.com

Sound cards, PCMCIA cards, MIDI keyboards, powered speakers, and music software

Rose Electronics
10707 Stancliff
Houston, TX 77099
(281) 933-7673, (800) 333-9343
fax (281) 933-0044
http://www.rosel.com

Keyboard and video control products, print servers, and data switches

S & S Software International
17 New England Executive Park
Burlington, MA 01803
(617) 273-7400, (888) 377-6566
fax (781) 273-7474
http://www.drsolomon.com

Dr. Solomon's Anti-Virus Toolkit

S. T. Research Corp.
8419 Terminal Rd.
Newington, VA 22122
(703) 550-7000

Palmtop computers

S3, Inc.
2841 Mission College Blvd.
P.O. Box 58058
Santa Clara, CA 95052-8058
(408) 588-8000
fax (408) 980-5444
http://www.s3.com

Graphics acceleration products

Sager Computer
18005 Cortney Court
City of Industry, CA 91748
(800) 669-1624, (818) 964-8682
fax (818) 964-2381

Notebook computers

Sampo Technology, Inc.
5550 Peachtree Ind. Boulevard
Norcross, GA 30071
(770) 449-6220
fax (770) 447-1109
http://www.sampotech.com

Monitors

Samsung America, Inc.
14251 E. Firestone Boulevard
La Mirada, CA 90638
(310) 802-2211
http://www.samsung.com

CPU cooler for the Pentium and P6

Samsung Electronics America, Inc.
Information Systems Division
105 Challenger Road
Ridgefield Park, NJ 07660
(800) 933-4110, (201) 229-4000

http://www.samsung.com

Notebook PCs, color monitors, hard disk drives, and laser printers

Samtron

A Div. of Samsung Electronics America
18600 Broadwick Street
Rancho Dominguez, CA 90220
(310) 537-7000

Monitors

Sanyo Energy (USA) Corporation

2001 Sanyo Avenue
San Diego, CA 92173
(619) 661-6620

Batteries and amorphous solar cells

Sanyo Fisher (USA) Corporation

Office Automation Products
21350 Lassen Street
Chatsworth, CA 91311
(818) 998-7322
http://www.sanyo.com

Multifunctional fax machines, CD-ROM drives, notebooks, desktop personal computers, monitors

Seagate Software

1098 Alta
Mountain View, CA 94043
(650) 335-8000
http://www.seagatesoftware.com

Seagate Technology

920 Disc Drive
Scotts Valley, CA 95066-6550
(831) 438-6550
(831) 936-1687
fax (831) 936-1685
http://www.seagatesoftware.com

Hard drives

Seattle Telecom & Data, Inc.

18005 N.E. 68th, Suite A115
Redmond, WA 98052
(208) 883-8440

Manufacturer of PS/2-compatible accelerator boards for most Micro Channel models

Sempro L.L.C.

2459 SE. T.V. Highway, Suite 133
Hillsboro, OR 97123
(503) 693-7894

PC gaming peripherals

Sharp Electronics Corporation

Sharp Plaza
Mahwah, NJ 07430
(201) 529-8200, (800) BE-SHARP
fax (201) 529-8425
http://www.sharp-usa.com

LCDs and LCD-based products

Shining Technology, Inc.

10533 Progress Way, Suite C
Cypress, CA 90630
(714) 761-9598

Parallel I/O products to EIDE (supporting HDD and CD-ROMs)

Shuttle Computer International, Inc.

1161 Cadillac Ct.
Milpitas, CA 95035
(408) 945-1480

Pentium 75-180MHz PCI motherboards with pipeline SRAM, EDO, and DRAM support

Shuttle Technology

43218 Christy Street
Fremont, CA 94538
(510) 656-0180

Parallel port interfacing technology

Sicos Products

SICOS Computer Vertrieb Deutschland GmbHAn den Hirtenäckern
9 - 63791 Karlstein
06188/95999-0
fax 06188/95999-59
http://www.sicos.com

Scanners

Sigma Interactive Solutions Corporation

46515 Landing Parkway
Fremont, CA 94538
(510) 624-4928

Simple Technology

3001 Daimler Street
Santa Ana, CA 92705
(714) 476-1180
(800) 4-SIMPLE or (800) 474-6753
http://www.simpletech.com

Memory and PC card products

SL Waber

520 Fellowship Road
Mount Laurel, NJ 08054
(800) 634-1485, (609) 866-8888
fax (609) 866-1945
http://www.waber.com

Uninterruptible power supplies

Smart and Friendly

20520 Nordhoff Street
Chatsworth, CA 91311
(800) 542-8838, (818) 772-8001
fax (818) 772-2888
http://www.smartandfriendly.com/

CD recording devices

SMART Modular Technologies, Inc.

4305 Cushing Pkwy.
Fremont, CA 94538
(510) 623-1231, (800) 956-7627
fax (510) 623-1434
http://www.smartm.com

DRAM, SRAM, and Flash memory modules and upgrade cards

Smile International, Inc.

175 Sunflower Avenue
Costa Mesa, CA 92626
(714) 546-0336, (800) USMILE-2
fax (714) 546-0315
http://www.smilekfc.com

Sony Corporation

One Sony Drive
Park Ridge, NJ 07645
(201) 930-1000
sales (800) 352-7669
tech support (800) 326-9551
http://www.sony.com

Digital technologies for computers, communications, audio, and video

Spider Graphics, Inc.

580 Charcot Avenue
San Jose, CA 95131
(408) 526-0535

Graphics and multimedia accelerators

SRS Labs, Inc.

2909 Daimler Street
Santa Ana, CA 92705
(714) 442-1070, (800) 243-2733
fax (714) 852-1099
http://www.srslabs.com

3D sound technology

Stac Electronics

12636 High Bluff Drive
San Diego, CA 92130-2093
(619) 794-4300, (800) 522-7822
fax (619) 794-4575
http://www.stac.com

Backup and disaster recovery products

STB Systems, Inc.

1651 North Glenville, Suite 210
Richardson, TX 75085
(214) 234-8750, (214) 669-0989
fax (214) 234-1306
tech support fax (214) 669-1326
BBS (214) 437-9615
e-mail: support@stb.com
http://www.stb.com

Storage Technology Corporation

2270 S. 88th Street
Louisville, CO 80028-4341
(303) 673-5151, (800) STK-2217
fax (303) 673-5019
http://www.storagetek.com

StorageTek storage products

Stracon, Inc.

1672 Kaiser Avenue
Irvine, CA 92714
(714) 851-2288

Memory upgrades for PCs, laptops, and workstations

Supra Corporation

Diamond Multimedia
2880 Junction Avenue
San Jose, CA 95134-1922
(408) 325-7000, (800) 468-5846
fax (408) 325-7070
http://www.diamondmm.com

Modems

Swan Instruments
Drive Division
3000 Olcott
Santa Clara, CA 95054
(408) 727-9711

Ultra High-Capacity (UHC) Flexible Disk Drives

Symantec Corporation
175 West Broadway
Eugene, OR 97401
(800) 441-7234, (541) 334-6054
outside the U.S. and Canada (541) 334-6054
tech support (541) 465-8420
fax (541) 984-8020
http://www.symantec.com

Norton Utilities, Norton Anti-Virus software

Synnex Information Technologies, Inc.
3797 Spinnaker Court
Fremont, CA 94538
(510) 656-3333, (800) 756-9888
http://www.synnex.com

SyQuest Technology
47071 Bayside Pky.
Fremont, CA 94538
(510) 226-4000, (800) 245-2278
fax (510) 226-4108
http://www.syquest.com

Removable storage products

Tagram System Corporation
1451-B Edinger Avenue
Tustin, CA 92680
(800) TAGRAMS, (714) 258-3222
tech support (800) 443-5761
fax (714) 258-3220
http://www.tagram.com

Tahoe Peripherals
999 Tahoe Boulevard
Incline Village, NV 89451
(800) 288-6040
fax (702) 832-3611

Tandberg Data
2685-A Park Center Drive
Simi Valley, CA 93065
(805) 579-1000, (800) 826-3237
fax (805) 579-2555
http://www.tandberg.com

SCSI QIC tape backup drives and kits

Tanisys Technology Corporation
12201 Technology Boulevard, Suite 160
Austin, TX 78727-6101
(800) 533-1744
http:// www.tanisys.com

Memory products

Tatung Company of America, Inc.
2850 El Presidio Street
Long Beach, CA 90810
(310) 637-2105, (800) 827-2850
fax (310) 637-8484
http://www.tatung.com

Monitors

Vendors Guide

TDK Electronics Corporation
12 Harbor Park Drive
Port Washington, NY 11050
(516) 625-0100, (800) TDK-TAPE
fax (516) 625-0171
http://www.tdk.com

Optical and magnetic recording media

TEAC America, Inc.
Data Storage Products Division
7733 Telegraph Road
Montebello, CA 90640
(213) 726-0303
tech support (213) 727-4860
tech support fax (213) 727-7674
http://www.teac.com

CD-ROM, tape, and floppy drives

Techmedia Computer Systems Corporation
7345 Orangewood Avenue
Garden Grove, CA 92641
(800) 379-0077, (714) 379-6677
fax (714) 379-6688

Monitors

Tektronix, Inc.
P.O. Box 7000 MS 63-580
Wilsonville, OR 97070
(800) 835-6100, (503) 682-7377
fax (503) 682-2980
http://www.tek.com

Tempest Micro
375 N. Citrus Avenue #611
Azusa, CA 91704
(800) 818-5163, (800) 848-5167,
(818) 858-5163
fax (818) 858-5166

Texas Instruments, Inc.
P.O. Box 650311
M/S 3914
Dallas, TX 75265
(800) 848-3927, (214) 917-6278
http://www.ti.com

ThrustMaster, Inc.
7175 NW Evergreen Parkway, #400
Hillsboro, OR 97124
(503) 615-3200
fax (503) 615-3300
http://www.thrustmaster.com

Thunder Max Corporation
15011 Parkway Loop, Suite A
Tustin, CA 92680
(714) 259-8800

TMC Research Corporation
631 S. Milpitas Boulevard
Milpitas, CA 95035
(408) 262-0888

Windows 95-compatible motherboards and SCSI host adapters

Toshiba America Information Systems, Inc.
9740 Irvine Boulevard
Irvine, CA 92718
(800) 457-7777, (714) 583-3000
sales (888) 598-7802
http://www.toshiba.com

CD-ROMs, hard drives

TouchStone Software Corporation

2124 Main Street
Huntington Beach, CA 92648
(800) 531-0450, (714) 969-7746
fax (714) 969-4444
http://www.checkit.com

CheckIt Pro, WinCheckIt 4 diagnostic software

Trend Micro Devices

10101 N. DeAnza Blvd. Suite 400
Cupertino, CA 95014
(408) 257-1500, (800) 228-5651
fax (408) 257-2003
http://www.trendmicro.com

PC-cillin anti-virus software

Trident Microsystems, Inc.

189 N. Bernardo Avenue
Mountain View, CA 94043
(415) 691-9211
http://www.trid.com

32- and 64-bit integrated graphics and multimedia video processing controllers for PC compatibles

Truevision, Inc.

2500 Walsh Avenue
Santa Clara, CA 95051
(800) 522-TRUE, (408) 562-4200
fax (408) 562-4200
tech support fax (317) 576-7770
BBS (317) 577-8777
e-mail: support@truevision.com
CompuServe: GO TRUEVISION
http://www.truevision.com

Tseng Labs, Inc.

6 Terry Drive
Newtown, PA 18940
(215) 968-0502
http://www.tseng.com

Graphics and video controllers

Turtle Beach Systems

5690 Stewart Avenue
Fremont, CA 94538
(510) 624-6200
tech support (510) 624-6265
fax (510) 624-6291
tech support fax (510) 624-6292
faxback (510) 624-6296
BBS (510) 624-6279
e-mail: support@tbeach.com
CompuServe: GO TURTLE, GO TBMIDI
http://www.tbeach.com

Tyan Computer

3288 Laurelview Court
Fremont, CA 94538
sales (510) 651-8868
tech support (510) 440-8808
fax (510) 651-7688
http://www.tyan.com

High-end motherboards and add-on cards

U&C AMERICA
5931 N. Reno Avenue
Temple City, CA 91780
(818) 287-4488
fax: (818) 287-4499
http://www.superpen.com

Makers of SuperPen

U.S. Robotics Corp.
3Com Corp
Great America Site
5400 Bayfront Plaza
Santa Clara, CA 95052
(408) 326-5000
fax (408) 326-5001
http://www.3com.com

UMAX Technologies
3353 Gateway Boulevard
Fremont, CA 94538
(800) 562-0031, (510) 651-9488
fax (510) 651-8834
http://www.umax.com

Unisys Corporation
Personal Computer Division
2700 N. First Street
San Jose, CA 95134-2028
(800) 448-1424
http://www.unisys.com

Notebook and desktop systems

Valitek
100 University Drive
Amherst, MA 01102
(413) 549-2700, (800) 825-4835
fax (413) 549-2900
http://www.valitek.com

Backup devices

Verbatim Corporation
1200 W.T. Harris Boulevard
Charlotte, NC 28262
(704) 547-6500, (800) 538-8589
http://www.verbatimcorp.com

Optical discs, tape products, floppy disks, CD-R and CD-ROM, and imaging products

Video Electronics Standards Association (VESA)
2150 N. First Street, Suite 440
San Jose, CA 95131
(408) 435-0333

ViewSonic Corporation
20480 East Business Parkway
Walnut, CA 91789
(800) 888-8583, (909) 869-7976
http://www.viewsonic.com

ViewSonic and Optiquest monitors

VLSI Technology, Inc.
VLSI Technology, Inc.
1109 McKay Dr.
San Jose, CA 95131
(408) 434-3000
http://www.vlsi.com

64-bit+graphics controller supporting SGRAM

Voyetra Technologies
5 Odell Plaza
Yonkers, NY 10701
(914) 966-0600
sales (800) 233-9377
http://www.voyetra.com

Multimedia sound products

WACOM Technology Corporation
501 S.E. Columbia Shores Blvd.,
Suite 300
Vancouver, WA 98661
(800) 922-9348, (360) 750-8882
fax (360) 750-8924
BBS (360) 750-0638 (300 to 14400 baud, 8 bis, no parity, 1 stop bit)
e-mail: sales@wacom.com, support@wacom.com
http://www.wacom.com

Pen tablets

Weitek Corporation
1060 E. Arques Avenue
Sunnyvale, CA 94086
(408) 738-8400
http://www.weitek.com

Processors

Western Digital
8105 Irvine Center Drive
Costa Mesa, CA 92718
(714) 932-5000
tech support (800) 275-4932
http://www.wdc.com

IDE hard drives, integrated circuits, and board-level products for the microcomputer industry

Wetech Electronics Inc.
14704 South Redburn Ave.
Santa Fe Springs, CA 90670
(562) 802-5960
fax (562) 802-3158
http://iready.com/wetech/

Monitors

Willow Peripherals
190 Willow Ave.
Bronx, NY 10454
(718) 402-0203, (800) 444-1585
fax (718) 402-9603
e-mail: peripherals@willow.com
http://www.willow.com

Manufacturer of video output and video capture products

Winner Products (USA) Inc.
21128 Commerce Pointe Drive
Walnut, CA 91789
(909) 595-2490
fax (909) 595-1483
http://www.joystick.com

Joysticks and other peripherals

Wyse Technology
3471 N. First Street
San Jose, CA 95134
(408) 473-1200, (800) GET-WYSE
http://www.wyse.com

Advanced video display terminals

Xerox Corporation

80 Linden Oaks Pky.
Rochester, NY 14625
(800) ASK-XEROX
tech support (800) 821-2797
http://www.xerox.com

Printers

Xircom

2300 Corporate Center Drive
Thousand Oaks, CA 91320-1420
(800) 438-4526
tech support (805) 376-9200
fax (805) 376-9311
http://www.xircom.com

Yamaha Corporation of America

CBX Group
6600 Orangethorpe Avenue
Buena Park, CA 90620
(714) 522-9011
http://www.yamaha.com

Computer sound products

Zenith Data Systems

2455 Horse Pen Road, Suite 100
Herndon, VA 22071
(703) 713-3000
http://www.zds.com

Desktops and wireless technology

Zoom Technologies

207 South Street
Boston, MA 02111
(800) 631-3116
fax (617) 423-3923
http://www.zoomtel.com

Data Recovery Vendors

The following vendors specialize in products for recovering data from damaged hard drives:

AA Computech

28170 Avenue Crocker #105
Valencia, CA 91355
(800) 360-6801, (805) 257-6801
tech support (805) 257-6804
fax (805) 257-6805
http://www.scvnet.com/~bobs

AMS (American Micro Solutions)

15461 Redhill Avenue, Suite E
Tustin, CA 92680
(800) 580-2525, (714) 258-8818
fax (714) 258-8918
e-mail: ams@calypso.com
http://www.calypso.com/ams

Aurora Electronics

1101 National Drive
Sacramento, CA 95834
(800) 767-9281, (916) 928-1107
fax (916) 928-1006
e-mail: sacrepair@aur.com

Data Recovery Labs

1315 Lawrence Avenue East
Unit 502-503
Don Mills, Ontario, Canada M3A 3R3
(800) 563-1167, (416) 510-6990
fax (416) 510-6992
e-mail: admin@datarec.com
http://www.datarec.com

Data Recovery Labs, Inc.

24705 US 19 North, Suite 312
Clearwater, Florida 34623
(813) 725-3818
fax (813) 712-0800
http://webcoast.com/drl/

Data Retrieval Services

1040 Kapp Drive
Clearwater, FL 34625
(813) 461-5900, (800) 952-7530
fax (813) 461-5668

Disk Drive Repair, Inc.

863 Industry Drive, Bldg. 23
Seattle, WA 98188
(206) 575-3181
fax (206) 575-1811

Disktec

5875 W. 34th Street
Houston, TX 77092
(713) 681-4691
fax (713) 681-5851

Drive Service Company

3303 Harbor Blvd., Suite E-7
Costa Mesa, CA 92626
(714) 549-DISK (714-549-3475)
fax (714) 549-9752
e-mail: jimc@driveservice.com
http://www.driveservice.com

DriveSavers Data Recovery

400 Bel Marin Keys Blvd.
Novato, CA 94949
(800) 440-1904, (415) 382-2000
fax (415) 883-0780
e-mail: recovery@drivesavers.com
http://www.drivesavers.com

Electric Renaissance

105 Newfield Avenue
Edison, NJ 08837
(908) 417-9090
fax (908) 471-9099

Excalibur Data Recovery, Inc.

101 Billerica Avenue, Bldg. #5
N. Billerica, MA 01862-1256
(800) 466-0893, (508) 663-1700
fax (508) 670-5901
e-mail: brnonteer@excalibur
.ultranet.com
http://www.excaliburdr.com

Lazarus

381 Clementina Street
San Francisco, CA 94103
(415) 495-5556, (800) 341-DATA
fax (415) 495-5553
http://www.lazarus.com

Micro Com

19011 Ventura Boulevard
Tarzana, CA 91356

(800) 469-2549, (818) 881-7417
fax (818) 881-8015

OnTrack Data Recovery, Inc.
6321 Bury Drive
Eden Prairie, MN 55346
(800) 872-2599, (612) 937-5161
fax (612) 937-5750
http://www.ontrack.com

Total Peripheral Repair
(a division of Technical Parts, Inc.)
4204 Sorrento Valley Blvd., Suite A
San Diego, CA 92121-1412
(800) 890-0880, (619) 552-2288
fax (619) 552-2290
e-mail (sales): sales@recoverdata.com
e-mail (service):service@recoverdata.com
http://www.recoverdata.com/

Valtron Technologies, Inc.
28309 Avenue Crocker
Valencia, CA 91355
(800) 2VALTRON, (805) 257-0333
fax (805) 257-0113

VANTAGE Technologies, Inc.
Four John Tyler Street, PO Box 1570
Merrimack, NH 03054
(800) ITS-LOST or (800) 487-5678,
(603) 429-3019, (603) 883-6249
fax (603) 883-1973
e-mail: recovery@vantagetech.com
http://www.vantagetech.com

Memory Vendors

Here are a number of computer memory dealers. Many will also buy your old memory; however, call and check first before sending anything.

Avalon Micro
688 #D Wells Road
Boulder City, NV 89005
(800) 610-1215, (702) 293-2300
fax (702) 293-4453

The Chip Merchant
World 1580 Oakland Rd #C208
San Jose, CA 95131
(408) 441-1477
fax (408) 441-1463
http://www.chipmerchant.com/

DMS (Data Memory Systems)
24 Keewaydin Drive
Salem, NH 03079
(800) 662-7466, (603) 898-7750
fax (603) 898-6585
e-mail: datamem@aol.com
http://www.datamem.com

H&J Electronics International, Inc.
2700 West Cypress Creek Road
Ft. Lauderdale, FL 33309
(800) 275-2447, (954) 971-7750
fax (954) 979-9028

Laptop, printer, and PC memory for name-brand computers

McDonald and Associates: The Memory Place

2544 South 156th Circle
Omaha, NE 68130
(800) 694-1307, (800) 306-8901,
(402) 691-8548
fax (402) 691-8548
e-mail: buymemory@aol.com
http://www.buymemory.com

Memory 4 Less

2622 West Lincoln, Suite 104
Anaheim, CA 92801
(800) 821-3354, (714) 826-5981
fax (714) 821-3361

Memory and CPU Warehouse

8361 East Evans Road, Suite 105
Scottsdale, AZ 85260
(800) RAM-7091, (602) 443-0696
fax (602) 443-0918

The Memory Man

7225 NW 25th Street
Miami, FL 33166
(800) 854-0067, (305) 418-4149
fax (305) 418-4277
http://www.memory-man.com

Worldwide Technologies

437 Chestnut Street
Philadelphia, PA 19106
(800) 457-6937, (215) 922-0050
fax (215) 922-0116
http://www.worldwidetechnologies.com

They carry motherboards and drives, too.

BIOS Upgrade Vendors

These are vendors who sell upgrade BIOS ROM to support new hard and floppy drive types, solve some compatibility problem, or add a new feature (such as built-in SETUP).

If you've got a clone, your clone may have a compatible BIOS written by Phoenix Technologies. Phoenix periodically updates their BIOS to speed them up, support new devices, and fix bugs. The person whom you bought the clone from, however, may have gone on to selling land in Florida. You can buy upgrades for your Phoenix ROM from Wholesale Direct.

Alltech Electronics Co.

1300 E. Edinger Avenue, Suite D
Santa Ana, CA 92705
(714) 543-5011
fax (714) 543-0553
e-mail: allelec.com
http://www.allelec.com

TTi Technologies, Inc.

1445 Donlon Street #9
Ventura, CA 93003
(800) 541-1943
e-mail: mike@ttitech.com

Unicore Software

1538 Turnpike Street
N. Andover, MA 01845
(800) 800-2467, (508) 686-6468

fax (508) 683-1630
http://www.unicore.com

Storage Device Vendors

In case you're looking specifically for a new hard drive or tape drive, here are a few vendors who specialize in storage devices:

AA Computech

28170 Avenue Crocker #105
Valencia, CA 91355
(800) 360-6801, (805) 257-6801
fax (805) 257-6805
http://www.scvnet.com/~bobs

Hard drives and data recovery

Ashtek, Inc.

2600-B Walnut Avenue
Tustin, CA 92680
(800) 801-9400
fax (714) 505-2693

Buy and sell hard drives and memory SIMMs

Bason Hard Drive Warehouse

(800) 238-4453, (818) 727-9054
fax (818) 727-9066
http://www.basoncomputer.com

Dirt Cheap Drives

3716 Timber Drive
Dickinson, TX 77539
(800) 786-1170, (713) 534-4140
fax (713) 534-6452

Hard drives, CD-ROMs, optical drives, tape backup units

Drive Outlet Center

3412 Milwaukee Avenue #445
Northbrook, IL 60062
(800) 260-5930
fax (847) 419-0705

Hard drives, CD-ROMs, optical drives, tape backup units

MegaHaus Hard Drives

2201 Pine Drive
Dickinson, TX 77539
(800) 786-1185, (713) 534-3919
fax (713) 534-6580
http://www.MegaHaus.com/

Drives, controller cards, drive accessories

Storage USA

101 Reighard Avenue
Williamsport, PA 17701
(800) 538-DISK, (717) 327-9200
fax (717) 327-1217
http://www.storageusa.com

Miscellaneous Computer Products Vendors

Many manufacturers also sell their own products. Here, however, are the dealers who sell a wide range of useful computer parts and peripherals:

1st Compu Choice

740 Beta Drive - Unit G
Cleveland, OH 44143
(800) 345-8880, (216) 460-1002
fax (216) 460-1066

A Matter of Fax

65 Worth Street
New York, NY 10013
(800) 433-3FAX, (212) 941-8877

Fax machines, printers, scanners, other components and peripherals

A+ Factory Outlet

526 S. Coralridge Pl.
City of Industry, CA 91746
(800) 717 7060, (818) 937-3090
fax (818) 937-3091
e-mail: info@datatrend.com

Computers and parts; a liquidator of computer products

A2Z Computers

701 Beta Drive, Unit 19
Mayfield Village, OH 44142
(800) 983-8889, (216) 442-9028
fax (216) 442-8891
http://www.a2zcomp.com

Computer components and peripherals

ABC Drives

8717 Darby Ave.
Northridge, CA 91325
(818) 885-7157
http://www.abcdrives.com/

Specializes in the sale and service of most major storage devices, including hard-to-find or obsolete drives

ACIS Corporation

2381 Philmont Avenue, Suite 219
Huntingdon Valley, PA 19006
(800) 223-9493, (215) 938-4288
tech support (215) 938-6482
fax (215) 938-4290

Motherboards, sound cards, video cards, RAM, hard drives, CPUs, CD-ROMs

AllMicro, Inc.

18820 U.S. Hwy 19 N, #215
Clearwater, FL 34624
(800) 653-4933, (813) 539-7283
fax (813) 531-0200
BBS (813) 535-9042
e-mail: allmicro@ix.netcom.com

Many computer products, including the AlertCard (power supply and temperature monitoring card)

Allsop Computer Accessories

4201 Meridian
Bellingham, WA 98226
(800) 426-4303
http://www.allsop.com

Ergonomic enhancements (drawers and glare filters)

Alpha Systems, Inc.

47000 Warm Springs Blvd, #455
Fremont, CA 94539-7467
(510) 249-9280
fax (510) 259-9288
e-mail: compu@alphasys.com
http://www.alphasys.com

American Computer Products (ACP)

Mercantile Medical Plaza
4015 SW Mercantile Drive, Suite 200
Lake Oswego, OR 97035
(503) 526-3551, (800) 623-7489
fax (503) 646-7631
http://www.acp1.com

American Computer Resources, Inc.

88 Long Hill Cross Road
Shelton, CT 06484-4703
(203) 944-7333
fax (203) 944-7370
http://www.the-acr.com/

American Micro Professionals

Corporate Center
5351 Naiman Parkway
Solon, OH 44139
(800) 857-3223, (216) 498-9564
fax (216) 349-6170

American Ribbon and Toner Co.

2895 West Prospect Road
Ft. Lauderdale, FL 33309
(800) 327-1013

Printer ribbons, toner cartridges, etc.

American Wholesale Center

817 New Churchman's Road
New Castle, DE 19720
(302) 845-4962

AMP Tech (American Micro Products Technology)

5351 Naiman Parkway
Solon, OH 44139
(800) 619-0508, (216) 498-9499
fax (216) 349-6170
e-mail: amptech@icgroup.net
http://www.amptech.com

Computers, motherboards, cases, drives, memory

Arlington Computer Products

851 Commerce Court
Buffalo Grove, IL 60089
(800) 548-5105, (847) 541-6583
fax (847) 541-6881

ARM Computer Inc.

1637 South Main Street
Milpitas, CA 95035
(800) 765-1767, (408) 935-9800
fax (408) 935-9192
e-mail: arm@armcomputer.com
http://www.armcomputer.com

ASI

48289 Fremont Boulevard
Fremont, CA 94538
(510) 226-8000

Distributor of computer hardware, peripherals, and private-label Nspire personal computers and multimedia kits

Aspen Imaging International, Inc.

1500 Cherry Street, Suite B
Louisville, CO 80027-3036
(800) 955-5555 (303) 666-5750
fax (303) 665-2972

Computer printer supplies including printer ribbons, printbands, and laser toner and inkjet supplies

Associates Computer Supply Co., Inc.

275 West 231st Street
Riverdale, NY 10463
(718) 543-8686
fax (718) 548-0343
http://www.associatescomputer.com

Motherboards, cases, video cards, hard drives, keyboards, memory, CD-ROMs

Astra Computer Corporation

7786 Metric Drive
Mentor, OH 44060
(800) 800-6047, (216) 974-7933
fax (216) 974-7939

Atlantic Logic

41 Canfield Road
Cedar Grove, NJ 07009
(201) 857-7878

ATronics International Inc.

44700-B Industrial Drive
Fremont, CA 94538
(800) 488-7776, (510) 656-8400
fax (510) 656-8560
http://www.atronicsintl.com

Parallel port CD-ROM adapter, BIOS enhancement card for IDE hard drive controllers

Aura Industries, Inc.

6352 N. Lincoln Avenue
Chicago, IL 60659
(312) 588-8722

CPUs, hard drives, memory, multimedia products, and computer accessories

Automated Tech Tools

851B Freeway Drive
Macedonia, OH 44056
(800) 413-0767

Autotime Corporation

6605 S.W. Macadam Avenue
Portland, OR 97201
(503) 452-8577
http://www.teleport.com/~autotime/

Memory recycling services and products

Barnett's Computers

417 Fifth Avenue
New York, NY 10017
(212) 696-4777

Battery Network

50 Tannery Road, Unit 2
North Branch, NJ 08876

(800) 653-8294
http://www.battnet.com/

Assembly, sales, and service of rechargeable batteries

Battery Technology, Inc.
5700 Bandini Boulevard
Commerce, CA 90040
(213) 728-7874

Battery products for laptop computers and portable peripherals

Battery-Biz Inc.
31352 Via Colinas, Suite 104
Westlake Village, CA 91362
(800) 848-6782, (818) 706-2767
http://www.battery-biz-br.com/

Distributes batteries for desktops, laptops, and notebooks, as well as for UPS systems and utility meters

Black Box Corporation
1000 Park Drive
Lawrence, PA 15055
(412) 873-6564
http://www.blackbox.com

Networking and data communication products

BNF Enterprises
134R Rt.1 South Newbury St.
Peabody, MA 01960
(508) 536-2000
fax (508) 536-7400
http://www.bnfe.com

Bulldog Computer Products
851 Commerce Court
Buffalo Grove, IL 60089
(800) 438-6039, (847) 541-2394
fax (847) 541-6988

Cable Connection
102 Cooper Ct.
Los Gatos, CA 95030
(408) 395-6700

Manufacturer of cable products and interconnect accessories

Cables America
(800) 348-USA4
fax (800) FAX-USA4

Cables To Go
1501 Webster Street
Dayton, OH 45404
(937) 224-8646, (800) 826-7904
fax (937) 496-2666, (800) 331-2841
http://www.cablestogo.com/

Cables, test equipment, toolkits

CAD & Graphics Warehouse
8515-D Freeway Drive
Macedonia, OH 44056
(216) 487-0485

CAD Warehouse
1939 East Aurora Road
Twinsburg, OH 44087
(216) 487-0485
http://www.cadwarehouse.com

Century Microelectronics, Inc.

4800 Great America Parkway,
Suite 308
Santa Clara, CA 95054
(408) 748-7788
http://www.century-micro.com/

Memory upgrades, with products ranging from industry-standard SIMMs and DIMMs to proprietary modules and memory cards

Chemtronics

8125 Cobb Centre Drive
Kennesaw, GA 30144
(800) 645-5244, (404) 424-4888
fax (800) 243-6003, (404) 423-0748

Ozone-safe compressed gas for cleaning inside PCs

CIRCO Technology Corporation

222 South 5th Avenue
City of Industry, CA 91746
(800) 678-1688
http://www.circotech.com

Cases, power supplies, removeable hard drive kits, motherboards

CMO Corporation

101 Reighard Avenue
Williamsport, PA 17701
(800) 417-4580, (717) 327-9200
fax (717) 327-1217
http://www.cmo.newmii.com

Compaq DirectPlus

P.O. Box 692000
Houston, TX 77269-2000
(281) 370-0670
http://www.compaq.com

CompUSA Direct

15167 Business Avenue
Addison, TX 75244
(800) COMPUSA
http://www.compusa.com

ComputAbility

P.O. Box 17882
Milwaukee, WI 53217
(800) 554-9950, (414) 357-8181
fax (414) 357-7814
http://www.computability.com

Computer City

P.O. Box 2526
Tempe, AZ 85280-2526
http://www.computercity.com

Computer Discount Warehouse (CDW)

1020 East Lake Cook Road
Buffalo Grove, IL 60089
(800) 726-4239
fax (847) 465-6800
http://www.cdw.com

Computers, parts, memory, monitors, printers

Computer Gate International

2960 Gordon Avenue
Santa Clara, CA 95051
(408) 730-0673
fax (408) 730-0735
e-mail: cgate@aimnet.com
http://www.computergate.com

Testers, cleaning products, cables, switches, computer assembly products

Computer Parts Outlet, Inc.

33 S.E. First Avenue
Delray Beach, FL 33444
(800) 475-1655

Buys all types of memory, including large or small quantities of working or non-working modules

Computer Products Corporation

1431 South Cherryvale Road
Boulder, CO 80303

Computer Things

27 Melken Court
Baltimore, MD 21236-3011
(410) 661-8613
http://www.computerthings.com

Inkjet printer supplies

Computers Direct

3613 Lafayette Road
Portsmouth, NH 03801

CompuWorld

24441 Miles Road
Cleveland, OH 44128
(800) 666-6294, (216) 595-6500
fax (216) 595-6565
http://www.compuworld.com

Core Components

9728 Alburtis Avenue
Santa Fe Springs, CA 90670
(888) 267-3266, (310) 654-2866
fax (310) 801-5630

Motherboards, controllers, video boards, memory

Corporate Raider

1449 39th Street
Brooklyn, NY 11218
(718) 453-3555

Dalco Electronics

275 S. Pioneer Boulevard
P.O. Box 550
Springboro, OH 45066
(800) 445-5342, (513) 743-8042
fax (513) 743-9251
BBS (513) 743-2244
CompuServe: GO DA
http://www.dalco.com

Data Impressions

13180 Paramount Blvd.
South Gate, CA 90670
(310) 630-8788
fax (310) 634-5033
http://www.di-wave.com

Computer supplies, printer supplies

DataVision
445 Fifth Avenue
New York, NY 10016
(800) 771-7466
http://www.datavis.com

Computers and multimedia components

DC Drives
1110 NASA Road One, Suite 304
Nassau Bay, TX 77058
(800) 473-0960, (713) 333-9602

Dee One Systems
1550 Centre Point Drive
Milpitas, CA 95035
(408) 262-8938

DellWare Direct
2214 West Baker Lane, Building 3
Austin, TX 78758-4053

Digital Micro, Inc.
901 S. Fremont Avenue, Suite 118
Alhambra, CA 91803

Diskette Connection
P.O. Box 1674
Bethany, OK 73008
(800) 654-4058, (405) 789-0888
fax (405) 495-4598

Disks, tapes, drive cleaning kits

Diskettes Unlimited
6206 Long Drive
Houston, TX 77087
(713) 643-9939
fax (713) 643-2722

Disks

DTP & Graphics
1175 Chess Drive, Suite C
Foster City, CA 94404
(415) 387-9945

Edmund Scientific Corporation
101 E. Gloucester Pike
Barrington, NJ 08007
(609) 573-6250
fax (609) 573-6295

Dual Function Digital Lab Thermometer

ELEK-TEK
7350 North Linder Avenue
Skokie, IL 60077
(800) 395-1000, (708) 677-7660

Envisions Solutions Technology, Inc.
47400 Seabridge Drive
Fremont, CA 94538
(800) 365-SCAN, (510) 661-4357
fax (510) 438-6709
http://www.envisions.com

Scanners, printers, graphics/OCR software

Expert Computers
2495 Walden Avenue
Buffalo, NY 14225
(716) 681-8612

FairFax

145 West 45th Street, Suite 1010
New York, NY 10036
(800) 932-4732, (212) 768-8300

First Computer Systems, Inc.

6000 Live Oak Parkway, Suite 107
Norcross, GA 30093
(800) 325-1911, (770) 441-1911
fax (770) 441-1856
e-mail: sales@fcsnet.com
http://www.fcsnet.com

Motherboards, computers, peripherals

First Source International

Seven Journey
Aliso Viejo, CA 92656
(800) 348-9866, (714) 448-7750
fax (714) 448-7760
e-mail: sales@firstsource.com
http://www.firstsource.com

Fry's Electronics

600 E. Brokaw Rd.
San Jose, CA 95112
(408) 487-4500

Galaxy Computers, Inc.

423 South Lyndhaven Road,
Suite 109
Virginia Beach, VA 23452
(814) 486-8389
http://www.galaxyusa.com/

Motherboards

GIFI Inc.

20814 Aurora Road
Cleveland, OH 44146
(216) 662-1910
http://www.gifi.com

Global Computer Supplies

2318 East Del Amo Blvd., dept. 73
Compton, CA 90220
(800) 829-0785, (800) 227-1246
fax (516) 625-6683

Global MicroXperts

6230 Cochran Road
Solon, OH 44139
(800) 676-0311, (216) 498-3330
http://www.microx.com

Graphics Warehouse

8515 Freeway Drive, unit C & D
Macedonia, OH 44087
(216) 487-0485

Harmony Computers

1801 Flatbush Avenue
Brooklyn, NY 11210
(800) 441-1144, (718) 692-3232
http://www.shopharmony.com/

Hartford Computer Group, Inc.

1610 Colonial Parkway
Inverness, IL 60067
(800) 617-4424, (847) 934-3380
fax (847) 934-9724
http://www.awa.com/hartford

HDSS Computer Products
2225 El Camino Real
Santa Clara, CA 95050

Hi-Tech Component Distributers, Inc.
59 S. La Patera Lane
Goleta, CA 93117
(800) 406-1275, (805) 967-7971
fax (805) 681-9971

Hi-Tech USA
1582 Centre Pointe Drive
Milpitas, CA 95035
(800) 831-2888, (408) 262-8688, (408) 956-8285
fax (408) 262-8772
BBS (408) 956-8243

HyperData Direct
809 South Lemon Avenue
Walnut, CA 91789
(800) 786-3343, (800) 380-1899, (909) 468-2933
fax (909) 468-2954
BBS (909) 594-3645
http://www.hyperbook.com

Laptops, accessories

Insight Computers
6820 South Harl Ave.
Tempe, AZ 85283
(602) 902-1176
http://www.insight.com

InterPro Microsystems, Inc.
46560 Fremont Boulevard, Suite 417
Fremont, CA 94538
(800) 226-7216, (510) 226-7226
fax (510) 226-7219
http://www.interpromicro.com

Jade Computer
18503 Hawthorne Boulevard
Torrance, CA 90504
(800) 421-5500, (310) 370-7474
fax (310) 371-4288

Parts and peripherals

Jinco Computers
5122 Walnut Grove Avenue
San Gabriel, CA 91776
(800) 253-2531, (818) 309-1108
fax (818) 309-1107
e-mail: jinco@wavenet.com
http://www.jinco.com

Cases and power supplies

Kahlon, Inc.
22699 Old Canal Road
Yorba Linda, CA 92687
(800) 317-9989, (714) 637-5060
fax (714) 637-5597
e-mail: kahlonmem@aol.com

IBM and Compaq parts and memory

Kenosha Computer Center
2133 91st Street
Kenosha, WI 53143
(800) 255-2989, (414) 697-9595
fax (414) 697-0620

KREX Computers

9320 Waukegan Road
Morton Grove, IL 60053
(800) 222-KREX, (847) 967-0200
fax (847) 967-0276
http://www.trcone.com/krexcom.html

Laitron Computer

1550 Montague Expressway
San Jose, CA 95131
(408) 888-4828

Lamberth Computer Services

3837 Northdale Blvd, #113
Tampa, FA 33624
fax (800) 876-0762
e-mail: john-lcs@intnet.net

Legend Micro

5590 Lauby Road, Suite 70B
N. Canton, OH 44720
(800) 366-6333, (330) 497-2444
fax (330) 497-3156

Motherboards and components

M.B.S.

7466 Early Drive
Mechanicsville, VA 23111
(804) 944-3808

Macro Tech Inc.

23151 Verdugo Drive, Suite 102
Laguna Hills, CA 92653
(714) 580-1822
http://www.macropc.com/

Magic PC

5400 Brookpark Road
Cleveland, OH 44129
(800) 762-4426, (216) 661-7218
fax (216) 661-2454

Motherboards, systems, components

Main Street Computer Co.

1720 Oak Street
Lakewood, NJ 08701-9885
(800) 333-9899
fax (908) 905-5731

Marine Park Computers

3126 Avenue U
Brooklyn, NY 11229
(719) 262-0163

Megacomp International, Inc.

261 N.E. 1st Street, #200
Miami, FL 33132
(888) 463-4226, (305) 372-0222
fax (305) 374-5040

Megatech Inc.

3070 Bristol Pike
Bensalem, PA 19020

Merritt Computer Products, Inc.

5565 Red Bird Center Drive, Suite 150
Dallas, TX 75237
(800) 627-7752, (214) 339-0753
fax (214) 339-1313

SafeSkin keyboard cover

Micro Assist

50 Harrison Street
Hoboken, NJ 07030
(888) 97-MICRO, (201) 459-0233
fax (201) 459-0283

Micro Time, Inc.

35375 Vokes Drive, Suite 106
Eastlake, OH 44095
(800) 834-0000, (216) 954-9640
fax (216) 954-9648

CPUs, memory, motherboards, peripherals

Micro X-Press

5646-48 West 73rd Street
Indianapolis, IN 46278
(800) 875-9737, (317) 328-5780

MicroniX USA, Inc.

23050 Miles Road
Cleveland, OH 44128
(800) 580-0505, (216) 475-9300
fax (216) 475-6610

Motherboards, memory, and other hardware

MicroSense, Inc.

370 Andrew Avenue
Leucadia, CA 92024
(800) 544-4252, (800) 246-7729,
(909) 688-2735
fax (619) 753-6133
e-mail: docdrive@microsense.com
http://www.microsense.com

MicroSupply, Inc.

(800) 535-2092
http://www.microsupply.com

Midland ComputerMart

5699 West Howard
Niles, IL 60714
(800) 407-0700, (847) 967-0700
fax (847) 967-0710
e-mail: sales@midlandcmart.com
CompuServe: 102404,327

Midwest Computer Works

180 Lexington Drive
Buffalo Grove, IL 60089
(800) 86-WORKS, (847) 459-9410
fax (847) 459-6933
http://www.mcworks.com

Midwest Micro

6910 US Route 36 East
Fletcher, OH 45326
(800) 537-1426, (513) 368-2309
fax (513) 368-2306
http://www.mwmicro.com

Midwestern Diskette

509 West Taylor
Creston, IA 50801
(800) 221-6332
fax (515) 782-4166
e-mail: salesinfo@mddc.com
http://www.mddc.com

Bulk disks

Millenium Technologies
35 Cherry Hill Drive
Danvers, MA 01923
(800) 251-3448

Motherboards, additional components

MMI Corporation
2400 Reach Road
Williamsport, PA 17701

Motherboard Discount Center
1035 N. McQueen, Suite 123
Gilbert, AZ 85233
(800) 486-2026, (602) 813-6547
fax (602) 813-8002

Motherboards, video boards, other hardware

Motherboard Express
333-B West State Road
Island Lake, IL 60042
(800) 560-1195, (847) 487-4639
fax (847) 487-4637
http://www.motherboardx.com

Motherboards and drives

Motherboards International (Shambis Corporation)
8361 East Evans Road, Suite 107
Scottsdale, AZ 85260
(800) 574-4000, 499-3970
(602) 596-5226
fax (602) 596-1554
http://www.motherboards.com

Motherboards & cases

Nationwide Computers Direct (NWCD)
110A McGaw Drive
Edison, NJ 08837
(800) 747-NWCD, (908) 417-4455
fax (800) 329-6923

Notebook computers, PCMCIA cards, printers, modems, scanners

NCA Computer Products
1202 Kifer Road
Sunnyvale, CA 94086
(800) NCA-1115, (408) 522-5066
fax (800) NCA-1666

NECX Direct
Four Technology Drive
Peabody, MA 01960
(800) 961-9208
http://www.necx.com

Network Express
1720 Oak Street
P.O. Box 301
Lakewood, NJ 08701-9885
(800) 333-9899
fax (908) 905-5731
e-mail: netexp@netline.net

Computers, peripherals, and test equipment

Next Generation
6230 Cochran Road
Solon, OH 44139

Next International
13622 Neutron Road
Dallas, TX 75244
(800) 730-NEXT, (214) 404-8260
fax (214) 404-8263
e-mail: next@fastlane.net

North American CAD Company
4A Hillview Drive
Barrington, IL 60010
(800) 619-2199, (847) 381-8834
fax (847) 381-7374
http://www.nacad.com

Graphics-related peripherals, including printers, monitors, video boards, digitizers, and scanners

Nova Computers, Inc.
1420 Lloyd Road
Wickliffe, OH 44492
(800) 461-5535, (216) 516-3035
fax (216) 516-3040

Computers, parts, accessories, motherboards

Odyssey Technology
5590 Lauby Road, Suite 70B
Canton, OH 44720
(800) 683-2808, (330) 497-2444
fax (330) 497-3156

PC Connection
Six Mill Street
Marlow, NH 03456
(603) 800-1111

PC Impact
(800) 853-9337, (800) 698-3820
fax (216) 487-5242

PC Importers
290 Lena Drive
Aurora, OH 44202
(800) 886-5155
fax (216) 487-5242

PC Importers
8295 Darrow Road
Twinsburg, OH 44087

PC International
290 Lena Drive
Aurora, OH 44202
(800) 458-3133
fax (216) 487-5242

Parts, systems, and components

PC Universe
2302 North Dixie Highway
Boca Raton, FL 33431
(800) 728-6483, (407) 447-0050
fax (407) 447-7549
e-mail: sales@pcuniverse.com
http://www.pcuniverse.com

Computers, peripherals, accessories

PCL Computer, Inc.
636 Lincoln Highway
Fairless Hills, PA 19030
(215) 736-2986

Cases

PComputer Solutions

130 West 32nd Street
New York, NY 10001
(212) 629-8300

Peripherals Unlimited, Inc.

1500 Kansas Avenue, Suite 4C
Longmont, CO 80501
(303) 772-1482

Supplies computer-related hardware and software products, specializing in mass storage and connectivity

Power Pros, Inc.

105 Cromwell Court
Raleigh, NC 27614
(800) 788-0070, (919) 782-9210
http://www.powerpros.com

Power protectors, UPSs

Price Pointe

Three Pointe Drive
Brea, CA 92621
(800) 840-7860
fax (800) 840-7861

Computers, peripherals, and software

Publishing Perfection

P.O. Box 307, dept. CS9608
Menomonee Falls, WI 53052-0307
(800) 716-5000, (414) 252-5000
fax (414) 252-2502
e-mail: cs9608@perfection.com

Digital cameras, scanners, multimedia hardware

Quark Technology

5275 Naiman Parkway
Solon, OH 44139
(800) 443-8807, (216) 498-7387
fax (216) 498-8857

Quick-Line Distribution

26001 Miles Road, Unit 8
Warrensville Heights, OH 44128
(800) 808-3606, (216) 514-9800
fax (216) 514-9805

Royal Computer

1208 John Reed Court
Industry, CA 91745
(800) 486-0008, (818) 855-5077
fax (818) 330-2717

Multimedia/graphics monitors

Seattle Data Systems

746 Industry Drive
Seattle, WA 98188
(206) 575-8123
fax (206) 575-8870
e-mail: sdsinc@seadat.com
http://www.seadat.com

Sky 1 Technologies

437 Chestnut Street
Philadelphia, PA 19106
(800) 294-5240, (215) 922-2904
fax (215) 922-6920

Motherboards, memory, drives, peripherals

Starquest Computers
4491 Mayfield Road
Cleveland, OH 44121
(800) 945-0202, (216) 691-9966

Systems, parts, peripherals

Sunshine Computers
1240 East Newport Center Drive
Deerfield Beach, FL 33442
(305) 422-9680

Sunway Inc.
(715) 483-1179
fax (715) 483-1757

Ergonomically designed computer accessories

Swan Technologies
3075 Research Drive
State College, MA 01680

TC Computers
P.O. Box 10428
New Orleans, LA 70181-0428
(800) 723-8282, (504) 733-2527
http://www.tccomputers.com

Motherboards, cases, peripherals

TDN Inc.
1000 Young Street, Suite 270
Tonawanda, NY 14150

Technological Innovations, Inc.
26 Main Street
East Haven, CT 06512
(800) 577-1970, (203) 488-7867

Technology Distribution Network
1000 Young Street, Suite 270
Tonawanda, NY 14150
(800) 420-3636, (716) 743-0195
fax (716) 743-0198

Motherboards and components

The PC Zone
15815 SE 37th Street
Bellevue, WA 98006-1800
(206) 258-2088

Tiger Software
800 Douglas, Executive Tower
Coral Gables, FL 33134

Top Data
574 Wedell Drive, #5
Sunnydale, CA 94089
(800) 888-3318, (408) 734-9100

Tri-State Computers
650 6th Avenue
New York, NY 10011
(800) 433-5199, (212) 633-2530
fax (212) 633-7718

USA Flex
444 Scott Drive
Bloomingdale, IL 60108
(800) 944-5599, (708) 582-6206
fax (708) 351-7204

Vektron
2100 N. Highway 360, Suite 1904
Grand Prairie, TX 75050
(800) 725-0009
http://www.vektron.com

Older PC Repair and Exchange

For those of you with older PCs, there are vendors who will repair and/or exchange parts for these PCs. Many vendors will not service all brands, so call to confirm that the vendor actually services your specific model of hard drive, motherboard, floppy drive, etc., before sending it off. Typically, vendors will not exchange damaged parts (i.e., the board is in two pieces or is water- or fire-damaged).

Computer Commodity, Inc.

1405 SW 6th Court, Suite B
Pompano Beach, FL 33069
(305) 942-6616
fax (305) 946-7815
e-mail: computer@gate.net
www.commodityinc.com

A full service dealer/broker/distributor of new, used and refurbished computer hardware

Computer Recycle Center, Inc.

303 East Pipeline
Bedford, TX 76022
(817) 282-1622
fax (817) 282-5944
e-mail: bert@recycles.com
http://www.recycles.com/

A world wide trading site and recycling center for used and surplus computer equipment and materials; provides upgrades for users of older equipment

Computer Recycler

670 West 17th Street
Costa Mesa, CA
(714) 645-4022
e-mail: maurer44@wdc.net
http://www.computerrecycler.com/

Buyer, seller, and trader of new and preowned Mac and PC equipment

Computer Recyclers

4119 Lindberg Road
Addison, TX 75244
(214) 774-0366
fax (214) 774-1161
http://www.comp-recycle.com

CPAC (Computers, Parts, and Commodities)

22349 La Palma Ave, #114
Yorba Linda, CA 92687
(800) 778-2722, (714) 692-5044
fax (714) 692-6680
e-mail: cpac@wavenet.com
http://remarketing.com/broker_html/cpac/

Crocodile Computers

240 West 73rd Street
New York, NY 10021
(212) 769-3400
http://www.crocs.com/

DakTech

4025 9th Ave. SW
Fargo, ND 58103
(800) 325-3238, (717) 795-9544
fax (717) 795-9420
e-mail: daktech@ix.netcom.com
http://www.gndi.com/shwcs/daktech.htm

Specializing in IBM and COMPAQ parts

Data Exchange Corporation

3600 Via Pescador
Camarillo, CA 93012
(800) 237-7911, (805) 388-1711
fax (805) 482-4856
http://www.dex.com/dexhome/

A leading full-service company specializing in contract manufacturing, end-of-life support, depot repair, logistics services and worldwide inventory management services for all high-technology industries; has an extensive inventory of spare parts for sale

Eritech International, Inc.

(800) 808-6242, (818) 244-6242
fax (818) 500-7699

Buyers of old CPUs and memory

NIE International

3000 E. Chambers
Phoenix, AZ 85040
(602) 470-1500
fax (602) 470-1540
e-mail: nie@nieint.com
http://www.nieint.com/

A leading supplier of micro-computer parts and systems to companies that maintain and support PC installations

Northstar

7101 31st Avenue North
Minneapolis, MN 55427
(800) 969-0009, (612) 591-0009
fax (612) 591-0029
http://www.northstar-mn.com/

A complete PC repair service

Oak Park Personal Computers

130 South Oak Park Avenue, Suite #2
Oak Park, IL 60302
(708) 848-1553
fax (708) 524-9791
e-mail: mlund@oppc.com
http://www.oppc.com/

OnLine Computing

3550-L SW 34th Street
Gainesville, FL 32608
(352) 372-1712
fax (352) 335-8192
e-mail: online@gnv.fdt.net

The Used Computer Marketplace

(part of the Affiliated ReMarketing Web)
http://www.remarketing.com

A place where you can list for-sale or wanted items for free in their confidential classifieds, which are then accessed by subscribing dealers

United Computer Exchange

2110 Powers Ferry Road, Suite 307
Atlanta, GA 30339
(800) 755-3033, (770) 612-1205
fax (770) 612-1239
fax info line (770) 955-0569
e-mail: united@uce.com
CompuServe: 73312,1224
America Online: UnCoEx
info on demand: uce-info@uce.com
http://www.uce.com/

A global clearinghouse for buyers and sellers of new and used microcomputer equipment

Computer Recycling Centers

After upgrading your PC, you might prefer to donate the older parts to needy organizations rather than sell them. Here are some organizations that help with the redistribution:

Computer Re-use Network (CoRN)

P.O. Box 1078
Hollywood, SC 29449
(803) 889-8247
e-mail: corn2000@juno.com
http://www.awod.com/gallery/probono/corn/

Computer Recycling Project, Inc.

http://www.wco.com/~dale/list.html
e-mail: dale@wco.com

A listing of additional organizations that deal with accepting old computers and funnelling them to nonprofit groups/individuals in need

Lazarus Foundation, Inc.

East Coast:
10378 Eclipse Way
Columbia, MD 21044
Donald Bard, President
(410) 740-0735
e-mail: lazaruspc@aol.com
West Coast:
30 West Mission Street, #4
Santa Barbara, CA 93101
Kenneth M. Wyrick, Western Regional Director
(805) 563-1009
e-mail: Recycle@west.net

This is a computer recycling center that accepts donated computers which they, in turn, refurbish. These computers are then donated to individuals, schools, and other non-profit organizations.

INDEX

Note to the Reader: Page numbers in **bold** indicate the principal discussion of a topic or the definition of a term. Page numbers in *italic* indicate illustrations.

NUMBERS

110 Twinalert heat sensor device, 729

A

ABCs of Microsoft Internet Explorer 4 (Ross), 527
ABCs of Windows 98 (Crawford and Salkind), 35, 57, 287, 371
Accessibility Options applet. *See also* Control Panel
    defined, *114*, **115**
    display options, 122–123, *123*
    keyboard options, 119–121, *119*
    mouse options, 123–126, *124*
    overview of, 118–119, *119*, 126–127, *126*
    sound options, 121–122, *121*
Active Accessibility program, **7**
Active Desktop feature, 49–50, 159, **792–793**, 803–804
adapters. *See also* video adapter cards
    in Dial-Up Networking, 337, *337–338*
    for RAM modules, 769
Add New Hardware applet. *See also* Control Panel
    accessing drivers, 128
    defined, *114*, **115**, **793**
    Install Hardware Wizard, 128–136, *129–130*, *132–134*
    overview of, 127–128
Add Printer Wizard, 181–184, *182–184*, 273–274
Add/Remove Programs applet. *See also* Control Panel
    creating startup disks, 795–796
    defined, *114*, **115**, **794**

installing Dial-Up Networking, 335–336, *335–336*
installing programs, 100–102, *101–102*, 137–138, *137–138*, 794
installing programs from networks, 796
installing Windows 98 SE components, 795
overview of, 136
removing existing programs, 138–139, 794–795
removing Windows 98 SE components, 795
Address Book
    address books, defined, **522–523**
    creating entries in, 797
    defined, **796**, **874–875**
    grouping entries in, 798
    importing address books into, 796–797
    in Netscape Messenger, 524
    opening, 796
    in Outlook Express, 523–524
Address toolbars
    defined, **798**, **874**
    on Desktop, 42
    in Internet Explorer, 534–536, 548
    in Windows Explorer, 813
addresses. *See also* Web addresses
    defined, **874**
    e-mail addresses
        defined, **457**, **886**
        finding on Internet, 524–525
        managing in address books, 522–524
        sending mail to, 494–495
    entering in Microsoft Wallet, 578–580, *579–580*
    Internet addresses, 456–458
ADSL (Asymmetrical Digital Subscriber Line), 467–469

Advanced Connection Settings dialog box, 268, 269
Advanced Display Properties dialog box. *See also* Display Properties dialog box
    Adapter tab, 164-165, 281-282, *282*
    General tab, 163-164, *163*
    Monitor tab, 166-167, *166*, 284-285
    overview of, 162-163
    Performance tab, 167-168, *167*, 285
Advanced tab of Find: All Files dialog box, 820-821
Advanced tab of Internet Options dialog box, 832
AJR NewsLink Web site, 550, *550*
aligning Web page images, 681-682
AltaVista search engine, **691-693**, *692*
alternatives to Web page images, 681
Andy's Art Attack, 678
animating menus, *157*, 158
APIs (Application Program Interfaces), 204
Appearance tab of Display Properties dialog box, 49, 51, 151-156, *151*, *154*, *156*
applets, **371-389**. *See also* Control Panel
    Calculators, 380-382, *381*
    Character Map, 377-378, *377*
    Clipboard, **375-376**, *375*, 382, 799, 879
    defined, **115**, **371**, **875**
    HyperTerminal
        creating connections, 383-385
        defined, **382**
        file transfer protocols, 385
        receiving files, 387, *387*
        saving sessions, 387-388
        sending files, 386, *386*
        starting, 382, *383*
        using connections, 388
    My Briefcase, 388-389
    Notepad, 372
    overview of, 371-372
    Paint, **376-377**, 420, **845-847**
    Phone Dialer
        overview of, 378-379, *378*
        speed dialing, 379-380, *379*
        telephone logs, 380
    WordPad
        defined, **372**

        dragging documents into, 373
        faxing and, 373
        formatting tools, 374, *374*
        opening screen, 373, *373*
        page setup and printing, 374
        starting, 372
        toolbars, 374, *374*
Application Program Interfaces (APIs), 204
applications, **875**. *See also* applets; Control Panel; programs
archives. *See also* saving; storing
    archiving images, 677
    defined, **875**
    restoring files in, 315-316, 855-857
    zip archives, **698**
art. *See* images; multimedia
ASCII standard character set, **404**, **876**
Asymmetrical Digital Subscriber Line (ADSL), 467-469
AT power connectors, 777-778, *777*
attaching to e-mail
    defined, **876**
    digital signatures, 513-515
    files, 506-508, *507*
    Web shortcuts, 562-563
attributes, 659, **876**. *See also* properties
ATX computer cases, **712-713**
ATX power connectors, **778**
AutoComplete feature, **535**
AUTOEXEC.BAT files. *See also* system configuration files
    creating DOS environments, 393-396, *394-395*
    editing DOS .PIF files, 403
    loading DOS drivers and TSRs, 393
    overview of, 392-393
    purposes of, 393
    storing DOS programs in .PIF files, 396-397
    viewing DOS .PIF files with DEBUG, 397-398
    warnings, 396, 397
AutoPlay feature, **207**
AutoScan feature, **535**

B

Back button
    in Internet Explorer, 542
    in Netscape Navigator, 629–630, 633
    in Windows Explorer, 812
background options
    for Desktops, 48–49, *48*, 143–147, *144*, *146*, 792–793
    for FrontPage Express Web pages, *668*, 669–670
backing up files, **308–316**. *See also* system maintenance
    with Backup, defined, **798**
    with Backup, starting, 308–309, *309*
    backup types, 310
    backups, defined, **876**
    creating backups, 312–314, *313*
    creating Desktop shortcut for, 315
    defining file sets for, 311
    with drag-and-drop, 315
    to floppy disks, 309, 311
    overview of, 308
    Registry files
        by exporting with REGEDIT.EXE, 414–416, *415–417*
        with SCANREG.EXE, 409–411, *410*
        with SCANREGW.EXE, 410, 413–414
    and restoring, 315–316, 855–857
    setting options for, 314–315
    to tape drives, 309–310
    warning, 309
    what to backup, 310–311
Backup Job Options dialog box, 314–315
Backup Wizard, 312–313, *313*
Bcc (blind carbon copy) in e-mail, **506**, **877**
binary files, 386, *386*
BIOS, **877**
BIOS upgrade vendors, 962–963
blocks, memory, 762
bookmarks. *See also* Favorites; links
    adding to Web pages, 675–676
    bookmark lists, **550**
    creating links to in Web pages, 674

    defined, **877**
    in Netscape Navigator, 633
borderless frames, **632**
broadcast-enabling features, **208**
Browse button, **798**
Browser Watch, 640
browsers, **877**. *See also* Internet Explorer; Netscape Navigator; Web browsers
bug fixes, 7
bugs, **877**
bulleted lists, 661–663
bulletin boards, **446**
busses, PCI, **717–718**
Busses, Universal Serial (USBs), **720**
Buttons tab of Mouse properties dialog box, 168–169, *169*
buying PCs. *See* computer vendors; PCs, buying
buying products online, **704–706**, *706*

C

cable connectors, removing, 779–780
cable modems, 468, **878**
cache in Netscape Navigator
    cache checking options, 634–635, *635*
    defined, **633**, **878**
    disk cache, **633**
    increasing disk cache, 635–636
    memory cache, **633**, 635, **895**
    overview of, 633–634
    warning, 635
Calculator applet, **380–382**, *381*
call forwarding properties, 270, *270*
cameras, digital, 272–273
Cc (carbon copy) in e-mail, **506**, **879**
CD Player, **240–248**. *See also* multimedia
    cataloging CDs, 244–246, *245*
    control buttons, 241–242
    creating play lists, 246
    defined, **219**, **240–241**, *240*, **799**
    display options, 242–243
    play order options, 243–244
    running, 241
    setting preferences, 247–248
    Toolbar, 242–243
    using play lists, 247

CD-PLUS specification—Computers and Internet page, Yahoo! 985

CD-PLUS specification, **208**
CD-R (CD Recordable) drives, 214–215
CD-ROM
    defined, **879**
    disks
        installing programs from, 98–99, *98*
        running programs from, 99–100, *100*
    drives
        power connectors, 778
        upgrading for multimedia, 213–214
CD-RW (CD ReWritable) drives, 214–215
certificates, **600–605**. *See also* Internet Explorer security
    defined, **600**
    downloading certified programs, 601–603
    managing, 831
    overview of, 597–598
    personal certificates, 600, 604–605
    publisher certificates, 600, 601–604
    security level settings, 603–604
    site certificates, 600, 604
    types of, 600
    warning, 600
CHAP (Challenge-Handshake Authentication Protocol), 366
Character Map applet, **377–378**, *377*
characters, **879**. *See also* special characters
Chat programs, 460
chips, memory, **895**
chips, RAM, **902**
Christiansen, Eric, 329, 391
client computers, installing DUN on, 336–344, *337–343, 345–346*
clients, **458**
Clipboard applet, **375–376**, *375*, 382, **799**, **879**
clock, internal system, **879**, **906**
clock on Taskbar, 41, 863
closed captioning, **122**
closing windows, 799–800, **880**. *See also* exiting; quitting
Coleman, Pat, 565, 567, 644
collapsing toolbars, 610
color
    in Desktop displays
        changing color palette settings, 160

creating colors, 155–156, *156*
loading color schemes, 152
modifying color schemes, 152–153
overview of, 49, 51, 151, *151*
editing in Registry, 418–421, *418–420*
for text in Netscape Navigator, 622–623, *623*
in Web page backgrounds, 669–670
color-refiner cursor, **156**, *156*
Columbia House online store, 706, *706*
cometizing, **608**
comments, adding to Web pages, 649
compatibility, **714**, **880**
The Complete PC Upgrade & Maintenance Guide (Minasi), 711, 725, 915
compressed files, **698**, **880**
compressed hard drives, installing Windows 98 SE onto, 28–30
compressing hard drives with DriveSpace 3, 303–308, *304*
Computer option on Find menu, 821
computer vendors, **916–981**
    BIOS upgrade vendors, 962–963
    computer/component vendors, 916–959, 963–978
    data recovery vendors, 959–961
    memory vendors, 961–962
    overview of, 916
    PC repair/exchange vendors, 979–981
    peripherals vendors, 916–959, 963–978
    recycling centers, 981
    storage device vendors, 963
computers. *See also* PCs
    cases
        in buying PCs, 712–713
        opening, 772–774, *774*
        in protecting from heat, 727–728
    client, defined, **458**
    client, installing DUN on, 336–344, *337–343, 345–346*
    and getting on the Internet, 458
    host computers, **457**, **890**
    leaving on all day, 740–742
    upgrading for multimedia, 212–213
Computers and Internet page, Yahoo!, 688–689, *688–689*

CONFIG.POL files, 399, 401, 402
CONFIG.SYS files. *See also* system configuration files
   creating DOS environments, 393–396, *394–395*
   editing DOS .PIF files, 403
   loading DOS drivers and TSRs, 393
   overview of, 392–393
   purposes of, 393
   storing DOS programs in .PIF files, 396–397
   viewing DOS .PIF files with DEBUG, 397–398
   warnings, 396, 397
conflict troubleshooter, 133
connecting to Remote Registry computers, 426, *426*
Connection tab of Internet Options dialog box, 831–832
Connection Wizard, 349–351, *349–351*, 476–478, *477*, **800–802**
connections. *See* Dial-Up Networking; Internet connections
Content Advisor, **582–592**. *See also* filtering Web site content
   blocking unrated pages, 587, 590
   creating passwords, 585
   disallowed pages, 588–590, *589*
   enabling, 584–587, *586*
   installing rating systems in, 590–592, *591*
   overview of, 582–583, 831
   rating systems, 583, 584
   setting ratings criteria, 587–588, 831
Content tab of Internet Options dialog box, 830–831
Control Panel, **113–173**. *See also* applets; Display applet
   Accessibility Options applet
     defined, *114*, **115**
     display options, 122–123, *123*
     keyboard options, 119–121, *119*
     mouse options, 123–126, *124*
     overview of, 118–119, *119*, 126–127, *126*
     sound options, 121–122, *121*
   Add New Hardware applet
     accessing drivers, 128
     defined, *114*, **115**
     Install Hardware Wizard, 128–136, *129–130*, *132–134*
     overview of, 127–128
   Add/Remove Programs applet
     creating startup disks, 795–796
     defined, *114*, **115**, **794**
     installing Dial-Up Networking, 335–336, *335*, *336*
     installing programs, 100–102, *101–102*, 137–138, *137–138*, 794
     installing programs from networks, 796
     installing Windows 98 SE components, 795
     overview of, 136
     removing existing programs, 138–139, 794–795
     removing Windows 98 SE components, 795
   applets
     defined, **875**
     listed, *114*, 115–118
     opening, 803
   Date/Time applet, *114*, 115, **139–140**, *140*, 806
   defined, **802–804**, **881**
   Desktop Themes applet, *114*, 115, **140–142**, *141*
   Fonts applet, *114*, 115, **824–825**
   Game Controllers applet, *114*, **116**, 278, *278*
   Infrared applet, *114*, **116**, 279, *279*
   Internet Options applet, *114*, **116**
   Keyboard applet, *114*, 116, **835–836**
   Modems applet, *114*, **116**, **837**
   Mouse applet
     defined, *114*, **116**, **838**
     double-click speed, 169, *169*
     left-right button reversal, 168–169, *168*
     overview of, 168, 838
     pointer schemes, 170–171, *171*
     pointer speed and trails, 171–173, *172*

Control Panel—deleting 987

Multimedia applet, *114*, **116**
Network applet
    access control settings, 367–368, *367–368*
    defined, *114*, **116**
    identification settings, 354–355, *355–356*
ODBC Data Sources applet, *114*, **116**
opening, 114, *114*
Passwords applet
    changing passwords, 353–354, 848–850
    defined, *114*, **117**, **847–848**
    enabling user profiles, 848
    remote administration options, 428–430, *428–430*, 850
    specifying passwords, 848
PCMCIA applet, *114*, **117**
Power Management applet, *114*, **117**
Printers applet, *114*, **117**
Regional Settings applet, *114*, 117, 806, **853–855**
Scanners and Cameras applet, 272–273
Sounds applet
    assigning sounds to events, 228, 229–231, *231*
    defined, *114*, 117, **218–219**, **859**
    deleting sound schemes, 232
    installing sound schemes, 228
    recording sounds, 228–229
    saving sound schemes, 231–232
    sound file sources, 229
    storing sounds, 230
    troubleshooting sound, 229
System applet, *114*, **117**, 136
Telephony applet, *114*, **117**
Users applet, *114*, 118, **866–867**
converting
    to FAT32, 301–303, *302*
    sound file formats, 239–240
cookies, 571–572, **881**
copying. *See also* Clipboard
    defined, **881**
    files and folders, 804–805
    floppy disks, 84, *84*

and pasting URLs, 596
shortcuts, 65
corrosion, 748–749
Cowart, Robert, 15, 111, 113, 175, 203, 462
CPUs (central processing units), **716–717**, **879**, **896**
Crawford, Sharon, 3, 13, 32, 35, 57, 73, 97, 285, 287, 319, 369, 371
credit cards, securing online, 577–578
cross-linked files, 290
crosstalk, **736–737**
Crumlish, Christian, 443, 489, 491, 492, 513, 685, 873
Currency tab of Regional Settings dialog box, 854–855
cursor, color-refiner, **156**, *156*
cursors, **881**
Customize This Folder Wizard, 814
customizing Windows 98 SE. *See* Control Panel
Cut command, 839, **881**
Cyber Patrol software, 583–584

D

data recovery vendors, 959–961
date, system, **906**
Date tab of Find: All Files dialog box, 820
Date tab of Regional Settings dialog box, 855
Date/Time applet in Control Panel, *114*, 115, **139–140**, *140*, 806
date/time settings on Taskbar, 41, 863
DCOM (Distributed Component Object Model), **7**
DEBUG program, 397–398
decoder cards, 223
decompressing files, 698, 702–703
decompressing hard drives, 306–307
deleting. *See also* Recycle Bin; removing
    defined, **882**
    e-mail, 500
    Favorites, 556–557
    files/folders, 806–807
    links, 675
    modems, 266
    print jobs, 196–197
    printers, 189, 275

deleting—devices

sound schemes, 232
undoing, 807
Desktop, **35-54**. *See also* Display applet
   accessing Internet from, 450
   Active Desktop, 49-50, 159, **792-793**, 803-804
   arranging icons on, 840
   defined, **807**, **882**
   display properties, 47-51, *48*
   help
      Offline Help, 52, 53-54, *53*
      overview of, 39, 51-53, *52*
      Web Help, 52, 54, 828
   My Computer tool, 45, 841-842
   overview of, 35
   Properties dialog boxes, **46**, *47*, 188, **852**, 901
   Recycle Bin, **87-95**
      bypassing, 90, 94-95, 807
      confirmation options, 94
      defined, **88**, **852-853**
      emptying, 95
      files not sent to, 90
      overview of, 45-46, 87-88
      properties of, 93-94, *93*
      recovering files from, 91-93, *92*, 865-866
      recovering files not in, 90
      sending files to, 89-90
      sizing, 93-94, *93*, 95
      warning, 95
   saving settings, 435-436
   shortcuts on
      to Backup program, 315
      to Dial-Up Networking, 348
      finding programs in, 105
      to floppy drives, 84
      to network home directories, 348
      to printers, 192
      to Start menu programs, 63-64
      to Windows Explorer programs, 75, 108
   Start menu
      adding program shortcuts to, 64, 109
      adding Registry Editor to, 407-408
      Desktop shortcuts to, 63-64
      Documents, 37, **809**
      Favorites, 37
      Find, 38-39, *38*
      Help, 39, 52, *52*, **827-828**
      Log Off, 39, **836**, **894**
      opening, 36
      overview of, 36, *36*, 860
      Programs option, 37, **105**, *105*, **851-852**
      reducing size of, 863
      removing programs from, 64
      Run, 39, **857**
      Settings, **37-38**, 858
      Shut Down, 39, 436-437, **859**
      Start button, **36**, *36*, 41, 862
      Windows Update, **297-298**, *298*, 860, **870**
   Taskbar
      adding toolbars to, 864
      Address toolbar, 42, **798**, 864
      clock, 41, 863
      configuring toolbars on, 44
      creating toolbars on, 43, *43*, 865
      defined, **861**
      Desktop toolbar, 42, 864
      hiding, 40, 863
      icons on, 41, 861-862
      Links toolbar, 43, 864
      moving, 40
      overview of, 40, 41
      Quick Launch toolbar, 41, **42**, **109-110**, 862, 864
      selecting toolbars on, 41
      setting properties for, 863-864
      shortcuts to programs on, 862
      sizing, 40, 44
      Start button, **36**, *36*, 41, 862
      warning, 44
   warning, 47
Desktop Themes applet, *114*, 115, **140-142**, *141*
Device Bay Support program, **7**
Device Manager tab of System Properties dialog box, 276-277, *277*
devices. *See* hardware

Dialer applet, Phone—disk drives 989

Dialer applet, Phone, **378-380**, *378-379*
Dial-Up Networking (DUN), **329-369**,
   478-488
   advantages, 329-330
   connection protocols, 333-334
   connection setup options, 332
   defined, **329**, **883**
   Desktop shortcuts to, 348
   direct serial connections and, 368-369
   DUN connections, **338-348**
      comparing, 359
      configuring on clients, 336, 338-339,
         338-339, 342-344, *342-343*,
         345-346
      editing, 341
      to NT domains via WINS, 352-359,
         355-356, *358*
      PPTP DUN connections, 339-341,
         340-341, 353, 359
      running applications on, 341-342
      testing, 347-348, *347*
      using for data access, 341-342
   DUN connections to Internet, **478-488**
      altering, 351, *351*
      changing defaults, 482-483, *483*
      creating profiles of, 480-482,
         481-482
      installing DUN software, 479-480,
         479
      Never Dial A Connection option,
         483-484, *483*
      overview of, 11, 344, *345*
      sample ISP information, 352
      setting up, 349-352, *349-351*,
         478-479
      sharing on networks, 485-488,
         487-488
   installing, **335-346**
      on client machines, 337-344,
         337-343, *345-346*
      Dial-up Server, 359-364, *360-363*
      for Internet connections, 479-480,
         479
      on networks, 335-336, *335*, *336*
      overview of, 335
   network protocols, 334

overview of, 330-331
remote access, defined, **331-332**
remote control, defined, **332**
security, **364-368**
   via CHAP protocol, 366
   for Dial-up Server, 361-362, *361-363*
   overview of, 364
   via PAP protocol, 364-365
   share-level security, 366-368,
      367-368
   via SPAP protocol, 366
   user-level permissions, 367-368,
      367-368
server type settings, 342-344, *342-343*,
   345-346, 352, 480-481, *481*
WINS connections to NT domains,
   352-359
   versus DUN or PPTP connections,
      359
   firewalls and, 353
   LMHOSTS files and, 356-357
   setting up, 352-355, *355-356*
   synchronizing passwords, 353-354
   troubleshooting, 357-359, *358*
digital cameras, 272-273
digital signatures, **513-515**, 601, **883**, **905**
DIMMs (Dual Inline Memory Modules),
   766-769, *767-769*, 781-782, *781*, 784
DIP (Dual-Inline Pins) memory chips, **761**,
   765. *See also* RAM
direct serial network connections, 368-369
directories
   defined, **10**, **883**
   installing Windows 98 SE to, 24-25
   searching the Web via, 548, **687-690**,
      688-689, *691*
DirectShow feature, **207-208**
DirectX feature, **207**
discussion groups on Internet, 446
Disk Cleanup program, **293-295**, *293-294*,
   808
Disk Defragmenter program, **291-292**, *292*
disk drives. *See also* system maintenance
   buying, 719
   CD-R drives, 214-215
   CD-ROM drives, 213-214, 778

CD-RW drives, 214–215
defined, **883–884**
DVD drives, 215–216, 220–223
floppy disk drives
    buying, 719
    Desktop shortcuts to, 84
    power connectors, 778, *779*
shortcuts to, 67
tape drives, backing up to, 309–310
Zip drives, 912
disk drives, hard
    buying, 719
    compressed, installing Windows 98 SE onto, 28–30
    compressing, 304–306, *304*
    creating shortcuts to, 67
    defined, **889**
    freeing up space on
        changing shell folders, 438–439, *439*
        with compression, 303–306, *304*
        creating partitions, 307
        with DriveSpace 3, 30, 303–308, *304*
        with Fat32, 299–303, *302*
        overview of, 29
        removing Uninstall files, 28
        turning off XtraDrive write cache, 30
    increasing cache size of, 635–636
    naming, 842–843
    partitions, **299**, 307, **899**
    power connectors, 778
    printing files to, 199–200
    versus RAM, 758
    saving files to
        filenames and, 626
        images, 627, 628
        links, 627–628
        overview of, 624
        and viewing offline, 628–629
        Web pages, 625–627, *626*
    sharing
        disconnecting from mapped drives, 83
        mapping drives, 82–83, *83*
        overview of, 77, 80–82, *81*
        setting up networks, 77–80

space on
    checking amounts of, 808
    freeing up, 28–30, 299–308, *304*, 438–439, *439*
    sound files and, 237
uncompressing, 306–307
disks
    CD-ROM disks, 98–100, *98*, *100*
    floppy disks
        backing up to, 309, 311
        copying, 84, *84*
        creating startup disks, 795–796
        defined, **888**
        formatting, 84–86, 825
        naming, 842–843
        overview of, 84
    passwords for sharing, 849
    space on, checking amounts of, 808
display accessibility options, 122–123, *123*
display adapters. *See* video adapter cards
Display applet, **142–168**. *See also* Control Panel; Desktop; video
    accessing, 142
    Active Desktop options, 49–50, 159, **792–793**, 803–804
    background options, 48–49, *48*, 143–147, *144*, *146*
    color options
        changing color palette settings, 160
        creating colors, 155–156, *156*
        loading color schemes, 152
        modifying color schemes, 152–153
        overview of, 49, 51, 151, *151*
    defined, *114*, **115**, *808*
    Desktop icon options, 50, 157–158, *157*
    font options, 49, 51, *151*, 153–154, *154*
    overview of, 142–143
    screen element size options, 155
    screen saver options, 49, 147–150, *148*, 858, **903**
    video driver settings, **159–168**
        adapter cards, 164–165, 281–282, *282*
        changing drivers, 281–282, *282*
        color palettes, 160

fonts, 163–164
graphics speed, 167–168, *167*
monitors, 166–167, *166*, 284–285
overview of, 50–51, 159, *159*, 280, 283–285, *283*
refresh rates, 162, 164, 217–218
resolution, **50–51**, **160–164**, *161*, **217–218**, 283–284, *283*
display options in CD Player, 242–243
Display Power Management Signaling (DPMS), 148
Display Properties dialog box, **143–168**
Advanced Settings page
Adapter tab, 164–165, 281–282, *282*
General tab, 163–164, *163*, 284
Monitor tab, 166–167, *166*, 284–285
overview of, 162–163, 284
Performance tab, 167–168, *167*, 285
Appearance tab, 49, 51, 151–156, *151*, *154*, *156*
Background tab, 48–49, *48*, 143–147, *144*, *146*, 792–793
Effects tab, 50, 157–158, *157*
opening, 792, 808
Screen Saver tab, 49, 148–150, *148*, 858
Settings tab, 50–51, 159–162, *159*, *161*, 283, *283*
Web tab, 49–50, 159, 793
Distributed Component Object Model (DCOM), **7**
Documents option on Start menu, 37, **809**
domain names, **457**, 458, 494, **884**
DOS. *See* MS-DOS
DoubleSpace software, 30
downloading files
certified programs, 601–603
content ratings files, 591–592
and decompressing, 698, 702–703
defined, **885**
in Internet Explorer, 695–697, *696*
Netscape software, 608
overview of, 460–461, 695–697, *696*
from Shareware.com, 703–704, *703*
virus protection for, 697–698
warning, 697
WinZip software, 698–699, *699*

DPMS (Display Power Management Signaling), 148
Dr. Watson tool, **321**, *322*
dragging-and-dropping
backing up files by, 315
defined, **885**
documents into WordPad, 373
documents to printers, 192–194, *193*
moving files and folders by, 839
overview of, 809
Show window contents while dragging option, 157, 158
DRAM (Dynamic Random Access Memory), **763**, **885**
Drive Converter FAT32. *See also* system maintenance
converting to, 301–303, *302*
defined, **13**, **299**
versus FAT16, 299–300
limitations of, 300–301
returning to FAT16, 303
warning, 302
drivers. *See also* video drivers
accessing, 128
mouse drivers, 276–277, *277–278*
multimedia drivers, 220, 260
printer drivers, 180–181, 186–187
drives. *See* disk drives
DriveSpace 3. *See also* system maintenance
compressing hard drives, 304–306, *304*
Compression Agent, 307–308
creating drive partitions, 307
defined, **30**, **299**
overview of, 303–304
settings, 306
uncompressing drives, 306–307
warning, 305
DUN. *See* Dial-Up Networking
dust, 732–733
duty cycles, **730–731**
DVD Player. *See also* multimedia
creating passwords, 224
defined, **208**, **219–220**
DVD drives, 215–216, 220–223
ending, 227

language options, 226-227
running, 223-225
searching in, 225-226
subtitle options, 226-227
Dynamic Random Access Memory (DRAM), **763**, **885**
Dyson, Peter, 873

E

ECCDRAM (Error Correcting Circuit Dynamic RAM), **764**
Edit menu options, 804-805, 811, 839, 850
editing. *See also* Registry
    defined, **886**
    Desktop patterns, 145-146
    DOS .PIF files, 403
    DUN connections, 341
    images, **376-377**, 420, 847
    sound files, 238-240
    SYSTEM.INI files, 435
    text with Notepad, 86-87, **372**
    text with WordPad, 372-374, *373-374*
    Web pages
        adding comments, 649
        adding line breaks, 647
        adding special characters, 647-648
        finding and replacing text, 648
        HTML source code, 649-650, *650*
        overview of, 646-647
        previewing changes, 650-651
    WIN.INI files, 435
EDO RAM (Extended Data Out RAM), **763**, 783
Effects tab of Display Properties dialog box, 50, 157-158, *157*
electromagnetism, stray, **735-747**. *See also* PCs, protecting
    electromagnetic interference
        crosstalk, 736-737
        overview of, 735
        radio frequency interference, 737-739
    electrostatic discharge, 743-747, 771-772, 784, *785*
    overview of, 735

power noise
    leaving computers on and, 740-742
    overview of, 739-740
    overvoltage, 742
    transients, 742
    undervoltage, 742-743
Electronic Frontier Foundation, **461**
electronic packaging for software, **601**
e-mail, **491-524**. *See also* Outlook Express
    addresses
        defined, **457**, **886**
        finding on Internet, 524-525
        managing in address books, 522-524
        sending mail to, 494-495
    attaching to
        defined, **876**
        files, 506-508, *507*
        signatures, 513-515
        Web shortcuts, 562-563
    Bcc lines, 506, **877**
    Cc lines, 506, **879**
    defined, **886**
    deleting, 500
    exiting mail programs, 502
    filing in folders, 515-517
    filtering, 497, **517-521**, *520-521*, 888
    formatting with HTML, 509-510
    forwarding, 508-509, **888**
    links in, 499, 505
    managing in multiple accounts, 522
    Netiquette, 459, **500-502**, 897
    in Netscape Messenger
        address books, 524
        attaching files, 507-508
        attaching signatures, 514-515
        filing in folders, 516-517
        filtering, 519-521, *520*, *521*
        formatting with HTML, 510
        in multiple accounts, 520-521, *521*
        overview of, 503-505, *504*, 509
        spell checking, 513
    in Outlook Express
        address books, 523-524
        attaching files, 507, *507*

attaching signatures, 514
creating identities, 575
defined, **844**, **899**
filing in folders, 516
filtering, 518–519
formatting with HTML, 510
new message window, 493, *494*
overview of, 5, *6*, 11–12, 502–503, 509
spell checking, 512
overview of, 11, 444–446, *445*, 491–493
reading, 497–498, *498*
replying to, 498–500, **902**
running mail programs, 493
saving as text files, 516
sending
with attached files, 506–508, *507*
to multiple recipients, 505–506
to other networks, 495–496, *496*
overview of, 493–495, *494*
spell checking, 512–513
subject lines, 496
warnings, 501, 506, 510, 513
writing in word processors, 511–512, *511*
EMI (electromagnetic interference). *See also* electromagnetism
crosstalk, 736–737
overview of, 735
radio frequency interference, 737–739
encrypting online transfers, **597–600**
Entertainment menu, **810**
EPA Energy Star monitors, 147–148, 150
Error Correcting Circuit Dynamic RAM (ECC-DRAM), **764**
error messages, 636–638, **886**
euro glyph fonts, 7
Excite Web address, 695
.exe files, **698**
exiting. *See also* quitting
e-mail programs, 502
Netscape Navigator, 640
program windows, 799–800
expanding toolbars, 610
Explorer. *See* Internet Explorer; Windows Explorer

exporting Registry files, 414–416, *415–417*
The Expert Guide to Windows 98 (Minasi, Christiansen, and Shapar), 329, 331, 391
Extended Data Out RAM (EDO RAM), **763**
extending RAM with swap files, 757–758
extensions, file, viewing, 75–76, *76*
Ezzell, Ben, 753

F

fans in PCs, 726–727, 728–729
Fast Page (FP Mode DRAM) Dynamic RAM, **763**
FAT32. *See also* system maintenance
converting to, 301–303, *302*
defined, **13**, **299**
versus FAT16, 299–300
limitations of, 300–301
returning to FAT16, 303
warning, 302
Favorites list, **550–559**. *See also* bookmarks; Internet Explorer; links
accessing, 37, 815
adding hot list pages to, 557–558
adding Web pages to, 552–553, 554, 815–816
defined, **887**
Favorites bar, 540, 551–552, *552*
Favorites menu, 551, *551*
Make Available Offline option, 558
organizing, 553–557, *554*, *556*, 816
overview of, 540, 550–551, *550*, 815
viewing, 551–552, *552*
Favorites menu in Windows Explorer, 812
Favorites option on Start menu, 37
Fax feature
composing faxes, 817
overview of, 12, 816
requesting faxes, 818–819
reviewing outgoing faxes, 819
WordPad applet and, 373
fax modems, **887**
File menu in Windows Explorer, **810–811**
File Transfer Protocol (FTP), **460**, **888**
file transfer protocols of HyperTerminal, 385

File Types tab in Folder Options dialog box, 823–824
files. *See also* system configuration files
    attaching to e-mail, 506–508, *507*, 513–515
    binary files, 386, *386*
    compressed files, **698**, **880**
    copying, 804–805
    cross-linked files, 290
    decompressing, 698, 702–703
    defined, **887**
    deleting, 806–807
    disk files, printing to, 199–200
    DOS .PIF files, 396–398
    .exe files, **698**
    extensions, viewing, 75–76, *76*
    file fragments, 290
    file sets in backups, 311
    filing mail in folders, 515–517
    LMHOSTS files, 356–357
    moving, 838–840
    naming, 843
    signature files, **513–515**, 601, 883, 905
    swap files, 757–758
    synchronizing with My Briefcase, 388–389
    temporary, in Internet Explorer, 537–538, *537*, 598
    text files
        defined, **908**
        saving e-mail as, 516
        sending/receiving, 386–387, *386–387*
Files and Folders option on Find menu, 819–821
filtering e-mail, 497, **517–521**, *520–521*, 888
filtering keystrokes with FilterKeys, 120
filtering Web site content, **580–597**. *See also* Internet Explorer security
    with Content Advisor, **582–592**
        blocking unrated pages, 587, 590
        creating passwords, 585
        disallowed pages, 588–590, *589*
        enabling, 584–587, *586*
        installing rating systems in, 590–592, *591*
        overview of, 582–583, 831
        rating systems, 583, 584
        setting ratings criteria, 587–588, 831
        warnings, 587, 590
    with Cyber Patrol, 583–584
    defined, **888**
    overview of, 580–582, 583–584
    with security zones
        assigning sites to, 596–597, *597*
        changing security levels for, 594–596, *594–595*, 603–604, 830
        defined, **830**
        overview of, 592–594
        warning, 596
    Web page authors and, 583, 584
Find: All Files dialog box
    Advanced tab, 820–821
    Date tab, 820
    Name & Location tab, 38, 39, 106, *106*, 820
    opening, 39, 819
    overview of, 38, *38*
Find dialog box, 408–409, 418–420, *418–420*
Find menu
    Computer option, 821
    defined, **819**
    Files and Folders option, 819–821
    On the Internet option, 821
    People option, 822
Find option on Start menu, 38–39, *38*
finding. *See also* searching
    computers on networks, 821
    files and folders
        using Find: All Files, 38–39, *38*
        using Find menu, 819–821
        using My Computer, 841–842
        in Windows Explorer, 815
    people in Internet directories, 822
    programs
        in Desktop shortcuts, 105
        on Program menu, 105, *105*
        using Find: All Files, 106, *106*
        in Windows Explorer, 106, *107*
    and replacing Web page text, 648

Web pages/sites on Internet, 821
    words in Registry, 408-409, 418-420, *418-420*
firewalls, 353, **888**
flaming, **501**, **888**
floppy disks
    backing up to, 309, 311
    copying, 84, *84*
    creating startup disks, 795-796
    defined, **888**
    drives for
        buying, 719
        Desktop shortcuts to, 84
        power connectors, 778, *779*
    formatting, 84-86, 825
    naming, 842-843
    overview of, 84
Folder Options dialog box, **822-824**
folders
    archived, restoring, 315-316, 855-857
    copying, 804-805
    creating, 561, 805-806
    customizing, 814
    defined, **10**, **888**
    deleting, 806-807
    filing mail in, 515-517
    finding, 38-39, *38*, 815
    moving, 838-840
    My Documents folder, **842**
    naming, 843
    passwords for, 849
    sharing, 77-83, *81*, *83*
    for Web shortcuts, 561
Folders bar in Internet Explorer, 541, *542*
fonts
    adding to computers, 825
    in Desktop displays, 49, 51, *151*, **153-154**, *154*, **163-164**, 824
    in FrontPage Web pages, 663-666, *664*
    in Netscape Navigator, 620-622
    overview of, 7, 824
    printing samples of, 825
    smoothing, 157, 158
    viewing samples of, 825

Fonts applet in Control Panel, *114*, **115**, **824-825**
formatting
    e-mail with HTML, 509-510
    floppy disks, 84-86, 825
    Web pages, **663-672**
        with <META> tags, 671-672
        background color, 669-670
        background images, 670
        background sound, *668*, 669
        browsers and, 663
        fonts, 663-666, *664*
        margins, 670
        overview of, 663
        page properties, 668-670, *668*
        paragraph properties, 666-668
        titles, 668, *668*
forms, Netscape Navigator and, 623-624
forums, **446**, **888**
Forward button
    in Internet Explorer, 542
    in Netscape Navigator, 629-631
    in Windows Explorer, 812
forwarding e-mail, **508-509**, 888
Forwarding tab of Modems Properties dialog box, 270, *270*
FP (Fast Page) Mode DRAM (Dynamic RAM), **763**
frames in Netscape Navigator
    borderless frames, **632**
    framesets, **673**
    overview of, 631-633, *632*
    printing, 639
freeware, **461**, **704**, **888**
FrontPage Express Web pages, **643-683**. *See also* home pages; Web pages
    adding
        bookmarks, 675-676
        bulleted lists, 661-663
        headings, 661
        horizontal lines, 658-660
        numbered lists, 661-663
    creating
        overview of, 652-653, *653*
        from templates, 653-654
        with Wizards, 654, *655*

creating links in
    automatically, 673
    to bookmarks, 674
    and deleting, 675
    and navigating, 656
    overview of, 672–673
    and revising, 674
    warning, 676
defined, **826**
editing
    adding comments, 649
    finding and replacing text, 648
    HTML source code, 649–650, *650*
    inserting line breaks, 647
    inserting special characters, 647–648
    overview of, 646–647
    and previewing changes, 650–651
formatting
    with <META> tags, 671–672
    background color, 669–670
    background images, 670
    background sound, *668*, 669
    browsers and, 663
    fonts, 663–666, *664*
    margins, 670
    overview of, 663
    page properties, 668–670, *668*
    paragraph properties, 666–668
    titles, 668, *668*
HTML source code, viewing, 649–650, *650*
HTML tags, creating attributes for, 659
images in
    aligning, 681–682
    alternatives to, 681
    archiving, 677
    background images, 670
    choosing type of, 680–681, *680*
    inline images, 678–679, **891**
    inserting, 656, 660
    moving, 679
    properties for, 679–683, *680*
    sizing, 682–683
    sources for, 677–678

navigating, 645–646, *645*, 656
opening, 655–656
overview of, 644–646
printing, 651–652
saving, 657
starting FrontPage, 644
WebBots and, 654
FTP (File Transfer Protocol), **460**, **888**

G

Game Controllers applet in Control Panel, *114*, **116**, 278, *278*
games programs, 826
Gates, Bill, 754
gateways, **445**, *445*
generic PCs, **712–713**
GIF image format, 677
Go button in Internet Explorer, 535
Go menu in Windows Explorer, **812**
graphics. *See* images; multimedia

H

hard disk drives. *See* disk drives, hard
hardware, **263–285**. *See also* computers; disk drives; PCs; printers; video
    digital cameras, 272–273
    game controllers (joysticks), 278, *278*
    infrared devices, 279, *279*
    installing, 128–136, *129–130*, *132–134*
    modems, **264–272**
        cable modems, 468, **878**
        defined, **896**
        deleting, 266
        fax modems, **887**
        installing, 264–265, *265*, *266*
        internal modems, **891**
        overview of, 264
        properties for, 266–271, *267–271*
        replacing, 267
        speed, 456
        troubleshooting, 268, 271–272, *272*
    overview of, 261, 263–264
    peripherals vendors, 916–959, 963–978

hardware—images 997

printers, 273–276, *275*
requirements for Web TV, 248–249
scanners, 272–273, 678
headings, adding to Web pages, 661
heat protection for PCs. *See also* PCs, protecting
    case design and, 727–728
    causes of heat, 726–727, 731
    duty cycles and, 730–731
    with fans, 726–727, 728–729
    with heat sensor devices, 729
    with heat sinks, 727
    overview of, 726
    safe temperatures, 729–730
    from sunbeams, 731
    from thermal shock, 731
Help
    in dialog boxes, 828, 869
    in Internet Explorer, 833
    Offline Help, 52, 53–54, *53*
    overview of, 39, 51–53, *52*, 826–827
    Troubleshooters feature, 133, 827–828
    Web Help, 52, 54, 828
    What's This?, 869
    in Windows Explorer, 812
hiding
    Internet Explorer toolbars, 531
    network computers, 439
    Taskbar, 40, 863
History lists
    defined, **890**
    in Internet Explorer, 540, *541*
    in Netscape Navigator, 629–630
HKEY subtrees in Registry, 399, **405–407**
home pages. *See also* FrontPage Express Web pages; Web pages
    changing, 543–545, *545*
    creating, 654, *655*
    defined, **890**
    returning to, 609–610
horizontal lines, adding to Web pages, 658–660
host computers, **457**, **890**
host drives, **305**
hot keys. *See* keyboard shortcuts
hot links. *See also* links
    hot lists of, 557–558, **890**

    in Internet Explorer, 536–537
    in Netscape Navigator, 615–617
HotBot Web search tool, 693
Hotmail.com, 493
HTML (Hypertext Markup Language)
    defined, **890**
    formatting e-mail with, 509–510
    hypertext, defined, **447**, **890**
    overview of, 644
    source code, editing, 649–650, *650*
    tags, creating attributes for, 659
hue, **156**
hyperlinks. *See* links
HyperTerminal applet. *See also* applets; Internet connections
    creating connections, 383–385
    defined, **382**
    file transfer protocols of, 385
    receiving files, 387, *387*
    saving sessions, 387–388
    sending files, 386, *386*
    starting, 382, *383*
    using connections, 388

I

I/O (input/output) hardware, 13, **713**, **891**
icons
    defined, **891**
    on Desktop
        moving, 840
        My Computer icon, 45
        options for, 50, 157–158, *157*
    of shortcuts, changing, 62–63
    on Start menu, sizing, 863
    on Taskbar, 41, 861–862
    of Web shortcuts, changing, 560–561, *561*
ICS (Internet Connection Sharing), **8**, **465**
identification settings in Network applet, 354–355, *355–356*
Identities feature in Outlook Express, **575**, **891**
identities of Web sites, verifying, **600–605**. *See also* certificates
images. *See also* multimedia
    animating menus, *157*, 158

images—installing

creating with Paint applet, **376**, 420, **845–847**
editing with Paint applet, **376–377**, 420, 847
excluding downloads of, 834–835
loading in Netscape Navigator, 612, 630–631
speed options for Desktop, 167–168, *167*, 285
in Web pages
    aligning, 681–682
    alternatives to, 681
    archiving, 677
    background images, 670
    choosing type of, 680–681, *680*
    inline images, 678–679, **891**
    inserting, 656, 660
    moving, 679
    properties for, 679–683, *680*
    sizing, 682–683
    sources for, 677–678
importing
    address books, 796–797
    saved Registries, 421–422, *422–423*
Infoseek Web address, 695
Infrared applet in Control Panel, *114*, **116**, 279, *279*
.INI (initialization) files, 402, **431**, **891**. *See also* SCANREG.INI files; system configuration files
inline images, **678–679**, **891**
input/output (I/O) hardware, 13, **713**, **891**
Install Hardware Wizard, 128–136, *129–130*, *132–134*
installing. *See also* uninstalling
    content ratings files, 591–592
    defined, **891**
    Dial-Up Networking, **335–346**
        on client machines, 337–344, *337–343, 345–346*
        Dial-up Server, 359–364, *360–363*
        for Internet connections, 479–480, *479*
        on networks, 335–336, *335*, *336*
        overview of, 335
    hardware, **128–136**, *129–130, 132–134*

local printers, **178–187**
    choosing ports, 183, *183*, 185
    local, defined, **893**
    naming and, 183–184, *184*
    overview of, 178–179
    printer drivers, 180–181, 186–187
    reasons for, 179–180
    uninstalling, 189, 275
    when printer not listed, 185–187
    Wizard for, 181–184, *182–184*, 273–274
memory chips, 765–767, *766–768*
modems, 264–265, *265*, *266*
mouse drivers, 276–277, *277*, *278*
network printers, 274–275, *275*
programs, **97–105**
    from CD-ROMs, 98–99, *98*
    from Control Panel, 100–102, *101–102*, 137–138, *137–138*, 794
    directly from networks, 796
    overview of, 97–98, 828
    reinstalling, 139
    uninstalling, 103–105, *104*, 138–139, 866
RAM, **771–786**
    deciding amount needed, 782–783
    dismounting power supplies, 776–778, *777*, *779*
    EDO RAM chips, 783
    locating memory sockets, 775–776, *775*
    memory access speed and, 783
    in motherboard/daughterboards, 780
    opening computer cases, 772–774, *774*
    overview of, 771, 786
    removing ribbon cable connectors, 779–780
    static electricity and, 771–772, 784, *785*
    steps in, 784–786, *785*
    tin or gold contacts and, 784
    types of chips, 783
    warnings, 772, 773, 778, 782, 785
rating systems in Content Advisor, 590–592, *591*

installing — Internet connections

Remote Registry, 425
sound schemes, 228
Web TV for Windows, 248
Windows 98 SE, **15-32**
    components, 795
    finding/fixing problems before, 25-26
    multi-booting with Linux, 32
    to new directories, 24-25
    onto compressed drives, 28-30
    over OS/2, 31
    over Windows 3.*x*, 95, or 98, 18-24, *19*
    overview of, 15-17
    removing Uninstall files, 28
    reverting to previous OSs, 26-27
    saving system files during Setup, 27-28
    ScanDisk and, 25-26
    and uninstalling, 26-27
    warnings, 17, 25, 29
    on Windows NT or 2000 computers, 31
Intellimouse, 125-126
interactivity, **205-206**
interfaces. *See also* Desktop
    defined, **909**
    in FrontPage Express, 645-646
    in Netscape Navigator, 610-614, *611*, *614*
internal modems, **891**
Internet, **443-462**. *See also* World Wide Web
    defined, **444**, **891**
    downloading files from, 460-461
    features
        building Web pages, 460
        in business applications, 451-452
        Chat programs, 460
        Desktop access to, 450
        discussion groups, 446
        e-mail, 11, 444-446, *445*
        File Transfer Protocol, 460
        overview of, 450
        PointCast Network, 450-451, *451*
        search engines, **459**, 524-525, **690-693**, *692*, 904
        Usenet newsgroups, 459, **909**

    getting on
        at home, 453-455, *454*
        Internet addresses and, 456-458
        modem speed and, 456
        overview of, 452
        warnings, 453, 456, 461
        at work, 452-453
    history of, 447-449, *449*
    overview of, 440, 443-444
    using with other platforms, 458
    Web sites about, 461-462
    versus World Wide Web, 446-449, *449*
Internet Connection Sharing (ICS), 8, 465, **485-488**, *487-488*, 892
Internet Connection Wizard, 349-351, *349-351*, 476-478, *477*, **800-802**
Internet connections, **465-488**
    via Dial-Up Networking, **478-488**. *See also* Dial-Up Networking
        altering connections, 351, *351*, 801-802
        changing default connections, 482-483, *483*
        creating connection profiles, 480-482, *481-482*
        installing DUN software, 479-480, *479*
        Never Dial A Connection option, 483-484, *483*
        overview of, 11, 344, *345*
        sample ISP information, 352
        setting up, 349-352, *349-351*, 478-479, 801
        sharing on networks, 485-488, *487-488*
    via HyperTerminal applet
        creating connections, 383-385
        defined, **382**
        file transfer protocols of, 385
        receiving files, 387, *387*
        saving sessions, 387-388
        sending binary or text files, 386, *386*
        starting, 382, *383*
        using connections, 388
    via Internet Service Providers
        defined, **454-455**, *454*, **892**

e-mail and, 506
local ISPs, 472-473, 475-478, *477*
national ISPs, 471-472
questions to ask, 469-471
sample ISP information, 352
types of accounts, 455-456, *456*
to Netscape Navigator, 609
via online services, **454-455**, *454*, **473-475**, 898
overview of, 11, 465, 831-832
speed of, 467-468
types of, 466-469
warning, 475
The Internet Dictionary (Crumlish), 873
Internet Explorer, **527-565**
AutoComplete feature, 535
AutoScan feature, 535
configuring, 834
default browsers and, 564
defined, **4-7**, *5-6*, **833**, **892**
downloading files, 696-697, *696*
excluding multimedia downloads, 834-835
Favorites list, **550-559**
adding hot list pages to, 557-558
adding Web pages to, 552-553, 554
Favorites bar, 540, 551-552, *552*
Favorites menu, 551, *551*
Make Available Offline option, 558
organizing, 553-554, *554*, 555-557
overview of, 540, 550-551, *550*
viewing, 551-552, *552*
Folders bar, 541, *542*
Go button, 535
Help menu, 833
History bar, 540, *541*
home pages, changing, 543-545, *545*
main screen, 528-531, *529*
moving around Web, **534-543**
via Back and Forward buttons, 542
via Explorer bars, 538-541, *539*, *541-542*
via hot links, 536-537
overview of, 534
returning to visited sites, 537-538, *537*
by typing addresses, 534-536
viewing multiple windows, 543
Netscape Navigator and, 624-625
overview of, 527
returning to favorite Web pages, **549-563**
via Favorites list, 550-559, *550-552*, *554*, *556*
overview of, 549-550
Temporary Internet Files and, 537-538, *537*
via Web shortcuts, 559-563, *561*, *563*
saving Web pages, 558-559
Search bar
customizing searches, 548, *548*, 693-694, *694*
defined, *5*, **540**
opening, 4, 547, 695
using, 547-548, *547*
speeding up, 834-835
starting, 528
Temporary Internet Files, 537-538, *537*, 598, 834
Tip of the Day bar, 541, *542*
toolbars
Address bar, 534-536, 548
hiding/displaying, 531
Links bar, 531-533
moving, 531
overview of, 528-529
Radio toolbar, 5, *6*, 530-531
viewing Web pages offline, 558-559, 834
warnings, 546, 564
Web shortcuts
changing icons for, 560-561, *561*
creating folders for, 561
opening from keyboard, 562, *563*
overview of, 559
sending to other users, 562-563
to Web pages, creating, 560
Internet Explorer security, **567-605**
certificates, **600-605**
defined, **600**
downloading certified programs, 601-603
managing, 831

overview of, 597–598
personal certificates, 600, 604–605
publisher certificates, 600, 601–604
security level settings, 603–604
site certificates, 600, 604
types of, 600
warning, 600
Content Advisor, **582–592**
blocking unrated pages, 587, 590
creating passwords, 585
disallowed pages, 588–590, *589*
enabling, 584–587, *586*
installing rating systems in, 590–592, *591*
overview of, 582–583, 831
rating systems, 583, 584
setting ratings criteria, 587–588, 831
warnings, 587, 590
encrypting transfers, 597–600
filtering site content, **580–597**
with Content Advisor, 582–592, *586*, *589*, *591*
with Cyber Patrol, 583–584
overview of, 580–582, 583–584
with security zones, 592–597, *594–595*, 597, 830
Web page authors and, 583, 584
guarding privacy, **568–580**
with cookie settings, 571–572
overview of, 568–569, 705–706
with passwords, 569–571
with Profile Assistant, 572–575, *574*
with Wallet, 576–580, *577*, *579–580*
overview of, 565, 567
securing connections, **597–600**
Security Alert messages, 599–600
security zones, **592–597**
assigning sites to, 596–597, *597*
changing security levels for, 594–596, *594–595*, 603–604, 830
defined, **830**
overview of, 592–594
warning, 596
verifying Web site identities, **600–605**
warnings, 598

The Internet: No Experience Required (Crumlish), 443, 491, 492, 685
Internet Options applet. *See also* Control Panel
Advanced tab, 832
Connection tab, 831–832
Content tab, 830–831
defined, *114*, **116**, **829**
General tab, 829
opening, 829
Programs tab, 832
Security tab, 830
The Internet Society, **461**
ISDN (Integrated Services Digital Network), 332, 466, 467, **892**
ISPs (Internet Service Providers). *See also* Internet connections
defined, **454–455**, *454*, **892**
e-mail and, 506
local ISPs, 472–473, 475–478, *477*
national ISPs, 471–472
questions to ask, 469–471
sample ISP information, 352
types of accounts, 455–456, *456*

J

joysticks. *See* Game Controllers
JPEG image format, 677
Juno.com, 493

K

Keyboard applet in Control Panel, *114*, 116, **835–836**
keyboard shortcuts. *See also* shortcuts
defined, **904**
listed, 68–70, *70*
opening Web shortcuts with, 562, *563*
removing, 66
starting programs with, 66–67, 862
as Web TV controls, 258–259
Windows keys, **911**
keyboards
accessibility options, 119–121, *119*
language options, 835–836
protecting, 747
speed options, 835

keys, Registry, **405–406**
Kienan, Brenda, 607

L

language options. *See also* HTML
    in DVD Player, 226–227
    for keyboards, 835–836
line breaks, 647
lines, horizontal, 658–660
links. *See also* bookmarks; Favorites
    creating in Web pages
        automatically, 673
        to bookmarks, 674
        and deleting, 675
        and navigating, 656
        overview of, 672–673
        and revising, 674
        warning, 676
    defined, **457**, **893**
    on Desktop to Web, 49–50, 159, **792–793**, 803–804
    in e-mail messages, 499, 505
    hot links
        hot lists of, 557–558, **890**
        in Internet Explorer, 536–537
        in Netscape Navigator, 615–617
    visited links, **617**
Links toolbar
    in Internet Explorer, 531–533
    on Taskbar, 43, 864
    in Windows Explorer, 814
Linux operating systems, 32
liquids, PCs and, 747–749
LMHOSTS files, 356–357
Log Off option on Start menu, 39, **836**, **894**
logon security, 836
lost file fragments, 290
luminosity bar, **156**, *156*
lurking, **459**, **894**
Lycos Web address, 695

M

Magellan Web address, 695
magnetism, PCs and, 733–735

mail. *See* e-mail
Maintenance Wizard, **295–297**, *296*
Make Available Offline option, 558
mapping drives, 82–83, *83*
margins in Web pages, 670
Mastering Microsoft Internet Explorer 4,
    (Weisskopf and Coleman), 567, 644
Mastering Windows 98 Second Edition
    (Cowart), 15, 113, 175, 203, 465
Maximize button, **837**, **894–895**
MCI (Media Control Interface) devices, **260**
Media Player program, **219**, **233–234**, **837**
memory, **895**. *See also* RAM
memory cache, 635, **895**
memory vendors, 961–962
menus. *See also* shortcut menus
    animating, *157*, 158
    defined, **896**
    Edit menus, 804–805, 811, 839, 850
    in Paint program, 847
    preventing from following mouse, 437
    in Windows Explorer, 810–812
<META> tags, 671–672
Mickeys, **171**
Microsoft
    address, 941
    Download Service (MSDL), 128
    Fax
        composing faxes, 817
        overview of, 12, 816
        requesting faxes, 818–819
        reviewing outgoing faxes, 819
        WordPad applet and, 373
    NetMeeting, **843**, **897**
    phone numbers, 128, 941
    Wallet, **576–580**, *577*, *579–580*
    Web addresses
        accessibility support, 119
        digital TV integration, 249
        getting ISDN, 466
        ordering CDs, 3
        search site, 821
        Web Gallery, 660
Microsoft Windows. *See* Windows
MIDI Mapper program, 220

MIDI (Musical Instrument Digital Interface) — multimedia 1003

MIDI (Musical Instrument Digital Interface), 206
Minasi, Mark, 327, 331, 391, 711, 722, 725, 750, 915
Minimize button, **837**, **896**
modems, **264-272**
    cable modems, 468, **878**
    defined, **896**
    deleting, 266
    fax modems, **887**
    installing, 264-265, *265-266*
    internal modems, **891**
    overview of, 264
    replacing, 267
    setting properties
        call forwarding, 270, *270*
        connections, 268, *268*, *269*
        dialing locations, 270, *271*
        distinctive rings, 269, *269*
        overview of, 266-267, *267*
    speed, 456
    troubleshooting, 268, 271-272, *272*
Modems applet. *See also* Control Panel
    Connection tab, 268, *268*, *269*
    defined, *114*, **116**, **837**
    Distinctive Ring tab, 269, *269*
    Forwarding tab, 270, *270*
    General tab, 266-267, *267*
monitor display. *See* Desktop; Display applet
monitors. *See* video monitors
motherboard/daughterboards, 780
motherboards, **713**, 718
Mouse applet. *See also* Control Panel
    Buttons tab, 168-169, *169*
    defined, *114*, **116**, **838**
    Motion tab, 171-173, *172*
    Pointers tab, 170, *171*
mouse options, **168-173**
    for accessibility, 123-126, *124*
    buying mice, 719
    double-click speed, 169, *169*
    installing mouse drivers, 276-277, *277-278*
    left-right button reversal, 168-169, *168*
    overview of, 168, 838
    pointer schemes, 170-171, *171*

pointer speed and trails, 171-173, *172*
preventing menus from following, 437
moving
    Desktop icons, 840
    files and folders, 838-840
    Internet Explorer toolbars, 531
    Programs menu shortcuts, 109
    Taskbar, 40
    Web page images, 679
MSDL (Microsoft Download Service), 128
MS-DOS. *See also* AUTOEXEC.BAT files
    defined, **884**, **897**
    Memory utility, 758-759, *759*
    programs, shortcuts to, 67
    RAM and, 754-756
multimedia, **203-261**. *See also* images; sound
    CD Player, **240-248**
        cataloging CDs, 244-246, *245*
        control buttons, 241-242
        creating play lists, 246
        defined, **219**, **240-241**, *240*, **799**
        display options, 242-243
        play order options, 243-244
        running, 241
        setting preferences, 247-248
        Toolbar, 242-243
        using play lists, 247
    default settings, 841
    defined, **205**, **897**
    drivers for, adding, 220
    drivers for, managing, 260
    DVD Player, **220-227**
        creating passwords, 224
        defined, **208**, **219-220**
        DVD drives, 215-216, 220-223
        ending, 227
        language options, 226-227
        running, 223-225
        searching in, 225-226
        subtitle options, 226-227
    excluding downloads of, 834-835
    features, 207-208
    Media Player, **219**, **233-234**, **837**
    MIDI Mapper, 220

overview of, 203–207
photos, 213–214
Sound Recorder, **235–240**
    converting sound file formats, 239–240
    defined, **219**, **235**
    disk space and, 237
    editing sound files, 238–240
    memory and, 238
    playing sound files, 235–236
    recording sound, 236–238, *237*
Sounds applet, **228–232**
    assigning sounds to events, 228, 229–231, *231*
    defined, *114*, **117**, **218–219**
    deleting sound schemes, 232
    installing sound schemes, 228
    recording sound, 228–229
    saving sound schemes, 231–232
    sound file sources, 229
    storing sounds, 230
    troubleshooting sound, 229
upgrading to, **208–218**
    CD-R drives, 214–215
    CD-ROM drives, 213–214
    CD-RW drives, 214–215
    computers, 212–213
    DVD drives, 215–216
    methods of, 209–212
    monitors, 217–218
    overview of, 208–209
    sound boards, 217
    speakers, 216
    video cards, 217–218
Volume Control, 220, **867–868**
Web TV for Windows, **248–259**
    adding channels to listings, 253, *253*
    adding channels to toolbar, 258
    avoiding Channel 1, 254
    benefits of, 249–250
    defined, **7**, **248**
    hardware requirements, 248–249
    how it works, 250
    installing, 248
    keystroke controls, 258–259

    online documentation, 253
    reading about programs, 256–257, *256*
    remote controls, 258–259
    removing channels, 253, *253*
    running, 250–252, *251*, *252*
    scrolling displays, 254, *255*, **903**
    searching for shows, 254–256
    setting reminders, 257
    sizing displays, 254
Multimedia applet in Control Panel, *114*, 116, **841**
Musical Instrument Digital Interface (MIDI), 206, 220
My Briefcase applet, **388–389**
My Computer tool, 45, **841–842**
My Documents folder, **842**

N

Name & Location tab of Find dialog box, *38*, 39, 106, *106*, 820
names, domain, **457**, 458, 494, **884**
names, user, **457**, 494, **909**
naming
    bookmarks, 676
    files and folders, 843
    hard or floppy disks, 842–843
    My Computer icon, 45
    printers, 183–184, *184*
    shortcuts, 61
nanoseconds (ns), **762**
navigating
    defined, **897**
    in Internet Explorer, 542
    in Netscape Navigator, 629–631, 633
    Registry, 408
    Web pages/links, 645–646, *645*, 656
Net, **897**. *See also* Internet
Netiquette, **459**, **500–502**, **897**
NetMeeting program, **843**, **897**
Netscape Communicator, downloading, 608
Netscape Messenger. *See also* e-mail
    address books, 524
    attaching files to mail, 507–508

attaching signatures to mail, 514–515
filing mail in folders, 516–517
filtering mail, 519–521, *520*, *521*
formatting mail with HTML, 510
multiple mail accounts, 520–521, *521*
overview of, 503–505, *504*, 509
spell checking mail, 513
Netscape Navigator, **607–641**
   Back button, 629–630, 633
   cache in
      cache checking options, 634–635, *635*
      defined, **633**, **878**, **895**
      increasing disk cache size, 635–636
      overview of, 633–634
      warning, 635
   changing fonts, 620–622
   changing text color, 622–623, *623*
   downloading, 608
   error messages, 636–638
   forms and, 623–624
   Forward button, 629–631
   frames, 631–633, *632*, 639
   getting information on, 640
   History list, 629–630
   home page, returning to, 609–610
   image loading, 612, 630–631
   interface, 610–614, *611*, *614*
   Internet connections to, 609
   Internet Explorer and, 624–625
   launching, 608–610
   navigating in, 629–631, 633
   opening Web pages
      and bookmarking, 633
      and exiting all at once, 640
      via hot links, 615–617
      and jumping among, 629–631
      overview of, 615
      and printing, 638–639
      and reloading, 630, 634, 637
      security and, 613, 619–620
      and switching between, 619
      by typing URLs, 613, 617–618, *617*
   overview of, 448, *449*, 607
   printing frames, 639
   quitting, 640, **901**
   saving files to hard drives
      filenames and, 626
      images, 627, 628
      links, 627–628
      overview of, 624
      and viewing offline, 628–629
      Web pages, 625–627, *626*
   security features, 613, 619–620
   shortcut menus, 629
   Stop button, 630, 640
   toolbars
      collapsing/expanding, 610
      Component bar, 614, *614*
      hiding/displaying, 610
      Location toolbar, 613
      menu bar, 610
      Navigation toolbar, 609, 610–612
      overview of, *611*
      Personal toolbar, 613
      scroll bars, 614, **903**
      status bar, 613
   warning, 640
Netscape Web addresses
   Assistance, 615
   Customer Showcase, 620
   Navigator, News of the Day, 639
   Web Security Solutions, 613
NetShow feature, **208**
NetWare Connect software, **333**, 343
Network applet. *See also* Control Panel
   access control settings, 367–368, *367–368*
   defined, *114*, **116**
   identification settings, 354–355, *355–356*
networks. *See also* Dial-Up Networking; sharing
   browse lists, 439
   direct serial connections, 368–369
   hiding computers on, 439
   installing DUN on, 335–336, *335–336*
   passwords in, 353–354, 849–850
   refreshing print queue information, 196
   setting up, 77–80
Never Dial A Connection option, 483–484, *483*
newbies, **446**

newsgroups, **446**, 459, 844, **898**
NewsLink Web site, AJR, 550, *550*
newsreaders, **898**. *See also* Outlook Express
Niko Mak Computing, Inc., 698, 699
Notepad applet, **86-87**, **372**
ns (nanoseconds), **762**
Number tab of Regional Settings dialog box, 853-854
numbered lists in Web pages, 661-663
numbers, calculating. *See* Calculator applet

O

ODBC Data Sources applet in Control Panel, *114*, **116**
Offline Help, 52, 53-54, *53*
offline, viewing Web pages, 558-559, 834, **898**
On the Internet option on Find menu, 821
online, **898**
online buying, **704-706**, *706*
online documentation for Web TV, 253
online services, **454-455**, *454*, **473-475**, 898
Online Services feature, **11**, 844
operating systems. *See also* MS-DOS; system; Windows
    defined, **898-899**, **906**
    environments, **898-899**
    Linux, 32
    RAM requirements, 755-757
    reverting to previous systems, 26-28
Outlook Express. *See also* e-mail
    address books, 523-524
    attaching files to mail, 507, *507*
    attaching signatures to mail, 514
    configuring, 845
    creating identities, 575, **891**
    defined, **844**, **899**
    filing mail in folders, 516
    filtering mail, 518-519
    formatting mail with HTML, 510
    new message window, 493, *494*
    newsgroups, 844
    as newsreader, 844, **898**
    overview of, 5, *6*, 11-12, 502-503, 509
    spell checking mail, 512

output devices, 13
overvoltage, **742**

P

packaged DIP chips. *See* RAM
Paint applet, **376-377**, 420, **845-847**
Paint Shop Pro software, 377
PAP (Password Authentication Protocol), 364-365
paragraphs in Web pages, formatting, 666-668
parallel ports, buying, 720
parity RAM chips, 764
Partition Magic program, **303**
partitions, hard drive, **299**, 307, **899**
passwords
    in Content Advisor, 585
    defined, **899**
    for Dial-up Server, 361, *361*, 849
    for DVD Player, 224
    in Internet Explorer, 569-571
    in networking, 353-354, 849-850
    for printers, 181, 849
    for screen savers, 149-150, 849
    for shared resources, 849-850
    synchronizing, 353-354
Passwords applet. *See also* Control Panel
    changing passwords, 353-354, 848-850
    defined, *114*, **117**, **847-848**
    enabling user profiles, 848
    remote administration options, 428-430, *428-430*, 850
    specifying passwords, 848
Paste command, 805, 839-840, 850, **881**
patterns for Desktop backgrounds, **143-146**, *144*
PB SRAM (Pipeline Burst Synchronous RAM), **764**
PC-100 RAM, **763**
PC Complete, 753
PC Power and Cooling, Inc., 729
PC User's Essential Accessible Pocket Dictionary (Dyson), 873
PCI busses, 717-718
PCMCIA applet in Control Panel, *114*, **117**

PCs, buying, **711-722**. *See also* computer vendors
    choosing computer dealers, 720-722
    choosing market niches, 715
    choosing PC parts
        cases, 712-713
        CPUs, 716-717
        disk drives, 719
        floppy disk drives, 719
        I/O, 713, **891**
        mice, 719
        motherboards, 713, 718
        overview of, 716
        parallel ports, 720
        PCI busses, 717-718
        printers, 720
        RAM, 718, 782-784
        ROM BIOS, 718
        serial ports, 720
        USBs, 720
        video boards, 713, 719
        video monitors, 719
    compatibility and, 714, **880**
    criteria for, 714-715
    generic PCs, 712-713
    overview of, 711-712
    price/performance and, 714-715
    proprietary PCs, 713-715
    serviceability and, 714
    upgradability and, 714
PCs, protecting, **725-750**
    from corrosion, 748-749
    from dust, 732-733
    from heat, **726-731**
        case design and, 727-728
        causes of, 726-727, 731
        duty cycles and, 730-731
        with fans, 726-727, 728-729
        with heat sensor devices, 729
        with heat sinks, 727
        overview of, 726
        safe temperatures, 729-730
        sunbeams, 731
        thermal shock, 731
    keyboards, 747
    by leaving on all day, 740-742
    from liquids, 747-749
    from magnetism, 733-735
    overview of, 75, 749-750
    from smoke, 733
    from speaker magnets, 735
    from stray electromagnetism, **735-747**
        crosstalk, 736-737
        electromagnetic interference, 735-739
        electrostatic discharge, 743-747, 771-772, 784, *785*
        overview of, 735
        overvoltage, 742
        power noise, 739-743
        radio frequency interference, 737-739
        transients, 742
        undervoltage, 742-743
    from viruses, 697-698, 910
    while cleaning, 781
    X-rays and, 733-734
People option on Find menu, 822
peripherals. *See* hardware
personal certificates, 600, **604-605**
Personal Home Page Wizard, 654, *655*
Phone Dialer applet
    overview of, 378-379, *378*
    speed dialing, 379-380, *379*
    telephone logs, 380
phone numbers
    BIOS upgrade vendors, 962-963
    computer/component vendors, 916-959, 963-978
    data recovery vendors, 959-961
    memory vendors, 961-962
    Microsoft Corporation, 128, 941
    national ISPs, 472
    PC repair/exchange vendors, 979-981
    peripherals vendors, 916-959, 963-978
    recycling centers, 981
    storage device vendors, 963
photos, 213-214
PICS content ratings, **583**

pictures — programs

pictures. *See* images; multimedia
.PIF files in DOS, 396–398
Pipeline Burst Synchronous RAM (PB SRAM), **764**
PnP (Plug-and-Play) feature, **127–128**, 204, 264, **850**, **900**
PointCast Network feature, **450–451**, *451*
Pointers tab of Mouse Properties dialog box, 170, *171*
ports
    defined, **900**
    for local printers, 183, *183*, 185
    parallel or serial ports, 720
POTS (Plain Old Telephone Service), 466, 467, 468
Power Management applet in Control Panel, *114*, **117**
power noise. *See also* electromagnetism; PCs, protecting
    leaving computers on and, 740–742
    overview of, 739–740
    overvoltage, 742
    transients, 742
power supplies, dismounting, 776–778, *777*, *779*
Powers, J. Tarin, 607
PPP accounts with ISPs, **455–456**, *456*
PPP (Point-to-Point Protocol), **333**, 343, **900**
PPTP DUN connections, 339–341, *340–341*, 353, 359
PPTP (Point-to-Point Tunneling Protocol), **333**
preferences, CD Player, 247–248. *See also* properties
print queues
    canceling all jobs in, 197
    defined, **176**
    deleting files from, 196–197
    pausing/resuming jobs in, 198–199
    refreshing network information on, 196
    viewing, 194–195
printers, **175–200**
    accessing, 181, 273
    buying, 720
    default printers, 190
    deleting, 189, 275
    installing local printers, **178–187**
        choosing ports, 183, *183*, 185
        local, defined, **893**
        naming and, 183–184, *184*
        overview of, 178–179
        printer drivers, 180–181, 186–187
        reasons for, 179–180
        when printer not listed, 185–187
        Wizard for, 181–184, *182–184*, 273–274
    installing on networks, 274–275, *275*
    overview of, 175–177
    passwords for, 181, 849
    Printers applet, *114*, **117**
    Printers command, 851
    properties, 187–188, *188*, 275–276
    shortcuts to, 64, 192, 194
    uninstalling, 189, 275
printing
    to disk files, 199–200
    documents from programs, 190–194, *191*, *193*
    by dragging to printers, 192–194, *193*
    font samples, 825
    FrontPage Web pages, 651–652
    in Netscape Navigator, 638–639
    overview of, 175–177
    Print Manager, 176, 177–178
    shortcuts to, 64, 192, 194
    troubleshooting, 276
    in WordPad, 374
privacy, guarding, **568–580**. *See also* Internet Explorer security; security
    with cookie settings, 571–572
    overview of, 568–569, 705–706
    with passwords, 569–571
    with Profile Assistant, 572–575, *574*
    with Wallet, 576–580, *577*, *579–580*
processors, **716–717**, **879**, **896**
Profile Assistant, **572–575**, *574*
profiles, user, enabling, 848
programs, **97–111**. *See also* Add/Remove Programs applet
    closing, 799–800, **880**
    defined, **901**
    finding
        in Desktop shortcuts, 105

with Find: All Files tool, 106, *106*
on Program menu, 37, 105, *105*, **851-852**
in Windows Explorer, 106, *107*
freeware, **461**, **704**, **888**
installing
    from CD-ROMs, 98-99, *98*
    from Control Panel, 100-102, *101-102*, 137-138, *137-138*, 794
    directly from networks, 796
    overview of, 97-98, 828
    reinstalling, 139
    uninstalling, 103-105, *104*, 138-139, 866
removing via Control Panel, 138-139, 794-795
removing from Start menu, 64
running from CD-ROMs, 99-100, *100*
running on DUN connections, 341-342
shareware, **695**, **704**, **904**
shortcuts to
    on Desktop, 63-64, 75, 108
    via keystrokes, 66-67, 862
    overview of, 107
    on Programs menu, 108-109, *108*
    on Quick Launch toolbar, 109-110, 864
    on Send To menu, 110, *111*
    on Start menu, 109
    on Taskbar, 862
Programs menu, 37, **105**, *105*, **851-852**
Programs tab of Internet Options dialog box, 832
Programs window, 63-64, 108-109, *108*
Properties dialog boxes, **46**, *47*, 188, **852**, 901
properties for. *See also* preferences
    Desktop, 47-51, *48*
    fonts
        in Desktop displays, 49, 51, *151*, 153-154, *154*, 163-164, 824-825
        in FrontPage Web pages, 663-666, *664*, 824
    mice, 168-173, *168-169*, *171-172*
    paragraphs, 666-668
    printers, 187-188, *188*, 275-276

Recycle Bin, 93-94, *93*
shortcuts, 61-63, *62*
SNAP.EXE, 393-396, *394*, *395*
Taskbar, 863-864
Web page images, 679-683, *680*
Web pages, 668-670, *668*
proprietary PCs, **713-715**
protecting PCs. *See* PCs, protecting
protocols
    defined, **444**, **901**
    in Dial-Up Networking, 333-334, 364-366
    File Transfer Protocol, **460**, **888**
    HyperTerminal file transfer protocols, 385
    Point-to-Point Protocol, **333**, 343, **900**
    Secure Sockets Layer protocol, 597-599
    TCP/IP networking protocols, **466**, **907**
proxy servers, **832**, **901**
publisher certificates, 600, **601-604**

Q

Quarterdeck Cleansweep software, 138
queues. *See* print queues
Quick Launch toolbar. *See also* Taskbar
    adding shortcuts to, 109-110, 864
    defined, **42**
    overview of, 41, 862
    Show Desktop icon, 42, 110
quitting. *See also* exiting
    defined, **901**
    e-mail programs, 502
    Netscape Navigator, 640

R

Radio feature, Internet Explorer, 5, *6*, 528-529, **530-531**
radio frequency interference (RFI), **737-739**
RAM (Random Access Memory), **753-787**
    buying, 718, 782-784
    checking installed amounts of, 758-761, *759-760*
    chips, **895**, **902**
    defined, **753-754**, **895**, **902**
    extending with swap files, 757-758

RAM (Random Access Memory) — Registry

versus hard drives, 758
history of, 754–756
installing, **771–786**
    deciding amount needed, 782–783
    dismounting power supplies, 776–778, *777*, *779*
    EDO chips, **763**, *783*
    locating memory sockets, 775–776, *775*
    memory access speed and, 783
    in motherboard/daughterboards, 780
    opening computer cases, 772–774, *774*
    overview of, 771, 786
    removing ribbon cable connectors, 779–780
    static electricity and, 771–772, 784, *785*
    steps in, 784–786, *785*
    tin or gold contacts and, 784
    types of chips, 783
    warnings, 772, 773, 778, 782, 785
memory access speed, 783
memory blocks, 762
memory speed, 762
module adapters for, 769
older, using in newer computers, 769
operating system requirements, 755–757
overview of, 787
packaged DIP chips
    defined, **761**, **765**
    in DIMMs, 766–769, *767–769*, 781–782, *781*, 784
    DIP chips, defined, **761**
    in SIMMs, 765–766, *766–767*, 781–782, *781*, 784, **905**
parity RAM chips, 764
planning requirements for, 770–771, 783
Sound Recorder and, 238
sources, 771
types of, 761, 763–764
vendors, 961–962
virtual memory, 438, 758, 759–761, *760*
warnings, 761, 765, 768
RAS (Remote Access Service), 332, 334, 359–360

ratings, content. *See* Content Advisor
reading e-mail, 497–498, *498*
Read-Only access, *81*, 82, **902**
recording sounds. *See also* sound
    controlling volume, 868
    in Sound Recorder, 236–238, *237*
    in Sounds applet, 228–229
Recreational Software Advisory Council (RSAC), 583, 584
Recycle Bin, **87–95**. *See also* deleting; restoring
    bypassing, 90, 94–95, 807
    confirmation options, 94
    defined, **88**, **852–853**
    emptying, 95
    files not sent to, 90
    overview of, 45–46, 87–88
    properties of, 93–94, *93*
    recovering files from, 91–93, *92*, 865–866
    recovering files not in, 90
    sending files to, 89–90
    sizing, 93–94, *93*, 95
    warning, 95
recycling centers, 981
refresh rates, 162, **164**, 217–218
Regional Settings applet in Control Panel, *114*, 117, 806, **853–855**
Registry, **398–439**. *See also* system configuration files
    anatomy of, 405–406, *405*
    backing up
        by exporting with REGEDIT.EXE, 414–416, *415–417*
        with SCANREG.EXE, 409–411, *410*
        with SCANREGW.EXE, 410, 413–414
    CONFIG.POL files, 399, 401, 402
    contents of, 401–403, *401*
    defined, **398–400**, *399*
    editing local Registry, **409–424**
        backing up before, 409–416, *410*, *415–416*
        contents, 418–421, *418–420*
        duplicate entries and, 423–424
        versus editing remote Registry, 425
        editing SCANREG.INI, 411–412
    local, defined, **893**

overview of, 409
reducing size of, 416-417
restoring after, 413, 414, 421-422, *422-423*
warnings, 404, 410, 436
editing remote Registry, **424-431**
    adding remote administrators, 428-430, *428-430*
    connecting to remote computers, 426, *426*
    editing, 430-431, *430*
    versus editing local Registry, 425
    installing Remote Registry, 425
    preparing for, 424-430, *426-430*
    purposes of, 424
    troubleshooting connections, 427-428, *427*
    warnings, 430, 436
editing, uses for
    changing system shell folders, 438-439, *439*
    hiding network computers, 439
    preventing menus from following mice, 437
    removing Shut Down from Start menu, 436-437
    saving Desktop settings, 435-436
    saving disk space, 438-439, *439*
    turning off zooming windows, 437-438
finding words in, 408-409, 418-420, *418-420*
HKEY subtrees, 399, 405-407
importing, 421-422, *422-423*
keys and subkeys, 405-406
navigating, 408
opening, 407
overview of, 391-392
purpose of, 400
.REG files, *401*, 402
restoring, 413, 414, 421-422, *422-423*
shortcut, adding to Start menu, 407-408
SYSTEM.DAT files, 399-402, *401*
trees, 405
USER.DAT files, 399-402, *401*

values, 406
versus Windows NT Registry, 403-404
remote access, **331-332**, **902**. *See also* Dial-Up Networking
Remote Access Service (RAS), 332, 334, 359-360
remote administration options, 428-430, *428-430*, 850
remote control, **332**
remote control for Web TV, 258-259
remote Registry. *See* Registry
removing. *See also* deleting
    keyboard shortcuts, 66
    memory chips, 766, 768
    power connectors, 776-778, *777*, *779*
    programs via Control Panel, 138-139, 794-795
    programs from Start menu, 64
    Shut Down option from Start menu, 436-437
    Uninstall files, 28
    Web TV channels from listings, 253, *253*
    Windows 98 SE components, 795
replying to e-mail, 498-500, **902**
resolution, screen, **50-51**, **160-164**, *161*, **217-218**, 283-284, *283*
Resource Meter tool, **325-326**, *325*
restoring. *See also* Recycle Bin
    archived files, 315-316, 855-857
    defined, **902-903**
    Registry, 413, 414, 421-422, *422-423*
RFI (radio frequency interference), **737-739**
ribbon cable connectors, removing, 779-780
ROM BIOS, buying, 718
Ross, John, 527
RSAC content ratings, 583, 584
Run option on Start menu, 39, **857**
Russel, Charlie, 3, 13

S

Salkind, Neil J., 32, 35, 57, 285, 287, 369, 371
saturation, **156**
saving. *See also* archives; storing
    Clipboard contents, 375-376
    defined, **903**

Desktop settings, 435-436
e-mail as text files, 516
HyperTerminal sessions, 387-388
sound schemes, 231-232
system files during Setup, 27-28
Web files to hard drives
    filenames and, 626
    images, 627, 628
    links, 627-628
    overview of, 624
    and viewing offline, 628-629
    Web pages, 625-627, *626*
Web pages
    in FrontPage Express, 657
    in Internet Explorer, 558-559
    in Netscape Navigator, 624-629, *626*
ScanDisk, 25-26, **288-291**, *289*, **857**
scanners, 272-273, 678
SCANREG.EXE files, 409-411, *410*
SCANREG.INI files, 411-412
SCANREGW.EXE files, 410, 413-414
screen display. *See* Desktop; Display applet; video
screen saver options, 49, 147-150, *148*, 858, **903**
scroll bars, **254**, *255*, **614**, **903**
SCSI (Small Computer Systems Interface), 209, **903-904**
SDRAM (Synchronous Dynamic RAM), **763**
searching. *See also* finding
    in Help topics, 827
    for shows in Web TV, 254-256
    for titles in DVD Player, 225-226
searching the Web, **685-695**
    with AltaVista, 691-693, *692*
    via directories, 548, **687-690**, *688-689*, *691*
    for e-mail addresses, 524-525
    with HotBot, 693
    in Internet Explorer
        Address bar, 548
        customizing searches, 548, *548*, 693-694, *694*
        via directories, 548
        Search bar, defined, 5, **540**

Search bar, opening, 4, 547, 695
Search bar, using, 547-548, *547*
    in online buying, 704-706, *706*
    overview of, 524-525, 545-546, 685-686
    via search engines, **459**, 524-525, **690-693**, *692*, **904**
    warnings, 546, 705
Web addresses of search sites, 695
with Yahoo!
    Computers and Internet page, 688-689, *688*, *689*
    for graphic images, 678
    by keyword, 689-690, *691*
    overview of, 687, *687*
    by topic, 687-689, *688*, *689*
    for virus protection software, 697
    for what's new on the Net, 640
    for Windows programs, 688-689, *688*, *689*
Secure Sockets Layer (SSL) protocol, 597-599
security. *See also* Internet Explorer security
    in Dial-Up Networking
        via CHAP protocol, 366
        for Dial-up Server, 361-362, *361-363*
        via PAP protocol, 364-365
        share-level security, 366-368, *367-368*
        via SPAP protocol, 366
        user-level permissions, 367-368, *367-368*
    logon security, 836
    in Netscape Navigator, 613, 619-620
    in online buying, 704-706, *706*
Security Alert messages, 599-600
security patches, 7
Security tab of Internet Options dialog box, 830
Send To menu, 64-65, 86-87, 110, *111*, **858**
sending
    e-mail
        with attached files, 506-508, *507*
        to multiple recipients, 505-506
        to other networks, 495-496, *496*
        overview of, 493-495, *494*
    files in HyperTerminal, 386, *386*

sending—ShowSounds feature 1013

files to Recycle Bin, 89-90
Web shortcuts to other users, 562-563
Serial Line Interface Protocol (SLIP), **334**, 343, **455-456**, *456*, **905**
serial network connections, direct, 368-369
serial ports, buying, 720
Server Type DUN settings, 342-344, *342-343*, *345-346*, 352, 480-481, *481*
servers
    defined, **458**
    proxy servers, **832**, **901**
    Web servers, **911**
serviceability in PCs, **714**
Settings option on Start menu, **37-38**, 858
Settings tab of Display Properties dialog box, 50-51, 159-168, *159*, *161*, *163*, *165-167*, 283-285, *283*. *See also* Advanced Display Properties dialog box
Shapar, Kristina, 329, 391
shareware, **695**, **704**, **904**
sharing. *See also* networks
    drives or folders
        disconnecting from mapped drives, 83
        mapping drives, 82-83, *83*
        overview of, 77, 80-82, *81*
        setting up networks, 77-80
        DUN Internet connections, 485-488, *487-488*
        resources, passwords for, 849-850
Shiva Password Authentication Protocol (SPAP), 366
shopping online, **704-706**, *706*
shortcut menus
    copying files using, 805
    defined, **904**
    moving files using, 839-840
    in Netscape Navigator, 629
    printing documents using, 194
    What's This? option, 869
shortcuts, **57-70**. *See also* keyboard shortcuts
    changing icons of, 62-63
    copying, 65, 108
    creating, 59-60, *59*
    defined, **858**, **904**

on Desktop
    to Backup program, 315
    to Dial-Up Networking, 348
    to disk drives, 67
    finding programs in, 105
    to floppy drives, 84
    to network home directories, 348
    to printers, 192
    to Start menu programs, 63-64
    to Windows Explorer programs, 75, 108
finding targets of, 62
naming, 61
overview of, 10, 57-58, *58*, 70
to printers, 64, 192, 194
to programs
    on Desktop, 63-64, 75, 108
    DOS programs, 67
    overview of, 107
    on Programs menu, 108-109, *108*
    on Quick Launch toolbar, 109-110, 864
    on Send To menu, 86-87, 110, *111*
    on Start menu, 109, 407-408
    in StartUp folder, 65-66, 861
    on Taskbar, 325, *325*, 862
properties for, 61-63, *62*
to Registry Editor, 407-408
to Resource Meter, 325, *325*
on Send To menu, 64-65, 86-87, 110, *111*
warning, 67
Web shortcuts
    changing icons for, 560-561, *561*
    creating folders for, 561
    opening from keyboard, 562, *563*
    overview of, 559
    sending to other users, 562-563
    to Web pages, creating, 560
Show Desktop icon on Quick Launch toolbar, 42, **110**
Show settings icon on Taskbar, 162, *163*
Show window contents while dragging option, 157, 158
ShowSounds feature, 121

Shut Down option on Start menu, 39, 436–437, **859**
signatures, digital, **513–515**, 601, **883**, **905**
SIMMs (Single Inline Memory Modules), **765–766**, *766–767*, **905**
site certificates, 600, **604**
sites. *See* Web sites
sizing
    fonts in FrontPage Express, 665–666
    fonts in Netscape Navigator, 620–622
    increasing disk cache size, 635–636
    Recycle Bin, 93–94, *93*, 95
    reducing Registry size, 416–417
    screen elements, 155
    Start menu and icons, 863
    Taskbar, 40, 44
    Web page images, 682–683
    Web TV displays, 254
SLIP (Serial Line Interface Protocol), **334**, 343, **455–456**, *456*, **905**
smoke, protecting PCs from, 733
smoothing fonts, 157, 158
SNAP.EXE Properties dialog box, 393–396, *394–395*
software publisher certificates, 600, **601–604**
sound. *See also* multimedia
    accessibility options, 121–122, *121*
    background, in Web pages, *668*, 669
    boards, upgrading to multimedia, 217
    volume control options, 220, 867–868
    WAV files, 228, 229, 230
Sound Recorder
    converting sound file formats, 239–240
    defined, **219**, **235**
    disk space and, 237
    editing sound files, 238–240
    memory and, 238
    playing sound files, 235–236
    recording sounds, 236–238, *237*
SoundBlaster software, **204**
Sounds applet. *See also* Control Panel
    assigning sounds to events, 228, 229–231, *231*
    defined, *114*, 117, **218–219**, **859**
    deleting sound schemes, 232
    installing sound schemes, 228
    recording sounds, 228–229
    saving sound schemes, 231–232
    sound file sources, 229
    storing sounds, 230
    troubleshooting sound, 229
SoundSentry feature, 121–122
space on hard drives. *See* disk drives, hard
SPAP (Shiva Password Authentication Protocol), 366
speakers
    protecting PCs from, 735
    upgrading for multimedia, 216
special characters
    in Character Map applet, 377–378, *377*
    in Symbol dialog box, 647–648
speed
    of Desktop images, 167–168, *167*, 285
    of Internet connections, 467–468
    keyboard options for, 835
    memory access speed, 783
    memory speed, 762
    modem speed, 456
    mouse double-click speed, 169, *169*
    mouse pointer speed, 171–173, *172*
    speed dialing, 379–380, *379*
    speeding up Internet Explorer, 834–835
spell checking e-mail, 512–513
spooling, **175–176**
SRAM (Static Random Access Memory), **763**, **906**
SSL (Secure Sockets Layer) protocol, 597–599
Stacker-compressed hard drives, 29
Start button on Taskbar, **36**, *36*, 41, 862
Start menu. *See also* Taskbar
    adding program shortcuts to, 64, 109
    adding Registry Editor to, 407–408
    Desktop shortcuts to programs on, 63–64
    Documents option, 37, **809**
    Favorites option, 37
    Find option, 38–39, *38*
    Help option, 39, 52, *52*, **827–828**
    Log Off option, 39, **836**, **894**
    opening, 36
    overview of, 36–39, *36*, *38*, 860

Programs option, 37, **105**, *105*, **851-852**
reducing size of, 863
removing programs from, 64
Run option, 39, **857**
Settings option, **37-38**, 858
Shut Down option, 39, 436-437, **859**
Start button, **36**, *36*, 41, 862
Windows Update option, **297-298**, *298*, 860, **870**
startup disks, creating, 795-796
StartUp folder, adding program shortcuts to, 65-67, 861
static electricity, **743-747**, 771-772, 784, *785*. *See also* electromagnetism
Static Random Access Memory (SRAM), **763**, **906**
StickyKeys feature, 119-121
Stop button in Netscape Navigator, 630, 640
storage device vendors, 963
storing. *See also* archives; saving
    DOS programs in .PIF files, 396-397
    sounds, 230
subject lines in e-mail, 496
subkeys, Registry, **406**
subtitles in DVD Player, 226-227
sunbeams, protecting PCs from, 731
SuperStor-compressed hard drives, 29
Surfing the Internet with Netscape Communicator 4 (Tauber and Kienan with Powers), 607
Surround Video feature, **208**
swap files, **757-758**
symbols. *See* special characters
sync links, **388**
Sync SRAM (Synchronous Random Access Memory), **764**
synchronizing files with My Briefcase, 388-389
synchronizing passwords, 353-354
Synchronous Dynamic RAM (SDRAM), **763**
system, **906**. *See also* operating systems
System applet in Control Panel, *114*, **117**, 136
system configuration files. *See also* Registry
    AUTOEXEC.BAT and CONFIG.SYS, **392-398**
        creating DOS environments, 393-396, *394-395*

editing DOS .PIF files, 403
loading DOS drivers and TSRs, 393
overview of, 392-393
purposes of, 393
storing DOS programs in .PIF files, 396-397
viewing DOS .PIF files with DEBUG, 397-398
warnings, 396, 397
overview of, 391-392
WIN.INI and SYSTEM.INI, **431-435**
    contents of, 431-432
    defined, **906**, **912**
    disadvantages of, 434
    editing, 435
    .INI files, defined, **431**
    overview of, 391-392, 402, 431
    purpose of, 434-435
    versus SYSINI.W31 files, 432-433
    versus WININI.W31 files, 433-434
SYSTEM.DAT files in Registry, 399-402, *401*
system date, **906**
System File Checker tool, **322**, *323*
System Information tool, **320-321**, *320*
system maintenance, **287-316**
    backing up files, **308-316**
        with Backup, defined, **798**
        with Backup, starting, 308-309, *309*
        backup types, 310
        creating backups, 312-314, *313*
        defining file sets for, 311
        Desktop shortcut for, 315
        with drag-and-drop, 315
        to floppy disks, 309, 311
        overview of, 308
        and restoring, 315-316, 855-857
        setting options for, 314-315
        to tape drives, 309-310
        warning, 309
        what to backup, 310-311
    with Disk Cleanup, 293-295, *293*, *294*
    with Disk Defragmenter, 291-292, *292*
    with Drive Converter FAT32
        converting to, 301-303, *302*
        defined, **13**, **299**

versus FAT16, 299–300
limitations of, 300–301
returning to FAT16, 303
warning, 302
with DriveSpace 3
  compressing hard drives, 304–306, *304*
  Compression Agent, 307–308
  creating drive partitions, 307
  defined, **30**, **299**
  overview of, 303–304
  settings, 306
  uncompressing drives, 306–307
  warning, 305
with Maintenance Wizard, 295–297, *296*
overview of, 287, 316
with ScanDisk, 25–26, **288–291**, *289*, **857**
with Task Scheduler, 297
troubleshooting tools
  Dr. Watson, 321, *322*
  overview of, 319, 326, *327*
  Resource Meter, 325–326, *325*
  System File Checker, 322, *323*
  System Information, 320–321, *320*
  System Monitor, 323–324, *323*, *324*
with Tune-Up Wizard, 869–870
with Windows Update, **297–298**, 297–298, *298*, 860, **870**
System Properties dialog box, 276–277, *277*
system shell folders, 438–439, *439*
system time, **906**

T

tape drives, backing up to, 309–310
Task Scheduler program, **297**, **865**
Taskbar. *See also* Desktop; Start menu
  adding program shortcuts to, 325, *325*, 862
  adding toolbars to, 864
  Address toolbar, 42, **798**, 864
  clock, 41, 863
  configuring toolbars on, 44
  creating toolbars on, 43, *43*, 865
  defined, **861**
  Desktop toolbar, 42, 864
  hiding, 40, 863
  icons on, 41, 861–862
  Links toolbar, 43, 864
  moving, 40
  overview of, 40, 41
  Quick Launch toolbar
    adding shortcuts to, 109–110, 864
    defined, **42**
    overview of, 41, 862
    Show Desktop icon, 42, 110
  selecting toolbars on, 41
  setting properties for, 863–864
  sizing, 40, 44
  Start button, **36**, *36*, 41, 862
  warning, 44
Tauber, Daniel A., 607
TCP/IP protocols, **466**, **907**
telecommuting, **330**
telephone logs in Phone Dialer, 380
telephone numbers *See* phone numbers
Telephony applet in Control Panel, *114*, **117**
temperatures. *See* heat
templates for Web pages, 653–654
Temporary Internet Files, 537–538, *537*, 598, 834
testing DUN connections, 347–348, *347*
text. *See also* fonts; special characters
  editing in Notepad, 86–87, **372**
  editing in WordPad, 372–374, *373–374*
  text files
    defined, **908**
    saving e-mail as, 516
    sending via HyperTerminal, 386, *386*
  in Web pages. *See also* HTML
    coloring, 622–623, *623*
    finding and replacing, 648
thermal shock, **731**
threads, **500**, **908**
Time applet in Control Panel, Date/, *114*, 115, **139–140**, *140*, 806
time, system, **906**
Time tab of Regional Settings dialog box, 855
time/date settings on Taskbar, 41, 863

Tip of the Day bar, Internet Explorer, 541, *542*
titles
    formatting in Web pages, 668, *668*
    searching for in DVD Player, 225–226
    sub, selecting in DVD Player, 226–227
ToggleKeys feature, 120
toolbars
    Address toolbars
        defined, **798**, **874**
        on Desktop, 42
        in Internet Explorer, 534–536, 548
        in Windows Explorer, 813
    CD Player Toolbar, 242–243
    defined, **908**
    in Internet Explorer
        Address bar, 534–536, 548
        hiding/displaying, 531
        Links bar, 531–533
        moving, 531
        overview of, 528–529
        Radio toolbar, 5, *6*, 530–531
    in Netscape Navigator
        collapsing/expanding, 610
        Component bar, 614, *614*
        hiding/displaying, 610
        Location toolbar, 613
        menu bar, 610
        Navigation toolbar, 609, 610–612
        Personal toolbar, 613
        scroll bars, 614, **903**
        status bar, 613
    Paint toolbar, 846–847
    on Taskbar
        adding, 864
        Address toolbar, 42, **798**, 864
        configuring, 44
        creating, 43, *43*, 865
        Desktop toolbar, 42, 864
        Links toolbar, 43, 864
        Quick Launch toolbar, 41, **42**, 109–110, 862, 864
        selecting, 41
    Web TV toolbar, 258
    in WordPad, 374, *374*
Tools menu in Windows Explorer, 812

transient power, **742**
trees, Registry, **405**
troubleshooting. *See also* system maintenance
    modems, 268, 271–272, *272*
    printing, 276
    remote Registry connections, 427–428, *427*
    sound, 229
    tools for, **319–327**
        Dr. Watson, 321, *322*
        overview of, 319, 326, *327*
        Resource Meter, 325–326, *325*
        System File Checker, 322, *323*
        System Information, 320–321, *320*
        System Monitor, 323–324, *323*, *324*
    with Troubleshooters, 133, 827–828
    WINS connections, 357–359, *358*
TUCOWS, 704
Tune-Up Wizard, Windows, **869–870**
TV Viewer. *See* Web TV for Windows
Twinalert heat sensor device, 729

U

undeleting, **908**. *See also* Recycle Bin; restoring
Underdahl, Keith, 465
undervoltage, **742–743**
Undo Delete option, 807
Unicode, 404
uninstalling
    local printers, 189, 275
    programs, 103–105, *104*, 138–139, 866
    and reinstalling programs, 139
    Uninstall files, 28
    utilities for, 138–139
    Windows 98 SE, 26–27
Update Device Driver Wizard, 277, *278*, 281, *282*
Update program, Windows, **12**, **297–298**, *298*, 860, **870**
updates, 7
upgradability of PCs, **714**
upgrades, 7, **909**
upgrading to multimedia, **208–218**
    CD-R drives, 214–215

CD-ROM drives, 213-214
CD-RW drives, 214-215
computers, 212-213
DVD drives, 215-216
methods of, 209-212
monitors, 217-218
overview of, 208-209
sound boards, 217
speakers, 216
video cards, 217-218
Upgrading to Windows 98 (Russel and Crawford), 3
URLs (Uniform Resource Locators). *See also* Web addresses
   copying and pasting, 596
   defined, **909**
   in Internet Explorer, 534-536
   in Netscape Navigator, 613, 617-618, *617*
USBs (Universal Serial Busses), 720
Usenet newsgroups, **459**, **909**
USER.DAT files, 399-402, *401*
user interfaces. *See* Desktop; interfaces
user profiles, enabling, 848
usernames, 457, 494, **909**
Users applet in Control Panel, *114*, 118, **866-867**

V

values, Registry, **406**
vendors. *See* computer vendors
verifying Web site identities, **600-605**. *See also* certificates
Verisign, Inc., 604
VGA (Video Graphics Display) boards, **713**
video adapter cards
   buying, 713, 719
   changing, 280-281
   defined, **713**
   settings, 164-165, 281-282, *282*
   specifications, 164-165
   upgrading for multimedia, 217-218
video drivers, **159-168**. *See also* Display applet
   adapter card settings, 164-165, 281-282, *282*

changing, 281-282, *282*
color palette settings, 160
font settings, 163-164
graphics speed settings, 167-168, *167*
monitor settings, 166-167, *166*, 284-285
overview of, 50-51, 159, *159*, 283-285, *283*
refresh rate settings, 162, 164, 217-218
resolution settings, **50-51**, **160-164**, *161*, **217-218**, 283-284, *283*
video monitors
   buying, 719
   settings, 166-167, *166*, 284-285
   specifications, 164-165
   upgrading for multimedia, 217-218
Video Random Access Memory (VRAM), **764**, **910**
View menu in Windows Explorer, 811
View tab in Folder Options dialog box, **823**
viewing
   file extensions, 75-76, *76*
   files saved in Netscape Navigator, 628-629
   font samples, 825
   HTML source code, 649-650, *650*
   in Internet Explorer
      Favorites, 551-552, *552*
      multiple windows, 543
      Web pages offline, 558-559, 834
   print queues, 194-195
virtual memory, **438**, 758, **759-761**, *760*
viruses, **697-698**, **910**
visited links, **617**
Volume Control program, **220**, **867-868**
Voxware plug-in, 239
VRAM (Video Random Access Memory), **764**, **910**

W

Wake-On-LAN program, **7**
Wallet, Microsoft, **576-580**, *577*, *579-580*
wallpapering Desktop, 143-147, *144*, *146*, **910**
WAV files, 228, 229, 230. *See also* sound
wave tables, 217

Web. *See also* Internet; World Wide Web
Web addresses. *See also* addresses
   AJR NewsLink, 550
   Andy's Art Attack, 678
   Bigfoot, 822
   BIOS upgrade vendors, 962–963
   Browser Watch, 640
   Columbia House, 706, *706*
   computer/component vendors, 916–959, 963–978
   data recovery vendors, 959–961
   defined, **457**
   Electronic Frontier Foundation, 461
   Excite, 695
   Four11, 822
   high-speed Internet connections, 468
   HotBot, 693
   Hotmail.com, 493
   icon sources, 560
   Infoseek, 695
   The Internet Society, 461
   ISPs, national, 472
   Juno.com, 493
   Lycos, 695
   Magellan, 695
   memory vendors, 961–962
   Microsoft
      accessibility support, 119
      digital TV integration, 249
      getting ISDN, 466
      ordering CDs, 3
      search site, 821
      Web Gallery, 660
   Microsystems Software, 583
   Netscape
      Assistance, 615
      Customer Showcase, 620
      Navigator, News of the Day, 639
      Web Security Solutions, 613
   Paint Shop Pro, 377
   PC repair/exchange vendors, 979–981
   peripherals vendors, 916–959, 963–978
   PICS content ratings, 583
   recycling centers, 981
   RSAC content ratings, 584
   SafeSurf Ratings, 591
   search tools, 548, 687, 695
   storage device vendors, 963
   TUCOWS, 704
   Verisign, 604
   WhoWhere?, 822
   WinZip, 698, *698*
   World Wide Web Consortium, 461
   Yahoo!, 640, 687
Web browsers, **447–448**, *449*, **910–911**. *See also* Internet Explorer; Netscape Navigator
Web connections. *See* Internet connections
Web Help, 52, 54, 828
Web pages. *See also* FrontPage; home pages; Internet Explorer; Netscape Navigator
   Active Desktop links to, 49–50, 159, **792–793**, 803–804
   defined, **911**
   finding on Internet, 821
Web sites. *See also* filtering Web site content
   defined, **911**
   finding on Internet, 821
   verifying identities of, **600–605**
Web tab of Display Properties dialog box, 49–50, 159, 793
Web TV for Windows, **248–259**. *See also* multimedia
   adding channels to listings, 253, *253*
   adding channels to toolbar, 258
   avoiding Channel 1, 254
   benefits of, 249–250
   defined, **7**, **248**, **911**
   hardware requirements, 248–249
   how it works, 250
   installing, 248
   keystroke controls, 258–259
   online documentation, 253
   reading about programs, 256–257, *256*
   remote controls, 258–259
   removing channels, 253, *253*
   running, 250–252, *251*, *252*
   scrolling displays, 254, *255*
   searching for shows, 254–256
   setting reminders, 257
   sizing displays, 254

WebBots, 654
Weisskopf, Gene, 565, 567, 644
Welcome to Windows program, **868–869**
What's This?, **869**
WIN.INI files. *See also* system configuration files
  contents of, 431–432
  defined, **912**
  disadvantages of, 434
  editing, 435
  .INI files, overview, 402, 431
  overview of, 391–392, 402
  purpose of, 434–435
  versus WININI.W31 files, 433–434
Windows 3.*x*
  defined, **911**
  installing Windows 98 SE over, 18–24, *19*
  RAM requirements, 755–757
  versus Windows 98 SE, 8–9
Windows 95
  installing Windows 98 SE over, 18–24, *19*
  RAM requirements, 755–757
  versus Windows 98 SE, 9–13
Windows 98: No Experience Required (Crawford), 73, 97, 287, 319
Windows 98
  installing Windows 98 SE over, 18–24, *19*
  RAM requirements, 756–757
Windows 98 SE, **3–13**
  defined, **3**
  FAT32, 13
  fax capability, 12
  folders, 10
  input/output devices, 13
  Internet e-mail, 11–12
  logon security, 836
  new features, **4–8**, *5*, *6*
  obtaining, 3
  Online Services, 11, **844**
  photos and, 213–214
  power management, 13
  shortcuts, 10
  system tools, 12
  updates, 7, 12
  upgrades, 7
  warning, 12

Web connections, 11
  versus Windows 3.1, 8–9
  versus Windows 95, **9–13**
  Windows Update, 12
Windows 2000, 31
windows
  closing, 799–800, **880**
  defined, **911**
  multiple, viewing, 543
  zooming, turning off, 437–438
Windows applications, **911**
Windows Explorer, **73–87**, **810–815**
  creating Desktop shortcut to, 75
  customizing folders in, 814
  defined, **810**
  finding files/folders in, 815
  finding programs in, 106, *107*
  floppy disks and
    copying, 84, *84*
    Desktop shortcuts to, 84
    formatting, 84–86
    overview of, 84
  menus, 810–812
  overview of, 73–75, *74*
  Send To menu, 86–87
  sharing drives or folders
    disconnecting from mapped drives, 83
    mapping drives, 82–83, *83*
    overview of, 77, 80–82, *81*
    setting up networks, 77–80
  toolbars, 812–814
  viewing file extensions, 75–76, *76*
  window, 814
Windows keys, **911**
Windows NT. *See also* WINS connections to NT domains
  defined, **911**
  installing Windows 98 SE in, 31
  RAM requirements, 756–757
  Registry, 403–404
  Remote Access Server, 332, 359–360
Windows OS/2, 31, 755–756
Windows programs, searching Yahoo! for, 688–689, *688–689*

Windows Radio feature, 5, 6, 528–529, **530–531**
Windows, reverting to previous versions of, 26–28
Windows swap files, **757–758**
Windows Tune-Up Wizard, **869–870**
Windows Update program, **12**, **297–298**, *298*, 860, **870**
WINIPCFG utility, 357–358, *358*
WINS connections to NT domains, **352–359**.
   See also Dial-Up Networking; Windows NT
   versus DUN or PPTP connections, 359
   firewalls and, 353
   LMHOSTS files and, 356–357
   setting up, 352–355, *355–356*
   synchronizing passwords, 353–354
   troubleshooting, 357–359, *358*
WinZip
   downloading, 698–699, *699*
   installing, 700–702
   unzipping files with, 702–703
Wizards
   Add Printer Wizard, 181–184, *182–184*, 273–274
   Backup Wizard, 312–313, *313*
   Connection Wizard, 349–351, *349–351*, 476–478, *477*, **800–802**
   Customize This Folder Wizard, 814
   defined, **912**
   Install Hardware Wizard, 128–136, *129–130*, *132–134*
   Internet Connection Wizard, 349–351, *349–351*, 476–478, *477*, **800–802**
   Maintenance Wizard, **295–297**, *296*
   Personal Home Page Wizard, 654, *655*
   Tune-Up Wizard, 869–870
   Update Device Driver Wizard, 277, *278*, 281, *282*
word processors, writing e-mail in, 511–512, *511*
WordPad applet. *See also* applets
   defined, **372**
   dragging documents into, 373
   faxing and, 373
   formatting tools, 374, *374*
   opening screen, 373, *373*

page setup and printing, 374
starting, 372
toolbars, 374, *374*
World Wide Web. *See also* Internet; Web
   defined, **912**
   versus Internet, 446–449, *449*
   Web sites about, 461–462
World Wide Web Consortium, **461**

X

X-rays, 733–734
XtraDrive compression, 30

Y

Yahoo! Web searches. *See also* searching the Web
   on Computers and Internet page, 688–689, *688–689*
   for graphic images, 678
   by keyword, 689–690, *691*
   overview of, 687, *687*
   by topic, 687–689, *688*, *689*
   for virus protection software, 697
   for what's new on the Net, 640
   for Windows programs, 688–689, *688–689*

Z

Zip drives, **912**
zip files, unzipping, **698–703**, *698–699*
zooming windows, turning off, 437–438

The PC Problem-Solving Wonder!

Completey revised and updated by Mark Minasi and a team of gurus, the 11th edition now includes easy-to-find Troubleshooting and QuickSteps sections in addition to valuable instructional videos by the engaging author.

ISBN: 0-7821-2800-9
$59.99 US
Available August 2000

Includes A+ certification test engines with more than 350 practice questions!

Check out this valuable bonus material:

- An extensive major hardware vendor resource guide
- Chapter on using the Internet to upgrade PCs and peripherals
- An online chapter that covers storage devices
- A comprehensive glossary

www.sybex.com   SYBEX®

Evolve to a Higher Level!

"I Didn't Know You Could Do That™....," is a new Sybex™ series for beginners through intermediate users. Each book covers a popular subject certain to appeal to the general consumer. Written in a light, conversational style, well-known authors teach users cool, fun, immediately useful tips and secrets. Each companion CD is loaded with valuable software and utilities.

MP3!
$19.99
ISBN: 0-7821-2653-7

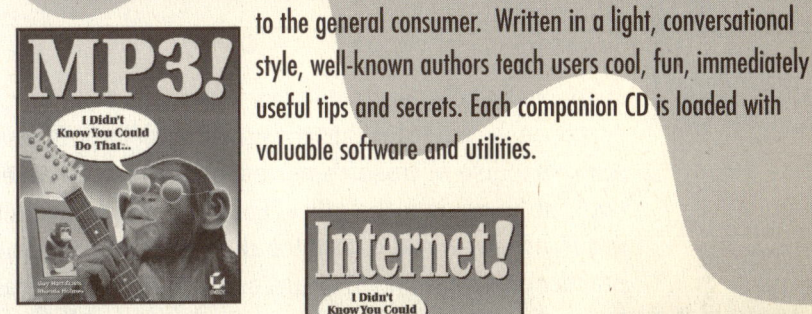

Internet!
$19.99
ISBN: 0-7821-2587-5

PalmPilot!
(and Palm Organizers)
$19.99
ISBN: 0-7821-2588-3

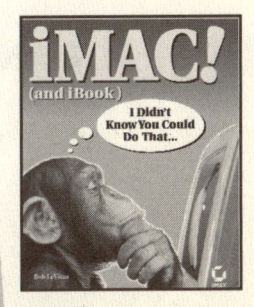

iMac™!
$19.99
ISBN: 0-7821-2589-1

Home Networking!
$19.99
ISBN: 0-7821-2631-6

Linux!
$19.99
ISBN: 0-7821-2612-x

SYBEX®
www.sybex.com

WINDOWS 98: NO EXPERIENCE REQUIRED.
Sharon Crawford

544pp; 7½" x 9"
ISBN:0-7821-2128-4
$24.99 US

Every user who's new to Windows 98 needs this book. This no-nonsense guide teaches the essential skills necessary for readers to use Microsoft's newest operating system effectively at home or at the office. Each chapter presents hundreds of real-world examples that let readers learn the practical skills they need to succeed in today's marketplace. Not only is Windows 98 completely explained, but so is Microsoft's Internet Explorer browser, which now built into the operating system. When you learn Web View, the wide world of the Web is as close as your Windows 98 Desktop—and this book shows you how to take advantage of both!

THE COMPLETE PC UPGRADE AND MAINTENANCE GUIDE, 10TH EDITION
Mark Minasi

2 CDs
1,664pp; 7½" x 9"
ISBN: 0-7821-2606-5
$49.99 US

The Complete PC Upgrade and Maintenance Guide is a problem-solving wonder—in simple, easy-to-follow language, it shows you how to prevent disasters and fix them when they occur. Based on author Mark Minasi's extremely popular, worldwide PC upgrade and repair seminars (course price: $800!), this book gives PC owners or support people all they need to know to handle 99 percent of their PC problems.